Third Edition

Check In · Check Out
Principles of Effective Front Office Management

Jerome J. Vallen

College of Hotel Administration
University of Nevada
Las Vegas

ωcb

Wm. C. Brown Publishers
Dubuque, Iowa

Book Team

Kathleen L. Loy Editor
Mary C. Murphy Assistant Editor
Vickie Blosch Production Editor
Kevin Pruessner Designer
Mavis M. Oeth Permissions Editor
Faye M. Schilling Photo Research Editor

**wcb
group**

Wm. C. Brown Chairman of the Board
Mark C. Falb President and Chief Executive Officer

wcb

Wm. C. Brown Publishers, College Division

Lawrence E. Cremer President
James L. Romig Vice-President, Product Development
David A. Corona Vice-President, Production and Design
E. F. Jogerst Vice-President, Cost Analyst
Bob McLaughlin National Sales Manager
Marcia H. Stout Marketing Manager
Craig S. Marty Director of Marketing Research
Eugenia M. Collins Production Editorial Manager
Marilyn A. Phelps Manager of Design
Mary M. Heller Photo Research Manager

TO
Thirty-five Years

Contents

2   **The Structure of the Front Office   24**

3   **Room Reservations   42**

12 Credit and Credit Procedures 236

13 The City Ledger 257

14   The Mechanical Night Audit 281

15 The Electronic Night Audit: Computer Reports 308

16 The Smart Switches 335

Preface

Printing three editions in eleven years allows us to offer a very current text. The degree of change during the production of this text has been astonishing (it takes approximately one year to rewrite and almost another year to review, edit, and publish). This is testimony, apparently, to the oft-repeated adage about the speed of change experienced by our society and also by our industry.

The areas of change can be identified without difficulty, but ranking them in importance is not so clear-cut. With call accounting and deregulation, telephones are poised for a decade of major overhaul. The text covers that. Computerization continues its march through the industry, but leaves many properties untouched. The text treats this by integrating computers into the chapters, while leaving the old systems intact as they still are in many, many hotels.

Old friends of the text will recognize the changes, and the non-changes too, in static areas like statistics or the American plan. New users must keep a perspective. Although the content touches on all the operational facets of the hotel, this is not a marketing text, an accounting text, a book on security, nor a tome on architecture. Thus, locks are discussed, but there is not a chapter on security. Group reservations and billing are also discussed, but group marketing is left for another time. Rooms management is the title and focus of the work.

Cognizance has been taken of the shift in rooms management: from concern about the mechanics of the front desk to management conceptualization of causes and systems. The reader will sense this in the discussions of reservations, room rates, communications, and credit, among others. One mechanical note about the text: reference to the numerous illustrations has been increased in an effort to improve clarity and understanding.

Chapter 6 identifies the stationers who have contributed forms and photographs, and other individual acknowledgments are made throughout the text. Special thanks go to Mr. Robert Bennett, Jr. of Delaware County Community College in Pennsylvania for his ideas, forms, and questions.

I would like to acknowledge the contributions of the following reviewers who provided me with many helpful comments and suggestions for this edition of *Check In/Check Out*.

Robert C. Bennett, Jr., Delaware County Community College

K. Michael Haywood, University of Guelph

Dennis H. Pitters, Georgia State University

Jeffrey M. Wachtel, Florida State University

Thomas E. Walsh, Iowa State University

Comments from the users have always been encouraged and I appreciate the changes and content suggestions that have been received.

Jerome J. Vallen
Las Vegas, Nevada

Check In·Check Out

1

The Scope of the Industry

Hotelkeeping is a dynamic institution. Resilient from centuries of change, it approaches the millennium with the surety of tradition and the confidence of progress. The very tempo of its change, that which so easily entices proselytes to its fold, makes difficult a simple definition of the business of hotelkeeping.

Indeed, hotelkeeping is many businesses. It is broadly segmented, catering to the rich and the poor, to the sophisticated and the naive, to the well-traveled and the homebody, and to the foreigner and the indigene.

The current of change tests the mettle of management. Shifts in purpose and function coinciding with changes in procedures and technique. No part of the hotel structure is immune. The impact of innovation has fallen heavily on the concept and operation of the front office, for if the industry and its components are in flux, so certainly is the front office, which is so often identified as the nerve center of the entire hotel.

Physically, the front office is an easily identifiable area of the lobby. Functionally, it is much less so despite constant reference to it as the "hub" and the "heart" of the hotel. The overuse of such terms should not detract from the real importance of the front office. It is indeed the heart and the hub and the nerve center of guest activity. Through it flow communications with every other department; from it emanate instruction and direction for the care and service of the guest; to it come charges for final billing and settlement.

Organizational interdependence is not the only reason for the preeminent position of the front office. It is equally a matter of economics. Room sales produce over half the total revenue of the average hotel. And much of the revenue that comes from food and beverage originates in meetings and convention groups, whose search for site selections begins with rooms. More revenue (about 60 percent) is derived from room sales than from the total of the next three departments: food, beverage, and telephone.[1] Furthermore, rooms are more profitable than these departments. Every dollar of room sales produces approximately 70 cents in departmental profit. Food and beverage combined average out to about 15 cents per dollar sale, and telephone has often shown a loss. (Although telephone deregulation is still new, there are strong indications that this traditional cost center will be recording hefty profits.)

Hotel guests relate with the front office and this adds another facet to its importance. Guests who rarely see their housekeepers, who never see the accountant or the cook, who deal with sales and credit only on occasion, know the hotel by its desk. They are received at the desk and they depart from the desk. It is toward the desk that guests direct complaints and from the desk that they expect remedies. Guest identification, as much as profit or interdepartmental dependence, accounts for management's overriding concern with the front office.

CLASSIFICATIONS

The front office cannot be identified independently of the hotel nor the hotel separately from the hotel industry. Even the industry lacks a single identity, comprised as it is of diverse services and facilities. And as each hotel attempts to maximize its particular assets and solidify its share of a particular market, it grows to be less and less a prototype of the whole industry and more and more its own entity. No common template fits each of the 52,000 hotels and motels (up 25 percent since the last census) scattered across the United States. No hotel or front office functions exactly like any other. And the differences grow more apparent.

The basic concepts of food, shelter, and hospitality are much the same. The means of assuring their availability has undergone some marked revisions however. Change in the outward appearance of the inn has been apparent over the years, far more so than the subtle changes taking place within. In many cases, new concepts have been marked by nothing more than shifting terminology: hostel, tavern, public house, inn, guest house, hotel, resort, motel, motor lodge, motor inn, airtel, boatel, hometel.

The inns of old evolved from private homes that were convenient to the traveler. Today's hotel, even the mom-and-pop variety, is not represented as anyone's home. It is conceived as a point of destination as well as an accommodation for those in transit. Yesterday's tavern offered the family meal to all who came. Dining today is a created experience in design, decor, and menu. The ordinary, the old inn of New England, was almost indistinguishable from its neighbors. Today's edifice is a sharp contrast in style and packaging.

These many changes notwithstanding, certain definitions and classifications have withstood the test of time. Hotels are classified into several definitive categories. Some of these are subject to more objective measures than others and none are self-excluding. Hotels can fall into every category or only into some. Moreover, there are degrees of belonging, since one property may be well within a classification whereas another may exhibit some characteristics but lack others. Each category has an impact on the scope and function of the front office.

---

1. The sequence is subordinated in casino hotels where casino revenue accounts for 60 percent of the gross and rooms only 15 percent. Food is 12 percent, beverage is 9 percent and other is 4 percent.

Size

The size of a hotel is a measure of its guest rooms. Height of the building, acreage of the property, gross sales, net profits, and similar measures are disregarded, although there is an obvious relationship between them and the number of guest rooms. Other relationships are evident to a knowledgeable hotelier, ranging from the probable number of employees to the estimated cost of replacing the structure.

Although size is the most objective of the several classifications, there is uncertainty even here. Advertised size and actual size are rarely the same. Often, more rooms are listed than are actually available for sale. Old hotels, for example, have many rooms that are just not salable. Even newer properties may have rooms converted for other uses, including quarters for the manager's family. Rooms, especially those on lower floors, may be converted into offices and leased to businesses and associations. Still others are converted to storage facilities, maintenance areas, or other operational facilities as defects in the original design or unanticipated needs become evident. Generally, the older the hotel, the fewer the available rooms in relation to total rooms.

It is evident that the number of rooms in a hotel is not the same as the number of rooms available for sale to paying guests. During poor business periods when rooms are vacant, employees, middle managers especially, are encouraged to live in the hotel in return for lower salaries. Good times obviously reverse the arrangement. Thus, the number of rooms available is not static; it changes as other needs arise.

Hotels are grouped by size for purposes of study, for financial reporting, for membership dues, and also by the U.S. Department of Commerce. Although the Bureau of the Census uses several categories (figure 1.1), a quick and easy classification considers 100 rooms or less to be a small hotel, between 100 and 300 rooms an average hotel, and over 300 rooms a large hotel. Even these are generous definitions.

Most of the industry's statistics depend on computations prepared by two accounting firms: Laventhol & Horwath, and Pannell Kerr Forster. Each has its own classification system for presenting data (figure 17.5 offers a sample), which makes the interchange of information almost impossible. In seeking a more general definition, another federal agency, the Small Business Administration (SBA), has defined "small" for hotels or motels seeking government business loans, as properties doing 3.5 million dollars or less in annual receipts. Inflation undermines any definition based on dollar values, so the SBA considered (but dropped after strong AH&MA opposition) replacing the more volatile dollar volume with the number of employees.

Hotels and motels have been getting larger. The American Hotel and Motel Association (AH&MA) reports the average size of its member hotel to be increasing annually at a rate of about 5 percent. Still, the reported size of the AH&MA figure (less than 150 rooms) is surprising. One thinks of hotels in terms of the Americana (Sheraton Centre) in New York (1,850 rooms), the Conrad Hilton in Chicago (2,270 rooms), or the St. Francis in San Francisco (1,200 rooms). This isn't the hotel industry at all. It is still an industry of small hotels in which a 350-room property is a good size and anything over 500 rooms large. Figure 1.1 illustrates the contrasts in size for hotels, motels and motor hotel properties giving special attention to the changes in size over a decade.[2]

2. For contrast, just a bit over 1 percent of all the British hotels have more than 100 rooms. (Hotel and Catering Economic Development Committee, 1976.)

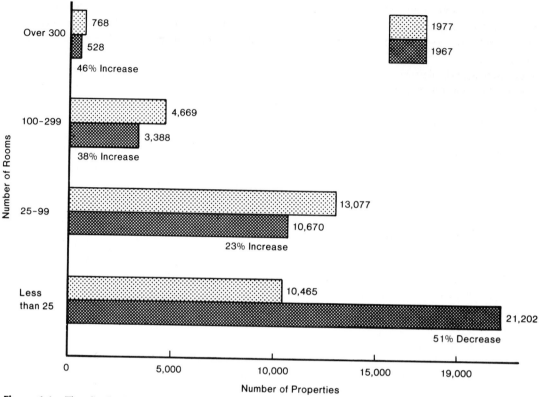

Figure 1.1. The distribution of U.S. hotels by size (as measured in rooms), contrasting a decade of change in which the mom-and-pops have declined dramatically. *Source: Census of Hotels, Motels, and Motor Hotels. U.S. Department of Commerce, 1971 and 1981.*

Motels

Attempts to distinguish hotels, motels, and motor inns (motor hotels, motor lodges) by the size of the property have been abandoned long ago. Many motor hotels have in excess of 300 rooms and many hotels less than 25. Even the Census Bureau is wise enough to allow each property to assign its own classification rather than attempt a nationwide definition. Still, the subconscious distinction remains that motels are smaller than hotels. The annual motor hotel census performed by Helmsley-

Spear, Inc., one of the nation's best-known real estate firms, supports the concept. It defines a motor lodge as a property containing at least fifty rooms, as well as several other characteristics.

At one time the now named American Hotel & Motel Association excluded motels and clung to the term American Hotel Association. One would think that the distinction, which generated a great deal of heated debate three decades ago, would be blurred and almost ignored by now. But it is more than an exercise in semantics. Palm Springs, California insists there is a difference between hotels and motels and has a law to prove it. Legally, none of the city's 200 resort properties are motels. City ordinances prohibit the use of the term in advertising and display signs. Hotel, lodge, and inn are the only terms acceptable to the city fathers.

An opposite viewpoint lies on the opposite side of the continent. The Canadian Provincial Conference on Tourism has developed three working definitions: a hotel is a commercial establishment in which the units (rooms) are accessible from the interior; motel units are accessible from the exterior; and motor hotels (or motor inns) have units which are accessible from both the interior and exterior.

Many years ago, the Florida tourism department offered a cash prize for a workable definition of hotel and motel. The money is still waiting. A more recent tempest was averted when American Telephone and Telegraph agreed with an AH&MA recommendation to list hotels, motels, and resorts separately in the yellow pages of the directory. The telephone company had planned to consolidate the three because a survey showed that nearly three-fourths of AT&T's customers looked under motels when in need of accommodations.

Mom-and-Pops

There are certain economics of size that account for the decline of the small hotel. It starts with financing and construction and involves every aspect of the operation from group solicitation to purchasing. Size determines the quality of management that the property can afford. A motel with less than 100 rooms cannot budget management talent at the same level as a competitor with 300 rooms or a chain controlling several 100-room properties in the same area.

How then does the mom-and-pop establishment (the small, family owned and oper-ated motel) continue to survive? It does, although less and less, in the same way that small grocery stores, tailor shops, and clothing outlets do. It offers individual attention and almost all of this attention is provided by the owners and their families. Guests deal directly with the owners and the owners with the guests. Guests receive the personal attention that is impossible with any other kind of organizational structure. Labor costs are almost nonexistent because the proprietor and the family baby-sit the establishment twenty-four hours per day, 365 days per year.

As the mom-and-pop motels become less able to compete for location and financing and less willing to serve the unremitting demands required of the operation, their numbers will continue to decline (figure 1.1).

Class

Assignment of class to motels and hotels is not as arbitrary as it might first appear. One hears customers, employees, and the general public refer to certain properties as high-class or low-class establishments. Most often this is a subjective evaluation based on a particular incident the individual has experienced.

Class is the level of elegance and service that a motel or hotel provides. Since elegance and service are reflected in the room price, the average rate per occupied room (room income ÷ number of rooms occupied) becomes the yardstick for the class of hotel. Large rooms, costly construction, and expensive furnishings mean larger finance costs, depreciation, taxes, power usage, etc., all of which is recovered by a higher room rate. If towels are elegantly large and thick, the higher costs of purchase and laundering (by weight) are recovered by a higher room rate. Similarly, a high level of maintenance, twenty-four-hour room service, sauna baths, and other extra services represent both a better class hotel and a higher

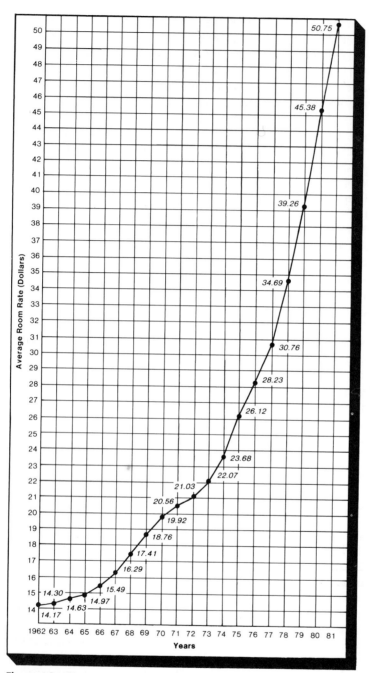

Figure 1.2. Twenty-year average room rate for
800 hotels and motels. *Courtesy: 1982 Trends,
Pannell Kerr Forster & Company.*

room rate. Even more than size, class determines the number of employees on the staff.

Average room rate has been increasing at a very noticeable pace (figure 1.2). But the increase is not solely a measure of increased service or elegance, rather it is a reflection of increased costs (particularly of labor and interest). Although increased efficiency and better planning have offset some of the increases, costs have been met in the main by increased room rates. In many instances, increased costs have also meant a decrease in services, in housekeeping, and in the general upkeep of the property. The danger of equating average room rate with the level of service (class) becomes evident when it is coupled with inflation. This is especially so when rating the same hotel or motel over a period of time. An average room rate $35 higher today than ten years ago does not necessarily mean a corresponding rise in class. However, at a given time and with a judicious concern for size and type of hotel or motel, the rate per occupied room, once called the average room rate, seems to be as fair a measure of class as is available.

Full-service (Luxury) or Limited-service (Economy)

Hotel/motel facilities are as diverse as the traveling public. Despite the composite profile that has been derived from analyses of travel data, there is no single picture of the traveler.[3] Handling the enormous range of guest needs has created a very heterogeneous industry,

from the plush, full-service high-rise to the squat, limited-service motel. It is this diversity that precludes a simple, universal definition of the hotel/motel business.

On the one hand is a group of operator-investors who maintain that guests need and want nothing more than a room with a good mattress and a clean bath. Guests get along nicely without swimming pools, pictures on the wall, closets, and even television sets according to this viewpoint. Therefore, the wise hotelier offers limited service and limited charge. There is such a market, of course, and the $25 to $30 room rate of the budget motel services it nicely.

One hundred and eighty degrees away is another market, the full-service hotel. Not only does this hotel include superior facilities, it also offers a full complement of employee services. Expense account executives patronize the full-service hotel while on business, although something less costly may be as satisfactory when traveling with the family.

In between the two extremes lies the bulk of the industry, adding services where competition and costs allow, paring them as market shifts and acceptable self-service equipment appear.

Part of that in-between market is the newest segment of the industry, the all-suite hotel. Many guests, especially commercial travelers (in contrast to conventioneers) have been attracted to this 1980s phenomenon. Names like Guest Quarters, Granada Royale Hometels, and Park Suites represent a new middle group. By locating on less costly real estate and reducing the amount of public space, these chains offer more guest room space (figure 1.3) at prices substantially less than the luxury properties. Reorganizing the room design allows all the rooms to be advertised as suites. That product seems to have meshed perfectly with guest demand. A Holiday Inns' survey, for example, pointed out the

3. One chain recently identified its typical guest as a forty-four-year-old male with a median income of $51,600. This typical guest travels by air, switches to an auto at the destination, and spends 4.9 room nights per month in hotels. Either he is self-employed, or he is a salesman or white-collar professional. One might presume that this definition fits most of the hotel industry's business travelers.

Figure 1.3. The all-suite hotel is both a new type and a new class of hotel that reflects the industry's move toward greater segmentation.
Courtesy: Guest Quarters, Washington, D.C.

increased use of guest rooms for entertainment and business during the past decade.

Budget motels are not immune from competition, and as a result they are being pulled both ways. To counter pressures from other budget properties and to attract market share away from the full-service facilities, budgets are offering services not usually associated with minimum rates. Among these services are toll-free reservation systems, in-room telephones, acceptance of credit cards, and payment by personal check. All of which are reminiscent of motel history. Introduced with price, convenience, and minimum service as their goals,

motels evolved into motor inns as guest expectations and competition forced motels to add the same type of services that budgets are now falling heir to.

Self-service hotels are at the other end of the budget continuum. Rooms are being sold without any services. Guests handle their own linen and towels, which they receive along with a key for their initial payment and deposit. There are no pass keys, which increases security, because hotel employees enter the rooms to clean only between guests. None of this quite meets the minimal facilities reported in Japan where capsule rooms (5 feet by 5 feet by 6.5 feet) for sleeping are stacked like tubes that look much like clothes washers turned on their sides. Common locker rooms round out the facilities. Capsule rooms are not unlike the railroad sleeping cars of a generation ago. Rooms are aligned along a corridor with sliding doors for privacy and ladders to reach the upper bunks.

Still the generalization remains that average room rate (the rate per occupied room) is the best measure of service and of the quality of accommodations.

Ratings

Although degrees of class have never been formalized in the United States, four categories are often used. First class is just that, the best category; fourth class is the flophouse of the Bowery bum. European hotels have a more generally accepted rating system than their American counterparts. Indeed, some three-fourths of the member nations of the World Tourism Organization (WTO) have adopted the five recommended classifications. Deluxe (or luxury) is first, followed by first class, which is only a medium-range property despite its name, and finally by tourist (economy or second) class. Third and fourth class are usually not for tourists. Most third and fourth class hotels have no private baths, no carpeting, and often no centralized heat. Europe's four-star hotels always have restaurants and bars; those with three stars may or may not; and two-star properties almost never do. *Garni* means that no restaurant is available, however a continental breakfast is informally served. In England, hotel garni is the American version of bed and breakfast.

Just recently, the French have expanded the five categories. Bottom up, there are still the one- and two-star categories. Two-star N (French for nouveau, new) has been inserted to represent hotels under renovation, on their move up to three stars. Four star L is now the epitome of luxe (luxury) at the top of the scale.

A new, five-category rating system has been developed by the Swiss Hotel Association to replace the single category, price, that had been used until recently to classify Swiss properties. It is probably the first time a private hotel organization has undertaken a self-classification, and it follows from several regional ventures among cooperating Swiss hotels.

The American Automobile Association (AAA) has also changed its rating system by replacing good, very good, excellent, and outstanding with a five-diamond rating plan. One diamond meets basic AAA standards; two diamonds means some categories have been exceeded; and so on up to five diamonds. Only four or five dozen properties in the entire United States and Canada earn that coveted five-diamond designation.

Mobil, another widely respected rating system, also uses a five degree rating, however their levels are designated by stars. Top rating goes to only about two dozen hotels, motels, and resorts each year, although some 20,000 are rated in the guides published by Rand McNally. Figure 1.4 identifies the criteria for earning Mobil's stars.

European auto associations add an extra to the ratings of standards and quality of service by classifying properties as private-owned or government-run. Government publications in Europe go an extra step too, rating facilities according to location: seaside/countryside; small town/large city.

Worldwide there are about eighty rating systems, from the self-evaluation plan of Switzerland's hoteliers to the mandatory grading and tax plan of South Africa's, where tax incentives encourage properties to upgrade their services. Sometimes, however, rating systems work in the opposite way. Deluxe Parisian hotels have threatened to close their dining rooms

The key criteria are: cleanliness, maintenance, quality of furnishings and physical appointments, service, and the degree of luxury offered. There will be some regional differences, as customers have different expectations for a historic inn in northern New England, a dude ranch in the Southwest, and a hotel in the center of a major city.

★

A one-star establishment listed in the Guide should be clean and comfortable and worth the prices charged when compared to other accommodations in the area. If they are below average in price, they may receive a checkmark for good value in addition to the one star. They offer a minimum of services. There may not be 24-hour front desk or phone service; there may be no restaurant; the furniture will not be luxurious. Housekeeping and maintenance should be good; service should be courteous; but luxury will not be part of the package.

★★

Two-star accommodations have a little more to· offer than one-star and will include some, but not necessarily all, of the following: better quality furniture, larger bedrooms, restaurant on the premises, color TV in all rooms, direct dial phones or 24-hour switchboard service, room service, swimming pool. Again, luxury will usually be lacking, but cleanliness and comfort are essential.

★★★

Three-star motels and hotels will almost always include all of the facilities and services mentioned in the preceding paragraph. If some are lacking, and the

place receives three stars, it means that some other amenities are truly outstanding. A three-star establishment should offer a very pleasant travel experience to every customer.

★★★★

Four-star and five-star hotels and motels make up a very small percentage (less than 2%) of the total number of places listed; therefore they all deserve the description of "outstanding." Bedrooms should be larger than average; furniture should be of high quality; all of the essential extra services should be offered; personnel should be well trained, courteous, and anxious to provide customers with everything they need and expect. Because the standards of quality are high, prices will often be higher than average, also. A stay in a four-star hotel or motel should be memorable. No place will be awarded four or five stars if there is a pattern of complaints from customers, regardless of the luxury offered.

★★★★★

The few five-star awards go to those places which go beyond comfort and service to deserve the description "one of the best in the country." A superior restaurant is required, although it may not be rated as highly as the hotel or motel. Twice-daily maid service is standard in these establishments. Lobbies will be places of beauty, often furnished in fine antiques. If there are grounds surrounding the building, they will be meticulously groomed and landscaped. Each guest will be made to feel that he or she is a Very Important Person to the employees.

Figure 1.4. Representative criteria for rating properties. *Courtesy: Mobil Travel Guide, Mobil Oil Corporation.*

on several occasions because that would allow them to pay taxes at the lower rates of the first-class hotels.

Yugoslavia has one of the world's few alphabetical systems, employing a five-letter classification. L, luxury, denotes a deluxe property using the international standards proposed by the International Union of Official Travel Organizations (IUOTO), now the WTO. Expectations rank downward from A, first-class hotel, to D, which promises no more than hot and cold water.

Another alphabetical system is employed jointly by the Irish Tourist Board, Bord Failte, and the Irish Hotel Federation. Here the sequence is A-star, A, B-star, B, C, and D — A-star is the deluxe designation. A separate classification is used for guesthouses; that distinction gives the whole rating system some extra validity.

Spain, too, has standardized its paradors (stopping places) despite their great range of physical facilities and furnishings. This government-operated chain of nearly 100 inns maintains approximately one-third at the four-star level. All but a few of the remaining group are in the second or three-star category.

Japanese ryokans are rated according to the excellence of guest rooms, kitchens, baths, and — of all things (to Western values) — gardens. These very traditional hotels usually serve two meals, which are often taken in the uncluttered guest rooms that open into the gardens. Nearly 100 ryokans are identified and ranked by the Japan Travel Bureau.

Even the People's Republic of China is considering a rating plan. However, the unique political structure of the United States makes a government rating system in the United States highly unlikely. The diversity of the American hotel industry makes a single, privately-operated system equally unlikely, but doesn't foreclose individual companies from making the effort. And, in a way, several have.

Representing the decision as part of a market-segmentation plan, Quality Inns, Ramada, and others have classified their properties. Trust Houses Forte, for example, has three categories: deluxe, first class (unique); inns (historical); and post houses (motor inns).

This method of broadening the market appeal — brand stretching — was introduced in 1981 and 1982. It permitted the middle-range hotels, which suffered most from the fall in occupancies, to stretch into the other segments of the industry, budget and quality, while holding onto their traditional market. So Ramada introduced Ramada Inns, Ramada Hotels, and the Renaissance Hotels; Quality Inns have Comfort Inns, Quality Inns, and Quality Royales. Whether this range clarifies or confuses the market place is yet to be seen.

Certainly, for the immediate future, price remains the best measure of class, especially in the broad markets and free economy of the United States.

Type

Tradition has typed hotels into three groups: commercial, resort, and residential. As with the hotel/motel question, distinctions have never been sharp and are becoming less so. Although different studies produce different percentage distributions, the commercial guest is by consensus the backbone of the industry. Tourism is changing this, so that statement may not be true by the close of the millennium. Indeed, the traditional designations used here are becoming less and less descriptive of a changing industry. They make no provision for the airport hotel, the miniprice or budget hotel, or the condominium. Neither do they provide for the newest concept of all, timesharing. For the time being, each new concept must be worked into the standard definition of commercial, resort, or residential hotel.

Figure 1.5. Commercial hotel serving transient guests. *Courtesy: The Hershey Hotel, Philadelphia, Pa.*

Commercial Hotels

The transient, or commercial, hotel (figure 1.5) caters to the transient guest — one who is on the move and one who is usually a commercial person. To a great degree the conventioneer, the company executive, the consultant, and the engineer have replaced the drummer and salesperson of a previous era. But not entirely; the commercial hotel, and the smaller motel as well, still relies heavily on this particular market.

A true commercial hotel is located close to its market — the business community — which means it is in an urban area. As the population center has left the downtown area, so has the commercial hotel. Arterial highways, airports, and even suburban shopping centers have become favorite locations. This helps explain the poor weekend occupancy (businesspersons are not working) of the urban hotel. Attempts to offset this weekend decline with tourists, conventions, and special promotions have been largely unsuccessful.

Once the transient hotel was all things to all people; now it has lost much of its function as the social-political center of the community. It remains the business center, catering to the various groups that have been enumerated, hosting trade shows, and serving as company training centers and meeting places.

Residential Hotels

In contrast to the commercial guest, the guest of the residential hotel takes up permanent residency. This creates a different type of legal relationship between the guest and the landlord and it is usually formalized with a lease.[4] Many residential hotels accommodate transient guests and even assign a percentage of rooms for that purpose. *Semiresidential* is the term used to describe this arrangement. Similarly, transient hotels have a number of permanent guests, some with and some without leases. The Towers of the Waldorf-Astoria are a good example of this. About 65 percent of all hotels reported both transient and permanent guests in the last census, accounting, however, for less than 5 percent of all guest room sales.

Apartment hotels are another type of residential hotel. They offer fewer hotel services than residential hotels, so they usually provide facilities for the guest to prepare meals. Many transient hotels that have outlived their com-

4. This legal distinction was further emphasized by the provisions of the 1971 Phase II price policy, which established separate controls for residential and transient accommodations.

mercial use have found new life in residential facilities for the aged, for welfare recipients, and as college dormitories.

Front desk facilities are very limited or nonexistent in residential hotels.

Resorts

Transient hotels have their commercial guests, residential hotels their permanent guests, and resort hotels their social guests. As resorts have lengthened their operating period from the traditional summer or winter season to a year-round operation, they have been forced to market to the group and convention delegate, often at the expense of their social guest. As this was happening, the commercial hotel shifted its design and markets toward the resort concept, dulling once again the distinctions between types.

Many feel the modified resort hotel (figure 1.6) is the hotel of the future. It is certainly in keeping with the nation's move toward increased recreation and leisure. It is compatible with the informality that characterizes the traveling, vacationing family. Unlike the early vacationist and the early resort, today's vacationist is a participant and today's resort a center of action. Skiing, riding, golfing, diving, boating, surfing, and a host of other activities are at the core of the successful resort. These features have given rise to many specialty resorts. None are quite like Britain's holiday camps, for which there really is no U.S. equivalent, despite our efforts to equate British holiday-makers to U.S. tourists.

Geographic location is to the resort hotel what commercial location is to the transient hotel and population location to the residential hotel.

Plan

Unlike the uncertainties and overlap that are apparent in hotel types, the plan under which a hotel operates is rather clear-cut. The "plan"

Figure 1.6. Resort hotel serving destination guests. *Courtesy: Saddlebrook, The Golf and Tennis Resort, Tampa, Fla.*

of the hotel is the basis for its room charge. Some hotels do offer more than one plan, but even then there is no confusion as to the meaning of each or to the identity and particular plan of the individual guest.

European Plan

Very few American hotels operate on anything but the European plan (EP), which came to North America with the French chefs who fled the French Revolution to New Orleans. In 1855, the Parker House introduced the plan to the Bostonian society and things were never the same again. Rates quoted under this plan apply to the room accommodations only. Extra charges at the prevailing menu prices are made for each meal taken. Evidence of the widespread use of the European plan is the lack of designation. Quoted rates always assume the European plan unless otherwise stated. The European plan is usually, but not always, offered as an alternative when guests object to other plans.

The European plan is less common in Europe than it is in the United States.

American Plan

Rates quoted under the American plan (AP) include room and all three meals: breakfast, luncheon, and dinner. At one time this uniquely American concept was offered by just about every resort hotel. In fact, further back in history, nearly every hotel in the United States had the American plan.

The resort industry held on to the American plan for a long time because resorts were isolated and guests were restricted to the general area. The automobile gave tourists more mobility and made other dining rooms more convenient, if not actually appealing. Guests found the American plan too restrictive (those who go elsewhere for meals must still pay the full AP charge) and the plan fell because of a lack of patronage. The American plan is limited today almost exclusively to the resort hotel and then only to those strong enough or isolated enough to insist on it.

Full pension or *en pension* is the European designation of our so-called American plan, except a continental breakfast, not a full breakfast, is served. Full pension is characteristic of the residential hotel of Europe as distinct from the transient hotel. Indeed, the residential hotel of Europe is sometimes called a pension, but guest house or boarding house is still the preferred term in Britain and the United States. Because pensions are usually long-term facilities, they are limited in services and the guest almost becomes a member of an extended family. *Inclusive terms* is another phrase used to designate this plan in Europe.

Modified American Plan

The modified American plan (MAP) is an attempt by the hotel to get the advantages of the American plan and still mollify the guest. Under this plan, guests get breakfast and dinner as part of the room rate quote, but not luncheon. This opens the middle of the day for a flexible schedule of activities. Guests need not return for an inconveniently scheduled luncheon nor suffer the cost of a missed meal. In turn, the hotel retains the obvious benefits of a captive market for the dinner hour. As with the American plan, the schedule of dining-room hours is the guests' major complaint. Vacation plans usually call for late breakfasts and unusual dining hours, and the hotel's schedule too often accommodates neither.

Half pension or *demi-pension* (DP) is the European equivalent of the modified American plan. It includes lodging and breakfast, and sometimes one other meal, which may or may not be specified. Granting either luncheon or dinner gives the guest still greater flexibility.

One major hotel recently announced another modification of the American plan. The rate includes so many dollars per day for food or beverage, which can be used in any dining room or cocktail lounge at any hour of the day. This hotel generates additional income with a minimum amount of restriction on its guests.

Some resort areas have experimented with still another modification, the dine-around plan. Guests are permitted to dine at any of several independent but cooperating hotels. This compounds the bookkeeping procedures and requires a great deal of communication between properties, but it takes advantage of what the guests are going to do anyway.

Continental Plan

On the European continent, breakfast is sometimes included with what the American calls the European plan. This continental breakfast, consisting of coffee or chocolate, roll, and a bit of cheese (cold meat or fish in Holland and Norway), is on the wane even in Europe. (A hearty English breakfast is served in Ireland and the United Kingdom. It usually includes cereal, eggs with a choice of meat, toast with butter and jam, and tea or coffee, but no juice. However, it is not always included in the room rate.)

Hence the Continental plan is the European plan plus an abbreviated breakfast of coffee, sweet rolls, and juice. In some parts of the world, this plan is known as *bed-breakfast* and, with the same line of reasoning, the modified American plan becomes *half-board.* Neither plan should be confused with the Bermuda plan, which is the European plan and a full breakfast. *Café complet,* a midmorning or afternoon coffee snack, is sometimes mistakenly called a continental breakfast. The distinction being neither the time of day nor the menu items, but the manner of payment. *Café complet* is not included within the room rate.

The appearance of late afternoon tea as a pleasant supplement to the overworked happy hour is certain to bring further confusion in terminology. Many top U.S. hotels have latched on to that quintessential British ritual, *afternoon tea.* Delicate sandwiches and a small sweet served with tea, or even sherry, comprise this light snack. It is not to be confused with *high tea,* which is a supper, a substantial meal almost always served with meat. High tea is a rarity today, even in British hotels.

The Continental plan experienced a brief surge when motor inns without restaurants began to feel the pressure from competitors with on-premise coffee shops. Guests prefer to stop where food is available. To counter the competition, guests were treated in the proprietor's own quarters to hot coffee and doughnuts, and the motel advertised ''Continental plan.'' Guests still prefer motels with coffee shops and few are built today without one — another reason for the development of larger operating units and the gradual disappearance of what was the United States' fling with the Continental plan. Automatic, in-room coffee makers hastened the decline. They relieved the owner of the burden and still provided the service after a fashion.

AP and MAP hotels employ a variation of the Continental plan. A continental breakfast is provided on a self-service basis after the dining room closes for breakfast. Late risers are accommodated, usually to their satisfaction, without pressure on the dining room or kitchen. A coffee urn with the continental fixings is left in the lobby or the dining room foyer when the crew goes off duty. A similar early morning set-up near the registration desk of a convention group or in the rear of a meeting room during a speaker's talk is usually listed on the convention program as continental breakfast.

Continental plans are occasionally offered by European-plan hotels as a means of promoting business.

Bed and Breakfast

B&B, bed and breakfast, has surged onto the American scene so strongly that the uninitiated might think it to be a whole new concept in hotelkeeping. It's hardly that. Bed and breakfast in the United States takes its cue from the British B&B, the Italian pensiones, and the German zimmer frei: lodging and breakfast offered by families in their own homes. Domestically, B&B is just a new version of the 1930 rooming house business. B&B was born from much the same reasons as its depression-era predecessor: the landlord's need to supplement income and the lodger's hunt for less costly accommodations. The acceptability of the B&B concept gets a boost from the experience of a generation of owner-renters sharing condominium and timeshare facilities.

Under the plan, guests take rooms with private families, who often furnish camaraderie and concern along with the mandatory breakfast. The lack of privacy — shared bath, conversation at breakfast — forces the host and guest into a level of intimacy that brings new friendship along with the business relationship.

National tourist agencies across Europe refer B&B establishments and in many cases even rate them by price and accommodations. Since the U.S. government has never entered the tourist business, several private rating and reservation systems have developed domestically. As with any new venture, the rating systems have come and gone quickly, lacking the staying power of government-backed systems ala Europe. Indeed, many of the B&B's themselves lack staying power. Advertising, even a sign in the window, may be ruinous because zoning laws may prohibit ''rooms for let.'' One positive sign is the yellow-page listing of referral organizations under B&B rather than under their previous categories of hotels, motels and tourist homes.

Boutiques, or urban hotels, are a different species altogether. They are not someone's home, not a B&B. They are very, very small inns, perhaps ten to thirty rooms, with all the room amenities of a fine inn but without the full services of a large hotel. The need to earn a return on investment pushes rates toward the level of more traditional hotels.

PATTERNS

Several new patterns have supplemented the old ones in recent years. Perhaps because they are still new, they are not usually included among the other four classifications: size, class, type, and plan. They are, nevertheless, important indices of change and harbingers of the new direction toward which the hotel/motel industry is apparently headed. Some of the patterns have more meaning for marketing, some for ownership and finance, some for operations and management, but all have significance for growth and profits.

Purposes

Guests come to a hotel for many reasons but actually for only two purposes. Either it is their destination or it offers them transient accom-modations. Although there are similarities, this transient-destination category is not the same as the commercial-resort grouping. A transient hotel is used as a passing-through facility for persons en route to somewhere else: tourists en route to a national shrine; business executives en route to a corporate meeting; families en route to weddings and reunions; or ball teams taking an extra overnight stop in anticipation of the big game. Rarely does the transient hotel hold the guest beyond one night.

In contrast, the destination hotel is the objective, the very purpose of the trip. It is the hotel that houses the convention or corporate meeting, it is the family's temporary residence while they seek housing in their new locality, and it is conveniently located near the large medical center for persons visiting sick friends and relatives. More and more, the destination hotel is part of the destination resort complex, which is so well typified by the Disney properties.

The role of any hotel changes from guest to guest. In this context, the transient hotel is obviously not the commercial property of our previous category nor is the destination hotel necessarily a resort. It would appear, moreover, that the destination guest of a commercial hotel would be more interested in the American plan than a transient guest at a resort.

Location helps fix the classification. Hotels of Atlantic City and Miami Beach are unquestionably destination points. Equally certain is the transient nature of many a motor inn. There, on the outskirts of town near the freeway, it awaits the traveler en route to the megalopolis still a day's ride away. Most hotels are not so clearly this or that, those of New York and San Francisco for example.

Condominiums and Timeshares

There is no categorizing of condominiums (condos) and timeshares because they cross over the traditional segmentation of the industry. They have blurred the lines between owner and manager and between manager and guest: guest, manager, and owner might all be the same person. Although often viewed by entrepreneurs as alternative financing, these new ownership patterns are possible only because the destination resorts are so attractive. Condos and timeshares require a long-term commitment from the guest to the destination. Guests buy into the future of the establishment in an attempt to build equity and profit, and simultaneously make a residential commitment to the destination.

The condominium concept had its birth in the same destination resorts (Florida, Hawaii, etc.) as timesharing, but it is older by two decades. Condominium units are purchased outright and owned by the guests as second homes. They are usually complete with bedrooms and kitchens. Owners place their units in a common rental pool and share the profits on a pro rata basis. The complex might be part of a large resort facility acting as a management company, or the condo owners might employ their own staff to operate and manage. There are endless permutations to the basic plan. In its simplest form, the guest owns the condominium, reserves so many days per year for personal use, and places the unit into the rental pool for the balance of the time. Changes in the income tax law altered the benefits of ownership and brought an end to the condominium spiral.

Timesharing is less costly to enter than condominium ownership. That's because one doesn't buy the real estate, but only the right to use the space so many days each year for a fixed period. Times range from ten years or so upward to forty years. The buyer gets a given date for each year. The more desirable the season, the higher the timeshare fee. In theory, the entrepreneur could sell each unit, which may be no more than a hotel guest room, for fifty-two weeks per year to fifty-two separate individuals.

Unlike the condo owner, the timeshare participant owns nothing when the interval of ownership is over. Even vacationing at the resort during the ownership period, which might require a five- or ten-year loan to finance, isn't without charge. The up-front payment merely assures the timesharer of access to the property. Occupancy carries additional costs, as much as half of a regular hotel room, but service is apt to be less than that of a standard hotel. Housekeeping may be curtailed, restaurant facilities nonexistent or restricted, and there may only be a few front desk employees about.

Timesharing has come under scrutiny by both the SEC and state consumer agencies. We can expect more standardized contracts, fuller disclosure, and probably reduced sales as a result.

Affiliations

The hotel chain is not new by modern reckoning, but it is a very young concept for an ancient industry. Both its appearance and its success find their cause in our modern, mass economy. The chain makes efficient use of labor and management; it thrives on the economics of mass production, broad financing, and wide advertising. And these are possible only when many properties are owned or managed by one company.

Rather than owning properties outright, some chains merely manage properties owned by others. This involves either a management fee or a lease arrangement. Under the fee arrangement, management is paid by the owning company, and profits or losses from the chain's management accrue to the owners. Usually, the chain name is used. Under the lease arrangement, which is far less common, the chain pays the owning company a rental for the property and keeps the profits or losses. Again, the chain name is used. Either plan might provide percentage payments as well as flat fees or rentals. Many companies operate under arrangements taken from both plans. Hilton is its own chain, for example, but has franchised the name to independent parties. At the same time, it is also a management company, earning a fee for managing hotels owned by others.

Referral

The growth of chains, with their interlocking reservation systems and single identity, placed independent operators at a competitive disadvantage. They joined with other independents to form referral groups. Referrals are cooperatives organized somewhat along the lines of cooperatives in other industries, except they are usually structured to provide one service only — marketing. Common reservation systems, standardized quality, joint advertising, and a recognizable logo were and still are the limited objectives of most referral groups. There is no interlocking management, no group buying, no common financing — nothing but a unified sales effort. But this effort has proved successful enough for some referrals to broaden their activities.

The referral is a means for the small entrepreneur to compete, and it has been especially popular with small motel and motor lodge owners. Cooperatives represent the consensus of the membership. Rapid decision making and aggressive positioning are difficult to achieve under committee management. Therefore, referrals have never reached the popularity and success of the franchises.

Franchising

Franchising has its roots in many of the same causes that brought the referrals together. But the franchise serves the absentee investor as much as the independent owner-operator. Franchising allows the small business to remain independent and yet gain many of the advantages of the chain, certainly more than just re-

ferrals. The individual adopts the franchisor's name and receives services in turn, including the preparatory steps of feasibility, site selection, financing, design, and planning. Indeed, almost all the advantages of the chain are available for the fee: mass purchasing, management consultation, wide advertising, central reservations, and systems design.

In fact, the franchise and the parent company are so alike that the guest cannot distinguish between them, which works to the advantage (or disadvantage) of both. Only the ownership-management structure is different. The chain does not own the franchise property, the franchisee does; the chain does not manage the property, the franchisee does. The success or failure of the franchisee is still determined by individual business acumen, except that now there is the support of the chain. For this support, the franchisee pays both an initial franchise fee and a continuing charge of so much per room per night plus certain other costs such as the purchase of the company sign.

Like the referral organization, both the franchisor and the franchisee pursue independent goals. Each can develop separately within terms of the franchise contract, although they appear as one company to the outside observer.

Seasons

Throwing the front door key away is the traditional ceremony for opening a new hotel. This act implies that the hotel remains open around the clock and throughout the year, as indeed most hotels do. It is not surprising, therefore, that few guests realize how seasonal the business of hotelkeeping is, even for the commercial hotel. If anything, the cyclical ups and downs of the commercial hotel are more pronounced today than ever before. The commercial hotel becomes more seasonal at the very time that the traditionally seasonal hotel, the resort, begins to overcome its cyclical limitations.

The Four-day Season

The cyclical trough strikes the commercial, transient hotel every seven days — a once-a-week season. As the five-day workweek became the norm of the business community, the weekend business of the commercial hotel declined, slowly at first, and more dramatically over time. Not only is the trend irreversible, but the pace is quickening. Already the ten-hour, four-day workweek is upon us and the eventual reduction to the eight-hour, four-day workweek is inevitable.

Hotel historians invariably trace the development of the early inn to the development of trade and commerce. This relationship is no less evident today and will again be demonstrated if national union officials achieve their program of a four-day workweek before the end of the century. The federal holiday law, which assigned long weekends (short workweeks) to five national holidays, set the pattern. It was certainly not the commercial-urban portion of the hotel-restaurant industry that pushed this legislation!

The continual decline in industry-wide occupancy during the past twenty years — although there was a turnabout from 1976 to 1980 — can be traced in part to the four-day season. This is mathematically true because commercial properties include the bulk of hotel rooms. Reduced occupancy reflects reduced weekend occupancy more than a general decline in room demand. Given the usual occupancy pattern of the downtown hotel/motor hotel (figure 1.7), it is practically impossible to exceed a 70 percent weekly occupancy. This is so even if we assume four days of 100 percent occupancy. And the approaching four-day workweek is certain to play havoc with the Thursday figures. Hotels that operate on

	%
Monday	100
Tuesday	100
Wednesday	90
Thursday	90
Friday	40
Saturday	20
Sunday	20
Total	460
Average per seven days	66%

Figure 1.7. Typical occupancy pattern of a downtown hotel with a weekend slump.

the four-day season may actually be worse off than those on the four-season year. At least the latter have a higher double occupancy.

Annual cycles compound the problem. Occupancy for commercial properties is low even in midweek during two periods of the year: Thanksgiving to New Year's Day and May through Labor Day.

The ultimate solution is unquestionably the most difficult to believe. Hotels in the urban area will operate on the same five-day week that their customers, their employees, and their purveyors do. They will close for the weekends and managers will no longer throw away the key.

The Resort Season

Resort cycles follow the seasons of the year, and this makes the cycle more recognizable. America's summer resorts were born in the spas and mountains of New England and matured with the railroads. Later came the winter resorts of Florida and the Southwest, which were born with the railroads and matured with the convention boom of the postwar years. Now the young, outdoor enthusiast is opening the summer resort to a year-round market just as the conventioneer did for the winter resort.

The occupancy pattern of the resort is just the opposite of the commercial pattern. Weekends are busy and midweek less so. These are the hotels that favored and benefited from the federal holiday law. May through Labor Day, the slack period of the commercial hotel is, of course, the resort season. At one time, resorts opened in June and closed Labor Day afternoon. Even then, the season really began July Fourth. This one hundred-day pattern made the hotel as dependent upon the weather as the farmer and often made the results as disastrous. Two weeks of rain or cold are devastating when the breakeven point is seventy-five to ninety days of near-full occupancy.

The dates of the winter season differ, but not the basic pattern. There are the same one hundred days between December 15 and March 15, the dates of the winter social season, as between the opening and closing of the summer resort. However, air conditioning and snow-making machines are lengthening the seasons of both.

Unlike commercial hotels, the resort has benefited from the work-leisure pattern of American business. First, it was the work pattern that extended the operating season with the convention market. Now it is the vacation-leisure pattern that holds new promise for the resort segment of the industry. Resorts straddle the whole range of leisure-recreation activities, from outdoor sports to indoor entertainment. A longer season is only the first step in the rebirth of the resort industry.

Mass Markets

It has taken a long time, but the travel and hotel industries have finally embarked on the kind of mass production and mass service that has brought increased efficiency and rising levels of production to the manufacturing industries. The delay was unavoidable for, as we men-

tioned earlier, the large hotel is of recent origin and only the large hotel is interested in and able to service large groups. Now that it is here, there is a new awareness of and a new concern for the mass movement of travelers.

The appeal of the mass market to the hotel coincides with similar developments in industries allied to the hotel business — airlines and travel packaging. A new entrepreneur has appeared on the travel scene, the travel wholesaler. Heretofore, the hotel — and the airline and travel agent as well — catered to and solicited the individual traveler; now the wholesaler has seen the advantages of mass movement. Rising economic wherewithal and broader travel horizons have made travel appealing to almost every level of American society, including the blue-collar worker.

Group business through mass marketing has meant many new customers. Customers have come despite the lack of individual service that many said would discourage them. Indeed, they have come because of it. With the group, they find safety and security as they move into areas and experiences that are alien to them. Inexperienced travelers find comfort among those they know or those with whom they have a common bond, while experienced travelers find irrefutable savings.

Mass packaging enables the customer to buy the services of the airlines, the ground transportation companies, the tour operators, the hotels, and the restaurants at a fraction of their separate, individual costs. But there is a loss of guest identity — there almost has to be — and even a reduced feeling of the hotel's responsibility when guests deal through third parties. Group customers accept the accommodations booked for them by the wholesale buyers. They make no demands upon the hotel's reservation system and have little call to use the front office. More and more, the front office deals with the group, and less and less with the individual guest.

QUERIES AND PROBLEMS

1. Identify the advantages and disadvantages to the personal career of a student who takes a job after graduation with a Holiday Inn franchise, and passes up an offer from Holiday Inns, Inc., the Memphis-based parent company.
2. Create a checklist of two dozen items that could be used by an evaluator inspecting guest rooms for a national rating system.
3. Through personal observation on the site and an examination of advertising media (telephone directory, billboards, etc.), classify one hotel/motel in your home area as to type, plan, class, pattern, and affiliation. Itemize any other sources that were used and explain the conclusions that were drawn.
4. Some 25,000 new hotel rooms were built annually during the 1970s. That number jumped 400 percent, to almost 100,000 rooms annually, through the first half of the 1980s. Occupancy fell to about 65 percent. What stance might an executive of a medium-sized chain adopt for the 1985–1995 decade? Respond in one or more areas of concern: operations, finance, control, marketing, location, construction, services, etc.

2

The Structure
of the
Front Office

The organizational structure of a hotel is determined in part by its objectives and in part by the classifications and patterns into which it falls. The 1,000-room chain hotel with heavy banquet and convention business is a far cry from the mom-and-pop highway motel. The seasonal resort that caters to a young, informal crowd needs a completely different structure than the New York City hotel whose towers house residential guests even as it solicits bus tours and senior high school classes. There is, nevertheless, a certain similarity of organization and a common denominator of front office procedure whether the hotel is AP (American plan) or EP (European plan), commercial or resort, first or second class. Size makes it possible to separate some of the jobs performed by the front office and creates some specialization among the larger work force. The change is one of degree more than of kind because there are certain functions that every front office must carry out.

THE HOTEL FRAMEWORK

The front office is only part of the whole organizational structure, which includes a great many supporting personnel. The more limited the services of the hotel, the larger the percentage of employees assigned to the desk. In other words, each hotel needs a basic front office staff. A full-service hotel, one with many employees in many different service segments, has a smaller percentage of its employees at the front office.

Each division of the hotel, or *department* as it is called, is responsible for a segment of the guest's stay, and any one of them can destroy the best efforts of all the others combined. It is the job of the hotel's manager to coordinate these departments and direct their joint efforts.

The General Manager

Management titles vary from hotel to hotel just as hotel organizations do. The chief executive

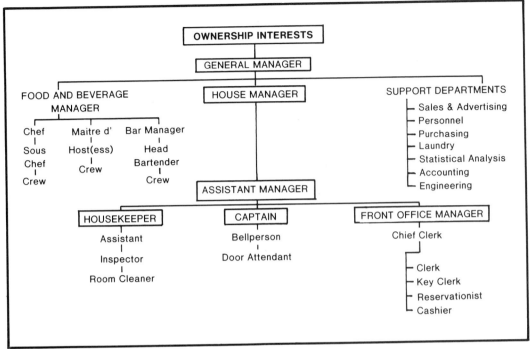

```
                        ┌──────────────────────┐
                        │ OWNERSHIP INTERESTS  │
                        └──────────────────────┘
                                  │
                        ┌──────────────────────┐
                        │   GENERAL MANAGER    │
                        └──────────────────────┘
                                  │
   ┌──────────────────────┬───────────────────┬────────────────────────────┐
   │                       │                   │
FOOD AND BEVERAGE    ┌───────────────┐   SUPPORT DEPARTMENTS
     MANAGER         │ HOUSE MANAGER │     └ Sales & Advertising
                     └───────────────┘     ┌ Personnel
 ┌───────┬──────────┬──────────┐           ┌ Purchasing
Chef   Maitre d'  Bar Manager              ┌ Laundry
 │        │           │                    ┌ Statistical Analysis
Sous   Host(ess)   Head                    ┌ Accounting
Chef      │        Bartender               └ Engineering
 │       Crew         │
Crew                 Crew
                           ┌───────────────────┐
                           │ ASSISTANT MANAGER │
                           └───────────────────┘
   ┌──────────────────────┬──────────────────────────┐
┌──────────────┐   ┌─────────────┐      ┌────────────────────────┐
│ HOUSEKEEPER  │   │   CAPTAIN   │      │  FRONT OFFICE MANAGER  │
└──────────────┘   └─────────────┘      └────────────────────────┘
   Assistant         Bellperson              Chief Clerk
      │                  │
   Inspector        Door Attendant           ┌ Clerk
      │                                       ┌ Key Clerk
  Room Cleaner                                ┌ Reservationist
                                              └ Cashier
```

Figure 2.1. Simple organizational chart locating the house manager (rooms manager) relative to the food and beverage manager and the support departments.

officer (CEO), the person responsible for all the departments (figures 2.1 and 2.2) and for the general profitability of the operation, uses one of several names. Better service and more individualized attention is expected when the manager is also the owner. The term *owner-manager,* or a variation of it, is used to communicate this situation.

A similar arrangement is possible with a corporate structure if the general manager holds a corporate office; hence the title vice-president and general manager. When the general manager merely sits on the corporate board of directors without holding a corporate position, the title could be director and general manager, or managing director. Man-

aging director has a European flavor (directeur is French for manager), so it may be employed for ambience as much as for organizational clarity.

Standing alone, the term *general manager* infers no ownership affiliation other than that of an employee of the company. When several properties are in one city or area, the general manager (GM) may be responsible for all and the term *manager* assigned to the chief executive of each of the units. Chain organizations use regional executives with titles like executive vice-president, eastern division. Whatever the title, the GM is the top executive of the hotel, reporting to ownership either directly or through operational or regional of-

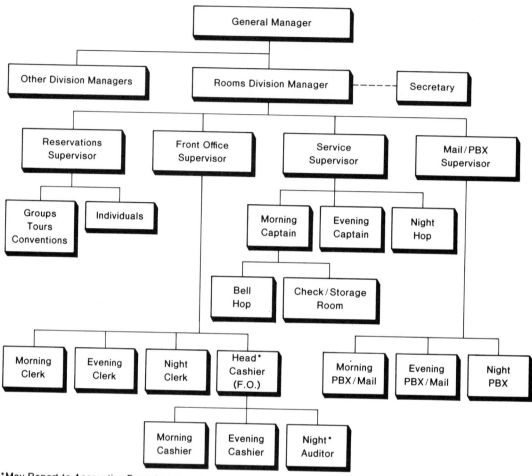

*May Report to Accounting Department

Figure 2.2. Typical organizational chart illustrating the rooms manager's span of control but without the housekeeping department. *Courtesy: Robert Bennett, Jr.*

ficers. Ownership vests its authority in the GM and, in turn, holds that person responsible for all that happens.

Large hotels support the general manager with an assistant who usually holds the title of *assistant to the manager,* or *executive assistant manager.* The term *assistant manager* is often reserved for the front desk and is normally not used in reference to the general manager's as-

sistant. Assistant managers in other departments usually carry that department's terminology, for example, assistant laundry manager.

Support Departments

Some departments of the hotel have no direct contact with the guest; their main function is to service those departments that do. As with so many facets of the hotel business, nothing is 100 percent this or 100 percent that. There are occasions when nonservice departments make guest contact, as when accounting corresponds with a guest about an overdue bill or engineering dispatches someone to repair a television set.

Sales, personnel, advertising and publicity, purchasing, and laundry are support departments in addition to accounting and engineering (figure 2.1). Sometimes a department's interests cross directly into the interests of other departments. Personnel and accounting's payroll responsibilities are obvious examples of this. These two functions touch every employee and thus bring these two departments into contact with every other department, service and nonservice alike.

Other functions are not quite as pervasive. The laundry, the engineering department (building manager), and the statistical department are less likely to be involved with every other department.

Food and Beverage Departments

Two major divisions are responsible for guest service. The front of the house will be examined shortly, and one portion of it, the front office, which is the thrust of this text, will be discussed in detail. Catering, or the back of the house, is the other service division. It encompasses all food and beverage functions.

This division is headed by a food and beverage manager (figure 2.1), sometimes called a catering manager, and divided into several subdivisions. Food preparation is one of these and is the responsibility of the chef. Food service falls under the jurisdiction of the maitre d'hotel. The bar manager heads another area of this division and the food and beverage purchasing agent still another.

Each of these department heads has one or more assistants, who are responsible for certain areas of operation. The chef has a *sous*

(under) chef and a steward. Subordinate to the maitre d' are hosts and hostesses, who supervise the dining rooms. Bars have head bartenders. So the organization grows, becoming larger and larger as lower organizational levels are added. At the bottom rung is the potwasher in the kitchen, the dining room attendant, the banquet porter, the kitchen runner, and the refuse handler.

The Hotel Manager

The hotel manager is the counterpart of the food and beverage manager. Here, too, there are department heads and assistant department heads. All operating departments, except those dealing with food and beverage, report to the front of the house manager. Resident manager, rooms manager, or house manager are the names most often used to designate this position. The jurisdiction may range from two or three departments in a medium-size hotel to six or seven in a large property.

Figure 2.2 outlines the divisions of the front of the house and positions the hotel manager in relation to the balance of the hotel organization. Departments that deal with the guest in either room assignment or final accommodations fall within the house manager's purview. The job is one of coordination. Presenting the services of several different departments as a one-company image requires a great deal of cooperation and harmony.

Housekeeping

Housekeeping is generally the largest hotel department. It is charged with the general cleanliness of guest rooms and public space. According to the type of organization, the housekeeper, who heads this department, may also supervise maintenance and repair and even the laundry. More and more, the housekeeper reports to the rooms manager, but there are still numerous instances where this manager reports to the GM directly.

Working with the housekeeper are assistant housekeepers, floor supervisors, inspectors, and, at the end of the line of command, room cleaners. Special attendants may be assigned to public washrooms, parlors, and bathhouses. Houseworkers are available to help with some of the heavier work and to move equipment.

Coordination between the front office and the housekeeper is essential. Hundreds of persons arrive at and depart from a large hotel daily. Rooms must be serviced quickly to placate waiting guests and information on the status of rooms must be furnished accurately and immediately to the room clerk, who uses the reports to make new room assignments.

This department handles lost and found, visits the sick, maintains linen storage and inventory, makes linen repairs, and issues uniforms to other departments. It handles all housekeeping assignments from dry-cleaning draperies, to disinfecting after animals, to the cleanup that follows a fire.

Service

The ranks of this once large department are on the wane. Where formerly it included baggage porters, transportation clerks, and elevator operators for both guest and service cars, it is now composed chiefly of bellpersons and door attendants, and even these are decreasing in number.

Several causes explain the decline. Changing travel habits and restrictive licensing by the Air Traffic Conference (ATC) have eliminated the service department's role in travel reservations and arrangements. Secondly, guests travel lighter today than they did a generation ago. Suitcases are built lighter, many have wheels, and shorter stays mean less clothing is carried by the guest. But labor costs have been

the major reason for the decline in the service department. Now a minimum wage is paid whereas tips alone constituted the salary of an earlier era. Fringe benefits increase the burden, which forces management to eliminate many jobs where output and productivity are difficult to measure. So the hotel that services the entrance door around the clock is rare; the motel without bell service is popular and becoming more so.

The service department makes first contact with the arriving guest through the attendant at the door. Parking, garaging, and auto service are offered at this time, although more and more urban hotels lease their garages on a concession basis. (Still another reason for a smaller department.) Handling baggage for arriving and departing guests, especially groups, is the major function of the service department. Laundry and valet service, ice, and transportation were once part of the department's duties, but they are less so today. Once roomed, few guests use bell service. Loudspeakers, telephones, and computer systems have even preempted the paging and message-service roles of the department. In small hotels, bellpersons handle room service and lobby cleaning along with their other duties.

Bell captains direct the service department, or "the uniformed services," as it is sometimes called. Large hotels title the department head superintendent of service and the bell captain then becomes the shift supervisor, subordinate to the superintendent.

Telephone

Mechanical telephone equipment has reduced the size of this department just as automatic elevator equipment has reduced the size of the service department. Outgoing local and long-distance calls are handled by automatic, direct-dial equipment. Calls between guest rooms or from guest rooms to departments such as room service no longer require an operator. Busy hotel boards once used as many as twelve or fourteen operators per shift (figure 16.7), but even the busiest board now gets along with four to six positions. Still, the number of telephones in a large hotel often exceeds the number found in small cities throughout the United States.

Supervising this department is the head operator or chief operator, sometimes called the telephone supervisor. Additional crew might include a message operator, a shift supervisor, and possibly a toll (long-distance) operator. Automatic equipment has reduced the billing and charge duties of this department as well as the mechanical duties that it once performed. In no other area of the hotel has the introduction of costly and complex computer equipment been so rapid and so complete.

The telephone department is responsible for message service, including morning wake-up calls and paging on the public address system.

Incoming calls must be handled correctly and pleasantly, for often the caller's sole contact with the hotel is the disembodied voice of the operator.

Other Departments

Security is another of the resident manager's responsibilities. It may be one person walking fire watch in a small hotel or a full-time police force, including plainclothes officers in large properties. As crimes against persons and property increase, larger and better-trained security forces appear. The security department is charged with the protection of the guest and the employee. It is responsible for the property of both the hotel and the guest. Casino hotels have additional security needs, but even here safety, including fire control and prevention, is the department's major responsibility.

Security helps the credit manager with lockouts and luggage liens. It also handles drunks and prostitutes, reports on accidents, and carries out investigations, including deaths and suicides, when necessary. Uniformed security serves first as a deterrent, then as a restraint, and only rarely as a police force.

Although the hotel manager is responsible for the swimming pool, that responsibility is guest service at the pool rather than sanitation problems, which are left to the engineer or housekeeper. Lifeguards and pool attendants, who furnish towels, rafts, and lounge chairs, make up the staff of this department, although there may be a pool manager in some of the larger operations.

The hotel manager handles day-to-day relationships between the hotel and its many tenants: stores, shops, offices, public stenographer, house physician, and airline ticket desks. Negotiating the lease contracts and rental arrangements by which these relationships are established is another of the hotel manager's responsibilities.

THE FRONT OFFICE FRAMEWORK

The front office must be defined as a bundle of duties and guest services rather than as a fixed area located behind the front desk. Some divisions of the front office, reservations for example, can be located elsewhere without affecting either their function or their membership within the front office. Large hotels have easily identifiable departments, which become less so as the hotel gets smaller and the various duties are taken over by a reduced number of employees.

Someone once said that the front office was so named because it was close to the front door. Simple enough, but many companies have taken up the term *guest service area*. By extension, the front office manager becomes

```
┌─────────────────────────────────────────────────────────────────────────────┐
│                              Job Title: Hotel Clerk                            │
│                             (DOT Number 242.268)                               │
│                                                                                │
│     The hotel is personified in its clerks. The clerks receive the guests, service them throughout their  │
│   stay, and handle their departures with efficiency and aplomb.               │
│                                                                                │
│        . . .  Acts as host(ess) and receptionist.                              │
│        . . .  Accepts reservations.                                            │
│        . . .  Quotes rates and sells rooms.                                    │
│        . . .  Keeps records of vacant and occupied rooms.                      │
│        . . .  Registers arrivals and assigns them rooms.                       │
│        . . .  Ascertains credit-worthiness of hotel guests.                    │
│        . . .  Controls and issues keys.                                        │
│        . . .  Coordinates activities of both the bell service department and the housekeeping department. │
│        . . .  Helps protect the guest's person, and the guest's and the hotel's property. │
│        . . .  Responds to guest inquiries and gives information and direction about the hotel and the locale. │
│        . . .  Dates, sorts, and files incoming mail, messages, packages, and telegrams. │
│        . . .  Receives and acts upon guest complaints.                         │
│        . . .  Maintains guest bills by posting charges and credits to individual guest accounts. │
│        . . .  Collects in cash or credit from departing guests.                │
│        . . .  Uses telephones, telewriters, pneumatic tubes, switchboards, video display terminals, and │
│               other computer equipment.                                        │
│                                                                                │
└─────────────────────────────────────────────────────────────────────────────┘
```

Figure 2.3. Job description for a hotel/motel clerk.

the guest service manager. Front office manager is still more common, however, although the title of assistant manager is also used. Small properties do without this management position and assign the duties to a chief room clerk.

Divisions of the Front Office
Room Clerks

Room sales and assignments are the chief duties of the room clerk, but coordinating the activities of the housekeeper, the uniformed services, and the other divisions of the front office is almost as important (figure 2.3). The room clerk is part salesperson, part psychologist, and part bookkeeper; it is difficult to say which of these roles is the major one. Recognizing this range of duties, Hyatt, and some other hotel chains also, have adopted the European term *receptionist.*

Receptionists initiate a great deal of the front office paperwork, all of which requires a high level of clerical accuracy. They adjust minor problems and buffer upper management from the first blasts of major complaints. As first-line employees, room clerks must carry out policy. Thus a management decision to increase room sales gives the clerks the responsibility of pushing the guest from a $56 reservation to a $60 room rate. Additional duties are assigned as a matter of course whenever the hotel is too small to staff the other front office positions.

More than any other individual, the room clerk is the hotel in the eyes of the guest. This same visibility subjects the clerk to an inordinate amount of criticism. On the one hand, desk personnel are the hotel's best public relations representatives and on the other hand, the source of much complaint. The supercilious attitude that is often ascribed to the desk clerk makes the reception an irritating, frustrating experience for the seasoned traveler and a frightening one for the inexperienced. Patient, gracious, and diplomatic desk clerks make friends for themselves as well as the hotel.

Mail, Keys, and Information

The division handling mail, keys, and information is usually the starting point for new employees and the route to a room clerk promotion. Keys are issued from this section of the desk and, obviously, collected there as well. Departing guests, cleaning personnel, uniformed services, and house security route keys to the desk. Arriving guests in the company of their bellpersons are issued keys from this area. Extra room keys are inventoried here (figure 16.8).

Circumstances have lessened the importance of this division and reduced the number of its employees. Management is happy to have the reduction and has, in fact, contributed to it. Guests are encouraged to keep their keys temporarily rather than return them to the desk each time they leave the property. Electronic locks with disposable keys have been widely adopted. Mail, including telegrams and telephone messages, has also changed in character. Few guests remain long enough to receive mail. Communications by telephone and airplane are so rapid and so relatively inexpensive that even businesspersons have little need for mail service. Conventioneers and exhibitors with booths have much of their material shipped through the convention sales office.

Two kinds of information are furnished from this desk. Callers might obtain the room numbers of registered guests, although few hotels will give out this information, and registered guests inquire about a variety of things: bus routes, theaters, general city-wide information, and directions.

Concierge

A new front office position, concierge (ko'-syerzh), has been introduced into some 100 hotels in the United States. The position of concierge has always been popular overseas, especially in France. (In Britain, where the front office is called the front hall, the job identification is head hall porter.) Like a French idiom, however, translating the nuances of the job into an Americanism leaves something to be desired.

The concierge was originally a door attendant and porter. Responsibilities included cleaning and security; thus, the concierge was the keeper of the keys. These are still part of the European concierge's job, particularly in the small hotels. Controlling the keys enables the concierge to watch the comings and goings of guests and to furnish, thereby, a bit of extra protection and information. This is not the domestic interpretation of the job, except when a hotel offers a concierge floor, or luxury floor. Several hotel chains, Hyatt especially, have created limited access floors with special, extra services. One of these services is a floor concierge.

More often, though, the concierge is located in the lobby for easy guest access (figure 2.4). The concierge provides all types of miscellaneous information and a variety of personal, but minor services. Information and service shape the basic description of the concierge's job. Travel information, messages, tickets and reservations to a broad range of events, baby-sitters, language translation, and notary and secretarial sources all fall within the purview of the concierge.

As hotels retrench some services and automate others, the post of concierge becomes increasingly important because guests can no longer turn to transportation desks, floor clerks, and elevator and telephone operators for questions and service. The computer, impersonal as it is, will probably be the concierge of the future for all but luxury-class

Figure 2.4. The concierge at the lobby location in the Westin Benson, Portland.   *Courtesy: Front Magazine, Westin Hotels.*

hotels. Electronic concierges in lobby kiosks are quite likely now that touch-sensitive CRTs (computer-input devices) are available. Guests who would never use a keyboard will be comfortable making one-touch inquiries. And hotels that could not afford a real live person will still have a concierge on board, after a fashion.

A professional organization, The International Union of Concierges, was founded in Paris in 1952 and brought to the United States in 1978. Members of both the European and American chapters wear with pride the Golden Keys (Clefs d'Or) that are their symbol of professionalism.

Room Reservations

Room reservations are received, processed, and confirmed by this division of the front office. They come in by letter, telephone, and telegram, directly across the front desk and, more and more, by means of central reservation systems maintained by the chains and other affiliate groups.

Keeping records of who is arriving, when, at what time, and for how long is the job of the reservationists under the supervision of the reservations manager. This information, along with the type of facilities wanted, must be communicated to the room clerk. Keeping track of the number of rooms sold and the number available for sale is the biggest headache of the reservation department. Groups and individual guests must be balanced to achieve a full house without overselling.

Reservations are maintained on a day-to-day basis for a year and in less detail for three to five years. Much of this information is now being computerized, as explained in the following three chapters.

Cashiers

Cashiers are actually members of the accounting staff. Their location in the front office and their relationship to many of the front office positions and functions place them in direct contact with the front office manager, who exercises a great deal of control over them on a day-to-day basis.

Billing, posting guest charges to accounts, and handling cash transactions are the major duties of this position. As the room clerk is the guest's first contact, the cashier is usually the last. The cashier's window is a frequent point of irritation due to lengthy delays and long lines, neither of which ever seems to attract sufficient management attention.

Several banking services are handled by this department. Checks are cashed, advances and loans are processed, safe-deposit boxes are provided, and cash is collected from both current guests and reservation deposits.

Other Positions

Other positions at the front desk depend on the size and organizational structure of the property. There are clerical positions such as computer operators, typists, and filing clerks.

Very large hotels with huge group and convention business may employ preregistration clerks who handle only group and VIP arrivals. Rack clerks have responsibility for the room rack, which is a record of room inventory, when the rack is too large to be located close to the room clerk.

Similarly, some hotels have attempted to separate the clerk's receptional duties by creating the post of receptionist. The receptionist, who is in a position between the desk and the concierge, greets guests from the front of the desk and deals with very minor problems and general reception while the clerk handles the registration procedure. Sometimes this position is part of the bell-captain's staff.

The assistant manager in charge of the shift is frequently seated in the center of the lobby in an attempt to make at least one executive readily available for guest contact (figure 2.6).

Design of the Front Office

Like so many other aspects of the front office, its design and location are also undergoing change. The bankteller look of the old-fashioned front office has given way to an open style that is less formal and more inviting (figure 2.5). New equipment, especially computerized reservation and billing systems, has reduced the amount of paper and much of the clutter that typified the usual front office.

New or old, the desk must still accommodate several needs. Hilton Hotels has earned a reputation for one of these: making economical use of costly lobby space. Heavy pedestrian traffic and the generally high-priced realty that hotels occupy make ground level shops and concessions an important income-producing division of the hotel. The more space taken for clerical use by the front office, the less available for rental. Good economics and better systems have joined to shrink the floor space of the front office.

Figure 2.5. The modern, inviting front office is open to the lobby, Holiday Inn, Monterey, Calif. *Courtesy: Jerome B. Temple and Lodging Magazine.*

Security is another important consideration in the design of the modern desk. The cashier must be secured (figure 2.6) and the desk must be positioned to monitor the sweep of the lobby and the traffic in the elevator bays. Security is enhanced by a design that provides front office personnel an unobstructed view of the lobby (figure 2.7).

Communications, particularly internal communications, must be the major consideration in the final design of the front office. Despite the many new marvels in communication, face-to-face interaction behind the desk remains the chief means of handling the front office's daily business. Most designs focus the room clerk as the hub of activity, the room rack location in figure 2.8.

From this location, the clerks coordinate the flow of business from reservations to cashiering. Group desks are the exception. Hotels with heavy group business often build

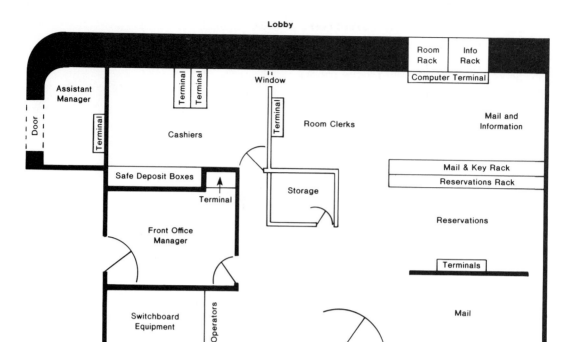

Figure 2.6. Typical front office design (not to scale).

Figure 2.7. An open front office, which enables desk personnel to watch the lobby and elevators, is a byproduct of property management systems (computers). *Courtesy: Wilcox International, Inc., Division of American Hotel Register Co.*

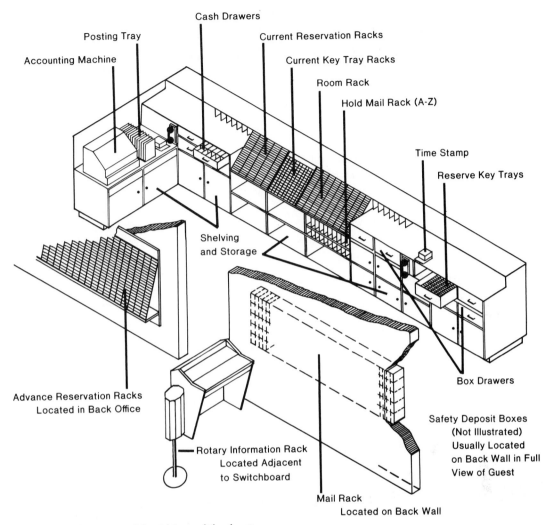

Accounting Machine
Posting Tray
Cash Drawers
Current Reservation Racks
Current Key Tray Racks
Room Rack
Hold Mail Rack (A-Z)
Time Stamp
Reserve Key Trays
Shelving and Storage
Box Drawers
Advance Reservation Racks Located in Back Office
Rotary Information Rack Located Adjacent to Switchboard
Mail Rack Located on Back Wall
Safety Deposit Boxes (Not Illustrated) Usually Located on Back Wall in Full View of Guest

Figure 2.8. Content and furnishings of the front office schematically presented. *Courtesy: Wilcox International, Inc., Division of American Hotel Register Co.*

separate reception desks where busloads of arrivals can be accommodated without interfering with the smooth flow of normal front office traffic. Indeed, agencies handling group business are demanding this of hotel companies.

Working Hours of the Front Office

Unlike the rest of the hotel, the front office never closes. Work schedules must provide for this continuous operation and for variations in volume by time of day and day of the week. Applicable wage-and-hour laws also need to be considered when bringing employees back for a return shift.

The Shift or Watch

Most desk employees work an eight-hour shift, five days per week with two successive days off. As yet, there is no sign of the ten-hour day and four-day week spreading to the hotel business. Eight hour watches provide three equal shifts per day. Although there are variations, the model is seen in figure 2.9. The day shift follows the pattern of most other businesses. Graveyard is the slowest watch, and the swing shift is the tie between the other two.

The night audit, which is a more specialized task than other front office duties, is completed during the graveyard shift. Thus, night auditors cannot take advantage of the general policy that allows senior employees to select their shifts. Few workers prefer graveyard, and this is one explanation for the general shortage of night auditors. Employees choose the day shift except when there is an expectation of tips. Clerks do get tips, especially at resorts. Tips give the swing shift first preference since it includes the hours of heaviest arrivals.

Although not a common arrangement, day and swing shifts are sometimes switched en masse. This is done at the start of each month

Day Shift	7:30 A.M. – 3:30 P.M.
Swing Shift	3:30 P.M. – 11:30 P.M.
Graveyard Shift	11:30 P.M. – 7:30 A.M.

Figure 2.9. Typical working hours of a hotel front office; schedules might vary by thirty minutes or so.

as employees' days off allow. It is unwise to make the switch on two successive work days because the swing shift would close at 11:30 P.M. and the same employees would report for work at 7:30 A.M. the following morning to assume the day shift. Not only is this procedure burdensome in a large city where employees need commuting time, but it may also be illegal under state labor laws. Rotating personnel and shifts whenever possible, and where union contracts allow, enables employees to know one another and it reduces the chance of collusion among employees who always work together.

Members of the uniformed service department are usually scheduled along with the front desk. Since tips are the major portion of service income, bellpersons prefer the swing shift when arrivals are heaviest. Although the day shifts have the morning checkouts, they are not as profitable as arrivals. People handle their own baggage when checking out, something that cannot usually be done when checking in.

Most front office positions follow the same work pattern. Mail handlers, cashiers, clerks, and even supervisors change shifts in concert. A fifteen-minute overlap offers a continuity that is lost with an abrupt change of shifts. If there are several persons in each job, individuals could leave in fifteen-minute intervals. If not, complementary jobs could be changed every quarter hour. Cashiers might change at 3 P.M. and billing clerks at 3:15 P.M.; room clerks might change at 3:15 P.M. and rack clerks at 3:30 P.M. A more deliberate overlapping of shifts is known as *forecast scheduling*.

Forecasting

Demand for labor at the front desk varies during the day and even within the same shift. Cashiers are busy in the morning handling checkouts and are less busy in the afternoon when the room clerks are busy with arrivals. Overlapping starting and stopping times provides a more economical use of labor. Employees need not start and stop at the same time merely because they work the same shift!

Proper scheduling begins with a forecast of business for the next week or two weeks or month, depending on the period of the work schedule. This information is a by-product of the reservation forecast discussed in chapter 4. Varied schedules allow each employee an occasional holiday or free weekend. Part-time personnel can cover unusually busy periods. The accounting staff might supplement the cashiers during the morning rush as part-time employees.

With forecasting and advance scheduling, employees are given their days off during the slowest part of the week. Several may be off on one day and none on a busy day. The pattern differs somewhat for different jobs at the desk. Cashiers at a commercial hotel are slower on Mondays, when clerks are busier, and busier on Thursdays, when clerks are slower. An employee can be hired as a cashier for some days and as a clerk for others. Buyers of computer hardware should be certain that registration terminals are interchangeable with cashier terminals if job assignments are to be scheduled in response to traffic patterns.

Split Shift

Even as late as post World War II, front office employees were being scheduled in two, twelve-hour shifts. Although this was more common in small or isolated hotels, larger hotels employed an equally unpopular schedule — the split shift. Split shifts are not exclusive

Employee A	7:00 A.M. – 12:30 P.M.
Employee B	12:30 P.M. – 6:30 P.M.
Employee A	6:30 P.M. – 11:00 P.M.
Night Auditor	11:00 P.M. – 7:00 A.M.

Figure 2.10. Typical split watch, resort hotel. Employees A and B would swap shifts weekly.

to the front desk, having been used in the kitchen, the dining room, and the housekeeping departments as well.

Unionization, wage-and-hour laws, and just plain physical distance have seen the decline of the split shift. Seasonal resorts still use it, or variations of it, where wage-and-hour laws exempt seasonal workers. Seasonal resorts have largely remained free of unionization because of the short employment period and the transient nature of the work force. Moreover, employees live on the resort property or nearby so that one of the major disadvantages to the employee — commuting time — is alleviated.

The split shift has a real advantage for the small resort hotel where only one person staffs the desk. Employees need not be relieved for meals but eat either before or after the shift. Figure 2.10 illustrates the long and short day commonly used at the resort desk. It is customary for employees A and B to switch shifts daily or weekly. Here again, the night auditor does not rotate watches.

To cover American plan meals, the dining room and kitchen work a variation of the split shift. Breakfast is scheduled from 7 A.M. to 10 A.M.; luncheon from 12 P.M. to 1:30 P.M.; and dinner from 6:30 P.M. to 9:30 P.M. Except for preparation and clean up, dining room employees work each meal (or sometimes just two meals) and are free between service.

Resorts that do turn-downs — replacing bathroom linen and preparing the bed for use — may require the housekeeper to return in the evening for still another variation of a split shift. In most other instances, turn-downs are handled by a second shift. It's a nice touch if the night attendant leaves all the messages that have come in that day with a piece of candy on the pillow.

THE FRAMEWORK OF GUEST SERVICE

Physicians treat *patients,* professional people have *clients,* and retailers service *customers.* The terms *buyer, patron,* and *purchaser* identify the customers of American business. Only in innkeeping is that customer a *guest.* Too often, of course, there is no relationship between the term and the fact. It is a cultural distinction more than a semantic accident that England and other European countries refer to the front office as the reception desk and the front office clerk as the receptionist. Reception is much wider in scope than the brief interchange between an arriving guest and the clerk behind the desk. It begins with the reservation communication and pervades all guest relations through the billing. True reception structures the front office for the service of the guest.

The Antiservice Syndrome

The hotel industry considers itself part of a vast hospitality industry loosely defined to include all types of lodging, food, beverage, and entertainment facilities. Within that definition, hotel leaders see their industry as a service industry, their product as hospitality, and their customers as guests. Because this position has been verbalized so often, hotel patrons are confused with the antihospitality-antiguest-antiservice syndrome that is part of many hotels.

Every hotel is not structured for the same degree of service as chapter 1 explained. Lumping all hotels together as members of the hospitality-service industry leads to the misconception that every property is equally charged with a high degree of service. This is not so, but neither does the converse hold true. Minimal service cannot be equated to antiservice; lack of personnel should not result in discourtesy. The economic inability to provide a product or physical service does not justify an antiguest attitude. Management's failure to distinguish minimal service, justified by minimal rates, from antiservice, shown by employee negativism, has led to the antiservice syndrome that many hotels demonstrate and many guests anticipate.

Meeting guest expectations is the foundation of guest services. The budget guest and the luxury guest have different expectations. The guests themselves know this and so does the host. Hoteliers can deliver at different levels of expectation and earn appreciation and loyalty from their guests, so long as basic courtesy and cleanliness are integral products. Quality, according to one hotel executive, is the guest's perception of the gap between expectation and actual product. The concept applies equally well for one hotel or the entire industry.

Complaints

As the hotel's front line of vision, the desk is also the first place guests register their complaints. Too often the response is weak and unsatisfying. Inadequate preparation — a failure to structure for the complaint — is the major reason for the desk's unsatisfactory reaction. Mistakes will be made and remedies will be sought, no matter how complete the training or how well managed the operation. Preparing for both the error and the complaint is structuring for a framework of guest service.

For most guests, making the complaint is as traumatic as receiving it is for management. So clerks must avoid the semantic solutions that attribute the problem to "standard orders" or "customary procedures." The old cliché about "company policy" satisfies no one. Honest admission of error takes the sting out of most complaints and apology administers the balm.

Because guests with complaints rarely voice them (they just don't come back again), there is an iceberg effect that helps managers beguile themselves. Each complaint should be investigated since it portends many that are left unsaid. Besides, a complaint that is ignored festers in the mind of the complainer while a properly handled complaint has the potential for making new friends.

Complaints should never be glossed over. For one thing, there is that hidden iceberg, and for another, the remedy is usually simple and easily administered. Arguments and positive statements of fact accomplish nothing but irritation. A simple situation is soon magnified into a major issue. Listen and avoid arguments. Save the clever retort for later. Tact, courtesy, and a quiet voice reduce the anger in the guest and open the way toward a satisfactory adjustment. The louder and more abusive the guest, the softer and more reconciliatory the clerk must become. The ability to satisfy a complaint, especially one that has no real solution after the fact, often rests with the attitude of the person receiving it.

The desk clerk, or even the supervisor, may not be able to resolve the complaint. The problem area might be out of the desk's jurisdiction, or the solution demanded by the guest might be outside the authority of the individual. Such complaints must be referred to a higher management level. By merely being present, higher levels of management indicate interest and concern, and this might be enough to mollify the situation.

Many front offices maintain log books in which complaints are recorded and immediate remedies noted. The guest's name and address are entered along with the circum-

stances. Showing the guest that there is sufficient concern to record the matter is often all that is needed. In addition, the assistant manager reviews the form daily. Management takes remedial action and writes the guest as to the solution or disposition of the case.

Mail and Telephone

Hotels have seen a decline in the volume of incoming guest mail during recent years. Understandable cuts in the mail department's labor force have been accompanied by a less understandable lack of concern about mail. Less mail has been interpreted as less important mail. On the contrary, the reduced use of mail has made each piece more important since the user finds mail the best agency for that particular item. Nowhere is the antiservice syndrome more apparent than in the hotel's indifference toward business mail that has not arrived, convention materials that are "lost enroute," and exhibitor's merchandise that is locked up for the weekend on some freight dock or shipping van.

Delayed mail represents real financial costs as often as not. Business deals cannot be consummated, convention programs cannot be delivered, and exhibitors' booths are less effective without the missing mail or freight. Invariably, the mail clerk refers the repeated inquiries to the receiving clerk, who is hidden in the bowels of the hotel, while the convention coordinator, who may well have the material in a corner of the office, shrugs and curses the shipper.

Telephone messages and morning wakeup calls are other sources of irritation, but they are becoming less so. Solutions are materializing in the form of telephone message lamps, in-room alarm clock systems, and hotel-wide paging devices. The installation of automatic, direct-dial telephone equipment has caused additional complaints in some cases. This equipment reduces the number of telephone operators as well as the amount of calls coming through the switchboard. It does not reduce the number of morning calls to be made and this becomes a problem with fewer operators.

Who Knows Why?

Dozens and dozens of little irritations face a guest each day. Many of them pass unrecognized by the management and some are just unavoidable. Some irritations seem intentional, as if management were saying that it is easier to inconvenience the guest than it is to inconvenience the operation. These are especially annoying when they seem to be without reason.

> Who knows why bellpersons must escort new arrivals to their rooms while groups are permitted to room themselves?
> Who knows why guests without baggage are subjected to loud lobby conversations between bellpersons and clerks?
> Who knows why American plan dining hours are established with the hotel's needs in mind and not the vacationing guest's?
> Who knows why it is necessary to tip the housekeeper for extra hangers (that should be there) when the bellperson was just tipped?
> Who knows why rooms are sold as double or triple occupancy but only have one room key?
> Who knows why the dress code in hotel dining rooms is more rigid than the accepted social standards?
> Who knows why the pool closes during the hours that most guests are in the hotel and opens when most guests are away?
> Who knows why check-out hours are set around the housekeeper's schedule rather than the guest's?
> Who knows why guests are asked not to take towels to the pool although there are no towels there?

> Who knows why guests with advance reservations must furnish the same information at registration that they have already provided?
> Who knows why room cleaners tap on the door hours before they are ready to make up the room?
> Who knows why informational signs are curt and inhospitable when it is just as easy to say, "For more rapid service please allow our host to seat you," rather than, "Wait here for host."
> Who knows why guests cannot be seated while they register, or while they wait in line to register?

Who knows why? What about the anti-service syndrome, the poorest of all front office structures.

QUERIES AND PROBLEMS

1. With special attention to front office activities, prepare a list of duties carried out by one (or more) of the fictional staff in the book *Hotel* by Arthur Hailey (Garden City: Doubleday & Company, Inc., 1965. Also available through Bantam Books).
2. From interviews with the traveling public, and/or hotel personnel, construct a list of irritants that careless or indifferent management inflicts upon unsuspecting guests, "Who Knows Whys."
3. Sketch, but not to scale, the lobby and front office area of a nearby hotel/motel. Comment on the efficiency of the design regarding traffic flow, security, reception, communications, employee work area, and space utilization.

4. Using the typical occupancy pattern of an urban hotel (see figure 1.7), plot the biweekly work schedule for the desk of a 300-room hotel that has separate room clerk and cashier positions. The switchboard is not at the desk. Strive for efficient coverage with minimum payroll costs. All full-time employees receive two successive days off and work an eight-hour day, five days per week.

3

Room Reservations

The arrival of a request for room accommodations, a request that may precede the guest by weeks or even months, begins a process called room reservations. Reservation procedures are undergoing dramatic change as more and more guests request accommodations through third parties and less and less by direct contact with the hotel itself. This separation of the traveler from the destination hotel is one of the most significant changes to have touched the hotel business in the decade of the 1970s. There is a dichotomy for hotel-keepers. On the one hand, they are more marketing oriented than ever before, and on the other hand, they are less involved than ever before in the actual room sale, abdicating their role to a host of intermediaries.

Since rooms continue to be both a highly perishable commodity and the most profitable division of the hotel, room reservation systems continue to bear a heavy burden for the success of the operation. These systems contribute substantially to profits: directly by maximizing occupancy; indirectly through improved guest relations. However, *Operation Breakthrough,* a study by the American Hotel & Motel Association, reports that "reservation systems are often unreliable and inefficient." Optimum levels of occupancy are not achieved and bungled service as often results in loss of goodwill as in new friends.

The need for reservation reform sparked the development over the years of many automated reservation systems. Their appearance coinciding with the introduction of computers to the hospitality industry. Some have focused on space banks for an entire geographic area. Others are operated for one specific group: business travelers in luxury hotels for example. Still others are quasi-public agencies like tourist or convention bureaus.

Unfortunately, these systems have been developed independently, and only limited efforts have been made to integrate the reservation systems of allied industries such as airlines and ground transportation. This reflects, no doubt, the mistaken belief that hotel reservations are separate transactions and not part of an integrated process called travel.

Integrated reservation systems will ultimately emerge as the best and simplest means of communication between the guest and the hotelier. We are not at this point yet, and competing efforts to achieve the goal leave both the guest and the hotel a little bewildered at times.

Ultimately, however, all hotels, affiliated or not, will be computer linked. Through this system, guests will find vacancies in common carriers and in hotel space, using the facilities of computer centers. Retail companies, like Sears, Roebuck and Co., or airline subsidiaries (figure 3.4) may be the nucleus of this new service agency, or the catalysts might be the family television sets in tandem with home computers.

A slightly different concept, that of passing the reservation request through the central answering number directly to the property itself, has been proposed by some entrepreneurs. Whether this proves to be the magic formula or not, the industry is moving toward an integrated reservation system. Credit card companies with their banks of computer information and a capability of guaranteeing reservations may prove to be the ultimate structure.

The next stage will begin once the hotel industry is as computerized as the airline industry is today. Accelerating the hotel industry's move toward full automation are two major trends: increasing size of the individual hotel and, therefore, of the records to be handled; decreasing length of stay, resulting in more frequent room turnover (figure 3.1).

The ultimate stage will link hotel properties with other services within the travel/tourism field. It will be an integrated reservation system with airlines, car rental companies, travel insurance, foreign exchange, and travel

agencies on line with hotels and motels. Until electronic equipment is installed and these new systems are functional, hotels will rely upon the slower, less complete, and occasionally faulty procedures now in use.

THE RESERVATION REQUEST

As with so many techniques outlined in this text, reservation handling depends on the size, class, and nature of the individual property. Some hotels, nonaffiliated motor hotels especially, depend almost exclusively on transient walk-ins. Others — resorts, for example — sell a large portion of their rooms by reservation. Convention hotels have the special problem of balancing group reservations with commercial accounts. The greater the hotel's dependence on reservation business, the more systematized its procedures must be. The more frequently the house fills, the more refined the system must be. Differences notwithstanding, some elements are common to every system, including those electronically run.

To make a reservation, the needs of the guest must be communicated to the hotel. This is done in a variety of ways including letter, Teletype, telegram, and telephone. Sometimes the guest makes the request in person, sometimes through a travel agent, sometimes with an airline, or sometimes through a group. The inquiry may be addressed directly to the hotel or indirectly through referral organizations, chain reservation systems, or private reservation companies. The request may first be processed through a convention headquarters or by the city's housing and convention bureau (chapter 5). A third party (friend, relative, secretary, or business associate) may make the arrangements or they may originate in the executive offices of the hotel itself, as when the sales manager offers accommoda-

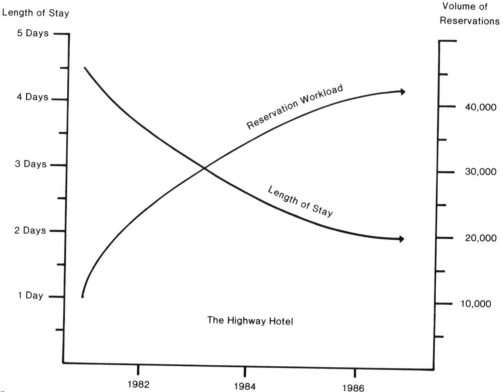

Length of Stay

5 Days

4 Days

3 Days

2 Days

1 Day

Reservation Workload

Length of Stay

The Highway Hotel

1982   1984   1986

Volume of
Reservations

40,000

30,000

20,000

10,000

Figure 3.1. The rush toward front office automation has its roots in increased reservation workload; reduced length of stay; desire to maintain service; the need to replace electromechanical equipment; and pressure on front office space.

tions to a potential buyer. Although not common, some hotels maintain sales offices in distant cities, shunting reservations from these offices to the hotel. Hotel "reps" (representatives) are more common as agents in other cities and, although individual reservations are not their primary mission, they do accept them for relay.

Accepting the Reservation

Before the 1960s, reservation requests came primarily by mail and telegram, and hotels generally responded by letter or wire. Written replies were not, and still are not, expected when the request arrives too close to the anticipated date of arrival. Today's reservations are made chiefly by telephone, so the reply is instantaneous, with written verification following by mail a few days later.

Central Reservation Offices (CRO)

More and more reservations, as much as 95 percent of all reservations made for the franchisees of one chain, are passing through the "res" (reservation) centers of America's heartland. From such midwestern points as Omaha (Western International), Kansas City (Trave-

Figure 3.2. A national reservation center, some of which employ upwards of 200 employees.
Photo by Nancy Conroy.

Lodge), and Oklahoma City (Howard Johnson's), to identify just a few, the hotel chains have tied their properties and customers together in an instantaneous system of in-WATS calls and computer memories (figure 3.2).

The Midwest, especially Omaha, Nebraska, developed into a res center because of the excess toll-terminal equipment in the area. The Bell System had unused capacity as a result of the massive defense grid built to accommodate the armed forces. With a promise of exceptionally good service and the support of the telephone system, hotel companies began opening reservation centers in the late 1960s. This created a specialized labor pool, making the area even more attractive. Al-

though there are no special rate advantages to these central locations, they are states of low population. Since in-WATS numbers within the state were different from in-WATS numbers for all the other states, only a small percentage of the national population required the special in-state advertising. This distinction is disappearing as Expanded 800, which allows both interstate and intrastate calls to route through the same numbers, goes into service.

Guests simply call the advertised toll-free number (with the 800 prefix), which most companies staff on a round-the-clock basis. And call they have! Marriott reported that it handles 250,000 calls a month, booking some 74,000 reservations, and employing a staff of almost 200 persons.[1] That's up from a decade earlier when the figures were 45,000 calls monthly, with 12,000 reservations and a staff of only 22. The annual figure has risen to about 3 million calls, resulting in nearly 1 million bookings. Figures of these magnitudes are reported by many of the res systems. It is possible to translate reservation numbers into dollar values by using the average room rate figures given in chapter 1 and an estimated length of stay as given in figure 3.1. Sheraton provides this figure, citing in a recent annual report a $450 million yearly sales volume from its res center.

Processing the Call

Reservation agents receive the incoming calls (figure 3.2) and process them at slightly over two minutes each. They are helped in this by Automatic Call Distributor Equipment, which automatically holds and relays calls in a rotating sequence. The res center and the host computer may actually be thousands of miles apart. Where it is economically feasible, the video display screen is tied directly to the computer by telephone lines; where telephone lines are too costly, a minicomputer handles the individual res center and the host computer polls the minicomputer several times daily.

The calling party identifies the city and hotel requested. This property is called up on the screen of the CRT (Cathode Ray Tube) or VDR (Video Display Terminal) (figure 3.3). Information about the hotel, the availability of rooms, the rates, and the types of facilities is at the agent's fingertips. If the guest's needs (including dates of stay, number in the party, and type of room) are available, the agent types in the data, including the caller's name and address, and confirms. A confirmation is printed out at once and mailed to the guest.

1. *Marriott World,* Vol. 3, No. 3, Fall, 1981, p. 7.

Figure 3.3. CRT (Cathode Ray Tube) or VDT (Video Display Terminal) for taking reservations. First, room availability is displayed; then the individual reservation is taken, see mask of figure 3.6. *Photo by Nancy Conroy.*

An immediate update of facilities is made as the computer subtracts the rooms just sold from the availability status.

Reservations are also being taken at the property site. Therefore, information from the individual hotels must be furnished to the computer that services the reservation center. Sometimes, the hotel computer and the reservation computer are interfaced; they speak to one another. In other systems, each property has direct access to the central computer through an in-house terminal and a periodic update is made. Telephones are used in still other systems, with the reservation manager of each hotel being responsible for updating the res center. A different in-WATS line is used for this internal communication. Reservation centers will generally be cut off from accepting bookings when room availability falls below five. Important city-wide dates, trade fairs for example, also preempt the center.

Early complaints about the system had focused on the agent's lack of knowledge about the individual property. Callers are interested in the facilities of the property and in its location: How close to the airport? The convention center? The business district? Most systems have now incorporated this information into the computer display. They are also having the reservation agents visit some of the properties so that in all likelihood someone in the res center has been to the hotel that the guest is asking about.

Specialists have developed as the systems have grown. Centers now have reservation personnel who deal only with travel agents, or only with wholesalers, or only with corporate accounts. Others specialize in group business or tour packages, much like the individual hotel's tour and travel desk in the sales office.

Many of the chains offer TDD (Telecommunication Device for the Deaf) by which the hearing impaired communicate on a teletypewriter.

The work of central reservations has been made more difficult by the numerous promotional rates and special packages being offered by the industry. Some are separate and some are in conjunction with airlines or other carriers. Foreign properties mean problems in exchange rates, and foreign language callers want translation capabilities. All this must be done as quickly as possible because the res centers are paying for the call and the line. There is a need to be quick and efficient without being abrupt or tactless.

The Link-ups
The pressure to improve the services of the reservation centers has brought about several important links in the integrated reservation system. Travel agents have been the initial focus. First, CROs assigned special operators to handle only travel agent calls. Then entire reservation centers were created for travel agents only. (Sheraton has a large one in Raleigh.) It is not a surprising move since travel agents may represent 50 percent to 90 percent of a chain's total bookings!

Hooking the hotel properties to the travel agents' offices through the airline computer is the phase presently under way. It is happening so quickly that the several stages have overlapped. Much of the speed is attributable to the airlines' expansion of their computer network. Room inventories are now accessed either by airline agents or by travel agents who have entry into the airline computer systems. Most of the systems have names (figure 3.4), and the skilled reservationist can tick off the acronyms with ease.

Several hotel chains have bypassed the airlines by putting their reservation terminals directly into the offices of the travel agencies. This is fine for large agencies. Smaller agents are serviced by a new middleman, a minireservation service. Acting as an intermediary, this minicenter has terminals for all hotel and carrier systems. For a fee, it acts as the communication hub for buyer and seller.

A very large portion of the nation's travel agents are mom-and-pop type operations. They are like the small hotel/motel. As long as they remain unautomated, the demand for the 800 toll-free number will remain high. Some hotel chains are creating separate 800 numbers for each division of the chain: deluxe, intermediate, and budget. This increases the segmentation mentioned in chapter 1.

Hilton, Marriott, and other chains have given the handicapped access to their computer systems. Using VuPhone Telecommunications and other systems, the hard of hearing and the speech-impaired can communicate electronically with the reservation systems.

No charge is made to the user for any of the services provided by the reservation cen-

Apollo	United Airline
ARINC	Central Communications for all Airlines
Datas II	Delta Airline
Hiltron	Hilton Hotels
Holidex II	Holiday Inns
INTELNET	International Telex
MARS	Marriott
NORTH	Compass Computer Services, Inc.
Pacer	USAir
PARS	Transworld Airline Co-host: Marriott
Prestel	European In-home TV Access
Reservatron III	Sheraton
Roomfinder	Ramada Inns
Sabre	American Airlines
SODA	Eastern Airlines
Starsystem	Best Western International
Sunburst	Quality Inns
Westron	Westin Hotels

Figure 3.4. Reservation system names. Reservation link-ups tie together airline and hotel res systems, causing distress over reservation bias (whose name or schedule appears first on the screen).

ter — neither to the agent nor to the individual caller. The system pays the costs. That is, the individual hotel is assessed pro rata to cover the costs of operating the center. The rate is usually skewed in favor of the large user. Although there is a per booking charge, the hotel also pays a flat per room and/or gross room sale fee. This becomes less costly if the basic charge is spread over many bookings. That is just the opposite of what will happen if airlines do more and more of the bookings. Not only will there be fewer reservations through the res systems, but the hotel will pay an additional fee to the airlines. Assume that the fee is $2. If 2.5 room nights are booked at an average room rate of, say, $80, the $2 fee represents a 1 percent surcharge $\left(\dfrac{2}{2.5 \times \$80}\right)$.

Hotels are actually paying almost $3 per booking placed by the res center.

The Hotel's Reservation Office

The res centers notwithstanding, the individual hotel, either the independent or the single property of the large chain, still takes a great many direct reservations. All inquiries, whether by WATS or mail or telephone or by guest or travel agent, are directed to the reservation department. They are processed here and eventually forwarded to the front desk for use by the clerk on the guest's day of arrival. Some of the larger reservation departments employ as many as one or two dozen persons. The size scales downward until the room clerk alone functions as the reservation department of a small hotel.

Larger operations, usually headed by a reservations manager, permit a degree of specialization. Telephone operators (answering incoming calls), Teletype operators, typists, and file clerks are all separate positions. Checks and money orders for advance deposits are handled by a deposits clerk and convention reservations are handled by still other employees. Reports and room status computations may be the responsibility of one group of employees and others may tend solely to tour groups. More often, several of these jobs are combined into one or two positions.

Regardless of the size of a hotel, detail is important and accuracy essential. Accuracy begins with information, giving rise to another reservation platitude: get as many facts as possible. Figure 3.5 is a representative form that is completed as the caller is telephoning or is abstracted from the correspondence. Letters arrive on all kinds and shapes of stationery and in all degrees of detail. This form, or one like it, organizes the data in a uniform presentation and condenses several pieces of communication into one brief form. Although the format of figure 3.5 is typical, efforts are underway by the HSMA and ASTA to create a standard reservation form to be used with the standard travel agency form. A standard-

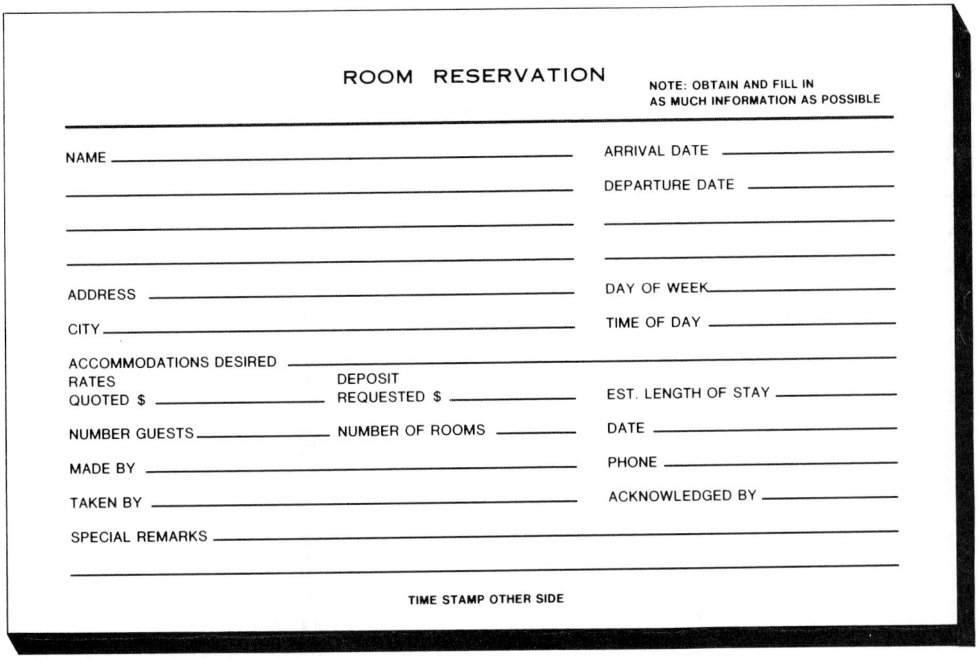

ROOM RESERVATION

NOTE: OBTAIN AND FILL IN
AS MUCH INFORMATION AS POSSIBLE

NAME _____

ARRIVAL DATE _____

DEPARTURE DATE _____

ADDRESS _____

DAY OF WEEK _____

CITY _____

TIME OF DAY _____

ACCOMMODATIONS DESIRED _____

RATES
QUOTED $ _____

DEPOSIT
REQUESTED $ _____

EST. LENGTH OF STAY _____

NUMBER GUESTS _____ NUMBER OF ROOMS _____

DATE _____

MADE BY _____

PHONE _____

TAKEN BY _____

ACKNOWLEDGED BY _____

SPECIAL REMARKS _____

TIME STAMP OTHER SIDE

Figure 3.5. Typical form for recording room reservations. Additional lines could provide for travel agency designation, credit card number, or other means of guaranteeing the reservation. Might be used as a backup even with a computer system.

ized form has been a long time in coming and will more likely materialize from the gradual adoption of electronic reservation systems than from negotiations among these organizations.[2]

The reservation form includes the minimum information needed by the hotel: name and address, arrival date, length of stay, number in the party, type of accommodations, rate, even means of transportation, and other special bits of information. Included among the latter would be a very late arrival hour, a spe-

2. ASTA unveiled a form in 1981 that the AH&MA rejected despite its input into the development. Objections focused on the legalities of antitrust arising from the cooperation of the two national organizations and on the use of the term "voucher," rather than "confirmation," to describe the form.

cial situation, or a particular type room — by the pool, lower floor, near the elevator, ocean front, on the same floor as the hospitality suite, or whatever.

Additional detail is added whenever further information is available. Company affiliation and anticipated method of payment are important to the credit department. Special rates (e.g., commercial rates) are noted on the reservation where applicable. Suites should indicate the number of bedrooms required and multi-room requests should indicate their proximity — same floor, adjoining, or connecting.

With the computer the procedure is essentially the same except there is no separate form. The form (called a mask) appears on the television screen when the operator signals a

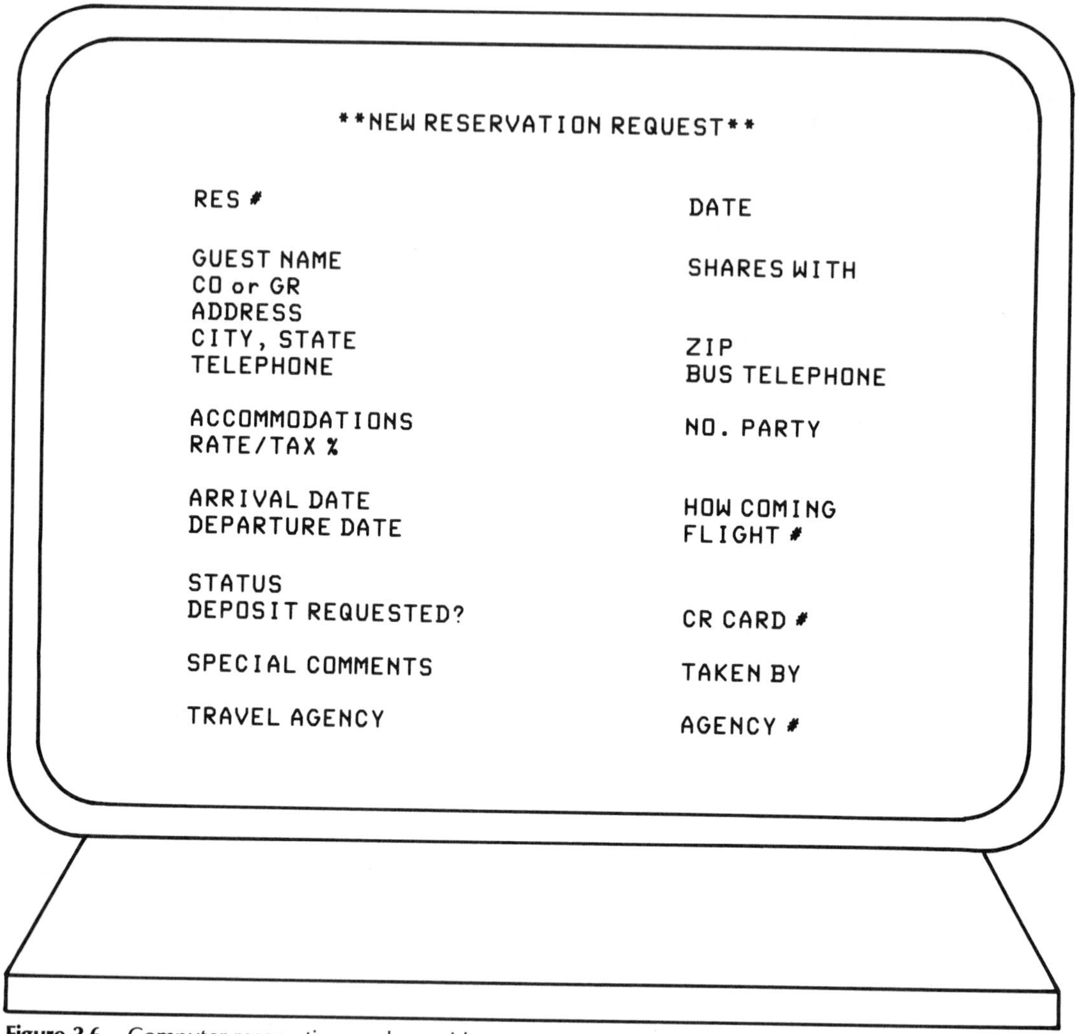

```
            **NEW RESERVATION REQUEST**

        RES #                        DATE

        GUEST NAME                   SHARES WITH
        CO or GR
        ADDRESS
        CITY, STATE                  ZIP
        TELEPHONE                    BUS TELEPHONE

        ACCOMMODATIONS               NO. PARTY
        RATE/TAX %

        ARRIVAL DATE                 HOW COMING
        DEPARTURE DATE               FLIGHT #

        STATUS
        DEPOSIT REQUESTED?           CR CARD #

        SPECIAL COMMENTS             TAKEN BY

        TRAVEL AGENCY                AGENCY #
```

Figure 3.6. Computer reservation mask provides a user-friendly format and assures complete detail for processing the reservation request. Res centers would also need to identify the individual hotel, not shown.

reservation input (figure 3.6). The same information, name of the party, dates of arrival, and so on, is now typed into the computer rather than being written on a form. Computers are programmed to request the information in a particular sequence, which the operator poses to the guest over the telephone. A small light, called a cursor, moves across the screen to direct the operator.

Mail reservations are entered in the same manner, but can be done at the most convenient time. As a backup for computer failure, some reservation offices record the request on a written form first, although it is obviously a duplication of work.

Reservations are nontransferable and are listed under the name of the arriving party even if someone else made them. Occasionally, the name of the party is unknown, as when a company books permanent reservations for its representatives. Reservations placed by a member of the hotel staff are flagged (specially designated to alert the clerk). The desk then prompts that executive so a proper courtesy call can be made as the party arrives.

Either verbally or by means of the reservation reply form, guests are told of advance deposit requirements and the cutoff hour. Reservations are cut off (taken down) at 6 P.M., plus or minus an hour or so depending upon the hotel and its traffic pattern, and released to walk-in traffic. They are held as late as 7 or 8 P.M. if the guest requests a late arrival. Reservations secured by advance deposits are held all night, but the deposit is forfeited if the guest is a *no-show*. When required, deposits (chapters 11 and 13) are expected to be on hand at least twenty-four hours before arrival. Refunds are allowed if the cancellation is received at least twelve hours in advance. All of these are, of course, matters of individual hotel policy. Another general rule is that guests who fail to specify their length of stay are booked for one night only.

Reservation or not, advance deposit or not, special request or not, hotels never promise a specific rate or room. A rate range is quoted with the requested price at the bottom of the range. A request for a $72 per night double is answered in the range of, say, from $72 to $78. If the hotel is unable to meet that range when the guest arrives, a higher priced room is assigned and the top figure of the quoted range is charged. Long stays and seasonal rates are exceptions. In many long-stay situations—resorts and residential hotels, for example—the assignment of a given room is most important and the hotel will meet its commitment. Similarly, long-term rates are negotiable and once decided, they too are met.

Denying the Reservation

Whether the reservation is accepted or not depends upon the occupancy forecast for the day or days in question. Even if only one day of the sequence is closed, the reservation is refused and an alternate arrangement is suggested. A tentative booking is made awaiting a final reply from the guest. This is also the procedure when the rate request cannot be met and a substantially higher range must be quoted. Telephone inquiries are obviously settled without delay. And that is when good sales tactics become important. Regrets are easily expressed. The challenge is to make the reservation when guests are rate resistant, when certain amenities (suites, waterbeds, etc.) are not available, or when closed dates are requested.

Requests for accommodations are sometimes denied even if the house is not full. The hotel's advertised package (a special, all-inclusive offering at a reduced price) is refused if the forecast shows that the house is likely to fill at standard rates. The inverse of this is also true. Reservationists must be taught to sell discounted packages or other reduced rates (weekend, commercial, governmental) only on request, or when encountering rate resistance.

With a full house, requests from travel agents, to whom the hotel pays a commission, are regretted. A low priority is assigned to requests from agents who are slow in paying. All reservations are refused if the particular agent has a low credit rating, regardless of the occupancy forecast. Busy hotels give preference to double occupancy requests over single occupancy.

Casino hotels give preferential treatment to those who are likely to gamble. Noncasino hotels do the same, allotting their scarce space to reservations from certain areas or markets that the hotel is trying to develop. Whatever the cause, guests are never told why there is no room. It is bad form, for example, to suggest that a group or convention has preempted all the hotel space.

Quick decisions are needed if the reservation clerks are to give meaningful replies to reservation requests. Computer systems automatically accumulate the mass of reservations and that information is available at once to the agent using the CRT terminal. Manual techniques are less facile. Room status in manual systems is communicated to the reservation clerks by chalkboards and monthly calendars visible around the room (figure 3.7). Based on information that will soon be discussed, the reservation manager flags busy days. The clerk can tell the daily room status by a glance at the calendar. Depending on the lead time of the particular property, room status is posted anywhere from six months to a year in advance. Closed dates are indicated by color, by a ring around the calendar date, or in any other convenient manner. Different colors are used for different conditions: one color may indicate that absolutely no rooms are available or to check with the supervisor

Figure 3.7. Reservation calendar, posted above the reservation rack, highlights special dates and rates for the res operators. *Courtesy: Radisson South, Minneapolis, Minn. Photo by Nancy Conroy.*

before committing. Closed-out rate or facility classifications — no queen-sized beds, for example — are also indicated.

Chalkboards supplement the calendars. Critical days, sometimes as much as a year or two in advance, are recorded there. These are important dates either for the hotel or for the entire city. Less often, off-days are listed in hopes that the staff can make a special selling effort there. Names and dates of convention groups are written on these chalkboards. Hotels reserve a given number of rooms for the convention and individual reservations are assigned against that block of rooms. It is possible, therefore, to accept conventioneers' requests while refusing rooms to outside persons.

A full house results in a rejection or, at best, an alternate date. Chain or group reservation systems provide alternate hotels as well. Non-affiliated hotels could make the same arrangement with other properties in the vicinity on an informal basis, but this is rarely done.

Reservationists accept or reject the requests for space according to the information on the calendar (figure 3.7) of a manual system, or in the computer (figure 3.3) of an electronic system. What goes into the systems is decided by the reservation manager using space availability forecasts, which is the topic of our next chapter.

QUERIES AND PROBLEMS

1. Develop a comprehensive list of questions to be asked in sequence by a reservationist responding to a guest who has telephoned for accommodations in one of the chain's hotels.

2. Many cities have several hotels of the same chain; some might be company owned, and some franchised. As sales manager of one of these sister hotels, what would you do to increase the number of referrals to your hotel from the central reservation office?

3. The communication/reservation separation of the traveler and the destination hotel is typified today by the travel agency. Look ahead a decade or so and identify the likely middlemen or communication linkups that will be in place at that time. Do you see a closer or more distant relationship between the hotel and its customer? Explain.

4. Computerized res systems can do more than just automate reservation procedures. Important information can be gathered for management review. Without concern for costs, list ten extras that could be incorporated in the system for management's benefit. For example, an inventory of bed selection would be helpful for future expansion plans.

4

Reservation Forecasting

SPACE AVAILABILITY FORECASTS

Somewhere within the reservation procedure a decision is made to accept or reject the reservation request. This may be as early in the sequence as the initial inquiry or as late as the minute before the registration. The decision, which is made by a front office executive, is based on everything from sophisticated electronic equipment to nothing more than a feeling derived from past experience.

Two methods with several variations are used to control reservations. Because of the greater number of variables, large hotels rely more on mathematics, an aggregate control method, than small hotels, which allocate reservations on a room-by-room basis.

Individual Assignments

Blocking individual rooms is the simplest of the several methods used to control reservations. The room rack is blocked with an appropriately colored flag at the time the reservation is received (plate 1, room 911). This could be weeks or even months in advance. In a small hotel, this is the sole record of the reservation other than the correspondence, which is filed alphabetically.

As the number of reservations grows, it is desirable to supplement the individual room block with a day's journal like that in figure 4.1. Without the journal it is difficult to keep track of all the reservations because the blocks are hidden behind the current room rack slips (plate 1). Even with the journal, however, reservations are not in perspective. Consequently, a guest who overstays may be forced to move when the room being occupied is on reservation. This is done at considerable inconvenience when the reservation could just as easily be moved to another vacant room before the incoming guest's arrival. This system does not provide the overall view necessary for reordering the reservations. It is difficult to see how to combine several reservations in sequence (figure 4.2) and thereby open another room for a single, longer period.

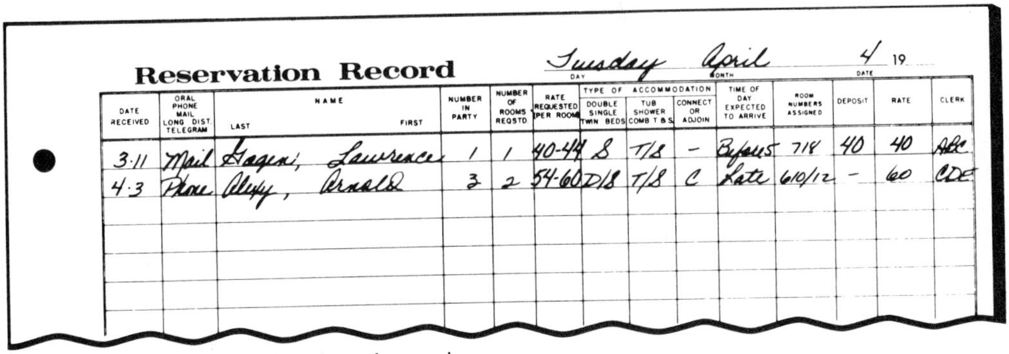

Figure 4.1. Room reservation sheet for use by the small hotel/motel. A separate sheet is used for each day's arrivals.

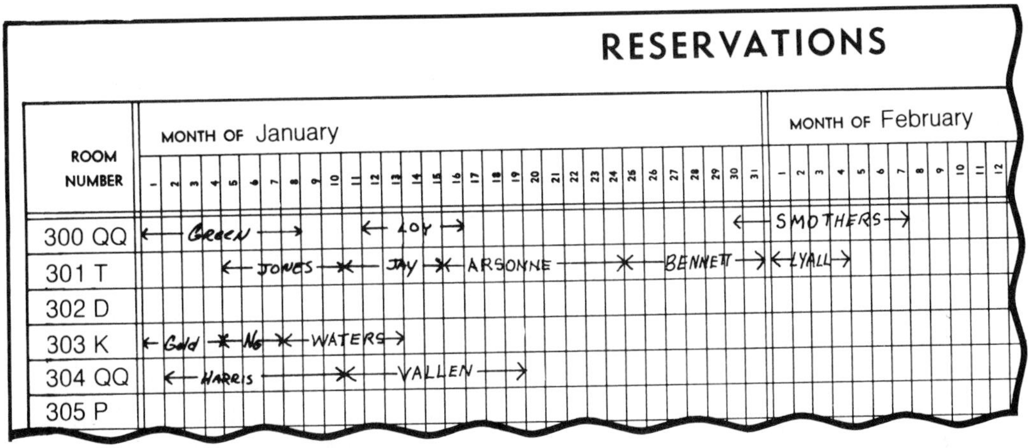

Figure 4.2. Reservation chart (or board) for the small or medium sized hotel with heavy reservations. Entire hotel is displayed for one to three months. Color identifies type of guest: deposit, tentative reservation, etc.

Yet simplicity offsets the disadvantages of this system and if reservations are few or the hotel is very small, it is a satisfactory procedure.

The Reservation Chart

Figure 4.2 shows a simple reservation chart. Rooms are listed vertically down the left side of the page and described by standard rack symbols (chapter 8). Listed horizontally are the days of the month with several months in se-

quence. Special dates are flagged in color. Each reservation is plotted on the chart as soon as it is confirmed and assignments are made immediately. The total picture is apparent at once and new requests can be honored by reference to the chart.

Continual updating of the chart is important for accuracy. Each extension or reduction of the original reservation must be recorded. Walk-ins are added to reflect both current and future occupancy. Colored pencils communicate the same kind of information as colored rack slips. Limited space and frequent changes, which involve erasures and revisions, lead to errors, so plastic covered charts have replaced the paper type and crayons have replaced the colored pencils. Not only is the wax more easily erased for changes but the charts can also be reused again and again.

Large, plastic covered wall charts serve nicely for hotels up to 100 rooms or so. Beyond that, the system is awkward, although track-mounted boards can be used for two or three hundred rooms. Colored masking tape substitutes for the pencils and colored rack slips. The tape is easily removed and relocated over the plastic. Where a portable reservation system offers special advantages, the whole idea can be adapted to loose-leaf form, provided the hotel is small enough.

Reservation charts best serve hotels where most bookings are made by advance reservations and where the stay is relatively long; that is, social resorts. Extending the chart for four months covers almost any resort season.

Forecasts by Totals

Unlike the chart system, mathematical forecasts do not assign reservations room by room. Control is maintained in totals and actual assignments are made on the day of arrival.

Density Charts (Boards or Graphs)

One system combines the format of the individual reservation with the aggregate forecast approach to produce a rather accurate control of room availability. Figures 4.3 and 4.4 illustrate this system. Figure 4.3 utilizes a density chart with the days of the month across the top and the kind and number of rooms vertically along the left side. Each room type is identified — single, twin, queen, etc. — and the number of each, but not the room number, is

listed. As a reservation is made, the appropriate room type is checked off. If the reservation is for several days, each room is checked off by a stroke under the appropriate date opposite the particular accommodation. For further information, the first day of the reservation is sometimes indicated with a stroke and subsequent days are indicated by a cross or other symbol. With the rooms listed in reverse sequence, it is a simple matter to determine the number available on any given day: for example, four twins available on November 1, two singles on November 5, etc.

Figure 4.4 offers another format for the basic concept. Here, unlike figure 4.3, information is gathered daily. Reservations for sequential days require the reservationist to flip pages, but the stroke and cross system described above can still be used. With a daily record, space can be set aside for the occasional, specific assignment that needs to be made, as shown on the bottom of the form in figure 4.4.

Density charts are also made in board form and look somewhat like a cribbage board with holes and pegs replacing the pencil and stroke. Reservations add a peg, cancellations remove one. It is easier than using pencil and eraser and a full column means a full house.

Another variation accumulates the reservations (by strokes) in groups of five in much the standard way of counting, ||||| |||||. All that is needed is a list of room types and the number in each category. A stroke is recorded for each reservation and the accommodations are closed when the total strokes equal the total rooms of that category.

Density charts may be used as a supplemental tool when another system of forecasting is in place. Then the chart controls convention bookings only, serving as a subsystem to the total forecast of all reservations. In none of these variants is the specific room assign-

NOVEMBER

Twins	1	2	3	4	5	6	. . . .	30
10	/	/	/	/	/			
9	/	/	/	/	/			
8	/	/	/	/	/			
7	/	/	/	/	/			
6	/	/		/	/			
5	/	/						
4		/						
3		/						
2								
1								

Doubles	1	2	3	4	5	6	. . . .	30
7	/	/	/	/	/			
6	/	/	/	/	/			
5		/	/		/			
4		/	/		/			
3		/			/			
2		/						
1								

Suites	1	2	3	4	5	6	. . . .	30
4	/	/		/				
3	/							
2	/							
1								

Singles	1	2	3	4	5	6	. . . .	30
5	/	/	/	/	/			
4	/	/		/	/			
3	/	/			/			
2	/	/						
1	/	/						

Figure 4.3. Room availability chart (or density chart) tracks reservations in the aggregate for the month, see figure 4.4.

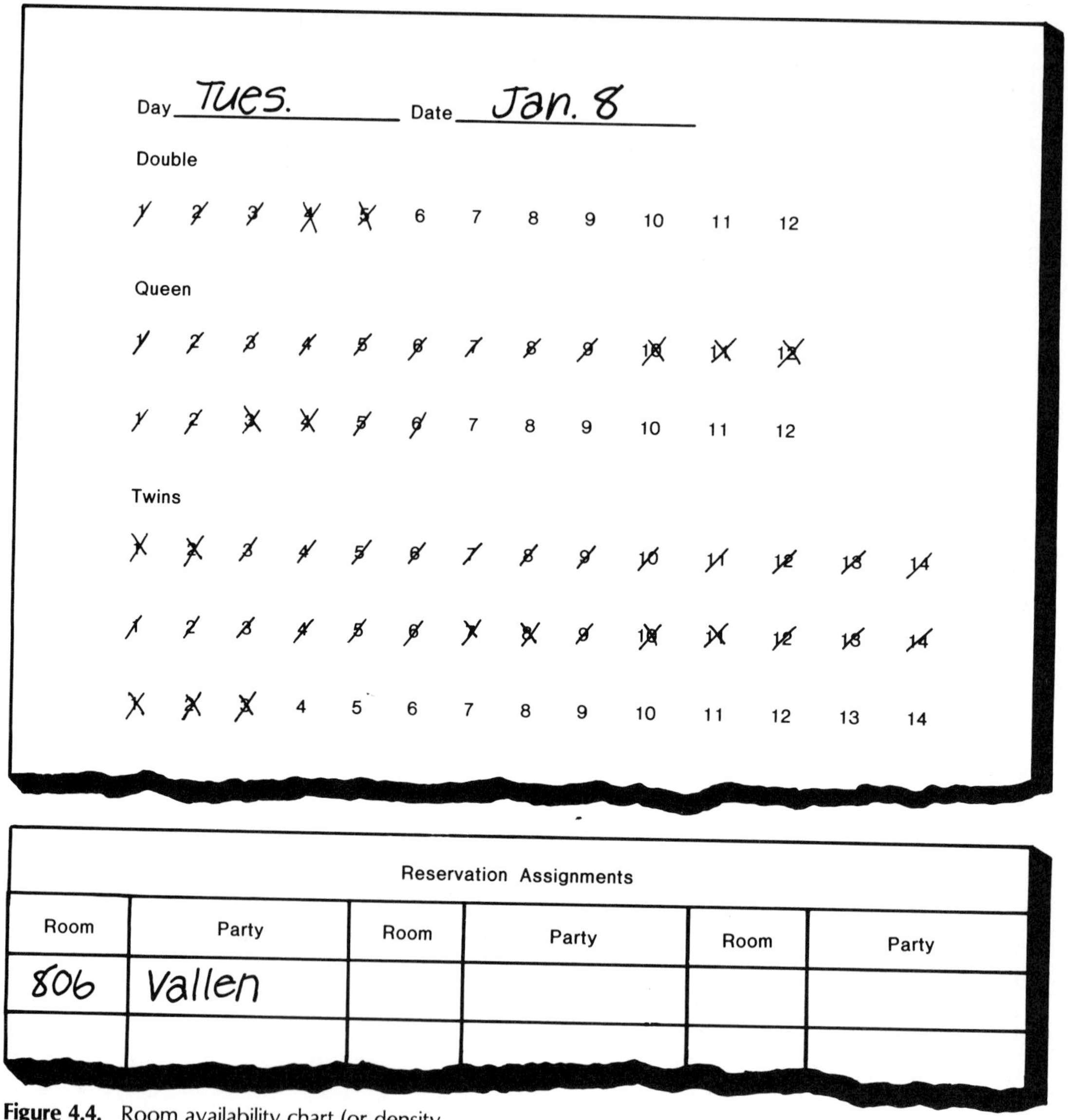

Day **_Tues._** Date **_Jan. 8_**

Double

~~1~~ ~~2~~ ~~3~~ ~~4~~ ~~5~~ 6 7 8 9 10 11 12

Queen

~~1~~ ~~2~~ ~~3~~ ~~4~~ ~~5~~ ~~6~~ ~~7~~ ~~8~~ ~~9~~ ~~10~~ ~~11~~ ~~12~~

~~1~~ ~~2~~ ~~3~~ ~~4~~ ~~5~~ ~~6~~ 7 8 9 10 11 12

Twins

~~1~~ ~~2~~ ~~3~~ ~~4~~ ~~5~~ ~~6~~ ~~7~~ ~~8~~ ~~9~~ ~~10~~ ~~11~~ ~~12~~ ~~13~~ ~~14~~

~~1~~ ~~2~~ ~~3~~ ~~4~~ ~~5~~ ~~6~~ ~~7~~ ~~8~~ ~~9~~ ~~10~~ ~~11~~ ~~12~~ ~~13~~ ~~14~~

~~1~~ ~~2~~ ~~3~~ 4 5 6 7 8 9 10 11 12 13 14

Reservation Assignments					
Room	Party	Room	Party	Room	Party
806	Vallen				

Figure 4.4. Room availability chart (or density chart) tracks reservations in the aggregate for each day, see figure 4.3.

```
● *** SCREEN # 26/ PRINTER # 5   7:17:14   6/16/
  BOOKINGS BY ROOM TYPE - 06/16/        SAT
●       AVAIL  O/M  % OCC  STAY  C/O   C/I  GRP  #GST
   AB     27    0   92.3   310    45    18    0   562
●  ST     20    0   96.2   430   100    78    0   851
   PAR -   1    0  104.5    22     0     1    0    36
   SUI     4    0   92.3    35     6    13    0    81
●  AMB     1    0    .0      0     0     0    0     0
   PRS     1    0    .0      0     1     0    0     0
   PNT     0    0  100.0     1     0     0    0     6
●  TOT    52    0   94.5   798   152   110    0  1536


●  *** SCREEN # 26  PRINTER # 5   7:17:21   6/16/
       DAILY BOOKINGS FOR PERIOD BEGINNING=06/16/

●  DATE     AVAIL  O/M  % OCC  STAY  C/O   C/I  GRP  #GST
   SAT 16     52    0   94.5   798   152   110    0  1536
●  SUN 17  -  31    0  103.2   386   525   605    0  1542
   MON 18  -  35    0  103.6   805   186   190    0  1535
●  TUE 19  -  43    0  104.4   880   115   123    0  1532
   WED 20    199    0   79.2   594   409   167    0  1220
   THU 21    337    0   64.8   417   344   206   39   984
●  FRI 22  -  21    0  102.1   368   255   613   70  1626
```

Figure 4.5. Computerized status report is an electronic variant of the manual density board. Upper half of the report provides availability, stayovers, group numbers, etc., by kinds of accommodations (AB and ST are sections of the hotel). The lower report displays the same information for the upcoming week. Note that the first line of the weekly report is today's totals. *Courtesy: Sahara Hotel, Las Vegas, Nev.*

ment made until the day of arrival. The reservation department keeps track of total numbers, not individual rooms or persons.

That is also true of a computer, which is actually a rapid density board. The total number of rooms is fed into the machine by types. As reservations are made, the machine subtracts the sale from the availability, but individual assignments are not recorded. When a given facility is requested, the computer reports the status. This status report (figure 4.5) is very similar to the density chart.

Some computer programs prepare a variation of the reservation chart. The property usage map (figure 4.6) combines several facets of the discussion. It is a reservation chart with some of the aspects of figure 4.2, and it is a room rack, permitting a visual inspection of the assignments and vacancies. The property usage map is also a density chart, computer activated, developed as a by-product — as many of the reports prepared by computers are — of reservation and assignment input.

Computing Room Availability

Density charts are abandoned once the property reaches several hundred rooms. Simple

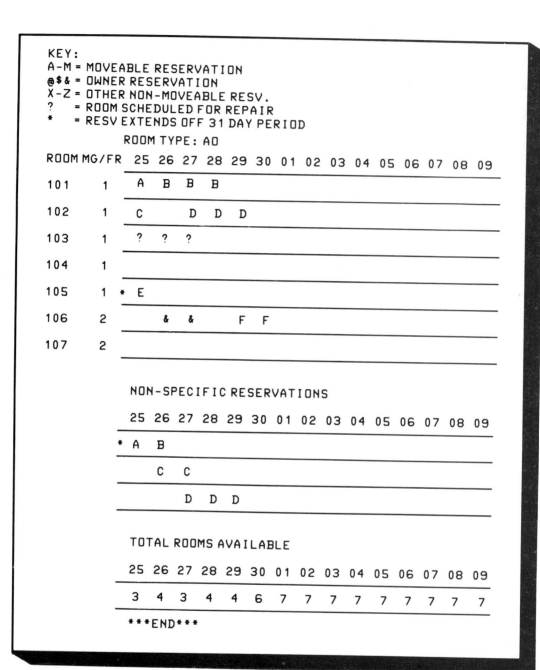

KEY:
A-M = MOVEABLE RESERVATION
@$& = OWNER RESERVATION
X-Z = OTHER NON-MOVEABLE RESV.
?   = ROOM SCHEDULED FOR REPAIR
*   = RESV EXTENDS OFF 31 DAY PERIOD

ROOM TYPE: AO

ROOM	MG/FR	25	26	27	28	29	30	01	02	03	04	05	06	07	08	09
101	1	A	B	B	B											
102	1	C		D	D	D										
103	1	?	?	?												
104	1															
105	1	* E														
106	2		&	&		F	F									
107	2															

NON-SPECIFIC RESERVATIONS

25	26	27	28	29	30	01	02	03	04	05	06	07	08	09
* A	B													
	C	C												
		D	D	D										

TOTAL ROOMS AVAILABLE

25	26	27	28	29	30	01	02	03	04	05	06	07	08	09
3	4	3	4	4	6	7	7	7	7	7	7	7	7	7

END

Figure 4.6. Computer-prepared property usage report: combines the characteristics of a room rack, a density chart, and a room status report. *Courtesy: Knox Data, Reseda, Calif.*

mathematics is used to determine room availability with hotels that large. The formula looks like this:

Rooms Occupied Last Night		1,121
Less Departures Today		− 444
Stayovers		677
Reservations Expected	498	
Plus Rooms Out of Order	+ 3	+ 501
Total Rooms Committed		1,178
Rooms Available for Sale		− 1,206
Space Available		28

Because the computation is a simple series of additions and subtractions, the mathematical steps are not always performed in the same order. By changing the language, the format, and the final figure to be derived, the illustration above can be made to appear as still another formula for projecting room availability. Above, the computation is directed toward the number of additional walk-ins the desk could accommodate today, which is twenty-eight. In the illustration that follows, the estimate of walk-ins is projected at twenty and the room count estimated thereby. This illustration, an actual procedure in some hotels, is confusing. The number of departures is computed, for example, but not used. And the final figure, estimated room count, is really meaningless without the number of rooms available for sale:

Rooms Occupied Last Night		1,121
Less Estimated Stayovers		− 677
Number of Departures Today		444
Reservations Expected	498	
Plus Estimated Walk-ins	+ 20	
Estimated Arrivals		518
Add Stayovers from Above		+ 677
Tonight's Estimated Room Count		1,195

Mathematics carries an aura of exactness that deceives any reservation department that relies on unadjusted figures. Most of the figures must be modified on the basis of experience. The reservation department collects data over the years and this information allows for more exquisite projections. But even the adjustments change from day to day depending on the day of the week and the week of the year. Percentages change with the weather, with the type of group registered in the house, and even with the news. Gathering the data is the first step and interpreting it is the second.

Each element in the formula can be altered enough to change the final figure, the estimate by which the desk accepts new reservations and walk-ins, by several times over. Rooms available for sale is discussed further in chapter 17. Rooms occupied the previous night is an exact figure except in those hotels where comp (complimentary) rooms are not listed as being occupied. Where policy excludes them from occupancy counts, comp rooms must be included in the "Rooms Occupied Last Night" figure to avoid an error in the projection. Similar errors pop up when the computer is programmed to count suites as two-room units even when the suite is not divided. The mistake comes in counting either two rooms as occupied or two rooms as checked out.

Very early arrivals, 5 A.M.–6 A.M., present a special problem. In all likelihood, they were omitted from the previous night's count, having been handled by the night auditor before the day shift arrived. Overlooking them as part of today's arrivals, even though for them it is almost tomorrow, causes an embarrassing error on busy days.

Overstays and Understays
Guests who were registered the previous night and remain the next night are called *stayovers.* Those who plan to leave − *departures* − are identified by the anticipated departure date that appears on each room rack slip (figure 9.1 and plate 1). The clerk gets the figure by going down the rack counting the departures. That's why reconfirming departure date at check-in

time is so important. This is a room count not a house (person) count! Departures are subtracted from the previous night's occupancy to determine the number of stayover rooms needed today.

Guests may not always leave on the departure day they had indicated upon arrival. Those who stay beyond this indicated date are *overstays.* Those who leave before this indicated date are *understays,* sometimes called *earlys.* Too many earlys and the house will not fill. The res center (and even neighboring competitors, who might send business) must be informed when a large number of unexpected departures create space in what had theretofore been a full house.

Each property collects data with which to project its understays and overstays. If the understay rate were estimated at 6 percent and the overstay rate at 2 percent, a net difference of eighteen rooms results from a recomputation of the first table:

Rooms Occupied Last Night		1,121
Less Adjusted Departures:		
Announced Departures	444	
Plus Understays @6%[1]	+ 27	
Total	471	
Less Overstays @2%	− 9	
Adjusted Departures		− 462
Adjusted Stayovers		659

Cancellations, No-shows, and Early Arrivals

Experience suggests the same type of uncertainty for arriving guests as for departing ones. Here again, situations as diverse as weather, labor strife, dishonest room clerks (who solicit tips to accept walk-in guests on sold-out days), and the nature of the group — physicians are notorious no-shows — affect the results by several percentage points. Assuming a 2 percent cancellation rate, no-shows at 5 percent, and early arrivals (reservations expected at a later date) at 0.5 percent, the answer fluctuates significantly:

Rooms Occupied Last Night			1,121
Less Adjusted Departures			− 462
Adjusted Stayovers			659
Plus Adjusted Reservations:			
Announced Reservations		498	
Plus Early Arrivals @0.5%[2]		+ 2	
Total		500	
Less Cancellations @2%	10		
No-Shows @5%	+25	−35	
Adjusted Reservations			+ 465
Total Rooms Committed			1,124
Rooms Available for Sale			−1,206
Space Available			82

With the same three rooms out of order, the hotel can now accept seventy-nine walk-ins, or fifty-one more guests than was originally estimated. The table could just as easily have projected a change in the opposite direction, with fifty rooms overbooked. Second-guessing the actions of the guest is the reservation department's burden. Projections are made from the data gathered for the property and forecasted on the basis of experience. At best, it is a composite of many previous days and may prove disastrous on any given day. A cautious projection with too few walk-ins accepted results in low occupancy and empty rooms despite guests who were turned away earlier in the day. An optimistic projection allows the desk to accept so many walk-ins that the reserved guest who arrives late in the day finds no rooms.

This then is the dilemma of overbooking: the need, on the one hand, to maximize occupancy and profits, and the pressure, on the

---

1. Although understays and overstays alter the day's actual departures, they may be computed as a variable of stayovers.

2. Although early arrivals alter the day's actual arrivals, they may be computed as a variable of the next day's reservations.

other hand, to keep empty rooms for guests who may never arrive. Hotels with heavy walk-ins, similar to the airline's standbys, are more flexible than isolated properties. Judicious overbooking, 5 to 15 percent depending on individual experience, is the hotel's major protection against no-shows, double reservations, and "guaranteed reservations." Judicious overbooking begins with a collection of data, made easier by a well-programmed computer, and a regular update of projections.

Data collection must be structured and accurate so the reservations office can rely on the figures. The computer can furnish the information if the data base for accumulating the report was planned for in the programming. Mechanical or electronic, attention to the relationships is the starting point. Cancellations, no-shows, etc., must be expressed relative to the reservation count, not to the hotel's room count.

It is a simple matter to create still another chart as a means for gathering the data (figure 4.7). Charts may be kept in chronological fashion, day after day and month after month. A more meaningful statistic is derived by charting similar days of the week (figure 4.7), so that the second Tuesday, say, in April appears on the second-Tuesday-in-April sheet, irrespective of the dates of those Tuesdays.

Dates do have importance, of course. The 4th of July holiday is a more important date than the day on which it falls. Similarly, the days before and after such a holiday must be identified with other before and after days of previous years. For the data to be useful in forecasting, it must be accurate. Therefore, thought and flexibility need be employed in developing a bank of data; it dare not be a mechanical process left to an untrained hand.

Periodic Recounts

Room forecasting starts with an annual budget and ends with an hourly report. In between are monthly, biweekly, weekly, three-day, and daily forecasts. Ten-day reports are sometimes used in place of the biweekly projections, but most reservation managers prefer to see two weekends included in a report.

Every department of the hotel uses the projections, but the longer the period between the preparation of the forecast and its use, the less reliable it is. Without periodic updating, the desk acts on information that is no longer accurate. Monthly projections are needed, nevertheless, to integrate the work of the sales department and the front desk. Group sales and room reservations are projected jointly to identify periods of weakness and overbooking and to bring a total management effort to the critical days. Sub-monthly forecasts are a tool for labor planning throughout the entire hotel with each department making sales and labor projections from the anticipated house count. Details are clarified and final planning is resolved by a week or ten days before arrival. The three-day forecast permits a final push for sales and a tightening of labor scheduling to maximize occupancy and net revenues.

By the time hourly projections are being made, responsibility has focused almost entirely on the front office. Overbooking problems, additional reservations, walk-ins, and stayovers are being resolved by the front office executives, including the reservations manager. Smaller properties may take the count throughout the day, 8 A.M., 11 A.M., 2 P.M. and 6 P.M., for example. Large hotels strike hourly totals from, say, 6 A.M. to about 7 P.M. Frequent totals are almost automatic when a computer is available (figure 4.8) and easy enough even with a manual system.

It is a simple matter for the desk or reservation department to keep a tally sheet (figure 4.9), marking a stroke for each walk-in accepted, cancellation received, stayover determined, and early checkout identified. Keeping the record by room rate ties it to a density chart. An additional tally is kept for *last-day*

MASTER MONTHLY RECORD SHEET
R1-12 F2320 REV. 3-63

Hotel _____ City _____ Month _____ Year _____

DATE	Rooms Alloted Arr	Rooms Alloted Out	No. Rooms Used	Name of Convention Group	Checkout Date	1st Count	2nd Count	Chk Date	Estimated Final 1st Count	2nd Count	Final Checkout Count	Computed Departure	Actual Departure	% Off + or −	Final Book Count	Actual Resv Count	Last Day Additions	Last Day Hotel No Show / %	Rooms Sold over Counter	Total Room Arrival	Vacant Rooms	Dishon'd Res.	Out of Order	House Count	% Occupancy	Dbl Occ	GTD
SUN. 31			1187	Jewelers of America	29	334	30		355	375	400 350	370	362	−.97	449	450	32	82 / 17.1	49	448	19	0	1	3133	97.7	51.39	6
MON.																											
TUE.																											
WED.																											
THUR.																											
FRI. 1					29	220	30		343	550	530 450	520	337	−5.19	360	361	50	111 / 27.1	33	332	886	0	388	1356	57.32	77.01	3
SAT. 2					30	130	1		225	300	320 300	330	337	−12.12	367	368	38	74 / 18.3	72	403	979	0	225	1563	59.95	86.44	5
SUN. 3					1	150	2		270	400	400 357	360	358	−0.56	154	155	19	65 / 37.6	14	122	647	0	793	1176	29.74	86.08	7
MON. 4					2	80	3		267	275	275 247	252	260	−13.17	440	441	45	112 / 23.1	48	421	595	0	684	1321	37.88	64.10	7
TUE. 5					3	150	4		184	200	200 218	225	217	−3.56	608	609	68	151 / 22.3	112	637	355	0	504	1835	51.15	51.15	18
WED. 6					4	83	5		194	325	375 218	375	392	+4.53	490	491	85	118 / 20.5	86	543	329	0	379	2022	56.76	49.23	12
THUR. 7					5	249	6		353	700	725 642	725	677	−7.09	397	398	60	102 / 22.3	40	395	588	0	402	1704	50.35	39.75	21
FRI. 8	800			Krenz Family Reunion 656	6	227	7		353	525	500 475	510	542	+6.24	921	922	56	118 / 23.6	118	972	336	0	224	2793	70.68	85.95	53
SAT. 9	700				7	170	8		195	300	300 220	290	297	+2.41	374	315	21	69 / 17.0	16	352	284	0	221	2454	72.70	92.58	3
SUN. 10	800				8	350	9		1170	1140	1170 1105	1160	1161	0	886	887	32	115 / 12.5	72	815	654	0	125	1802	52.24	43.93	18
MON. 11			599	Meeting World	9	80	10		160	270	250 200	240	225	−6.25	481	482	83	127 / 22.6	60	497	379	0	128	2226	71.57	40.38	12
TUE. 12					10	125	11		300	440	450 430	455	507	+11.43	360	361	67	97 / 22.7	66	396	501	0	135	1944	66.53	38.50	8
WED. 13					11	530	12		685	850	850 725	795	759	−4.53	366	367	84	99 / 22.0	52	403	846	0	187	1559	49.90	40.38	13
THUR. 14	900	100			12	260	13		365	530	520 440	500	499	−0.20	351	352	70	91 / 21.6	63	393	953	0	180	1458	44.61	55.14	7
FRI. 15					13	280	14		340	490	490 445	467	503	+7.71	433	434	49	94 / 19.5	129	517	997	0	190	1471	41.46	63.76	4
SAT. 16					14	140	15		270	325	310 310	333	341	+2.35	466	467	51	74 / 14.9	66	489	822	0	198	1802	48.42	76.84	11
SUN. 17					15	150	16		297	400	380 350	390	338	−0.51	800	801	38	106 / 12.7	41	773	407	0	202	2330	68.7	60.10	12
MON. 18	740			Veterinary Medicine	16	125	17		200	330	320 300	301	320	+6.31	525	526	84	117 / 19.2	41	533	243	0	154	2599	78.9	55.74	7
TUE. 19					17	120	18		240	380	350 350	400	445	+11.25	428	429	97	98 / 18.7	49	476	287	0	127	2660	80.28	36.68	11
WED. 20					18	390	19		500	700	700 650	700	800	+14.29	470	391	90	72 / 15.0	64	472	512	0	180	2164	64.99	57.66	2
THUR. 21					19	530	20		750	795	825 720	790	789	−0.13	360	361	85	95 / 21.4	72	422	869	0	195	1586	47.12	57.72	11
FRI. 22	900	900			20	230	21		250	510	500 503	546	551	+1.0	394	395	67	105 / 22.8	58	414	1001	0	200	1334	44.51	78.23	6
SAT. 23					21	130	22		242	300	320 310	334	329	−1.5	535	536	34	132 / 22.2	99	536	758	0	228	1951	51.25	80.86	22
SUN. 24					22	177	23		380	445	460 450	475	499	−3.37	809	810	23	105 / 24.7	60	797	507	0	152	2261	67.2	57.40	22
MON. 25				Clinical Chemists	23	104	24		170	270	270 247	250	263	+5.2	853	854	87	105 / 17.6	146	921	0	0	4	3003	98.11	44.52	17
TUE. 26			964		24	255	25		350	525	489 489	550	536	−2.55	529	530	51	125 / 21.2	27	484	49	0	3	2892	95.61	42.74	11
WED. 27	1225				25	266	26		475	650	700 576	625	680	+1.8	470	479	79	112 / 20.1	40	485	247	0	4	2666	86.49	45.05	12
THUR. 28			900		26	525	27		657	850	875 756	825	887	+7.52	552	553	74	157 / 21.9	26	515	620	0	2	2223	65.99	32.53	18
FRI. 29					27	614	28		687	850	850 664	725	733	+1.10	1095	1096	61	115 / 14.3	79	1010	246	0	33	2862	84.85	59.49	24
SAT. 30					28	202	29		377	400	400 355	384	382	−.95	578	579	42	142 / 22.9	91	569	91	0	9	3096	0.65	56.23	20
TOTAL	4525	3300	4146									15,218 / 15,442	−.98	16,229	16,260	1812										

Monthly Rooms Alloted 4525 % Pick-up 91.62 No. Rooms Used 4146
Monthly Statistics: Gross Rooms Income: $ 4,112,211 Number Trans Guests 65,182
Number of Occ. Trans. Rooms 41,798 Number of Occ. Trans. Rooms
Average % Off −.98 Total Res. 16,260 Total Rooms 15,957 Total Vacant 0.000
Average Room Rate $ 98.38 Net % Occ. 63.45 Average % Occ.
Total 33,218,206 989 10,662 / 15957
−.98 Unclaimed 208 Total / Total Vacant

Figure 4.7. Monthly master data sheet used to collect reservation data as the starting point for projections and decisions. *Courtesy: Hilton Hotels Corporation, Beverly Hills, Calif.*

```
  ***  SCREEN # 26 PRINTER #  5  7:16:19  6/16/
       HOUSE STATUS REPORT      07:16

  RMTYP   OFF   VAC   /   INS   OCC   C/O   C/I   AVL
  AB       0     8    /    0    347   37    18    27
  ST       1    10    /    0    517   86    81    15
  PAR      0     0    /    0     22    0     1    1-
  SUI      6     1    /    1     45    7    10    2-
  AMB      1     0    /    0      0    0     0     0
  PRS      0     0    /    0      1    1     0     1
  PNT      0     0    /    0      1    0     0     0

  TOTALS   8    19    /    1    933  131   110    40


  ***  SCREEN # 26 PRINTER #  5  7:16:25  6/16/
       EXPECTED DEPARTURE REPORT   07:16

  ROOM         COUNT
  TYPE

  AB            37
  ST            86
  PAR            0
  SUI            7
  AMB            0
  PRS            1
  PNT            0

  TOTALS       131


  ***  SCREEN # 26 PRINTER #  5  7:17:08  6/16/
       06-16-   EXPECTED ARRIVAL SUMMARY   07:17

  RM  TYPE  6PM*  7-12*  6PM  7-12  DAY  IN  TOTAL
       AB    11     5     2    0    0    0    18
       ST    38    36     7    0    0    5    86
       PAR    1     0     0    0    0    0     1
       SUI    0    10     0    0    0    0    10
       AMB    0     0     0    0    0    0     0
       PRS    0     0     0    0    0    0     0
       PNT    0     0     0    0    0    0     0

  TOTALS     50    51     9    0    0    5   115
```

Figure 4.8. The computer makes periodic reservation reports easy work, providing current room availability (top), expected departure (center) and arrival (bottom) summaries.
Courtesy: Sahara Hotel, Las Vegas, Nev.

adds—reservations that are received on the day of arrival (in some hotels, also the day prior to arrival). Tally sheets are necessary even with a batch computer since the reservation work is current only to that morning. Another reason to go on-line, because on-line systems accept the changes as they occur.

Room rack slips can be used to communicate the changes to whomever is computing the hourly count: arrivals are indicated by an extra copy of the room rack slip and departures by the old rack slip, which is otherwise destroyed. Care must be exercised to count the number of rooms, not persons, on each

	Rate Classifications				
	46–50	52–56	56–62	Suites	Totals
Walk-ins	////		//		6
Overstays	//	THL /			8
Understays			////		4
Arrivals	THL THL //	////		/	17
Departures			THL		5
Cancellations	//				2
Adds		////			4

Figure 4.9. Reservation tally sheet; pencil counterpart of figure 4.8.

slip. Reservation requests lend themselves to similar errors of count because more than one room may be requested on one slip.

Periodic or hourly forecasts improve the system in two ways. Obviously, the information is more current. Less obvious is the increased accuracy in percentage variations as the day wears on. Were it known, for example, that 80 percent of all the checkouts were usually gone by noon, a better guess of understays and overstays could be made at noon each day than at 7 A.M. Similar refinements are possible with cancellation percentages, no-show factors, and so on. In fact, it is possible to improve the accuracy of no-show forecasts by separating the total reservations into paid, guaranteed, and regular categories before applying a no-show percentage (figure 4.7).

Just as daily accuracy increases by making hourly updates, long-range forecasts also need updating. Each day's computation begins with the previous day's balance (figure 4.10). When that balance is only an estimate, the forecasts get less reliable day by day. Projections of all types become less certain. Users of forecasts, and these include the food, beverage, sales, and housekeeping departments, must be cognizant of the time limitations inherent in long-range forecasts.

Accuracy can be improved by attention to the character of the market. The type of group clues the reservation department to the no-show percentage. For example, teachers are very dependable. Tour groups are nearly always full because volume is as important to the tour operators as it is to the innkeeper. Market research may prove that bookings from certain localities are more or less reliable depending upon transportation, weather, distance, and the kind of guest the hotel is attracting. Commercial guests have a different degree of dependability than tourists, who differ again from conventioneers or referrals. A large permanent guest population needs to be recognized in any percentage computation involving stayovers and anticipated departures.

Rate Selectivity

Through a selective choice of room rates, the reservation department marries the markets of its guests to the availability of its rooms. Casino operations offer an extreme example of this illustration. Reservation requests from casino players, who in all likelihood will occupy free accommodations — where legal — are always accepted more readily than those from nonplayers, who would pay the full rate. Ca-

ROYAL HOTEL

Weekly Forecast for February 3 to February 9

	3	4	5	6	7	8	9
Rooms Available for Sale	1206	1206	1206	1206	1206	1206	1206
Rooms Occupied Last Night	1121	1190	1193	890	480	140	611
Less Anticipated Departures	444	396	530	440	350	55	20
Stayovers	677	794	663	450	130	85	591
Reservation Expected	498	386	212	25	10	501	552
Estimated Out of Order	3	3					
Rooms Committed	1178	1183	875	475	140	586	1143
Estimated Walk-Ins	12	10	15	5		25	63
Rooms Occupied Tonight	1190	1193	890	480	140	611	1206

Group Arrivals

	3	4	5	6	7	8	9
National Water Heater Co.	80	140					
Play Tours of America			68				
Chevrolet Western Division					5	183	
PA Library Association						251	396
Chiffo-Garn Wedding Party							23

Figure 4.10. Weekly forecast of space availability. Forecasts, which depend upon the cumulative results of previous days' forecasts, grow less reliable day by day.

sinos might even turn away certain convention groups if they are unlikely to play.

By no means is rate selectivity limited to the casino hotel. As accommodations tighten, requests for many of the hotel's special rate categories are denied although full rack price reservations are still available. Included among these special rates (explained in later chapters) are daily discounts for the military, the clergy, students and faculty, and government workers on a per diem. Travel agencies, commissionable IT (inclusive tour) packages, and special airline bookings will also be refused. There is no reason to pay a commission if the house fills without that expense. Nondiscount special rates like family plan accommodations would likely be accepted.

Restricting certain rates outright is the other side of the same coin. Working to maximize revenues as well as occupancy, the reservations manager orders that only the upper range of rates be quoted. Thus, rooms selling for a range of, say, $68 to $74 are quoted only at the upper figure, or the upper portion of the range, $72 to $74. Rate availability charts are then needed to supplement room availability charts. On some days, all rooms are blocked and no reservations are taken. But on other days, only certain rates are blocked and accommodations can be had, for a price.

Boxing dates (no through bookings) is another control device open to the reservations manager. Reservations on either side of the boxed day are not allowed to spill into that date. Dates are blocked in anticipation of a mass of arrivals, usually a convention or group movement, that could not be accommodated through the normal flow of departures. With such heavy arrivals, no one is permitted to check in before that day and stay through a series of subsequent days, even though there is more than enough space on those later dates. A less extreme measure closes the day to arrivals, but allows previous-day arrivals to stay through. Boxed dates are very costly, losing revenue for several days on either side of the boxed period. Every effort should be made to close the date to arrivals, but to allow sell throughs (sometimes called pass throughs).

Computer people describe the selectivity process with a word from their own jargon, *algorithm,* which is a mathematical procedure that involves repetition. The computer will suggest rooms for assignment in a given order, depending upon management's instructions. Rooms can be displayed by exposure, for energy zoning; by floor, for labor planning; by rate, for selling; or by alternation, to assure equal wear and tear. All of these can be manually overridden by the clerk.

Clerks can also override the computer when it indicates the house is full. Using a special code, the clerk can add reservations beyond the full house designation. More often a different procedure is used; an excessive number of rooms is built into the original program. That excess is the probable number of overbookings that management can live with. It then takes a management decision to override the adjusted full house.

If the forecast system is working properly, a full house should be achieved with few overbooking incidents. Indeed, many feel that the overbooking trauma causes more harm to the industry and its guests than the industry and the individual property gain from a few nights of 100 percent occupancy.

OVERBOOKING

Overbooking — selling more rooms than are actually available — is probably the most aggravating experience to which the hotel subjects its customers. Tired and irritated, the guest receives the announcement more as a personal affront than as an inconvenience.

The burden of walking an arriving guest — sending that person away — falls to the room clerk. Too often management leaves it at that — although it is a major management problem — making no provision for either the clerk or the guest. Where this is a frequent affair, the staff becomes immune to the protests and even finds a bit of humor in walking one guest after another. As with most guest problems, it is better to face the matter openly and try to set things right. The situation must not be treated lightly no matter how often it has happened that day. For each guest, it is a first.

Most frustrating of all for the hotel guest is the pretense of no reservation and the inference that there never was one. Mysterious documents are consulted, secret phone calls completed, and hidden room racks examined while the guest waits ignored. Finally comes a proclamation of "nonperson" — someone the hotel has never heard of and seems to care nothing about. Playing this lost-reservation parody is bad enough when there are no rooms — sometimes a reservation really does get lost. But too often the clerk worries the guest needlessly when rooms are vacant and a simple assignment would remedy the situation.

This chapter deals in part with the mechanics of reservation systems. Interesting as they may be to the hotelier, they are of no concern to the guest. Within this difference lies

Our Pledge to You

We will not knowingly offer for rent, space on which we already have an advance deposit or credit-card guaranteed reservation from a customer. If, for any reason beyond our control, a room should not be available for a customer who has either an advance deposit reservation or a credit-card guaranteed reservation, we shall arrange for at least comparable accommodations at another hotel or motel in this area.

The Management

Figure 4.11. Non-overbooking pledge.
Courtesy: American Hotel & Motel Association.

the distinction between service and nonservice. The guest's sole interest in reservations is getting into the room with the accommodations and price that were promised. Hotels that understand this provide service. Those hotels that do not understand explain their inability to meet the reservation commitment in terms of their own problems. It is no wonder unhonored reservations continue to surprise the arriving guest and confound the hotel's management.

Some hotels with a low rate of repeat business or a high level of occupancy assign a low priority to customer goodwill lost through unhonored room reservations. Their handling of the situation marks it as a negligible matter. For the majority of hotels, however, promising rooms when there are none is a serious matter. This group of hotels tries to minimize the frequency of overbooking; the other group deems the problem insolvable.

Who's at Fault?

As a national issue, overbooking appears and disappears as occupancies rise and fall. That it became a national issue at all is testimony to the strength of the consumer movement. A deemphasis of governmental regulation, falling occupancies in the early 80s, and the industry's recognition of the problem combined to stave off the regulatory policies that were almost enacted in the late 1970s. But threats of legislative intrusion have moved much closer to reality in the past decade.

Severe cases of overbooking especially in resort areas prompted investigations by the Federal Trade Commission (FTC). Action by the FTC was held off, in part, by the industry's belated decision to act. At long last, recognition of the problem was acknowledged, responsibility was accepted (figure 4.11), and a program to educate the public was begun. The burden is not the hotel/motel industry's alone. Travel agents who earn commissions, conference committees who pledge room blocks, and individual travelers who don't show are all to blame. Each, the hotel included, attempts to maximize its own position at a minimum of risk.

Tour operators, who bring planeloads of tourists to a town, contribute to the problem. The group is usually divided among several hotels, with the guest's selection determining the cost of the tour. The tour operator is playing the numbers also, estimating that a given number in each plane will opt for the different hotels in the same ratio that the tour operator has committed rooms. When too many people select one property and too few select another, the hotel is blamed for overbooking when, in fact, the hotel and the tour operator agreed on the numbers months before.

Guests too are to blame! They are notorious no-shows. Many guests will make reservations in more than one hotel and, if they do show, will change their length of stay without notifying the desk. The reservation department is always second-guessing guests' moves and this means occasional errors no matter how carefully previous statistics and experiences are projected.

Airlines have had similar overbooking problems, which have led to CAB (Civil Aeronautics Board) regulations and penalties. Regulatory legislation can be expected for hotels, too, unless a combined effort at industry policing, improved reservation systems, and public relations can avert it. Florida has already enacted just such legislation. In addition to monetary penalties, the law requires the hotel to reimburse the guest for prepaid reservations whether paid directly to the hotel or to a travel agency. New York requires travel agents to warn clients in the form of a rubber-stamped message that, "this hotel has been known to overbook in the past."

Although states like New York and Georgia have legislated mere refunds for unaccommodated guests, Pennsylvania, Michigan, and Florida permit punitive damages. Hawaii and Puerto Rico have enacted an eviction law permitting the physical ejection of guests who overstay their reservation. The legal and public relations ramifications of this means of combating overbooking are frightening.

Overbooking is as understandable to the hotelier as it is incomprehensible to the customer. Why it is understandable has already been discussed. Simply put, it is a matter of guessing. Although the guesses can be sharpened and refined, they are still guesses and no amount of legislation can change that.

No-shows

Any overbooking discussion invariably focuses on no-shows: reservations that never arrive and never cancel. No-shows, which reach as high as 25 percent in some cities on some occasions, leave a great many rooms in doubt every single night. A margin, says the industry, that might well resolve the overbooking issue once and for all. Educating the public and penalizing it for its failure to learn is the carrot and whip approach. Convention managers are taught to pair their members at the meeting site as the individuals arrive. This reduces the number of single rooms created when previously paired delegates do not show. Failing this, the hotel levies a compulsory room charge for no-shows.

No-shows are also attributable to the hotels. Inadequate reservation systems are the most obvious cause. Unattractive grounds may also hurt, especially for motor inns. Uncared for lawns, dirty windows, poor lighting and a low level of maintenance may actually turn away a guest at the door.

Until recently, there has been no way to enforce the guest's side of the reservation understanding. The guest often didn't show and often didn't cancel. Guaranteed reservations were no help either. The rate of collection on guaranteed reservations is less than 25 percent. Some see the hotel industry's rather cavalier attitude as a bit of tit for tat. In truth, it is a concerned professional trying to maximize profits in the face of much uncertainty.

What Are the Solutions?

Solutions to the overbooking problem — if, in fact, there is a problem — must come from individual hotels and chains acting discreetly. The decision to act may be self-generated, or it may be urged upon the member properties by the industry acting in concert. This will avoid intercession by the FTC or other governmental agencies, who perceive the issue more strongly than the public. An AH&MA study on customer satisfaction ranked overbooking nineteenth in the frequency of guest complaints.

No matter how well managed the hotel, no matter how well made the forecasts of this chapter, overbooking will occur. Preplanning for overbooking mollifies the guest somewhat and offers some chance of retaining the business. Finding substitute facilities is the least that courtesy and good business demand, but this is ignored by a good number of properties. At a minimum, baggage storage should be offered. Some managers pay for the cab to the substitute property and back again the following day when space becomes available. Others proffer an outright sum to minimize the inconvenience. A free room on the next visit helps to bring a walked guest back.

Plagued by bad publicity from overbooking, the Bahamas Hotel Association (BHA) formalized these general solutions into an area-wide policy. After all, being stranded on an isolated island without a room is not going to encourage tourism. The BHA policy carried the cab ride one step further, guaranteeing air taxi to another island if all accommodations in the host area were fully booked.

The real problem of overbooking lies with those properties that do nothing: they either pretend that the reservation was never received or act as if the person's inconvenience is of small consequence. Publicity, and it is bad publicity, pinpoints the weaknesses of individual reservation systems or the unconcern of inept management. Even the chief investigator of the FTC noted that it was not overbooking per se that concerned the Commission, it was what happened — actually what didn't happen, that is what the hotel didn't do to help — when the guest was turned away. This is the antiservice syndrome.

Arranging substitute accommodations at other nearby properties is the least the clerk should be taught to do. Providing the telephone numbers is the least that management should do. Then, preliminary calls are made to neighboring properties as the situation becomes obvious — overstays are exceeding projections — and are confirmed when the guest arrives. Many satellite properties depend on this overflow. Other less ethical ones pay the room clerk for each walked guest the clerk sends their way. At times the arrangement is more formal, as when group business that has been overbooked is "farmed" out to other properties.

The Third-party Guarantee

Traditional room guarantees, where payment is pledged by the guest or the guest's company, have not worked. Hotel management is hard pressed to insist on payment from a regular customer who didn't use the room. Especially since insisting results in more lost business than can ever be recovered from one-night collections. And from those guests unknown to the hotel, there certainly is no collection. Enter the third party. The very same intermediaries who caused the dramatic changes in room reservation systems are about to solve the overbooking/no-show dilemma.

Hotel companies have been moving away from the guaranteed reservation for some time. Advanced payment by credit card was first thought to be the solution, but credit card companies were as reluctant to enforce the billing as were the hotels. Billing protests were charged back to the hotels, with little attempt to verify the cancellation. (Reservationists issue a code when the guest cancels, and that code should be furnished if the guaranteed billing is challenged.)

As with many other industry changes, solutions lie in external forces more than internal

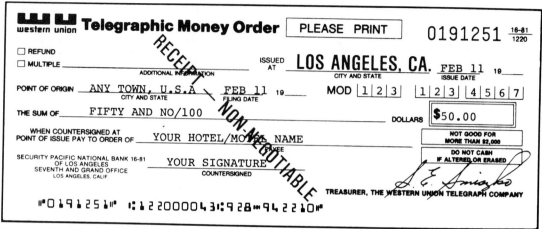

Figure 4.12. Third-party money orders can be used to guarantee reservations. The hotel draws the check, which is used as a reservation deposit, leaving the collection between the guest and the third party. *Courtesy: Western Union.*

ones. It is in the future of the cashless society that the solution to overbooking appears. Prepaid reservations is the probable answer. Not prepaid in cash with the burdensome accounting procedures that we have known in the past, but prepaid nevertheless. The number of resorts requiring prepayment has risen substantially in the past decade. If the new procedures fall in line, the figure might reach 100 percent.

Two forms of the guarantee are materializing. One is the credit card company, except now the company is guaranteeing payment and removing the hotel from the collection problem. This service is being extended by the travel and entertainment cards, particularly American Express. Undoubtedly, the bank cards, Visa and MasterCard, will soon follow. It is merely a clearer understanding of the old arrangement: "no-shows" will be paid by the credit card company; "no rooms" require the hotel to refund the deposit and furnish free accommodations elsewhere.

Although the second procedure is part of the reservation discussion, it also has ramifications for check cashing. Consequently, banks as well as special service companies have entered the field. Western Union is probably the best known. When the hotel signs with Western Union (or the other agencies), it receives an inventory of blank checks drawn on the participating company (figure 4.12). These checks are paid to the order of the hotel and need only be countersigned by authorized hotel personnel, which occurs when the participating company calls the desk with a reservation. The hotel has its money immediately. The servicing company (say, Western Union) bills the guest's bank card (for example, MasterCard or Visa) for the room charge plus a service fee, thus relieving the hotel of the collection hassle. The reservation passes through the system in the usual manner.

Third-party guarantees suggest several reservation innovations still to come. All reservations will probably be guaranteed in this manner. Therefore, standby prices (reduced room rates offered to walk-in guests) may exist someday. Similarly, just as some airlines offer discounted rates without refund possibilities, hotels may enter a new pricing formula era. For certain, hotels have entered a new reservation era. How that reservation is made was the topic of the last chapter. Committing the space has just been reviewed. Now let's move on to the processes that bring the reservation system together.

QUERIES AND PROBLEMS

1. In the order of their complexity, itemize and describe three reservation systems that a reservation manager might install; include information about the size and characteristics of each hotel.
2. Who is (are) the real culprit(s) in overbooking? What brings the issue periodically to the public's attention? And what can be done to forestall such cyclical review by consumer advocates?
3. A chain's corporate office launches a national campaign advertising its policy of honoring every reservation. Each property is notified that overbooking

will not be tolerated. What policies can be implemented at the hotel level to meet corporate goals and still generate the maximum occupancies on which professional careers are built?
4. Two hours before the noon check-out hour, a walk-in party requests five rooms. The following data (scrambled) has just been completed as part of the desk's hourly update. Should the front-office supervisor accept the walk-ins?

General no-show factor	10%
Rooms in the hotel	693
Group reservations due (rooms)	250
Number of rooms departed so far today	211
Rooms occupied last night	588
Total reservations expected today from all sources	320
No-show factor for groups	2%
Understays minus overstays as a percentage of occupied rooms	8%
Early arrivals (rooms)	2
Nonsalable rooms and rooms that are out of order	7
Comp rooms not counted in last night's occupancy	4
Forecasted departures for the day	211

5

The Reservation Process

Once the decision to accept the guest is made — a decision fraught with uncertainty as chapters 3 and 4 explained — the processing machinery of the reservation system begins to fall in place. Ultimately the guest will be assigned to an acceptable room at an acceptable rate. Occasionally there is a problem and the arriving guest finds no room. Space for that individual will be unavailable even though earlier arrivals, who may well have made their reservations later, will have been accommodated. Sensitive to the public's criticism, the hotel industry has begun resolving some of the causes for overbooking. Many of the causes are not of the industry's making, as chapter 4 has explained.

Electronic data processing is one new tool that the hotel industry has employed. Reservation systems generate a staggering amount of recordkeeping. Before the event of the computer, manual systems required the same bits of information to be reproduced over and over. Some information was used for room availability projections, some for reservation records, some for registration, and some for billing. Electronic data processing has simplified this process and in that simplification is seen the potential of computerizing the entire front office. For once the information is entered into the computer, much of the work is done. Reservations, registration, billing, and reports are all prepared from the same initial entry made at the time of the reservation.

PROCESSING THE SINGLE RESERVATION

The reservation sequence begins either in the reservation center or in the hotel's own reservation office. Procedures vary depending on whether the system is centralized or not and whether the system is computer based or not. More reservation systems operate without computers than with them.

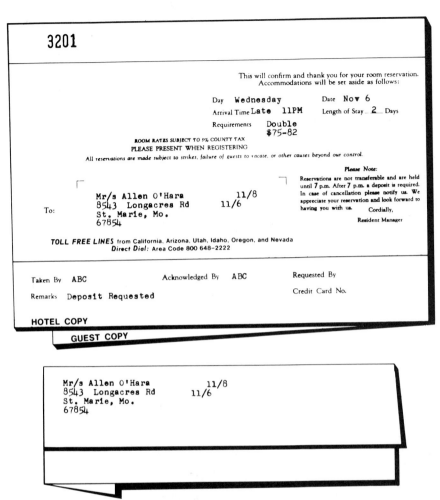

Figure 5.1. Typical reservation acknowledgment. One copy mailed to the guest and one copy maintained in the correspondence file, supported by the rack slip filed chronologically in alphabetical sequence (figure 5.4).

Acknowledging the Reservation

When there is no res center, reservation calls and mail come directly to the office of the hotel. A reservation packet (including the reservation form of figure 3.5), the correspondence, and the reservation number, if used, is created and given to a typist for processing. One copy of the acknowledgment prepared by the typist is sent to the guest (figures 5.1 and 5.2). A second copy, sometimes called the "hard copy," is added to the reservation packet. What happens from this point on differs from hotel to hotel but involves the same general procedures and objectives.

The reservation acknowledgment can take one of many, many forms (figure 5.9). It might be a simple postcard unrelated to the internal

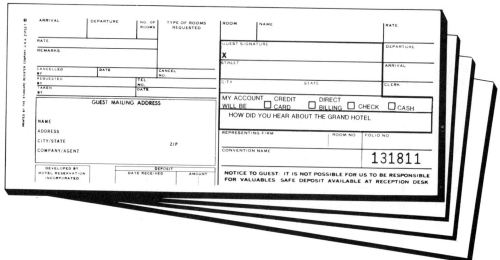

Figure 5.2. Reservation packet with carbonized slips to handle the reservation, the reservation deposit, the registration, and the express checkout. *Courtesy: Grand Hotel, Anaheim, Calif.*

processes of the reservation. It can be used to prepare the reservation rack slips that are part of the internal reservation procedure or it can incorporate the registration card that the guest eventually signs on arrival. Electronic data systems accomplish both by printing the rack slips and the registration card either as the reservation confirmation is being prepared or on the night before the anticipated arrival.

Figure 5.2 illustrates the less common of the two formats, a combination reservation-registration form (see also figure 5.12). This particular format has four parts. Copies two and three are for reservation confirmations. One copy confirms the reservation and asks for the deposit, and the other reconfirms when the deposit check arrives. Copy four is an express checkout (given the guest on arrival) and copy one is an express checkin. All registration information except the guest's signature and the actual room/rate assignment is completed as part of the reservation process.

Figure 5.1 illustrates the more common noncomputerized form. When this confirmation is prepared, a rack slip is duplicated using carbon or NCR paper. This reservation rack slip is similar in size and form to the room rack slips. It is filed alphabetically by anticipated date of arrival, using a shelf with cubbyholes for each day or an alphabetic rack like those in the telephone department (figures 5.3 and 5.4). Large properties may use separate racks with different colored slips for group or convention reservations. When a shelf with cubbyholes is used, the slips are racked two or three days before the anticipated arrival dates for easier visibility.

Small hotels do away with the reservation racks by using a form like that of figure 5.5. Reservations are distributed daily on one or more reservation sheets. If walk-ins are added to the sheet and cancellations struck from it, the reservation sheet also serves as an arrival sheet.

Figure 5.3. Reservation rack: confirmations filed vertically by alphabet and horizontally by date.

Figure 5.4. Reservation rack: alphabetized daily for the month of June.

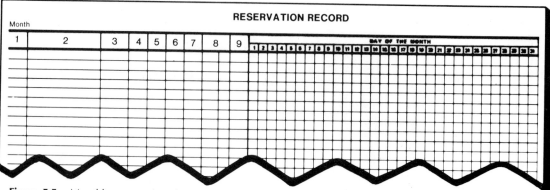

Figure 5.5. Monthly reservation sheet; reservation record is maintained in sequence as requests arrive. See also figure 4.1. *Courtesy: Wilcox International, Inc., Division of American Hotel Register Co.*

1. Room No.
2. Name of Party
3. City
4. State
5. No. in Party
6. Answered Date
7. Deposit Due Date
8. Deposit Received Amount
9. Deposit Confirmed Date

A completely computerized system would have neither the shelf of figure 5.3 nor the rack of figure 5.4. All information would be stored in computer memory. The only paperwork would be the correspondence file, including a computerized copy of the reservation confirmation that was mailed to the guest.

Thus, pending the guest's appearance, two records are maintained: a list of daily arrivals and a supporting packet of correspondence. With a noncomputerized rack system of reservations, the list is maintained alphabetically by date (figure 5.3). With a computer, the information is maintained in memory to be called forth by individual name on the CRT screen (figure 5.6) or printed out each day in advance of arrivals (figure 5.7). For the small hotel using the journal sheet (figure 5.5), the arrival list is maintained randomly in the order in which the arriving reservations are entered.

In those hotels using electronic reservation systems, the request is given an identification number that serves as a reference code. The code might be numerical, but it is more likely to be the guest's name or the first several letters of the name. Thereafter, the reservation information can easily be called up from the storage bank. Most computers maintain a reservation horizon of about two years. Beyond that, reservations are maintained manually. Depending upon need, reservation lists can be alphabetically prepared for arrival lists or chronologically prepared for reservation control (figure 5.8).

The computer can be programmed to prepare a confirmation letter from the same entry that records the reservation and stores it for future use (figure 5.9). An additional step is required if the reservation originates in a central office. Information about the reservation must be transmitted to the hotel. If the computers are interfaced (which is unusual), the information is transmitted electronically. If the hotel has no computer, a written duplicate of the confirmation letter is sent to the hotel from the res center. There the confirmation letter enters the hotel's reservation process and is attached to the correspondence packet. Sometimes the hotel has a terminal that is connected to the res center computer. Then the res center sends the information electronically, and the hotel feeds that printout into its own system, either manually or by reentering it into its in-house computer.

```
EXPECTED ARRIVALS 4/4/ MAGNA ONE HOTEL
PAGE 4
```

RES #	NAME	CONV GRP	NO. RMS	TYPE RM	RATE CAT	RES TYPE	ARRIV	SPL SVC
0261	ONITO, RANDAL		2	K	2	4		
0005	OTTA, M/M ALPREDO		1	K	2	2	11:00P	25
0616	OUVIA & FMLY, MRS JACK		1	D	3	2	11:00P	
R111	RAMLETT, M/M JOHN		1	K	2	2	8:00P	
R260	ROADWATER, M/M REX		3	K	1	2		26 13
R312	RODEY, M/M FRED	ZTUK	1	K	3	2		B1
R406	ROWN, M/M MIKE		1	K	2	2	7:00P	
R234	RUCHER, WM/SON		1	D	3	1	10:00P	63
					W/KNIGHT			
R400	RUDNICK, M/M DUANE		1	D	2	3		
R422	RUNKER, M/M WM	00E	1	D	1	1		
R713	RURNSTEIN, M/M SCOTT		1	K	2	2		
R646	RYANT, MS CISSY		1	K	1	2	5:00P	
R456	RYER & FAM, M/M WAYNE		1	K	2	2		
S121	SAMPBELL, M/M KRONE		1	K	1	2		
S216	SAPP & PTY, M/M DONALDO		1	K	1	2		
S200	SAREY, TOMITHAN		1	S	4	2		
S617	SARNIVELE, NICHOLAS	JOIN	1	S	4	1		
S836	SARPENTER, MRS JULYE	WK	1	D	2	1	12:31P	
					W/SMITH			
S855	SASTELLI, MONSIEUR		2	K	3	4		02
T202	TATO, D/M LOUIS	ITUK	1	K	2	2	3:51P	
T008	TENTER & FAM, M/M DEAN		2	D	2	3	5:00P	25
T361	THANDLER, MR HAL		1	S	2	1		

```
                        **MORE**
```

Figure 5.6. CRT display of the daily reservation list. See also figure 5.7.

```
        EXPECTED ARRIVALS 4/4/  MAGNA ONE HOTEL
        PAGE 4

   RES #  NAME                    CONV    NO.   TYPE   RATE   RES    ARRIV    SPL
                                  GRP     RMS   RM     CAT    TYPE            SVC

   0261   ONITO, RANDAL                    2    K      2      4
   0005   OTTA, M/M ALPREDO                1    K      2      2      11:00P   25
   0616   OUVIA & FMLY, MRS JACK           1    D      3      2      11:00P
   R111   RAMLETT, M/M JOHN                1    K      2      2       8:00P
   R260   ROADWATER, M/M REX               3    K      1      2               26 13
   R312   RODEY, M/M FRED        ZTUK      1    K      3      2               B1
   R406   ROWN, M/M MIKE                   1    K      2      2       7:00P
   R234   RUCHER, WM/SON                   1    D      3      1      10:00P    63
                                                      W/KNIGHT
   R400   RUDNICK, M/M DUANE               1    D      2      3
   R422   RUNKER, M/M WM         00E       1    D      1      1
   R713   RURNSTEIN, M/M SCOTT             1    K      2      2
   R646   RYANT, MS CISSY                  1    K      1      2       5:00P
   R456   RYER & FAM, M/M WAYNE            1    K      2      2
   S121   SAMPBELL, M/M KRONE              1    K      1      2
   S216   SAPP & PTY, M/M DONALDO          1    K      1      2
   S200   SAREY, TOMITHAN                  1    S      4      2
   S617   SARNIVELE, NICHOLAS    JOIN      1    S      4      1
   S836   SARPENTER, MRS JULYE   WK        1    D      2      1      12:31P
                                                      W/SMITH
   S855   SASTELLI, MONSIEUR               2    K      3      4               02
   T202   TATO, D/M LOUIS        ITUK      1    K      2      2       3:51P
   T008   TENTER & FAM, M/M DEAN           2    D      2      3       5:00P
   T361   THANDLER, MR HAL                 1    S      2      1               25
```

Figure 5.7. Hard copy printout of the daily reservation list. See also figure 5.6.

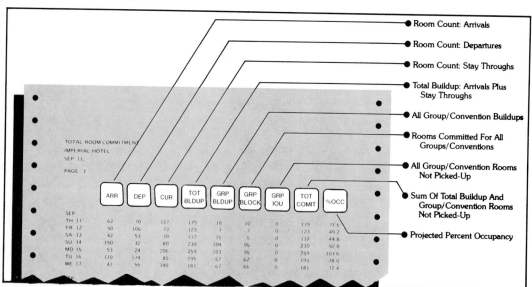

Figure 5.8. Room commitment report with a four-week horizon. Compare to figure 4.10.
Courtesy: Compass Computer Services, Dallas, Tex.

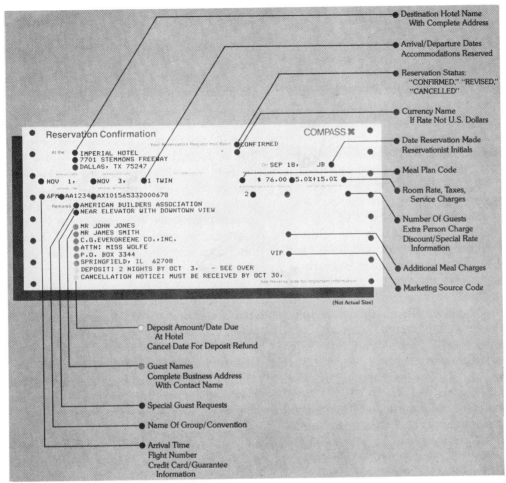

Figure 5.9. Computer-prepared confirmation letter, an automatic by-product of reservation input, including reservation changes and deposit receipts. *Courtesy: Compass Computer Services, Dallas, Tex.*

Changing the Reservation

Once made, the reservation remains undisturbed in the file, either the computer file or the manual file. Data about the aggregate reservations may be retrieved for report purposes, but the individual record remains unaltered unless the guest initiates a change. Changes involve the same type of data that was obtained during the original booking: dates or times of arrival or departure, changes in accommodations or rate levels, number of persons or rooms needed, guest response to a deposit request, and others.

A change in reservation follows the same sequence as that of the reservation itself. Except now the process must first locate the original request. This is done electronically by calling up the original date of arrival and locating the guest alphabetically. Making the change there updates the entire data base. For additional security, the change information, like the original computer reservation, may be recorded first on a hand-written form (figure 3.5), perhaps in a different color. Another confirmation, also frequently in a different color, is mailed to the guest.

Hand-based systems require some additional steps when a reservation change occurs. Another reservation form like figure 5.1 is completed, usually in a different color or format; the correspondence is located and the form is attached to the packet. The reservation slip is changed and relocated in the rack (figure 5.4), and appropriate changes are made in the forecasting and control system. Also, a new confirmation is mailed to the guest.

Reservation deposits usually arrive in response to the hotel's request (figure 5.1), and they require special cash handling and control, which is discussed in chapter 11.

Filing the Reservation

Each packet of reservation correspondence is maintained chronologically, with the latest communication on the top of the pile. Included in the packet are the original reservation, which could be from a travel agency, a deposit verification, and subsequent changes to the original request.

Each morning, the reservations office furnishes the desk with a list of anticipated arrivals (figure 5.7) backed up with their correspondence. If the correspondence is filed alphabetically without being separated by date of arrival, a cross-reference of date and name is possible. A reservation can then be traced through the guest's name even if the date of arrival is not known. When both the correspondence and the daily arrival list are filed by the anticipated date of arrival, tracing the reservation is not possible unless that anticipated

date is known. To overcome this, a second reservation slip can be prepared and filed alphabetically without regard to date (figure 5.4). Because of the extra work, this is not always used. As a result, most systems, including computerized ones, require both the name and the date of arrival in order to locate the reservation. The arrangement shown in figure 5.3 narrows the search, but is too awkward for more than one month.

Subdividing the correspondence keeps it manageable. One category—inquiries—includes only provisional reservations or those for which the final confirmation is pending, request for reservation deposit, for example. Reservations are moved from this category to a confirmation or booking classification when a definite commitment is received. Many times reservations are filed in the second category immediately and the first category is eliminated. Past reservations is a third grouping.

Correspondence for the current day is separated and kept near the desk for quick reference. Normally no room assignments are made at this stage of the reservation process, but there are exceptions.

Color Coding

Color plays the same important role in reservations that it does in the room rack. Each hotel has its own code although each experiences the same type of reservations. Different colored rack slips (figure 5.4) are used to communicate the guests' circumstances. One guest can fall into several categories but only the major category is flagged. A colored celluloid placed over the reservation slip, however, makes a second flag possible.

Regular Reservations

White is the color used by all hotels for the standard reservation. Although the long list of possibilities that follows implies otherwise, most guests fall into this classification. These regular reservations are sold to walk-ins if the guest does not arrive by the stated cutoff hour. Naturally, a late arrival is accommodated regardless of the time if there is still space.

Advance Deposit

Many hotels are not interested in reservations with advance deposits since they require an additional amount of paperwork as chapters 11 and 13 explain. Commercial hotels do not solicit such reservations. Although the room is paid for whether the guest arrives or not, it sometimes happens that there are no rooms for even this category of guest.

Late Arrivals

Sometimes the guest has indicated a later-than-usual arrival although the room is not covered by an advance deposit. Even so, the hotel may need to let the room go early. Late arrival notification is some protection that a room will be available, but guests assume it to be more than the reservation implies.

Guaranteed Rooms

Guaranteed rooms are held without advance deposit but payment is guaranteed. Because these reservations are usually made by business firms for their representatives, they are sometimes called *company-made* reservations. In case of a no-show, the room charge is run through the company's regular charge account, called a city ledger account, and billing takes place in the usual manner.

Credit card companies are rapidly replacing private companies as the guarantor. It is a new market for the companies and a new service to their card holders. Most important, it is the probable solution to the problem of overbooking.

Convention Delegate

Group affiliation is a better term than convention delegate because the members of a group need not be part of a convention. Hotels cater to tours, company delegations, wedding parties, and other groups that need to be identified. Several colors are needed when several groups are booked at one time. The color can also indicate a master billing in which all accounts are charged to one folio.

Inquiries Only

This reservation slip corresponds to the provisional reservation file. It is prepared in the event that the guest does come even though the reservation is unconfirmed. Such guests receive preference if possible. "Inquiries only" and "regrets" are treated similarly.

Regrets

Regrets are reservations that have been denied. Preparing a reservation slip gives the clerk additional information should the guest decide to come anyway. Special consideration can be given if circumstances allow. This slip also enables the front office to report how many reservations were turned away on a given day, something that most reservation departments do not know. This slip is rarely prepared.

Travel Agents

Color coding travel agencies expedites the internal office procedure and the payment or billing of each agent. It also helps the front office manager gather information: What percentage of business originates with travel agents? How much with each agent? What days of the week is the agent selling? What is the percentage of no-shows? Cancellations?

Special reservation confirmation forms or at least special colored forms are used for travel agencies. Hotel "reps" have their own color. To maintain accountability with the agency, the hotel sends a notice whenever one of its clients does not show.

VIPs

Important guests are flagged by color. These may be well-known dignitaries, other hoteliers, or important members of an association that the hotel hopes to book later. VIP designations are made by a member of management or by the sales department. *Star reservation* is another term that is sometimes used. A *contact reservation* is a VIP that should be met (contacted) and escorted to his or her room by the management.

"Riding" Reservations

Reservations for which the date of arrival is vague or uncertain are allowed to "ride." The probable date is booked and then the reservation is carried until the guest shows or an allotted period of time passes, usually less than one week.

Permanent Reservations

Guests who return to the hotel periodically make a permanent reservation. Frequently, a particular room that the guest favors is saved for a given night or nights each month. Commercial travelers use this type of reservation.

Computer Coding

With a manual reservation board of the type shown in figure 5.4, the colored rack slips are immediately visible, alerting the clerk to the special circumstances of the reservation. With a computerized system, the information is held in computer memory. It is not easily viewed since it is displayed on the CRT only upon request and then limited to a space of about 8" by 11." It is necessary, therefore, to build a code series into that display to communicate

the kind of information that the colored rack slips convey. The possibilities are almost endless as figures 5.7 and 5.10 illustrate.

PROCESSING THE GROUP RESERVATION

The hotel business has entered a new era. Mass travel and group reservations are replacing the individual traveler as the hotel's largest source of business. More than ever before, the industry is now oriented toward the group market. Incentive travel, tour groups, conventions, and trade shows have become the mainstay of hotel sales both at home and abroad. There is economy in group selling. Mass merchandising reduces the overhead per guest. The sales manager's assiduous pursuit of a single tour operator or account executive produces anywhere from dozens to hundreds of room nights. The savings carry through all departments, including accounting, billing, reservations, and registrations. Front office operations and reservation procedures have changed somewhat in the face of mass market demands, but the revisions have been very slow in coming.

Kinds of Group Business

Americans are gregarious and their natural inclination to gather has been facilitated by the speed and ease of modern transportation systems. The need to communicate an ever-increasing amount of information has given further impetus to the convention concept as has the expense account structure of the federal income tax. Meetings and conventions did not originate with the hotel business, but in three to four decades they have come to dominate the hotel marketplace.

The recency of the convention market notwithstanding, a new trend is already evident — group travel for pleasure. Lacking the

Code	System Meaning	Print Out on Guest Confirmation
11	VIP	
12	Group Buyer	
13	Honeymooners	
14	Comp	
20	Connecting Rooms	Connecting rooms, if possible.
21	Adjoining Rooms	Adjoining rooms, if possible.
22	Rooms on Same Floor	Same floor, if possible.
23	Need Individual Names	Please advise names of individuals in your party.
24	PS	Petit suite
25	RS	One-bedroom suite
26	LS	Two-bedroom suite
30	Send Liquor	
31	Send Champagne	
32	Send Flowers	
33	Send Gift	
34	Send Fruit	
40	Require Deposit	Please send one night's deposit to guarantee your reservation.
41	Due Bill	
42	No Credit, Require Advance Payment	
43	Walk-in	
50	Special Rate	Special rate
51	Airline Rate	Airline rate
52	Press Rate	Press rate
53	Convention Rate	Convention rate
54	Non-convention Rate	Convention rate applies to convention dates only.
55	Travel Agency	Travel agency
60	Cot	Cot will be provided.
61	Crib	Crib will be provided.
62	Bedboard	Bedboard will be provided.
63	Wheelchair	Wheelchair will be provided.
70	Casino Guest	
80	See Correspondence for Very Special Instructions	
99	Print Special Message	(Whatever that message is.)

Figure 5.10. Computer reservation code; code numbers communicate on black and white CRT screen the information provided by colored reservation rack slips. See right column of figure 5.7.

tax advantages of the conventioneer, the tourist looks chiefly for economy. Price is the big appeal. Whereas convention business is sold as a group and handled individually, tour business is sold as a group and handled as a group. One sale, one reservation, one registration,[1] one service, and one billing provide the savings on which the tour concept is built.

Conventions and Shows

Our propensity to gather has produced an astonishing variety and number of organizations. People come together for many reasons: business, union, fraternal, social, historical, veteran, health and medical, educational, religious, scientific, political, service, athletic, and so on without end. Each classification translates into numerous organizations, societies, clubs, and associations and each of them meets, holds shows, and stages conventions. Functioning at local, state, regional, national, and international levels, these groups offer business to every hotel regardless of its size or location.

Conventions

Conventioneers assemble to promote their common purpose. These purposes are as diverse as the list of associations that hold conventions. During the gathering of two, three, or four days, papers, meetings, speeches, and talks are given on a range of topics. Some are professional and some merely entertaining. The members interact individually, discussing common goals and problems with colleagues. Professional conventions also serve as informal job placement forums.

Arrangements for the convention are made by a representative or committee of the organization and confirmed with a letter of agreement. Large associations have permanent, paid executives in addition to the annually elected officers. These account executives are so numerous that they have their own organization — ASAE, the American Society of Association Executives. The negotiated arrangements, which are completed between the organization and the hotel's sales staff, include housing, meals, and meeting facilities. Because of the large sums that conventions represent to a community, estimated at over $100 per day per delegate, city-wide, tax-supported convention bureaus work with hotels and convention groups in many ways.

The organization contracts for certain services that it buys as a unit from the hotel, such as meeting space and association rooms, and certain services that the hotel sells directly to the guest, such as individual room reservations. In other instances, the organization acts as an intermediary, for example, making food arrangements for various social functions.

The association sells function tickets to the membership; the organization pays the hotel for only those who partake of the function but usually guarantees a minimum number. Therefore, members who buy tickets and do not attend represent profit to the association called *breakage*. If the association had 100 members buy food tickets, but only eighty-eight eat, the breakage is the dollar value of those twelve tickets.

The organization is responsible for its own entertainment (although it may hire people through the hotel), its own speakers, films, etc. For this, it charges the attendees a registration fee. Although some of the fee goes toward the costs of the program, the association usually profits here again. Further gains may be made through the room rate arrangements. Sometimes organizations require the hotel to charge the attending members more than the room rate and to refund that excess to the group treasury. This raises many ethical con-

---

1. Massachusetts was the last state to pass legislation allowing preregistration of groups. Prior to 1975, each member of the group had to register separately.

cerns, particularly if the convention guest is unaware of the arrangement. Unfortunately, it has also led to a more serious abuse, that of rebating the excess to the individual who books the group into the hotel.

In no way does the association contract for rooms except for those directly related to association headquarters, such as officers' and speakers' rooms. Room reservations are individually contracted between the hotel and each delegate. Billing is handled the same way and collections become a personal matter between the conventioneer and the hotel. Reservations, paper work, registrations, and folio preparations are no different for the convention delegate than for any individual, nonconvention guest.

Trade Shows

Trade shows are exhibits of product lines shown by purveyors to potential buyers. Conventions and trade shows are often held together. Shows require a great deal of space, particularly if the displays are large pieces of machinery or equipment. Space requirements and the difficulty of handling such products limit shows to a small number of hotels. Here again the city convention bureau has a role. It builds halls to accommodate the exhibits, leaving the housing and guest service to the local hotels. Goods of small compass — perfume shows, for example — can be housed in almost any hotel. Although less common today, it is still a practice to assign several guest floors to such a trade show and convert guest rooms into exhibit space. The purveyor also occupies the room as a registered guest.

The trade association acquires space from the hotel or convention center and leases it to the exhibitors at a profit. Guests and exhibitors are invited by the association, with the hotel playing the same role it had with conventions except that it may also be renting exhibit space. The length of guest stay is longer with a show

because the displays, which are costly and elaborate, require set-up and tear-down time. Otherwise, reservation and front office procedures are the same as for a convention or an individual guest. More city ledger charges may occur because the exhibitors are usually large companies that request that type of billing.

Tour Groups

Tour or package plans come in a variety of wrappings, some reminiscent of the old American plan. Indeed, the very breakage that the guest objects to in the American plan is accepted with fervor in the tour package. Undoubtedly, the one price quote for the whole package holds great appeal. Rooms, food and beverage, entertainment, and, in some cases, transportation, are packaged in with tips and baggage handling for one price. Breakage profits materalize because guests do not take every meal and drink nor use every service provided by the plan. Breakage belongs to the travel promoter or, in some cases, to the hotel itself.

A new entrepreneur has appeared to handle the mass movement of travelers and it is this travel wholesaler, rather than the individual guest or even the individual travel agent, with whom the hotel does business.

By mass marketing the travel package, the wholesaler prorates the cost of the aircraft over all the seats, bringing the per seat cost far below that of the commercial airline. Special room and meal rates are negotiated under the umbrella of a planeload of customers. With the promise of year-round, back-to-back charters, the hotel sales manager and accountant sharpen their pencils. One sale books hundreds of rooms, one correspondence confirms all the reservations, and one billing closes the books. There is no commission to credit card companies and there is a minimum loss from bad debts. It is a bargain buy for the traveler, a profitable venture for the wholesaler, and a basic occupancy for the hotel.

Throughout, the hotel deals with one party — the wholesaler. The wholesaler leases the plane, books the rooms, commits land transportation and entertainment, and then goes out to sell the package. Travel agents are the wholesaler's major sales outlets. Each agent receives a commission for the sale — from the wholesaler, not from the hotel — and the wholesaler combines them into one group. In so doing, the workload of the front office is reduced considerably.

IT Packages

The popularity of tour packages lured the hotel industry into the lucrative business. Why leave all the profits to the wholesaler? By eliminating the airfare portion and concentrating on the hotel's portion of the package, much of the risk was reduced. Everything else was included: rooms, meals, drinks, tips, tickets to events, use of recreational facilities, and so on.

Marketing the inclusive tour (IT) requires communication with the travel agents. Sometimes this is done through a direct mailing. It is also accomplished through the Consolidated Air Tour Manual (CATM), which lists the tours so that travel agents, airlines, and other intermediaries can sell the product. Then, of course, it is the hotel that pays the commission. But it is also the hotel that gets the sales and the breakage. With IT packages, the hotel competes with itself, selling discounted rooms with extra services at a lower price than the regular rack rate of the very same room.

IT numbers are the codes used on the hotels' tour folders to identify the packages. Some hotels have several different IT packages, each with its own price structure. The codes are used by the agents to book the packages. Keeping track of all the different rates within the hotel is a responsibility of the reservation department or res center. The computer can make the distinction, but it takes a well-trained

operator to sell rates from the top down, especially when the caller is pressuring and the IT rates are being displayed.

However, several studies indicate that the res centers are not selling the upper rates — not aggressively selling from the top rates down. Yet the res centers are the front line of hotel sales and the major reason for franchise membership. Too often the res center clerks are ignored by a sales team attempting to improve occupancy or rate per room sold.

Excess rate categories might be part of the explanation. Ten, twelve, fourteen rate categories plus the special rates like the ITs are so confusing that reservationists either avoid the property (if there are several in town) or, being unable to discriminate, sell at one easily identifiable rate.

Group Records
Convention Groups

Associations book their shows and conventions as much as five to ten years ahead — two to three years advance planning is the norm. A *blanket* reservation is negotiated at the time arrangements between the hotel and the group are completed. As the date approaches, perhaps five to eight months before the convention arrives, the total room commitment is identified as to number of single rooms, doubles, suites, and so on. These are estimates based on the group's historical experience with its convention. About two months before the event, the association distributes the hotel's reservation form (figure 5.11) through its mailing list, which could number anywhere from dozens of persons to thousands. These self-addressed postal cards piggyback the general convention mailing that details the program, the activities, and the cost.

If properly designed with name, address, rate information, arrival and departure times,

Associated Tailors of America

May 4-8

Herald Square Hotel
Reservation Department

Please make the following reservations quoted on European Plan.

Reservations must be received by Herald Square no later than April 15.

☐ Guest Rooms—Single $60

☐ Guest Rooms—Double $64

☐ Suites: Petite $84
Deluxe $98

Will Arrive ______ Time ______

Will Depart ______ Time ______

Name ______

Address ______

City ______

State ______ Zip ______

Reservations will not be held after 6 P.M. unless otherwise requested

Associated Tailors of America

May 4-8

Herald Square Hotel
Reservation Department

Please make the following reservations quoted on European Plan.

Reservations must be received by Herald Square no later than April 15.

☐ Guest Room—Single $44 $48 $52 $58

☐ Guest Rooms—Double $50 $54 $58 $66
(Please circle rate choice)

☐ Suites: Petite $84
Deluxe $98

Will Arrive ______ Time ______

Will Depart ______ Time ______

Name ______

Address ______

City ______

State ______ Zip ______

Reservations will not be held after 6 P.M. unless otherwise requested.

Figure 5.11. Group confirmation cards showing run-of-the-house (flat) rates (left) and spread rates (right). Spread rates offer a range of choices not provided by flat rates.

etc., the reservation request, as completed by the conventioneer, becomes the registration form upon arrival (figure 5.12). Countless clerical hours are saved and guest reception is expedited during the crush of convention arrivals.

As individual requests arrive at the hotel, they are charged against the blanket reservation. The hotel and the association reexamine the room commitment forty-five, thirty, and twenty days before the convention begins. (Critical dates are kept in color on the reservation chalkboard.) Reservations received after the close-out date, usually from twenty to thirty days before the convention starts, are accepted only if general space remains—"availability basis only." In all cases, reservations are confirmed individually with an additional copy sometimes going to the association for count control. One night's deposit may be required, especially at isolated resorts where there is little chance that walk-ins would fill no-show rooms.

Rooms are added or deleted from the blanket reservation by mutual agreement.

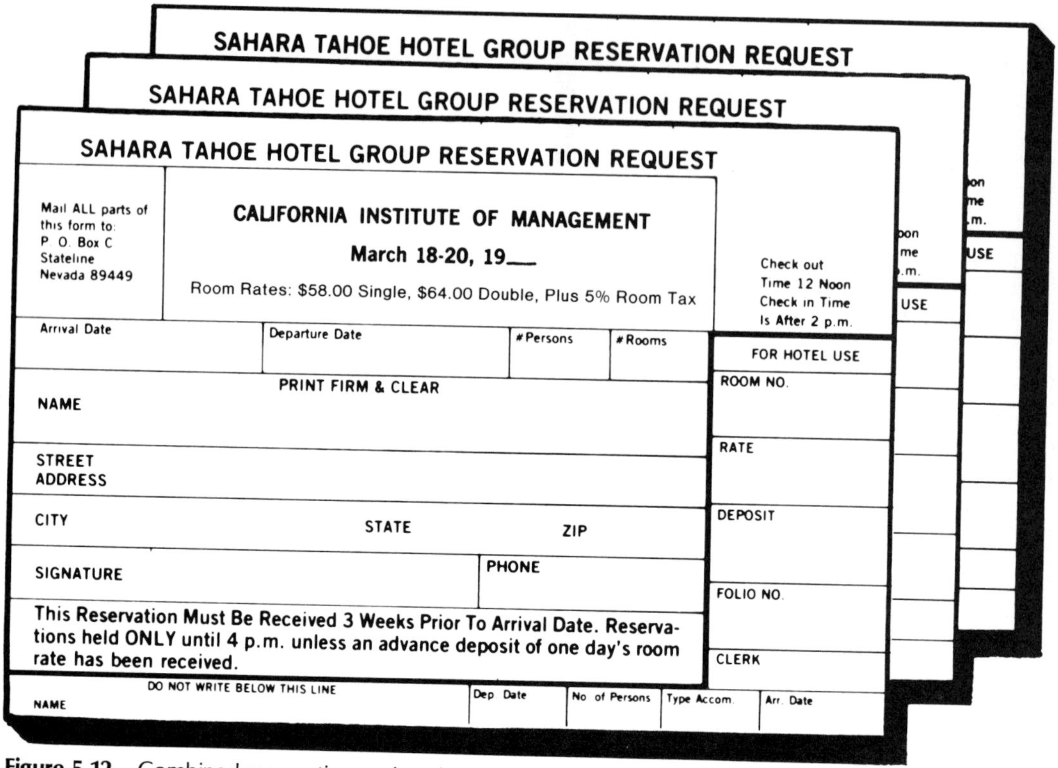

SAHARA TAHOE HOTEL GROUP RESERVATION REQUEST

Mail ALL parts of this form to:
P. O. Box C
Stateline
Nevada 89449

CALIFORNIA INSTITUTE OF MANAGEMENT

March 18-20, 19__

Room Rates: $58.00 Single, $64.00 Double, Plus 5% Room Tax

Check out Time 12 Noon
Check in Time Is After 2 p.m.

Arrival Date	Departure Date	# Persons	# Rooms

PRINT FIRM & CLEAR

NAME

STREET ADDRESS

CITY — STATE — ZIP

SIGNATURE — PHONE

This Reservation Must Be Received 3 Weeks Prior To Arrival Date. Reservations held ONLY until 4 p.m. unless an advance deposit of one day's room rate has been received.

FOR HOTEL USE
ROOM NO.
RATE
DEPOSIT
FOLIO NO.
CLERK

DO NOT WRITE BELOW THIS LINE

NAME	Dep. Date	No. of Persons	Type Accom.	Arr. Date

Figure 5.12. Combined reservation-registration card. The third copy serves as a rooming slip. See also figure 5.2. *Courtesy: Sahara Tahoe Hotel, Lake Tahoe, Nev.*

Rarely are they added. Association planners are an optimistic breed and the hotel sales force may release space unilaterally after ascertaining the organization's experience in previous years at other hotels.

Convention hotels usually cooperate by furnishing each other historical information about numbers, no-shows, and the like. They do this because conventions usually move annually. A hotel in one section of the state or nation is not competing with another if the organization has already decided to meet in another city. Similar information is available through local convention or tourist bureaus, which report to and have access to the files of the International Association of Convention and Visitor Bureaus. The IACVB gathers data from its members about the character and performance of each group handled by the member bureaus.

Practices of this type are just now coming under the scrutiny of various federal agencies. Hoteliers must remain cautious to possible charges of restraint of trade.

Reservation problems occur despite the best predictive efforts of the marketing and reservations departments. Association memberships change over time, and certain cities prove more or less appealing than previous sites. The casualty factor (cancellations plus no-shows) also varies from group to group, reducing the value of generalized percentage figures. Two special cases help defeat the best planned approach to group reservations. One is the unidentified conventioneer; the other is the package plan.

Many conventioneers make room reservations by telephone or on business stationery rather than using the reservation postal cards. One of two things happens with these unidentified conventioneers. Either the reservation is denied (the convention block is open but general reservations are closed) and the guest goes elsewhere, or the reservation is accepted (both the block and the nongroup reservations are open) as a nonconvention guest and the hotel ends up holding duplicate space.

IT packages also compete with convention bookings. Unless the convention takes all of the rooms, the hotel continues to sell its special packages. Package prices may be more attractive than convention rates. Keen shoppers may book the packages. If a travel agency is used, identity is further blurred and a commission is paid to boot. Either way, the count is duplicated once again. Dummy reservations complicate the count still further. In an effort to protect themselves against the unexpected, convention planners often reserve rooms in dummy names, which undermines the count and weakens the executive's credibility.

Reservations and sales must keep on top of developments. Convention managers, or tour brokers, must be asked for guarantees, explanations, or room releases on a regular basis.

Rates

Except for the color assigned to the rack slips of the groups, there are no procedural differences at the front desk for convention reservations versus individual reservations. Special convention rates may be negotiated, how-

ever. The more food and beverage functions the group buys, the greater their percentage of double occupancy,[2] and the slower the business period, the more the sales manager negotiates the room price to assure the booking.

Complimentary rooms for use by the association are included at a rate of about one comp unit per fifty sold, with a bedroom-parlor suite equaling two units. Recent negotiations have involved parking spaces: two free spaces for every seventy-five to one hundred rooms sold. But they have also involved a hard look at how the comps are earned and used. No-shows and cancellations are not counted; only the number of rooms actually sold during the convention are counted. Use of comps is also being restricted, usually to the period of the convention.

Rates are quoted as *flat* or *spread*. Under the flat arrangement all guests pay the same convention rate which is usually less than the rack rate. Except for suites, rooms are assigned on a best-available basis called *run-of-the-house*. Some pay more for the room than its normal price and others pay less. Run-of-the-house implies an equal distribution of room assignments. If one-half the rooms are ocean-view and one-half not, the convention group should get a 50/50 split with a run-of-the-house rate. A fair distribution includes an equitable share of standard, medium, and deluxe accommodations.

A spread rate uses the standard rate distribution, although sometimes the level is reduced several dollars below the rack rates. Assignments are made over the entire rate spread according to individual preferences.

2. Double occupancy runs higher than normal for resort conventions. One rule of thumb sets it at 70 percent, room occupancy is multiplied by a 1.7 factor to determine the number of persons. It depends, of course, on the nature of the group and the location of the meeting.

Large conventions find spread rates more desirable; small groups tend toward the flat rate quotation. Figure 5.11 shows both examples.

Housing Bureau

Once the convention or show outgrows the capacity of a single hotel, a reservation center is established. Convention bureaus or chambers of commerce frequently take over this job. Each hotel commits rooms toward the blanket reservation and a city-wide commitment is made to the association. Rates remain the prerogative of the individual properties.

Reservation requests arrive at the housing bureau, which relays them to the guest's first, second, or third choice depending upon which hotel still has space. The hotel replies and a copy of the confirmation goes to the housing bureau as well as to the association's headquarters. Sometimes the housing bureau itself makes the confirmation, sending informational copies to the hotel and the association. Unless the bureau is notified otherwise, requests are honored until the blanket reservation of that particular hotel has been reached.

In their enthusiasm, hotel sales offices sometimes sell to other groups between the time the city-wide pledge is made and the convention's arrival, which can be months, or even years, later. They assume some other hotel will pick up the slack. If one or more hotels renege, the city-wide convention is jeopardized. This emphasizes the need for a close working relationship between the individual hotels and the city's convention or tourist bureau.

Two properties may join forces if the convention is too large for one hotel but does not need a city-wide commitment. The property that booked the business becomes the headquarters site and the booking office, with the second hotel honoring the other's convention rate. This practice is now considered a possible violation of the antitrust laws. Joint housing

of delegates is permissible, but each property should be careful to negotiate its own rates.

Convention buyers sometimes solicit bids from several hotels with different rate classifications. So long as the properties are in close proximity, the rate spread of $10 to $25 per night will appeal to some conventioneers. It is a service for that portion of the membership and it reduces congestion at the headquarters hotel.

The Single Entity

The *single entity* group is not a tour package nor a convention/trade show. It differs from the first because costs are borne by the charterer and not by the individual members. It differs from the convention or trade show because there is only one buyer, although there are many individuals being served.

Hotels cater to various kinds of single group bookings. A visiting athletic team is one example. Company sales and technical meetings, new product line showings, incentive tours, and training sessions exemplify the range. Gambling junkets are the hotel/casino's own form of single entity. Airlines promote single entity charters, but the transportation arrangements are unimportant to the hotel except as arrival and departure times bear on the work of the front office and the readiness of the rooms.

Tours, be they single entity, alphabetic, or as yet undefined, are the tourist markets of tomorrow. One can anticipate a growth of vertical integration with holding companies owning the transportation, the tour company, and the hotel or resort. Airlines are moving in this direction as a result of the Airline Deregulation Act of 1978 and the demise of the CAB's authority in 1984. It has been estimated that one bed night sold by a vertically integrated company is worth five to seven times more than it represents to a hotel company alone. The future is clear!

QUERIES AND PROBLEMS

1. What response should a desk clerk be taught to make when a walked guest insists that the reservation be honored because nine weeks have elapsed since the acknowledgment, and that's plenty of time to arrange the accommodations.

2. Differentiate between guaranteed reservations, credit-card reservations, advance deposits, and third-party payments.

3. Under what circumstances should what particular type of group buyer be urged to accept run-of-the-house rates? Under what circumstances split rates?

4. One hears that, ''IT packages are self-competing; I would never have them.'' Argue with the statement explaining when it has foundation and when it does not.

6

Registration and Assignment

The arriving guest — who may or may not have a confirmed reservation — is received at the desk, registered into the hotel, and assigned to a room. The three steps are not in distinct, chronological order but overlap with several variations of the sequence possible. With some advance reservations, for example, room assignments are made even before the guests arrive. Once these three steps have been completed, the balance of the registration process, including rooming by the bellperson and billing by the cashier, follows in a more or less prescribed order.

REGISTRATION

The Guest Arrives

Unless there have been some changes in the reservation, the original request with its supporting documentation remains undisturbed in the file (or in the computer) until the guest arrives. Early each morning the reservation office forwards that day's arrival list along with other pertinent materials to the front desk. Sometimes the transfer is made the previous night, or even as early as the previous afternoon. The arrival list takes one of several forms. It might be printed (figure 5.7). It might be an entire section of the reservation rack (figure 5.4) moved intact to the front desk. Moving the list might be nothing more than transferring the data from reservation memory in the computer to registration memory. Or, finally, it might require the reservation slips in the cubbyholes (figure 5.3) to be racked near the room clerk. Other than the reservation journal (figure 5.5), all the lists will be alphabetically arranged.

If everything is functioning properly and if the reservation procedure preprints the registration card (figure 6.4), the guest's delay at the desk should be limited to a signature and a welcoming comment from the clerk. This service should also occur even if the guest's reservation has been misplaced, provided there is ample space. It is another matter if the reserving party arrives and there are no rooms. Very early arrivals — those before the checkout hour — are asked to wait for a departure. Even then the room must still be cleaned. Sometimes the hotel offers a complimentary beverage to help pass the time. Anticipating space, the clerk has the guest register, using a "RNA" (registered, not assigned) designation.

At other times it is immediately apparent to the desk that there are insufficient rooms and that some of the reservations cannot be accommodated. It then becomes a first-come-first-served situation except for special reservations and VIPs. On close counts — the desk is never positive who will or who will not check out — a guest may be kept waiting for hours only to be told that there are no rooms after all. To force departing guests to leave, a card explaining that the room is reserved and that the guest is expected to vacate on the stated departure date is placed in the room or hand-delivered at registration time (figure 6.1). Notifying an in-house guest to leave and forcing him to leave are two different matters, however.

The Registration Card

Registration is not essential to the creation of a legal guest-hotel relationship. In several states it is not even a statutory requirement. In contrast, many other countries not only require registration cards but also use them as police documents. Guests furnish foreign innkeepers with passports and a great deal of personal information that has value only to the authorities (figure 6.2). Age, sex, next destination, previous stop, and nationality are never found on registration cards in the United States. Legally required or not, registration remains the best means of acknowledging the arrival and recording and processing the guest's stay.

Please be advised that your room is on reservation to another on the date you indicated as your checkout date. Checkout time is 1:00 P. M.

Please see the Assistant Manager if your needs differ. **When possible,** he will issue a Late Checkout Approval form. After 1:00 P. M., a ½ day charge will apply until 6:00 P. M. After 6:00 P. M., a full rate will apply.

Please enjoy your stay.

Figure 6.1. Notice of room on reservation. *Courtesy: The Capital Hilton, Washington, D.C.*

Even the eventual automation of much of the front office recordkeeping will not eliminate the registration form, although it may well alter its format (contrasted in figure 6.5). That format has already undergone one major change. At one time guests registered in a book. These books are still seen in B-grade movie thrillers in which the private detective traces the suspect by inspecting the registration book as it lies open on the desk. Various codes were necessarily employed to screen private information. Room rates were recorded much as today's retailers mark merchandise with cost prices that they do not wish the customer to know. A ten-letter word is used to represent the ten digits. Rates are then recorded in code using the appropriate letter. For example,

```
B L A C K    H O R S E
1 2 3 4 5    6 7 8 9 0
```

According to this code, LB would be $21; BR, $18; and so on. Care in selecting a word or phrase that has no repeating letters is all that is required to make the code.

Individual registration cards, which offer privacy, speed in registering, and better appearance, have replaced the book. NCR (no

东方宾馆外国人临时住宿登记表

Tung Fang Hotel Registration Form of Temporary Residence for Foreigner

姓　名 Name in full	中　　文 In Chinese		性　　别 Sex	
	原　　文 In original language		生　　年 Date of birth	
国　籍 Nationality		来华身份或职业 Identity or occupation		
签证或旅行证号码及期限 Visa or travel document number and date of validity				
停留事由 Object of stay		抵达日期 Date of arrival		
何处来何处去 Where from and to		拟住日期 Duration of stay		
房号或住址 Room number or address				

Figure 6.2. Foreign registration card, Tung Fang Hotel, Canton, People's Republic of China.

carbon required) paper and a new awareness of systems as a management technique have produced still another format — the registration packet. Electronic data processing (EDP) systems have brought about further changes in the format and composition of the registration form. Guests of the next decade will probably register by computer. They will be provided a room key after identifying themselves to the computer and signing — with some styluslike instrument — a registration form that will be reproduced on a CRT screen.

Today there are as many shapes and sizes of registration cards as clerical needs and advertising considerations require. Although room rack slips (figure 9.1) and guest bills (figure 10.1) are usually prepared from information contained on the registration card, small hotels use the card as a combination of all three forms (figure 6.3). When EDP equipment is used, much of the information on the registration form is preprinted at the time of reservation and the guest merely signs in on arrival (figure 6.4). Figures 6.3 and 6.4 represent the simplest and most complex of the range of registration cards.

Stock registration cards, as well as other standard forms, are available from several stationery companies that service the hotel industry.[1] Custom-printed forms are needed when special information is required or when it is desirable to create an individuality or mood that is incongruous with a stock form. Irrespective of form, several essential bits of information are common to almost every registration. Some of the items are completed by the guest and some by the room clerk after the guest has signed in.

Name and Number in the Party

The number of registration cards used to register a party depends on the character of the group more than its size. Except for an immediate family, a separate registration card is

1. Catalogs are available from: American Hotel Register Co., 2775 Shermer Rd., Northbrook, Ill. 60062; Kayco Systems, 583 Monterey Pass Road, Monterey Park, Calif. 91754; John Wiley and Sons, 605 3rd Avenue, New York, N.Y. 10016; Whitney Duplicating Check Co., 406 W. 31st St., New York, N.Y. 10001; William Allen and Co., 121 W. 27th St., New York, N.Y. 10001; Wilcox International, Inc., 564 W. Randolph St., Chicago, Ill. 60606.

Guest Registration

THE PROPRIETOR WILL NOT BE RESPONSIBLE OR LIABLE FOR ANY LOSS OF VALUABLES, JEWELS, MONEY OR PERSONAL PROPERTY.

NAME *Ms. Janet R. Wing*

STREET *Feather Wing Road*

CITY *Canyon Park* STATE *Arizona*

MAKE OF CAR

LICENSE NO. STATE

ROOM	RATE	TIME ARRIVED	FOLIO
706	35	6 ☑A.M. ☐P.M.	

DATE	ROOM TAX	NO. IN PARTY	CLERK
12-6	1.40	1	RK

REMARKS

Kayco Form No. 1105MA

ROOM ~~706~~ 316

Wing, Janet R. Ms.

Canyon Park, Ariz.

MONTH	ARRIVE	DEPART	NO. DAYS	RATE	FILE NUMBER	ACCT. RENDERED
Dec	6	9	3	35	71274	12.9

ROOM CHANGE	DATE 12/7	FROM ROOM 706	TO ROOM 316	NEW RATE 35

DATE	ITEM	CHARGE		CREDIT		BALANCE	
12.6	Room	35	—				
	Tax	1	40			36	40
12.7	Telephone	1	70			38	10
	Bar	6	—			44	10
	Tip		75			44	85
	Room	35	—			79	85
	Tax	1	40			81	25
12.8	Coffee Shop	2	20			83	45
	Room	35	—			118	45
	Tax	1	40			119	85
12.9	C.O. Cash			119	85		

AMOUNT FORWARD

Figure 6.3. Combination registration card, room rack slip, and folio for use in small hotels.

prepared for each person. Thus, two adult brothers sharing a room register separately, but one card handles the registration of a husband and wife. One card also serves if the couple has children in the party, the signature being "Mr. and Mrs. John Doe and Family."

Three women sharing one room require three registration cards, whereas a couple with several children assigned to a three-room suite needs only one. Adult children, who have established their own identity, register separately even when accompanying their parents.

Although a separate card is used for each person, one member of the party can complete the cards for others in the group. And in some cases, as with unmarried siblings at the same address, two names could be listed on one card.

Like the rest of society, innkeepers face the dilemma of new social mores toward sex and marriage. They find themselves in the untenable position of accommodating unmarried couples even though it opens them to prosecution under the laws of every state. Still, few police agencies would act so long as the innkeeper does not hold out a disorderly house. Unless the room clerk is absolutely certain from some information that the desk possesses, it is unwise to challenge a represented relationship on the mere suspicion that the couple is not husband and wife or brother and sister. Most innkeepers would take the couple in unless they blatantly flout the relationship. Under today's standards, it seems better to admit them than to challenge them.

Having accepted the guest, the room clerk completes the registration card. Using Arabic numerals, the clerk records the number of persons who have registered on the card (figure 6.5). The number of persons (the house count) has importance for statistics, which are developed in a later chapter, as well as for rate determination and general control of traffic in the room. Some American plan hotels charge half price for children's meals. This half price for billing purposes should not be confused with the party count, in which the child still counts as one.

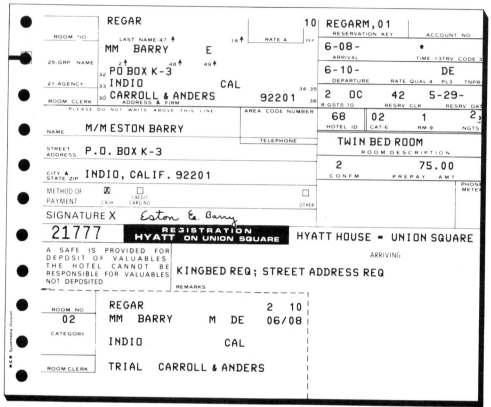

Figure 6.4. Computer-prepared registration card and rack slip (lower left corner). *Courtesy: Hyatt on Union Square, San Francisco, Calif.*

Guest signatures are notoriously illegible. As the clerk records the number in the party, the guest's name is also printed on the registration card (figure 6.5). By checking pronunciation, the clerk is ready to state the name when the bellperson comes forward to room the party. If the registration card is part of a prepared packet, printing the name on the registration card also completes the rooming slip, which is then given to the bellperson (figure 6.6).

Pets

Registering pets has some serious potential costs, including the discomfort of other guests. Some hotels refuse all animals except Seeing Eye dogs. Others seek out pet owners as a distinct portion of their market. Most pet owners appreciate the innkeeper's problems and make restitution for damages done. Additional protection is provided by the contract shown in figure 6.7. It is a light attempt at a serious agreement in which the owner accedes to leash the animal and to pay for damages, if any, in consideration of the animal's admission to the property.

Address

An accurate and complete address is needed for credit and billing and for the development of mailing lists for future sales promotions. A complete address includes such things as zip

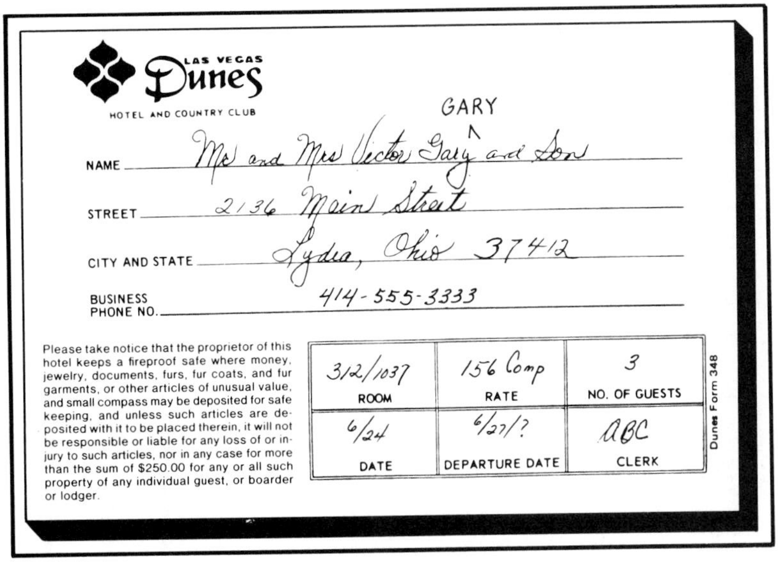

LAS VEGAS Dunes

HOTEL AND COUNTRY CLUB

NAME Mr and Mrs Victor Gary and Son (GARY)

STREET 2136 Main Street

CITY AND STATE Lydia, Ohio 37412

BUSINESS PHONE NO. 414-555-3333

Please take notice that the proprietor of this hotel keeps a fireproof safe where money, jewelry, documents, furs, fur coats, and fur garments, or other articles of unusual value, and small compass may be deposited for safe keeping, and unless such articles are deposited with it to be placed therein, it will not be responsible or liable for any loss of or injury to such articles, nor in any case for more than the sum of $250.00 for any or all such property of any individual guest, or boarder or lodger.

ROOM	RATE	NO. OF GUESTS
3/2/1037	156 Comp	3
DATE	**DEPARTURE DATE**	**CLERK**
6/24	6/27/?	ABC

Dunes Form 348

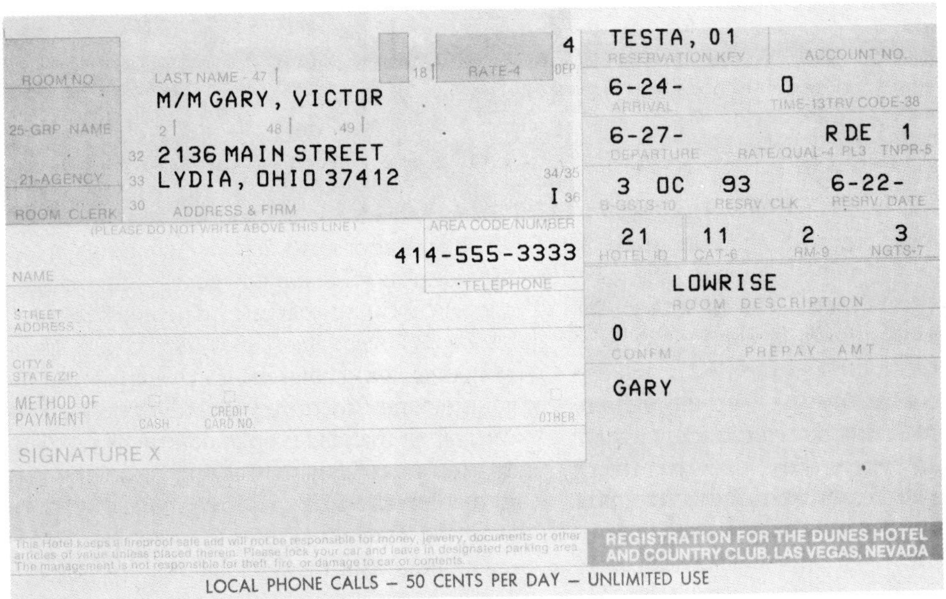

ROOM NO	
LAST NAME - 47	M/M GARY, VICTOR
25-GRP. NAME	
21-AGENCY	32 2136 MAIN STREET
	33 LYDIA, OHIO 37412
ROOM CLERK	30 ADDRESS & FIRM
RATE-4	4
AREA CODE/NUMBER	414-555-3333
TELEPHONE	

(PLEASE DO NOT WRITE ABOVE THIS LINE)

NAME

STREET ADDRESS

CITY & STATE/ZIP

METHOD OF PAYMENT — CASH — CREDIT CARD NO. — OTHER

SIGNATURE X

RESERVATION KEY	TESTA, 01
ACCOUNT NO.	
ARRIVAL	6-24-
TIME-13TRV CODE-38	0
DEPARTURE	6-27-
RATE/QUAL-4 PL3 TNPR-5	R DE 1
8-GSTS-10	3
RESRV. CLK	OC 93
RESRV. DATE	6-22-
HOTEL ID	21
CAT-6	11
RM-9	2
NGTS-7	3
ROOM DESCRIPTION	LOWRISE
CONFM	0
PREPAY AMT	
	GARY

This Hotel keeps a fireproof safe and will not be responsible for money, jewelry, documents or other articles of value unless placed therein. Please lock your car and leave in designated parking area. The management is not responsible for theft, fire, or damage to car or contents.

REGISTRATION FOR THE DUNES HOTEL AND COUNTRY CLUB, LAS VEGAS, NEVADA

LOCAL PHONE CALLS — 50 CENTS PER DAY — UNLIMITED USE

Figure 6.5. Contrasts the style of registration cards before and after the installation of a property management system (computer).
Courtesy: Dunes Hotel, Las Vegas, Nev.

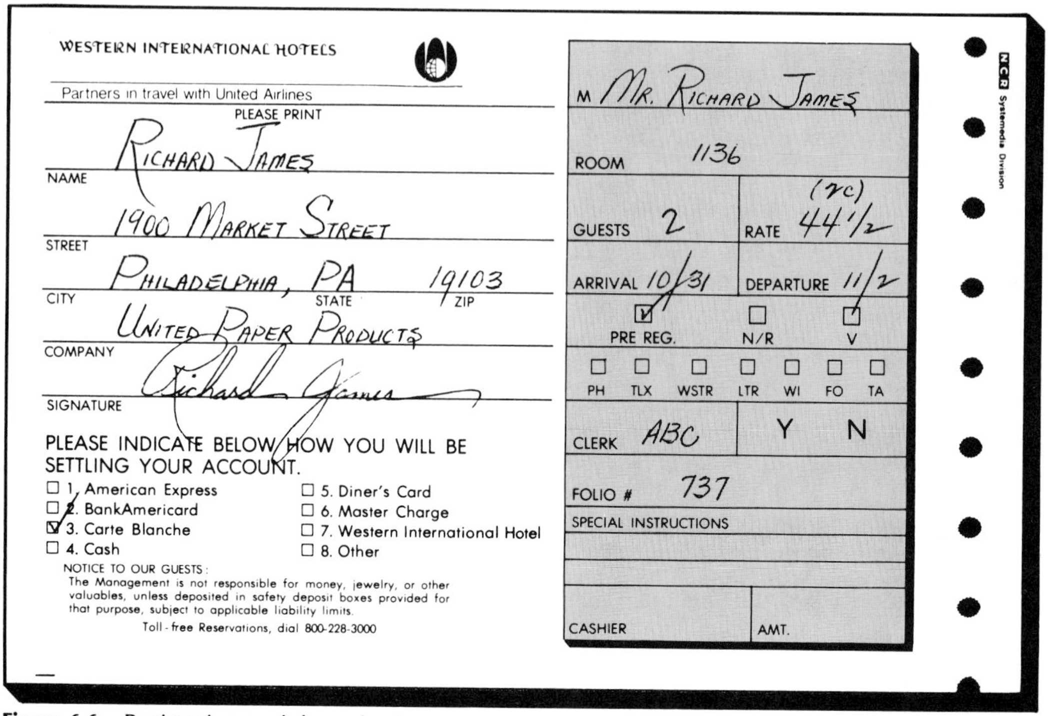
WESTERN INTERNATIONAL HOTELS

Partners in travel with United Airlines

PLEASE PRINT

NAME Richard James

STREET 1900 Market Street

CITY Philadelphia, STATE PA ZIP 19103

COMPANY United Paper Products

SIGNATURE Richard James

PLEASE INDICATE BELOW HOW YOU WILL BE SETTLING YOUR ACCOUNT.

☐ 1. American Express ☐ 5. Diner's Card

☐ 2. BankAmericard ☐ 6. Master Charge

☑ 3. Carte Blanche ☐ 7. Western International Hotel

☐ 4. Cash ☐ 8. Other

NOTICE TO OUR GUESTS:
The Management is not responsible for money, jewelry, or other valuables, unless deposited in safety deposit boxes provided for that purpose, subject to applicable liability limits.

Toll-free Reservations, dial 800-228-3000

M Mr. Richard James

ROOM 1136

GUESTS 2 RATE (rc) 44 1/2

ARRIVAL 10/31 DEPARTURE 11/2

☑ PRE REG. ☐ N/R ☑ V

☐ PH ☐ TLX ☐ WSTR ☐ LTR ☐ WI ☐ FO ☐ TA

CLERK ABC Y N

FOLIO # 737

SPECIAL INSTRUCTIONS

CASHIER AMT.

NCR Systemedia Division

Figure 6.6. Registration card shows business affiliation and method of payment. Part of a packet including the rooming slip. *Courtesy: Arizona Biltmore, Phoenix, Ariz.*

codes, apartment numbers, and even state of residence, for the names of many cities are common to several states. The clerk requests this information if it is not furnished.

Greater credit can be extended to a guest whose address has been verified through an exchange of reservation correspondence than to a walk-in. Whereas those intent on fraud will use false addresses, vacant lots, or temporary box numbers, unintentional skippers can be traced, billed, and subsequently collected from if an accurate address is on file. Experience and tradition has made suspect the address of another hotel. Nevertheless, there are persons who reside permanently in hotels just as there are still cities and towns in the United States small enough to have neither street addresses nor street names.

Rising labor costs and an increasingly mobile population have made guest-history cards passé in all but special cases. The guest history is a record of the guest's stay and of any special needs and preferences. This information is sometimes recorded on the registration card rather than on a separate form. Filing registration cards alphabetically makes all the information about a particular guest readily available. The labor expense of continual updating has offset the benefits of guest-history cards, especially since guests' loyalties to a given property have diminished and addresses are frequently out-of-date. Even the computer, with its great storage capacity, is not likely to revitalize the guest-history record. There are just too many travelers who are one-time visitors to justify the effort. Casinos main-

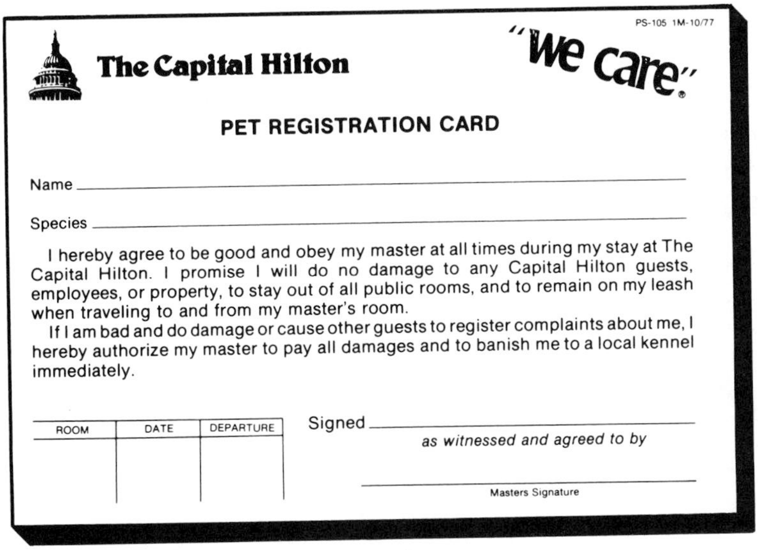

PS-105 1M-10/77

The Capital Hilton "We care"®

PET REGISTRATION CARD

Name ______________________

Species ______________________

I hereby agree to be good and obey my master at all times during my stay at The Capital Hilton. I promise I will do no damage to any Capital Hilton guests, employees, or property, to stay out of all public rooms, and to remain on my leash when traveling to and from my master's room.

If I am bad and do damage or cause other guests to register complaints about me, I hereby authorize my master to pay all damages and to banish me to a local kennel immediately.

ROOM	DATE	DEPARTURE

Signed ______________________

as witnessed and agreed to by

____

Masters Signature

Figure 6.7. Pet damage agreement. *Courtesy: The Capital Hilton, Washington, D.C.*

tain a guest history for credit players, but this is a casino cashier's record, a cage record, not a hotel form.

Commercial hotels – and resorts too – ask for the patron's business address and sometimes organizational title in addition to the residential address (figure 6.6). Again, the purpose is better credit control and more effective sales promotion.

Room Number

Courtesy, guest service, and cordiality notwithstanding, the guest is known as much by room number as by name. Room number is the major means of locating, identifying, and billing the guest. The room number or numbers to be occupied by the party are recorded on the card by the clerk. When a suite of rooms is assigned, the entry appears as "702/4/6," representing connecting rooms 702, 704, and 706 (figure 6.8).

It may be necessary to separate the party or even to room the guests on separate floors when connecting or adjoining rooms are not available. This is done intentionally, although far less today than heretofore, when the group is composed of unmarried persons of both sexes. Both room numbers would be shown if the entire party has registered on one card (figure 6.5). When the party uses more than one registration card, room numbers might be cross-referenced. This is also done, especially in small resorts, where friends come together and where the proprietor plans to capitalize on this fact during later promotions. Since it is important for the innkeeper to remember that the Joneses came with the Smiths, names as well as room numbers are cross-referenced to create a guest history from the registration card.

Identification

The clerk's initials are affixed to the registration card for identification. This carries through the balance of the rooming procedure. Initials appear on the rooming slip, the room rack slip, and the top of the guest's folio (figures 6.17, 9.1, and 10.1).

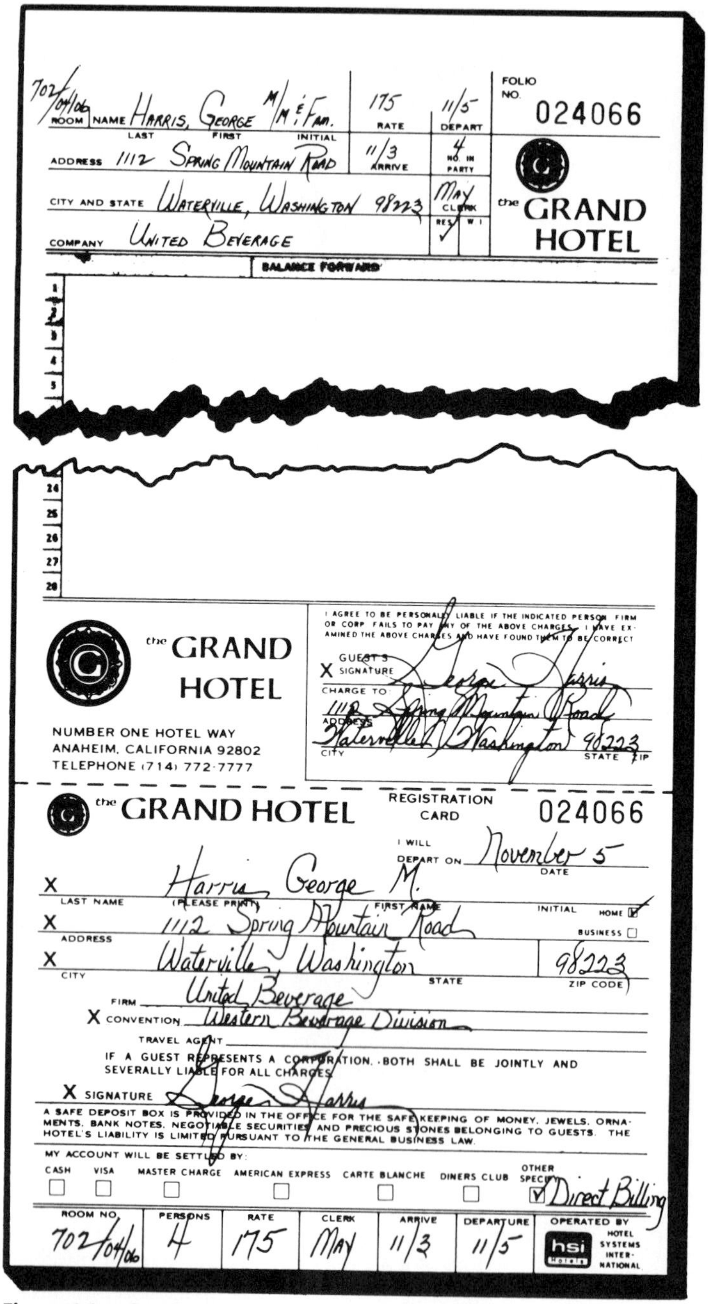

Figure 6.8. Combined registration card and guest folio, numerically matched. *Courtesy: Grand Hotel, Anaheim, Calif.*

Account Number

Numbered registration cards and numbered guest folios are more important in smaller hotels than in larger ones. Numbering serves as a control device when one employee is clerk, cashier, and supervisor all in one. It is possible for such an employee to sell the room as clerk, pocket the money as cashier, and cover the discrepancy as night auditor. When the staff grows large enough to permit a separation of duties, form control becomes less important. In fact, numbered registration cards actually become burdensome as the front office staff grows larger. Care must then be exercised to assure the sequence and to account for missing numbers without the offsetting advantage of a control function. Sequentially numbered forms also cost considerably more than unnumbered ones.

Electronic systems have no bills. Data is kept in memory, not on a prenumbered form, and printed on request. Several printings may be needed during the guest's stay. In fact, many hotels print all of the accounts nightly to protect against loss of data from a computer malfunction.

Unless registration cards and guest folios are bound in a packet, as shown in figure 6.8, it is almost impossible to keep them number coordinated. If they need to be numbered for control, it is better to have numbered folios and cross-reference them on unnumbered registration cards (figure 6.6). Used folios are then filed in numerical sequence, which almost corresponds to chronological order, and used registrations are filed alphabetically. If the guest's name is known, it is possible to locate the folio through the cross-reference registration. According to some management consultants, registration cards may be destroyed after three years.

Disclaimer of Liability

Almost every registration card carries a statement concerning the hotel's liability for the loss of guest valuables. Several such disclaimers are shown in figures 6.3 through 6.6. The form and content of the statement is prescribed by state statute and, consequently, varies among the states. If the innkeeper meets the provisions of the statute, and public notice on the registration card is usually one such provision, liability for the loss of valuables is substantially reduced. Were it not for the dollar limits set by state legislatures, innkeepers would be liable under common law. Common law is far more stringent than statutory law; it makes the hotel responsible in full for the value of guests' belongings. Most states, but not all, limit the innkeeper's liability to a fixed sum even when the guest uses the safe provided. Other statutes prevent recovery against the hotel if the guest fails to use the safe, provided the hotel has complied with every provision of the law. See figure 6.9.

Since state laws require hotels to furnish safes, these laws are sometimes called iron-safe statutes. State legislatures have extended this principle of limited liability to checkrooms and to goods that are too large for the ordinary safe, salesperson's samples for example. A few hotels have begun to provide closet-sized safes or walk-in safes to house larger items like fur coats and cameras.

Safe-deposit Box

The method of securing guest valuables depends upon the type of safe provided. If the hotel has safe-deposit boxes similar to those used in banks,[2] the guest places valuables in a

2. The safe-deposit box originated in a hotel — the New England Hotel — not in a bank. Introduced in Boston about 1848, it was used to protect money left at the hotel by local business interests.

NOTICE

When checking out please notify Front Office before ________ to avoid charges for another day.

Thank You!

(1) Please take notice that the proprietor of this hotel, inn, boarding house, or lodging house keeps a fireproof safe where money, jewelry, furs, fur coats, documents or other articles of unusual value and small compass may be deposited for safe-keeping and unless such articles are deposited with him to be placed therein, he will not be responsible or liable for any loss or injury to such articles, nor in any case for more than the sum of $250.00 for any or all such property of any individual guest, or boarder or lodger.

(2) Section 1863: Civil Code of California. (a) Every keeper of a hotel, inn, boarding house or lodging house shall post in a conspicuous place in the office or public room, and in every bedroom of said hotel, boarding house, inn or lodging house, a printed copy of this section, and a statement of rate or range of rates by the day for lodging. "(b) No charge or sum shall be collected or received for any greater sum than is specified in subdivision (a). For any violation of this subdivision, the offender shall forfeit to the injured party one hundred dollars ($100.00) or three times the amount of the sum charged in excess of what he is entitled to, whichever is greater. There shall be no forfeiture under this subdivision unless notice be given of the overcharge to such keeper within 30 days after payment of such charges and such keeper shall fail or refuse to make proper adjustment of such overcharge."

(1) Section 537: California Penal Code. Any person who obtains any food or accommodations at a hotel, inn, restaurant, boarding house, lodging house, apartment house, bungalow court, motel or auto camp, without paying therefor, with intent to defraud the proprietor or manager thereof, or who obtains credit at a hotel, inn, restaurant, boarding house, lodging house, apartment house, bungalow court, motel or auto camp by the use of any false pretense, or who after obtaining credit, food accommodations, at a hotel, inn, restaurant, boarding house, lodging house, apartment house, bungalow court, motel or auto camp, absconds, or surreptitiously, or by force, menace, or threats, removes any part of his baggage therefrom without paying for his food or accommodations is guilty of a misdemeanor.

Evidence that such person left the premises of such a hotel, inn, restaurant, boarding house, lodging house, apartment house, bungalow court, motel, or auto camp, without paying or offering to pay for such food or accommodation shall be prima facie evidence that such person obtained such food or accommodations with intent to defraud the proprietor or manager.

RATES	ROOM No. ________
SINGLES - ONE PERSON	$ ________ To $ ________
DBLS. / TWINS - TWO PERSONS	$ ________ To $ ________
SUITES	$ ________ To $ ________

Kayco Form No. 1024 California

Figure 6.9. Notice limiting the liability of innkeepers in California.

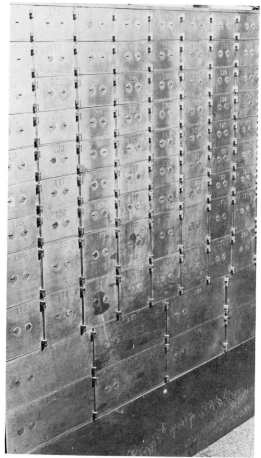

Figure 6.10. Typical safe-deposit box installation. Two keys (one of which is held by the guest) are needed to open the box.

box (figure 6.10), signs a register or card (figure 6.11), and takes the key as a receipt. Goods are retrieved by signing the register again (to allow for a comparison of signatures) and presenting the receipt—the key. Intermittent access to the box is also handled by the sign-in card pictured.

The number of the safe-deposit box is recorded on the safe-deposit register and sometimes on the folio. Cashiers are then able to remind departing guests about their boxes, and the notice also alerts the cashier to the deposit refund if a key deposit was required when the box was issued. A lost key requires the service of a locksmith. Not only do guests pay the locksmith's charges for drilling them open, but they must also satisfy management that the contents of the boxes are theirs.

A different procedure is used if the hotel has a large, noncompartmentalized safe. Valu-

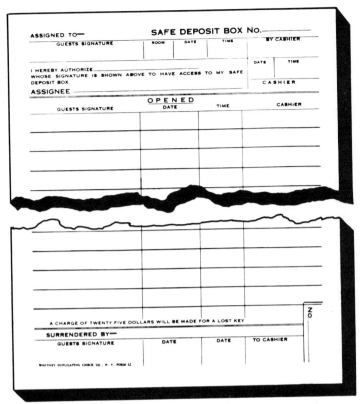

Figure 6.11. Safe-deposit signature form; also used for intermittent access.

ables are stored in individual envelopes (figure 6.12) rather than in individual safe-deposit boxes. The envelope has two tags, both with the same number and each with a place for the guest's signature. The guest signs one and is given the other numbered but unsigned slip when the valuables are left. Deposits are retrieved by signing the blank receipt slip in front of the cashier. After signatures and numbers are compared, the guest is given the sealed envelope that had been stored in the safe.

Envelopes are also used when the item to be safeguarded is too large for the safe-deposit box. The same procedure is used, except the original signature is removed from the envelope and taped to the large item that is being stored.

In no instance does the cashier know what the guest is depositing either in the envelope or in the box. The weakness of both procedures is obviously in the reliance that the systems place on the cashier's ability to differentiate valid signatures from forgeries.

Although the legal position is still to be tested, some innovative hotels are experimenting with in-room safes. Special bolts, which fasten the safe to the wall, provide initial security. They are further protected by a tilt device that signals a loud alarm when they are moved (figure 6.13).

Bolting a safe-deposit box to a table in the room is another variation. All sides are intact except the front panel. This panel, along with the key, is checked out by the guest. The desk

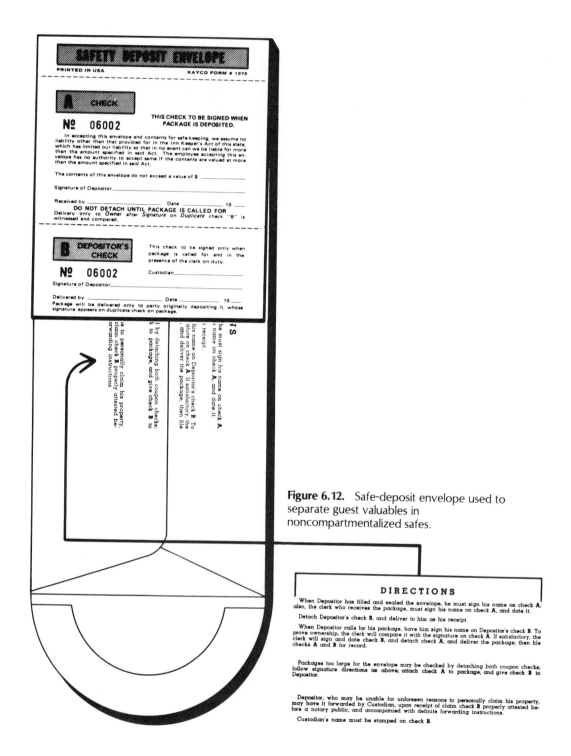

SAFETY DEPOSIT ENVELOPE

PRINTED IN USA   KAYCO FORM # 1070

A CHECK

N° 06002

THIS CHECK TO BE SIGNED WHEN
PACKAGE IS DEPOSITED.

In accepting this envelope and contents for safe-keeping, we assume no
liability other than that provided for in the Inn Keeper's Act of this state,
which has limited our liability so that in no event can we be liable for more
than the amount specified in said Act. The employee accepting this envelope has no authority to accept same if the contents are valued at more
than the amount specified in said Act.

The contents of this envelope do not exceed a value of $ _____

Signature of Depositor_____

Received by _____ Date _____ 19 ____
DO NOT DETACH UNTIL PACKAGE IS CALLED FOR
Delivery only to *Owner* after *Signature* on *Duplicate* check "B" is
witnessed and compared.

**B DEPOSITOR'S
CHECK**

N° 06002

This check to be signed only when
package is called for and in the
presence of the clerk on duty.

Custodian _____

Signature of Depositor_____

Delivered by _____ Date _____ 19 ____
Package will be delivered only to party originally depositing it, whose
signature appears on duplicate check on package.

Figure 6.12. Safe-deposit envelope used to separate guest valuables in noncompartmentalized safes.

DIRECTIONS

When Depositor has filled and sealed the envelope, he must sign his name on check **A**;
also, the clerk who receives the package, must sign his name on check **A**, and date it.

Detach Depositor's check **B**, and deliver to him as his receipt.

When Depositor calls for his package, have him sign his name on Depositor's check **B**. To
prove ownership, the clerk will compare it with the signature on check **A**. If satisfactory, the
clerk will sign and date check **B**, and detach check **A**, and deliver the package; then file
checks **A** and **B** for record.

Packages too large for the envelope may be checked by detaching both coupon checks;
follow signature directions as above; attach check **A** to package, and give check **B** to
Depositor.

Depositor, who may be unable for unforseen reasons to personally claim his property,
may have it forwarded by Custodian, upon receipt of claim check **B** properly attested before a notary public, and accompanied with definite forwarding instructions.

Custodian's name must be stamped on check **B**.

Figure 6.13. An in-room safe, a new amenity in many hotels, reduces guest losses and guest demands on the front desk. *Courtesy: Elsafe of Nevada and Elsafe International, Vanvikan, Norway.*

levies a charge if the panel is not returned when the guest departs. But do in-room safes meet the provisions of the various state statutes? Until the matter is resolved in court, cautious managers are posting disclaimers that remind the guest of the availability of the more traditional safe in the lobby. Levying a charge for using the in-room safe, which innkeepers are doing, compounds the legal question.

Additional Contents

The registration procedure is completed quickly when there is no waiting line. Empty spaces and lines are filled in by the guest (name, address, and signature), or by the clerk (dates and time of arrival and departure, room and rate assigned, folio reference if any, and the

clerk's identification). With a computer, much of the data is preprinted during the quiet hours of the previous night, so there is even less to do at registration. Noncomputerized reservation/registration packets also expedite the arrival process.

Extra messages are being added to the reg card even as management struggles to expedite the often frustrating delay inherent in registering. The message content differs among the hotels and chains and reflects their unique problems and growing legal concerns. It's an unusual guest who would read any message printed on the registration card during the hurried minutes of registration, but the presence of the message meets the niceties of legal requirements. Besides, the registration card is usually part of a packet that includes the rooming slip, which is left with the guest at the end of the rooming sequence.

Questions about credit are the most common items found on the cards. How do you intend to pay: with cash, credit card (and which one), or personal check? Guests paying by personal check are advised to clear the arrangement in advance with the assistant manager. Guests paying by credit card must proffer the card so that it may be imprinted on the rear of the registration card or on the credit card form (figure 13.11). One sometimes finds a statement above the guest's signature agreeing to personal liability for the bill if the company or association fails to pay (figure 6.8). Motor inns have long required auto identification to be recorded on the registration form (figure 6.3).

Legitimate misunderstandings occur quite often: a misunderstanding about the rate of the room, a misunderstanding about the date of departure, etc. In a rather unusual turn, some hotels have guests initial the registration card indicating their agreement to its content. The check-out hour is frequently included with a notice of additional charges for overstaying. Misunderstandings are not eliminated by the system; the hotel just gains the satisfaction of blaming the guest. Printing the messages in several languages accents both the cautionary attitude of the management and the hotel's quest for foreign business.

ASSIGNMENT

Making the Room Selection

Soon after the day shift begins, a housekeeper's report (figure 14.8) arrives at the front desk. The vacant and occupied rooms reported by the housekeeper are compared to the status of rooms shown by the room rack. With that information in hand, the clerks assign a room number to each anticipated arrival listed on the reservation sheet, which was forwarded to the desk that morning or even earlier.

The number of anticipated arrivals is compared with the number of vacant rooms and expected departures. It is at this point that the first determination is made whether to accept walk-ins or not. That decision is not firm and may be changed once or several times throughout the day.

If many vacant rooms are available, either from current vacancies or anticipated departures, there is no reason to make assignments before the guest arrives. Special requests for limited facilities is the exception, and these are assigned early to assure availability. Regardless of vacancies available, a cautious manager will generally block connecting rooms, early arrivals, guaranteed reservations, management-made reservations, special rates, suites, and VIPs.

A crowded hotel with few vacancies or estimated departures requires different handling. Some assignments, including special requests, may need to wait for checkouts. The desk clerk knows who will be leaving on a particular day, although this too may prove surprising, but doesn't know at what time they are checking out relative to the guests who are arriving. So the special requests are assigned to the vacant rooms first, and then arriving guests are assigned on a first-come, first-served basis as vacancies occur.

Room numbers are written on the reservation material as part of the preassignment process. Guests can then be roomed quickly when they arrive. Colored flags are placed in the room rack (plate 1) to block those rooms. Blue flags normally signal standard assignments — accommodations that are plentiful and can be reshuffled as new circumstances develop throughout the day. Other colors flag limited facilities whose blocks are moved only if comparable accommodations are available. Still other colors are used for blocks that may not be changed at all except on approval of higher authority. When a bin system is used, the stock cards are attached to the reservation slips and the rack is blocked with an appropriate flag.

Assignment changes are made because new information becomes available — the arriving guest plans to stay a longer or shorter time than the reservation stated, or the party is larger or smaller than anticipated. The original room might not be available if the previous guest has not vacated or if some emergency has placed it out of order. By playing "solitaire" with the rack, scattered reservations can be combined and additional rooms can be opened with greater flexibility. It is difficult to make this manipulation with a computerized system. Only portions of room status can be seen on the CRT at any one time. Because of this limitation, many large properties maintain a room rack even though it duplicates computer memory. In fact, they do this because it serves as a backup in case of computer failure.

Eventually the guest arrives. Even if a particular room has been earmarked for the party by the preassignment process, the clerk makes the actual room assignment only after verifying needs. This information is obtained from the guest as part of the reception process, or from reference to the reservation that the guest holds, or from both sources. The room or rooms assigned will depend upon the character (couple, children, friends) of the arriving party, its size (number of persons), and the rate and facilities (bed, bath) needed.

Unless there is a change in the reservation request, the clerk rooms the arrivals in the facilities that were preassigned and blocked earlier in the day. The room number and rate are then recorded on the reg card. In all likelihood, no special room has been blocked even if the guest has a reservation. In that case, and in the case of a walk-in, the room clerk makes the assignment from the available rooms, completing the registration card in the usual manner. All registration cards are time-stamped.

Room assignments are selected from the room rack or from stock cards that represent the room rack. As the following chapter explains, the room rack contains information about the facilities and price of each room. The same information is available with a computerized system. The procedure is the same; only the mechanics are different. The list of available rooms is displayed on the CRT screen after the clerk inputs the request for a given accommodation and rate. The clerk matches the needs of the arriving party with the available facilities and makes the assignment. Obviously, the better the clerk knows the product being sold, the more rapidly and satisfactorily the assignment will be made. It has been jokingly said that the fewer the rooms available, the easier it is to make assignments, implying that with few rooms available the guest must take what's offered or have no room. Whenever possible, and it's possible more than it's practiced, the clerk should attempt to *sell up* — to sell the guest a higher

priced room than what the guest reserved or planned to buy. Good selling is the keystone to rooms profits.

As a salesperson, the clerk must be sensitive to changing guest demands and expectations. For example, higher floors (away from street noise) with better views have always been more desirable and more expensive. But after several major fires swept through hotels across the land, guests demanded lower sleeping floors, and hotels changed reservation processes and rates to conform.

A similar shift has developed in the market because of the increase in women travelers. Hotels have worked hard to develop a market segment from traveling career women. Women-only floors, furnished with make-up mirrors, skirt hangers, blow-dryers and the like, have often pulled higher occupancy than the overall property. Still, room preference is an individual thing. One person wants a room near the elevator for security reasons; another wants the end of the corridor to be away from the noise.

The best way to sell a product is to show it. At resorts, where longer stays are the norm, guests may prefer to see the room before signing in. That can be done — and has been — with a screen monitor at the desk. In the not too distant future, the image will be projected into the home to sell the reservation directly to the buyer.

Completing the Reception

Many things are going on simultaneously at the front desk: the reservation is being located; the guest is being welcomed; accommodation needs are being determined or reevaluated; some small talk is taking place; the clerk is trying to sell up; the guest's identity, including the correct spelling of the name and address, is being verified; quality of the luggage is being noted; certain public rooms, services, or events in the hotel may be pitched; anticipated departure date is obtained or verified; both the guest and the clerk are completing their portions of the registration card; and mail or messages are handed over. Finally, a bellperson is called and a temporary block is made on the assigned room so no other party will be roomed there inadvertently (plate 1).

All this activity notwithstanding, the clerk must remain alert to certain problem areas. The room assigned must meet the rate reserved. Arrangements for special rates must be identified early enough to be properly assigned. Discounted package plans, for example, must be collected in advance and the proper coupons issued. Special rates for conventioneers must be watched because sometimes the reduced rate is allowed before and after the convention dates, and sometimes it isn't. Many of these special situations require different registration cards or different handling to assure the special billing that comes later on in the guest's stay. This is especially true of trade advertising contracts.

Room clerks also perform accounting functions. Advanced deposits must be verified. Color on the reservation form or on the reservation rack slip alerts the receptionist to the prepayment. If it is an electronic system, the information is in the computer or has been printed out on the preprinted reservation form awaiting the guest's signature. Guests speak up quickly enough if the clerk errs in handling the reservation deposit.

Travel agency vouchers require special handling if the booking agency is to be properly credited. Here again, color and computer printout flag the need. Often the guest carries the agency's travel voucher (figure 13.5), which is indication enough.

Throughout the procedure, which could take anywhere from one to ten or fifteen minutes, the clerk must remain calm, dignified, and friendly. Some feel that the clerk's attitude is the most important part of the whole registra-

tion process. Room clerks were historical figures in the late 1800s and early 1900s. Perhaps this is the explanation for their supercilious posturing, which still haunts the profession today. It is bad enough to have a room or a reservation denied; it is inexcusable to have it done in a humiliating manner. As one travel writer said, "Ship off to the Siberian Sheraton the room clerk who greets poor tired me, having come 3,000 miles, lost my suitcase, and been delayed three hours, by fumbling around with the papers and asking icily, 'now when did you make that reservation?' "

Assignment Variations

Several variations alter the otherwise simple assignment procedure. If there are no rooms and the guest has a reservation, accommodations must be found elsewhere. This was discussed in the overbooking section of chapter 4. Many hotels go a step further and search out accommodations for every guest who inquires whether or not a reservation had been made.

Special handling is also needed if no rooms are available at the rate reserved. The clerk might sell up, convincing the arrival to take a better room at a better rate. More frequently, the guest is given the better room at the lower rate. If the differential is large, the guest is moved the next day when the lower rate opens.

Did Not Stay

DNS, "did not stay," means just that. The party registered, may even have gone as far as the room, and then left. Dissatisfaction with the accommodations, the rate, or the attitude of the staff may precipitate a hasty departure. Sometimes the guest first seeks remedy in the form of a different room assignment and sometimes just leaves without ever saying why. Emergency messages, either by telephone or in the mail that the guest finds on arrival, account for some of the immediate departures. Usually no charge is made if this occurs within a reasonable time after arrival, even if the room was occupied for a short period.

As a control device, registration cards are marked "DNS" and approved by a member of the management. Weaknesses in the reservation system or hotel service are uncovered thereby and areas that need attention made a bit more evident. Control is also important if the registration cards and/or folios are being kept in numerical sequence. Voided cards that carry a manager's signature maintain the internal control.

Registered, Not Assigned

Immediate room assignment is not always possible. Guests who arrive far in advance of the check-out hour may find that no rooms are available even though they have reservations.[3] Either the house is full or the needs of the arriving party are so specific that those limited facilities are not yet open. Unable to accommodate the guest at that moment, the clerk completes the registration nevertheless and marks the card "RNA," which means "registered, not assigned."

The RNA registration card is kept in the work area of the desk and the guest is asked to wait. As soon as a room is vacated, the assignment is made, but the guest may be held in the lobby until the housekeeper reports the room ready for sale. Guests are not usually sent to unmade rooms. Guests who arrive after the room is vacated but before it is readied by the housekeeper — that is, while *on change* — are assigned at once but not sent to the unmade room. This is not a RNA.

3. A publication of the Hotel Sales Management Association says that occupancy may not be possible until after the established check-out hour, usually 1 P.M. Loew's Anatole in Dallas goes further, posting 3 P.M. as the check-in hour.

RNAs were commonplace during World War II and immediately thereafter, when limited hotel facilities were in demand. It occurs today when there are simultaneous arrivals and departures of large convention groups or when bus or tour groups overlap. Busy holidays give rise to nonassignment, especially when it is the type of resort where arrivals come early and departures stay late.

On some occasions it may be necessary to assign guests temporary rooms, changing them to a permanent assignment later on. This type of costly duplication should be avoided except in special circumstances. At the least, clerks should offer to have baggage checked for the waiting guest. Waiting for a room is a distressing experience and some innkeepers make it less painful by offering complimentary coffee or cocktails. Most computers are able to accept RNAs and allow the guest to create charges even though no room identification is possible.

Paid in Advance

Under the law, room charges may be collected in advance. Hotels have rarely resorted to this heretofore, limiting their requests for advance payment to guests with no baggage or light baggage. An intermediate position between paid in advance and paid at departure has now been broadly adopted. Most hotels require credit identification and imprint the card on the folio for credit reference. Guests with no credit card and no baggage must still pay in advance. Motels are an exception and almost always collect in advance because the physical design of the property permits guests to leave unnoticed.

Under the law, innkeepers also have the right to hold luggage for nonpayment. This traditional prejudgment lien is presently under court challenge. Rather than testing the issue in court, hotelkeepers are relying more and more on the credit card and on their right to collect in advance.

Paid-in-advance guests are "flagged" to prevent charges being made from other departments. Once the room is paid in advance, all other departments must collect cash for services rendered. Communicating that to the other departments is easier said than done. It is one problem that the computer easily solves. Collecting an additional deposit, say $100, eliminates the problem entirely.

Paid-in-advance guests are checked out automatically the following day at the checkout hour unless other arrangements have been made beforehand.

Special Attention

Reservations may carry the symbol SPATT, which means "special attention." VIP, "very important person," and "star guest" are terms also used. They all mean that the guest is an important person and the clerk should provide service in keeping with the visitor's stature. He or she could be the executive officer of a large association, for example, that is considering the hotel as a convention site.

The special designation is transferred to the room rack slips, which are prepared from the registration card. SPATT sometimes requires the assistant manager to accompany the arriving guest to the room. It sometimes means that the guest need not register. It may also mean that no information about the guest will be given out to callers without first being screened.

There is a difference between a VIP and DG, "distinguished guest," according to one professional publication. The VIP represents either good publicity for the hotel or direct business, whereas the DG is honored because of position rather than economic value. Presidents, kings, and tycoons rate a DG designation. Meeting planners, company presidents, or committee chairpersons get the VIP treatment and then only during the tenure of their office. VIPs are treated to comp rooms, baskets of fruit, or bottles of liquor. Thoughtful-

ness and imagination sustained by personal consideration are more important to the DG than the amount of money spent, this publication explains.

The Rooming Procedure

Once the registration card is completed, a rooming slip is prepared for the use of the bell department, and the guest is dispatched to the room. The rooming slip is either part of the registration packet (figure 6.6) or it is a separate form (figure 6.17). While the bellperson, who has received the rooming slip from the clerk, is directing the guest to the room, the completed registration card is being processed. From it comes the guest bill and the room rack slips. Figure 6.14 represents the process schematically.

Bell Service

The uniformed services are an integral part of the registration and assignment process. This department attends the guest from the time of arrival at the front door, where the door attendant makes the greeting, to the final room destination, accompanied by the bellperson. In the performance of their duties, service personnel have an extraordinary opportunity to sell the facilities of the hotel and portray its character.

Several innovations have had an impact on the service department's functions and means of livelihood. Self-service items, such as floor icemakers, vending machines, and in-room refrigerators and liquor dispensers, have reduced the kind and number of service calls that bellpersons make. Group arrivals, where individuals room themselves, further reduce the service functions of this department.

Rotation of Fronts

Tips comprise the bulk of the bell department's earnings. According to a study done by the American Hotel & Motel Association, the

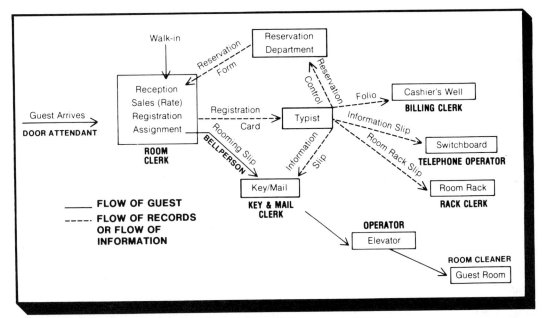

Figure 6.14. Schematic presentation of the registration procedure. For property management systems, substitute "information flow" for "record flow."

bellperson's cash salary was the lowest of any hotel employee. Despite this, total earnings usually exceed that of most other front office employees, including some management positions. Each opportunity for earning a tip is carefully monitored.

The bellperson who comes forward to take the rooming slip from the clerk and room the guest is called a *front*. Fronts rotate in turn. The one who has just completed a front is called a *last*. Lasts are used for errands and deliveries that are unlikely to produce gratuities. They are used as runners between the front office and other departments when no other communication system is available. Housekeeping the lobby is a responsibility of the last. Lasts are also assigned dead room changes with no chance of a gratuity such as lockouts, deaths, and moves carried out in the guest's absence.

Between the front and the last, positions rotate in sequence, moving forward in the rank as each new front is called. At one time, each position in the sequence was represented by a particular post in the lobby. One station might be by the front door to receive incoming luggage; another across the lobby; a third by the elevators.

The procedure is much less formal today, although fronts still wait by the bellstand, which is usually, but not always, in the lobby adjacent to and visible from the front desk. The bellstand at the Camelback Inn in Scottsdale, Arizona is outside near the parking circle. At this particular inn the road doesn't go to the lobby; since all the units are in outbuildings, luggage is never carried to the desk.

As the clerk completes the registration, the front is summoned to the desk by lights or signals or verbally by the clerk calling "Front!"

Aware of the routine, the front rarely needs prompting. Computerized front offices employ a remote printer at the bellstand. The rooming slips are printed at the bellstand, so the bellperson approaches the guests aware of their names. By coding the printout with color or symbols, the desk communicates additional information (VIP, light luggage, etc.) to the bell department.

Today's traveler comes with less luggage and lighter luggage than was the custom a few years ago. Not only are stays shorter but clothing and bags are also lighter in weight. Since the bellperson uses handcarts in hotels and scooters for motel properties, it is rarely necessary to call more than one person for a front.

A record of fronts is maintained at the bell captain's desk to assure each individual a proper turn, although the sequence may be altered if a guest requests a specific person. The record also enables the captain to keep track of the crew, which is the most mobile department in the hotel. By noting the bellperson's presence on various floors at various times, the record offers protection from accusations in the event of theft or other trouble. It fixes responsibility if problems arise about the rooming procedure or lost luggage. Their comings and goings, the purposes of their errands, and the times elapsed are recorded in the record that is maintained as a book, a card, or a duplicate of the rooming slip. All are time-stamped. (As yet, there is no special computer program.)

Duties of the Bell Department

Despite the bellperson's independent earnings and entrepreneurlike spirit, they are still employees of the hotel. They are in a position to carry the hotel's message to the guest and the guest's reaction to the management. Bellpersons are often the first to note light baggage and they must discreetly inform the clerk of this. They act as hosts to the arriving guest and as sales representatives for the hotel. In addition to escorting guests to their rooms, the bell staff services guests in the lobbies and public areas, runs errands, and assists at departures. They act as the eyes and ears of the security department, watch for skippers, and make inspections as they room their charges. Depending on the organization, the service department either operates the garaging facilities or coordinates them with the independent operator. Small hotels use bellpersons to make room service calls, especially from the bar.

There are certain matters that they should not handle. The service department does not quote rates or suggest room assignments. Bellpersons call the room clerk for a second assignment whenever the guest is dissatisfied with the first or when the original room is occupied or on change. Sometimes bellpersons become involved in services that are neither legal nor condoned by the hotel. Strict management vigilance holds such practices to a minimum. Bellpersons, or sometimes just the captains, share in other incomes. Auto rentals, tickets to local attractions, bus tours, and the like are available at the captain's desk. Each of these companies pays a commission (10 to 15 percent) that more often accrues to the benefit of the uniformed services than to the hotel. This may also hold true when the hotel contracts an outside laundry or dry cleaner for guest service. Then, too, there is a percentage from the illicit services that flourish despite management's best vigilance.

The chief function of the bell staff is to room arrivals, although they also assist departing guests and those making room changes. Many hotels still insist that each new arrival be accompanied to the room. Ostensibly, this is to avoid embarrassing situations when the previous guest has not yet gone. Motels have been able to eliminate bell service and even those hotels that insist on it give group arrivals, such as bus tours, their own keys for self-rooming.

Luggage. The department's reception, sales, and inspection services begin when the guest is turned over to the bellperson by the room clerk. Baggage is identified and retrieved, and the party heads for the elevators. The guest should get on and off the elevator first. Sometimes bellpersons use service elevators even when the party is small, but especially if the front elevators are very busy. The guest is told which floor to go to and is met there at the elevator lobby by the bellperson who takes the bags up the service elevator.

Several very large hotels employ a unique system of baggage handling. The luggage of arriving guests is taken at the curb by the door attendant, who gives the guest a baggage check. The luggage goes into a receiving area adjacent to the door and behind the bell stand. There it waits while the guest enters the lobby and registers. A room key and an extra copy of the rooming slip (the bellperson's copy) are given to the guest by the room clerk as the registration is completed. The guest gives the bell captain, or a clerk at the bell stand, the rooming slip (showing room number and name) along with the luggage stub obtained from the door attendant. The guest goes to the room unescorted. A few minutes later the baggage is delivered, having been matched at the bell stand using the stub delivered by the guest and the tag attached by the door attendant.

Baggage losses for the world's airlines exceed $100 million per year. Some of the best minds in the industry are now focusing on the cost, delay, and inconvenience of handling baggage throughout the travel system. Talk of delivering luggage directly to the guest's room from the airport has been precursor to the fact. Special baggage systems that make such deliveries are now being tested in several large cit-

ies. Although there is a delay of four to six hours and additional cost, the concept is being developed. The systems have their origin in the baggage handling developed for groups because package plans almost always include airport transportation and baggage transfer.

Group Handling

Tour groups, including single entity groups, are relatively easy for the desk to handle. Instead of numerous reservations, registrations, assignments, and rooming procedures, there is only one for the entire group. Reservations come together considerably in advance of the arrival date, although some tour companies negotiate a twenty-four-hour cancellation provision. Using the guest list furnished by the group, the desk preregisters the party by making room assignments before its arrival. Roommates are matched, room rack slips are prepared, and keys are readied in small envelopes for quick distribution (figure 6.15). Roommates nearly always know their companions and room themselves without benefit of service from the bell department. Delegates to company meetings might register individually but tour groups rarely do. Preregistration for all guests is being done more frequently now that data processing equipment has become available.

The computer will print the key envelopes coded by group identification, the rooming lists showing who is with whom and where (so important to the tour guide or the company meeting planner), labels showing room numbers for mail distribution, credit cards for in-house use, baggage tags, and every other form needed for a successful group meeting. All of these items are derived from the same basic information, which is fed into the computer only once.

Special desks and even special lobbies are being used by hotels with large group business. Here the group receives attention and last minute changes are resolved. To minimize

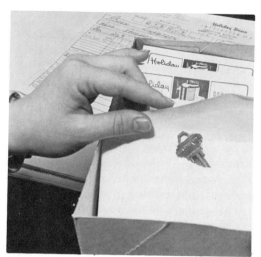

Figure 6.15. Tour group keys readied for distribution. Holiday Inn, Minneapolis, Minn. *Photo by Nancy Conroy.*

lobby confusion, final arrangements with tours are made on the bus before the group disembarks. Communication is nigh impossible once the captive audience is lost. The room and certain charges are included in the price of the tour. Extras are the guest's responsibility and a notice to that effect is frequently enclosed in the key envelope of figure 6.15.

A preregistration of sorts is also utilized by convention hotels. Each conventioneer is mailed a preprinted registration form (figure 5.12) with the reservation mailing from the group's headquarters. By returning the form with the reservation request, the guest has preregistered. The form includes rates (different for each group), deposit requirements, guarantee information, and so on. Different colors identify different groups. Since keys can be distributed in the lobby or at a special desk, registration is quick and pleasant.

Group baggage handling is a headache as well as a backache, but it can be made easier. One method is to give each traveler a supply of brightly colored tags to attach to his or her baggage. The color identifies the group, thus expediting baggage handling in and out of the airport. The individual's number is written on each tag, and that number corresponds to the individual's place on the master rooming sheet (copies of the list have been given to every hotel on the tour). The number, which is easier to read than a name, helps the bell staff match the bags with room numbers.

There is another variation. Each bag — which was tagged in advance with the guest's name — is marked with the correct room number from a computer printed list of adhesive-backed labels. The bellperson removes the guest's name and room number from the printed list and slaps it on the bag for delivery.

In some instances, baggage is delivered only to the floors, where the guests pick up their own bags. Assigning tour groups to one floor or one wing facilitates baggage handling and rooming procedures and also contains the noise to one area of the hotel. When group luggage is handled en masse, tips are levied by the hotel — a provision of most union contracts — for later distribution to the bell department.

Regardless of the method utilized, group baggage delivery takes time. Guests are impatient and the bell crew knows there is no extra tip coming. At best, the bag is placed in the room without the usual service.

In rooming individual guests, the bellperson performs a room inspection. Luggage is placed on the luggage rack, loose clothing is hung up, temperature controls are checked, and the room is inspected, checking for cleanliness, towels, soap, toilet tissue, and other bathroom needs. Lights, hangers, television sets, and furnishings are examined. Special features of the hotel are explained: for example, how to get to the pool or the closing hours of the dining room to a late American plan arrival. The ice machine and other self-service items are pointed out. Connecting

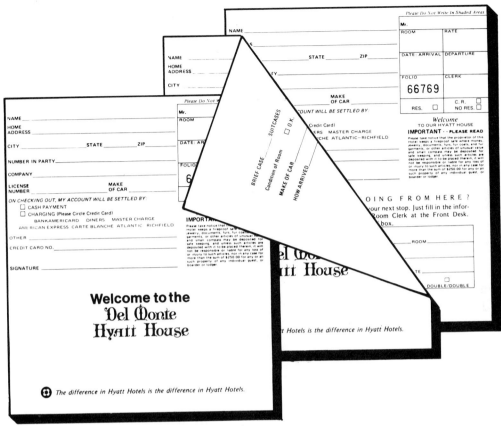

Figure 6.16. Combination registration card and rooming slip. Copy one to the desk; copy two to the bellperson (note bell information on the rear of copy two); copy three to the guest. *Courtesy: Del Monte Hyatt House, Monterey, Calif.*

doors are unlocked if the party is to share several connecting rooms. Unless there is a special request for service, the bellperson leaves the key and the rooming slip and accepts the proffered tip, if any. Before leaving, there may be a final sell for a particular dining room or lounge and a final good day.

The Rooming Slip

The rooming slip serves as a means of communication between the room clerk and the bellperson and later between the hotel and the

guest. It contains the same information as the registration card and is often prepared as a carbon when the clerk completes the hotel's portion of the card. To accomplish this, the clerk records the guest's name, room number, dates of arrival and departure, rate, and initials the form (figure 6.16). When more than two or three copies are prepared, a separate rooming slip form is used rather than a carbon of the registration card (figure 6.17).

The rooming slip identifies the guest and the room destination to the bellperson. The bellperson's copy may be used as authority to

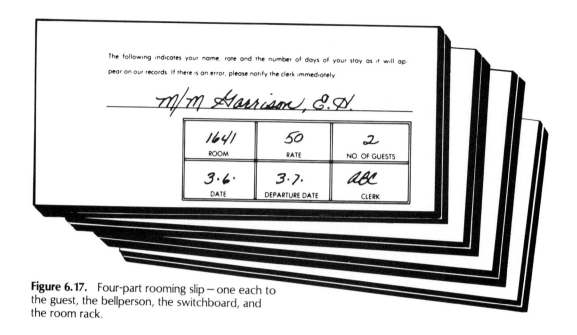

Figure 6.17. Four-part rooming slip — one each to the guest, the bellperson, the switchboard, and the room rack.

Figure 6.18. The flip sides of European rooming slips serve as advertising media. *Courtesy: Insel Hotel, Bad Godesberg, Germany.*

draw a key from the mail, key, and information desk, although few hotels are so formalized. Additional copies are used as temporary room rack flags and temporary information rack slips. In an American plan hotel, still another copy may be used for dining room identification; the guest presents it to the headwaiter(waitress) when coming to the dining room the first time. This accounts for as many as six rooming slips: one for the guest; one for the bellperson; one for the key clerk; one for the room rack; one for the information rack; and one for the American plan dining room. There could even be another for the concierge. In most cases only two rooming slips are used.

The first copy is left with the guest along with a key when the rooming procedure is complete. It is hoped that any errors in name, rate, or date of departure will be questioned and reported to the desk. A statement to that effect is included on the rooming slip. The disclaimer of liability may be repeated there as well.

The final copy of the rooming slip is kept by the bellperson, who records on it information about the checkin (figure 6.17). Included are the guest's type of auto, the license plate number, and the number and kind of bags, including golf bags and tennis rackets. The bellperson also initials and time-stamps the slip. This copy is used to resolve complaints, trace lost luggage, and aid the credit department. It is also used to control the rotation of fronts.

Although not intended for that purpose, the slips have been used by the Internal Revenue Service on occasion. Estimating the average tip per front and counting the number of fronts according to the rooming slips provides a fair estimate of tip income, which is then compared to that reported by the employee.

Hotels abroad use the rooming slip as a sales device. Not only are hotel facilities mentioned on it, but also local, noncompeting businesses are sold space on the slip, which can measure as much as eight by twelve inches when opened (figure 6.18). American hotels haven't as yet taken to selling ads on their rooming slips. With their more extensive services and facilities, they need all the space themselves. The American rooming slip is an eclectic mix of selling, services, and legal safeguards. Depending on management's inclination, the rooming slip is either a simple, carbon scribble on the rear of a scratch pad or a complete, elaborate sales tool in a variety of colors. Caesars Palace in Las Vegas has a rooming booklet of twenty pages! Figure 6.19 lists the range of information that might be included in

Informative

Floor Plan of the Property
Aerial View of the Property
Telephone Directory of Services
Kinds of Lobby Shops
Foreign Language Capabilities of the Staff
Airline, Taxi, and Limousine Telephone Numbers
Local Sites to See and Things to Do
Airport Bus: Times of Operation and Rates
Currency Exchange Capabilities
Map of the City with Highway Designations

Marketing

List of Restaurants: Prices, Hours of Operation,
    and Menu Specialties
A Message of Welcome or a Note of Appreciation
WATS Number for Other Hotels in the Chain
Recreational Facilities: Tennis, Golf, Pool, Sauna

Regulatory

Check-out Hour and Check-in Hour
Rate of Gratuity Applied to the Room Charge
Regulations for Visitors
Limitations on Pets
Dress Code
Availability of the Safe for Valuables
Settlement of Accounts
Expectations for Guaranteed Reservation Holders
Deposit of Room Keys When Leaving the Property
Fees for Local Telephone Calls

Identification

Clerk's Identifying Initials
Identification of the Party: Name, Number of
    Persons, Rate, Arrival and Departure Dates
Room Number
Key Code—Where Room Access Is Controlled by
    a Dial System Key

Instructional

Express Check-out Procedure
Electrical Capacity for Appliances
What to Do in Case of Fire
How to Secure the Room
Notification to the Desk if Errors Exist on
    the Rooming Slip
How to Operate the In-room Films; Their Cost
How to Operate the In-room Refrigerator; Cost
Rate of Tax Applied to the Room Charge

Figure 6.19. U.S. rooming slips contain a host of regulations and market appeals for the guest who takes time to read them.

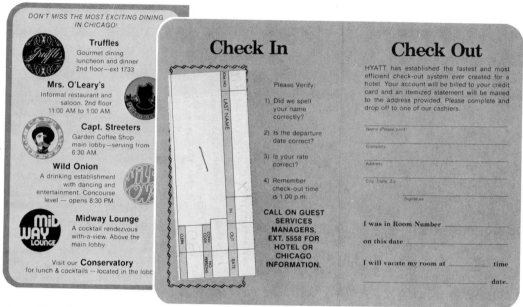

Figure 6.20. Rooming slips for Hyatt Hotels include advertising (over) and express checkout.
Courtesy: Hyatt Regency, Chicago, Ill.

any given slip. Certain properties color code the booklets (figure 6.20), which must be presented in dining rooms and bars if charging, to identify the guest's credit status: paid-in-advance, group tour, etc.

Quick Checkout

Rooming slips, which service arrivals, have also become a vehicle for expediting departures. Figure 6.20 illustrates one of the systems in use. The program is available to guests with hotel credit, or users of the major credit cards. Having established credit, the guest leaves without the inconvenience of check-out lines. Figure 6.20 is a bit open-ended to encourage anyone to try the system. Usually it isn't quite that easy.

The quick check-out guest must be identified at checkin. Then one of several systems is put in place. The credit card is imprinted on a credit card voucher (figure 13.11) and also on a departure form similar to that of figure 6.20. Room number, name, departure time,

and the date are recorded by the guest. When leaving, the guest deposits the departure form in a box near the cashiers. Periodically the cashiers retrieve the forms and process the departures. Instead of standing in line to sign the credit slips at departure, the guest processes them on arrival. The bookkeeping is identical.

A variation has the guest notify the desk of intended departure on the preceding day. Everything else is much the same, except that the guest finds a copy of the folio in the mailbox — the folio was placed there by the night auditor. A final folio is mailed with the bill. This poses no problem for computer prepared folios, which are printed individually on call. Hand or machine forms would require an additional carbon of the folio to be included in the packet.

Having arrived, been registered, and roomed, the guest is ready to accumulate charges; one of which is room charges.

QUERIES AND PROBLEMS

1. Ten weary, footsore travelers,
    All in a woeful plight,
   Sought shelter at a wayside inn
    One dark and stormy night.
   "Nine beds — no more," the landlord said,
    "Have I to offer you;
   To each of eight a single room,
    But number nine serves two."
   A din arose. The troubled host
    Could only scratch his head;
   For of those tired men, no two
    Could occupy one bed.
   The puzzled host was soon at ease —
    He was a clever man —
   And so to please his guests devised
    The most ingenious plan:

   | A | B | C | D | E | F | G | H | I |

   In Room marked A, two men were placed;
    The third he lodged in B.
   The fourth to C was then assigned,
    The fifth went off to D.
   In E the sixth he tucked away.
    In F the seventh man;
   The eighth and ninth to G and H.
    And then to A he ran.
   Wherein the host, as I have said,
    Had lain two travelers by.
   Then taking one — the tenth and last,
    He lodged him safe in I.
   Nine single rooms — a room for each —
   Were made to serve for ten,
   And this it is that puzzles me
    And many wiser men.*

2. Consult the statutes of your state and compare their provisions of the innkeeper's liability law to the content of California's regulations, cited in the text as figure 6.9.

3. Intentional bias can be programmed into the room selection sequence of a property management system. Rooms will then appear in a prescribed order, rather than in sequence or at random. Certain rooms can be offered first, or not, depending on management's criteria. What criteria might management establish to decide which rooms appear in which sequence in order to direct the clerk's selection?

4. Reorder the jumbled sequence of events, persons, forms, and job activities to suggest the normal flow of guest arrival and assignment.

a. Sell up	j. Door attendant
b. Rack clerk	k. Rooming slip
c. Luggage	l. Room rack slip
d. Housekeeper's report	m. Temporary rack block
e. Reception	n. Bellperson
f. Walk-in	o. Stock card
g. Registration	p. Assignment
h. Key and messages	
i. Credit verification	

Hotel News, Winnipeg (1935).

7

Room Rates

RECORDING THE RATE

As we have just seen, entering the room rate on the registration card is just another task for the clerk as the arriving guest is registered. This is not so for management, which focuses considerable attention on this particular section of the registration card.

The Clerk's Entry

The rate entered on the registration card is the total charge for all the rooms shown on the one card. Figure 6.8 illustrates a suite, "702/04/06," assigned to one party, with the charge for the three rooms at "175." Rates are listed as daily costs, usually in whole dollars. Hence, "175" means $175 per day for three rooms. When the rate is less than an even dollar, the 25-cent multiples are written as fractions, so that "69½" means a $69.50 daily rate. Dollar signs are not used on any of the front office

forms, including the guest bills. Rates are always quoted on the European plan unless the American plan, or some other plan, is specifically stated. European hotels frequently include the Continental breakfast, especially for international tourists.

The rate block on the registration card usually presents no special difficulty. A single occupant will pay his or her own bill and a parent or spouse will be responsible for charges of the family unit. It is not this simple when two or more persons share the room and divide the charge. Assume that a Marty Ross and a Richard James share one room at an $89 double rate. Each is billed $44.50, although the single occupancy on the room might be as much as $65.00.

There are several ways of handling this type of split-rate billing on the registration card and folio. One method records the full $89 charge on one card (also, therefore, one folio) and merely records "info" in the rate square of the other registration card and other folio.

By another method, $44.50 is recorded in the rate square of both registration cards along with the name of the other member of the party. Marty Ross's card would have "44½/R.James" in the rate square; vice versa for James's card. The bills would show the same information as the cards.

A third method indicates in the rate square the number of persons dividing the rate, but does not name them. Thus, "2/44½" on Richard James's card means that there are two persons each paying $44.50 for a total of $89.00. Another means of showing the same information is "44½ (2c)," interpreted as $44.50 each on two cards (figure 6.6). Still another technique provides a "shareswith" blank on the registration card.

However accomplished, it is necessary that those preparing the bill from the registration card and those interpreting the bill are able to translate the information into the proper room charge and assign responsibility for that charge to the proper guest.

When the folio is to be transferred to a master account — company meetings, for example — the guest may be required to pay incidental charges so that only room and tax are charged to the master folio. Both the registration card and the guest's bill would be marked "room and tax only" with no dollar value shown. Sometimes a second folio, entirely independent of the first, is opened for the guest's personal charges from the same registration card.

What Is a Full Day?

Arrival and departure dates, and arrival and departure times are the bases for computing total room charges. Calendar and clock are the measurements, but management must determine the criterion for a full day's charge. What is that criterion? Pose this question to most hoteliers and the answer is simply a night's lodg-ing.[1] The termination point of a night's lodging is set by the hotel and called the check-out hour. Guests' arrivals are obviously less structured although some hotels have started to advertise an official check-in hour.

Arrival and Departure Times

The actual time of arrival is more critical to the American plan hotel, in which billing is based on meals taken, than to the European plan hotel. The day of arrival can be recorded in one of three possible places on the registration card. Strangely enough, dates are often recorded in all three places. Either the guest writes the date or the clerk completes the date box or a time clock is used. A time clock is a small piece of desk equipment that records the time and date on the registration card or on any other form that is inserted in the mechanism (figure 7.1). Computerized equipment usually contains its own built-in clock.

The actual hour of arrival has little importance to the European plan hotel except for the occasional complaint about message service or the rare police inquiry. Very, very late arrivals are the exception. Somewhere in the early morning (four, five, or six in the morning) comes the break between charging for the night just passed or levying the initial charge for the day just starting.

If rooms are vacant, guests are generally assigned as soon as they arrive. But many hotels are tightening up on arrival time; they tighten and ease as occupancies rise and fall. Roadside motels and minipriced properties pay stricter attention, as a rule, to in and out times. Under current industry practices, a stay of several hours can cost as much as a stay of a full day or longer (figure 7.2).

The check-out hour still receives the most attention. Either the guest vacates the room by

1. A full day at a Japanese ryokan is defined as noon to noon.

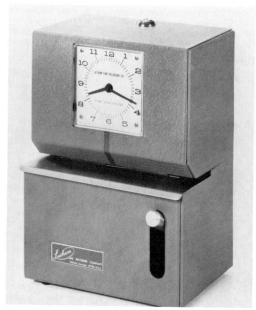

Figure 7.1. Time clock prints time and date on forms inserted in the aperture. *Courtesy: Wilcox International Inc., Division of American Hotel Register Co.*

	Jan. 1 Arrival	Jan. 2 Departure	Time
Guest A	12 midnight	7:00 A.M.	7 hours
Guest B	6:00 P.M.	11:00 A.M.	17 hours
Guest C	10:00 A.M.	3:00 P.M.	29 hours

Figure 7.2. Each guest pays the same although use of the room varies by more than 400 percent.

then or is charged for an additional day. The check-out hour varies from hotel to hotel. Many times it is established without any rationale or by selecting the same hour as that of nearby competitors. The proper hour is a balance between the guest's need to complete his or her business and the hotel's need to clean and properly prepare the room for the next patron.

The seasoned traveler is well aware that check-out extensions are readily granted by the room clerk if the house is light. Under current billing practices, the effort should be cheerfully made whenever the request can be accommodated. When anticipated arrivals require the hotel to enforce the check-out hour, luggage can be stored in the checkroom for the guest's convenience.

Incentive rate systems have been suggested as a means of expediting checkouts (figure 7.3). First, the check-out period for a normal day's charge would be established, say between 11 A.M. and 1 P.M. Guests who leave before 11 A.M. are charged less than the standard rate and those who remain beyond 1 P.M. are charged more. Flexible charges of this type require a new look at the unit of service, shifting from the more traditional measure of a night's lodging to smaller blocks of time.

Resorts are under more pressure than commercial hotels to expedite checkouts. Vacationing guests try to squeeze the most from their holiday time. American plan houses usually allow the guest to remain through the luncheon hour and a reasonable time thereafter if the meal is part of the rate. Some 90 percent of the resorts surveyed in an AH&MA study identified their check-out hour as between noon and 2 P.M. These same properties made assignments to new arrivals on a "when available" basis.

Special techniques besides that of figure 7.3 have been tried to move the guest along. On the night before departure, the desk, the assistant manager, or the social host(ess) can call the room to chat and remind the guest of tomorrow's departure — a task that even today could be assigned to a computer. A more personal touch is a note of farewell left by the floor housekeeper who turns down the bed the night before.

Unlike most other service industries, hotels have given little consideration to time as a factor in rate. Yet time is a major component of any service. Arrival and departure times establish broad parameters at best. We can expect these to narrow as hotelkeepers become

Checkout time: 1 PM

We would like to ask your cooperation in checking out by one pm so that we may accommodate travelers who are beginning their stay. If you require additional time, you may request a two-hour grace period (until 3 pm) from the Assistant Manager or the Front Office Manager. If you wish to check out later, we regret that there must be an $8.00 per hour charge, from 3 until 5 pm, for this added service. An additional half-day rate will be charged to guests who delay their departure until between 5 pm and 8 pm. After 8 pm, a full-day rate will be charged. Of course, you are then welcome to remain until the following afternoon at one pm.

As in incoming guest, your comfort and convenience depends on these stipulations. We hope you will visit again soon.

Figure 7.3. Permanent bureau tent card left in each guest room. A specific reminder provides more impact if left only on those days the house is actually full.

more concerned with the role of time in rate structuring. Taken to the other extreme, it is possible that the hour will eventually become the basic unit for constructing room rates.

Once the guest is registered, it is the hour of departure that concerns the hotel, but during the registration process, it is the date of departure that holds the hotel clerk's attention. The date of departure—actually the anticipated date since guests often change their minds—is important to reservations and room forecasting. It is ascertained at the time of registration or reconfirmed then if furnished earlier during reservation correspondence.

The anticipated departure date is recorded on the registration form. From there, it is eventually copied onto the bill and the room rack slip or fed into the computer if a data processing system is in use. If only a tentative date is given, it is recorded but followed by a question mark, for example, "6/27/?" (figure 6.5). When even an estimated departure time is not possible, a solitary question mark is placed in the appropriate square. Obviously, some estimate is better than none, and an effort to get one should be made.

The actual date of departure may not agree with the original estimate. Posting the actual date on the registration card is especially helpful when the card becomes part of the guest-history system. The procedure in some front offices is to attach the registration card to the folio during the guest's stay. Then it, too, is stamped at the time of departure, providing both arrival and departure dates on the same record.

Dual Occupancy

Room charges have traditionally been based on the number of persons occupying the room. The price spread between single and double occupancy has been narrowing, however. This narrowing reflects the high fixed costs that the room represents to the hotel and the relatively small additional costs of having a second or third occupant in the room. Although it is far from a common arrangement, there is some movement, especially with conventions, toward establishing a fixed room charge regardless of the number of occupants. Almost all suite charges are made that way already. Then the room, rather than the guest, becomes the unit of pricing. Travelers without reservations frequently encounter this arrangement in busy resort areas. The room will carry a given price whether the party is one, two, or three persons. The guest's angry reaction to this arrangement is evidence enough that the practice is not widespread.

Perhaps the first step in this new direction is the movement toward a percentage rate differential rather than a flat dollar spread. Adding a fixed amount to a single rate in order to convert it to a double rate may be the traditional practice, but it has less justification than a percentage increase. On a $45 single, a $15 charge for dual occupancy represents a 33 percent increase. On a $60 room the same $15 is only 25 percent and on a $75 room only 20 percent. Yet a higher priced room infers higher investment costs, greater service, and better facilities, all of which create the basis for a greater return, not a smaller one. It has been suggested that as a minimum, double occupancy should be approximately one-third more than single occupancy.[2] Then:

Single Occupancy	Double Occupancy	Rate Spread
$45	$ 60	$15
60	80	20
75	100	25

Even this is a far cry from the usual European structure in which the double rate, logically enough, is twice the single rate.

Package plans and tour arrangements always quote prices based on shared accommodations. Hotels can then shave the rates because the second occupant represents a very small additional expense. This is even

2. Joseph H. Nolin, "Pricing Policy in the Hospitality Field," *The Horwath Accountant*, Vol. 47, No. 7, 1967, p. 5.

more so with a third party. Most third party rates are quoted as a flat extra charge rather than a percentage increase. The surcharge is smaller if the extra person or persons share the same bed than if a rollaway cot is requested, requiring extra handling and linen. Guests opt for double occupancy during slow economic periods, taking one room instead of two. Higher rates per room offset somewhat the decline in occupancy, which delays the impact of a falling economy during the early period of the decline.

Except intermittently, occupancy, the number of rooms sold relative to the number of rooms available for sale, has been in decline for the past thirty years. Income from room sales has risen despite this decline in rooms sold. This is why the industry has focused its attention on room rate rather than on room occupancy. Hotel executives seem to have a greater control over the rate per room than over the percentage of occupancy.

Special Rates

Special rates should not be confused with the dubious practice of "sizing up" the guest and charging whatever the traffic will bear. Ethical hotels adopt standard rates that apply equally to all. In fact, many states require room rates to be posted, and these usually appear behind the guest room door along with the notice of limited liability that was discussed earlier (figure 6.9). There are no legal restrictions on charging less than the posted rate. However, it is good salesmanship to explain why the hotel can offer lower rates. Equally good explanations are needed to sell the guest up to the next rate. Clerks should have a repertoire of reasons for special rates: The room has just been refurbished, higher rate. You are vacating early in the morning, lower rate. Spectacular view! sell up. Just had a cancellation! we can take less.

Posted rates can be changed or they can include seasonal variations. Season and off-season rates are quoted by most resort hotels with incremental increases and decreases coming as the season approaches and wanes. The poor weekend occupancy of urban hotels makes them only too happy to offer an off-season rate during the doldrums of the weekend.

Certain activities, such as a bowl game, the Mardi Gras, etc., will push demand to capacity and encourage some questionable rate practices. Not only will rates be increased, but guests will also be required to take the room for three nights whether or not they plan to remain that long.

Properly designed reservation systems contain rate adjustment mechanisms. A second pricing tier is triggered when occupancy reaches a predetermined level. Rates increase because of the imbalance between supply and demand. Profits are impacted twice: once because the break-even point has been reached; twice because the rate structure reflects the incremental step.

Occasionally, one hears a weekly rate quote of something less than seven times the daily rate. The daily loss in revenue is recovered by the longer stay, which includes an increase in spending on food, beverage, greens fees, and the like. Both the daily rate, assume $60, and the weekly rate, assume $375, are recorded by the clerk on the registration card and, later, on the guest bill. The $60 rate is charged daily until the final day, when a $15 charge is posted. In this way, the daily charge is earned until the guest meets the weekly commitment. If one-seventh of the weekly $375 charge were posted daily, the hotel would be at a disadvantage whenever the guest left before the week was up, as is frequently done.

Strangely enough, some hotels increase the rate the longer the guest stays. There are some indications that per diem spending decreases the longer the guest remains. In an area where there is an unusually high demand for rooms, as in a resort area during the height of the season or at a gambling spa, this reverse technique has some justification. Still another variation discounts services such as valet and laundry, greens fees, and the like for weekly or monthly stays but leaves the room rate constant.

Category of Guest

By the same tradition that gives police officers discounts in the coffee shop, clergy, reporters, and military personnel are given special room rates. One hotel chain has special rates for teachers; others have special rates for government employees whose allowable per diem is below the minimum room rate of the chain. This is so important to government employees that the General Services Administration publishes a lodging directory of hotels offering these rates. Similarly, special rates are frequently extended to employees of the chain when they travel to other properties. These special rates are almost always sold on a space available basis. Space available means they are not confirmed in advance by reservation and are accepted only if rooms are vacant when the employee guests present themselves.

Advocates of special rates have extended the idea: why not offer a walk-in rate similar to the reduced rates that airlines sometimes offer standbys? Full rack rate could be charged for the convenience of the reservation, and an incentive rate could be offered for the last-minute decision that helps carry the hotel toward a full house. Carried further, the later the walk-in arrives, the cheaper the room.

Reservation Rates
Special rates are also used to honor reservations because reservations are always confirmed in a rate range. A request for a $72

Hotel Stapleton

Special Rate Authorization
House Promotion Authorization

Name ____________________ Room __________

Affiliation ____________________

Reason for Special Rate or Comp ____________________

____

Regular Rate $ __________ Special Rate $ __________

Other Comps: Food __________ Beverage __________ Other __________

Date In __________ Date Out __________

Authorized by: ____________________
(name) (title)

Figure 7.4. Special rate and complimentary rate authorization form.

room will be answered with a reservation in the range of \$72 to \$76. Even so, a room in this rate range may not be available when the guest arrives. The assignment is then made to a higher priced room, perhaps an \$84 room, and quoted at a \$76 special rate. In the rate square on the registration card the clerk marks "76 SPEC." Special rates are so marked to assure management that no errors have been made and to emphasize the special nature of the rate. Guests should not expect that same \$84 room for \$76 the next time around.

Some hotels use special rate-authorization forms (figure 7.4), especially if the discount is being authorized by some other department of the hotel for business reasons. For example, sales might be entertaining an association manager who is considering a convention, or the casino a good table player. Depending on the circumstance, the form could be forwarded on either the day of arrival or the day of departure. Rate discrepancy reports should be prepared for management by the night auditor. These reports are readily available when data processing systems are used, but with other systems this information is usually not accessible unless the special rate-authorization forms are meticulously used.

Commercial Rates

Commercial rates are a variation of the special rate given to meet reservation commitments. It is assumed that commercial travelers always reserve a room at the minimum rate. It does not matter that the actual reservation has not even been made. When the commercial person arrives, the reservation, real or assumed, is honored at the minimum rate. Commercial rates are usually lower than the going charge. Similar treatment is offered other regular guests by charging them the same rate each time they come irrespective of the room assigned. The guaranteed maximum rate plan is another variation of the commercial rate. Business firms are guaranteed a maximum rate charge even if the value of the room assigned is higher. And with especially good customers, the assignment is always upgraded.

Any commercial rate, or corporate rate as it is sometimes called, presumes a given volume of business. Large corporations seeking a chain-wide arrangement might need to commit a minimum of 500–1,000 room nights per year. One major chain dropped its 600 room nights commitment to a mere 150 room nights during the slow years of the early 80s. A small motelkeeper might be happy with 5 room nights per year from a manufacturer's representative traveling on a personal expense account. Travel agencies may not be able to get commercial rates for their business clients unless the agency generates a given number of total room nights for the hotel or hotel chain. Agents quoting corporate rates may not be eligible for commissions.

Group Rates

Special rates are also extended to groups. The sales staff will quote special run-of-the-house (flat) rates to entice group meetings and convention business. Everyone in the group pays the same rate, usually about the middle of the price range, and room assignments are made on a best available basis. Some members of the group get the better rooms at a lower price, but others get poorer rooms at a higher price. This is not recorded on the registration card as a special rate since the whole convention is viewed as a special arrangement.

Not all hotels sell flat rates. In fact, several large chains disdain them since these run-of-the-house rates make no provision for quality. Instead, group rates of 10 to 15 percent off net rates are used to encourage conventions. And here is where terminology gets sticky. Rack rates are full commissionable rates, gross rates. Commissions of 10 to 15 percent are paid to third parties, travel agents, who make rack rate sales. Net rate is the rack rate less commission, thus net rates are noncommissionable by definition. Convention buyers attempt to negotiate group rates of 10 to 15 percent off net rates, while convention sales executives try to maximize revenue. Since the convention negotiation is carried out at arm's length, neither one quite achieves individual goals.

When competition heats up, as it did during the first part of the 1980s, innkeepers pay travel agent commissions even on net corporate rates. Similarly, when inflation cools, as it did during the first part of the 1980s, hotel sales departments resume quoting guaranteed convention rates even for bookings two to four years ahead — something that is impractical to do in rapid inflationary periods.

Package plans are another form of group discount. These plans, which are operated by travel agencies, transportation companies, or the hotels themselves, are based on volume. Sales volume and operating expenses are spread among large groups rather than based on individual room sales. The savings makes special rates both possible and profitable. The special rates are not recorded as a dollar figure in the rate square of the registration card. Since the total charge includes more than the room rate, the clerk writes in the name of the package, for example, "San Francisco Holiday." Guests are not told what portion of the package relates to the room charge only, and cashiers post the total package charge.

The certainty and regularity of airline crew business have enabled the airlines to negotiate good room rates for their personnel and for the occasional planeload of passengers that may be stranded.

A variety of special associations have come into being recently under an umbrella of terminologies: leisure clubs, retirement clubs, and golden-years clubs. Their members are fixed-income persons and their clients are hotels and chains feeling the pressure of poor economic times. By promising volume for the hotelier, the clubs receive rate discounts for their members, sometimes in the form of the second night free.

Hawaii's *kamaiina* rate (literally, an old-timer's rate) is an interesting case of special rates. A class action suit, filed by a Californian and predicated on the grounds that the 25 percent discount granted to Hawaiian residents was discriminatory, was denied by the court. The judge found that "offering a discount to certain clients, patrons, or other customers based on an attempt to attract their business is (not) unlawful." The decision is important because it shows the other side of the issue. Rates that are raised to discourage business from certain persons might well be judged as discriminatory. Rates that are lowered to attract certain persons are viewed quite differently, at least by one court.

Complimentary Rates (Comps)

The hotel manager should be as reluctant to give comp rooms as the auto sales manager is to give away free cars. But the perishability of the room and the low variable cost of an occupant in an otherwise vacant room allows a degree of latitude. Consequently, complimentary rates are by no means uncommon. Custom has extended complimentary rates to other hoteliers. This courtesy is reciprocated, resulting in a general industry-wide fringe benefit. Such comps rarely include food or beverage, even in American plan operations.

Comps are used to promote business. Travel agents and travel writers are frequently entertained as guests of the hotel to provide familiarization (hence, "fam trips") with the property. Their business cards should always be attached to the reg card and forwarded on to the marketing department. Fam trips by the airlines are no longer prohibited as they were

before deregulation. Hotels should see more requests for fam trips now that the airlines may grant free or reduced-rate tickets for site inspections.

Executives of associations or trade groups also make site inspections when considering the property as a possible meeting place for their groups, and they are comped. Notoriety comes to those association executives who abuse the industry standard by using the site inspection opportunities to vacation with their families.

Comps are also given to famous persons whose presence has publicity value. Comps are used as promotional tools in connection with national, regional, or local contests in which the winners receive so many days of free accommodations. In gambling casinos, comps extend to food, beverage, and even airfare from the player's home. Parking is so difficult and costly in Atlantic City, that it too has become part of the high-roller's comp package. After all, in a brief period of table play, such individuals can lose many times the cost of this promotion, which on close inspection proves to be surprisingly inexpensive.

Internal control of comps is important. In some hotels, the night auditor is required to submit a report of comps granted each day and by whom. It is also desirable to include this information in the accounting records. To that end, the room rate is recorded in the rate block on the registration card and marked "COMP" (figure 6.5). Daily, or more often at the end of the stay, the charge is removed with an allowance. Under this procedure, a daily room charge is made so that the room and the guest are both counted in the room and house counts. The total allowances at the end of the accounting period provide statement evidence of the cost of comps.

Recording no value in the rate square but only the word COMP is another method for handling free accommodations. No dollar value is charged each day and, therefore, no allowances are required to remove the charges. Neither is a permanent dollar record of comps available. Comps are not usually recorded in room and house counts under this procedure.

Day Rates

Except under the American plan, which provides for meal hours, room rates are based on overnight stays. Special rates exist for stays of less than overnight, and these are called *part-day rates, day rates,* or sometimes *use rates.* Day rate guests arrive and depart on the same day. Since rooms sold by the day are serviced and made available again for the usual overnight occupancy, the schedule of the housekeeping staff has a great deal to do with the hours to which the day rate applies. If there are no night room cleaners, the day rate must be closed off early enough to allow room servicing by the day crew. On the other hand, low occupancy would allow a day rate sale even late in the day since nothing is lost if an additional empty room remains unmade overnight. Day rates need not be limited to short daytime stays. Six hours is a common maximum allowed for day rates, and these six hours could conceivably come at any time of the day or night.

Day rates obviously make possible an occupancy of greater than 100 percent. The additional amount of business is important, but the possibilities have not been fully exploited by the industry. Sales of use rates have been marketed to suburban shoppers and for meetings. Airport hotels have attempted to get travelers who are between planes but have been far more successful in promoting their locations as central meeting places for company representatives coming from different sections of the country.

A new day rate market is just now becoming evident. Motels near campsites and along the roadways are attracting campers as a wayside stop during the day. A hot shower,

an afternoon by the pool, and a change of pace from the vehicle are great appeals when coupled with the low day rate. Although some purists insist that the day rate should be half of the regular rate, there is good reason to negotiate a lower charge whenever the market warrants.

The rate square on the registration card carries the amount of the charge and the identifying phrase "Day Rate." As a later chapter indicates, day rate information must be left for the night auditor to help in the preparation of the room report.

ESTABLISHING THE RATE

The Proper Rate

Because a sound room rate structure is fundamental to a sound hotel operation, the average manager is sooner or later faced with the question of what is the proper room charge. It is a matter of exceeding complexity because room rates reflect markets and costs; investments and rates of return; supply and demand; accommodations and competition; and not least of all, the quality of management.

Divided into its two major components, room rates must be large enough to cover costs and a fair return on invested capital, and reasonable enough to attract and retain the clientele to whom the operation is being marketed. The former suggests a relatively objective, structured approach, which can be analyzed after the fact. The latter is more subjective, involving many factors from the amount of local competition to the condition of the economy at large. There is little sense in charging a rate less than what is needed to meet the first objective; there is little chance of getting a rate more than that limit established by the second.

Room Rate Formula
Transient and Residential Hotels

SCHEDULE I

TO DETERMINE THE AMOUNT NEEDED FROM ROOM SALES TO COVER COSTS AND A REASONABLE RETURN ON THE PRESENT FAIR VALUE OF PROPERTY

Example

OPERATING EXPENSES:

Rooms Department	$244,273.00
Telephone Department	9,490.00
Administrative and General	79,160.00
Payroll Taxes & Employee Relations	48,685.00
Advertising & Business Promotion	24,625.00
Heat, Light & Power	36,757.00
Repairs & Maintenance	42,804.00
Total Operating Expenses	$485,794.00

TAXES, INSURANCE, ETC.

Real Estate & Personal Property Taxes	$29,624.00
Franchise Taxes	13,300.00
Insurance on Building & Contents	14,922.00
Total Taxes, Insurance, Etc.	$57,846.00

DEPRECIATION (STANDARD RATES ON PRESENT FAIR VALUE):

	Value	Rate	
Building	$_____	at ____%	$149,240.00
Furniture, Fixtures and Equipment	$_____	at ____%	136,160.00
Total Depreciation			$285,400.00

REASONABLE RETURN ON PRESENT FAIR VALUE OF PROPERTY:

	Value	Rate	
Land	$_____	at ____%	
Building	$_____	at ____%	
Furniture, Fixtures and Equipment	$_____	at ____%	
Total Fair Return	$_____	at ____%	$415,000.00

TOTAL	$1,244,040.00

DEDUCT:—Credits from Sources Other Than Rooms

Income from Store Rentals	$ 85,259.00
Credit from Food and Beverage Operations (if loss subtract from this group)	144,864.00
Net Income from Other Operated Departments and Miscellaneous Income	7,524.00
Total Credits from Sources Other Than Rooms	$237,647.00

AMOUNT TO BE REALIZED FROM GUEST ROOM SALES TO COVER COSTS AND A REASONABLE RETURN OF PRESENT FAIR VALUE OF PROPERTY	$1,006,393.00

Figure 7.5. Mechanics of the Hubbart Room Rate Formula. *Courtesy: The American Hotel & Motel Association.*

COMPUTATION TO DETERMINE AVERAGE DAILY RATE REQUIRED PER OCCUPIED ROOM

		Example
(1) Amount to be Realized from Guest Room Sales to Cover Costs and a Reasonable Return on Present Fair Value of Property (From Schedule I)		$1,006,393.00
(2) Number of Guest Rooms Available for Rental		70
(3) Number of Available Rooms on Annual Basis (Item 2 Multiplied by 365)	100%	25,550
(4) Less: Allowance for Average Vacancies	25%	6,388
(5) Number of Rooms to be Occupied at Estimated Average Occupancy	75%	19,162
(6) Average Daily Rate per Occupied Room Required to Cover Costs and a Reasonable Return on Present Fair Value (Item 1 divided by Item 5)		$ 52.52

Figure 7.5. *Continued*

The Hubbart Room Rate Formula

Hubbart offers a standardized approach that structures the decision making involved in assigning room rates.[3] The Hubbart Formula proceeds from the needs of the enterprise and not from the needs of the guests. The average rate, says the formula, should pay all expenses and leave something for the investor, which is valid enough, for a business that cannot do this is short-lived.

Figure 7.5 illustrates the rather simple mechanics of the formula. Estimated expenses are itemized and totaled. These include operational expenses by departments ($485,794 in the illustration), realty costs ($57,846), and depreciation ($285,400). To these expenses is added a reasonable return on the present fair value of the property: land, building, and furnishings ($415,000). From the total expense package ($1,244,040) is subtracted incomes from all sources other than room sales

3. *The Hubbart Formula for Evaluating Rate Structures of Hotel Rooms*, 1952, is available from the American Hotel & Motel Association, 888 Seventh Ave., New York, New York, 10019, and is used here with the Association's permission.

($237,647). This difference ($1,006,393) represents the annual amount to be realized from room sales. Estimating the number of rooms sold annually (19,162), it becomes a simple matter to compute how much each of these rooms must produce on the average ($52.52). The computations are simple enough.

Of course, the formula is only as good as the assumptions that precede it. Several come immediately to mind. What is a reasonable return on the present fair value of the property? Indeed, with what accuracy can we estimate the fair value of the property? It is interesting to note that although the Hubbart Formula was promulgated in 1952, it called for depreciation to be computed on present fair value, something the accounting profession and the SEC have just gotten around to doing.

The formula leaves the rooms department with the final burden after profits and losses from other departments. But inefficiencies in other departments should not be covered by a high, noncompetitive room rate. Neither should unusual profits in other departments be a basis for charging room rates below what the market will bring.

There is some justification in having rooms subsidize low banquet prices if these low prices result in large convention bookings of guest rooms. (Incidentally, this is one reason why the food and banquet department should not be let on concession.) Similar justification could be found for using room income to cover unusually high dining room repairs and maintenance or advertising costs if these excessive expenditures produced enough other business to offset what is lost through the higher room rates that result.

Additional shortcomings become apparent as the formula is studied. Among them is the projected number of rooms sold. This estimate of rooms sold is itself a function of the very rate being computed. Rate, in turn, is a function of double occupancy (with the one-third differential discussed earlier implicit in the Hubbart Formula), but that is not even projected. Of course, the average rate that is ultimately derived is not the hotel's actual rate. The average rate is a weighted average of all the rooms sold. Reflected therein are the range of accommodations that the hotel offers and the competition that the neighborhood establishes.

The Hubbart Formula can be executed in another computation: average rate per square foot. Assume, for example, that the illustrated hotel of 70 rooms has 28,000 square feet of room rental space. With occupancy of 75 percent (figure 7.5), there would be 21,000 square feet nightly to meet the daily share of the $1,006,393. That daily share is $2,757 ($1,006,393 ÷ 365 days). Thus, a 300-square foot room would generate a room rate of about $39 daily ($2,757 ÷ 21,000 × 300).

Whichever system is used, the formula's average room rate assures a minimum operating result. Management might well select another average room rate with corresponding levels of occupancy to achieve a different return on investment. There is a great interdependence between sound rate policy and sound operating policy. The Hubbart Formula is a guide through the complexities of rate structuring, but no single formula can replace balanced business judgment.

The Building Cost Rate

Time and repetition have created an industry axiom that says rate can be evaluated by a rule of thumb. The rule states that the average room rate should equal $1 per $1,000 of construction cost. For a 200-room hotel costing $12 million (including land and land development, building, and public space but excluding furnishings and equipment), the average rate should be $60 ($12 million ÷ 200 rooms ÷ $1,000).

The building cost rate is still widely quoted despite some very radical changes over the years. Not long ago, Marriott reported its per room construction costs between $83,000 and $115,000. This in contrast to their 1957 figure of $8,000 per room. Stephen Brener traces similar changes in motel values. A 1960 room cost $7,500 to build and earned a $10 rate. That moved to $15,000 by the close of the 1970s with a $20 rate, and to $30,000 with a $50 rate by the start of the 1980s.[4]

Cost is a composite of many factors: size, type of construction, location, highrise-lowrise, and the cost of borrowed money. Luxury properties can cost five times as much per room as economy hotels. Land costs vary greatly across the nation. Comparing California and Arkansas is a lesson in futility. New York City may be stretching toward the $125 room night, but that is not the expectation of the manager in Dubuque, Iowa. Economy chains have stopped advertising a minimum, national rate because each locality has its own special cost problems: building costs, interest, labor, and taxes. Budgets are therefore aiming for a percentage rate below their competitors. Advertising a flat, national rate as part of the company logo is no longer popular.

4. *Lodging Hospitality*, July, 1981, p. 20.

Variations in value are equally evident among old hotels that change hands. Marriott acquired Mountain Shadows in Scottsdale for nearly $86,000 per room. In the same year, the Chiu Family of Hong Kong bought the 505-room Warwick in New York for $69,000 per room. Internationally, Princess Hotels sold at $3,380 per room, while the Inter-continental Chain was going at twenty times that, about $58,000 per room.

As pressure against rising room rates builds, actual room rates tend to be less than that suggested by the rule. The general rise in land and construction costs, which drives the average rate upward, has been only partially offset by improvements in design and reductions in the labor force. There have been noticeable increases in operating costs, financing, and taxes so that the relationships in the rule seem less reasonable today than when it was initiated some time ago. Since the building costs of older hotels — which ask lower rates — are tied to historical prices, these hotels have lower financing costs to recover (and probably lower realty taxes, too) and find that the rule has more application.

Its shortcomings notwithstanding, the rule is widely quoted and efforts are being made to modernize it: a $1.50 rate per $1,000 of construction costs has been suggested. Except it is the rate that has not kept up. Changing the rule won't increase the rates. A square footage rule has also been offered, but nothing as simplistic as the $1 per $1,000 has emerged. Rapidly rising room rates will help keep the figures in perspective; it is, after all, only a rule of thumb.

The concept behind the rule can be applied to marginal additions of room construction according to Irving Sicherman.[5] For example, a decision whether to add an extra, say, $1,500 to units under construction could be quantified. Assuming a 12 percent constant to amortize principal and interest, annual costs of $180 ($1,500 × 12 percent) are needed to meet capital payments. If occupancy is projected at 70 percent, there will be 256 days (365 × 70 percent) to recover the annual costs or an average extra charge of $.70 ($180 ÷ 256) per rental. With that kind of information, management can evaluate the likelihood of the additional investment being competitive in the eyes of the buyer.

The Ideal Room Rate

The firm of Laventhol & Horwath designed the Ideal Room Rate as a means of testing the room rate structure.[6] According to this approach, the hotel should sell an equal percentage of rooms in each rate class instead of filling from the bottom up. A 70 percent occupancy should mean a 70 percent occupancy in each rate category. Such a spread produces an average rate identical to the average rate earned when the hotel is completely full, that is, an ideal room rate.

Figure 7.6 illustrates the computation used to derive the ideal rate. At a given level of single and double occupancy, the hotel is assumed to fill first from the top down and then from the bottom up. (The computations resemble those of inventory pricing: LIFO, last-in, first-out and FIFO, first-in, first-out.) The minimum and maximum rates generated by the two computations are averaged by twice the number of available rooms.

If the actual average rate is higher than the ideal average rate, the hotel has failed to provide its customers with a proper number of high priced rooms. The particular market of that hotel is interested in rooms selling above the average, and the rates should be adjusted upward. An average room rate lower than the ideal, and this is usually the case, indicates sev-

5. *The Investment in the Lodging Business*, Scranton: Irving Sicherman, 1977, p. 104.

6. Used with permission.

Determining the Ideal Average Room Rate

Number of Rooms	Single Rate	Double Rate
200	$50	$65
300	$65	$84
100	$70	$92
600		

At 70% occupancy and 10% double occupancy, the ideal rate is computed:

From the bottom up

200 rooms @ $50 +	20 rooms @ $15	= $10,300
220 rooms @ $65 +	22 rooms @ $19	= 14,718
420 (70% occupancy)	42 (10% double occupancy)	$25,018

From the top down

100 rooms @ $70 +	10 rooms @ $22	= $ 7,220
300 rooms @ $65 +	30 rooms @ $19	= 20,070
20 rooms @ $50 +	2 rooms @ $15	= 1,030
420 (70% occupancy)	42 (10% double occupancy)	$28,320

Total Revenue $53,338

Total Revenue ÷ Twice the Occupied Rooms = Ideal Rate
$53,338 ÷ 840 rooms = $63.50 The Ideal Average Room Rate

Figure 7.6. Showing the derivation of the Ideal Room Rate. *Courtesy: Laventhol & Horwath.*

eral problems. There may not be a sharp enough contrast between the low and high priced rooms. Guests will take the lower rate when they are buying nothing extra for the higher rate. If the better rooms do, in fact, have certain extras — better exposure and newer furnishings — the lack of contrast between the rate categories might simply be a matter of poor housekeeping. If a hotel has very poor housekeeping, all rooms look alike.

Poor selling at the front desk is another reason for not achieving the ideal room rate. Rooms can be sold up with that magic repertoire that we suggested earlier: newly furnished, spectacular view, etc., just $3 more! But essentially the failure might be due to a totally improper rate structure for the actual market that is being entertained. Rates can be marketed by raising and lowering them daily during the week depending on variations in supply and demand.

The ideal room rate can be used to adjust the spread between rate categories using the internal features that were mentioned before: size, furnishings, etc. Rate increases should be concentrated in those rooms on those days for which demand is highest, according to the authors who designed the formula.

What the hotel furnishes and what the guest requires are not always the same. The discrepancy can be pinpointed with a simple bar chart or graph on which the guest's demands and the hotel's offerings are plotted side by side. Guest demands can be determined by a simple survey of registration card rates over any given period of time. Like the ideal room rate, the survey should not include days of 100 percent occupancy when the guest had no rate choice. Special rate situations would also be excluded. Using elementary arithmetic, the percentage of total registrations is determined for each rate class. Figure 7.7 illustrates the

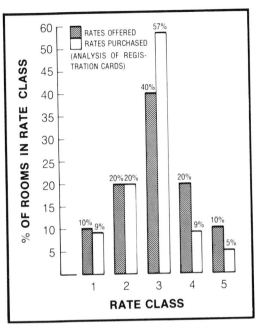

Figure 7.7. Highlights the need for rate adjustments by contrasting the supply and demand of different rate categories.

contrast between what the guest buys and what the hotel offers. It also points out the rates that need adjustment.

In figure 7.7 the hotel has five rate categories with 40 percent of the rooms assigned to the average room rate and the balance 20 percent and 10 percent, respectively, on both sides. Hilton Hotels use five rate categories much like the illustration. Holiday Inns, on the other hand, recently simplified its rate structure using three classes: economy, standard, and luxury. Special values like poolside or oceanview carry an additional premium. For contrast, 107 different rates were uncovered in the 1,076-room Roosevelt Hotel in New York City during a major renovation project!

Lower priced rooms are in greatest demand. It is the sad history of our industry that hotels fill from the bottom up. This means that low occupancy is accompanied by a low average rate per room sold. It is felt, therefore,

that there should be more categories at the lower end of the price scale. These lower categories would be bunched together while the higher rates would be spread over fewer categories. That might be the reason that Hilton advises its franchises to concentrate on the minimum single rate as the key in competition. They also recommend that double occupancy be 50 percent higher than single rates.

Competitive Factors in Rate

Just as the Hubbart Formula establishes the minimum floor the hotel can afford to charge, competition sets the ceiling it can expect to get. External competition from neighboring facilities prescribes the general price range, and internal physical differences within the rooms determine the rate increments.

Supply and demand, the degree of saturation, and the extent of rate-cutting in the community fix the rate parameters. Some localities have "established" rates and, especially in small towns, it is almost impossible to charge more than that traditional rate.

External competition requires a comparison of services and accommodations. It is easy to contrast pools, color television, charge for local calls, central air conditioning, dual lavatories, and so on. These can be determined by competitive shopping or by direct inquiry to the other property. Differences in service are less obvious, but they are reflected in cost as directly as capital outlay. Twenty-four-hour room service, a pool guard, lounge entertainment, and similar services must be valued when contrasting one's rates with those of the locality.

Room size, furnishings (including types of beds and baths), physical condition of the property, location, and exposure all bear on the distribution of the rates around the desired average. Other factors include noise, accessibility, and decor. Newer hotels have more uniform rooms, furnishings, exposure, maintenance, and decor so they generally have fewer rate classes than older properties. Older hotels have had a varying degree of maintenance over the years. Moreover, room differences were accentuated when these hotels were built. All told, older hotels generally have more — sometimes far too many — rate classes than newer properties.

Interest rates have been the innkeepers' own worst competitor. As borrowing costs increased, hoteliers were forced to raise rates higher and higher just to meet the ballooning costs of interest. With interest rates at 15 percent, for example, a million dollar loan costs $150,000 annually. Amortization is slow in the early years so that figure remains for quite a while. Some $75,000 extra is added to the room rate burden when compared to a competitor with, say, half that rate of interest. Spread over 100 rooms, there is an extra $750 per year. For a new property with 50 to 60 percent occupancy, there is a $4+ extra (per million dollars borrowed), noncompetitive amount laid on the basic room charge.

Ignored in this simple illustration are the higher land costs, construction costs, and furniture costs, which add increments to the rising room rate. No wonder so many hotel companies have decided to go into the luxury market. Rate forecasts were so high that only a luxury-class hotel could sustain them. Decisions that should have been marketing derived were predetermined by construction and financing costs.

Rate Cutting

Rate cutting, which is not to be confused with special rate promotions, is a phenomenon of the industry's concern with occupancy. Although room income is the product of occupancy and rate, only the number of rooms sold has been the bellwether of industry success. It will not be so hereafter, for not only was room

income maintained during the low occupancy periods of the 1960s, early 1970s, and 1980s, it was improved through increased room rates. This indicates that room demand is relatively inelastic.

Elasticity is the degree of demand resulting from changes in price. Large demand changes that result from price changes mean that demand is elastic; no changes mean the demand is inelastic. Rate reductions in an elastic market generate new business; rate reductions in an inelastic market do not. The hotel industry has always felt that reductions in rate produce less new business than is lost from lowering the unit price.

Elasticity of demand for hotel rooms is exceedingly complex.[7] An inelastic property can actually increase rates during an economic slump with profitable results. Rate changes can be disastrous — or very beneficial — depending on the elasticity of demand and the direction of change chosen by management. Different markets have different degrees of sensitivity. Tour properties are more elastic, and commercial demand is more inelastic. Hotels experience different degrees of elasticity throughout the year; that is what seasonal rates are all about. A given hotel may have numerous seasons throughout its annual cycle.

The industry began to rethink its position on inelastic markets during the first part of the 1980s. Hoteliers realized they were also retailers, and they moved toward incremental rates. Discounting, which swept the industry after it was introduced, meant that hotel executives were finally viewing their industry from a marketing perspective rather than from the traditional operational one. Thus the rationale that selling a room for any price above

7. It has been suggested that demand is elastic to about fifteen points above the average occupancy and almost inelastic thereafter. Frank D. Borsenik, "The Lodging Market . . . Phase I," *Hotel Bulletin*, November, 1966, p. 14.

THE PRICE OF RATE-CUTTING

Reduction in Present Rate

Present Occupancy	5%	10%	15%	20%	25%
			Occupancy Required to Make Up for Reduction		
76%	81.4%	87.7%	95.0%	103.6%	114.0%
74	79.3	85.4	92.5	100.9	111.0
72	77.1	83.1	90.0	93.2	108.0
70	75.0	80.8	87.5	95.5	105.0
68	72.9	78.5	85.0	92.7	102.0
66	70.7	76.2	82.5	90.0	99.0
64	68.6	73.8	80.0	87.3	96.0
62	66.4	71.5	77.5	84.5	93.0
60	64.3	69.2	75.0	81.8	90.0
58	62.1	66.9	72.5	79.1	87.0
56	60.0	64.6	70.0	76.4	84.0
54	57.9	62.3	67.5	73.6	81.0
52	55.7	60.0	65.0	70.9	78.0
50	53.6	57.7	62.5	68.2	75.0

(Based on cost of operating additional occupied rooms equal to 25% of present rate)

Figure 7.8. The price of rate cutting showing the increases in occupancy required to offset decreases in room rate. *Courtesy: The Horwath Accountant, v. 47, no. 7, 1967, p. 3.*

the direct cost of the room (housekeeping, heat, linen, etc.) was better than leaving it vacant.

Rate cutting, on the other hand, presupposes an inelastic market where unwarranted rate reductions generate new business for individual properties only by luring customers away from other properties. Competitors, who are the source of the new business, counter with rate cuts and the price war is on. A general decline in price per room and in gross sales, rather than the hoped-for increase in occupancy, is the net result. Some resort localities outlaw price wars of this type by making it a misdemeanor to post rates outside the establishment. Printed rate schedules are permitted; it is advertising on the marquee that is not allowed. The real test of any rate-quoting plan is whether it will bring new guests to hotels or whether it is a form of rate cutting, which diverts existing business from other hotels with benefit accruing only to the bargain-hunting guest.[8]

Figure 7.8 illustrates the difficulty of recuperating from any substantial cut in prices in an inelastic market. At 70 percent occupancy, it takes a 7 percent rise in occupancy (five percentage points) to offset a 5 percent reduction in rates.

8. Glenn M. Walker, "The Cost of Rate Cutting," *Transcript*, Vol. XXV, No. 4, April, 1968, p. 1.

A 100-room hotel with an average rate of $60 offers a simple example. With a 70 percent occupancy, $4,200 is generated each day (70 rooms × $60). Were the average rate cut to $50, occupancy would need to rise fourteen percentage points to assure the same gross sales (84 rooms × $50 = $4,200). If the occupancy were to reach only 80 percent, or $4,000 per day, the property would suffer an annual loss in gross sales of $73,000 ($200/day × 365 days/year). There would also be additional operating costs to maintain the extra occupancy, estimated in figure 7.8 at 25 percent of the original rate.

The long list of special rates proves that not all rate variations are viewed as rate cutting by the industry. Perhaps they must merely stand the test of time. The family plan, in which all children roomed with their parents are accommodated without charge, caused a great deal of dissension when it first appeared. It is today a legitimate business builder. So, too, is the free room given to convention groups for every 50 or 100 paid rooms. Like any good sales inducement, special rates should create new sales, not make the product available at a lower price. For once sold at a lower rate, it is almost impossible to get the buyer to pay the original price again. Some new properties in New York City discovered this when increases in their introductory rates met resistance several months later. Yet upgrading regular guests into otherwise empty rooms is a practice of long standing.

Rates are not easily adjusted once they have been established. Increases must be undertaken slowly if they are not to affect patronage. This is true even if they were too low to begin with. Rate reductions will bring no guest complaints, but the damage may already be done before that action is taken. Excessive rates create bad word-of-mouth advertising that takes time and costly sales promotion to counteract.

Rate Incentives

Motivated room clerks are better selling tools than cut-rates and giveaways. They are probably less expensive too. The fact that clerks will sell up if given the proper training and incentive is often overlooked. Incentive systems stimulate interest and make the front office aware of the goal, which makes the system effective. Clerks must be rewarded, but especially so during rate discounting periods when the guest knows that rates are running at less than rack values. Unlike their European counterparts, American clerks do not share in any mandatory service charge. A special cash pool is needed to make the system work.

Incentive systems require an accurate and easily computed formula. Flat goals can be established, or the focus can be on improvement from last year, or last month, or last week for that matter. Most front office incentives are keyed to average rate per room sold. Occupancy is a factor in total revenue, which suggests other bases for setting goals. Most systems establish a pool that is shared by the team. Individual competition is restricted to the clerks, but selling up is a function of the reservation office, the telephone operators, the bellpersons, and others. That's why the team pool, with its spin off in morale and teamwork, is preferred.

The cash pool is generated from a percentage, say 10 percent, of room sales that exceeds what management projects as the total room sales or the average rate per room sold. Management projections might be based on the ideal room rate (figure 7.6) or the budget forecast. If actual sales exceed target sales, the bonus becomes payable. The bonus period is important. It must be long enough to reflect the true efforts of the team, but short enough to bring the rewards within grasp.

All special discounts must be accounted for and removed from the computation. There are so many of these discounts, including convention rates, package plans, tie-in sales, and others, that total room revenue, rather than the average room rate, may be preferred.

Measuring the change in higher room sales attributable to the incentive system requires a standard, some yardstick by which success is computed. A trend line for previous periods or the full rack rate can be used. Then the measure is a ratio of actual total room sales over maximum revenues at full rack rates.

Any reasonable incentive plan will encourage the clerk to record a larger-than-average figure in the rate space of the registration card. When this rate space and all of the other spaces on the card have been completed, and the guest has been assigned a room, the front office begins the internal recordkeeping that keeps track of the guest and the guest's charges.

QUERIES AND PROBLEMS

1. There are many explanations for the wide range of prices quoted for any given room. The apparent simplicity of the basic rack rate disappears before this variety of special rates, discounted rates, and oblique techniques for quoting rates. Prepare a list of these rate variations and briefly describe each.

2. Using the data from problem 3 below, compute what the typical room charge should be according to the building-cost, or rule-of-thumb, rate.

3. The Hubbart Room Rate Formula calls for an average room rate that will cover expenses and provide a fair return to the investors. Compute that rate from the abbreviated, but scrambled, data.

Investment (also Fair Market Value)	
Land	$ 3,000,000
Building	25,000,000
Furniture and Equipment	6,000,000
Nonappropriated expenses such as advertising, repairs, etc.	1,200,000
Income from all operating departments except rooms, net of losses	3,200,000
Rooms available for sale	563
Nonoperating expenses such as insurance, taxes and depreciation	510,000
Desired return on investment	16%
Interest on debt of $25,000,000	14%
Percentage of occupancy	71%

4. Explain in detail and in sequence how to set the room rate for each of the 386 rooms in a hotel approximately eight months before opening.

8

Constructing
the
Room Rack

Just as the front office is the coordinating center of the hotel, the room rack is the focal point of the front office. From it rooms are sold, identifications are made, and countless questions are answered about both the guest and the guest room. On the one hand, it identifies the guest's party and its tenure, and on the other, it identifies the room, its condition, and its facilities.

BASIS FOR THE ROOM RACK

Room racks are representations of the sleeping rooms. By employing colors, codes, and abbreviations, information about each guest room is condensed into a small metal pocket or a line on the computer screen. Each pocket or line represents one room. Room clerks refer to the pocket of a particular room as a means of recalling the room's accommodations. Thus, guest needs and room facilities are matched for the best assignment.

Figure 8.1 illustrates several room rack types. Combined here in one illustration, they provide a good instructional tool. In reality, it is more likely that the rack would be of one variety or the other rather than the mix shown in figure 8.1.

All but two rooms of the illustration have windows. Symbols, abbreviations, and other information are printed on the window slips and protected by celluloid. That makes them more costly initially, but far more permanent than the windowless type. Rooms 45 and 46 are without windows so the information must be written on a slip that is placed in the rack. These information slips soil more easily and are less concise, but they are also less costly. Plate 1 contrasts the window and windowless racks and also shows (room 901) how to remove the pockets for changing room numbers or symbols.

Other modifications of the rack are available in more expensive models. These are the signal racks with built-in "flags" that are intended to call the clerk's attention to a partic-

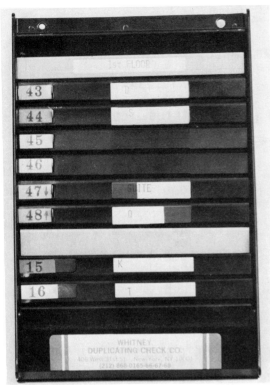

Figure 8.1. Room rack segment illustrating window and windowless type, with and without "flags." The flag is on the window for rooms 47 and 48. The flag is adjacent to the room number for rooms 15 and 16. *Courtesy: Whitney Duplicating Check Co., New York, N.Y.*

Racks may be purchased with any number of pockets, since they are sold by pocket cost. The standard pocket holds a 4-by-1½-inch card, but they do come in larger sizes, up to 4 by 6 inches. The combination registration-rack card illustrated in figure 6.3 fits a 4-by-4¾-inch pocket. It serves two functions and is a satisfactory size for the mom-and-pop operation. It is not a satisfactory size for the large hotel that requires many pockets and an efficient use of costly lobby area. Here the smaller pocket is favored even though the greater overlap makes less of the card readable at first glance. Whatever information is hidden from immediate view is available when the rack slip is lifted (plate 1, room 905).

The Computerized Rack

Since the room rack is a bank of basic, unchanging information, it lends itself well to computerization. Beds, baths, rates, and all of the other information that goes onto the rack can be programmed into the computer and called up with the typing of a few code words (figure 8.2). Furthermore, the equipment needn't be in the front office. It could be in another part of the hotel, in another part of the city, or even in another city altogether. The desk needs only a small keyboard and a CRT screen or a printer (figure 3.3). When properly programmed, the computer will furnish a wide range of information. All of the vacant rooms on a given floor can be listed, all of the king-sized beds available in the tower building can be identified, or a list of connecting rooms can be printed out. Facts that would take many minutes to ascertain from a manual rack can be flashed on the screen in microseconds. Simply put, the computer can do away with the kind of room rack illustrated in figure 8.3. And it has.

Larger hotels — 1,500 rooms and up has been suggested as the magic figure — seem to be using both the computer and the traditional

ular room. Chapter 9 discusses the use of rack flags, which are illustrated in rooms 47 and 48 and in rooms 15 and 16 of figure 8.1. In the first pair (47/48) the signal slides over the center window. The signal of the second pair is adjacent to the room number.

Since other means of flagging the rack are available and since the signals are not always dependable, they have not been popular. They are also more expensive. Light signals adjacent to the room numbers do the same type of flagging, but with the age of computers, they have all but disappeared.

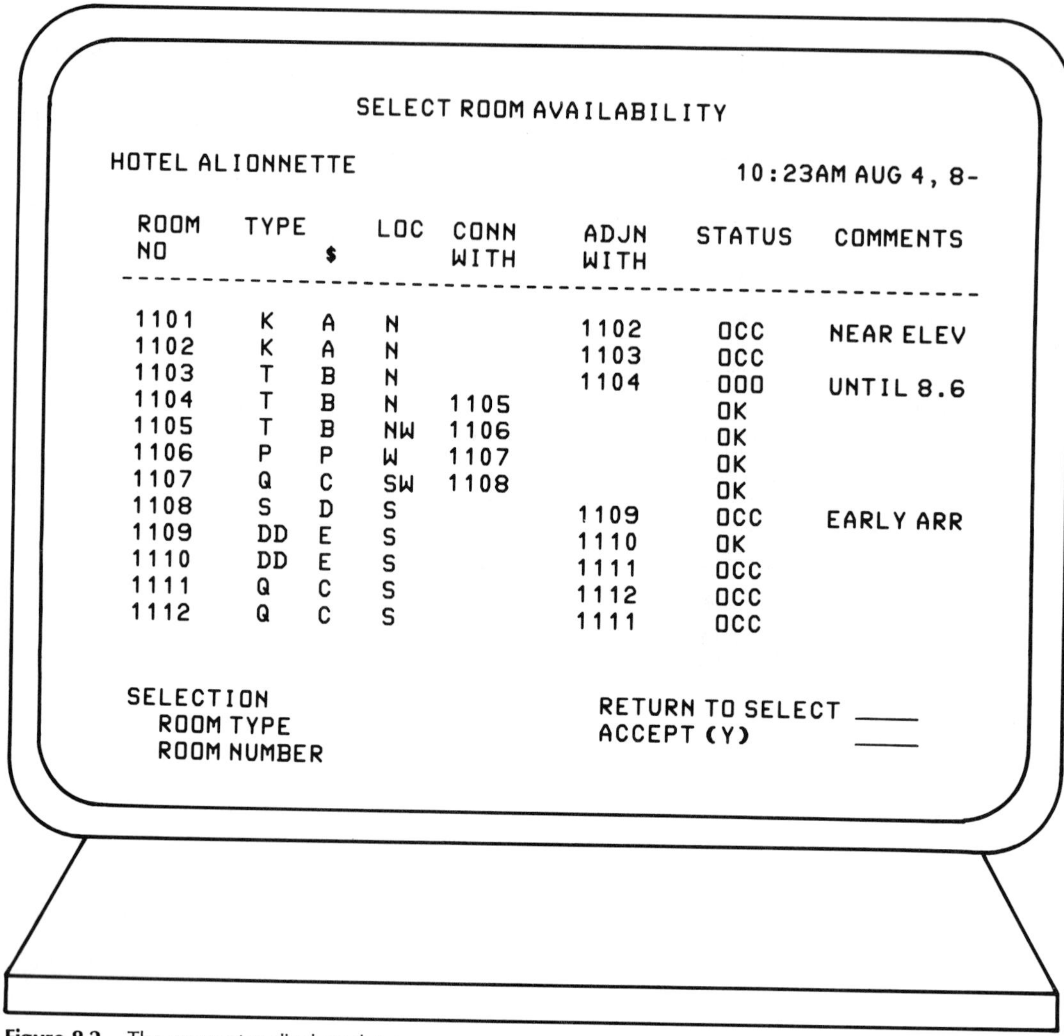

```
                    SELECT ROOM AVAILABILITY

HOTEL ALIONNETTE                            10:23AM AUG 4, 8-

   ROOM     TYPE      LOC   CONN      ADJN    STATUS    COMMENTS
   NO          $            WITH      WITH
   - - - - - - - - - - - - - - - - - - - - - - - - - - - - - - - - -
   1101     K    A    N               1102    OCC       NEAR ELEV
   1102     K    A    N               1103    OCC
   1103     T    B    N               1104    OOO       UNTIL 8.6
   1104     T    B    N    1105                OK
   1105     T    B    NW   1106                OK
   1106     P    P    W    1107                OK
   1107     Q    C    SW   1108                OK
   1108     S    D    S               1109    OCC       EARLY ARR
   1109     DD   E    S               1110    OK
   1110     DD   E    S               1111    OCC
   1111     Q    C    S               1112    OCC
   1112     Q    C    S               1111    OCC


   SELECTION                     RETURN TO SELECT _____
      ROOM TYPE                  ACCEPT (Y)
      ROOM NUMBER                                 _____
```

Figure 8.2. The computer displays the room
rack, including room type, rate class, location, and
status. Clerk's selection (lower left) must agree
with previous input of room type. If all is
satisfactory, clerk exits with Y (Yes), lower right.

Figure 8.3. Room rack installation for a large hotel. Ideally installed, it would have the same room number on each floor on the same horizontal plane. Also see figure 2.5.

rack. Certainly a lack of confidence from inexperience with the equipment is part of the explanation, but there are several, more legitimate reasons. Back-up is one. Hoteliers like the assurance that the manual rack represents in case of equipment downtime or power failure. The screen, with its limited perimeter, just doesn't seem to provide the broad view that comes from looking at the rack. So in numerous instances the systems have been married. Each time the computer prints a registration card and a rooming slip, it also prints a room rack slip that helps keep the manual board up to date. Increasing confidence from technical improvements and better screens should bring reductions in the number of duplicate systems.

Stock Cards

The rack should be arranged in an orderly, logical manner. Keeping one or two floors to a section makes it possible to locate a given room quickly. It is easier to work the rack this way since similar numbers on each floor are in the same horizontal plane (figure 8.3). Limited space and lack of uniform floor plans often dictate less usable arrangements. A section of three to four feet (seventy-five to one hundred pockets) is already too long when installed at the recommended fifty-five to sixty-five degree angle. The optimum is forty to fifty pockets and about twenty-two to thirty inches long (figure 2.5). Size limitations are less restricting when the room rack is moved out of the im-

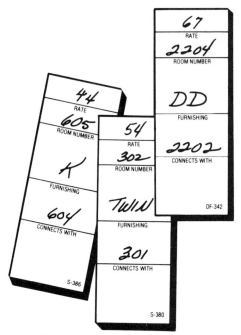

Figure 8.4. Sales tickets, stock cards, or "ducats." Each represents a pocket of the room rack and is used when physical space prevents the clerk's direct access to the rack.

mediate front desk area. Then, of course, the room clerk cannot use the room rack itself but sells from stock cards that represent the pockets of the rack. This system also requires another employee to maintain the rack — a rack clerk.

The stock card, or *ducat*, serves as a means of communication between the desk and the distant rack. It is a piece of heavy stock paper with the same symbols, colors, and identifying information as are contained in the room rack itself (figure 8.4). There is one stock card for each pocket.

Stock cards of available rooms are stored at the front desk in small wells (figure 9.9) by type of room (single, twin, etc.) and rate class. As the rooms are sold, the stock cards are returned to the pocket in the rack. Their very

lack of availability prevents the clerk from selling the same room twice. When the guest vacates the room, the rack clerk returns the stock card to the room clerk and the process begins again.

HOW TO BUILD THE RACK

An effective use of the rack presupposes some knowledge of the rooms since the rack is no more than a representation of those rooms. Hotels differ greatly in design and facilities. These differences are even apparent floor to floor, especially in older hotels. That's why the clerk's experience in one hotel offers no special advantage to another hotel in this respect. New room clerks should inventory the hotel on a room-by-room basis as the best means of learning a rack that is already in use. Old employees should be required to inspect a certain number of rooms per week to increase familiarity and check on housekeeping. It is impossible to do an adequate job of selling and assigning rooms without visualizing the facilities and accommodations. Yet, few front office clerks are required to inspect guest rooms and few front office managers seem concerned about the omission.

Three parts comprise the source of the rack's information: the floor number, the room number (the design), and the content.

The Floor Number

Floors are almost always numbered in sequence. Although an occasional thirteenth floor or room number 13 exists, these are not popular by custom, even though famous hotels like the Plaza in New York have them. Numbers are more important to the people of the Far East than to Americans. Seven, for example, is considered to be luckier than six, and four is to the Oriental what thirteen is to the Occidental — room and floor numbers reflect this.

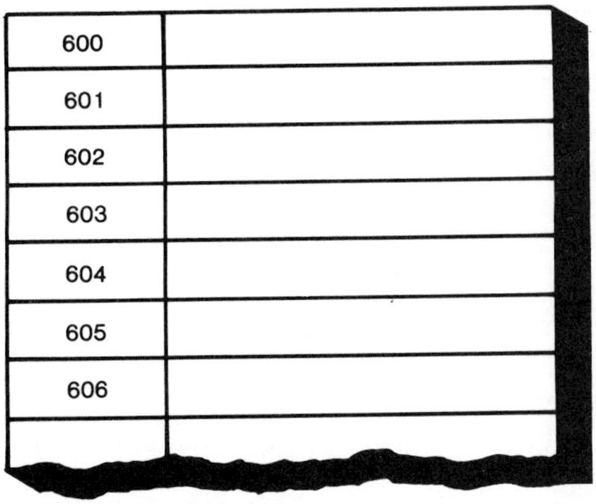

Figure 8.5. Construction of a room rack segment. Step one: identify the floor number and the room numbers.

Americans are accustomed to numbering floors from the street up. The second floor is two even if the first is called lobby or ground. Throughout much of the world, however, floor number one begins above the street level; for example, what would be the tenth floor in the United States would be numbered as the ninth floor elsewhere. Adding to the confusion is a proliferation of intermediate floors between the street level and the first numbered floor. Floors like mezzanine, upper ground floor, and shopping level are interspersed without any standard order.

Motel properties or resorts with separate low-rise units require a different numbering approach. Either all of the numerous three- or four-story units are numbered identically and each building is identified by a different name, or the floors are numbered sequentially so that one or more ground floors might actually be numbered in the teens or even the twenties.

Figure 8.5 is the first of several illustrations (figures 8.9 and 8.13) that shows the construction of a room rack segment. Building the rack requires each room to be identified, first by its floor (six in this illustration) and then by its number.

The Room Number (Floor Design)

Room numbers are less standardized than floor numbers. That's because old hotels, which reflect the life style of a past era, are still around, and new hotels, which reflect changing techniques in design construction and public tastes, are always abuilding. New hotel rooms are larger and new designs require more land per square foot of room space. Space, uniformity, and desirability are contrasted in the old of figure 8.6 and the new of figure 8.7.

The most noticeable change is the disappearance of the inside room, which followed the public and semiprivate bath into oblivion. Rooms 58 to 97 in figure 8.6 form a U of inside rooms around the light court. As illustrated, inside rooms face a court enclosed by wings of the building. Contrast the view to the outside rooms, numbered 02 to 28 and 72 to 98, or to the entire design of figure 8.7. The view from the inside room is down, and the roof on the lower floors is often dirty and unsightly. Inside rooms are also affected by the changing position of the sun, which casts shadows into these rooms even early in the day. The light courts and the design of this hotel produce some unusually shaped rooms, note rooms 60 to 66, for example. Of course, smaller rooms and inside rooms are more economical in construction and land costs.

Other features contrast the floor plans of the old and the new hotels. Modern retail practices have all but eliminated the demand for the large sample rooms of figure 8.6, room numbers 40 and 41. Salespeople used to move their heavy goods into the sample room for display, hence the proximity to the service elevators, so local buyers could examine the season's line. The room also served as the salesperson's sleeping quarters.

Businesspeople still use their hotel rooms as offices. Surveys indicate that women spend more time in their rooms than men do and prefer to do business in a more office-like set-

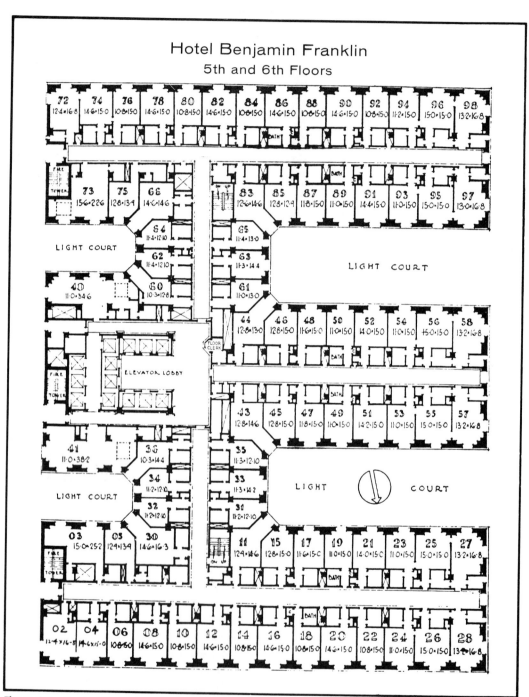

Figure 8.6. Typical floor plan of a 1925 hotel. (This structure is no longer a hotel, having been converted recently.) *Courtesy: The Benjamin Franklin Hotel, Philadelphia, Pa.*

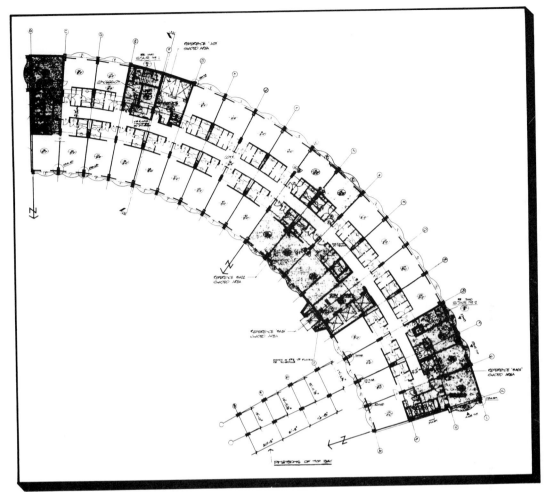

Figure 8.7. Floor plan for the last half of the century is an open style with more square footage and better exposure. Guest rooms in the new addition of this hotel measure fifteen-by-thirty-three feet with a modified king bed, seventy-two-by-eighty inches. *Courtesy: Alameda Plaza, Kansas City, Mo.*

ting. This has brought a small renaissance to the Murphy room (figure 8.11), but has impacted more heavily on the all-suite hotel (figure 1.3). Executives find it less costly to take a suite and use the parlor as a meeting place than to separately rent a small meeting room.

One bedroom and a parlor constitutes a suite, but there may be many rooms in the apartment. Second or third bedrooms are easily added. More luxurious accommodations include formal dining rooms, swimming pools, and even libraries. In addition to the executive suites and display suites that have already been mentioned, hotels feature other uses for suites: hospitality suites, bridal suites, lanai suites, and even one-room suites.

Floor clerks, who once occupied offices near the elevator on each floor (figure 8.6 opposite the elevator foyer), disappeared with the shortage of labor during World War II.[1] Except in limited instances, such as in the towers of some prestigious hotels, the rising cost of postwar labor prevented their return. Now the practice has gone full circle again with the concierge floor: a special, high-priced facility with limited access and an upgraded floor clerk, the concierge.

Terms like *inside room* and *outside room,* and *semiprivate bath* and *private bath* have disappeared from the professional vocabulary as new designs relegate these accommodations to the past. Corner rooms — those with double exposure — are still found in hotels of every age (figure 8.6, room 98 and figure 8.7) and still command premium prices. So, much of the clerk's selling lexicon remains.

---

1. The 775-room Palace Hotel in San Francisco claimed to have the first floor clerk (1875) to communicate to the front desk through speaking tubes. The idea was adopted by eastern hotels, reversing the usual trend of hotel innovation from East to West. Horace Sutton, *Travelers: The American Tourist from Stagecoach to Space Shuttle,* New York: Wm. Morrow and Company, Inc., 1980.

Good salesmanship requires knowledge of the product. Knowing the floor plan enables the clerk to communicate the differences in rooms and in rates. It also enables the clerk to answer the guest's questions. "How far from the elevator?" is a simple query that has haunted hotel architects. It is essential that the noise from the elevator, the ice machine, and the soda dispenser be insulated from adjacent bedrooms. On the other hand, guests dislike a long trek from the elevator to their rooms. Not only is the population aging, but a long, empty corridor instills a feeling of insecurity. Some architects have adopted the service core design (figure 8.8) in one form or another. Here, the wings of the building radiate from a central service area that contains guest and service elevators, linen and maintenance closets, and fire stairwells. Central linen storage on each floor means savings for both the linen runners, who stock the linen closets from the main linen room, and the floor attendants, who service individual rooms from the same central point. Decorators also find central core hotels easier to treat than the long, unbroken corridors that were once the norm.

Obviously, the initial design, which sets the room sizes, the number of suites, and the exposure (the view, and hence the location and land cost), determines the room rate long before the hotel opens.

Sequence of Rooms

Room numbers appear on the room rack in the same sequence in which the rooms are ordered on the floor. Thus, it is very unlikely that they would appear in numerical order. Since the rooms are usually numbered odd and even on different sides of the corridor, one group usually follows the other in the room rack (plate 1), although promulgating such a rule would be very misleading. More and more, the number plan seems to follow a sequence along the

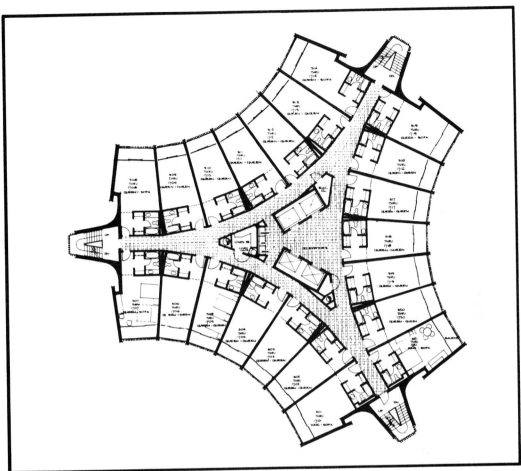

Figure 8.8. The popular tri-arc (center core) configuration as used in Buena Vista, Fla.
Courtesy: TravelLodge, El Cajon, Calif.

right wall from the elevator back to the starting point. Even then, there is no assurance of sequential numbering. Whatever order is needed to place the pockets of adjacent rooms adjacent in the rack is the order that the rack assumes. Look at the sequence of room numbers in figure 8.6!

Room numbering runs into real difficulty when a new wing or ell is added to the original structure. Should the entire floor, old rooms and new, be renumbered in sequence? Should the new wing be numbered sequentially from the old even though the floor numbers would not be in a logical order? Should the addition duplicate the old numbers but contain an identifying prefix or suffix, like N, north?

Problems like these are more difficult if there are more than 100 rooms on the floor. Some computer programs are limited to four digits in room identification, which then makes computer identification almost impossible for hotels with new wings or floors with over 100 rooms when the building height exceeds nine stories. For instance, some equipment cannot distinguish the 119th room on the first floor (1119) from the 19th room on the eleventh floor (1119).

Computer racks usually display the rooms in sequence without regard to floor plan (figure 8.2). The viewer is limited, of course, to the dimension of the CRT screen. Since it is impossible to view the full rack, displaying the rooms out of floor sequence, which is apt to be different than the displayed numerical sequence, places a heavy burden on the memory of the room clerk. That's why a simple request for adjacent rooms or rooms close to one another may be undeliverable in a computer controlled front office. Traditionalists trying to preserve the room rack along with the computer terminal find support here for their position.

The old adage that every horse is a quadruped but not every quadruped is a horse can be paraphrased to read that every connecting room adjoins, but not every adjoining room connects. It is, therefore, necessary to indicate which of the adjoining (adjacent) rooms connect and which do not. This is usually done by an arrow pointing toward the connecting room or rooms (plate 1, rooms 909 and 911; figure 8.1; figure 8.9).

Connecting rooms could be shown equally well by printing their numbers in a common color different from that of the nonconnecting rooms. Since connecting rooms would be color coded, a lack of color would indicate adjoining rooms. If most of the rooms connect, it makes no sense to code all of them. It is easier to code the fewer rooms that merely adjoin. This type of exception coding is frequently used to reduce the number of rack symbols. If every room in the hotel but one had a double bed, for example, only that one room would need an identifying symbol.

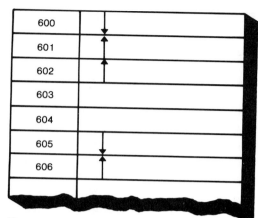

Figure 8.9. Construction of a room rack segment. Step two: rooms that adjoin on the floor abut on the rack; rooms that connect on the floor are connected with arrows on the rack. Rooms 600, 601, and 602 form a suite; rooms 605 and 606 connect.

There was a time when rooms were connected by a bath that was shared. This was shown by changing the color of the connecting arrow from the usual black to, say, a red. The computer age has not done away with the connecting room, but in many cases it has replaced the connecting arrow with a memorandum notation on the screen, "connects with . . ." (figure 8.2).

Room Shape and Size

The shape and size of the sleeping room weigh heavily in product acceptability and demarcate clearly the market to which the hotel is catering. As chapter 7 explained, the physical room remains the major factor in determining rate differences. But the room clerk, who is responsible for selling the rooms, is not able to get information about size and shape from the room rack. That's what makes the physical inspection so important.

In contrast to marketing's tremendous impact on room size, there has been little overall change in the shape of guest rooms. As concave, square, and round structures are built, corresponding changes will occur in the interior shapes and dimensions. Research may eventually show advantages in guest satisfaction or in reduced wear and tear from certain shapes. Until then, the parallelogram remains, and while it may be "old hat," there are certain problems with other shapes. A round building of very small diameter, for example, produces rooms in which there are no parallel walls. The outer wall is circular and the inner walls are angled this way and that to accommodate the bath and the central service core within the limited cross section of the small diameter.

For all of this century, the bath has been used as a sound barrier between the room and the corridor. Abutting the bath to the corridor has also provided constructional advantages. Finally, it has left the most desirable outside wall for windows and balconies.

Room shape is primarily an architectural decision; room size is derived from financial and marketing factors. (Neither explanation accounts for the 325-square-foot minimum dictated by New Jersey law for guest rooms in Atlantic City casinos.) Although the trend has been toward larger and larger rooms, some companies have capitalized on smaller accommodations and smaller rates.

Larger beds — the popularity of queen- and king-sized beds — is one reason for the increase in size. Another part of the explanation is the growing affluence of the modern traveler, who not only wants better facilities but is also able to pay for them. In the final analysis, it is the market that determines the rate structure and consequently the average size room. That market varies from hotel to hotel so that the twin-double of the family-oriented hotel might be quite unacceptable to a property servicing the business traveler.

A comparison of accommodations points up the differences in guest expectations and in the facilities being offered by an international industry. As pointed out earlier, Japan's cap-sule rooms are nothing more than stacked tubes measuring about 5 feet high and 5 feet wide by less than 7 feet deep. Guests change in common locker areas and crawl into their own capsules for sleeping. These capsule inns (that's a grand marketing euphemism) are less than 4 square feet. Japanese budget inns, the Washington chain, for example, offer a 14-square-foot room, about 10 square meters.

Most budget facilities are larger than the Japanese facilities and range in size from the Ibis chain (a new European entry into the American market) with rooms of approximately 130 square feet to groups like Econo or Super 8 with rooms of about 190 square feet. Day's Inns add almost another 100 square feet. The surprise comes when comparisons are made between the budget accommodations and the rooms of the Benjamin Franklin Hotel (figure 8.6), which was a first-class facility for its era. With 150–175 square feet, the rooms of the prosperous 1920s were smaller than many of today's economy facilities.

The Far East contributes to the other end of the scale as well. It has many of the world's opulent hotels, with large rooms and many extras. Hong Kong's Shangri-La Hotel offers a 500-square-foot facility (bath included). That may be somewhat extreme, but when the standard hotel room measures almost 300 square feet, without bath or closet, it takes a minimum of 400 square feet to have a luxury facility. All-suite hotels accelerate the trend toward more space. Although the bedrooms are smaller than the typical hotel room, total space is greater by as much as 25 percent.

Increases in the size of the room have been matched by increases in the size of the bath. Not only is the bath larger but the ancillary space has grown as well. Dressing areas and second lavatories outside the bath proper have added floor space to the overall dimensions. Bathing and dressing areas may be assigned as much as 20 percent of the total space allotted to the room. Some saving has been

Figure 8.10. Typical guest room for the hotel of the last half of the twentieth century. Note exposure, balcony, and bed sizes. Figure 8.7 shows the floor plan for this room. *Courtesy: Alameda Plaza, Kansas City, Mo.*

effected by the elimination of large closets, which have been replaced by open hanger space much as large bureaus have been replaced by second baggage racks. All of which reflects the two nights' stay and garment bag luggage of today's traveler.

Good design and careful location of furniture can make a room appear much larger, especially when complemented by careful interior decorating (figure 8.10). Nevertheless, it takes a differential of about 20 square feet to convince the guest of the justification of a rate increase.

Different kinds of guests require different amounts of space for the functions within the room, regardless of the overall dimensions. A destination hotel needs to furnish proportionately more storage space than a transient property. A transient property allocates more space to sleeping and less to the living area than a destination facility. Such would be the case with New York City hotels where the average use of the room is for seven or eight hours. Heavy use requires different space ratios and different furniture. In China and the Middle East, the room serves as the company's office;

in California, it might be a meeting room. Very cold or very hot climates increase the use factor and the wear and tear.

Researching guest uses and expectations is an ongoing project with most chains since they are building constantly and altering their basic accommodations to catch trends and anticipate demands. Not too long ago, Holiday Inns announced the results of one such study. Three-fourths of their guests travel alone and well over half arrive by auto. Guests are a 4:1 male-female ratio. The room is used for sleeping and about two additional hours daily. Almost every guest watches television, about 75 percent while in bed. Data of this nature suggests all types of bed and room configurations, with most of the ideas substantially different from the average room that one encounters in traveling.

Clearly, there is no standard size room. The hotel industry is not monolithic; it is moving in several directions at once. Miniprices are using module units that measure 12 feet center to center. Luxury operations are moving toward 15-foot centers and lengths of 15 to 20 feet, 300 square feet, without bath. (The standard carpet sizes of 12 and 15 feet dictate the limits in room size unless the plan calls for an expensive custom job.) Costs of energy, of housekeeping and of maintenance limit the expansion that competition pushes for. Comparisons, therefore, begin with the marketplace. (To make those comparisons still more difficult, metric figures will be in use as the century draws to a close.)

ORGANIZATION OF THE ROOM RACK

Once it is understood that the room rack represents the guest floors and the sleeping rooms, it is a simple matter to establish symbols or codes to represent the possible variations. So long as room clerks are able to interpret the individual codes, the lack of standardization from hotel to hotel is not serious. Although there is no uniform code, custom and practice have standardized the symbols somewhat. The colors are less standardized, although they play as important a role as symbols at the front desk.

Similarly, the sequence in which the various symbols appear is customary at most. No regulatory codicil exists and no national, professional organization has yet prescribed either the symbols or their order of appearance. And they may never need to since the computer is rapidly replacing the room rack. Computers employ none of the symbols described below; they are not fixed in a given sequence as discussed next; they rely on none of the color used in rack abbreviations. Some of the following material obviously then has no relevance to a computerized front office rack.

Symbols for Beds

If every room were a replica of every other, there would be no need for rack symbols. When all but a few rooms have the same furnishings, only the exceptions need be noted on the rack. Hotels had been approaching that point, but new developments in bed sizes have reversed the trend for the time being. Hotel rooms passed from the double bed era through the twin bed era into the long-twin and queen-size period that we are now enjoying. As the choice of models explodes in autos and soap powders, we can anticipate an increasing variety of beds, including a choice of mattresses: foam, spring, hard, soft, orthopedic; a range of types: adjustable, vibrating; and a selection of newcomers: flotation, futons.

A *single* bed, which appears in the room rack as an *S*, sleeps one person. A true single bed is 36 by 75 inches but is rarely found in a hotel room. It is too small. Instead, single rooms (rooms furnished for one person) are furnished with one twin bed, one double bed, or one studio bed. When the room is furnished with one twin bed, the symbol *S* is still used. Single beds must measure at least 39 by 72 inches to win an AAA rating.

A *twin* room, which shows on the rack as *T*, contains two beds that are each capable of accommodating one person. Two persons could also be roomed in a double bed or in two studio beds. A twin bed usually measures 39 by 75 inches and uses linen 72 by 108 inches. Mattresses of only 75 inches have lost popularity in recent years due, no doubt, to the increasing height of the average citizen. They are being replaced by the extra-long twin, which measures 39 by 80 inches and requires linen 72 by 113 inches. One also encounters lengths of 79 or 81 inches.

Beds are being lowered as well as lengthened. The usual mattress and spring is 22 to 24 inches high, in contrast to the average chair of some 17 inches. Lowering the bed to 17 inches makes the room appear larger because all the pieces are on the same horizontal plane. It also makes the bed easier to sit on, and most hotel beds are used for that purpose. Modern guest rooms provide adequate seating to reduce the unusually heavy wear on mattresses when beds are used as chairs.

Because twin beds offered a degree of flexibility, most hotel rooms were once furnished with them. In the past, twin beds accounted for as much as 60 to 70 percent of total available rooms in some hotels.

Eventually the trend shifted away from the twin bed as the double-double and queen-double became more popular. The current trend is toward the single queen- or king-size bed. Decreasing family size, increasing travel by the elderly, and increasing single occupancy — as much as 50 to 75 percent of the rooms are being single occupied — have spurred this movement toward single, queen- or king-size beds.

The *double* bed, which appears in the rack as *D*, sleeps two persons. Like the twin, it, too, has grown from the traditional 54 by 75 inches to a length of 80 or 81 inches. Occasionally, one sees a double bed that is 57 inches wide. This bed needs linen wider than the usual 90-inch double width just as the California length (80 inches) increases the standard 108-inch linen length to 113 inches. Even then, half of a 57-inch width provides each occupant with about as much space as a narrow cot. As in the case of the twin room, nothing prevents the sale of a double to one person. It was this very versatility that first made the double bed popular for small rooms.

All of this leaves the public confused. Very confused. Single or double refers with equal ambiguity to (1) the room rate, (2) the number of guests housed in the room, (3) the number of persons the room is capable of accommodating, or (4) the size and type of the beds. It is possible to have a single occupant in a double bed being charged a single rate although the room is designated as a double, meaning it could accommodate two persons. A single occupant in a twin room often needs assurance that no additional charge is being made for the extra, unused bed. The single room configuration, that is, one single bed for one person, is almost unknown today. Thus, to the innkeeper, "single" means single rate almost without exception.

Fortunately, the confusion is usually limited to the single, double, and twin, although the twin-double gives occasional problems. The *twin-double* or *double-double,* as it is sometimes called, appears in the rack as *DD*. Both the *U* and the △ symbols are also used, but not very consistently. The twin-double is merely a pair of doubles instead of the usual pair of twins. Because the twin-double sleeps four persons, it is also called a family room. Motel owners sometimes sell twin-doubles to a couple at a reduced rate with the stipulation that only one bed be used. In fact, a survey done by Sheraton's franchise division showed that the second bed of a double-double was used only about 15 percent of the time. Thus encouraged, they created a minisuite from the standard 12-by-19-foot double-double. A sleeper sofa was substituted for one of the beds, and a movable curtain divider separated the living-entertainment area from the sleeping quarters.

In an attempt to clarify the terminology, one of the trade associations adopted the following standardized descriptions: single — one person, one bed; double — two persons, one bed; twin — two persons, two single beds; double-double — one room, two double beds; suite — two rooms (one sleeping, one parlor); studio — studio couch to be converted into bed; efficiency — contains some type of kitchen facility. Although commendable, they indicate how confusing meanings are even to the professional. Imagine the problem facing the guest or the meeting planner who is the communication intermediary between the guest and the hotel. The success of the meeting depends on the accommodations that three different persons might be calling by three different names.

The *queen* and *king* are extra long, extra wide doubles. As to be expected, *K* and *Q* are the rack symbols for these large beds. Although designed for two persons, some families squeeze in three or even four. The queen measures 60 by 75 inches and the king 78 by 75 inches. In both cases, the 80-inch California length has gained sway and, in some cases, the king has stretched to 84 inches. Both require larger rooms (the critical distance between the foot of the bed and the furniture — a three-foot minimum — remains) and larger sheets, 108 by 122½ inches. Since laundry costs are calculated by weight, larger sheets mean larger laundry bills. A larger room with extra laundry

costs can only mean a higher room rate even without consideration for the additional cost of the larger bed, mattress, and linen. A higher rate dictates, in turn, the class of patron.

A *cot* or *rollaway* is a portable utility bed that is added to the usual room furnishings on a temporary basis. Since it is moved in and out of different rooms, it is not marked on the rack. A cot sleeps one person, and a comfortable one measures 34 by 75 inches and uses twin sheets. Cots usually come smaller — 30 by 72 inches with linen 63 by 99 inches. Only if the clerk knows the property well will he or she know which rooms are large enough to take a rollaway. Cots are costly in housekeeping time, so an effort to room the party properly should be made at the start. Figure 8.8 illustrates storage areas in which premade cots can be stored until needed. Rarely is cot storage so adequately planned for in the original design.

Twin beds joined by a common headboard is a *hollywood* bed. A hollywood bed appears as twins on the rack, since that's what they are. They are difficult beds to make because the room cleaner cannot get between them. To overcome this, the beds are placed on rollers and swing apart, resulting in rapid carpet wear. Because the dimensions of this bed are 78 by 75 inches (two twins), it can be converted into a king by replacing the two mattresses with one mattress laid across both springs.

A *studio* bed is a sofa by day and a bed by night. During the day the bed is slipcovered and the pillows are stored away. There is neither headboard nor footboard once the studio sofa is pulled away from the backrest, which usually holds the unused pillows. Today's guest room must serve a dual bedroom-living room function, so studio rooms that contain one or two studio beds are popular with businesspersons. They can be used as conference rooms or offices during the day. Despite the great strides made in dual purpose pieces, surveys indicate that most hotel guests prefer regular beds.

A wide studio is more comfortable for sleeping, but a narrow one is better to sit on. The best of both worlds is reached by using the dimensions of a single bed, 36 by 75 inches, which is pushed under a deep backrest to convert it into a narrower sofa.

The studio room, sometimes called an executive room, has proven ideal for redoing small, single rooms in older hotels. It appears on the rack as an *O* but sometimes as an *S* if that letter isn't being used as a single bed designation. *UP*, undersized parlor, is also used. In Europe, a parlor that has no sleeping facilities is called a *salon*.

A *sofa* bed is similar in function to the studio bed except that it is a sofa first of all, which makes it more comfortable to sit on. It is usually 17 inches off the floor whereas the studio bed may be as high as 22 inches. Unlike the studio bed, which rolls away from its frame, the sofa bed opens in accordion fashion from the seat. Since it unfolds, the sofa bed is less convenient and requires more space than the studio. Parlors are generally equipped with sofa beds as part of a suite, but a studio bed is usually a room unto itself. Sofa beds can be single, double, or even queen size, although the single is more like a three-quarter bed (48 by 75 inches). Sofa beds are often called hideabeds and, thus, carry an *H* designation on the rack. Large rooms that contain both standard beds and hideabeds are junior suites. The rack would show both kinds of beds, for example *DH*.

The *Murphy* bed, *M* (figure 8.11), is making a comeback after many years of absence. This bed folds up into the wall, improving still further on the dual sleeping-living room. It is ideal for working executives who prefer to conduct their business in a bedless room. The Murphy bed's edge over the studio is sleeping comfort.

Operators have begun to furnish still another bed variety, the water bed. In one decade water beds have passed through the novelty stage to offer a viable alternative to innerspring and foam mattresses. The bed goes back historically to the nomadic tribes of pre-Christianity, who filled goatskins with water. Even Queen Victoria is reported to have had a water bed. It was rediscovered by a Californian who first tried starch and gelatin as a filler. The water bed is still primarily a western phenomenon. Broader usage can be expected as manufacturers reduce the size and weight of the bed and overcome the wavelike motion. This is being done with stabilizing chambers that make flotation sleep in hotels/motels a possibility for the near future. And for the long range? Possibly air beds — air cushions that support the sleeper without bedframe, mattress, or linens.

The Japanese futon, which is an adaptable, cotton-quilted "bed," is a recent addition to the American sleeping design — so recent that no U.S. hotel has yet reported using one. (No need for rack symbols either.) They come in regular mattress sizes. The thick layers of batting are easily stored and readily adapted to service as a couch or bed.

Figure 8.12 summarizes the symbols and plate 1 shows their use. Although the symbols are relatively standard (the British use — for single, = for twin, and + for double), they are not absolute by any means. Similarly, the bed symbols often precede the bath symbols in the rack, but one sees them the other way around almost as frequently.

Symbols for Baths

Bath is a confusing term. A bath is a room that houses the bathing and toilet facilities. It is not, as the inexperienced traveler is surprised to learn, a bathtub. The bath contains the tub (or shower), the water closet (toilet), and the lavatory (sink or basin).

Figure 8.11. The versatile Murphy bed provides
a dual sleeping-living facility, ideal for the business
person who uses the room as an office.
Courtesy: Murphy Door Bed Co., New York, N.Y.

At one time public baths served whole floors or even entire wings, and tubs were the only type of bathing facility. As old hotels began converting rooms without baths to rooms with baths, stall showers, which occupy little space, gained favor. These showers fit easily into old closets or corners of large rooms.

As the life style changed again, tub and shower combinations were installed. This is a fortunate compromise, since some persons generally prefer the shower and others the bath. Japanese tourists favor tubs very definitely, just as they prefer twin beds over double beds. The bidet has not found acceptance in the American home and, thus, is rarely found in the hotel bath.

If each room has a tub and shower combination, as many new hotels do, it is an exercise in futility to list this in each rack pocket. Symbols are needed only if the facilities differ from room to room.

Bed	Symbol
Double	D
Double-Double	DD
Hideabed	H
King	K
Murphy Bed	M
Parlor	P
Parlor sleeps one	P–1
Parlor, sleeps two	P–2
Queen	Q
Queen-Double	QQ
Single	S
Studio	O
Twin	T
Long-Twin (or California Twin)	LT
Water Bed	W

Figure 8.12. Rack symbols used to identify sleeping accommodations in guest rooms.

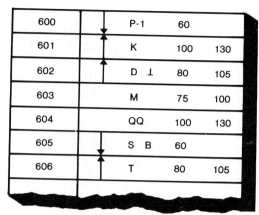

Figure 8.13. Construction of a room rack segment. Step three: bed symbols are followed, where applicable, by bath symbols and by rates, single and double occupancy. Baths are signalled by exception; all but rooms 602 and 605 have tub and shower combinations.

S for shower and *T* for tub are not satisfactory symbols because of the probable confusion with the *S* and *T* of single and twin beds. Although these are used nevertheless, *B* is preferred for bathtub and ⊥ an inverted *T*, for shower. A *Z* is also used for shower. In their book *Hotel Accounting*, Horwath, Toth, and Lesure (Ronald Press) recommend an *X* for tub and shower combination.

No symbol has yet been suggested for a dual lavatory. It wouldn't be needed, of course, if all the rooms had them. Perhaps the letter *V* would do.

The chapter illustration concludes with figure 8.13, which represents the completed room rack segment using the symbols identified throughout the discussion.

Rate Symbols

Usually, single and double occupancy rates are given. Listing the single rate first and the double rate next makes further explanation unnecessary. The rate for a third person is usually a fixed dollar amount above the double rate and is rarely shown. Similarly, the double rate could be eliminated if the hotel had a flat fee above the single occupancy or if all rooms were sold at a given price regardless of occupancy. No dollar signs are used in the rack and parts of a dollar are usually expressed as fractions, not decimals (plate 1, room 913).

Other Symbols

The facilities of hotel rooms have changed along with their shapes and sizes. Hotels once advertised telephones in each room; today's room may actually include a second telephone in the bath. Circulating ice water was advertised in the Statler era, which was as unique to that period as the in-room vending machine is today. Radio and television are common to every room and no longer require special symbols. Personal computers, in-room liquor dispensers, and gas masks for fire protection are likely to join a host of telecommunication devices as the special accoutrements of the next decade. So make up your symbols and be ready.

Cluttering the rack with symbols reduces the speed of the clerk. Symbols are needed only when the facility is not available in every room, as at a mountain resort where only a portion of the rooms are air conditioned. In *Hotel Accounting,* the authors recommend that no more than six to seven symbols be used even though the rack will accommodate nine or ten.

A great deal of information can be communicated with color. Corner rooms are shown by printing the room number in a particular color. Suites that contain a wet bar may be numbered with a special color. If one side of the hotel has an especially desirable exposure, that series of room numbers might be color coded. In fact, resort racks are sometimes set up with rooms in order by exposure. These could be identified either by direction — north, south, east, and west — or by other designations — lakeside, mountainview, golf course, and so on. Color identifies sample rooms, efficiencies, cabanas, lanais, junior suites, rooms with dual lavatories, parlors, and other special facilities.

Color codes are not limited to room numbers. By printing one or more of the symbols in color, other symbols can be eliminated. If, for example, the *T* that represents twin beds were printed in red, it would mean that the room had a bathtub and no tub symbol would be needed. Green could be shower and blue a tub and shower combination.

Windowless room racks show the information on permanent rack cards rather than with symbols (plate 1, right side). Even here color has a function because the color of the permanent rack card can be used to indicate the type of bed or bath.

The room rack is likely to be a historic relic by the close of the century. Rapid technical breakthroughs in electronics can only hint at the still more amazing developments to be made before the turn of the millennium. Such developments are certain to bring computer costs and applications within the range of every type of lodging facility. Until that happens, the rack will remain the center of communications for the desk. The focus of concepts that it provides will be no less valid because of new equipment.

QUERIES AND PROBLEMS

1. Clarify the confusion from mixed terminologies by distinguishing single bed from single room from single rate; similarly, double bed from double room, from double rate.
2. Prepare stock cards reflecting the three separate givens below:
   a. Twin room with tub and shower selling for the standard $72 single and $88 double that is the charge for every room in the hotel. Room 1012.
   b. Queen room adjacent to a connecting parlor with a sofa bed. The bedroom has a step-in tub and a separate stall shower. The parlor is $100 nightly; the queen is $80 for single occupancy, $100 for double occupancy. Rooms 806 and 807.
   c. Rooms 404, 406, and 408 are a three-room suite with Room 406 being the parlor. Both bedrooms have double queens and tub and shower. (The entire hotel has tub and shower in every room.) The parlor has a wet bar and a Murphy bed. As a corner room, 404 is 50 percent more than the price of 408, which sells for $76 and $100. The parlor can be assigned to either room and has a daily rate of $90.

3. Using a room rack facsimile similar to that shown on page 164, build the room rack from the floor plan shown on p. 163. Every room has a tub and shower combination. Northern exposure rooms have kings and face the pool. They sell for a flat $10 more than the twins of the southern exposure, whose rack rate is $48 single and $60 double. Parlors, which contain a double hideabed, are $60 per night, but they are not usually sold separately from the bedroom. Rooms located in the cross piece of the "T" are all double beds with a rack rate of $45 single and $50 double, except rooms 142 and 145, which have double queens and are priced the same as the kings.

4. Reconstruct the floor plan from the segment of room rack that is given.

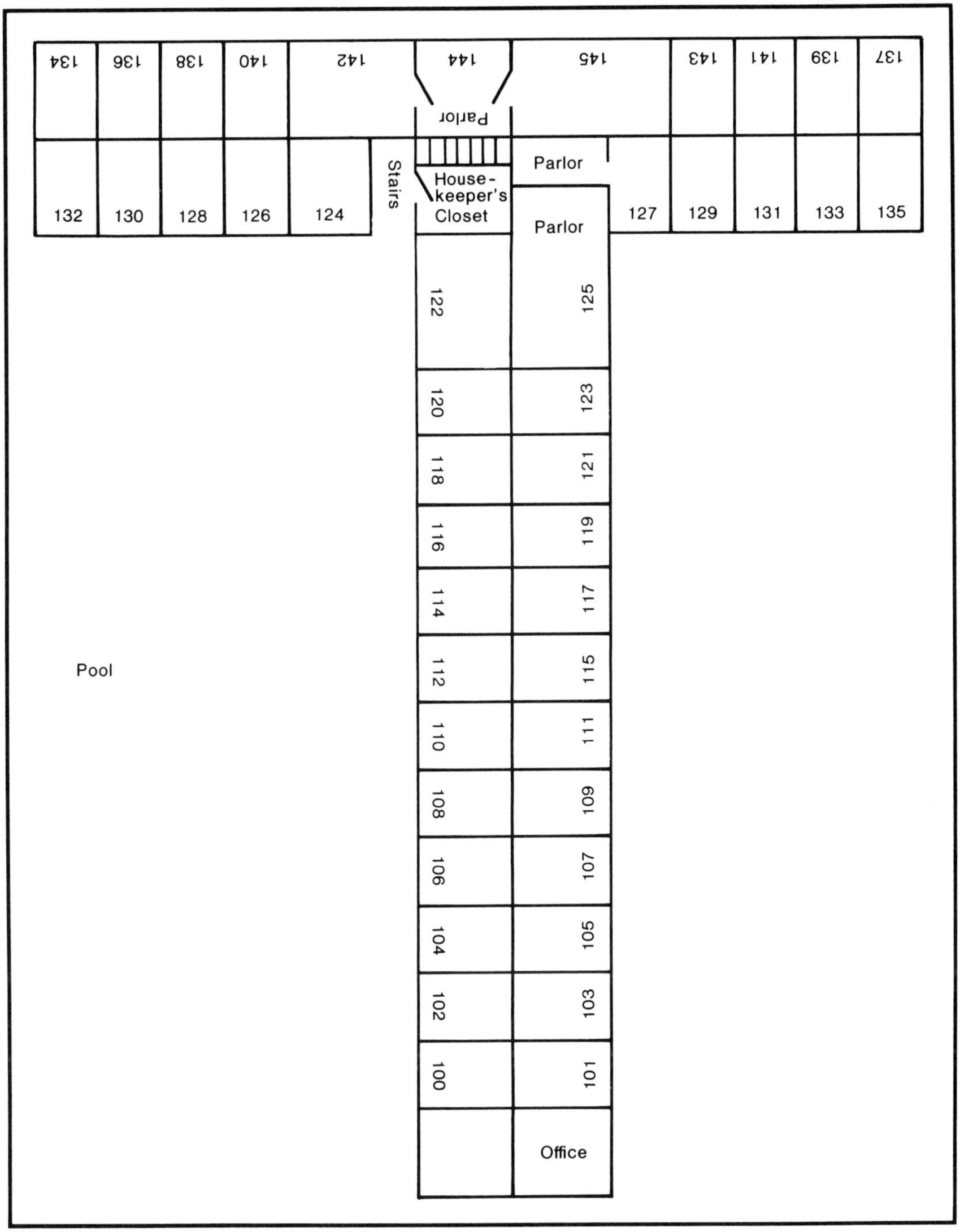
134
136
138
140
142
144
145
143
141
139
137
Parlor
Parlor
Stairs
House-
keeper's
Closet
Parlor
132
130
128
126
124
127
129
131
133
135
122
125
120
123
118
121
116
119
114
117
112
115
110
111
108
109
106
107
104
105
102
103
100
101
Office
Pool

FACSIMILE OF A ROOM RACK

Northern Exposure		Southern Exposure	
1600	QQ H	1601	QQ O
1602	K	1603	K
1604	T	1605	T
1606	T	1607	T
1608	T	1609	T
1610	↓ K	1611	↓ K
1612	↑ S	1615	↑ O
1616	D Eastern	1617	QQ H Double Exposure
1618	D Eastern	1619	↓ D Eastern
1620	↓ D Eastern	1621	↑ P M Three Exposures
1622	↑ P H2 Three Exposures	1623	↑ D Western
1624	↑ D Western	1625	D Western
1626	D Western	1627	D Western
1628	D Western	1629	D Western

9

Communication Systems

From the very first page of the textual material, the responsibility for communication has been assigned to the front office:

> Through it [the front office] flow communications with every other department; from it emanate instruction and direction for the care and service of the guest; to it come charges for final billing and settlement.

Developing the communication system has been a major activity of front office planners. And that responsibility remains despite the implementation and promise of electronic magic. The very excitement of the computer and of its communication kin lies in the ability to structure information for the hotel business far more rapidly, in newer forms, and with far more detail than the traditional room rack and its communication kin are able to achieve. Chapter 9 points up the transition of the system from the now to the new.

THE NOW: HOTEL RACKS

Hotel racks give order to the information that the front office staff must have at its fingertips. The room rack structures only one type of information. Other racks, including the telephone and information racks, provide cross reference to the room rack and facilitate the other duties of the front office staff. As the use of electronic data processing becomes more widespread, racks will become less important because the information they contain will be immediately recallable from on-line computers. This will be some time in coming for the small- to medium-size properties. For them, the racks, and especially the room rack, are the now.

The Room Rack

Once constructed, the room rack communicates several types of information. The physical facilities and the rate have been discussed

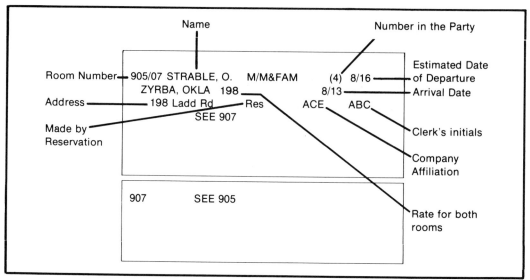

Figure 9.1. Typical room rack slip. Bits of information may be relocated according to the front office manager's own preference. (See also plate 1, room 905/907.)

already. The room rack also tells which rooms are occupied, which are vacant, and which of the vacant ones are ready for sale. In addition, the rack serves as a directory of the guest population, telling who is where and who warrants special service. Most of this information comes from the room rack slip.

The Room Rack Slip

The room rack slip is prepared by a typist working from the registration card. Often it is prepared by hand by the room clerk as part of the registration packet (figure 6.6). In other places, a temporary rack slip is prepared by the clerk until the typist can complete the permanent form.

Occasionally the form is computer prepared. At a hotel using both rack and computer, the computer prints out the rack slip from the information that was placed in the computer memory during either the reservation or registration procedure. From the infor-

mation on the rack slip, from its color, indeed from its very presence or absence, the room clerk keeps the rack updated and the desk informed (plate 1).

Content of the Rack Slip

Each occupied room is represented by a room rack slip in the pocket of the room rack. Figure 9.1 illustrates a typical rack slip. Since this party is occupying two rooms, a cross reference is necessary but it is sufficient to list all the details on one slip. Only one bill would be prepared even though two rack slips are needed. The presence of the rack slip in the pocket indicates that the room is sold; its absence indicates the room's availability.

Although a similarity of needs and uses to which the slip is put has created a general standardization, the format of the slip will not necessarily be identical to the illustration. Room number(s) and name will most likely be found in the sequence shown. Other items will or will not be included according to the needs of the individual hotel. The information is typed close to the top of the slip to assure maximum exposure in the overlapping room rack pockets. For the same reason, the top line usually contains what is adjudged to be the most important information.

Street addresses are sometimes omitted since the reg card contains the complete address; then the rack slip shows only the city of origin. Further information is helpful for credit decisions, however, so the complete address is shown in figure 9.1. The fact that the guest was a reservation whose address was verified by mail, rather than a walk-in, strengthens any credit requests still further. So does an association with the Ace Corporation, one of the hotel's city ledger accounts.

The anticipated departure date of August 16, "8/16," is used for reservation and occupancy forecasting. A question mark would follow the date if departure time were very uncertain, as in plate 1, room 917. The number of persons in the party "(4)" is helpful for both daily operational matters and the preparation of the night audit. If the hotel offers more than one plan, the room rack slip carries that designation along with the number of persons, "4 AP." (See plate 1, room 902.)

"M/M" means Mr. and Mrs., but "Mr/s" is also used. Ms., the abbreviation for both Miss and Mrs., is growing in popularity. The date of arrival, "8/13"; the clerk's initial, "ABC"; and the rate, "198," $198 for both rooms, rounds out the information normally found on the slip. The reader will recognize the registration card as the source of the data.

Color of the Rack Slip

Rack slips are prepared in many colors using colored paper or colored overlays. As with the room rack itself, color communicates a great deal of useful information. Each hotel sets its own meanings but the key is easy to learn.

White room rack slips are used for the normal guest who has no special identification. Other possible color codes are:

Aqua	Day Rate — guest will vacate before evening.
Blue	Paid-in-Advance — credit privileges not extended; no additional charges permitted.
Green	American Plan — only necessary when two or more plans are offered.
Orange	Weekly Rate — or other special situations, such as monthly or seasonal rate.
Pink	Conventioneer — several colors are used whenever several different groups are meeting at the same time; membership in each group is identified by its own color.
Gold	House Use — occupied by manager or given over to housekeeping, etc.
Tan	No Information to Be Given Out — guest has requested privacy. Telephone calls to such rooms may be directed to the assistant manager.
Red	Permanent Guest — could be lease or other rental arrangement.
Violet	VIP — very important person entitled to special attention. Sometimes written SPATT.
Yellow	COMP — complimentary, no charge for accommodations. COMP RFB means complimentary for room, food, and beverage and might be a different color.

Color codes are limited only by the needs of the hotel and the spectrum of the rainbow. Some other color possibilities were discussed in the chapter on reservations.

Distribution of the Rack Slip

Room rack slips are generally prepared in three copies: one for the room rack, which is the topic of this immediate section, and one each for the telephone and information racks (figure 6.14). One copy may suffice if all three racks are one, as they are in a small hotel. The distribution is the same whether the slips are prepared manually by a clerk, on a machine by a typist, or automatically by a computer. Additional copies of the rack slip are made and distributed according to need. If manually prepared by the clerk at the time of registration, one copy may become the bellperson's rooming slip.

Less frequently, slips go to housekeeping and room service. Some information, rates for example, may be deleted in such cases. The carbon paper being so located that the impression does not pass through to the second or third copies. At one time, copies were given to the key and mail clerk for identification of guests requesting mail and room keys. The slips were filed in the key and mail rack so guests requesting keys could be asked to identify themselves. Copies still go to the floor concierge in the few hotels that have this position.

Status of Rooms

A brief summary will clarify several points. The room clerk has used the room rack, or the stock card, to make the room assignment. (Either the stock card was in hand, indicating the availability of the room, or the pocket was empty, exposing the accommodation and rate symbols.) The assignment completed, the registration card goes to the typist, if one is used, and the guest goes to the room in the company of the bellperson. The completed room rack slip is inserted in the rack pocket. The presence of the slip indicates that the room is occupied.

Flags

In the interim between the sale of the room and the completion of the rack slip, it is possible that the room could be sold again to another party. When several clerks are working the rack and when the delay in typing can be thirty minutes or more, the danger of a second assignment becomes very real.

To prevent the sale of the same room twice, a flag is used. Some window room racks have colored slides that are made for this purpose (figure 8.1). A temporary rack slip, one prepared by the room clerk as part of the registration packet, is another means of flagging the temporary assignment. A blank room rack slip inserted in the rack pocket at a forty-five-degree angle is probably the most common flag used. The angled slip indicates that the room has been assigned and is waiting for the preparation of the permanent room rack slip (plate 1, room 919).

Where stock cards are used, the stock card is returned to the rack as a flag. It is placed in the empty pocket until the final rack slip is prepared. The rack slip remains in front of the stock card until checkout when it is removed, exposing the stock card again. The card goes back to the clerk and the cycle resumes.

Other special situations are flagged by standing the rack slip on end until the matter is resolved (room 915). Included here are complaints about noisy rooms, questions about the number of occupants in a given room, temporary room assignments, and others. Temporary assignments should be avoided since they require extra housekeeping time, extra desk time, and extra time from the service department. Delaying the guest in the lobby or choosing a different room skirts the temporary assignment with its costly second move. This is more feasible for a transient hotel, where the stay is brief, than for a resort hotel, where the room becomes a significant item in the long-term stay. Guests dislike changing too. It's not only inconvenient but it's also frequently done by a second bellperson who expects a second tip.

On Change

The permanent room rack slip remains in the rack during the guest's stay. Because it is the cashier who checks out the guest, it is the cashier who notifies both the room clerk and the housekeeper of the guest's departure. The room is put *on change* by the room clerk during the period between the checkout and the point at which the room is ready for occupancy again. It is ready for occupancy when the housekeeper has completed the job and notified the room clerk to that effect. Rooms may be sold and assigned during the on-change period, but guests are not usually sent to unmade rooms.

There are several methods of flagging the rack during the on-change period. With the windowless rack, the permanent rack card is turned over to expose the side that reads on change. Room 912 of plate 1 shows this and another very popular technique. The old room rack slip is removed, folded in half, and returned in a vertical fashion to the pocket. When the housekeeper notifies the desk that the room is ready for sale, the slip is removed. In some hotels it is simply discarded, but in others it is put to one of several uses. Reservations may get the slip and use it to update the day's departure count, or it may be used to communicate the departure to other office personnel as a basis for clearing the other racks. Finally, it may be used as a list of the day's departures.

Some window racks (figure 8.1) have dual signals: one for on change and one for flagging until the permanent rack slip is prepared.

Out of Order

On-change rooms and out-of-order rooms are not the same. On-change rooms are temporarily unavailable, but out-of-order rooms are inoperative for some reason. It might be an unexpected mechanical breakdown in plumbing, electrical, or heating equipment. Or it might be a planned shutdown to complete routine maintenance, such as painting and wall washing or major refurbishing. There are many conditions that force the loss of room income

for a day or more. Among these are fire, fumigation after disease or occupation by an animal, a death that requires public investigation, and so on. Seasonal resorts usually open one floor at a time, leaving the others out of order.

Although a special out-of-order card is available, a blank room rack slip is used just as often by marking it "000," as shown in room 904, plate 1. It is helpful to inform the desk of the reason for the room's out-of-order status and the approximate date of its return to service. Conversely, if the desk puts the room out of order, it must notify the department that is responsible for the repair.

Double-up

Several room rack slips will fit into one room rack pocket. Whereas one rack slip is sufficient when all of the occupants are in one family, several slips are needed when unrelated friends with different surnames share a common room. Several slips are also helpful for flagging separate billing requests or identifying the company name on hospitality suites.

The additional rack slips are not always visible at first glance because they are identical in size. To avoid overlooking the extra slips, a double-up card is sometimes used. Since it is another form and another task, it is more often ignored than used. Plate 1, room 913, shows both means of doing the same thing. The first rack slip is folded in half (window rack side), exposing the slip behind it.

Unauthorized double-ups require special diligence by the hotel staff. Groups arrive and willingly pay for two or three occupants but sleep an additional two or three on the floor. The practice prevails at hotels where sleeping bags are common. Ski areas, summer resorts, and highway motels encounter the problem more frequently than downtown or suburban properties. An identification and collection policy needs to be established by management and made effective through an alert room clerk, a conscientious bell staff, and a trained housekeeping department.

Cots and cribs for members of the same family are not considered to be double-ups.

Blocks

Pockets in the rack are blocked when circumstances prevent the assignment of rooms in the ordinary course of events. A room on reservation for an arriving guest is blocked. But blocks come in degrees. Room reservations that are blocked in the morning may be shuffled at the discretion of the clerks during the day (plate 1, room 911). Other blocks are inviolable, requiring permission of higher authority before they can be moved (room 918). Reservations for members of incentive tour groups fall into that classification. Incentive tour guests have all won the trip by superior performance, and they must be treated identically. Care in the initial assignment cannot be undone in a last-minute change by someone who is unaware of the group's nature.

Reservations are blocked with a standard form; restrictive blocks are made either by a note on the reservation form, on a blank rack slip, or by a colored plastic overlay. Temporary blocks are used when rooms are being shown as part of the sales effort.

Coordination

The coordinating role of the front office, which uses the room rack as one of its tools, becomes clearer as one understands the functions and procedures of the desk. Through the presence or absence, the color and content, and the location and position of the room rack slip, the clerk ascertains the status of rooms, identifies the populace, and determines the facilities of each room. All of these tasks need to be done regardless of the means employed. Reservations must be blocked, rooms placed on change, and out-of-order facilities communicated whether the room rack or the computer is the tool.

A constant flow of information is needed to keep the front office up-to-date on the arrivals, departures, and room changes that are taking place. The room clerk, the cashier, and the housekeeper (the linen room) are the three major terminals in the communication triangle. Until recently, the rack has been the method used to coordinate the three. It is rapidly being replaced by the computer system, which offers instantaneous communication throughout the hotel. The objectives remain the same, however, only the tool and the techniques have changed.

The Typical System

Under the usual procedure, new arrivals are communicated to the cashier and to the other stations by the room clerk. While the arriving guest is being roomed by the bell staff, a carbonized packet of room rack slips, including the guest bill, is being prepared by the typist. As explained earlier, this packet may be prepared instead by the room clerk as the registration card is being completed and the guest is waiting (figure 6.8). Although the second procedure eliminates the cost of a typist, it slows down the registration procedure. Either way, the rack slips are distributed to each rack and the guest bill is sent to the cashier.

Housekeeping is not notified of the specific room assignment and normally learns of it only when the floor attendant makes rounds the following day. An exception to this would be a crowded hotel where a registered guest is waiting for the assigned room to be readied. The clerk might call the housekeeper to expedite the cleaning. Even then, housekeeping remains unaware of the guest's actual identity. During the guest's stay, a daily report from the housekeeper to the room clerk keeps tabs on the status of the room (figure 14.8).

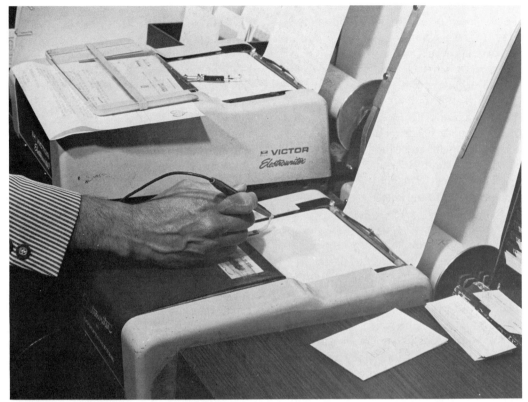

Figure 9.2. A telewriter reproduces the handwritten messages at one or more stations. For example, the number of a room that has been checked out is written by the clerk and appears in the linen room.

A computerized front office shortcuts much of this "typical" system as we shall soon see.

Whereas the room clerk initiates the arrival information pattern, the cashier begins the departure communication. At checkout, the registration card, which was stapled to the bill at arrival, is removed and passed to the room clerk. A special form, or just the room number noted on a pad, is used if the registration card was not attached to the guest folio initially. The clerk immediately puts the rack on change and notifies the other racks of the departure.

The cashier reports checkouts to the linen room as well. A special machine that transmits written messages over the telephone lines, in this case the room number, is used by the cashier. The receiving portion of this telewriter (figure 9.2), located in the linen room, reproduces a facsimile of the written message with a special pen.[1] When the floor housekeeper next checks with the linen room, in person, electronically, or by telephone, the checkout is relayed. In large installations, an

1. TelAutograph is a trademark of the TelAutograph Corporation.

additional receiver is located in the linen closet on each floor so that the floor housekeeper learns of the checkout sooner.

Years ago the cashier relied on the last bellperson to carry the departure lists to the linen room. In turn, the linen room dispatched a runner to the housekeeper on the floors. Later came corridor lights on each floor, which alerted the floor housekeeper to the checkout, and the need to call the linen room by telephone for the room number. Of course, the housekeeper sometimes sees the guest leaving or learns of the checkout when entering the vacant room.

After the room is readied by the housekeeper and approved by the inspector — again a delay in getting the inspector to the room — a machine message from the linen room notifies the desk clerk that the room is ready. The on-change notice is removed from the rack and the room is opened for sale. There is no need for housekeeping to notify the cashier of the ready status of the room. (Some very small motel properties, where all guests pay in advance, have departing guests leave their keys in the rooms. When the room is finished, the room cleaner delivers the key to the desk. A key in the key rack then indicates the room is ready for sale.)

The major delay in communication takes place between the linen room and the housekeeper on the floor. Almost everyone except the employee on the floor knows when the room is put on change and the reverse is true when the room is ready. The housekeeper's mobility makes a solution to the problem difficult, but several of the communication systems soon to be discussed have all but solved the problem. After all, this is the age of communications.

Room Changes

Occasionally it is necessary to move guests from one room to another. The first room may have been more costly than the guest's reservation and a temporary assignment made with the understanding that a room change would be made the following day. Changes also originate with guests who find the room unsatisfactory because of noise, location, bedding, and so on. Guests must be moved when hotel facilities fail and a long repair period is anticipated. Fire, flood, or other disasters warrant room changes. It is also possible that a portion of the party may leave and smaller, less expensive facilities are needed. Conversely, additional persons may join a party and require larger quarters. If the specific room is on reservation for the following day and no other room was available on the day of arrival, a room change must be made unless it is possible to shift the reservation. A RNA guest who was given a temporary room awaiting the vacancy of the permanent assignment requires a room change, too.

Whether guest requested or hotel initiated, room changes must be communicated to all concerned. A simple form often in a special color (figure 9.3) is prepared by the room clerk and sent to the other racks as well as to the cashier. In the room rack, the slip is moved to the appropriate pocket and the room number changed on the slip. (See plate 1, room 902.) Where applicable, rate changes and changes in the number or composition of the party will be noted on the rack slip. Similar changes will be made by the cashier and the bill moved to its new location in the well to maintain the room number sequence. A change sheet (figure 14.11) can be used for communication between the cashier and the clerk. Since the other racks are filed in alphabetical (figure 9.6), rather than numerical sequence, the room number on the information rack slip will be changed but not the location of the slip in the sequence.

As explained later, none of this is needed with a computer.

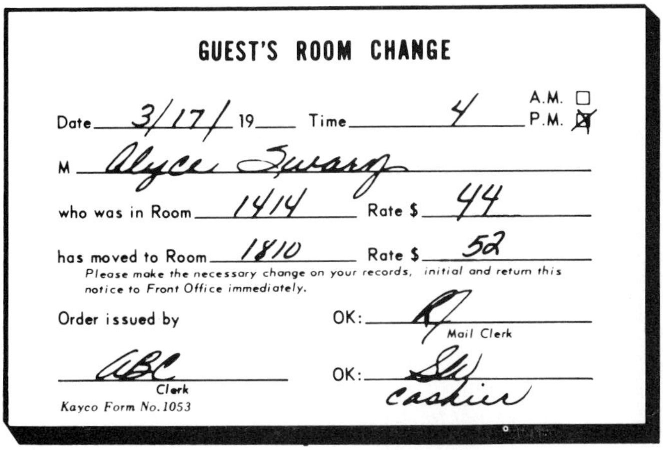
GUEST'S ROOM CHANGE

Date 3/17/ 19__ Time 4 A.M. ☐ P.M. ☒

M

who was in Room 1414 Rate $ 44

has moved to Room 1810 Rate $ 52

Please make the necessary change on your records, initial and return this notice to Front Office immediately.

Order issued by OK: _____ Mail Clerk

ABC Clerk OK: _____ Cashier

Kayco Form No. 1053

Figure 9.3. Room change notice initiated by the room clerk and circulated to the other racks. (See also figure 14.11.)

Timing the Change

Just as there are several reasons for a guest to move or to be moved, there are several times at which the change might take place. If the change takes place during the rooming procedure – the guest is unhappy with the assignment – the same bellperson completes the move. If caught soon enough, before the typist has done the rack slips and folio, the clerk simply changes the room assignment square on the registration card and allows the normal procedure to follow. The temporary flag on the room rack would be moved to the new room however. If the typist has already distributed the rack slips, the usual room change form is processed.

Other room changes involve the last bellperson if no tip is likely; especially if the guest isn't present. This isn't done often since most guests prefer to supervise the handling of their personal goods as much as the hotel prefers to have them do so. There is nothing that upsets a guest more than being moved without prior knowledge. Something – a pair of shoes, a favorite tie – is invariably lost when the owner is not present. Nevertheless, on rare occasions the hotel will move guests either without their prior knowledge or in their absence. This requires a bellperson to be accompanied by a security officer, the credit manager, or the housekeeper. Goods are inventoried by one member of the party and verified by another. This procedure is also followed in the event of deaths or other emergencies.

Changes arranged in advance of the actual move – a will-call change – require a slightly different procedure. The completed, but unprocessed change form is clipped to the stock cards of both the old and the new room and the package is flagged by standing it vertically in the rack pocket of the old room. There it remains until the guest is ready to move. The bellperson is dispatched; the old room is checked out; the old rack pocket is cleared; the change slip is processed; the old stock card goes back into circulation; and the new stock card blocks the room just assigned.

A waiting change – where the guest is waiting in the lobby or in the room for the change just agreed upon – merely requires the

Figure 9.4. Pneumatic tube system for carrying messages between stations.

old room to be checked out (and put on change perhaps) and the room rack slip to be placed in the new pocket. The change slip is then circulated.

All changes do not involve physical room changes. There could be a change in the size of the party and/or the rate and the room remain the same. Room change slips are also used to correct errors of the front office staff. These may involve rates, number of persons, or plans. Change slips are used whenever guests change from one plan to another in those hotels that offer more than one plan.

Stayover notices are sometimes used for the same reasons and circulated in the same manner as change notices in very busy hotels when guests remain beyond their original check-out day.

Since all changes affect the night audit, a separate change sheet record (figure 14.11) or a copy of the change slip is furnished to the night auditor; this will be considered further in a later chapter.

Pneumatic Tubes

Whichever communication device is used, the message flow follows the pattern just outlined. The telewriter (figure 9.2) may be partially or completely replaced by pneumatic tube systems. With these systems the clerk actually sends the discarded rack slip to the switchboard to indicate a checkout. The messages are carried between departments by a pneumatic system that moves cylinders in tubes between the message stations (figure 9.4).

Some installations use Teletype in place of either the telewriter or the tubes. Then messages can be sent simultaneously from, say, the cashier to the linen room, the front office, and the floor linen closet.

Although the telephone is an important supplement to either system, it has certain disadvantages by itself. The receiver must be at the post at all times if the message is to be completed. And if someone is there, the call

Figure 9.5. Rack with lighted panel board is a communication device that has all but disappeared. *Courtesy: RCA Service Company, Camden, N.J.*

must take priority over the immediate job at hand. Both the telewriter and the tube system leave written messages, which the telephone does not do.

Light Boards

Various electronic systems have been introduced to improve communication between the three communication stations and the floor housekeeper. Each has minor variations but they generally work as follows.

The room rack is equipped with a light panel so that each room pocket has a red, yellow, and green light. (Some systems use only two lights, figure 9.5.) A similar light board, numbered but without the rack pockets, is located in the linen room. A third series of lights is on the corridor wall near the guest room door or in an inconspicuous panel of four to six rooms strategically located in the hall. Motels without corridors either do without this

light or locate it over the entryway. An occupied room appears as a red light on the two panel boards.

When the guest departs, the cashier activates the system by changing the red light to a yellow one — on change. The new status is seen simultaneously at the room rack, in the linen room, and in the corridor by the floor housekeeper. The latter knows the room needs attention and the others know it is on change. When the housekeeper enters the room, the key activates a switch and the yellow light begins to blink. This locates the housekeeper for the supervisor in the linen room and tells the clerk that the room will soon be ready. After inspection, the light is turned to green; it remains green until sold, when the room clerk again activates the red light.

This light system was never widely adopted and never will be. Computers took over before the light system caught on.

Figure 9.6. Information rack in which guests'
names are filed alphabetically.

The Other Racks

Racks are nothing more than convenient means of filing information. Consequently, many racks in many forms are found throughout the hotel. Housekeepers, engineers, and even headwaiters(waitresses) have a need for racks. Some racks are hung, others swivel on a vertical axis; some are wood, others metal. All are more or less an adjunct to the front office procedure.

Information Racks

Information racks differ from room racks as figure 9.6 illustrates. The pockets are readily removable so they may be rearranged to accommodate the alphabetizing of guest names. Whereas room racks are maintained in room number sequence by floor, information racks are maintained alphabetically. Guests are traced by room number through the room rack and by name through the information rack. Room racks have one pocket per room, but information racks have extra pockets to accommodate the total number of individual guests. Husbands, wives, and families have only one listing since they register that way. Unrelated persons who share the same room — double-ups — are listed individually in the information rack although they occupy only one pocket in the room rack.

Large hotels customarily use two information racks: one for the telephone operators and one for the front office staff. Computerized properties have no racks: the information is stored in memory and displayed on CRTs.

Telephone Information Rack

Callers, both those from within the hotel and those from without, expect the hotel operator to identify the room number of the party being called. This is done by reference to the alphabetic list in the information rack. In very small hotels where the switchboard is located at the front desk and the clerk doubles as telephone

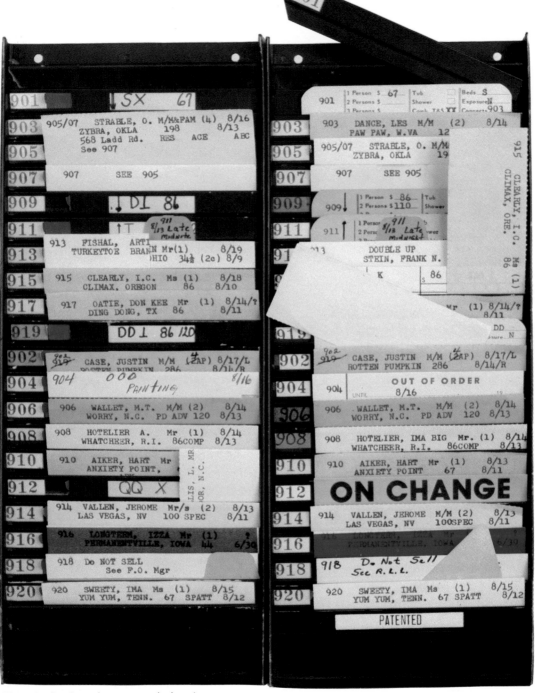

Plate 1. Section of a room rack showing rooms occupied, vacant, and on reservation in window and windowless racks.

operator, inquiries are handled by direct reference to the room rack. The operator always connects the call because the actual room number is never given out.

Even when the design of a medium-size hotel permits the switchboard to be in the front office, the number of guests soon necessitates an alphabetic listing in addition to the room rack. When the switchboard is in the front office, one information rack serves both the telephone operators and the front office staff.

Consideration should be given to moving the switchboard out of the front office whenever the volume of calls is large enough to require a separate telephone position. Such a move preserves valuable lobby space, reduces background noise, and increases the privacy of calls coming through the telephone operator. Room location information is then maintained on a separate information rack at the desk.

Before the advent of the computer, multioperator boards were serviced by a circuit operator who located guests' names on the telephone information board for the other operators. No such position exists today. The information is displayed on a small CRT screen, which is conveniently located by or between the operators (figure 16.7).

For protection and privacy, almost all hotels complete telephone calls or accept messages without revealing the guest's room number. Even where this is not general procedure, the service is available on request. It's initiated by the clerk who marks the reg card "No info." Clerks and operators are alerted by color coding the information rack slips, where still used, or by noting the special service on the chalkboard used by the telephone operators. Other color codes flag paid-in-advance rooms, guests who are ill, and VIPs.

Automatic dial systems, which are almost universal, allow guests to direct dial other guest rooms, outside calls, and hotel services. Guest room calls may still require location assistance, but a small directory near the guest's telephone usually takes care of most hotel service numbers. The city directory and the long-distance operators account for most outside calls. Incoming calls are still received by the hotel operator.

Mail Information Rack

The mail information rack is located in the front office area. Front office business, especially incoming mail and over-the-counter inquiries for registered guests, is handled from this information rack by the mail, key, and information clerk. When this position is not part of the staff, as in a small hotel, these duties fall to the room clerk.

Both the telephone information rack and the mail information rack are identical except for physical location. Both use a copy of the room rack slip, which is prepared as part of the carbonized packet. If the duplicates are on plain, white paper, their value is limited considerably. The user lacks some of the information available to the room clerk who sees a colored slip. The void is especially noticeable with paid-in-advance guests who are supposed to get no services on credit.

The slip remains in the information rack(s) until the guest checks out. Even then it may not be removed immediately as it is in the room rack. Sometimes the name of the departing guest is merely ruled out in colored pencil and the slip left for the night crew to remove. It then becomes possible to tell callers that the guest was registered and left. Were the slip removed, callers would be told the guest wasn't registered, which is an entirely different piece of information. By changing the color of the pencil every hour or so, an approximate time of departure can also be furnished.

The volume of guest mail has dropped substantially over the past decade or two. Inexpensive telephone calls, poor postage ser-

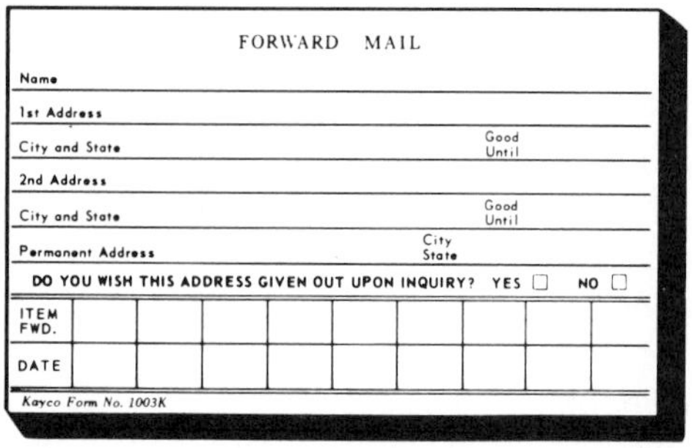

FORWARD MAIL

Name

1st Address

City and State — Good Until

2nd Address

City and State — Good Until

Permanent Address — City State

DO YOU WISH THIS ADDRESS GIVEN OUT UPON INQUIRY? YES ☐ NO ☐

ITEM FWD.									
DATE									

Kayco Form No. 1003K

Figure 9.7. Mail forwarding card. Reduced length of guest stay and increased use of cross-country telephoning have almost eliminated the request for mail forwarding.

vice, and ever-shorter stays by the traveler account for the decline. Nevertheless, departing guests will occasionally request that mail be forwarded. A special slip is inserted in the mail and information rack in alphabetic sequence and left there for ten days. When mail arrives, the usual alphabetic search uncovers the mail-forwarding information and the instructions are carried out (figure 9.7). The infrequency of the necessity for mail forwarding is pointed up by the rarity of such a program in the new rooms management systems.

Mail and Key Rack

The space-consuming, dust-gathering mail rack illustrated in figure 9.8 grows less and less important. It will probably disappear during the next ten years. Many front offices are now being built without them. Not only is the amount of guest mail declining, but electronic locks are replacing the present-day key. The telephone message lamp has further minimized the importance of the mail rack.

When mail or messages do come, the clerk time stamps them, locates the guest's name on the alphabetized information rack, and places the room number on the envelope. The mail is then placed in the pigeonhole corresponding to the guest's room. Packages that are too large for the pigeonhole are stored elsewhere and a notice is placed in the appropriate box. Unlike the information rack's alphabetic order and the floor-plan design of the room rack, the mail and key rack is in numerical sequence, from left to right in horizontal rows. A symmetrical arrangement of rooms and floors enables clerks and guests to locate the desired box with minimum delay.

Much space is saved and nothing is sacrificed if this rack is reduced to a key rack only. The mail is then filed together alphabetically rather than in separate pigeonholes by room number. Guests can be notified about their mail by the telephone message lamp, or not at all. That is, except for alphabetizing, the mail would be unsorted until the guest inquired, telegrams and special delivery letters excepted. This is not especially good service, but it is consistent with the present procedure of filing mail by room number and then waiting until the guest asks for it.

Mail that arrives for nonregistered guests is handled much the same way. Unable to locate the name on the information rack, the mail clerk files the letter in alphabetical sequence. The letter can be retrieved by the incoming guest upon request or it is placed in the box after arrival. Periodically, the mail clerk compares the alphabetized packets of mail to the information rack. If this is done frequently enough, delay in delivery is minimal. Unclaimed mail is held ten days and then returned to the sender, as required by postal directives. Hotels that wish to handle valuables must prescribe to postal regulations. Registered, certified, insured, and COD pieces require special handling, including the use of safes and signatures.

Only the mail and key rack is exposed to the lobby and guest inspection. The room rack and the information rack, as well as other racks, are restricted to employee use. Each rack in the following list communicates information to a particular locale of the hotel, but it is the same information.

Figure 9.8. Mail and key racks are following many other front office racks into oblivion.

Dining Room Rack

As noted earlier, copies of the room rack slip are sent to the headwaiter(waitress) in an American plan hotel. These are filed alphabetically in the dining room rack. If the property is small, the rack can be located under the reception desk and in drawerlike fashion pulled forward and down to reveal the names. Any small rack located anywhere can be built in the form of a drawer.

Housekeeper's Rack

Sometimes a rack similar to the room rack is maintained in the linen room. A copy of the room rack slip may be provided for it. More often, the rack merely contains a permanent inventory of furnishings and equipment. It helps minimize theft and facilitates the transfer of equipment among the various guest rooms. Since it requires constant updating, it falls into disuse as often as not.

Figure 9.9. Sales rack for displaying ducats. (See also figure 8.4.)

Sales Rack

The sales rack is not a rack in the usual sense. It is a series of tiered wells (holes) in the front desk in which unsold stock tickets are kept. There are usually enough wells to separate the stock cards into various classes of room and rate (figure 9.9).

Floor Rack

In infrequent cases where a concierge floor is used, a copy of the room rack slip is forwarded to the floor. It is racked there and used for the distribution of keys, mail, and information on the floor.

Reservation Rack

Although reservation racks have a special use, they are physically like the information racks. These were considered earlier in the chapter on reservations (figure 5.4).

City Ledger Rack

The city ledger rack is an alphabetic listing of active city ledger accounts. It is accessible to the front office so that the validity of charges generated by someone who claims to be a city ledger account can be verified. It could also be kept by exception, listing only those city ledger accounts that are no longer honored. Then all hotel credit cards would be honored unless they were on the deadbeat list. Depending on the size, this listing may or may not be kept in informationlike racks.

Computerized, this rack offers immense savings in space and potential credit losses. Although national credit cards make it less so today than heretofore, many hotels maintained city ledgers of hundreds or thousands of accounts. There are far too many to preempt the important front office space needed to rack this number of accounts. Since accounting is not open twenty-four hours a day, many city ledger cards or accounts are accepted on faith. A small computer terminal, the very one used for other desk purposes, can display the entire city ledger regardless of size or time of day. Security needs may limit the display to bad accounts only.

Automation of these kinds of procedures has brought some dramatic changes to the front offices of American hotels. The impact on communication systems has certainly been one of the significant changes wrought by the computer.

THE NEW: ELECTRONIC COMMUNICATIONS

Electronic communications eliminate the need for racks, but leave intact the system that has just been outlined. The three stations of clerk, cashier, and housekeeper remain pivotal points in the communication triangle. Electronics does modify the process, of course. There are changes in the time that it takes to do the job, changes in the equipment being used, and changes in the format of the data. Still, all three message centers are handling the same information as before. Whether by rack or computer, arrivals, changes, departures, on changes, and out of orders are the essence of the communication process.

Electronics adds the element of speed. Speed involves more than the measure of the electronic impulse; the frequency that data and paperwork are handled and manipulated is also a factor that contributes to speed. Information is entered into the electronic data system but once. Instantaneously, the facts are available at every point of the triangle, and more. No wait for rack slips; no pieces of paper lost en route; no inconsistencies between the room rack and the cashier's well, or between the linen room status and the desk. All information is being reported from the same data base and internal communication is accelerated once the guest has checked in. Delay at the initial point, as the registration data is entered, is the major trade-off for electronic velocity.

The change in front office equipment is almost as dramatic as the increase in communication speed. New keyboards and screens are added to the furnishing (figures 2.5 and 2.7), and several old standbys are removed. The racks are eliminated (although some managers prefer to keep the room rack), along with typewriters, telewriters, pneumatic tubes, and light boards. Although the telephone is retained, it is no longer part of the internal communications system. The keyboard/screen and its interface with other keyboard/screens has replaced the telephone in this capacity.

Without the standard equipment and accoutrements of the front office in place, the means of providing information must also change. To understand the format in which the information appears, we must understand what the room clerk sees.

What the Room Clerk Sees

To understand the magnitude of the communications change, it is as important to be familiar with what the room clerk doesn't see as it is to be aware of what he or she does see. No longer is reference made to the reservation rack (figure 5.4) or to the room rack (plate 1). No longer does the clerk rely on the symbols of the room rack, the flags of the room rack slips, or the subtleties of color. In their place stands the screen of the computer, the video display terminal, VDT or CRT.

Computers have many functions as a later chapter explains. They do payrolls, statistics, audits, and direct-mail letters, as well as front office functions. Each VDT screen is restricted to the specific functions needed by a particular employee. Room clerks can call up several programs pertaining to the responsibilities of the front office, but they cannot call up, for example, information about food inventories. Similarly, the food and beverage clerk has no access to the front office programs. So to start with, the room clerk sees only what he or she needs to see.

The Menu

Depending upon the circumstances and the guest's specific needs, the room clerk selects the particular program needed to complete the task at hand: registration, room status, name inquiry, or whatever. A program is chosen from an array of programs called — appropriately for the hotel and food service industry — a menu. The menu (figure 9.10) is displayed on the screen when the clerk touches a keyboard button labeled *advance* or some other similar terminology. From the list on the menu, the room clerk selects the proper program. The identification of the program (a letter or number shown on the screen) is typed into the keyboard and the advance button activated. The old menu is then replaced on the screen either by another menu (if there are subparts to the main program) or by a program (a sequence of steps for the clerk to follow in completing the assignment at hand).

The program on the screen prompts the user to type in the data which that particular program requires to complete the task. So if

the clerk is in an inquiry program searching for a name that begins with *Mc* or *Mac,* that information is typed in and the advance or activate key is depressed. Immediately, the screen is filled with a list of names. Not all the *Mc* or *Mac* names will fit on the screen at the same time since the screen has a finite limit, two dozen lines perhaps. "More" appears at the bottom of the screen indicating additional names to come. The additional names can be advanced until the user finds the guest or reaches the end of the list.

User Friendly

A program that guides the user with ease and alacrity is said to be user friendly. Not only does the program indicate at the bottom of the screen that there is more to come, it also prompts the operator who fails to complete a procedure. A user-friendly program directs the operator by asking whether a particular function is required: Print? Meaning that the information can be printed as well as displayed if the operator types in "yes."

Program prompting minimizes the ill-at-ease feeling that neophytes experience at the terminal. What is to be done when the user completes the process — or thinks the process is complete — but the machine remains dumb? The user-friendly program prompts the user to set off the operation. User-friendly screens have dots of light or color called cursors that flow across the lines telling the operator where to move into the next step and where to skip along. These blinking cursors speed up the input of data and build confidence in the user.

Front offices use an amazing array of forms, as the reader must have noted already. By displaying a mask of a particular form (figure 9.11) on the screen, the computer builder attracts the novice user. Familiar with the form, the clerk establishes rapport with the equipment and with the processes needed to complete the task at hand. User friendly!

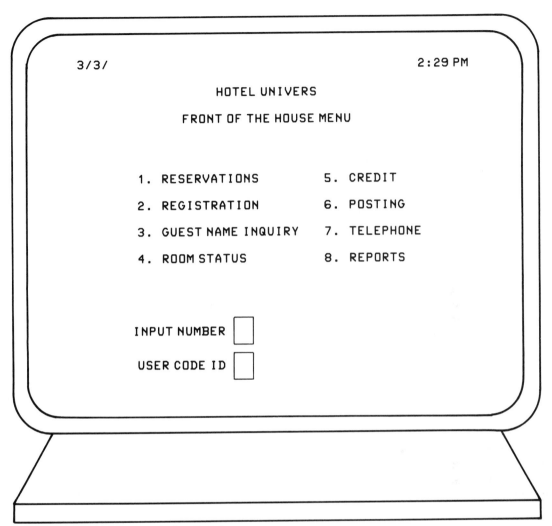

Figure 9.10. A major menu display. Each input number (6, for example) will display a second menu or mask (figure 9.11) with which to complete the entry.

A friendly keyboard reduces apprehension still further. Input keyboards resemble the standard typewriter, and this brings some comfort to the novice. Some keyboards have touch sensitive keys that require no pressure and invite even the nontypist to participate. Recently, more user-friendly equipment has been developed that allows the operator to call up programs without remembering computer codes. Depressing a ''Display Folio'' key is far less traumatic than calling up a menu by entering a two-, three- or four-digit code. Instructional keys like ''Display Folio'' may have other functions as well, depending upon the process being run. Colored keys help distinguish the functions.

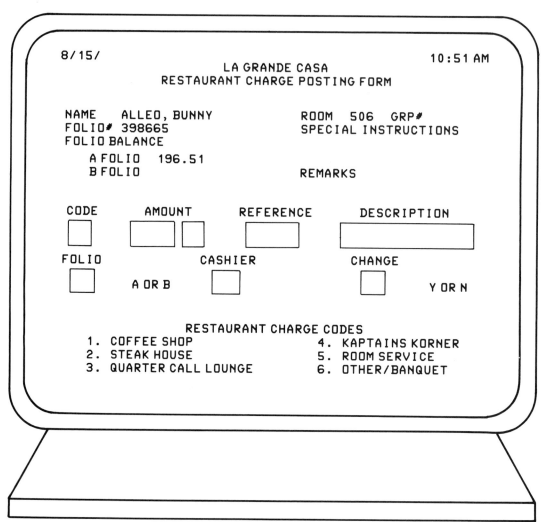

Figure 9.11. A computer display mask guides the clerk in a user-friendly atmosphere to complete the particular entry. This one being a restaurant charge to the guest bill. The posting could be done at the front office (off-line) from vouchers sent by the departmental cashiers.

User acceptability is as important to marketing the equipment as it is to improving operational procedures. Thus, some of the user-friendly features are more important to one aspect than to the other. Initially one feels more comfortable with an Apple computer than with a System 38. A variety of features are offered to attract the user and allay his fears, including colored keys, colored screen display, reduced glare on the screen display, ten-key numeric board to resemble a calculator, edit or correction keys, and more.

Audio-activated computers are the near-term ultimate in user-friendly equipment. Initial efforts have concentrated on developing computers that respond to voice commands rather than to typewriter terminals. Few doubt the ability of technology to reach the next plateau, a verbal response from the computer. Computer language is of more immediate concern. Low-level languages have been replaced by high languages that both the equipment and the untrained user can understand. The shift from scientific languages like FORTRAN, through business languages like COBOL and BASIC, toward a horizon of ordinary English testifies to the industry's concern for the end user.

The "Racks"

We have noted more than once before that the new electronic systems do away with the racks. What has not been noted are the differences in the room clerk's style and work pattern as a result of the change. All of the clerk's data now comes from a handsome console near at hand. The need to leave the front area to consult the reservation rack, the information rack, or the room rack has disappeared along with the racks themselves. Available and in view, the clerk is better able to play the role of host. And if the process is a little slower, at least it is being carried out in front of the waiting guest, who feels a greater sense of attention.

With no need to hide the space-consuming racks with their confidential information, front offices have been opened and made more pleasant for both the worker and the guest (figure 2.7).

The Room Rack and the Room Rack Slip

By restructuring the data, the computer separates into distinct programs the whole field of information that is visible to the user of the rack. Separate menus are needed to identify what previously had been one class of information: the room rack. From the presence or absence of the rack slips, from their colors, and from their locations and positions an experienced room clerk reads the entire house at one glance. One sees there the rooms vacant and occupied, the rooms out of order and on change, the names of the guests and their city of residence, the number in the party and their company or group affiliation, the rate on the room and the anticipated check-out date. Not so with electronic systems. Getting that information from a computer may require three or four different menu accesses. Room identification requires a different menu from guest identification, which differs again from the reservation menu, and so on.

No one computer program provides the bird's-eye view obtained from a glance at the room rack (plate 1). VDT's are too small to show the entire picture. Besides, the information is accumulated differently in order to be processed differently. When looked at in its totality, more information is available with the computer, and it can be processed more quickly and completely than with the racks. This is true for the whole despite the greater amount of time required to process one individual bit of datum: identifying that guest with the *Mac* or *Mc* name, for example.

Rack Content. Gone are the romantic symbols of the room rack; in their place is a program that displays the rooms of a given accommodation. Onto the screen (figure 8.2) comes a listing of all the rooms that are vacant (queen, double, single, etc.), and the selection is made. Many computers do not display adjacent rooms, as figure 8.2 does. So a family's request for a double and connecting single may give a new clerk some difficulty. Unless the VDT has split screens, it may be necessary to flip between the double and single programs, or even to write down some room numbers, until the match of facilities and needs is made.

Newer and larger hotels — and these are the ones employing computers — have fewer choices than older and smaller hotels. If every room on every floor has the same facilities and configuration, computers serve their public well without the host of symbols that comprise the older room racks.

Rack Slips. With no room racks, there are no room rack pockets, and hence, no room rack slips. All the writing or typing that rack slip preparation requires is saved. The information is there, nonetheless, having been entered at the time of the registration. It can be called up by the CRT user as often as necessary. Of course there's a difference in the range of view. CRT's display information about one guest: the party the clerk is asking about (figure 9.12). In contrast, the clerk who refers to the rack of plate 1, sees information about many guests.

Colors jump from the rack communicating instantaneously information that must be searched for on the monochromic computer screen. Numeric or alphabetic codes (figure 5.10) replace the rainbow of the rack slips but convey the same information — VIP, conventioneer, permanent guest, etc. — that an earlier part of this chapter reviewed.

Rack Slip Distribution

The beauty of the computer is its ability to communicate simultaneously and instantaneously with all the locations throughout the hotel. Data recorded during the registration is available at once — no delay in preparing, transporting, and filing rack slips — to the information clerk, the housekeeper, the cashier, the accounting department, the telephone operators, and the dining rooms. Management must decide whether each of these stations, and others like room service, should have this information. Whether telephone messages or hotel credit decisions, whether late charges or improved valet service, all areas realize improvements in speed and productivity because of the capability of the computer.

Lost room rack slips or information rack slips are no problem when there are no slips. Similarly, errors from failures to change information on one or more of the slips disappear; changes made in the computer appear at all the video display terminals. Not that computers are trouble free. They have their own special problems from a complete shutdown of the system, where no information at all is available to anyone, to an annoying "bug." Bugs are inexplicable glitches, aberrations in either the software or the hardware, that cause errors, which often remain undiscovered for some time. A guest's name might be lost; figures might misprint; or information might be unavailable under certain procedural sequences.

When the system is working well, and it usually is, only the rooming slip, the form with which the hotel communicates to the guest, is paper printed. It is easily conceivable to expect that information will one day be viewed on the television set in the guest room when the party arrives with the bellperson.

What the Room Clerk Does

Installing a computer doesn't materially alter the job of room clerk. Room clerks are still responsible for each and every heading in the first half of this chapter and throughout the text. They still make room assignments and

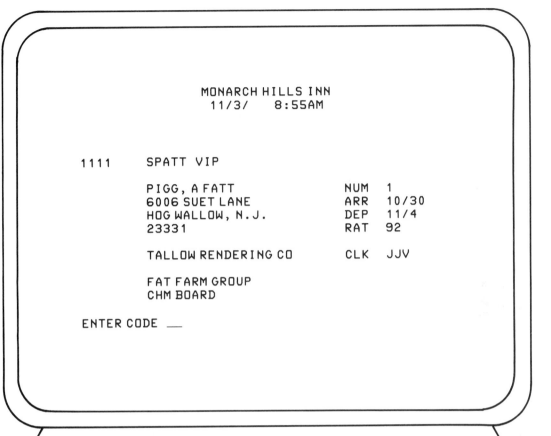

```
                    MONARCH HILLS INN
                    11/3/    8:55AM


      1111       SPATT VIP

                 PIGG, A FATT              NUM   1
                 6006 SUET LANE            ARR   10/30
                 HOG WALLOW, N.J.          DEP   11/4
                 23331                     RAT   92

                 TALLOW RENDERING CO       CLK   JJV

                 FAT FARM GROUP
                 CHM BOARD

       ENTER CODE ___
```

Figure 9.12. Video Display Terminal displays a computer version of the room rack slip. See also figure 9.1 and plate 1.

changes, double up guests, ascertain rates, communicate with housekeeping, and so on. And just as the procedure may vary from one manual system to another, so it varies from one computer system to another. Manufacturers build variations in their hardware and software, and hotels buy more or less complete systems.

At Arrival

Reservation listings are moved from the reservation rack (figure 5.4) to the front office prior to the guest's anticipated arrival. With a computer, this requires no such physical shift, merely the change from reservation to arrival programs. Registration cards (figure 6.4) are computer printed during the slow hours of the early morning so that arriving guests merely sign in. The room clerk makes the assignment and assigns the rate, using a VDT rather than a room rack or stock cards, and the guest is whisked away by the bell staff. Walk-ins, of course, still need to furnish the complete registration data at the time of arrival, as they would with a manual system. Room and rate assignments are made from information displayed on the CRT. The clerk calls up a list of a certain type of room (queen rooms or suites or whatever) or proceeds by rate determination if that is the more important criterion.

Data about the newly registered guest is available immediately to all terminals authorized to receive it. (Information isn't delayed while room rack slips are typed.) Callers inquiring about guests can be connected at once; a manual system might take an hour or more to get the guest name on the information rack.

CRTs (figure 9.12) display the information in a format different from that of the room rack slip (figure 9.1). The same information is furnished, but alphanumeric codes replace the symbols and colors of the more traditional rack. There are other differences also, because every computer cannot perform every function.

Hardware and software capabilities, especially the latter, distinguish one product from another. Buyers use an immense range of criteria with weighted checklists in an attempt to quantify the variables in an equally large number of products being offered. Ultimately, decisions are based on a ranking of priorities. How fast can a guest be registered? Can rates be split into two or three folios? Does the program accommodate RNAs (registered, not assigned)? Is storage capacity great enough to hold several different rates for the same room? Product selection depends as much upon management's astuteness in asking the correct questions as it does upon the computer's construction and program.

Through the Stay

Guest needs are not altered by the presence of a computer. It is unlikely that the guest is even aware of the hotel's electronic capability. The desk is still called upon for the same mundane services. An inquiry about rates and availability. Request for credit. Request for information about the room where the convention is meeting. Permission to remain beyond the check-out hour. A room change to be made for yesterday's arrival who was given a suite because the requested rate wasn't available. A DNS (did not stay). A bellperson returning with a party that was assigned to an occupied room. A request for television service in room 909. A stayover is identified. A guest has forgotten his or her room number.

And just as the arrival programs might lack certain capabilities, the through-the-stay system might not be able to handle certain functions that manual procedures handle with ease. Does a room change require the guest to be checked out and then reregistered? Some do. Can postings be made to B folios or master accounts? Some can't. Are the housekeeper's movements traced so that on-change and ready rooms are easily identified? Yes, for most systems. After management has asked and answered such questions, they are ready to furnish the desk with new communicative equipment.

As we already know, the video display terminal replaces both the alphabetized information rack and the sequential room rack. Charges to guest accounts are also computerized. The charges that a guest incurs in the dining rooms and lounges are transmitted immediately over wire. The guest's identity is verified and the charges are recorded simultaneously on the guest account, or folio. In place of a pencil and paper folio, the posting clerk has a CRT. Instead of pneumatic tubes (figure 9.4), the equipment has an electronic impulse. Instead of a cumulative folio balance, there is computer memory.

When tasks can be computer performed, they are executed electronically. Communication is terminal to terminal with each station accessing the information completely and immediately.

At Departure

Computerized systems replace the posting machine and pencil with still another CRT at the cashier's station. At checkout, the action is initiated by the cashier, who signals the other points of the triangle as soon as the billing portion of the transaction is completed. The on-change status of the room goes into memory. It's recallable in the linen room; a housekeeper is dispatched to clean the vacancy. It's recallable at the desk; the clerk adds it to the available inventory. It's recallable at the switchboard; the operator reports the guest's departure to the outside caller.

Completing his or her turn at the cashier's window, the guest is unmindful of what inquiry has gone into the system's installation. Can records of that departing guest be transferred automatically to the American Express account in the city ledger? Does the system distinguish tour group charges from individually incurred expenses? Are package plan components, including breakage, automatically computed? Will the room status be properly reported if one guest from among a party of several leaves?

Few systems can do everything they are supposed to do between checkin and checkout. Whether the system is complete or not, it represents an amazing improvement in communications within the front desk and between the desk and other service areas. What has happened in computer maturity happened quickly once the momentum started. The very special billing needs of the front office, the critical core of the entire system, de-

layed the introduction of data equipment. How that billing system works is the subject of the next chapter.

QUERIES AND PROBLEMS

1. Professionalism is measured, in part, by the proper use of technical vocabulary (jargon). Demonstrate your level of achievement by distinguishing between:
   a. Walk-in and walked guest
   b. On change and out of order
   c. Double rate and double-up
   d. Rack slip and rooming slip
   e. Guaranteed room and guaranteed rate
   f. VDT and CRT
   g. Understay and overstay
   h. Hotel and motel
   i. In season and off season
   j. American plan and European plan
2. Gain access to the terminal of a hotel computer system, or to a CRT of any computer, or even to a word processor. Describe the parts of the keyboard or the portions of the call-up segments of the system that are user friendly.
3. Color is used to speed communication and reduce paperwork throughout the front office. List and explain the applications of color to the front office, including illustrations from this and other chapters.
4. Diagram the communication flows within the front office and between the front office and the several stations of the communication triangle for a hotel using a stock card system when:
   a. A guest arrives.
   b. A guest changes rooms several days after arrival.
   c. A guest checks out.

10

Billing the Transient Ledger

An accurate and current guest statement is available at the front office on demand; it is available in spite of an almost total lack of information about the guest's intended checkout hour. Hotels have evolved a rather complete system that enables them to proffer the bill promptly. After all, the hotel is as anxious as the guest to have the bill ready. Payment for items not on the guest's statement is difficult to collect after the checkout and then is collected only with additional expense to the hotel and ill feelings by the guest. Incorrectly charged items delay the checkout procedure and create similar ill feelings.

ACCOUNTING FOR ACCOUNTS RECEIVABLE

Hotel patrons fall into two accounting-billing categories: transient guests and city ledger guests. Transient guests are those currently registered in the hotel. City guests are those

persons or companies who use hotel services without occupying sleeping rooms. City guests are of the charge account types common to other retail businesses. Guests can and do change status from transient to city and even occasionally from city to transient. Accounts are sometimes maintained in each category. A transfer takes place, for example, when a transient guest settles the outstanding account by using a credit card at checkout. The debt is still owed, but the guest is no longer in the hotel.

Both transient and city guests charge the cost of goods and services to their accounts. In accounting terminology, a charge customer is known as an *account receivable* and the aggregate of the individual accounts receivable is known as an *accounts receivable ledger*. Hotels maintain transient accounts receivable ledgers and city accounts receivable ledgers. In their shortened forms they are called the *transient ledger* and the *city ledger*. Because transient ledger guests are actually in the hotel, their accounts must be more readily accessible. Thus, the transient ledger is located in the front office and is sometimes called the *front office ledger. Guest ledger* or *rooms ledger* are other terms used for the transient ledger.

Timing is the chief billing difference between the ledgers. Charges are *posted* (recorded) immediately to the transient ledger since the bill may be rendered at any time. City guests, having established credit in advance, are billed periodically. This permits some delay in posting charges. Like many other businesses, city accounts are billed monthly unless the nature of the charge calls for an earlier billing. To accommodate these variations in time, each ledger differs in form and in the posting-billing procedure.

Accounting for the front office concentrates on only three areas: cash, accounts receivable, and income (or sales). Although an adequate understanding of accounting and of debits and credits makes easier the work of the clerk and especially of the night auditor, front office staffers may lack even a rudimentary knowledge of the subject. Front office forms and internal record keeping are designed to assure accuracy without accounting skills. A working knowledge of accounting is essential for a complete understanding, however.

Accounting parlance speaks of debits and credits. Meaningless in themselves, debits and credits represent the manner by which accountants increase and decrease the values of certain records. Under some circumstances, debits increase and credits decrease these values. This is true with cash, for example, and with accounts receivable. Cash received by the hotel from customers increase (debit) the cash record. Similarly, services provided to customers (accounts receivable) increase the amount these customers owe to the hotel. This increase is shown in the account receivable with a debit. Decreases in both cash and accounts receivable are handled by credits.

Each accounting event has two parts. Two things happen, for example, when the guest settles an account. The hotel gets cash (money) and the guest owes less. Since we have already mentioned that increases to cash are debits and decreases in guest debt (accounts receivable) are credits, an accounting entry has been created. This system of *double entry* always requires equal dollar amounts of debits and credits. Couched in accounting terminology, a debit to cash and a credit to accounts receivable is the entry required to record a guest's money settlement of an outstanding bill.

Under other circumstances, debits represent decreases and credits represent increases in the accounting records. This is true with departmental earnings (departmental income or revenue), for example. Thus, recording increases in room sales, food sales, bar sales, and so on requires a credit. Conversely, debits decrease these income accounts. All of which is just the opposite from the cash and accounts receivable examples of the previous paragraph. Now it is possible to make a second entry, this one for the guest who incurs service in any of these income-producing departments. A dinner, a drink in the bar, or the use of the room increases the amount that the account receivable owes to the hotel (debit: accounts receivable) and also increases the amount of earnings of the individual department (credit: rooms income, or food income, or bar income, or all three). Another double entry transaction.

Nature of the Transient Folio

Several names are used to identify the individual guest records that comprise the transient ledger. *Bill, guest folio, guest account card,* and *guest bill* are the most common. *Visitor's account* is the European version. Unlike the city ledger, which is maintained alphabetically in the accounting office the transient ledger is maintained numerically by room number at the front desk. More and more, both are maintained in computer memory, which means they are not even visible.

The folios are in the cashier's area of the front office. The cashier's position may be combined with that of the billing clerk or even the room clerk according to the size of the property. Very small hotels maintain the folio as part of the room rack. (See figure 6.3.)

The size of the hotel determines the number of folios in the transient ledger, which may be hundreds or even thousands of accounts. City ledgers are not limited by the number of rooms and in the pre-credit card era, numbered in the thousands or even tens of thousands for large properties. Small or medium-size hotels sometimes maintain their small city ledger at the front desk for convenience and economy, although it weakens the internal control system.

These restrictions in physically locating the transient or city ledger at a particular location apply only to noncomputerized systems. Computerized systems are limited by memory capacity, which is measured in kilobytes. Thus, 20K of memory is 20 kilobytes of storage capacity. With communication taking place electronically, the central processing unit of the system can be housed anywhere so long as the front office and the city ledger department of the accounting office have access to input/output terminals.

Preparation of the Folio

Increases and decreases in the guest's account balance are reflected on the folio. Increases are called *charges* by the front office staff, another name for debits. Decreases are called *payments*, another name for credits. At any given time the folio reflects the amount due the hotel from the guest (figure 10.1) or the debit balance of the guest account. It is possible, however, for the guest to have a balance due from

the hotel — a credit balance — as in the case of an advance deposit. The form that the folio takes is prescribed by the size of the hotel and the registration procedure employed, as described by previous chapters. The folio might be part of a handwritten package that includes the registration card, the rooming slip, and the room rack slips as discussed in chapter 6. Just as often, the registration card is passed to a typist for preparation of the rack slips. Then an additional carbon takes care of the heading on the folio, resulting in identical information on the folio and the rack slip (figure 10.1). Computerized folios are retained in the computer memory so there is no form at all.

Copies

Two copies of the folio are prepared. One eventually goes to the guest as a receipt. The other remains as the hotel's permanent record. Two copies are needed whether the folio is hand posted or machine posted. Hand-prepared bills use carbon to prepare the duplicate, whereas the older machine-prepared bills usually involve duplicate printing. The electromechanical machine, which was the generation before computers, returned to duplicate bills, using the no-carbon-required duplicating paper. Regardless of the type, the guest's copy usually contains less information than the hotel's copy.

Some hotels might use three copies of the folio. The third copy accommodates guests who use credit cards or have their bills mailed to their homes or offices. In effect, such guests transfer their transient accounts to the city ledger when they check out. The third copy of the folio serves this purpose. One copy goes to the guest at check-out time, one copy is mailed with the city ledger billing at the end of the month, and one copy remains with the hotel. Since most city ledgers use national credit cards, which have their own receipt form, rather than hotel credit cards, the third folio copy is not common.

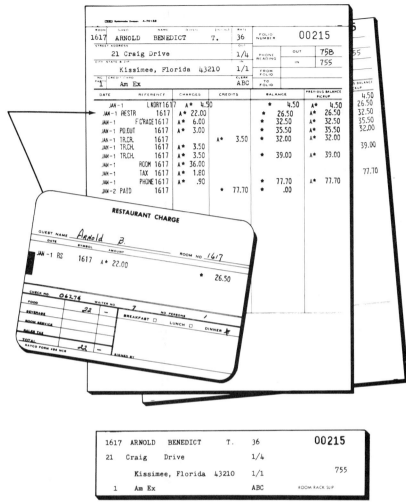

Figure 10.1. Machine-prepared folio showing both house and guest copies plus validated voucher; with corresponding room rack slip, it is part of a numerically controlled registration packet (note numbers 00215).

Since the computerized folio is printed on demand, at check out or at any other time as required by the guest or the hotel, there is no limit to the number of copies that could be produced.

Master Accounts. Tour operating companies, trade associations, convention groups, and private businesses incur charges that are not billable to any one individual. The master account permits the distinction between personal expenses and group charges. The master account is its own person, much like a business corporation, which has a legal identity separate from that of its individual owners. Master accounts are not city accounts, although eventually they might be, because the group is in the hotel and the master folio is in the cashier's well. At least it is there figuratively speaking, although in reality it might be in computer memory.

Many master account arrangements involve split billing, giving rise to *A folios* (the master accounts) and *B folios* (the personal folios of the individual guests). Both folios have the usual two copies: one for the guest and one for the hotel.

Billing decisions are made well in advance of the group's arrival. The hotel and the organization settle sales and credit terms for the group's occupancy. The group decides internally on the distribution of charges. A business company holding a regional sales meeting might have all of the charges of every delegate billed to the master account. A convention of, say, dentists has individual convention delegates responsible for room and personal charges, while the dental association covers banquet costs, cocktail parties, and meeting expenses. Rooms for visiting speakers are charged to the master account.

Tour groups do just the opposite. The master folio covers all the room charges and whatever meals were included in the tour price. No individual room rate postings are made. Personal expenses (a bar drink, green's fees, etc.) not offered by the tour package are charged to the B folio.

Numerous variations of master account billing occur. Large associations have member companies and association affiliates who sponsor functions for the general membership and/or cover the charges of their own staffs. These master accounts are obviously separate from that of the association. Charges are sometimes posted to individual folios and then transferred to the master account at the close of the convention. Since the accounts are usually hefty ones, including food and beverage charges for groups that may number in the thousands of persons, authorized signatures for master accounts must be identified and enforced in all cases, and the split billing must be clearly understood.

One arrangement might include the room rate, whatever it is, on the master folio. Another might include only the single rate. Delegates with attending spouses would be charged the spread between single and double rate on their individual folios. A flat dollar allowance per room is another modification. Onto the master folio goes a per diem allowance that includes any type of charge (room, meals, bar). Charges that exceed the lump sum figure are entered on the personal folio. Or the flat allowance might pertain to room only; then even single occupants would pay if they elected a room whose rate exceeded the room allowance. Add the complications of American-plan billing, of compulsory service charges, and of taxes, for a start, and the need for a clear understanding of who pays for what is very evident.

Casino hotels use the split billing procedure to account for comps, using the A folio (the primary folio) for the complimentary charges and the B folio for personal, noncomplimentary items.

Figure 10.2. The cashier's well, bucket, or pit. Folios are filed behind the heavy cardboard separators in room number sequence.

Filing

Folios are filed at the front desk in the cashier's work area in a folio file box, more often called a *well* or *bucket,* but sometimes called a *pit* (figure 10.2). This is merely an open file recessed in the work counter. In larger establishments, where the folios are moved during the night audit or to accommodate lines of guests checking out, the bucket is on a movable cart.

Within the well, folios are separated by heavy cardboard dividers of a larger dimension than the folio itself. These separators are in numerical sequence with the folio and its duplicate filed behind the number. Guest accounts are kept in room number sequence because room numbers are the major means of guest identification, even more so than names. Many charges arrive at the front desk from the other operating departments with only the room number for identification. Either the guest name is missing or it is illegible.

The folio is removed and replaced periodically during the guest's stay as the various charges incurred are posted to the account. It remains in sequence in the well until the guest checks out. At that time, it is filed along with other departures of that day in the front of the well for use by the night auditor. Following the audit, the folio is permanently filed in the hotel's records room.

Registration cards are frequently attached to and filed with the guest folio at the time it is prepared. At checkout the registration card is removed, time stamped, and used to communicate to the room clerk the on-change status of the room just vacated.

There is no bucket and no folios with a computerized system. All the information is stored in memory, including the various charges that are incurred, until the guest departs. At the close of the day, computer records are transferred to storage discs or printed and stored. The saving in posting time is very measurable. And, of course, there is no clerical time in preparing the folio headings.

Types of Folios

Folios reflect the type of billing and accounting system being used. There are really only three choices: hand-prepared bills, machine-prepared bills, and bills prepared by data processing equipment. Although one hears a great deal about the marvels of electronic data processing, the fact remains, as chapter 1 explained, that most hotels are small. Thus, although it is anachronistic in an age of space travel, the bulk of hotel accounting is still done by hand or machine. Even so, a 150-unit motel typically generates 500 to 600 transactions per day and larger properties proportionally more. A 400- to 500-room hotel handles upwards of 3,000 transactions daily.

Chapter 1 also pointed out that the economies of scale are causing investors to increase the size of the operating unit. Innovation and the same economies of scale applied to the manufacturer have forced down the cost of microcomputers. Even now, the 150-room property can economically employ the new generation of data processing equipment. The days of the folio are numbered.

Whether hand- or machine-prepared, the folio serves two purposes: it is the guest statement and it facilitates the reconciliation of total guest charges with other hotel records — that procedure is the night audit.

The Hand-prepared Folio

For the simplest of the three folio forms, the work is done in pencil using carbon. Because carbon always shows black, red figures are never used on the original copy; credits are shown instead with a circled figure (figure 10.3).

Hand-prepared bills are ruled with seven vertical columns representing a one-week period. The seven columns do not represent Sunday through Saturday, however. Guests arrive on different days and each folio is started with the date of that arrival. The first column is dated when the folio is prepared and subsequent dates are added by the night auditor (figure 10.3). Since the average stay in hotels/ motels is two or three days, a great deal of time, paper, and space could be saved with a newer, narrower form.

At right angles to the vertical date columns is a horizontal listing of departmental services. Intersecting vertical and horizontal columns enable items to be identified by department and day. This separation of charges by type and date is essential to the daily reconciliation that takes place during the night audit.

The larger, upper portion of the folio represents charges (for room, food, telephone, etc.) that guests incur, which increase their obligation to the hotel. These charges are debits to the folio, which is an account receivable, and credits to the respective departmental incomes. The bottom portion of the account reflects credits to the account receivable, that is the means by which guests discharge their obligations to the hotel, and debits to the cash (payments).

When the settlement is by credit card (city ledger transfer), the bottom of the transient folio (figure 10.3) represents a credit to transient accounts receivable, reducing the transient folio to a zero balance. Simultaneously, a charge (or debit) to the city account is made. That city account might be a new account, or it might be one of the standard credit card accounts that the hotel maintains permanently. The debit portion of this double-entry transaction takes place in the accounting office and is not visible on the front office records.

Each night the auditor determines the difference between the debits and credits and carries the balance forward to the next day. This balance is shown at the bottom of one column and at the top of the next. When the

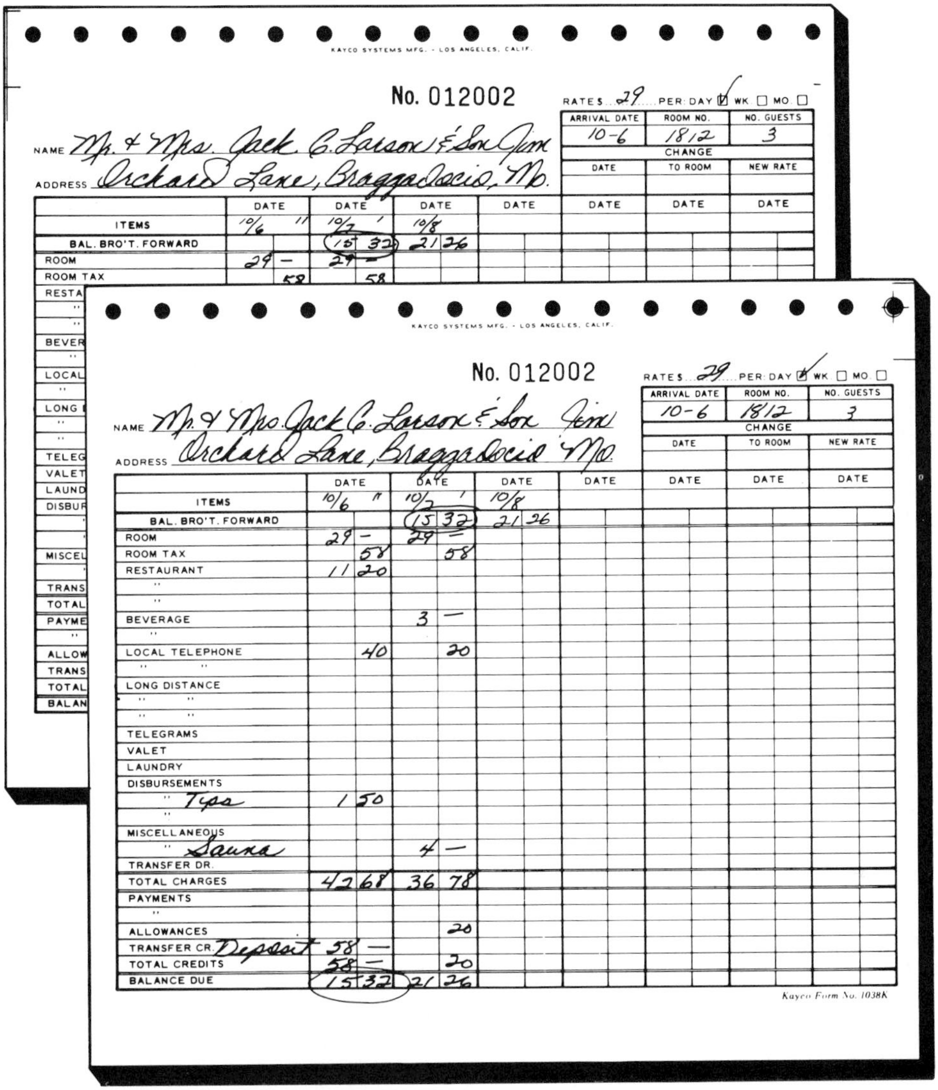
KAYCO SYSTEMS MFG. - LOS ANGELES, CALIF.

No. 012002

RATE $ 29 PER: DAY ☑ WK. ☐ MO. ☐

ARRIVAL DATE	ROOM NO.	NO. GUESTS
10-6	1812	3
CHANGE		
DATE	TO ROOM	NEW RATE

NAME Mr. & Mrs. Jack C. Larson & Son Jim

ADDRESS Orchard Lane, Braggadocio, Mo.

ITEMS	DATE 10/6	DATE 10/7	DATE 10/8	DATE	DATE	DATE	DATE
BAL. BRO'T. FORWARD		(15 32)	21 26				
ROOM	29 —	29 —					
ROOM TAX	58	58					
RESTAURANT	11 20						
"							
"							
BEVERAGE		3 —					
"							
LOCAL TELEPHONE	40	20					
" "							
LONG DISTANCE							
" "							
" "							
TELEGRAMS							
VALET							
LAUNDRY							
DISBURSEMENTS							
" Tips	1 50						
"							
MISCELLANEOUS							
" Sauna		4 —					
TRANSFER DR.							
TOTAL CHARGES	42 68	36 78					
PAYMENTS							
"							
ALLOWANCES		20					
TRANSFER CR. Deposit	58 —						
TOTAL CREDITS	58 —	20					
BALANCE DUE	(15 32)	21 26					

Kayco Form No. 1038K

Figure 10.3. Hand-prepared folio with carbonized guest copy. The October 6 "Balance Due" (circled) is a credit: the hotel owes the guest part of the original, unused deposit. The closing balance of October 7 is the more usual debit balance: the account receivable (the guest) owes the hotel.

guest departs, it is a simple matter to total the last column and quickly present the statement (figure 10.3).

Bills may be rendered and collected whenever management wishes, because credit is a privilege and not the right of a hotel guest. Motels carry this a step further and collect in advance. The hand-prepared bill is designed for weekly billing. Whenever the seven columns are completed, the duplicate is given to the guest (usually placed in the mailbox) and the original is attached to a new folio that is then prepared. Management also sets a limitation on credit, a predetermined amount beyond which no credit is allowed. As soon as a guest generates this predetermined amount, which varies with the class of hotel, the folio is rendered. Thus, with hand-prepared folios, guests are billed either weekly or when their credit reaches the given limit, whichever occurs first.

The Machine-prepared Folio

Machine-prepared bills differ from the hand-prepared ones because the machine, not the clerk, segregates charges by type and date. (This separation is essential to the nightly reconciliation of accounts and departmental charges known as the night audit.) Daily totals of each department are accumulated in the machine much like a large cash register. It is unnecessary, therefore, to do the departmental separation on the folio. Departmental charges and credits are printed on the folio and the duplicate (figures 10.1 and 10.4), and simultaneously accumulated in the machine total for that department.

Similarly, there is no need to use separate daily columns on the machine-prepared folio. Since machine totals are cleared daily after the night audit, each day's figures accumulate independently of what has gone before. Charges are posted chronologically down the page with the machine printing the date of each transaction. As the hand-prepared bill is

limited by the seven daily columns, so the machine-prepared bill is limited by the number of posting lines — twenty-four on the old electromechanical machines, more on the newer electronic models. Machine bills are rendered weekly, when the folio is full, or when the credit limit is reached, whichever comes first.

Charges are separated from credits vertically on the machine bill and horizontally on the hand bill. Some machines print credits in red; others indicate credits with a minus sign (figure 10.4).

The hotel's copy of the electromechanical folio (the NCR machine) is larger than the guest's copy and contains more information (figure 11.3).

On the left side of the hotel's copy is a memo column that permits handwritten explanations of unusual events, but it is rarely used. Opposite, on the right side, is a room number column. Printing the room number with each posting minimizes the chance of charging the wrong room. The additional letter or symbol contained in this column identifies the cashier who made the posting. Each cashier is assigned a key that activates the posting machine. The absence of this key prevents tampering with the machine and its presence identifies the user.

The hotel's copy of the NCR folio has still another extra column, the *pickup* (figure 11.3). This figure deals with the mechanics of operating the machine and has nothing to do with the account balance. In order to keep a running balance, the total of the previous line is picked up (punched into the machine) and the new posting is added or subtracted from the previous figure. Printing the pickup, like printing the room number, makes transactions easier to trace.

The electronic machine, of which the Micros is a good example (figure 10.4), has automatic pickup, considerably reducing the chance for error. Overprinting, which requires a good deal of involved corrections with the

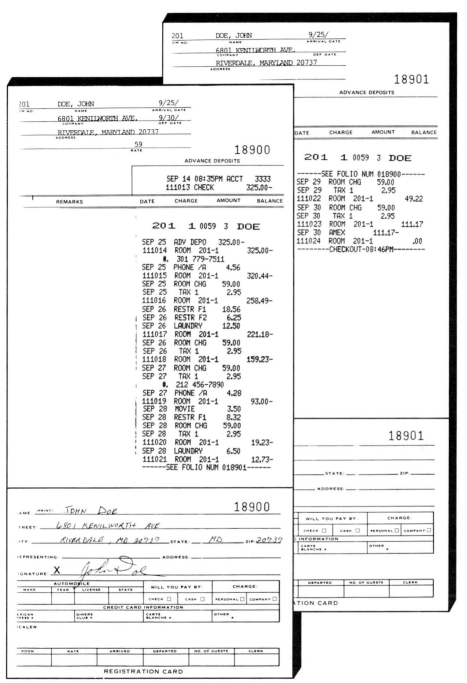

Figure 10.4. Electronically derived folio whose presentation is similar to the electromechanical machines because each posting is individually entered. A combined registration-folio packet with credits appearing as minus signs. *Courtesy: Micros Systems, Inc., Riverdale, Md.*

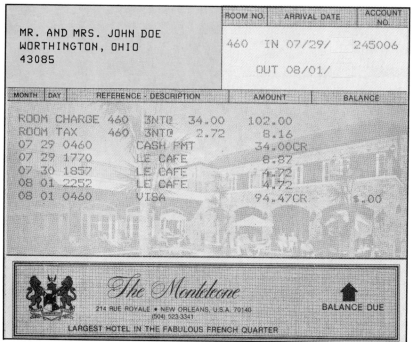

		ROOM NO.	ARRIVAL DATE	ACCOUNT NO.
MR. AND MRS. JOHN DOE WORTHINGTON, OHIO 43085		460	IN 07/29/	245006
			OUT 08/01/	

MONTH	DAY	REFERENCE - DESCRIPTION	AMOUNT	BALANCE
		ROOM CHARGE 460 3NT@ 34.00	102.00	
		ROOM TAX 460 3NT@ 2.72	8.16	
07	29	0460 CASH PMT	34.00CR	
07	29	1770 LE CAFE	8.87	
07	30	1857 LE CAFE	4.72	
08	01	2252 LE CAFE	4.72	
08	01	0460 VISA	94.47CR	1.00

The Monteleone

214 RUE ROYALE • NEW ORLEANS, U.S.A. 70140
(504) 523-3341

BALANCE DUE ↑

LARGEST HOTEL IN THE FABULOUS FRENCH QUARTER

Figure 10.5. Computer-prepared folio. Items are not posted individually; they are retained in memory and the entire folio is printed on demand.

N.C.R. machine (figure 10.8), is solved with electronic equipment that has automatic line-finder features, thus reducing the number of errors left for the night auditor.

The Data-prepared Folio

One sees more and more computer prepared statements. These are not folios in the traditional sense. There is no posting of individual items. They are, rather, stored in memory. A paper folio is printed only on call, usually at check-out time. Since the storage capabilities of data equipment are enormous, there is no machine limitation that would force the rendering of the bill. Unlike the hand-prepared and machine-prepared folios, which are rendered when full, a computer bill is tendered weekly or whenever the credit line is exceeded.

Contrary to previous implications, the average guest in the average hotel rarely sees the bill until checkout. The average guest does not stay a week, does not incur enough postings to fill the machine bill, and rarely overextends the credit line. Consequently, the guest is aware of the bill only at departure.

Completed, the data bill looks somewhat like its machine-prepared counterpart (figure 10.5). The only difference is that the data is stored in memory and reproduced in one quick printout at the conclusion of the guest's stay, whereas the machine bill is prepared item by item during the course of the stay.

Folio Numbering

In small operations it is important for the accountant to establish well-defined means of internal control. Folio numbering (figures 10.1

and 10.3) is one of these. In larger operations several persons are involved in the office procedure and internal control procedures may be relaxed somewhat with a proportionate saving in office detail.

Any numbering control system, be it food checks or registration cards, is purposeless unless verification is made. On any given day it is possible to verify the folios of the previous seven days because all the folios are returned by the end of the week. Either the guest has departed during the week or, having remained longer than a week, has been issued a new folio. However, some hotels keep the old folio in the well until the guest leaves, regardless of the length of stay.

Chapter 6 explained how the registration card and the folio are given identical numbers and how an attempt is made to coordinate their use. If they are bound together in one registration packet (figure 6.8), which might also include the rack slips, the arrangement works without too much difficulty. Guests who remain beyond a week present a special problem since they require a new folio but not a new registration card. Special folios are used to handle this, distinguished from the others either by color or by the term *transfer folio* printed in place of the number on the regular folio. Special folios are also used for master accounts or for group registration when individual members of the party do not sign in. Not numbered, these special folios are handled with less care and control, diminishing the effectiveness of the whole idea. More often than not, attempts to coordinate folio and registration numbers are scrapped. Numbered cards and folios are obviously more costly to print.

Computer systems have no prenumbered folios and often no registration cards either. This makes the "audit trail" more difficult to follow, and it reflects one of the disadvantages of computerizing the system. Control is maintained through the numerous reports that are generated by the computer and the inability of the clerk to tamper with those report-generating programs.

From Bill Number . . . To Bill Number

This phrase, or one like it, cross-references and identifies several folios assigned to the same guest during an extended stay (figure 10.4). Although few guests remain longer than seven days, folios often provide for that possibility. When the folio of the second week is prepared, its number is inserted on the original bill in the space marked "To Bill No." Similarly, the old folio number is referenced on the new folio in the space marked "From Bill No." There is obviously no need for such cross-referencing if no numbering system is in use or if the second folio is taken from a special, unnumbered pile of transfer folios. Similarly, the unlimited capacity of the computer and the absence of a weekly limitation make the phrase passé for data processing equipment terminology.

BILLING

It has been noted several times that there are two types of hotel receivables, transient and city. But the fact that the folio deals solely with accounts receivable has not been mentioned. Persons who pay cash for the services they use are not included in this discussion of front office billing. It makes no difference whether that person is a registered guest or a stranger; those who pay cash in the various departments are not accounts receivable. Only charged services will eventually involve the billing clerk at the front office, but it could be either a registered or a city guest.

Simplified, the procedure is this. The guest incurs a charge in some department of the hotel: coffee shop, cocktail lounge, telephone, laundry. A record of the charge is made at the department selling the service. Then the

Figure 10.6. Point of sale (POS) terminal allows cashiers throughout the hotel to enter charges directly and immediately into the guest's account. *Courtesy: Sahara Hotel, Las Vegas, Nev.*

charge is communicated to the desk, where it is posted to the guest account card and eventually is paid as part of the entire bill. During the night audit, guest account cards are reconciled with the departmental records in order to uncover and correct errors. The success of the entire system obviously rests on the communication between the department in which the charge originates and the front office, where the charge is posted. Although the communication devices are the same as those discussed for registration, their purposes are different.

With an on-line computer, the departmental (food, bar, etc.) charge goes immediately into memory (figure 10.6) bypassing the communication route through the front desk. Since the charge no longer passes through the front office billing clerk, there is a major change

in the night audit. Historically, the night audit has concentrated on proving that the charge made at the front desk was the same as that initiated by the particular department. A communication problem that the point of sale computer terminal solves.

Communication

Communication systems have matured a great deal since the day when all messages were hand carried to the desk. Hand-carried messages are slow, irregular, costly, and above all, unreliable. They are slow because they await the availability of a runner and because it is more economical to accumulate several charges before calling and dispatching that runner. They are irregular because it is too costly to assign the job to a full-time employee. They are costly when one compares foot speed with voltage and labor costs with kilowatts. And they are unreliable because employees pocket the slips of paper as they go off on other jobs to which they are normally assigned. This means uncollected income or lengthy investigation by the night auditor to uncover the missing charge.

Computers are at the other end of the historical continuum. No runners are needed here. Messages flow electronically and instantaneously. Charges made at the point-of-sale (POS) terminal (figure 10.6) in the dining room or bar are recallable immediately at the billing/cashiering terminals at the front desk. All the intermediate communication steps discussed next are replaced by the POS.

Pneumatic Tubes

Before computers, pneumatic tubes (figure 9.4) were the chief means of communication between the operating departments and the bill clerk. Unlike the other communication systems, this one transports the actual voucher, carrying it along in a cylinder. The same check that the guest signs in the dining room is sent to the bill clerk for recording on the folio.

The pneumatic tube system can grow quite large unless the front office acts as a communication center.[1] Dispatches between housekeeping and engineering, for example, are routed to the front desk for relay rather than being sent direct. This reduces the piping system but increases the work load of the front office.

Telephone

The versatility of the telephone compensates for its serious weakness in the billing procedure—lack of a written record. It is an ideal tool for resolving problems between the departments and the desk because it provides two-way communication. Similarly, charges that have not reached the desk by the time the guest departs can be obtained quickly by telephone.

Departmental cashiers use the telephone to alert the billing clerk of charges that are delayed, as would occur in a hand-carried system. Direct line telephones are used in the same manner. When new wings, roof gardens, and lounges are added to the hotel after construction, direct line telephones may be the best means of communication between the new department and the billing desk.

Telewriter/Remote Printer

The telewriter (figure 9.2) is another substitute for the pneumatic system. Charges are recorded by the departmental cashier and im-

mediately reproduced on the receiver in the front office. Unlike the telephone, the telewriter, or even teletype, produces a written record. Therein lies a special danger—that of recording the charge twice, once from the telewriter and once from the original voucher when it is finally received from the department.

The remote printer is an electronic variant of the telewriter. As the departmental cashier rings the charge on the point-of-sale register, the remote printer duplicates the information at the front desk on a tape similar to that used with an adding machine. Charges are posted immediately, but there is the danger of dual posting as with the telewriter. Moreover, the tape is small and easily lost, especially when it curls as it does when the tape roll gets small. Remote printers need not be that small, but increasing the size, and hence the cost, destroys whatever rationale existed for employing such an indirect electronic system.

Electronic On-line

Direct, on-line communication devices (POS terminals) are rapidly being introduced into the hotel business. These are located at the stations of the departmental cashiers, where the charge vouchers are generated. After the guest makes the charge, it is punched into the terminal by the departmental cashier. The impulse goes to the memory bank, from whence the front office can call it up as needed.

Optical card readers (OCR) are being tried as point-of-sale terminals. Small spaces on the rear of the guest check are blackened in by the waitress or waiter, bartender, cashier, or other employee to indicate the number in the party, the amount, the tip and tax, and the room number. The encoded check is fed into the OCR, which transmits the data to the computer.

Random is the best word to describe the current status of hotel computerization. With certain pieces and processes in place, and oth-

1. An interesting historical note is provided by the *Standard Practice Manual for Hotel Operation, I, Front Service Division*, p. 72, that was prepared in 1935 by Ralph Hitz in his capacity as president of the National Hotel Management Company, Inc. The manual contains a complete procedure for clearing the tubes, including a special tube-clear report. Once cleared, the tubes were not used between midnight and 7 A.M. the next morning.

ers not, POS terminals have not received first priority. Part of the fault lies with the manufacturers, who have marketed microcomputers capable of handling internal control and reports as well as communications with the host memory. The added cost for stand-alone POS's have relegated them to lower importance for the time being.

Charges

Charges, or debits, to the guest folio originate in services that the guest buys from one of the many hotel departments. Rooms, food, and beverage are the three major departments in which charges originate. Charges for laundry, valet, and telephone are referred to as minor departments. Depending upon the nature of the hotel, there are still other charges: greens fees, ski tows, parking fees, sauna baths, in-room films, and similar services.

Basic Forms

Except for room charges, the mechanics of the departmental charge and of its recording are similar for each department. Basically, there are three forms: the departmental record, the voucher, and the folio. The system provides for correct posting at the front desk of charges made by a guest at some distant department. The front office folio is the ultimate record. The voucher is the means of communication between the department where the charge originates and the front office. Departmental records are maintained to reconcile at day's end in the event of a lost or misposted voucher.

It is possible to do away with the voucher if the charge originates at the front desk itself, as it does with cash transactions that the cashier handles directly. Locating the switchboard at the front desk also eliminates the voucher since communication would be direct and the charge would be posted from the departmental control sheet.

With an on-line computer, there are none of these forms. All three records are the same computer entry, except when POS terminals are independent of the system.

Food and Beverage

After rooms, food and then beverage sales generate the largest gross income. Many of these sales are cash, but many are also charged to the folio under the following procedure.

The guest is presented with the check for the food or drink that was served. The guest signs the check and provides a room number. Depending upon the means of payment in that particular dining room or lounge, the server or cashier will challenge any illegible signature or room number. Though infrequently done, the employee should call the information clerk or room clerk to make certain the individual is actually registered in the house, or if a credit card is proffered, that it is still valid. Such verification is an automatic by-product of installations using electronic data equipment.

A record of the charge is made on a departmental form, similar to that shown in figure 10.7. According to the particular hotel, the charge may be rung on a cash register under a separate charge key. In this way, all departmental sales will be recorded on the register whether for cash or charge. Since the register record is incomplete, lacking the guest's name and room number, a written record is still desirable. Sometimes guest checks are prepared in duplicate. One copy is used as the voucher and the other remains as the departmental control sheet.

The signed check (the voucher) is forwarded by tube or runner to the front desk, or any of the other methods just described may be used.

Beverage charges are handled the same way. When the food and beverage originate from separate departments, each with its own cashier, the guest is sometimes presented with two separate checks to sign. For ease in sort-

DEPARTMENT CONTROL SHEET

NAME_____   DATE _____

VOUCHER NO.	ROOM NO.	GUEST NAME	AMOUNT	MEMO.
			$	

KAYCO NCR FORM NO. 118   **THIS REPORT MUST BE SENT TO NIGHT AUDITOR BY 12 O'CLOCK EACH NIGHT.**

Figure 10.7. Departmental control sheet is maintained by the departmental cashier as a control on vouchers forwarded to the front desk. The form is reconciled nightly with those vouchers by the night auditor. Note instructions at the bottom of the form.

ing and recording, different colored checks are used in each dining room and bar. These would be in keeping with the decor of that particular room. Separating the vouchers is necessary for the night audit, and separate totals are easily accumulated with the posting machine. Either a separate key is used for each dining room and bar, including room service, or an identifying code letter indicating the public room in which it originated is printed with the generic charge.

Posting

As each voucher is received by the billing clerk, it is posted to the guest's folio. The posting is completed on the hand-prepared folio by writing the charge in the proper daily column opposite the correct department (figure 10.3). On the machine-prepared folio, the charge is recorded on the next unused line (figure 10.1). The hand-prepared folio is totaled nightly or when the guest departs. The machine-prepared statement maintains a running balance (figure 10.4).

With POS terminals, there is no posting; charges go directly into computer memory from the departmental cashier. If the POS terminal is not integrated with the host computer

that contains the folio billing program, the transaction will need to be posted. In which case, the chance for communication and posting errors remains.

Once posted, the voucher is validated to prevent a second charge to the folio. On the hand-posted folio, this is done by pen or with a rubber stamp. The machine validates by printing the posting on the voucher at the same time it records the entry on the guest folio. A third printing takes place on a continuous journal record called the audit tape (figures 10.8 lower right and 14.3). The audit tape records the entries in sequence showing the room number, the department charged, the amount, the cashier's identification, the date, and the previous pickup, if any. All of this information is needed at the time of the night audit. The departmental record of sales also becomes an integral part of the night audit, arriving at the front desk for the use of the auditor at the close of the day (see statement on figure 10.7).

Minor Departments

The number of departments originating charge sales is limited only by the amount of service that the hotel wishes to provide. Sales records

Figure 10.8. Electromechanical front office posting machine, NCR model 4200. Although still in use, neither the machine nor its parts have been manufactured for years. *Courtesy: NCR Corporation, Las Vegas, Nev.*

and charge vouchers originate in room service, laundry and valet, cigar and newsstands, baggage and checkrooms, and all of the recreational facilities that a hotel is apt to maintain. Since many of these departments sell primarily for cash, the newsstand for example, there may be no provision at all for the charge sales that terminate at the front desk. Other minor departments, which sell exclusively on charge, use vouchers with carbonized sales records. The vouchers are forwarded to the desk periodically and the carbon remains as the control record.

Although the actual forms differ in format, the procedure for all the minor departments is the same as for food and beverage. The charge originates with the guest, who signs a voucher. A record of the charge is made in the department and the voucher is forwarded to the desk for posting. The charges are reconciled nightly by the night audit and the entire bill is paid when the guest checks out.

Whether the charge originates in the minor departments, in the food and beverage department or with concessionaires, the need for prompt communication with the front desk remains paramount because the manual system of handling the minor departments is likely to remain. Relatively few charges originate in the minor departments. Not enough, usually, to justify the costs of POS terminals.

Telephone is the exception. It was once treated as a minor department. So much is happening in decontrol and in automatic equipment that this one-time-money-losing department may prove to be the surprise sleeper of the next decade. Its true income-generating capacity is yet to be ascertained. The topic is treated later in the text.

Rooms

Unlike the charges from other departments, room rates are posted only once each day by the night staff as part of the audit. Day rate charges, charges for late checkouts, and advance payments are exceptions and are posted by the billing clerk. Again, unlike the other departments, no voucher is needed to initiate the room charge. Although there is no departmental record similar to the sales sheet that is maintained by other departments, there is a means of verifying the total room charges. Since room charges are a duty of the night auditor, the technique used is discussed in chapter 14.

"Plus" Rate

Several special situations affect the otherwise routine posting of room rates. On occasion, one guest joins another who is already registered. The registered guest has a folio that reflects the single room rate. When the new guest registers, the room clerk assigns the arrival to the already occupied room and indicates this on the registration card by writing "Joins Room 637" in the room assignment square. The rate on this additional guest is the difference between the single rate being charged the current guest and the double rate that they both will pay. This is noted in the rate square of the registration card by marking it, for example, "+18," where the $18 represents the difference between the two rates. A second folio is prepared at this "plus" rate and filed in the bucket with the other folio. Both rates are posted by the auditor, although one will be considerably larger than the other.

Rates may be split at the time of registration among several persons sharing a room. Then each folio is marked with the sharing symbol to clarify the situation to the night auditor. (See chapter 7, Rates.)

Rate changes must be called to the attention of the night auditor. This is done by crossing out the old rate and writing in the new one above it. Rate changes caused by new room assignments or changes in the number of guests in the party will be indicated by additional alterations on the folio heading. Rate changes may also reflect corrections in the original rate quotation. Sometimes a room and rate change form must be completed. This might be a change slip (figure 9.3), a change book, or a change sheet (figure 14.11).

Plus-rate transactions are not very frequent. Besides, there are other ways to post them, which usually becomes apparent with the first effort to handle a plus-rate transaction through the computer. The program may simply not accommodate a transaction like "plus-rate" or other equally rare activities. So it may be necessary to first check out the guest in residence, and then to register the two guests as if they were a new party just arriving.

Credits

Each departmental voucher increases the debit or charge balance of the account card. This is not so, of course, when the guest pays for departmental services in cash at the time of the purchase. But many departments, such as telephone, have no provision for cash sales even if the guest desires it. Even when no other departmental services are used, there is still a daily room charge and most likely a room tax as well. These charges must be settled by the guest at the time of checkout with sufficient credits to balance out the account.

Regardless of the means employed, the transient folio must have a zero balance, no debits and no credits, after the guest checks out. Several different kinds of credit may be applied, individually or jointly, to balance the charges. Cash, as a means of settlement, is treated in the next chapters. Allowances (sometimes called credits) and transfers, including the application of advance deposits, are the two other credits.

Allowances

Just as department stores allow the return of unsatisfactory goods, hotels grant credit al-

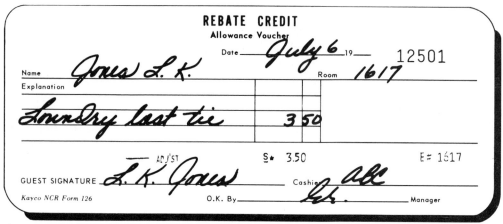

Figure 10.9. Allowance (or rebate) voucher is used to reduce the guest's folio balance. Correction might be an accounting correction or an adjustment for poor service.

lowances, or rebates. Having no goods to sell, hotel allowances are based on poor service, misunderstandings, and errors. Legitimate adjustments to guest complaints are considered so important that lease provisions usually allow the hotel to grant allowances for unsatisfactory service by concessionaires.

Still another form is needed to record an allowance (figure 10.9). Except in minor instances, allowances require the signature of the assistant manager or the front office manager or some other supervisor. Bringing the allowance to management's attention assures the guest of its importance and alerts management to possible problem areas. Allowances are prepared at the front office, so no control sheet like a departmental sales record is maintained. The allowance voucher, or rebate slip, itself serves this purpose and posting is done directly from the voucher to the folio, although some hotels do keep an allowance journal in the front office. Allowance vouchers are prenumbered and maintained in numerical sequence. Computerized desks still use allowance forms since they serve other than a clerical purpose.

Telephone

Complaints about telephone charges, particularly those involving local calls, are the source of most allowances. These protested calls are settled immediately by the cashier, who is usually authorized to do so. It's impossible to disprove the guest anyway. Besides, it doesn't pay to do so over small change. Larger long-distance allowances require approval in the usual manner, which relieves the cashier of responsibility. One allowance voucher may be used to record all local telephone allowances for the shift rather than completing the same paper work many times over.

Telephone deregulation has provided the incentive for large capital outlays in telephone equipment. Hotels are investing in automatic route selectors that choose least cost routing for each telephone call. Firm identification of the calling number is a byproduct of the new equipment, and this should reduce claims for telephone allowances.

Comps

Complimentary rooms are given at the discretion of management. "Visiting firemen" usually receive the courtesy of the house, one manager to another. It is so traditional that one salary study listed comp privileges as a fringe benefit for the industry. Other persons and groups receive complimentary facilities as well. Like so many items, comps are subject to abuse, and top management should require a compilation of comp charges. If, as is done in many instances, the guest is not recorded, not charged a rate, nor counted in either the house count or the room count, there is no accounting record of the stay and, consequently, no control. It is far better to charge the guest in full and grant an allowance at the end of the stay to cover the charge on the room.

What is better accounting may not be better service. If no rate is posted, the guest will certainly not be charged. Embarrassing and awkward situations occur when the charge is made and the comp reduction is either overlooked by or unknown to the cashier, who insists on payment. Accumulating comp allowances separately from normal room allowances permits an easy review of policy and procedure. Comp reports are a standard part of the night audit; a job handled by the computer in seconds.

Since the comp is authorized and approved at the time the rate is recorded, cashiers prepare the comp allowances without seeking a management signature.

Poor Service
Who has not witnessed coffee poured into a customer's lap or a woman's hose snagged on the cocktail booth? Room service leaves a leaky champagne bucket on the bureau top and water ruins a piece of clothing. A suit is lost by valet; the laundry scorches three shirts; the cot in the room is never made up. Countless irritating events are bound to occur in hotels serving thousands of persons per day.

Often the problem is caught immediately and management acts to remedy the situation. Just as often it isn't, and other than an apology

and corrective action for the future there is little management can do but pay. Allowances are an after-the-fact attempt to ameliorate the situation. Allowances of this type must be approved by management.

Correction of Errors
Allowances are also used to correct errors, since no amount of training can ever eliminate them entirely. Posting a charge to the wrong room is one of many kinds of errors. Room 1716 (Smith) might be erroneously charged with the room service check incurred by Jones in room 1617. If both are still registered at the time the error is discovered — most likely when Smith complains — a transfer is made, as will be explained shortly. Almost the same transfer procedure is used if Jones has left the hotel and the charge is large enough to warrant billing by mail. But if Jones has checked out and if the amount incorrectly posted to Smith is too small to attempt collection by mail, Smith will have the bill adjusted by an allowance. (The adjust key of the posting machine is used.)

Other errors of mathematics or procedure call for similar adjustments to the folio by an allowance. Many errors originate in misunderstanding or lack of attention. A couple arrives for several days but one spouse leaves after the first night. Although the desk knows of the situation, the double occupancy rate somehow continues for the entire stay and an allowance is eventually needed.

In theory it should not happen, but sometimes the guest folio is carried one night beyond the actual departure day and an allowance is used to correct the mistake. This happens most often with paid-in-advance guests who do not feel obligated to check out.

A rate could simply be recorded incorrectly or, more likely, the clerk and the guest did not communicate. Arriving with a $58 reservation, the guest does not expect to be assigned to a $62 room. The clerk understands the guest to agree; the guest understands the clerk to offer a $62 room for $58, or at least that is the position taken. Although the rooming slip is intended to prevent this situation, the assistant manager may accept the story at check-out time and authorize an allowance. (A $62 room that is sold for $58 should be marked "$58 SPECIAL.")

Every protested charge is not necessarily a hotel error. This is why it is helpful to have old vouchers accessible to the cashier. When shown a signed voucher, guests often recall charges that they vehemently protested only a few moments earlier. Large bar charges fall into this category when they are viewed with a sober eye the following day. This also happens when two persons share a room and one makes charges but the other pays. Especially when the first guest has already checked out is it necessary to prove to the remaining guest that the charge was, in fact, made and that payment is, indeed, due.

Offsetting guest complaints is more difficult with computer systems using POS terminals. There are no old vouchers to refer to. And when telephone charges, a frequent source of guest dissatisfaction, are posted electronically, there is no trace of paper to show to the unhappy guest. Although computer equipment minimizes hotel errors, it does not mitigate guest forgetfulness or honest misunderstandings.

Extended Stay

Some hotels and motels, especially resorts, allow a reduction in daily rate if the guest remains an extended length of time. To make certain of the guest's commitment to remain, the full daily charge is posted and not the per diem charge of the special rate. Either an allowance is given on the final day to adjust the weekly rate or, as explained in chapter 7, the charge of the final day is adjusted to balance the week.

Allowances for American plan meals are treated in the text's final chapter. Although meal allowances sometimes appear as separate items on the AP folio, the accounting procedure is the same for all allowances.

Method of Recording

Once the amount and type of allowance is determined, the posting is a simple mechanical procedure. A voucher is completed (figure 10.9) by the cashier and signed by the appropriate hotel officer when necessary. The amount of the allowance is then credited to the guest's folio (credits reduce accounts receivable), and the balance is collected if the guest is checking out. Each allowance will be charged (debited) against the department from which it originates — room, food, telephone, etc. — by the accounting department, not the night auditor, on the following day. The allowance vouchers serve as the basis for these charges.

Some properties may employ two types of allowances. The rebate allowance is used to make an accounting correction of an error that occurred on a previous day. The second type is used for errors that are caught and amended on the same day that they occur. The net results are, of course, the same.

Transfers

A transfer is an accounting technique used to move a figure from one folio to another. One folio balance gets larger (debit) as the new information is added, while the balance of the other gets smaller (credit) as the amount is removed. Each account changes by the same amount except one increases and one decreases. Hence the rule that each debit transfer must have an equal credit transfer — a rule that is important in balancing the night audit.

All or part of the account balance can be transferred. According to the circumstances, transfers are made between accounts in the same ledger or between accounts in the two

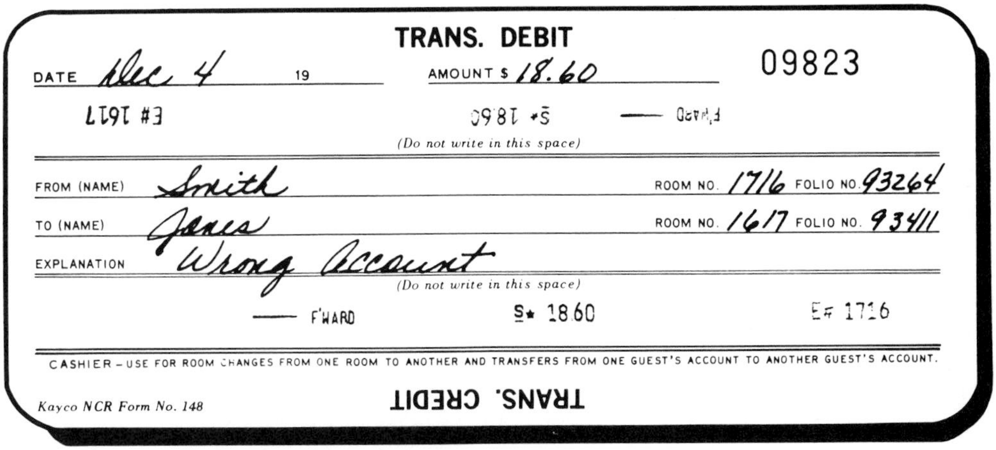

TRANS. DEBIT

DATE *Dec 4* 19 ___ AMOUNT $ *18.60* ___ 09823

E# 1617 ___ 5* 1860 ___ F'WARD ___

(Do not write in this space)

FROM (NAME) *Smith* ___ ROOM NO. *1716* FOLIO NO. *93264*

TO (NAME) *Jones* ___ ROOM NO. *1617* FOLIO NO. *93411*

EXPLANATION *Wrong Account*

(Do not write in this space)

___ F'WARD ___ S* 1860 ___ E# 1716

CASHIER — USE FOR ROOM CHANGES FROM ONE ROOM TO ANOTHER AND TRANSFERS FROM ONE GUEST'S ACCOUNT TO ANOTHER GUEST'S ACCOUNT.

Kayco NCR Form No. 148

TRANS. CREDIT

Figure 10.10. A transfer form used with machine-prepared folios for corrections of mispostings. Posting the correction is done twice: a credit to the account being repaired and a debit to the account being charged. (The correction would be just the reverse if the original posting error were a credit.)

ledgers. Machine folios use transfer debit and transfer credit keys to effect the movement.

Transient Ledger to Transient Ledger

Return to the illustration involving the incorrect charge that was posted to room 1716 (Smith) instead of to 1617 (Jones). Discovered at once, the error is simply voided and reposted correctly. (With a machine, a correction key is used.) This is not possible if the error is undetected for a day or longer. Once the day's balances are totaled and carried forward by the night auditor, the records of the day are closed. Although the charge was posted to the wrong guest account, it was posted to the correct category, room service. Therefore, the correction will not appear on the guest's folio as a room service charge. Not only would a charge to room service at a later date duplicate the record but it would also show a room service charge on a day when there was no such charge.

The correction is made with a transfer. The incorrect amount is removed from Smith's account as a credit transfer and charged to Jones' as a debit transfer. Folio numbers, names, and room numbers are cross-referenced on each folio. This information is noted in the memo column of the machine-prepared folio and a special transfer debit-credit voucher is validated along with the posting (figure 10.10). Usually no voucher is used on hand-prepared bills, but a transfer journal may be opened if the number of transfers gets too large. A transfer report is prepared by the computer as part of the audit procedure.

The technique is the same whether all or part of the balance is moved. When one party pays for another, the entire balance is transferred. No transfer is needed if both parties leave together and the sum of the two is paid by one. The proper amounts are posted to each folio in order to close the accounts and the cash is collected. A transfer is needed only if one party leaves before the other or if it is desirable to show the entire charge on one folio.

Holds

Changes in the public's travel patterns have decreased the number of hold transactions to almost none. These are charged to transient guests who are not registered. Either the guest has not yet arrived or has just left, expecting to reregister shortly. Collect telegrams and freight payments in advance of convention guests are examples of charges to the first category. Guests who return to the hotel on a regular schedule will sometimes leave laundry or valet work behind, and these charges will be posted to a folio temporarily. The hold folio is theoretically part of the city ledger, but it is kept in the front of the well because it has little activity.

Charges are posted to the hold card and held until the guest arrives. Then a credit transfer moves the charge from the hold card to the newly opened account, where it appears as a debit transfer. It is customary to post charges to the hold card on every other line so that each credit transfer will appear immediately below the particular charge and the balancing will be apparent. (Transfer charge keys and transfer credit keys are used with machine postings.) Transfer vouchers (figure 10.10) are used to support the entry.

Transient Ledger to City Ledger

Transfers also take place between ledgers: transient to city more often than the reverse. Even less frequently, transfers are made from one city account to another. Unlike transfers between transient accounts, a journal record is maintained for transfers between the ledgers. This form, called the *city ledger journal,* and the transfer procedures involving it are detailed in chapter 13. Transfers of late charges—those that arrive at the desk after the guest has gone—are also treated in that discussion.

Skippers—persons who leave the hotel without paying their bills—have their unpaid balances transferred to the city ledger. Some of these cases are accidental but many are preplanned, even though it is a crime in most states to intentionally defraud an innkeeper. It often takes a day or two to verify the skipper. Once discovered, the room is checked out and the balance is transferred to the city ledger. The police are notified in appropriate cases. These accounts are eventually written off as bad debts since collection is rare. Telephone companies in most states grant credit for telephone calls made by skippers but never paid for. Telephone companies are likely to renege on this under the deregulation climate.

Credit card (MasterCard, Visa, etc.) accounts that are carried in the city ledger but charged from the transient ledger require interledger transfers. Hotels also issue cards to individuals or companies who apply for credit, and a city account is opened for them. By this means a company executive can have the account sent to the central office, an individual guest can get home billing, and the convention executive can direct the bill to association headquarters. A city account also makes it easier to reserve rooms on a guaranteed payment basis.

National credit cards are handled in the same way as hotel cards, except any guest is apt to have them. Although a hotel maintains one city account for each of its own card holders, only one account is needed for each credit card company since the hotel expects payment from the company and not from the individual guest. In both cases, the transient folio is transferred to the city ledger and billing is made to either the individual or the credit card company.

By signing the folio, either in a prescribed place or across the face of the statement, the guest authorizes the transfer of the transient account to the city ledger. Guests who offer a national credit card as payment sign that company's form. Permission is also needed when one active account is transferred to another. Except in unusual circumstances, one guest should not be charged with the account of another unless the transfer is cleared first.

After the checkout, the transient folio balance must be zero. One way or another, all of the debits incurred during the stay—room, food, beverage, and the minor departmental charges—must be balanced through credits. Allowances may offset some of the charges. All or part of the folio may be transferred to another account in either the transient or the city ledger. (Settlement is also possible with a travel agent's coupon, which is a type of transfer.) Cash is the final means of settlement and this is discussed next. It is conceivable that future computer ties will provide payment through a bank card (called a debit card) that will reduce the guest's bank account and increase the hotel's account without any cash or checks exchanging hands. That topic is two chapters away.

QUERIES AND PROBLEMS

1. Differentiate:
   a. Debit from credit.
   b. Master account from split account.
   c. "A" folio from "B" folio.
   d. Transient guest from city guest.
   e. The billing frequency of hand-prepared folios from machine-prepared folios from computer-prepared folios.

2. Sketch a hand-prepared folio showing the following data.
   a. The Arthur Jones family, M/M and son George, arrived three days ago. When the opening balance was determined today, it was fixed at $79 after the application of a $200 advanced deposit.
   b. Breakfast charge of $12.90.
   c. Mrs. Jones hosted a small luncheon meeting for her company and a $260 room service charge was posted. A $30 tip was paid to the room service waiter by the front desk.
   d. The family requested and received a late check-out permission.
   e. Long distance call was completed, $8.
   f. The family checks out, settling the account with a credit card, but not until the front office manager granted a $15 allowance for failure to supply towels during the second day of their stay. The laundry was on strike.

3. Explain the meaning of each posting on the segment of the folio provided below. (The items are identified as a, b, . . . f, but these references would not appear on a real folio.)

a.	4-2	307	TRSF	150.00cr	150.00cr
b.	4-2	307	ROOM	75.00	
		307	TAX	1.50	
		307	TEL	6.65	66.85cr
c.	4-3	211	REST	32.76	34.09cr
d.	4-3	211	CADV	6.00	28.09cr
e.	4-3	211	ROOM	58.00	
		211	TAX	1.16	
		211	MOVIE	5.00	36.07
f.	4-4	211	CASH	36.07cr	00.00

4. Under which of the following circumstances would management grant an allowance? How much would the value of that allowance be? What else might be done if an allowance were not granted?
   a. Guest sets the room alarm clock, but it fails to go off, which causes the guest to miss a meeting that involves thousands of dollars of commission.
   b. Same circumstance as "a" but the guest called the telephone operator for a morning call.
   c. Guest checks out and discovers the room charge to be $15 more than the rate quoted two weeks earlier by the res center.
   d. Same circumstances as "c" but the discrepancy is discovered soon after the guest is roomed.
   e. Departing guest discovers that a $14 beverage charge was incorrectly posted to the folio yesterday.
   f. Same circumstances as "e" but the charge is posted today, the day of departure.
   g. Two days into the guest's four-day stay, the reservation department realizes the guest's advanced deposit was never transferred to the transient account.
   h. Same circumstances as "g" but the discovery is made by the guest, who writes in complaint about one week after checkout.

11

Cash: Charges and Credits

Cash paid-outs (cash advances made on behalf of the guest) are debits, increasing the guest account balance. Cash receipts (payments made by the guest to the hotel) are credits, decreasing the balance. So for accounting purposes, cash is no different than the other charges and credits discussed in chapter 10, except that cash can be both a charge and a credit. Cash is a volatile commodity and errors are not easily corrected after the fact. Front office cash is exchanged in the same area in which the posting takes place, making the departmental record as much a control device as a communicative one.

For years hotel guests have used the front office as a branch bank as well as a desk. They have come to expect cash advances almost on demand and even direct loans on occasion. Of late the hotel industry has shown great reluctance to play the banker's role. Large sums tied up in ever-growing accounts receivable and a

rising level of bad debts have contributed to this more restricted view of the desk's responsibility. Still, the daily cash sheet shows many transactions on both sides of the ledger.

THE CASH SHEET

The cash sheet is a departmental record much like the dining room departmental sales record. Each cashier maintains a cash record, which must be reconciled with actual cash on hand at the end of the watch. Figure 11.1 illustrates a typical front office cash sheet with provisions for paid-outs (disbursements) and receipts for both transient and city ledgers. A sheet is used with both hand-prepared and machine-prepared folios, but not always with the computer, which stores this information in memory. Figure 11.2 illustrates the display that the cashier would have if the system were computerized.

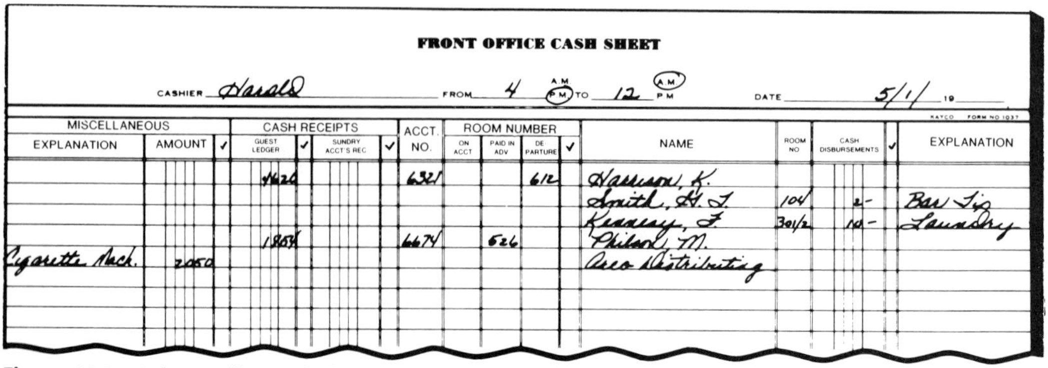
FRONT OFFICE CASH SHEET

CASHIER Harold FROM 4 PM TO 12 AM DATE 5/1/ 19

MISCELLANEOUS EXPLANATION	MISCELLANEOUS AMOUNT	✓	CASH RECEIPTS GUEST LEDGER	✓	CASH RECEIPTS SUNDRY ACCT'S REC	✓	ACCT. NO.	ROOM NUMBER ON ACCT	ROOM NUMBER PAID IN ADV	ROOM NUMBER DEPARTURE	✓	NAME	ROOM NO	CASH DISBURSEMENTS	✓	EXPLANATION
			46 26				6321			612		Harrison, K.				
												Smith, H. J.	104	2 -		Bar Tip
												Kearney, J.	301/2	10 -		Laundry
			18 54				6674		626			Philson, M.				
Cigarette Rack.	20 50											Area Distributing				

Figure 11.1. A front office cash sheet is maintained by each cashier. Cash receipts (debit cash, credit accounts receivable, or sales) are recorded on the left side; cash advances (debit accounts receivable and credit cash) on the right side. See also figure 11.2.

Paid-outs — Cash Advances

Notwithstanding their restrictive attitude toward credit in general, hotels still disburse funds in the guest's name. Like any other departmental service, this increases the debit balance of the bill. Paid-outs are recovered from the guest at check-out time since they are considered short-term advances.

Tips

Tips are the most common cash advance. They are paid to the employee at the request of the guest. A signed check from the dining room or bar is the usual method of request. The amount of gratuity is added to the check by the guest when signing for the service. When the signed voucher reaches the billing clerk, the departmental charges are separated from the tip. The latter is posted under the cash advance category, not the food or beverage category. After all, the tip is not departmental income, so it must not appear under a departmental heading. Acting on the guest's signature, the front office cashier pays the tip to the server, who signs for the money on a cash advance voucher (figure 11.3). An item reflecting the paid-out is entered on the cash sheet and posted to the guest's folio. Of course, the departmental charge is also posted.

Since this procedure is not an unusual one, it could pose a traffic problem at the front desk. This potential problem is usually avoided because in large hotels tips are paid by the cashier of the department from which the charge originates. A bellperson's tip would still go through the front office. This reduces front office traffic but decentralizes the paid-outs. The increasing use of national credit cards adds to the problem. Employees collect their tips when the charges are written but the hotel may wait weeks to be reimbursed. This ties up hotel funds, a particularly expensive cost during periods of high interest rates. And if the guest defaults, collecting from the employee months after the service was rendered is quite unlikely. This might one day be an issue for labor contract negotiations.

Other than credit card tips, there are very few cash advances made to city ledger accounts.

```
CASHIER NO.    99 REPORT
12/22/
CR-PAGE    1
                                                            CASH MINUS
LOCATION          CHARGES          CASH       PAID OUT       PAID OUT
   11                 .00            .00           .00            .00
   21                 .00         285.00           .00         285.00
   31                 .00            .00           .00            .00
  101                 .00            .00           .00            .00
  111                 .00          75.00           .00          75.00
  121               16.20            .00           .00            .00
  131              130.00            .00           .00            .00
  141              162.50            .00           .00            .00
  151                 .00          60.00           .00          60.00
  161                 .00         172.00           .00         172.00
  171               23.00            .00           .00            .00
  191                 .00          25.00           .00          25.00
  201            3,310.00       2,625.00           .00       2,625.00
  301                 .00         101.00           .00         101.00
  311                 .00            .00           .00            .00
  401                 .00            .00           .00            .00
  411                 .00            .00           .00            .00
  421               60.00          35.00           .00          35.00
  431                 .00            .00           .00            .00
  501               80.00            .00           .00            .00
  511                 .00            .00           .00            .00
  601               40.00            .00           .00            .00
  611              160.00            .00           .00            .00
  701                 .00            .00           .00            .00
  801                 .00            .00           .00            .00
  921                 .00            .00           .00            .00
  931                 .00            .00           .00            .00
  941               58.00            .00           .00            .00
                                SETTLEMENTS    LOCATIONS
AMERICAN EXPRESS                   4,081.70       140.00
SPARE**DO NOT USE**                    .00           .00


UNALLOCATED                            .00           .00
VISA/BANKAM/CB/CHARGEX                 .00           .00
CASH RECEIVED                     1,144.36
PAID OUT                             58.00
DIFFERENCE                        1,086.36
```

Figure 11.2. Cashier's report (or display) for all cashiers at every location, including the departmental cashiers who incur charges (second column). "Location" column is the guest room number or city ledger name (e.g., American Express). "Settlements" are folio settlements by credit card or coupon and "Locations" are credit card sales by the departmental cashier. *Courtesy: ECI, EECO Computer, Inc., Santa Ana, Calif.*

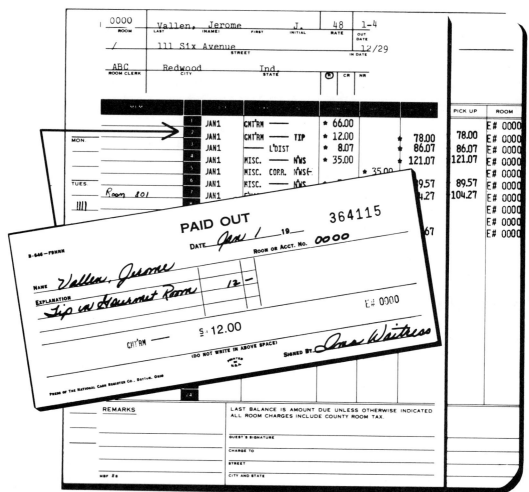

Figure 11.3. A cash-advance voucher posted on an electromechanical machine, NCR 2000. Signature of recipient shows evidence of payment.

Loans

Although one hears about the availability of loans for hotel guests, they are in fact quite rare and are made only to persons known to the management. It is now more difficult to cash a check than it was to obtain a cash loan years ago. This is especially true on weekends when banks are closed, although some hoteliers believe that it is better to have a small loan skip than to have a large check bounce and will grant the former if forced to choose. Companies that use the hotel on a regular basis may establish "loan" arrangements for their staffs by guaranteeing the advances.

Third-party Lenders

Two new lending procedures have surfaced as a result of the industry's unwillingness to act as banker for the millions of domestic and international travelers. Credit cards that conform to banking needs (magnetic stripes), retail outlets (optical-character readers), and supermarkets (zebra stripes) are being introduced. Not only will these cards bridge the gap between banking and retailing, they will allow cash withdrawals from one bank through the teller machines of another banking system. It is quite reasonable, therefore, to expect such machines in the lobbies of tomorrow's hotels. They would provide cash loans to guests, assigning the risk and collection to the expanded and deregulated banking industry. There may even be a rental fee to the hotel for the space in the lobby. If nothing else, guests could be encouraged to pay bills by cash (getting the money from the lobby machine) and thus reduce both the credit card fee and the cost delay in collection that hotels now experience.

Western Union's FlashCash, or similar money order services (e.g., Comcheck), offer a second banking alternative. It is an expansion of the advance room deposit procedure discussed in chapter 4. Guests send money orders to themselves. By calling Western Union and using their standard credit cards, the guests authorize payments to themselves. The guests need not go to a Western Union office if the hotel has signed up for the plan. Western Union authorizes payment by telephone and the hotel disburses the funds to the guest who has just made the telephone call. Western Union, not the guest, is now the account receivable. The hotel collects without cost, risk, or credit card discount. Fees paid by the guest to the third party range from 5 to 10 percent depending on the amount and the company plan.

Advances to Concessionaires

Small properties often arrange for a local merchant to supply services that the hotel is too small to offer. This merchant may or may not have a shop on the hotel premises. Laundry and dry cleaning are the best examples of this but recreational facilities, beauty parlors, florists, or specialty shops may also be involved. When the guest uses the service — sends out clothing through the bellperson — the concessionaire looks to the hotel for collection. Payment is made to the concessionaire when the service is completed and charged to the guest as an advance. The money is paid from the drawer and an appropriate entry is made on the disbursement side of the front office cash sheet. It is not an income to the hotel and is not listed on the folio as a laundry (valet, etc.) item.

A different method of handling is needed if the concessionaires allow the hotel to collect for them and make restitution periodically. It becomes necessary to separate the concessionaire's charges from other advances in order to identify them for later payment. Under those circumstances the laundry would be posted as a laundry charge, since no cash was advanced at the time the laundry was returned, and accumulated in that account. This represents the hotel's obligation to the concessionaire and is not income earned as it would be if the hotel had its own shop. The usual contract allows the hotel to retain a percentage of the sales as a commission and pay the balance monthly. In other words, the hotel collects from the guests as they depart and rebates monthly the total less commission to the concessionaire. Under this arrangement, the charge appears on the folio just as it would if the hotel owned and operated its own laundry (valet, etc.). Sometimes the commission goes to the bell captain.

Paid-outs to Checkouts

Although unusual, it is possible for the hotel to owe the guest at the conclusion of the guest's stay. This could happen in one of two ways. Either there was a substantial deposit with the reservation or a large payment was made after the arrival. If the guest shortens the stay, or there is a rate adjustment because of dissatisfaction, there could be a credit balance at the time of departure. This balance would show on the machine-prepared folio as a credit figure and on the hand-prepared one as a circled balance at the beginning of the day. Computers display it as a credit (cr).

Zeroing the credit balance of the account at checkout requires a debit or charge entry. A cash advance voucher is prepared for the guest's signature in the amount of the credit balance. An entry is made on the disbursement side of the cash sheet, posted to the folio as a cash advance, and the account is balanced. The guest takes the cash authorized by the voucher. Cash is not refunded if the original payment was not made in cash! The guest might have a credit payment as a result of an unused deposit made with a travel agency voucher or a credit card. A refund, if any, should be made by the travel agent to the guest, and the clerk should so explain.

Other Paid-outs

Certain minor departments of the hotel, especially of a small hotel, do not provide for credit sales even to registered guests. Nevertheless, it is sometimes advisable to accommodate the guest and sell on "credit." In reality, the department handles this like a cash sale by getting the money from the desk, where it is posted to the folio as a cash advance. To avoid confusing the guest, it may even be posted as a departmental charge, but it is not an income even though it has a departmental name. This is likely to be the way charge sales are handled by the newsstand, the barbershop, the limousine service, and other infrequent charges.

Signatures are not required on all types of advances, although loans require the guest's signature on a paid-out voucher and the approval of management. Hotels will accept collect telegrams, for example, without direct

authorization from the guest. Likewise, resort hotels pay shipping charges on trunks that arrive in advance of their owners. In both instances, paid-outs are recorded on the disbursement side of the cash sheet, and the delivery person who actually receives the cash signs the paid-out voucher, which is attached to the bill. When a shipping charge is paid, the advance is made to a city ledger account since the guest has not yet arrived.

Except for some convention materials, COD packages are almost always refused unless arrangements have been made beforehand and proper authorization and signatures have been obtained. Hotels have been known to accept worthless COD packages addressed to one of their guests by a collaborator. When the registered guest refuses to accept the package, the hotel is left with a worthless box and a large paid-out loss.

Cash Receipts
Receipts at Departure

Collections from departing guests are the most common entries on the front office cash sheet. (Credit card settlements merely substitute the account with the credit card company for the account with the guest and are not, therefore, cash collections although they are settlements.) The cash payment is recorded on the receipts side and a credit is posted on the folio to zero the balance. It is a quick procedure. The machine-prepared folio has a cumulative balance that indicates the amount due, and the hand-prepared folio merely requires the opening balance of the day to be added to the day's charges, which are usually few in number.

Unlike the hand-prepared and machine-prepared forms, the computer folio is not immediately evident. The cashier must first display the folio, or print a working copy for the guest's inspection, then request payment from the guest. After the payment is entered, the folio is printed. If the CRT is placed on a swivel, or an additional screen is available, the guest can examine the account before making payment. Using the room television for this pre-check-out display is a likely development for the next generation of hotel computers.

It is standard procedure for the cashier to inquire about recent, unrecorded services in an effort to minimize late charges.

Once the bill is settled, the folios are stamped "paid" and initialed by the cashier. The validated guest copy is given to the patron. A busy cashier may delay making the entry on the front office cash sheet, but the bill must be posted immediately in order to serve as the guest's receipt.

Receipts on Account

A different procedure is followed when a guest who is not checking out makes a payment against the account. In this instance, the folio is not totaled and the guest copy is not given away as a receipt; a standard receipt form like figure 11.4 is used instead. Because there is always the possibility of late charges being overlooked by a guest who thinks the account is paid in full, employees try to dissuade guests from making early payments. In fact, day-early payments require special attention by the cashier, who must be certain to collect enough to cover the upcoming room night, room tax, and local telephone calls that will not be posted until the auditor arrives. So the employee tries to convince the guest to wait until the next day rather than paying in full the previous day in anticipation of an early departure. Naturally enough, guests who are so convinced find it incomprehensible that they are unable to conclude their business early the next morning as they prepare to checkout. There is a clerk on duty all right, but the safe where the valuables are stored is programmed to open several hours later.

Weekly payments are an infrequent but possible type of receipt on account. At the close of a week, the guest's copy of the folio is placed in the mailbox to indicate that the account is due. A new folio is opened and the balance is carried over from the previous card. (If appropriate, the "from bill number" and "to bill number" sections are completed.) When payment is received, a record is made on the receipts side of the cash sheet and the guest's copy of the previous week's folio is receipted. The credit posting actually appears on the folio of the second week.

Collections are also made within the week if the folio balance is unusually high or if the guest's charge activities are outside the norm.

Some city ledger collections are made at the front desk and these, too, are recorded on the receipts side of the cash sheet. If the city ledger is actually kept in the front office, it is possible to post such payments directly to the individual city account. It is more likely that the account is not in the front office, and the posting is made to the city ledger journal sheet instead (figure 13.9).

Sometimes all city ledger receipts are recorded on the front office cash sheet, even those received by mail. This is more apt to be the case with small hotels, which lack a full accounting staff and which use this means to show the complete accounting sequence. The general cashier of a large property has a journal to record incoming checks, whether city ledger payments or miscellaneous receipts, without running the transaction through the front office cash sheet. Figures from this journal are combined with the cashiers' reports to complete the daily deposit (figure 11.9).

Paid in Advance

Guests without luggage and those with light baggage may be asked to pay in advance for their accommodations. With one exception,

CASH CREDIT

24901

DATE_____ 19 _____

NAME   ROOM

ACKNOWLEDGEMENT IS MADE OF RECEIPT OF AMOUNT PRINTED BELOW.
THIS HAS BEEN CREDITED TO YOUR ACCOUNT.   THANK YOU.
CASHIER: – USE THIS RECEIPT IN THE FOLLOWING INSTANCES: –
(1) IN CASE GUEST DOES NOT PRESENT WEEKLY BILL TO BE RECEIPTED.
(2) PAYMENT TO APPLY ON ACCOUNT.
(3) ADVANCE PAYMENT.

(DO NOT WRITE IN ABOVE SPACE)

Kayco NCR Form No. 130

SIGNED_____

Figure 11.4. Cash credit slip used with posting machines as indicated on the form in (1), (2), or (3).

the procedure is much like a normal cash collection. Entries are made on both the front office cash sheet and the folio; but rather than wait for the night auditor the cashier sometimes posts the room charges and tax, if any. Then the completed folio is receipted and a copy is presented to the guest. The hotel's copy remains in the bucket overnight, filed according to room number. Although no posting is required of the night auditor, the guest is listed on the audit of the arrival night and counted as part of the room and house count, appearing on the departure list the following day. Other times the cashier does not post the room charge and the guest is given a receipt like that in figure 11.4. To get a copy of the receipted folio, the guest must return to the desk at check-out time.

Unless an additional deposit is made, no charges are allowed against a paid-in-advance guest, who usually leaves without stopping at the desk. An additional charge is made and collected each succeeding day the customer remains. Unless this is tendered, someone on the desk automatically checks out advance

payments by the check-out hour of the following day. Some of the economy motels, where all guests pay in advance, actually lock out guests who remain beyond the check-out hour. Less extreme measures, including telephone message lamps, are usually used to communicate with the paid-in-advance guest.

Unless all guests pay in advance, collections of this nature should not be viewed as cash sales. They are not similar, for example, to cash sales made to a patron in the dining room. Paid-in-advance rooms are merely collections of the account receivable in advance of rather than at the conclusion of the stay. Like other room sales, paid-in-advance is an account receivable sale.

Room sales are recorded daily by a debit to accounts receivable (increase) and a credit to room sales (increase). Cash is collected at the end of the stay and recorded with a debit to cash (increase) and a credit to accounts receivable (decrease). With paid-in-advance sales, only the sequence is reversed. The cash is received and the account receivable settled even before the guest occupies the room.

Reservation Deposits

Although advance deposits are not often requested, many hotels, particularly resorts during their busy season, require them to confirm reservations. The public accepts this as a reasonable way of doing business. That's why dishonored reservations that have been paid in advance generate irreparable hostility toward the hotel and its management. To the public, it's just not equitable.

Variations in processing reservation deposits are chiefly a function of hotel size. One way of handling these deposits is to keep the check in the front office drawer until the guest actually arrives some days or weeks later. The check is then applied to a newly opened folio as if the money were just received that day. This procedure simplifies the bookkeeping but has little additional merit even for a small hotel. Lack of a proper record and the failure to clear the check through the bank indicate poor management of both procedure and funds.

Sometimes the actual folio that is to be assigned to the guest upon arrival is opened when the deposit check is received. This procedure is impractical for prenumbered folios and is awkward for large properties. The new folio is kept as part of the city ledger in the back of the well. When the guest arrives, a room is assigned and the folio is refiled in room number sequence in the well. This procedure may be very satisfactory for a small property since there is a record of the transaction and the check is cleared as soon as it is received. The check appears on the front office cash sheet on the day it arrives and is deposited. Under the previous plan, the cash sheet entry does not take place until the day the guest arrives.

Still another method of handling deposits is to create a special city ledger folio called "advance deposits." Each advance deposit is recorded on the cash sheet and posted to this special account, which obviously carries a credit balance since the hotel owes money to the guest. The balance of this card appears daily as part of the night audit. When the guest arrives, the deposit is transferred from the master deposit account (by a debit transfer) to the guest's newly opened folio (as a credit transfer).

Under a similar and more widely used method, the advance deposit account is maintained in the city ledger by the accounting office rather than on a folio in the front office. Paid-in-advance reservations are flagged, usually by a colored reservation slip, to alert the room clerk, who marks the amount of the deposit on the registration card. The typist includes the figure on the folio heading and the cashier posts it as a transfer credit. It is the same transfer described above but is less obvious since the debit portion is not made by the cashier but by the accounting office. In machine-prepared folios, the credit is posted in red using the transfer key. The daily total of these credits is charged against the city ledger advance deposit account by the general accounting office on the following day. This procedure is in contrast to the individual debit postings of the previous system.

As an added safeguard, the reservation office sends notices of each advance deposit to the accounting office and to the cashier's cage, where they are filed by anticipated date of arrival. Each day's list is compared to the actual arrivals, and oversights are corrected. At the close of the day the individual reservation notices, which should agree in total to the credit transfers, are returned to the accounting office by the cashier. These notices are matched to the original notices forwarded to the accounting office by the reservation department at the time the deposit was confirmed. Deposits applied that day become the basis of the city ledger transfer entry. Unclaimed deposit notices then serve as a subsidiary list to the advance deposit control account in the city ledger.

Regardless of which procedure is used, cash received through the mail must be recorded. The reservation office prepares a daily list of checks received. As with city ledger collections, these advance receipts enter the bank deposit either through the front office cash sheet or through the journal of the general cashier. Receipts from travel agents are treated similarly, as the discussion on travel agencies in chapter 13 indicates.

A computer system may or may not be simpler. If the reservation and accounting programs are interfaced, the deposit, which was being carried in the reservation program, is merely switched to the accounting program. Immediately the guest folio is updated with the deposit credit. If the two programs are not interfaced, and many are not, the transfer requires the same mechanical steps as a noncomputerized system. The reservation list, including deposits, is printed daily. Each deposit must be identified individually with each arrival and entered into the accounting program. This is not much different from the hand accounting procedure.

Miscellaneous Receipts

The front office of a small hotel may be the depository for cash from sources other than receivable collections. All kinds of monies are routed through the small front office simply because of convenience. The front office cashier might serve as dining room or bar cashier. Magazines, newspapers, and cigars may be sold across the desk. Coin collections from vending machines or sales of miscellaneous items, such as kitchen fat, and container deposits may all flow through the front desk. Meal tickets in American plan resorts are sometimes sold at the desk. It is simply a question of separating the cash flow on the front office cash sheet into sales (such as the newsstand), collections on account (such as checkouts), and miscellaneous income (vending machines).

Similarly, other cashiers may deposit their funds at the front office rather than at the accounting office. Although this is obviously not front office receipts, it is sometimes shown on the cash sheet just for the record. In this instance, the front office cashier merely acts for the general or chief cashier, both as a depository and as the source of original record.

Paid-outs — House Expenses

Just as the front office cashier handles cash receipts from miscellaneous sources, petty expenditures for house expenses may be made there as well. And just as some of the cash coming into the desk may not actually be receipts, some of the cash flowing out from the desk may not be treated as paid-outs. On the one hand, the front office cashier acts as a depository for the general cashier and, on the other hand, acts as the general cashier's disbursing agent. When the front office cashier is the intermediary for house paid-outs, the front office bank is reimbursed at the end of the shift. This trade-off (the disbursement voucher for a cash reimbursement) requires no entry on the front office cash sheet and no posting in the machine or the computer.

The person receiving the money signs a petty cash voucher (figure 11.5), which is kept in the drawer as if it were cash. It is cash because the general cashier "buys" the voucher with money from the petty cash fund, thereby reimbursing the front office bank. The transaction "washes out," leaving the front office bank as it would have been had the petty expenditure not been processed through the desk. The petty cash voucher is then in the general cashier's petty cash fund, where it would have been had the transaction been handled there initially.

Reimbursement of the front office bank could take place daily as part of the turn-in, or the front office cashiers themselves could hold the *imprest petty cash fund*, as this system is

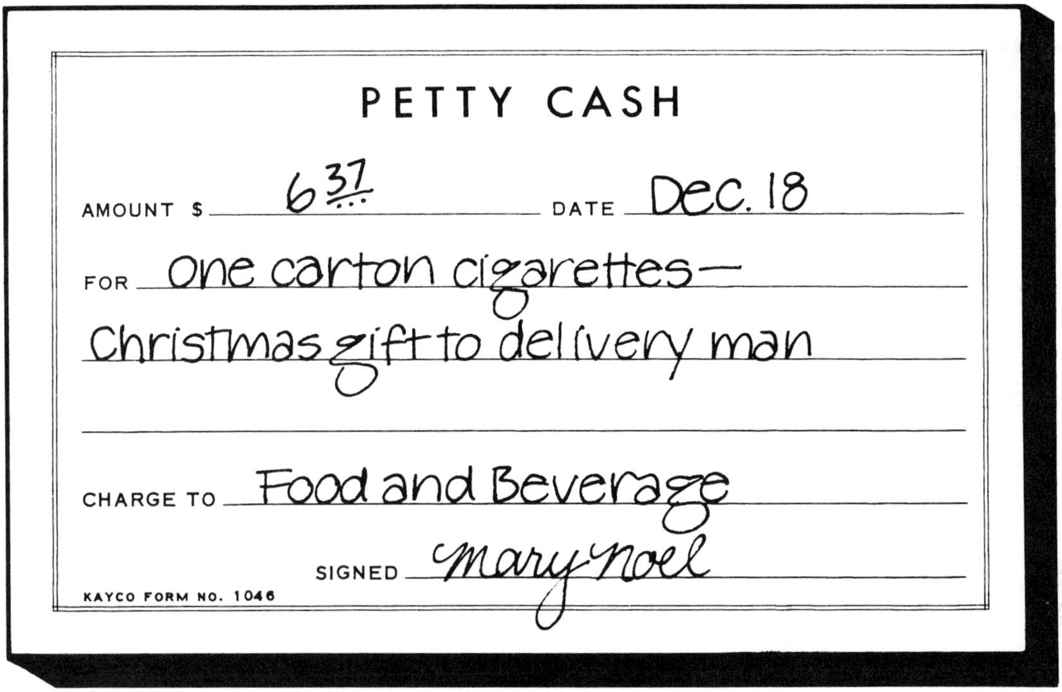

PETTY CASH

AMOUNT $ ___6 37___ DATE ___Dec. 18___

FOR ___One carton cigarettes — Christmas gift to delivery man___

CHARGE TO ___Food and Beverage___

SIGNED ___Mary Noel___

KAYCO FORM NO. 1046

Figure 11.5. Typical petty cash voucher for use with imprest petty cash fund system.

called. House vouchers would then be accumulated and kept in the drawer as part of the cash count. Weekly, biweekly, or monthly a check would be issued by the general cashier to the front office cashiers — or one cashier could buy the vouchers of all the others daily — for the total of the house vouchers. Issuing the check gives rise to the accounting entry by which the petty cash disbursements are placed in the books of account. No intermediate petty cash bank is used when the front office bank is itself the imprest petty cash fund.

Using another procedure, paid-outs for house expenses are recorded in the same manner as paid-outs for guests. An entry is made on the front office cash sheet in addition to the signed petty cash voucher. Although there is no difference in the actual cash flow between the methods, there is a difference in the recordkeeping. With this method the paid-out entry originates on the front office cash sheet daily instead of in the petty cash fund periodically.

House expenses range from normal petty items to payroll disbursements for terminated employees or those authorized to draw advances on their salaries. Some freight bills need immediate cash payment under ICC regulations. Stamp purchases, cash purchases from local farmers or purveyors, and other payments are handled through the front office of a small hotel.

THE CASHIER'S REPORT

Each cashier, whether at the front office or at one of the bars or dining rooms, makes a daily cash report and a deposit with the general cashier. These reports are audited and the total cash received is combined in a daily deposit. Thus funds received by the cashiers during the day are audited through the night audit and again the following morning by the income auditor before finding their way to a bank deposit.

Preparing the Report

The front office cash report is more complex than that of the dining room or bar because of the variety of transactions handled there. Departmental cashiers are reporting only cash sales, so both the recordkeeping and the cash proof are simpler.

The Bank

Each cashier receives and signs for a permanent supply of cash, called the *bank*. The amount varies depending on the position and shift that the cashier has. A busy commercial hotel needs front office banks of as much as $10,000, but the night cashier at the same hotel might get along with $250. It is partly a question of safety and partly a question of good financial management. Excessive funds should not be tied up unnecessarily; temporary increases can be made for busy periods. A careful review of all house banks may release sizable sums for more profitable use. Laventhol & Horwath report the total of house banks and cash on hand at about 2.0 percent of total sales, or about $600 per room. An excessive percentage suggests that cashiers are borrowing from their banks or that daily deposits and reimbursements are not being made, which means that extra funds are required to operate the banks. There are other reasons, of course—infrequent reimbursement of the petty cash fund, for example.

Cashiers lock their banks in the safe or hotel vault (figure 6.10) after each shift. Funds may not be taken from the bank for personal use. Surprise counts are made by the accounting office on these banks by taping the box closed and requiring the cashier coming on duty to summon an auditor before opening the box. Everyone handling money should be covered by a bond, which is written for individual positions or as a blanket coverage depending on the amount and kind of insurance that best meets the needs of the company. Unfortunately, common banks for several employees to share are not unusual. These are seen in every department from the bar to the front office. Control is difficult to maintain and responsibility almost impossible to fix. Custom and convenience seem to be the major reasons for continuing this poor practice, although it obviously releases extra funds as well.

The bank must contain enough small bills and silver to carry out the cashiering function. There is absolutely no value in having a $300 bank comprised of three $100 bills.

For the illustration that follows, assume a bank of $600.

Net Receipts

Net receipts is the difference between what the cashier took in and what was paid out. Since only front office cashiers are permitted to make advances, net receipts in the bar and coffee shop are the same as total receipts. Net receipts at the front office are computed by subtracting total advances, city and transient, from total receipts, city and transient. House paid-outs and miscellaneous receipts are not included, although they might be in some hotels as explained earlier.

For discussion, assume the totals of the front office cash sheet to be:

Receipts	
Transient Receivables	$ 900.30
City Receivables	190.00
Total	$1,090.30

Paid-outs			Should Have on Hand	
Transient Paid-outs	$ 40.00		Bank	$ 600.00
			Net Receipts	1,050.30
Total	$ 40.00		Total	$1,650.30

Net receipts: $1,050.30 ($1,090.30 − $40.00).

Does Have on Hand	
Checks	$1,158.30
Currency	310.00
Coins	182.11
Total	$1,650.41

Over and Short

No cashier is perfect, and the day's close occasionally finds the cash drawer over or short. Sometimes the error is mathematical and either the cashier finds it without help, or it is uncovered later by the auditor. (It is essential that the bank be verified when a report that is supposedly in balance is opened to question by the subsequent discovery of an error in the paperwork.) Errors caused by poor change-making techniques are usually beyond remedy except when the guest complains that the change received was for a smaller bill than was actually tendered. Restitution is possible if the cash count proves this to be so at the close of the shift.

Overages and shortages become a point of employee–management contention when cashiers are required to make up all shortages but turn in all overages. Other systems allow overages to offset shortages, asking only that each day's record balance. Both procedures encourage the cashier to reconcile at the expense of the customer. Shortchanging, poor addition, and altered records accommodate these management requirements. It is a better policy to have the house absorb the shortages and keep the overages. A record of individual performance is then maintained to determine if individual overages and shortages balance over the long run, as they should.

Over and short is the difference between what the cashier should have in the cash drawer and what is actually there. It is a comparison of a mathematical computation and the physical count of the money.

Overage: $0.11 ($1,650.41 − $1,650.30).

The cashier *should* have the sum of the bank and the net receipts. What money is on hand in the drawer is what the cashier *does* have. Over and short is the difference between the *should* and the *does*.

The cashier of our illustration has more in the drawer than should be there; thus, an 11 cent overage. If the amount on hand were less than it should be, say the count was $1,650 rather than $1,650.41, there would be a shortage of 30 cents ($1,650.30 *should have* minus $1,650.00 *does have*).

Turn-in

Each cashier begins the shift of each new day with an exact bank, and everything in excess of the bank is turned in to the accounting office at the close of the day. Except for the front office, each cashier closes the watch by retaining the bank and turning in everything else. This turn-in is compared to the cash register reading, which is usually taken by the night auditor, to determine overage or shortage. Some properties have cashiers total their own register or tally the checks to determine overage or shortage, but this procedure obviously reduces the effectiveness of internal control. A register that is used by several shifts must be totaled or subtotaled between cashiers.

The procedure differs at the front office where the bank is used to cash checks, make change, and advance cash as well as accept receipts. Assume, for example, that nothing took place during the watch except check cashing. At the close of the day the bank would contain nothing but nonnegotiable checks. It would be impossible to function the following day with a drawer full of guests' personal checks. So all the checks are turned in even though there are no net receipts and even though the dollar value of the bank is intact.

Turn-in involves every type of nonnegotiable money in the broadest sense of the term, including checks, traveler's checks, foreign funds, large bills, casino chips, cash in poor condition, and vouchers for house expenses, including refund slips for inoperative vending machines. (As explained previously, house vouchers are treated here as loans to the general cashier and are converted into cash from the petty cash fund.) If the total of all these items is still less than the net receipts of the day, enough cash is added to clear the drawer of all funds except the original bank. Were all the transactions of the day in cash only, the front office turn-in is simply the amount in excess of the bank, as it is with the other departments.

Our continuing illustration helps explain the turn-in. The only unusable funds in the drawer are the checks of $1,158.30. These are turned in. Since the remaining currency and coin total less than the original bank ($600), no cash is included in the turn-in. Cash would be included if the currency and coin totaled more than the bank. Phrased another way: check turn-in (including traveler's checks) exceeds net receipts so there is no reason to add additional cash.

Since the cashier always retains the exact bank, it is apparent that the turn-in includes the overage or allows for the shortage.

Due Bank

Turning in all the checks ($1,158.30) leaves the bank with only the cash ($492.11). But $492.11 is less than the original bank of $600. The front office cashier requests the return of the excessive turn-in. It is excessive because the net receipts of the day were only $1,050.30 in contrast to the $1,158.30 turned in. This spread between the net receipts and the turn-in is known as the *due bank*; it is also called the *due back*, the *difference returnable, U-owe-me's,* or the *exchange*.

Simply computed, when the exchange is added to the cash in the drawer, the bank should be reestablished at its original value. The bank is exactly right at the $600 of the example:

Due Bank Computation

Cash on Hand	$492.11
Due Back	107.89
Original Bank	$600.00

The fact that the due back allows for overages and shortages is made apparent in the following formula:

Due Back = Turn-In − (Net Receipts ±
$$\text{Over or Short})$$
Due Back = $1,158.30 − ($1,050.30 + $0.11)
Due Back = $1,158.30 − ($1,050.41)
Due Back = $107.89

This formula produces the very same answer.

To keep their banks functional, cashiers will specify the coin and currency denominations of the due bank. There is little utility in a due bank of several large bills. For the very same reason, the turn-in may be increased with large bills to be exchanged for more negotia-

```
Given:
      1. THE BANK AT $500
      2. THE FRONT OFFICE CASH SHEET SHOWS:
            Cash Receipts $444        Cash Advances $25
      3. COUNT IN THE CASH DRAWER AT THE CLOSE OF THE WATCH:
            Checks                        $403.99
            Currency                       390.00
            Coin                           109.00
            House Vouchers                  15.00
                                         _____
                                          $917.99

Computation:
      1. NET RECEIPTS (Gross Receipts Minus Advances)
            N.R. = $444 − $25 = $419
      2. OVERAGE AND SHORTAGE (What Should be in the Drawer
         Minus What is in the Drawer)
            O&S = ($500 + $419) − $917.99 = $1.01 Short
      3. TURN IN (Checks, Vouchers, Other Nonnegotiable Items
         and All Cash Except the Bank)
            T.I. = $403.99 + $15 = $418.99
      4. EXCHANGE (Amount Needed to Reconstitute the Bank)
            Ex = $500 − ($390 + $109) = $1.00
      5. VERIFICATION (The Excess of the Turn In Over the
         Amount Due)
            Ex = $418.99 − ($419 − $1.01) = $1.00
```

Figure 11.6. Preparation of the front office cashier's report (figure 11.7) requires an understanding of the computations.

able currency. More often, the change is made with the general cashier before the shift closes.

Figures 11.6 and 11.7 offer another example of the due bank and illustrate the completed cash envelope.

Foreign Funds

Foreign currency is not widely accepted in the United States; it has nothing near the degree of acceptability that the greenback has had worldwide. In contrast, tourists in countries behind the iron curtain may be required to make a daily exchange of various amounts into local currency. Even the Canadian dollar, with its stability and similarity of value, experiences exchange problems as it moves away from the Canadian–American border. But international tourism is increasing at an amazing rate with the full potential still years away. More and more foreign currencies are being tendered across the hotel desk and more and more hotel companies are developing language and exchange facilities to encourage the flow of foreign visitors and foreign funds. Exchange procedures are improving as individual hotels and agencies like the United States Travel and Tourism Administration begin to recognize the advantages of international tourism.

As of now, however, few American hotels accept foreign exchange. When they do, it is taken mainly to settle accounts, although

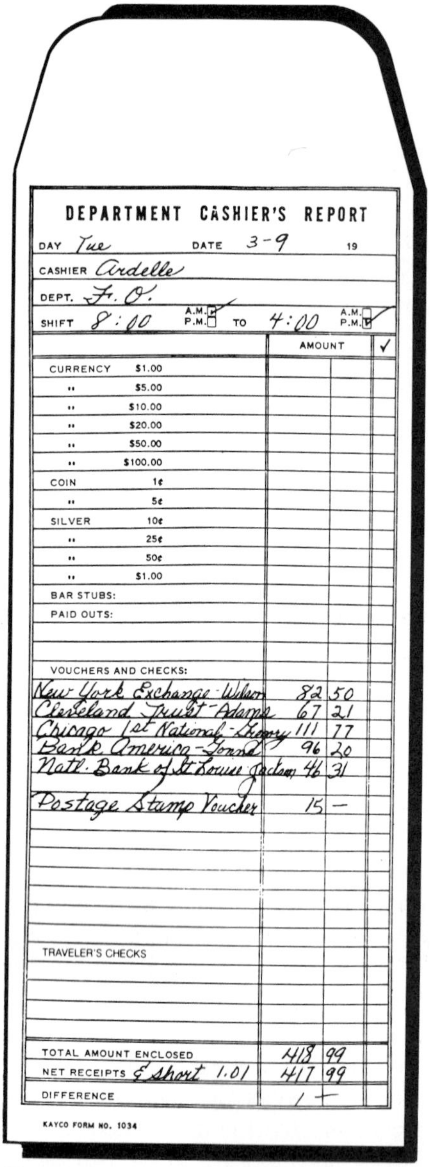

DEPARTMENT CASHIER'S REPORT

DAY *Tue* DATE *3-9* 19

CASHIER *Ardelle*

DEPT. *F.O.*

SHIFT *8:00* A.M. ☑ P.M. ☐ TO *4:00* A.M. ☐ P.M. ☑

	AMOUNT		✓
CURRENCY $1.00			
" $5.00			
" $10.00			
" $20.00			
" $50.00			
" $100.00			
COIN 1¢			
" 5¢			
SILVER 10¢			
" 25¢			
" 50¢			
" $1.00			
BAR STUBS:			
PAID OUTS:			
VOUCHERS AND CHECKS:			
New York Exchange-Wilson	*82*	*50*	
Cleveland Trust-Adams	*67*	*21*	
Chicago 1st National-Livony	*111*	*77*	
Bank America-Jones	*96*	*20*	
Natl. Bank of St Louis-Jackson	*46*	*31*	
Postage Stamp Voucher	*15*	*—*	
TRAVELER'S CHECKS			
TOTAL AMOUNT ENCLOSED	*418*	*99*	
NET RECEIPTS *Short 1.01*	*417*	*99*	
DIFFERENCE	*1*	*—*	

KAYCO FORM NO. 1034

Figure 11.7. Cashier's envelope for preparing the turn-in at the close of each shift.

sometimes, as a service, hotels will exchange United States currency for foreign funds (figure 11.8). Typically, both domestic and foreign hotels make the exchange at something less than the official rate. Even the official rate provides a spread between income and expense. Money brokers quote both a sell rate and a buy rate. Similarly, the hotel buys at a lower rate and sells to the broker at a higher rate. We might buy Nod dollars (₦), for example, at, say, 25 cents less than we sell them for, although the official spread might be only 15 cents.

The extra spread between buy and sell, which may be supplemented by an exchange fee, allows a small profit to be applied against bank charges for exchange or to offset unexpected variations in foreign currency value. The latter makes it especially important to process foreign currency quickly and to include it in the turn-in of every day. Obtaining daily quotes and avoiding banks that are not brokers themselves (rather, just middlemen) will maximize foreign exchange profits. In fact, the hotel could become an intermediary broker by also converting funds for taxi drivers, bellpersons, and servers throughout the community in addition to its own personnel. Of course, this opens a whole new business with the large risks that accompany foreign exchange.

Since it is not desirable to inventory foreign money, few hotels provide for the reconversion of American funds into foreign currency as the visitor prepares to go home.

It is a great help to the cashier if the accounting office furnishes a table of values for each major currency. (Several airlines quote rates, including foreign traveler's checks, as part of their res system service.) If this is not possible because values fluctuate over a wide range, a daily or even hourly quote is necessary to prevent substantial losses from certain currency exchanges. More likely, the hotel will just refuse that particular currency.

Canadian currency poses less of a problem than most other kinds. It is similar in form, divisions, and value to the American dollar. Consequently, hotels close to the border have accepted Canadian dollars at a par with the

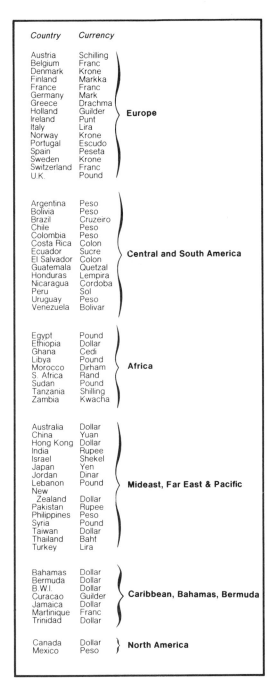

Country	Currency	
Austria	Schilling	
Belgium	Franc	
Denmark	Krone	
Finland	Markka	
France	Franc	
Germany	Mark	
Greece	Drachma	
Holland	Guilder	Europe
Ireland	Punt	
Italy	Lira	
Norway	Krone	
Portugal	Escudo	
Spain	Peseta	
Sweden	Krone	
Switzerland	Franc	
U.K.	Pound	
Argentina	Peso	
Bolivia	Peso	
Brazil	Cruzeiro	
Chile	Peso	
Colombia	Peso	
Costa Rica	Colon	
Ecuador	Sucre	Central and South America
El Salvador	Colon	
Guatemala	Quetzal	
Honduras	Lempira	
Nicaragua	Cordoba	
Peru	Sol	
Uruguay	Peso	
Venezuela	Bolivar	
Egypt	Pound	
Ethiopia	Dollar	
Ghana	Cedi	
Libya	Pound	
Morocco	Dirham	Africa
S. Africa	Rand	
Sudan	Pound	
Tanzania	Shilling	
Zambia	Kwacha	
Australia	Dollar	
China	Yuan	
Hong Kong	Dollar	
India	Rupee	
Israel	Shekel	
Japan	Yen	
Jordan	Dinar	
Lebanon	Pound	
New Zealand	Dollar	Mideast, Far East & Pacific
Pakistan	Rupee	
Philippines	Peso	
Syria	Pound	
Taiwan	Dollar	
Thailand	Baht	
Turkey	Lira	
Bahamas	Dollar	
Bermuda	Dollar	
B.W.I.	Dollar	
Curacao	Guilder	Caribbean, Bahamas, Bermuda
Jamaica	Dollar	
Martinique	Franc	
Trinidad	Dollar	
Canada	Dollar	North America
Mexico	Peso	

Figure 11.8. The world's currencies. Conversion rates for major currencies are quoted daily in local newspapers and the *Wall Street Journal.*

American dollar.[1] Although this practice sometimes involves a small exchange cost to the hotel, it has been a good advertising and public relations gimmick that has more than offset the expense.

Let's see what needs to be done when a guest from the Land of Nod tenders a ₦1,000 bill in payment of a $34 account. Each ₦ (Nod dollar) is exchanged at 5 cents United States money by the hotel although the official rate may be somewhat higher, say 5.1 cents. The ₦1,000 is exchanged at $50, which is $1 less than the official rate of exchange. The cashier would return $16 United States in exchange for the ₦1,000 and the charge of $34. If on the other hand, the guest had offered only a ₦500 bill, the cashier would have collected an additional $9 United States to settle the $34 account in full.

When payment is made by foreign check, the hotel makes an additional charge, passing on to the guest the bank's fee for foreign exchange. The amount of the fee is a function of both the size of the check and the variation in the rate of exchange.

Cities with large numbers of foreign tourists, New York, Las Vegas, and Miami among them, have established exchange facilities. Private in ownership, they have been supported by local tourist bureaus and chambers of commerce. These allow the hotel to service the guest with a reasonable ceiling on costs. A national clearing house for travel agencies has facilitated exchange there as well. Travel agencies have two needs. Commission checks from abroad need to be cashed and payments in domestic currency need to be sent overseas for foreign accommodations.

The Other Banks

Until now, the patron who pays cash for meals and drinks has been largely ignored. Whereas

1. Currency values fluctuate, which is the real problem with foreign exchange, and at the time of this writing, Canadian dollars are worth less than American dollars.

the record of the charge customer goes to the front desk for posting to the folio, the record of the cash customer remains with the departmental cashier (food, beverage, etc.) until the turn-in.

Unlike the front office, no advances, house paid-outs, or cashed checks are handled by the departmental cashiers. Therefore, total receipts are net receipts and the turn-in is always in cash except for an occasional traveler's check or credit card vouchers. Promotional vouchers, or chits, and tour coupons are other exceptions. Although departmental cashiers could use exchange to keep their banks manageable, they usually buy bills or rolls of coins from other cashiers during the day. Thus the main computation is over and short and this is not really computed.

Unless the cash register needs to be cleared between shifts, the cashier normally has no knowledge of the amount of cash due. Instead, the bank is counted out and retained. What is left is counted and turned in to the general cashier. The register tapes are accumulated later to be verified against the turn-in. This job is done by the auditing office.

Departmental cashiers cannot always bring their envelopes to the chief cashier, so a drop box at the front office is used instead. This practice gives the departmental cashier a witness, who signs a receipt form or book certifying that the departmental cashier did in fact deposit the envelope. The content of the envelope is not certified, merely its deposit. Lacking this type of protection, at least two members of the accounting department would need to empty the box to verify the envelopes therein.

An identical problem exists when the manager drops the day's receipts into the commercial bank's night depository. Without witnesses, the manager may subject the funds to an "Exculpatory Clause," which frees the bank of liability if the money isn't there the next

morning. Enforceable in some states and not in others, losses from this paragraph of the depository contract can be protected by extending the bonding coverage.

Tip Advances

A slightly different procedure is needed if the departmental cashiers advance tips to the waiters and waitresses for charge guests whose bills are recorded on the front office folio. As mentioned before, this procedure is designed to minimize traffic to the front office. Both the departmental charge and the tip advance are posted by the front office billing clerk from the signed restaurant (bar) check. The charge is posted to the department and the tip is posted to a tip designation that is separated from cash advances (tips) made by front office cashiers. The tip, which is paid to the server by the departmental cashier, is obviously not recorded on the front office cash sheet. It must, therefore, be separated from items on the folio that are recorded on and eventually reconciled to the front office cash sheet.

The cash advance voucher, which the server signs, is enclosed by the restaurant (bar) cashier as part of the cash turn-in to the general cashier. It is counted as cash for reconciling the amount due but recorded on the cash summary sheet (prepared by the general cashier) as an advance to receivables since the cash is not included as part of the day's deposit (figure 11.9, S. Gold).

Preparing the Deposit
Refunding the Due Bank

The daily bank deposit is comprised of yesterday's total net receipts plus or minus overages or shortages. As previously noted, front office cashiers often turn in more than these net receipts plus or minus overages and shortages. This excess (due back) is not for deposit but must be returned to the cashiers in a more negotiable form.

CASHIER'S NAME	DEP'T	CASH SALES	COLLECTIONS FROM RECEIVABLES		TOTAL RECEIPTS	ADVANCES TO RECEIVABLES		NET CASH RECEIPTS	PLUS OVERAGES MINUS (SHORTAGES)	TURN IN FOR DEPOSIT
			TRANSIENT	CITY		TRANSIENT	CITY			
Al White	Front Office		540 —	26 —	586 —	38 —		548 —	(1 —)	547 —
H Blue	Front Office		695 —	31 —	726 —	42 —		684 —	03	684 03
N Green	Front Office	566 —	1020 —		1020 —			1020 —	(21)	1019 79
J Black	Bar	3960 40			566 —			566 —		566 —
G Gold	Lounge	1822 20			3960 40	6 —		3960 40		3960 40
S Brown	Dining Room				1822 20			1822 20	1 42	1823 62
		11 44 60	2275 —	57	3476 60	86 —		3390 60	24	3390 84

Figure 11.9. Cash receipts summary recaps the records of all cashiers and serves as the basis for the daily bank deposit. It also serves as a worksheet for the daily entry into the books of account.

After each of the cash reports and envelopes has been verified, the general cashier refunds the excess to the front office cashiers. These funds are taken from the cash turn-in provided by the various dining rooms and bars. One might visualize the general cashier "selling" the excess turn-in checks to the cash-rich envelopes of the bars and dining rooms. The cash thus generated for the front office envelopes is used as due bank. Once this procedure has been completed, smaller bills and change can be made from the special change bank maintained by the general cashier and the whole is returned to the front office at the start of the new shift.

Refunding the House Vouchers

In a similar manner, the general cashier "sells" the house vouchers that are in the envelopes of the front office cashiers to the petty cash fund, a special cash reserve maintained by the general cashier. The cash is placed in the front office envelopes and becomes part of the deposit. This procedure is not necessary when policy requires all house expenses to go through the petty cash fund initially. Then no house expenditures are made at the front office.

Listing the Checks

A check list is prepared in support of each day's deposit. Each check is identified by the bank on which it is written, including the transit number that appears on the upper right corner of the check, the maker, the date, the payee, and the endorsers, if any. All checks are endorsed with a "For Deposit Only" stamp by the front office as soon as they are received. The value of each check is listed and the total should agree with the daily deposit. A complete listing of this type speeds the search for lost and returned checks.

The general cashier usually prepares the check list as part of the deposit, but in some properties lists are prepared by each cashier. The list would be computer-prepared if the software was programmed to accept the data (transit number, maker, etc.) when each check was presented for processing.

Completing the Summary Sheet

Whether forwarded directly or routed through the front office, all cash receipts find their way to the accounting office in the person of the general or chief cashier. So long as there are only a few cashiers, the deposit can be prepared directly from the cashiers' reports. As the staff grows larger, it becomes desirable to summarize the many reports and use the summary both as a means for preparing the bank deposit and as a worksheet for preparing the entry in the cash receipts journal.

Figure 11.9 illustrates a typical cash receipts summary form. As seen there, front office cashiers generate no cash sales unless they are responsible for sales outside the realm of the front office, such as newsstand sales or collections from the dining rooms. In turn, departmental cashiers generate no account receivable entries, since they neither collect from nor advance to accounts receivable. All departmental transactions are for cash. The exception to this is tip advances that the departmental cashiers might pay to employees, and these appear as advances to guests on the summary sheet. All this information is illustrated by figure 11.9. It is also apparent from the figure that the hotel absorbs both cash overages and shortages since the deposit is the net of both.

Accountingwise, the deposit is a debit to cash (increase), a credit to the various departmental incomes (increase) for the cash sales, a credit to accounts receivable (decrease) for the net figure of collections and advances, and a debit or credit to short or over.

Cash and cash transactions are becoming obsolete. Credit cards, debit cards, and instant electronic communications are returning us to that time before the ninth century when paper money was introduced. Credit and credit procedures have become more important to the front office than cash and cash procedures, as we shall see in the next chapter.

QUERIES AND PROBLEMS

1. Segments of two hand-prepared folios are given for April 1. Each guest checks out today; each settles the account with cash. Complete the April 1st column for each folio and explain what other forms or records the front office cashier uses for each. (Guest B requests and receives a $4 allowance as part of the final settlement.) Why does Guest A have a room charge, but Guest B does not?

	Guest A	Guest B
Opening Balance	298	82
Rooms	22	
Food		12
Beverage		
Telephone		
Cash Advance	10	
Valet		
Parking	6	
Transfers		
Total Debits		
Cash		
Allowances		
Transfers		
Closing Balance		

2. An international guest tenders $171 in U.S. funds and ₢#2000 from his native land to settle an outstanding account of $206.20. ₢#'s are being purchased by the hotel for 51.50 per U.S. dollar. What must the cashier do now to settle the account? Assume the guest has more American dollars; assume he or she doesn't.

3. Sketch and complete a cashier's envelope for October 11 showing the details of the turn-in and the amount of due-back. (City ledger collections are handled by the accounting office. No provisions are made for cash over or short; the cashier covers both.)

Given:

House bank	$1,800
Advances to guests	$181.15
House vouchers	$ 16.20
Vending machine refunds	$0.50
Collections from guests	$7,109.40
Cash in the drawer exclusive of other cash listings	$1,721.00
Traveler's checks	$2,675
Personal checks:	
Washington	$75.25
Lincoln	310.00
Jefferson	44.98
Carter	211.90
Kennedy	55.00
Others	1,876.85
One-hundred dollar bills	10 each
Torn and dirty currency	$62
Silver	$680.14

4. (a) Prepare a bank deposit slip for the morning of February 15th from the cash reports summarized below. Exchange is always handled in cash if possible. (b) In general journal form, prepare a cash receipts journal entry.

Given:

Cashier	Turn-in	Over (Short)	Cash Sales	Accounts Receivable Advances	Collections
Abel	43,060.00	(4.00)		756.00	43,820.00
Baker	8,263.98	(.12)	8,264.10		
Charleen	933.86		933.86		
Davis	21,800.88			19.00	17,350.88
Evans	9,116.26	16.00		800.70	9,400.50
Frankl	2,626.00		2,626.00		
Gray	64.00	(9.00)			73.00

12

Credit and Credit Procedures

Social and economic reasons set the stage for the credit revolution that began during the latter half of the 1900s. Credit in innkeeping predates the phenomenon by centuries and, like today's traveler's checks, was founded on the need for safety and security. Colonial and Roman innkeepers issued tokens that they would redeem on demand. Still earlier, knights used their signet rings in wax to guarantee payment and free them from the need to carry coins along the dangerous byways inhabited by highwaymen.

A CREDIT SOCIETY

Credit today is more than a way of life for American business; it is the American way of life. Some 90 percent of American business is done by check; credit card transactions may be as numerous as one hundred billion annually. Cash for service rendered is out of step with the times and especially with the cashless society that many foresee developing through interlocking computer and banking systems.

Several changes have coincided with the widespread use of credit in buying. Sales volume has increased because customers are able to spend what they have not yet earned. Unfortunately, a large part of the increase has been among the marginal credit risks, where losses run highest. This change has been accompanied by a general easing of credit standards made possible by new social attitudes toward credit. Debt is no longer a sin nor debtlessness a virtue. Debtor's prisons are not only illegal today but also socially inconceivable. Wage garnishees face the same extinction. Recent federal limitations on credit bureaus and agencies emphasize the new direction. Interest charged by hotels falls under these credit regulations, including those on full disclosure. Socio-legal changes favor the customer. No longer is credit a privilege granted by the seller; it is almost an inherent right of the buyer.

The hotel/motel industry is no exception to this new pattern. Estimates put credit card charges between one-third and three-fourths of total food and beverage business. Since resort and roadside properties depend less on credit cards, these average figures are achieved only by attributing 75 percent and up of volume in urban commercial hotels to credit card charges.

Total figures are staggering. Over 3 million establishments stand ready to accept the major charge cards from an estimated 150 million cardholders worldwide, and in so doing ring up some $175 billion in sales each year just in the United States. Figures are so fluid, information so proprietary, and food sales between hotels and restaurants so intertwined, that specific industry figures are estimates at best. Such estimates suggest the volume of credit card usage to be increasing at 10 percent per year. That certainly is in keeping with general trends. An increasing amount of travel agency volume is being reported on credit cards. Everyone is searching for new marketing gimmicks. Associations, for example, have begun to accept credit card charges to encourage early convention registration. This will probably mean greater convention attendance and thus a higher demand for hotel accommodations.

Interestingly enough, individual hotel/motel credit systems have declined. Beginning in the half decade of the early 1970s, many hotel chains — Sheraton, Loews, Marriott, and Treadway among them — went out of the credit card business. Costs of administration were high, as was the cost of money, and many other broad-based cards were finding more general acceptance. More than ten years earlier, Hilton had gone through a similar experience. Between 1959 and 1962, Hilton converted all of its credit cards twice: once to Carte Blanche for all Hilton and Statler card holders; and once back again to company cards only.

Only Holiday Inns appear to be bucking the trend, having reentered the credit card market with a preferred card for designated corporate executives. Their timing — during the economic doldrums of the early 1980s — suggests that the move was marketing driven, rather than financially sound. Generally, the hotel industry has been relieved that outside agencies have preempted the field of credit cards. Unfortunately, their appearance has coincided with a rising level of bad debts, which has increased faster than both room rates and room sales and at almost twice the rate of accounts receivable. Credit has been overextended; bad debts have increased; capital has been tied up in accounts receivable; and a larger portion of resources have been assigned to credit administration, including legal expenses, collection agencies, and management time. As an expense per occupied room, credit card commissions cost about $250 annually.[1]

Hotel credit and collection was deemphasized somewhat as the industry removed itself from the credit card business. The situation had changed. Questions that once dealt with the advisability of extending credit gave way to those dealing with the best means of minimizing losses and maximizing the marketing advantages of a credit system that was already here. For example, most of the reference guides, the *Red Book* included, list credit card data in their property descriptions and advertising.

Once again the pendulum is swinging back as industry managers take cognizance of their individual responsibility for controlling credit. And that management of credit begins at the front desk, where policies and procedures are put to the acid test. Before examining these in detail, let us review the direction in which our credit society is moving.

1. Laventhol & Horwath, *U.S. Lodging Industry,* 1981 (Philadelphia, 1981), p. 59.

A Credit Card Smorgasbord

A "family of products" is the terminology being used to explain the evolution of money and credit into a series of new products, none of which is either money or credit. Given impetus by the electronic age and the deregulation of banking, a new "transfer of value" business is emerging from the marriage of old banking systems and new credit card usages. Once there was barter, and then there was money; now there is credit, and soon there'll be debits. New traveler's checks and electronic fund transfers add to the buffet's variety.

The very segmentation of the marketplace that we are witnessing in the hotel business is taking place in the credit markets: debit cards and credit cards; regular cards and gold cards; free cards and fee cards; even cash is being used. Higher credit card fees have made cash popular with buyers who are able to negotiate higher discounts for cash from merchants who must otherwise pay high discount fees to the credit card companies. The trend has gained momentum from the formation of cash-buyer clubs, which have formalized the process with store directories, membership cards, and window decals.

A shakedown of product line began as soon as the banks started charging for credit cards. Customer needs were more sharply delineated than ever before. Credit cards are used as much for the convenience of buying without cash as for the extension of credit. The trend is very apparent: nearly 50 percent of all credit card users pay the statement within the grace period. Accepting convenience, not credit, as the major attraction for the cards provides a good rationale for the progressive development of electronic banking systems, interstate banking/credit hook-ups, and even external kiosks in hotel lobbies for a variety of financial services.

The Expanded Credit Card

Inflation — at a higher rate and for a longer period than Americans have ever experienced before — has produced a sophisticated consumer who knows the costs and benefits of the many financial services being proffered. Intense competition to attract that buyer has broadened the expectations of the user and produced an expanded credit card. The process is well under way, but is really an intermediate step to a new type of card and a new definition of what the card is and does.

MasterCard and Visa (bank cards) are now charging to issue cards. Although the fee is not as high, the bank cards are now more like the travel and entertainment cards (T&Es) of American Express and Diners. Although bank card fees have driven away many users, they have also brought the two classes of card into more direct competition. Adding to the rivalry is an effort by the bank cards to enter the affluent markets long held by the T&E cards. They have done this with new names like gold card and affluent card. Note the similarity to Ramada's move to Renaissance Hotels and Holiday Inns' new Crowne Plaza chain.

Adding new fees requires new services. Among these is the guaranteed reservation service that earlier chapters reviewed. There is an obvious impact here on the hotel's front office. Other services of the expanded credit card may or may not be reflected in the management decisions of the front office. Cardholders, who now get cash from banking machines, may turn to front office cashiers. Similar decisions may come from the removal of dollar limits on certain cards and the issuance of an unsecured line of credit to cardholders. Loans, check guarantees, and traveler's checks, including currency in foreign denominations, are all part of the expanded service. But there is even more being offered: rebates on purchases above a given amount; access to private and athletic club facilities across the nation.

Tying the cards to cash management accounts administered by Wall Street brokers, rather than to the traditional banks, is among the newest offerings. It presumes the already evident merger of banks, brokerage houses, retailers, and realtors. More important, it sets the stage for the next phase of credit card expansion, the debit cards and their electronic funds transfer (EFT).

Debit Cards (EFT)

Debit cards are the means to a cashless society. Unlike credit cards, debit cards immediately reduce the bank account of the user-buyer. There is no time lag (float) between the purchase and the payment. Paying for a credit purchase may lag thirty days or more after the purchase and use of the goods. Not so with electronic fund transfers, which transfer the funds instantaneously from the buyer's account to the seller's. Why would anyone use a debit card in preference to a credit card?

No one does, yet. Federal legislation does not now allow merchants to levy surcharges on credit card purchases. There is an opposite side. Current interpretations of federal and state usury and truth-in-lending laws also limit cash rebates to 5 percent. So long as the price of money remains high, earnings from the customer's float will continue to exceed the 5 percent allowance made for cash, and the consumer will remain a credit card fan. Both of these regulations may change by the time this paragraph reaches print. If so, there will be dual pressure to do away with the credit card. Increased discounts for cash will encourage cash buyers; fees levied on credit card holders will encourage debit card buyers.

Once a credit card purchase fee is added to the annual fee to get the card, debit cards grow more appealing. Buyers will opt for debit cards when administrative costs exceed the value of the float. Impetus for the change is based on the actual use of credit cards: they are as much a convenience as an instrument of credit. That theme is pushed by the companies who prefer convenience card nomenclature over credit card terminology. Convenience cards will remain credit cards until it is more economical to make them debit cards. (Debit because it reduces the buyer's account at the bank; the bank carries that depositor as a liability, that is, as a credit.)

Debit cards are technically in place, awaiting only consumer acceptance. Credit electronic fund transfers (direct deposits) are the opposite side of the debit cards and have been used for some time. EFT means savings in time, paper, accounting costs, and processing expenses, including the expense of bad checks. Supermarkets that now take checks, but not always credit cards — their markups are too small to absorb credit card fees — will likely lead the swing to debit cards.

Debit cards lack the charisma of smart card terminology. Smart cards have miniature microprocessors embedded in the plastic. Such cards act as credit cards or debit cards and interface with magnetic stripes, zebra stripes, or optical readers. They link a range of financial institutions with a range of retail outlets, including the hotel's front office. The more advanced the smart cards and the point of sale terminals, the easier the retailer can enter the clearing house machinery, bypassing the merchant bank, which is presently the hotel's major transit for bank cards.

Visa International (Visa) and Interbank Card Association (MasterCard) serve two roles. They market the systems, signing up cardholders and merchant banks, and they clear the paper. The merchant banks charge their merchant members a 2 to 3 percent fee and pay the bank issuing the credit card a 1 to 2 percent fee through the clearing houses. Whether the big retailers (grocery and hotel chains) will bypass the merchant banks and deal directly with a debit clearing house is still to be seen.

Schemers and scamers are out to beat the system, whatever it might be. The burden of protecting noncash transactions, be it today or sometime in the future, continues to fall on the credit manager and the entire front office staff.

CREDIT MANAGEMENT

Open credit, which is credit based solely on guest signatures, has long been the traditional authorization for charge sales of rooms, food, and beverage. Even more questionable has been the additional credit granted for third parties, on the same basis: advances to concessionaires; outlay for tips; acceptance of COD packages; and so on. Hotels extend more credit on this shallow documentation than any other business. This makes a close scrutiny of the identification that is the basis of open book credit both necessary and fair. Guests who find it otherwise signal caution.

Scrutiny is but one factor in establishing and administrating a credit policy. Since credit policy must encourage a healthy marketing approach even as it strives for prompt payment and bottom line returns, what is best for one hotel may not serve another. Resorts, for example, depend less on credit cards; there is less impulse buying at a resort. Besides, advance reservations, repeat guests, and an ability to trace addresses make payment by check acceptable and desirable at resorts.

Cost is another consideration in the credit decision. In fact, total cost was one factor that drove the hotel industry out of the credit business. Credit managers must weigh the gains in sales against the costs. Credit cannot be granted merely because the guest requests it. Nonpayment is the foremost cost, but bookkeeping costs, the costs of borrowed funds to finance the accounts receivable, and the loss of goodwill also have a place in the credit decision.

In addition to marketing and cost considerations, the hotel and its credit staff also focus on preventative procedures, which are administered at the front desk, and remedial procedures, which are put into place after the guest's departure.

At the Guest's Arrival

Collecting current or overdue accounts begins with guest identification, and guest identification starts with the reservation-rooming procedure. There can be no collection of accounts unless the hotel can identify the person and that person's resident or business address. Responsibility for guest identification is not vested solely in the front desk. Like marketing, credit is a pervasive function with the onus placed equally on housekeeping, the uniformed services, and serving personnel. Identification is as simple as legible signatures and room numbers on signed departmental checks.

Identification

Identification is more reliable when the guest has a reservation that involved correspondence. Then the name and address and perhaps even the company association have been verified by mail. Missing information is added during the registration procedure. This information includes the intended means of settling the bill at departure time as well as the guest's complete name and address: given name not initials, street address not city alone. Comparing zip codes to the post office list can uncover false addresses, as can the credit manager's general knowledge of a city. Some hotels include the auto registration number; this is verified by the bellperson, who reports it on the hotel's copy of the rooming slip (figure 6.16). Illegible signatures or addresses are clarified by the room clerk, who prints the information above the scrawl.

However, these procedures do place a heavy burden on the room clerk. Tact in selecting the right words and courtesy in voice intonations must be taught and practiced. Even good training programs often ignore this portion of the clerk's role. Many factors exacerbate the situation: the guest is tired or the reservation has been misplaced. Perhaps the clerk is unsure or pressing for more complete details, which he or she might do if the baggage is light or in poor condition. If the guest is nervous or poorly dressed, the clerk may ask for and photograph the driver's license. It's a thin line between information and invasion, between guest understanding and anger. The clerk must tread carefully.

No magic formula separates safe risks from poor ones. But for the guest with good intentions, collection is possible only if the hotel can identify the person and the address. Returned checks, late charges, credit card charge backs, and other open accounts cannot be collected, regardless of the guest's sincerity, without the facts. Unlike most industries, innkeeping has the opportunity to get the data; procedures should assure its collection.

The Walk-in

Because the walk-in requires special care, every hotel has some means of special identification. NR for no reservation, WI for walk-in, and OS for off the street are three of the more common flags. Telephone reservations, particularly those preceding the arrival by only a brief time (up to twenty-four hours), must be classified as walk-ins for credit purposes. Room rack slips, folios, and CRTs should be specially marked for walk-ins or be of a special color code. That information coming from a special notation made by the room clerk on the reg card.

The registration cards of NR guests are not filed with the folios until the credit manager has inspected them. Telephone directories and direct-dial to city information help verify name, address, and telephone in many instances. But the absence of a listed telephone number is not sufficient evidence of bad credit. Telephone companies report an increasing use of nonlisted numbers among their subscribers.

Suspicious walk-ins can, of course, be required to pay in advance — credit card or not — with corresponding limitations on their credit. Not every walk-in is suspect, of course, and the extra caution exercised with walk-ins should not be allowed to pervade a general negative attitude.

Means of Payment

A novelty a few short years ago, it has become standard practice to ask arriving guests to identify the means of payment. Signs, which are distributed by the trade associations, are conspicuously posted in the front office to call attention to the rule. And the question is standard content on most registration cards (figure 6.6). Each of the three methods (cash, checks, and credit cards) has advantages and disadvantages.

Cash is the most acceptable medium of exchange but it has certain procedural disadvantages. If payment is delayed until departure, the guest may choose to interpret a check as cash. At that late date, verification will not be possible. Additional identification — which will upset the guest to no end — is desirable if collection is made in advance of the stay. Collecting one day more than the anticipated stay forces the guest back to the desk at departure. The hotel is protected but at the cost of the guest's ire — the antiservice syndrome at work again — and the extra delay at refunding the excess collected.

Payment by check usually requires advanced approval at the time of arrival. This enables the credit manager or assistant manager to verify the check during normal business hours. Except in very unusual cases, approval is limited to the actual amount of the bill. Several check identification systems are in use.

Local and regional check-cashing cards have been in circulation for some time. The issuing bank guarantees the check provided the hotel (or other merchant) checks the expiration date, matches signatures, verifies the card number against the checking account number, completes several procedural routines, and holds the transaction below the dollar ceiling, perhaps $200. The cards are obviously not much help for an industry that draws its clientele from outside the immediate region.

Several national systems of check verification, trademarked under names like Telecheck or Telecredit, are available. Whereas the local guarantee cards are usually administered without charge to either depositor or merchant — the banks limit their issuance to favored credit risks only — the national systems, by their very nature, impose a fee. The hotel pays the fee on a per use basis if no intermediary bank is involved. Payment is made to the check guarantee company, which insures each check. When a bank is involved, the depositor pays either an annual fee for the card or a per use fee against the demand account, or both. Hotels could recover their costs by charging the guest to cash the check. Fifty cents to cash a check in a remote location doesn't seem unreasonable. The larger the check, the less costly the flat fee; even less expensive than the 1 percent traveler's check fee, which many travelers pay without complaint.

A complex system of computer interfaces and credit identification lies behind the apparently simple process of check verification. Using a telephone, but more and more a point of sale device (figure 12.1), the employee inputs the guest identification. In about a half minute, the answer returns. Verification is by exception. The check is OK'd unless there is

negative information on file. If the check is approved, a guarantee number, which is written on the face of the check, is furnished. It's the hotel's claim number if the check is returned.

Thus one of three types of check-guarantee cards might be offered the hotel: a local card, a bank card with national coverage, or a nonbank card administered by a check-guarantee company, complete with window decal and logo. By one means or another, the hotel is protected against noncollectible checks up to a predetermined level.

Greater and greater reliance is being placed upon credit card payment and, indirectly, upon identification. Clerks must be taught to ask for the card that charges the least fee rather than make an open-ended request. The credit card is imprinted on the rear of the registration card or on the proper credit card form (figure 13.11), which is then attached to the folio. The cashier is alerted by this means, or by some other marking on the folio, as to which credit card will be used.

During the guest's stay, the card is checked against the lengthy bad-card list but especially against the shorter hot-card list furnished by the credit card company. Since most cards guarantee payment up to a certain amount, the floor limit, the verification may not be made if the guest's intended stay is brief. Desk clerks are notorious for avoiding this tedious task. Telephone and teletype communication with credit clearing houses using computer records are replacing the long printed lists of bad credit cards. WATS lines (Wide Area Telephone Service — the 800 telephone numbers) make this a less onerous task for the clerk, so the likelihood of verification is improved. The clerk is probably unaware that the telephone inquiry is being answered by a computer voice.

Credit Alerts

Credit risks and intentional skippers can be identified by a pattern of things they do. In-

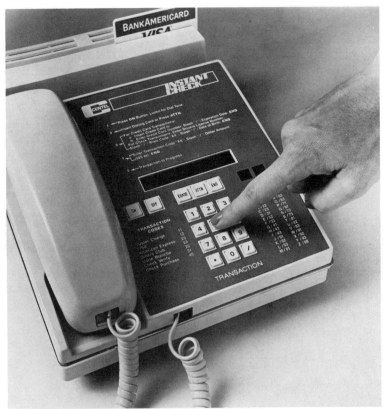

Figure 12.1. Point of sale check verification terminal. A transaction code appears to the left of the keyboard, and an alpha numeric conversion table (A=21) appears on the right. *Courtesy: Centel Transaction Services, Las Vegas, Nev.*

deed, the credit manager should be able to develop a standard description much like the airlines have done for the prototype hijacker. The typical skipper is male, from thirty to thirty-five years old, a late walk-in with light baggage and vague identification. He is a heavy tipper and usually a quick new friend of the bartender. The skipper makes no telephone calls that can be used to trace him. His address is usually a well-known one in a large city, but it proves to be false. He writes his name and address poorly and offers no business identification.

Obviously, it is not always that easy to identify skippers, so clerks, bellpersons, and housekeepers must be taught to watch for the pattern that alerts the credit manager. Since the discretion to act remains with the assistant or credit manager, the employee need only be taught to report conditions that have a possible meaning for credit or crime. These conditions would include luggage that was light or totally worthless, large quantities of blank checks and money orders, printing equipment, firearms and burglary tools, property belonging to other hotels, especially room keys, unusual amounts of cash or gems, gambling equipment, or just suspicious activities like heavy traffic to a room or loiterers in public areas or near house telephones.

Frequent charges to the account from all departments and in the small amounts that one usually pays in cash are a common sign of a skipper. Bad risks concentrate on weekends or holidays when the staff of the commercial hotel is reduced and the banks are closed. Charges begin very soon after arrival.

Skippers and bad check passers frequently work one area before moving on. A telephone or Teletype network among local hotels does much to identify the culprit even before he arrives. This system can be tied to a central credit bureau as well, but it is only as good as the regularity with which members report bad experiences.

A record of checks cashed should be maintained and filed with the folio. Note can be quickly made of any pattern that develops, especially that of cashing checks during different shifts when the authorizing manager would be unaware of previous approvals. With a computerized system, this information is at the credit manager's finger tips. A VDT quickly displays all checks previously cashed by the guest during this particular stay. Photographs and other identifying information will undoubtedly be displayed some day by computer terminals.

Credit personnel should not be lulled into a feeling of false security by the presence of a national credit card. Not only is there a market in stolen cards but there is a credit limit as well. When credit is extended beyond that limit, the card company's responsibility is voided for the entire amount, even that below the maximum limit.

More and more credit managers are turning to the three-day billing cycle in place of the traditional seven-day wait. This is not only consistent with changing credit patterns but with changing guest patterns in which three nights is already longer than the average.

Internal Procedures

Except in the smallest of hotels, upper management is not making hourly credit decisions at the desk. It must create, instead, a credit policy and procedure that will minimize losses and retain guest goodwill. Many properties handle this through a credit manual. Although every manual or handbook has some inherent shortcomings, they usually offer direction in check handling and credit card procedures.

Check Cashing

Being cheated by a skipper is irritating and frustrating. There is a limit to what one can do. Still, the loss is relatively small since the skipper is absconding with only the marginal cost required to deliver the services and goods. How much more exasperating is a bad check! The passer not only takes full value of the money, but he or she does so with the hotel's permission and blessing. That's why there is a new, more restrictive attitude toward check cashing today. It is due partly to the increasing size of the loss and partly to a new understanding of the hotel's rights and obligations in terms of credit. It can be no other way because bogus check passing is big business. Estimates put it at over $40 billion annually (and climbing) for American business, given impetus by color copiers that make the fraudulent and the real almost indistinguishable.

Rules and procedures must be established and followed. Exceptions, if any, cannot be based on a glib tongue or an expensive suit. Credit personnel must be firm and deliberate. Decisions must not be rushed no matter how loquacious the guest or how pressing his business. Credit managers must be pleasant but unintimidated. Indeed the more belligerent the guest becomes the more deliberate the manager should be. One cannot expect a fraudulent check passer to have scruples about using fraudulent identification. Delay will evoke concern and the bad check passer, using the pretense of pressing business, may hurriedly withdraw the request.

Procedural Protection

Closed-circuit television in banks and photographing procedures elsewhere affirm a hotel's right to use similar equipment. New dual lens cameras, which simultaneously record a picture of the instrument being negotiated and of the check passer, are available. Other systems allow the development of latent fingerprints without the use of ink or other messy substances. Just a sign explaining the equipment being used serves as a deterrent, as does a printed warning citing the penalty for passing bad checks.

Most hotels refuse to handle foreign checks because of the delay in clearing and the reduced chance of recovery. Uncertainty in foreign exchange rates increases the risk.

The American Hotel & Motel Association and the American Bankers Association have a long-time agreement intended to thwart the passer of bad checks, two-thirds of which are never collected. Banks will wire collect whenever a worthless check is cleared. Hotel personnel need continual reminders to accept these wires or calls. Some hotels also use the endorsement, "Communication by collect wire or telephone (800 number) authorized."

Other hotels collect a check-cashing fee, which is used to offset worthless checks. The rationale of penalizing honest guests is open to debate. It would be better to adopt and enforce a stringent procedure, irritating as it is to the honest guest, than to collect an unwarrantable fee. The procedure may include a telephone call at the guest's expense to his or her office or bank according to the circumstances and time of day.

Procedural protection requires proper and immediate endorsement after the check is received. This is particularly true if third-party checks are accepted (not recommended) with only an open endorsement containing the payee's name. The cashier should have a rubber stamp that reads:

> For Deposit Only
> The Hotel Name

The stamp should also contain space for identification, credit card number, room number, and the initials of the person approving the check.

Invariably, bank endorsements blot out much of the information recorded on the rear of the check. The data is unusable when needed most, if the check comes back. Other than the endorsement, data should be written on the front of the check. Examination of past checks may indicate the pattern of bank cancellations, if there is one, allowing careful placement of data on the check's rear.

A special endorsement is used for checks that are cashed. Otherwise the hotel falls prey to an old ruse by which the guest cashes a check in the exact amount of the bill and then leaves without paying. When the hotel attempts to collect by mail, the cancelled check is presented as evidence of payment and the guest generously accepts the hotel's apologies. Consequently, some hotels take all checks as receipts on account. Any cash given for the checks appears on the folio as a cash advance. This roundabout procedure can be avoided by an endorsement that reads:

> Received in Cash From
> The ABC Hotel

Checklist for Check Cashing

No one set of rules covers every circumstance, but a list of limitations and restrictions are a helpful guideline to those responsible for approving checks. Such a list follows. Modifications will depend on the class of hotel, the source of authority, and the circumstances surrounding the particular request.

Take checks only for the amount of the bill. Be particularly alert for the cash-back technique by which cash as well as services rendered are lost.

Allow no one to be above suspicion on weekends, holidays, and after banking hours.

Refuse to accept any check that is altered, illegible, stale (over thirty days), postdated, poorly printed, or from a third party (figure 12.2).

Be suspicious of checks slightly smaller than the statutory measure of grand larceny. If $100 separates petty larceny from grand larceny in the state, then a $107 check is safer than a $94 one (figure 12.2).

Compare the signature and address on the check with that on the registration card: are they similar? should they be? Compare the signature on the front with the endorsement on the rear. Ask the same questions!

Compare the age of the guest with the date on the driver's license. Has the license expired?[2] Compare the person's listed height and weight, hair and eye colors, and the photograph, if available, to the person standing before you.

Pay special attention to endorsements. Accept no conditional, circumstantial, or restrictive endorsements. Challenge endorsements that are not identical to either the printed name (in case of a personal check) or the payee (in the case of a third-party check).

Require endorsements on all bearer and cash payees. Require all endorsements to be made in your presence, repeating them when the check is already endorsed.

Refuse a check payable to a corporation that is endorsed by one of the officers seeking to cash it.

Obtain adequate and multiple identification and record it on the front of the check along with any other information that can help if the check is refused: address, telephone number, credit card number, auto plates, clerk's initials (figure 12.2).

Verify business names in telephone directories or listings like Dun & Bradstreet, Inc. Obtain military identification. Call local references. Request a business card.

Create fictitious information or names of company officers and see if the guest verifies them.

Make certain the check is complete, accurate, and dated. Watch for misspellings and serial numbers of more than four digits.

Keep a bank directory and check the transit and routing numbers against it. Verify the name of the bank with the directory listing, giving special attention to the article "the" and the use of the ampersand (&) in place of "and." City Bank of Laurelwood is not the same as The City Bank of Laurelwood; Farmers and Merchants Bank is not Farmers & Merchants Bank.

Personal and company checks are usually perforated but counter checks and copied checks are not.

2. Two manuals, *Drivers License Guide* and *U.S. Identification Manual,* can be used for validating identification and auto license cards.

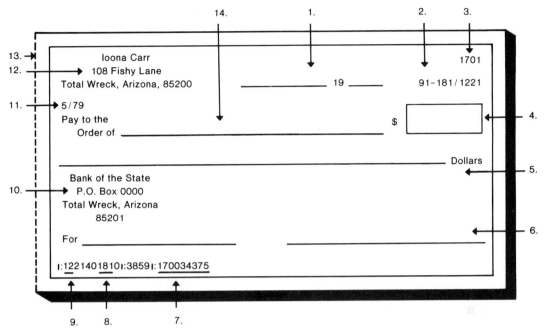

Figure 12.2. Fourteen locations flag a possible bad check: (1) Is the date current; (2) Do the routing numbers correspond to the magnetic numbers; (3) Has the account existed for some time; (4) Is the amount more or less than the statutory definition of grand larceny; (5) Are the values of the handwritten dollars and the numerical dollars identical; (6) Does the signature correspond to the registration card or the endorsement; (7) Are the account numbers in agreement with a bank card that is being proffered; (8) Is magnetic ink dull or reflective; (9) Is the number of the Federal Reserve Region accurate; (10) Does the bank directory list this bank as shown; (11) When was the account established; (12) How does the maker's identity compare with the hotel's records; (13) Is the check perforated; (14) Is the payee a third party, a corporation, or cash.

Remember cashier's checks (a check drawn on the bank by one of its officers) are spelled with an apostrophe "s," are full size, never pocket size, and are rarely ever prepared with a typewriter. Trust companies issue treasurer's checks, not cashier's checks.

Be cautious of certified checks since most persons do not use them. Certification numbers are written or stamped, rarely typewritten.

Check the signatures on bank drafts (a check drawn by a bank on its correspondent bank) with the bank directory and verify the bank's correspondent bank at the same time.

Note that because of withholding, payroll checks are almost never even dollar amounts.

Read identification; don't just look at it!

Ask questions: "What does your middle 'C' stand for?" Don't offer the answer: "Is your middle name Charles?"

Determine whether the guest is registered from the same city as the one in which the bank is located.

Be familiar with bank locations: the twelve federal reserve districts are numbered from one in the East to twelve in the West. Eastern locations being tendered Western checks (and vice versa) should be cautious since the delay in clearing allows the culprit extra time.

Locate the magnetic code on the lower left of the check (figure 12.2). The first two digits following the bracket (⊩) identify the federal reserve bank handling the commercial paper. Numbers greater than twelve (the federal reserve districts) are spurious. This is not true of NOW accounts or similar noncommercial checks.

Expect the magnetic code to be dull; shiny numbers that reflect light were printed with other than magnetic ink.

Recall that nearly three-quarters of all bad checks are passed during the holiday season, October to December.

Establish firm limits on the value of the check to be cashed.

Question emergencies. If airfare is needed to go home unexpectedly, why can't the airline take the check?

Ignore evidence of identity that consists of social security cards, library cards, business cards, or voter identification cards.

Personally deliver the check to the cashier without allowing the guest to retrieve it once it has been approved.

Watch check numbers (figure 12.2). Low digits mean a new account where the danger is greatest. The larger the number the safer the check. New accounts begin with 101.

Look for the small date on the left, upper section of the check (figure 12.2). This indicates the date the account was opened.

Do not write the check; insist that the check be written by the guest.

Machine, color-copied checks can be smeared with a wet finger; real safety-paper checks cannot.

Remember that bank cards do not cover cash losses, only merchandise purchased.

Limit check cashing to the front desk cashiers.

Note that credit managers have been known to eavesdrop on guest telephone calls.

Ask yourself how difficult it would be to create the identification offered.

Compare the numerical amount of the check with the written amount.

Watch the value of foreign traveler's checks. Foreign checks are issued in foreign currency. Don't cash twenty marks or francs as a twenty-dollar value.

Traveler's Checks

Traveler's checks are readily recognizable checks purchasd by the user from one of the larger issuers, who insures them against loss or theft. American Express (Am Ex) pioneered the traveler's check in 1891 and has retained its preeminent position in the field ever since. Although competition is grabbing a larger and larger share, American Express still holds better than 50 percent of the worldwide market.

Competition increased as the new banking-credit conglomerates reached out for the float. Large sums of interest-free money are available for short-term investments. The time lag between the purchase of the traveler's check and the use of the check might be weeks or even months. Between 15 to 20 percent of traveler's check sales remain unclaimed. Am Ex advertising encourages buyers to hold their checks for some distant emergency. Business is so lucrative that some issuing banks even waive the selling fee in order to enjoy the float.

Buyers sign the checks at the time of purchase and countersign when they cash the instruments. Signature comparison is the main line of defense against fraud. Checks must be countersigned under the scrutiny of the cashier or re-signed if they were initially endorsed away from the cashier's view. It is customary to cover the first signature if the guest is being asked to sign again. Traveler's checks are very acceptable and some hotels will cash them even for nonregistered guests. Other hotels are extra cautious and require additional identification or compare signatures to registration cards.

American Express Travelers Cheques have the words raised on the printing and this can be used to distinguish the real from the copies. Red dots are visible in the check if held to the light, but a wet finger is the acid test. It will smear the check when applied to the denomination on the back left side. But the wetness must be applied there. Like their commercial brothers, traveler's checks employ a magnetic code on the lower left portion of the paper. The first digits are always 8,000, which tells the clearing house computer it is a traveler's check. The next portion of the code identifies the type, e.g., 8000001 is Bank of America, 8000005 is American Express.

Prompt refund of lost or stolen checks is the major appeal. Hotel desks, with their twenty-four-hour service, represent a logical extension of the issuing company's office system. Hilton has already entered into such an agreement with Bank of America. It is both a service to the guest and a marketing device for the hotel chain, so we should see more announcements like this forthcoming.

Credit Cards

Credit cards have made possible the credit economy of modern America and the Western World. Growth and acceptance have been nothing less than astonishing. Diners Club introduced the concept in the early 1950s. Thirty-five years later, more than 100 million Americans use credit cards of one variety or another; over 90 percent of them bank cards. The phenomenon has spawned a whole new industry worldwide with special legislation, banking systems, and numerous ancillary services.

Proliferation of cards has been matched with a proliferation of uses: traffic fines, college tuition, and charitable contributions among the more exotic. Their pervasiveness raises the specter of privacy infringements even as it offers the solution to more mundane problems like overbooking.

Kinds of Cards

All credit cards are not the same. Although their number and variety seem almost endless, and probably are, they can be classified into three general types: bank cards, travel and entertainment cards, and others. Bank cards and T&Es dominate the field. Their differences growing less apparent as banking deregulation and competition forces one to take on many of the attributes of the other. Bank cards charge an annual fee, although they were initially offered without cost. T&Es, which traditionally required the merchant to wait a long time for reimbursement, have introduced express deposits ala the bank cards. Prestige cards with higher limits and special privileges have been added to the bank card lines to attract the affluent, long the purview of the travel and entertainment cards. T&Es have reacted with minicomputer cards to broaden their use and reduce fraud. And the battle has but recently been joined.

Bank Cards. Bank cards, as the name infers, are issued by banks. Issued in most cases to their own depositors, they encourage credit use among a lower economic group than holders of travel and entertainment cards. This generalization will prove false if the less expensive bank cards eventually offer as many services as the more costly T&E cards or if the spread in fees narrows to a less discernible gap.

Interest is paid, with rates of 1½ percent per month on the open balance, only if the purchase is financed over time. With prompt payment, the card holder has no costs whatsoever. Banks, being in the business of lending money, encourage the card holder to finance.

Banks finance the system through the discount fee charged to the merchant users. (Unlike hotel franchise fees, costs of signs and imprinters are insignificant.) The fee, which is sometimes a per unit charge, is usually negotiable, ranging from a 1–2 percent low to a high of 5–6 percent of dollar volume. The larger the volume, the smaller the fee, but charges also reflect the banker-customer (hotel) relationship: Banks charging less to good customers; or hotel customers willing to pay more for this service because of better rates offered by the bank for other services. The growth of large interstate banks may change this local appeal.

Obviously, chains, franchises, and affiliated groups, which combine their volumes for negotiating discount rates, have a competitive edge over independent properties. Efforts to umbrella independents have not been too successful since the flat charge levied by the umbrella organization may nearly equal the savings experienced by the low bank card volume. Be that as it may, bank charge fees are lower than those of the travel and entertainment card companies.

Immediate accessibility — charges to bank cards are treated as cash deposits by the hotel — has been one advantage of the bank cards over the T&Es and will remain so for some time to come. Both types guarantee collections, with some limitations, and both reduce the costs of skippers and bad checks. Some credit card companies levy their discount against tips that the hotel has paid out to service employees! But this, like the basic fee itself, is negotiable. Management might reduce the tips paid out to employees by the percent being paid to the card companies. Implementing such a policy obviously has personnel implications as well as financial ones.

Generally, employees are expected to refund tips if the credit card is dishonored or city accounts prove uncollectible. This becomes a serious morale problem and involves so much paperwork that although the reimbursement rule stands, it is often not enforced. Employee turnover and long delays in processing make restitution from the service employees look good in theory but work poorly in practice. Besides, no matter how well justified, recovery from employees creates ill will.

Concessionaires cause similar problems if guests are permitted to charge purchases to their folios. When the folio is paid by credit card, the hotel ends up paying the concessionaires' fees. Then too, there is the occasional charge back: the credit card company refusing the voucher. Both circumstances should be treated in the lease.

The two major bank cards, MasterCard and Visa, have grown to international scope. Reciprocal agreements with overseas banks have added additional customers on the one hand and additional outlets on the other. They do everything the regional cards do but have a universal acceptance. This acceptance is more than geographic; it includes a wide variety of goods and services. Among these are hotel and dining accommodations. With these two major cards, guests can complete an entire trip on credit and even obtain cash loans when the emergency arises.

Internationally or domestically, the system works much the same. The merchant deposits the sales tickets at the local bank for immediate credit to the company account. If the merchant's bank and the cardholder's bank are the same, the bank could charge the purchase against the customer's account. It is more likely with hotel customers that the account is in some other bank. Getting funds from the other bank involves a procedure called interchange. Authorization centers, not unlike the twelve federal reserve banks, facilitate the interchange. Computers have really made the system work, especially internationally. The interchange no longer includes the actual sales slips, which were returned at one time to the purchaser. Instead, the information is transmitted by wire or transhipped using magnetic tapes. Communication is extremely rapid and without the crunch of physically delivering huge quantities of paper.

Travel and Entertainment Cards. T&E cards differ in several ways from bank cards. First of all, the buyer faces a far more stringent credit check. Because of this, T&E holders number

less than 15 percent of bank card holders. There is, moreover, an annual fee that is levied without consideration for the amount of individual customer usage. But intent remains the basic difference between bank cards and T&E cards. The first encourages delayed payment and monthly interest charges. The travel and entertainment card companies, which rely on higher annual membership fees and higher merchant's commissions, expect the user to make a monthly settlement. Not only are the T&Es less concerned now with monthly settlements, but they are beginning to advertise extended payments.

Float, the access to interest-free money because of the delay between usage and billing, and billing and collection, typically averages sixty days. Companies and individuals have interest-free money for their near-term travel and entertainment expenses. Users enjoy the float between usage and payment. T&E companies enjoy the float between collections from card holders and payment to merchants, hotels included. The hotels not only pay a larger discount on T&E card purchases, but they wait a longer time for collection. A delay in payment is a very real cost in a tight money market. Extra prompt payment can be arranged at an additional surcharge of 2–4 percent over the usual 4–7 percent discount fee.

Although many hotels would prefer it, guest expectations make it nigh impossible to refuse the cards altogether. Bermuda hotels resisted for many years by acting in concert in a well-defined and isolated area. The ban was overturned eventually, but many small properties in Bermuda still refuse the cards. Despite the general grumbling, the number of outlets for T&E cards continues to increase.

Largest and best known of the travel and entertainment cards is American Express. Diners Club and Carte Blanche are now under one umbrella, both having been acquired by CitiCorp. It is likely that they will be combined under one name and begin competing somewhat more fiercely.

Retail Credit Cards. Retail credit cards are by far the most numerous of the three types and are best represented by the hotel's own card. Such private label cards are limited in scope and negotiability. Their chief purpose is the promotion of customer loyalty, but the 1½ percent charge on overdue accounts cannot be dismissed. Credit verification is minimal, since the objective is sales promotion as much as credit control. This is changing somewhat as the amount of bad debts rises.

Hotel companies may begin reentering the credit card business now that the economy of computerization has reached the industry. Costs were one of the reasons for surrendering an in-place credit card system to the upstart national companies in the first place. Hotel credit has some real advantages for customers seeking direct corporate billing without fees or cash advances to their traveling executives. Guaranteed reservations, express check-outs, and the addition of related travel services (made possible by computer link ups) may regenerate customer interest in proprietary credit cards. Especially if the large hotel chains can combine many hotel visits by many company executives across the nation into one monthly billing. Interest from the chains will focus primarily on costs.

But there is another side of the coin. Rich marketing data is a byproduct of account billing. American Express has been touting its assemblage and distribution of basic data for some time. It is the type of data that spins off from the computer processing of many, many credit card charges. Should the hotel companies return to the credit card business, they could offer marketing analysis both to their own management and to their client accounts.

Additional sales advantages can be obtained when noncompeting cards are interchanged. Gasoline credit cards for hotel rooms was one such arrangement. Other possibilities exist with local department stores or specialty shops, but hoteliers have never promoted such reciprocal agreements very diligently.

The gasoline shortages of the 1970s altered the marketing emphasis of the oil companies. That, along with the general availability of bank cards, eliminated the gasoline credit card as a factor in hotel credit.

Procedural Protection

The great volume spawned by the credit card systems has required the credit card companies to establish certain restrictions to protect themselves from unwarranted losses. The hotelier can do no less.

Credit card fraud is reaching unprecedented proportions. Part of the solution seems to be the elimination of paper records. Discarded papers and carbons have been used to match names and credit card numbers. For a price, front desk employees furnish the last of the crucial evidence to the fraudulent user, the address. There is little incentive for cardholders to fight fraud because they are responsible only for the first fifty dollars in charges fraudulently made to the card. It's up to the credit card companies and the merchants (the hotels) to combat credit card fraud.

Long-term solutions seem to lie in the technical ability of the card manufacturers. Holograms using laser readers to produce a three-dimensional effect are technically feasible, but the cost dissuades the licit as well as the illicit user. A less costly interim step is surfacing, which involves embossing the back of

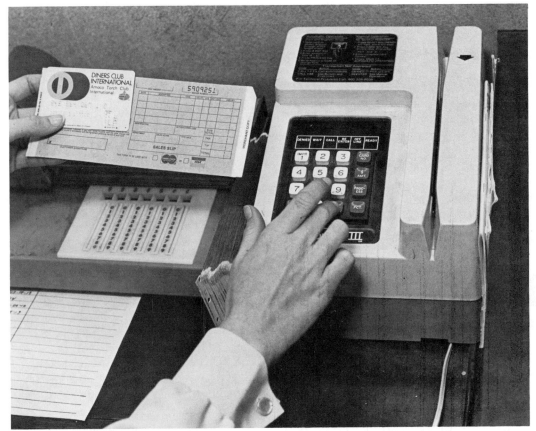

Figure 12.3. Credit card authorization terminal. Credit cards and check verification could be done on the same terminal, seé figure 12.1. *Courtesy: Radisson South, Minneapolis, Minn. Photo by Nancy Conroy.*

the card with the number. Counterfeiters would need to alter both sides of a card to make it machine-readable.

The machine that verifies credit cards is the credit authorization terminal (figure 12.3). It is to the credit card what the check verification machine (figure 12.1) is to the personal check. Both are, of course, spin-offs of computerization. A magnetic tape, which contains the guest's card number and identification, is on the rear of each credit card adapted to the

system. The authorization terminal reads the tape when it is inserted and sends this descriptive information along with the amount of the transaction over the telephone lines. It is read by a computer. Approval activates the terminal so that both the guest's identity and the amount of the transaction are printed automatically on the charge form.

Replacing as it does the tedious search for cancelled cards among long printed lists, this point-of-sale terminal promises reduced losses and better control. Costs seem to be the major obstacle. The expense of installation is high and rentals, paid monthly per terminal by the hotel, take almost two years for the pay back. Besides, at this time, no one terminal accepts every one of the major cards.

Until the credit card verification terminal is more widely used, innkeepers will rely on the in-WATS telephone service maintained by all the credit card companies. The direct dial number should be used whenever the staff is suspicious of the individual or the card. It must be used whenever the floor limit is reached. It could be used for every card presented but the realities of time make this unlikely.

Checklist for Credit Cards

As with personal checks, a list of do's and don't's can be prepared to guide the front office staff in handling credit cards and persons presenting those cards.

Be aware that every business is assigned a floor limit, which is the maximum dollar volume allowed on a single credit card. Insist that employees know that limit, for once exceeded, all charges including those below the floor are voided.

Negotiate a high floor to reduce the need to frequently call for authorization.

Require that every card be checked against the hot list. Insist that the cashier or night auditor who makes the search initials the voucher imprint to take responsibility.

Watch for altered cards, rearranged numbers, or replaced digits that will make a hot card usable. Clues are glue on the card, color variations, or unaligned numbers. Compare numbers on back and front sides.

Question credit card signatures made with a felt pen that could be used to cover an original signature.

Compare the signature on the sales ticket with the signature on the credit card. If uncertain still, compare with the registration card signature.

Compare the credit card and driver's license signatures when suspicious of the individual or the card.

Refuse credit cards whose expiration date has passed, the last day of the month specified. Watch on some cards for "from" dates; charges before that time will be rejected.

Make certain the card imprints completely on all copies of the voucher; check clarity of signature.

Use the proper voucher form. Each company has its own and may not accept its competitors.

Anticipate employee misuse: changed figures or additional charges that permit the employee to pocket some cash.

Insist that the guest sign the charge voucher at checkout to finalize the process started at checkin when the card was imprinted, and insist that the signature be witnessed by an employee.

Instruct employees not to apprehend anyone suspected of using an invalid card. Cardholders agree to surrender the card on request since it remains the property of the credit card company. Agents of the hotel should exercise no force in retrieving a card, nor should they destroy the card or humiliate the guest in public.

Carry insurance against false arrest based on incorrect information furnished by the credit card company. Better still, have the company provide the coverage.

Do not split charges on two or more vouchers to avoid the floor limits.

Never give a cash refund if the unused advance deposit was made through a credit card charge (or travel agency voucher, for that matter).

Bill credit card companies promptly.

Refuse to post fictitious items in order to give cash against the credit card.

Be it credit card or common check, change is the word that best describes the status of the instruments. To a large degree the check, and hence the bad-check passer, has been replaced by the card and hence the credit card fraud. Even as technology promises relief from their misuses, we teeter on the edge of the debit card era. By immediately transferring funds, debit cards promise substantial changes in old debtor-creditor relationships. Hotels have kept records of those relationships in the city ledger, but several major changes have already visited that ledger. Record-keeping has shifted from pencil to computer. Thousands of individual accounts receivable have been compressed into a handful of major credit cards. These have heightened, rather than diminished, the importance of the city ledger, as the next chapter explains.

QUERIES AND PROBLEMS

1. A front office clerk attempts to get additional credit information from an arriving guest. Write two dialogues to be used in a training manual. Include the proper choice of words to be employed by the clerk as well as the kinds of information to be asked if the guest: (a) has a reservation but the information is incomplete; and (b) is a walk-in with light baggage.

2. Approximately twenty months ago your hotel installed a new computer system. With all the start-up problems now far behind, the system is working very, very well. The high carrying charges of the national credit cards, the unused capacity of the computer, and the very capable computer staff suggest to management the possibility of introducing the hotel's own credit card system. You are asked to prepare comments (pro and con) as a basis for discussion during the deliberative phase of the proposal.

3. A guest, Owen Moore of Secaucus, N.J., is checking out and has offered a payroll check in payment for an outstanding folio of $239.46. He had a reservation and offers a credit card, a driver's license, and an ID badge from his place of employment, Midwestern Utility Services, as identification for the check being tendered. List at least ten reasons for cashing or not cashing this check, which is shown on page 256.

4. An interstate bank with which the hotel does business has proposed that a debit card (electronic fund transfer) system be installed at the hotel. Management is intrigued with this possible replacement for the credit card. As with many management decisions, timing is the key here. Develop a chronological series of events that comprise the scenario of American society's march toward the debit card. Management wants to know when to act, and your milestone markers will provide that information.

MIDWESTRAL UTILITY SERVICES
P.O. Box 1000
Grand Central Station
New York, New York 89103

103

6/7

19_____

91-181-1221

Pay to the Order of _____OWEN MOORE_____ $ 300 00/xxx

Three Hundred twenty and ~~~~~ no/000 Dollars

CORN BANK OF NEW YORK
333 Seventh Avenue
New York, New York 32409

⑈:0749218100:⑈7767:⑈66545432

Ima Henchman
Treasuror

13

The City Ledger

Credit, as discussed in the previous chapter, and city ledger, now to be considered, are almost synonymous in American hotelkeeping. Other than registered guests, all accounts receivable (individuals or firms using credit) are maintained in the city ledger. The term is misleading since these accounts may or may not reside in the city in which the hotel does business. Perhaps this is the reason the British call it a *sales journal*. Thus, the father of the new bride becomes a city account when he signs the banquet check for the wedding party. Guests who check out without settling their outstanding accounts become part of the city ledger. Hotel and private credit card balances are carried here as well. So, too, are bad checks that have not cleared; skippers; accounts of entertainers who are playing the hotel; airline accounts for employees and passengers; and any other nontransient accounts receivable.

STRUCTURE OF THE CITY LEDGER

The Physical Ledger

Except in small hotels, the city ledger is maintained in the accounting office. It is maintained there for reasons of both internal control: the handling of money should be separate from the handling of records; and space: the city ledger numbered at one time in the hundreds or thousands of accounts. Although obviously of an entirely different nature, casino credit accounts number upward of 250,000 in some of the larger Nevada casinos. This is one patent explanation for the very early introduction of computerization to the Nevada hotel industry. Numbers of this magnitude are much like the accounts receivable of any large retail business.

Whereas other businesses refer to their lists of customers as accounts receivable ledgers to distinguish them from the general led-

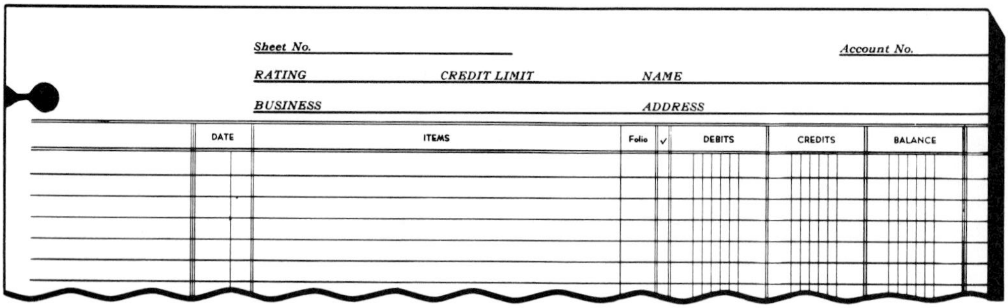

Figure 13.1. A city ledger account for manual recordkeeping. Even when the front office has not been computerized, widespread implementation of back office computerization has put most city ledger records on tape or disc.

gers or accounts payable ledgers, the hotel industry uses the term *city ledger*. Since the city ledger is more like the standard accounts receivable ledger, on which charges and credits are not posted immediately, its physical form (figure 13.1) is more like them than like the front office ledger (figure 10.1 or 10.3).

The more numerous the city ledger accounts, the more flexible the form of the ledger. One finds city ledgers as small as a permanently bound notebook, to tens of thousands of individually maintained ledger cards, to computer tapes. Computers being the most flexible of all. City ledger accounts may be maintained in the front office well using the transient form of the folio (figure 13.2) when they are very few in number and when the front office staff is responsible for their maintenance.

Early efforts to computerize the hotel industry were spin-offs from successes in other industries. Since electronic systems first concentrated on records like accounts receivable (what the hotel business calls back-office accounting), computerized city ledgers have generally preceded computerized front office systems. Delayed billing of this type (in contrast to the immediacy of the front office folio) also lends itself to shared, or rented, off-property computer service companies. For these reasons, city ledger accounting is sometimes computerized even before the balance of the house is. As with front office systems that have been computerized, city ledger information is kept on discs or tapes.

As the volume of city ledger accounting increases, functions are separated and several logical categories have evolved. Even when the work of the city ledger is not distributed throughout the accounting office, it may be subdivided. Whether it is subdivided or not, or computerized or not, a city ledger control account is maintained in the general ledger summarizing the city accounts, just as the transient ledger control summarizes the front office accounts.

Unpaid accounts are subject to bad debt losses, which are minimized by a system of billing and follow-up. Different kinds of city accounts have different billing needs but every account is billed at least once monthly. Standard ten-day, follow-up letters and notices of unpaid accounts supplemented by an occasional telephone call have been standard credit procedure for years. With bad debts running from 4 percent to 5 percent of accounts receivable, it may be time to try some new techniques.

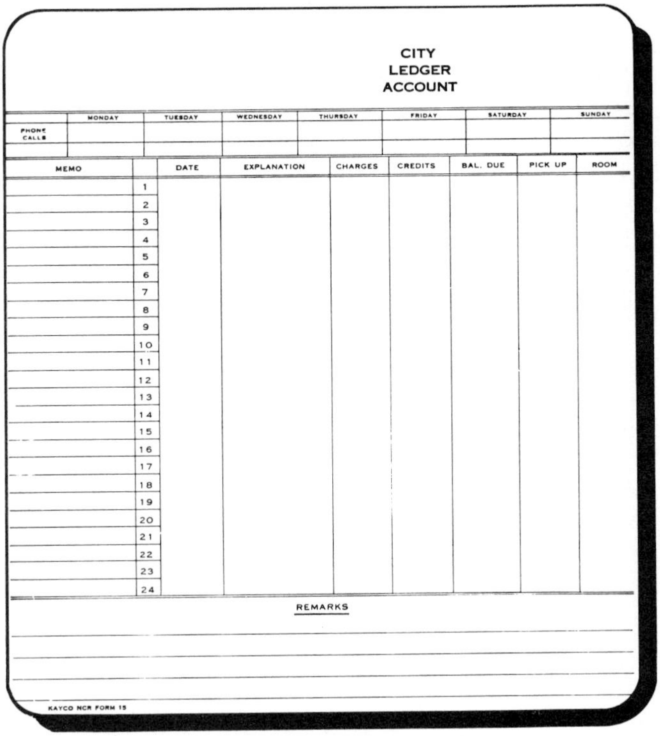

CITY
LEDGER
ACCOUNT

	MONDAY	TUESDAY	WEDNESDAY	THURSDAY	FRIDAY	SATURDAY	SUNDAY
PHONE CALLS							

MEMO		DATE	EXPLANATION	CHARGES	CREDITS	BAL. DUE	PICK UP	ROOM
	1							
	2							
	3							
	4							
	5							
	6							
	7							
	8							
	9							
	10							
	11							
	12							
	13							
	14							
	15							
	16							
	17							
	18							
	19							
	20							
	21							
	22							
	23							
	24							

REMARKS

KAYCO NCR FORM 15

Figure 13.2. Special city ledger folio used at the front office; compare to figure 11.3.

Categories of the City Ledger

The particular divisions of the city ledger depend upon the nature and quantity of the credit business being done.

City Ledger

Confusingly, one division of the city ledger is the city ledger, sometimes called the *city ledger proper* for clarity. The title identifies this portion as the usual, run-of-the-mill receivable. In this division are accounts with no special problems: guests and firms that are active and current in their payments. Also included here are hotel credit card holders, local firms that use the dining rooms and lounges, and transient accounts that were transferred from the front office ledger when the guest checked out. Some of these charge categories are large enough to warrant separate classifications within the city ledger, and that is the way they are discussed next. Obviously, separate classifications would not be necessary for every hotel; as often as not, one category would suffice—the city ledger (proper).

Late Charges

Charges made to a guest's account after checkout are called *late charges*. An excessive amount of late charges indicates poor procedures for handling charge vouchers. Management can minimize this cost even though it cannot be eliminated entirely except by using a POS on-line computer.

Guests sometimes create late charges intentionally by using a service after they have checked out or immediately before departure. Fortunately, this petty attempt to defraud is rare. Since both the hotel and the guest find late charges irritating, the cashier should always ask departing guests about recent charges. If the guest reports such a charge and if the voucher has not yet arrived at the desk, the cashier should telephone the indicated department and prepare a dummy voucher using the figure supplied. Unable to obtain the actual amount, the cashier should accept whatever value the guest recalls.

Late charges especially irritate business guests who must either amend their expense account reports or absorb the charges themselves. Some credit card systems are no better, since individual charge slips may not be altered after the guest signs. Other systems provide a special late charge section and keep the original charge unaltered. If the guest's address is available, the late charge is posted to the city ledger and the guest is billed. (When a disputed charge originated with a nonregistered guest in the dining room or bar, collection is less likely since credit card companies will not release guests' addresses.) Late charge vouchers are usually marked "LC" or "AD" (after departure).

Cash customers are as reluctant as national credit card companies to pay late charges. Collection is best with transient folios that have been transferred to the city ledger because the account is merely updated before billing. That is typically the express checkout guest. The experience is costly to the hotel no matter who the customer. Frequent correspondence with the guest (some studies put a $5.00 cost on each letter a company sends), accounting expenses, and loss of customer goodwill add extra costs to the departmental charge. Rather than billing every late charge, most hotels grant an allowance for all charges under a given amount—up to $3–$5.

There are two general procedures for handling the late charge allowance. Either the late charge is posted to the guest's closed folio and balanced off immediately with an allowance, or a special front office account is created. This account would be labeled "late charges" and all small late charges would be posted directly to it rather than to the account of the guest who just left. Daily, weekly, or monthly the charge balance of the card would be cleared with an allowance.

Previous comments notwithstanding, efforts to collect large late charges should be conscientiously pursued. In that case, the late charge could be posted to the guest's closed folio and immediately transferred to the city ledger for billing. This is not the only procedure, however. Rather, the late charge is posted directly to a special city ledger folio (figure 13.2) and a pencil notation is made in the memo column of the closed folio for later reference. This special city folio is transferred at the end of the day to the back office, where the guest is billed immediately. The results are the same, with the second method providing, at a glance, all of the late charges that were billed for the day.

Banquet Charges

There has been a decided reduction in the type of open-book credit that banquet charges once represented. Party givers and banquet chairpersons expected to sign for their charges the night of the party, and the hotel waited for collection. Catering managers still allow this when credit arrangements have been made in advance. When such arrangements have not been cleared, payment is expected at the conclusion of the affair. Payment is received by a member of the catering department, who channels it through the front desk or directly to the accounting office. When credit is extended, the signed food or beverage check enters the city ledger charge procedure. Banquet accounts are usually billed within three days of the affair.

Company-sponsored banquets are big business in Japan, about twice the U.S. volume of hotel earnings. Whether overseas or at home, company-sponsored affairs, and to a somewhat lesser degree, private receptions (weddings, bar mitzvahs, etc.) are less risky since the responsible party is known. Group, pay-as-you-go functions are credit suspects. Included in this group are school proms, political dinners, charitable fund-raisers, and other speculative functions where payment is based on ticket sales. At least a portion of the payment should be collected in advance, and a ticket accounting system should be part of the up-front agreement. The credit department should review the agreement and establish the identity and credit worthiness of the responsible individual.

Master Accounts

Master accounts are one facet of banquet billing, but they involve more than just banquets as chapter 10 explained. Included on the master account are items like room charges, entertainment activities, tips, large food and beverage (banquet) functions, and, sometimes, outside vendor charges (florist, orchestra, etc.).

Because the amounts involved are considerable, the hotel wants prompt payment. To help assure this, the master account is carefully examined and discussed by the two parties: the association manager (the client); and the hotel in the persons of the convention coordinator, the sales manager, and/or the accountant. Disputes do occur. Although it is best to resolve differences while they are fresh in everyone's minds and before the group leaves the property, it is not always possible to do so. Areas of agreement should be resolved and billed promptly without waiting for the resolution of the few differences. Otherwise a paltry sum will keep thousands of dollars unpaid.

Giving a small discount for prompt payment (ten days perhaps) accelerates collections even if some charges remain unresolved.

Vouchers are another component of the master account. Sometimes it is better for the group to take its meals separately in different dining rooms. If the conventioneer is given a voucher with which to pay for these meals (most exclude alcoholic beverages), additional charges to the master account materialize. Another variety of the voucher payment is discussed a few paragraphs on.

City accounts with other hotels are possible when overflow group business has been booked in a competing property and payment for the whole is through a master account. Or it may arise from guests of one hotel, usually master account guests, using the golf greens, entertainment facilities, or display space of a second hotel. The billing goes between hotels. In no event should there be any appearance of a restraint of trade by which one hotel seems to dictate the terms of the sale (rooms, golf greens, whatever) between the second hotel and the guest.

Contention is a frequent by-product of this arrangement. The prime hotel may make payment to the second hotel within ten days whether or not it collects from the guest. More likely, the prime hotel defers payment until it has been paid. The second hotel carries the prime hotel as a city ledger while the prime hotel settles the convention billing. Depending upon the number of challenges, it may take from thirty to sixty days to settle the account. In effect, the prime hotel borrows interest-free money.

Circumstances are very much the same when the hotel acts as an intermediary with outside restaurants, sightseeing bus lines, and outside entertainment organizations.

Single entity groups are also billed through a master account, room rates having been negotiated in advance. The single entity group (traveling athletic team, company product showing, incentive tours) is like neither a tour package nor a convention/trade show. There is only one buyer who assumes all the costs. Unlike the convention group, there are no comps, but this is, of course, negotiable.

On the back of the master account, or attached to it, is the preregistration list of names and room numbers. The group is also identified by colored room rack slips; one color being assigned to each group. Incidental charges made by individual members of the group are treated in one of two ways. Either they are paid by the individual or by the organization. If all charges (rooms, meals, and incidentals) are paid by the arranger, posting is made to the master account. But split folios are needed if the individual is responsible for the incidental charges (see chapter 10).

To assure collection, notices (some of which are computer printed) are inserted in the key envelope (figure 6.15) reminding the guest that personal charges must be settled individually upon departure. The master account is transferred to the city ledger for final collection from the tour company or other responsible party.

Wholesalers and mass tour movers add to their master accounts in other ways besides room charges. Additional services are purchased by the guest with coupons that are issued upon registering or as part of the tour package price. Guests pay for breakfast, dinner, drink, or whatever with one of these coupons, which the cashiers treat in the turn-in. The coupons are charged to the tour operator's account, from which eventually comes the bill. Breakage accrues to the wholesaler. That is, the wholesaler collects from the guest for the entire tour but only pays the hotel for actual tickets returned. By not using the services they have purchased, guests create this breakage profit for the promoter.

In the hotel's own package — *inclusive tours* (ITs) — breakage comes to the hotel. The package is sold to the guest and the money is collected in advance, minus a commission if it goes through a travel agency. Then if the guest fails to use a coupon, it is the hotel that has gained.

Hotel packages are paid in advance. A portion of the total is charged as room sales. The balance, equal to the value of the coupons, is credited as coupon income. (Debit cash; credit room sales, credit coupon income.) This is actually a wash account. As the coupons come into back office accounting, from the several operating departments, their income value is credited to that department and debited to the wash account. (Debit coupon income; credit food income, bar income, tennis income.) The balance of that account, a credit, equals the coupons outstanding, a portion of which is breakage. Coupons are dated to limit their use to the time of the tour or package.

Executive Accounts

Hotel executives can be city ledger receivables in their own hotel. Management people use the hotel for personal pleasure as well as for house business. Company policy or individual employment contracts dictate how charges are to be made. House entertainment might be distinguished from personal charges on the guest check by an "H" (house business) or an "E" (entertainment) added under the signature. Without these symbols, the accounting department bills the individual as a regular city account. Many times, though, the billing is only a percentage of the actual menu price, depending upon the employment agreement and the gross profit margin ratio of the dining room. Executive accounts are billed like any other city account, in thirty-day cycles usually by alphabetic rotation.

Delinquent Accounts

The delinquent division of the city ledger may contain only accounts that have already proven uncollectible and are awaiting final disposition as bad debts. Or it may include overdue city accounts that have not been thoroughly tested as to their collectibility but are likely to be difficult to collect.

Skipper accounts, one subdivision of the delinquent ledger, are not always bad. A regular guest with good credit may simply leave expecting the hotel to bill through the usual city ledger procedures. Indeed, some hotels compound the problem by marketing a checkout feature (figure 6.20) that exacerbates the occasional oversight. In this case, and in other skipper situations as well, there may be a delay of a day or even two before the condition is discovered. A one or two night allowance may be warranted under those circumstances before the skip account is finally settled. As often as not, skippers are intentional and bad debts are the final disposition.

Skippers are billed to the addresses on the registration cards as soon as they are discovered. And at this point, all the cautions that chapter 12 itemized on full information and identification pay off. Clerical errors and unintentional skippers are quickly clarified. The intentional skipper has committed a crime in the many states where fraud perpetrated on an innkeeper is so classified.

Returned checks is another division of the delinquent ledger. Rather than reestablishing the customer's old account, a new account is opened for each bad check caused by insufficient funds, illegible signature, incorrect date, no such account, etc. The bad check account is frequently larger than the original charge because of bank fees incurred while processing the bad paper. The check should be redeposited, subject to funds in the maker's account, since the shortage may have been a temporary one. That's when it is good to know someone at the hotel's bank who can make appropriate inquiries at the maker's bank.

Passing bad checks is a criminal offense, prima facie, under the statutes of most states. Police cooperation can be obtained under those circumstances, but the hotel should not expect the police to act as a collection agency. Even if the passer makes restitution, the criminal proceedings should continue. Notification should not be limited to the police. Local and state hotel/motel associations and neighboring properties should be alerted to the individual's description and modus operandi.

Adequate information is needed about each bad check, and either the form of the ledger is altered to provide for this or the check itself is stored in a special envelope with the information recorded on its face. The envelope then serves as a subsidiary to the regular account.

Dishonored checks cashed with a credit card are treated differently. Most of the credit card companies will honor the check, up to a ceiling if the hotel is participating in the plan. Then the collection task becomes a matter for the credit card company. The bad check is transferred to a city ledger account to await payment. It is best to separate this type of account from the usual credit card city account, which represents the balance due from normal credit card usage.

Credit cards can be used in another way if the delinquent debtor is willing: simply have the open, unpaid account paid with a credit card voucher. Collection is shifted then from the hotel to the credit card company.

Credit Cards

By far the largest section of the city ledger is the credit card accounts. Although individual hotel credit cards are still issued and are still an aspect of credit and customer relations, the national credit cards represent the largest single amount of outstanding receivables on the hotel's balance sheet.

The number of credit cards seems almost endless, but they can all be classified into the three general types discussed in detail in chapter 12: bank cards; travel and entertainment cards; retail charge cards. The retail cards have become far less important. Since the first oil embargo, the oil companies have made no aggressive marketing thrust. Almost immediately the spread of the oil cards halted and credit arrangements between the oil companies and the motor inn chains ceased. Credit card volume continues to rise nevertheless as the national credit card companies grow.

T&E cards are processed like other city accounts; bank cards operate much like a separate checking account for the hotel. T&E card companies are billed periodically, as are city accounts, and payment is received periodically, as are city accounts. Deposits are made for the bank cards using a transmittal form (figure 13.11), and checks are drawn in the usual manner. Deposits are net of the discount negotiated between the bank and the hotel.

Charge slip deposits, which are comparable to check deposits in a regular checking account, may bounce, that is, be charged back, for any of a number of reasons. These were outlined in chapter 12. Some charge backs are redeemable: illegible figures or the wrong credit card form, for example. Some are not: a canceled card or failure to get a release above the floor limit. Competition among the cards and between the T&Es and the bank cards has meant more flexibility from the companies during charge back negotiations.

Although not the general rule, charge back delays can be inordinately long. For a start, card holders are billed in thirty-day cycles. Sixty additional days are available for the card holder to complain. That's ninety days without even

allowing for the normal communication time between the hotel and its bank, between the customer and his or her bank, or between the two banks.

At one time, no-show tickets for room reservations led the charge back problem. The reservation caller uses a credit card number to guarantee the reservation. If the guest fails to arrive, the hotel initiates a no-show voucher. The hotel's representative signs in place of the guest and notes the order was by telephone, describing the merchandise as a guaranteed reservation. Only recently have the credit card companies assumed responsibility for the no-show. They now guarantee payment and negotiate with the guest.

The success of the credit card instrument, the increasing capability of computer equipment, and the acceptability by the consumer points clearly to the direction of the future: more of the same, until, or if, city ledger credit cards are replaced by cash debit cards.

Credit cards are the means of processing the quick check-out systems that each of the chains advertises under its own trademark. The mechanics of the procedure are simple (see chapter 6) and rely upon the credit card in all cases. Where the guest uses a national credit card, the procedure is the same as if the guest waited in line to check out. If the guest uses the hotel's credit card, the procedure is the same, but the charge goes into the city ledger as an individual account (personal or company) rather than to a major credit card company.

OTHER RELATED ITEMS

Due Bills

Airlines, theatres, sports events, and public media have highly perishable products, as do hotels. There is no means of recapturing an unsold airline seat, an unused television commercial, or a vacant hotel room. Swapping goods and services can be an effective management technique and prove mutually beneficial when both parties have unsold perishable products. The volume of trade is likely to grow now that the Civil Aeronautics Board has stopped regulating the airlines' participation. Hotels, however, have used trade outs to acquire advertising on radio and television stations, billboards, newspapers and magazines, and even capital goods since the 1930s.

These reciprocal trade agreements swap free advertising for free hotel facilities, except their use may be restricted to rooms only; food and beverage to be paid for in cash. This is understandable from the hotel's point of view. The cost of providing an otherwise empty room is minimal, estimated at $5 on the average. In contrast, the cost of food and beverage is high: from 40 percent to 50 percent of the selling price. Moreover, unused food and beverage, unlike unused rooms, can be sold the following day. The advertising media sets restrictions too, making no promise as to where the hotel's ad will appear in the printed matter or at what time it will be heard on the airwaves.

Figure 13.3 illustrates a due bill, but the excessive restrictions on it make it atypical. Whereas the hotel would like to limit the due bill to rooms, to use by certain individuals, and to given days of the week with advance reservations required, the facts of life may be otherwise. It is a matter of negotiation. The fact is that some due bills are so negotiable that they are traded on an open market. Discount houses buy the bills from the original receiver at reduced prices, or they may buy directly from the hotel by trading goods. (Remember that both the media and the hotel have negotiated at a selling price but deliver the services at a cost price.) Then the due bills are resold with an additional markup, still below the face value, to a third party who uses them in lieu of cash. One company has developed a due bill in the form of a seminegotiable check (figure 13.4).

Due bills are favored during periods of low or moderate occupancy and are less popular during busy periods. The poor economy of the early 1980s caused a new push in due bill usage.

The guest is required to present the agreement at the time of registration. This not only permits the clerk to assign high priced accommodations but also allows verification of the expiration date; amounts unused after that date are lost. And this is not uncommon. The benefits accrue to the hotel, which gets the advertising in the media but does not need to deliver the room accommodations. Less scrupulous hotel managers will take advantage of the expiration date to run the unused due bill through the front desk. The due bill is charged on the final day as if the media representatives used it. A number of improved statistics result: better occupancy and higher average room rate among them. It goes beyond a mere question of ethics if the front office manager takes the next step: removing cash from the day's turn-in and substituting the unused due bill.

The due bill is attached to the registration card and the rate is marked "due bill" along with the room charge. A standard guest folio, or sometimes one specially colored or identified as a due bill folio, is used. The due bill is attached to the folio and after the value of the accommodations used has been recorded on the form, it is returned to the holder at checkout.

The transient folio, which was used to accumulate charges during the due bill user's stay, is transferred to the city ledger in the usual manner. The city ledger account is the one treated differently. There is no billing. Instead, the account is charged off against the liability

TO BE PRESENTED TO ROOM CLERK ON ARRIVAL

COPY FOR HOTEL No.................... Expires.................................... 19.........

Trade Advertising Contract
with
HOTEL

NOT NEGOTIABLE . . . NOT TRANSFERABLE Not valid unless presented when registering

The...of ....

hereby agrees to insert.. of advertising in its pages for the

Hotel ....; as ordered at any time or times prior to

expiration date shown above at its regular rates. The net cost of such advertising space is $.............................;

to be paid for in room accommodations at the Hotel..
at daily transient rates **ONLY** as shown below, prior to expiration date, under the following conditions.

This trade order expires on date shown above. Any advertising space not used by the hotel and any hoted accommodations not used by the publication, before the expiration date shown above, are hereby waived and cancelled by both parties. No extension can be given by either party.

This trade order will be honored for room accommodations ....
when presented by the publisher or by authorized employees whose signatures have been filed in advance at

the hotel by the publisher. At no one time may more than ....
authorized persons, including immediate families, use this trade order except by special advance arrangement with the hotel.

Charges for all services rendered by the hotel, other than charges under this contract, are payable upon departure, or at the end of each week if stay is a week or longer. **The publication hereby agrees to be responsible for the payment of such services rendered, other than charges under this contract, and for all charges in excess of the amount of this trade order.**

The hotel cannot guarantee room accommodations without reasonable advance notice of arrival, but agrees to use its best efforts to provide accommodations at all times; except that this trade order will not be honored for room accommodations during the period when special events or celebrations occasion more than ordinary demands for room accommodations, without the specified written consent of the hotel.

This trade order will be cancelled by the hotel without further liability on its part if presented by other than an employee authorized to use it; thus preventing its use in the event of loss, theft or sale. The hotel accepts no responsibility in identifying the user other than to exercise due care. The publisher may at any time withdraw credit privileges extended to any individual by notifying the hotel in writing of such withdrawal, whereupon the signature of such individual shall be stricken from the hotel record of authorized persons. The publisher may also substitute names of new employees eligible for credit by communicating in writing with the hotel.

The hotel is not liable to the person presenting, using or otherwise availing himself of the use of this trade order, for any compensation or damages of any kind whatever for personal injury or property losses sustained while in the hotel, or loss or damage to property either as the result of the ordinary or gross negligence of the hotel proprietors or employees or otherwise.

VOID IF SOLD OR TRANSFERRED

Daily Rates: Single.. Double..

THE HOTEL DESIRES TO EXTEND EVERY COURTESY AND CONSIDERATION TO THE USER OF THIS TRADE ORDER, EXACTLY AS THOUGH ACCOMMODATIONS WERE TO BE PAID FOR IN CASH. THIS TRADE ORDER SHOULD, THEREFORE, BE PRESENTED TO THE REGISTRATION CLERK WHEN THE PERSON USING IT REGISTERS.

Signatures of authorized users of this Trade Order:

....

....

Publishers are advised to keep a record of names of persons authorized to use this trade order.
All conditions above are understood and hereby agreed to by the hotel and the publication.

HOTEL..

....
(Publication) (SIGNATURE) (Title)

....
(SIGNATURE) (Title)

Date ...., 19..........

Advertising agency

The use of this form by hotels and advertising agents is prohibited except by consent in writing from the

Hotel Association of New York City, Inc.

Figure 13.3. Due bill, or trade advertising contract, for trading hotel space for advertising or other services normally purchased with cash.
Courtesy: Hotel Association of New York City, Inc.

Figure 13.4. A due bill in check form accentuates the negotiability of many trade contracts that allow third-party users. *Courtesy: Courtesy Check, Inc., St. Louis, Mo.*

that was incurred by the contract. At the time of the agreement, an asset was created for the hotel in the form of unused advertising and a liability was created in the hotel's promise to furnish accommodations to the media or other trader. As hotel accommodations are furnished, the liability is decreased by balancing it off against the city ledger account that was created from the transfer at the time of checkout.

Advance Deposits

Resort hotels more than commercial hotels require advance deposits for guest reservations. Technically, the deposit is not a city ledger item. The hotel owes the guest service in the amount of the deposit rather than the guest owing the hotel. Nevertheless, advance deposits may be viewed as city ledger accounts since they reflect a guest-hotel relationship. It is an inverse relationship (a contra account receivable), with the hotel an account receivable of the guest rather than the other way around. Advance deposits usually appear on the balance sheet as a liability, although the guest accounts may be carried as a contra account receivable in the hotel's accounting office.

Chapter 11 explained the several methods of handling reservation deposits. Basically, the money is received in advance of the guest; it is run through the records as a contra city ledger receivable and transferred from the city ledger to the folio when the guest arrives sometime later. The deposit appears on the folio as a credit transfer, reducing the charges for the arrival day by the amount received, usually one night's charge.

Travel Agencies

Hotels pay a 10 percent commission — more in off-seasons to generate volume — for all room business booked into the hotel by a travel agency.[1] But fees are not regulated: not for the hotels, and not for the airlines. Amounts paid vary from property to property and even within the same property over time. Overrides, additional points of 10–15 percent, are paid to encourage high levels of business from one agency. IT packages, which involve airline reservations as well as rooms, generate two commissions for the travel agent in one booking.

Market forces can be seen in the flow of conflicting trade news. One resort complex announces no more commissions of any kind to travel agents. Another stops paying commissions on American plan meals. Simultaneously, a third holds out the carrot of commissions on all meals taken in the hotel,

American plan or not. A costly suggestion considering the small markup on food and the impossibility of accounting for the sale to the agency. How would anyone know that the guest who paid cash for breakfast was a travel agency account?

Guests pay no direct charge to the agency for its service. Neither do they pay a fee for airline or other bookings made by the agent in the guest's name. Two areas of contention emerge from this relationship. One is a marketing problem, the other a bookkeeping problem.

Hotels complain that travel agencies (TAs) send business chiefly during the hotel's busy periods, when additional reservations are not needed, certainly not if they require a commission. According to the agents, hotels befriend them only when there is no business and ignore them and their customers — who incidentally are also hotel guests — as soon as volume recovers. According to a recent study, TAs recommended clients to particular hotels based chiefly on whether the hotel honored the TAs reservation and paid the commission. Overbooking, hotel ads that bypass travel agencies, hotels directly soliciting agency customers, and discrimination in space assignment are all part of the ongoing love-hate relationship.

Procedures and Accounting

Bookkeeping is the other half of the dissension and it involves two parts: poor recordkeeping that fails to acknowledge the reservation, and sloppy accounting procedures that lose or miscalculate the agency's fee. Unhappily, all these matters catch the guest in the middle.

If time permits, both the agency's request and the hotel's confirmation are processed by mail. With an increase in the number of in-WATS lines (800 numbers) by the hotels and out-WATS lines by the agencies, much of the communication has shifted to the telephone.

1. Travel agency identification has been blurred by federal deregulation, which has left unresolved the legitimacy of nontraditional agencies, including in-house travel departments operated by companies buying travel for their own employees.

But the gains in speed are many times offset by the lack of written messages. TAs commissions could be as little as four or five dollars. They would prefer, therefore, not to process a great deal of correspondence and paperwork, expecting the hotel to generate their commission automatically. Hotel accountants haven't as yet accepted this completely.

Accounting for the travel agency commission starts with the reservation process. Commissionable reservations are so marked and the identification is carried onto the folios from the reg cards. These reservations are separated in the accounting office on the day following departure and specially treated before being permanently filed. DNAs, did not arrive, must be identified at once and a notice, frequently a postcard, immediately mailed to the travel agency. This should forestall a claim and the endless correspondence that usually follows.

A great deal of detail work takes place in this section of the accounting office. DNAs must be identified. Advance agency payments must be differentiated from unpaid agency accounts. Cumulative account balances are maintained by posting the amount of the commission due to an account with the travel agency. Each posting is identified by the guest's folio number, the date, and similar information.

If the reservation has not been prepaid, it is a city ledger account (a receivable) that the hotel maintains with the agency. Many hotels will not accept reservations that they must collect from the agency after the guest is gone. It is an account payable if the reservation has been prepaid and the hotel owes the commission. More often, the agency withheld the commission before it sent the deposit. Then, unless the guest changed the length of stay, all accounts have been settled at departure. Some agencies are both receivables and payables.

The sorting and posting completed, the hotel pays (or bills) the agency monthly. More frequent payments are made if the hotel is attempting to build agency business through prompt remittance. That's why care must be exercised in staffing the accounting department. Too few clerks mean inordinate delays in paying agency accounts, resulting in an unexpected, and often unsuspected, impact on the market forecast. Increased computerization will probably concentrate agency payments in chain headquarters. For now, members of chain hotels still settle agency accounts individually for the most part. Some even write checks daily. There's no better way of telling the agency you want its business!

The relationship of travel agency payments and the business' cash flow has yet to receive the management attention it warrants, but it is one reason that many hotels put travel agents on a prepaid basis only. That is, the agency supports its reservation request with a check for the full amount less commission. Accompanying the check is a reservation form like that in figure 13.5. By returning one copy of the form, the hotel confirms the reservation and awaits the guest. (The check is processed through the front office cash sheet or through the general cashier's deposit, depending on the hotel's procedure.) On arrival, the guest presents the reservation with a copy of the agency receipt, called a *coupon* or *voucher*.[2] Additional charges, if any, for food and beverage are paid at checkout but the guest receives credit for the prepaid room charges. For the hotel, this is the preferred procedure: the cash is on hand and there is no paperwork since the commission was taken in advance.

2. Travel agent's vouchers or coupons must not be confused with the host of marketing coupons that the hotel chains have distributed as promotional discounts or summer travel incentives.

Step 1. Agency types out as much of form as it can.
Step 2. Agency mails Parts 2 and 3 to hotel or completes form by phone.
Step 3. If Step 2 was done by mail, hotel fills out balance of form on both parts and returns

Part 3 to agency. If Step 2 was completed by phone, agency throws away Part 2.
Step 4. When form has been all filled out, remittance is attached to Part 4 and mailed to hotel.

Step 5. Part 3 is filed in client's folder and Part 1 is mailed or delivered to client.
Step 6. Part 5 is filed in date tickler for commission collection and/or is thrown out when commission has been collected.

AGENCY REQUEST FOR HOTEL/MOTEL ACCOMMODATIONS

Date_____ ☐ INITIAL REQUEST ☐ CANCELLATION ☐ CHANGE

CONFIRM TO AGENCY VIA ☐ RETURN MAIL ☐ AIR MAIL ☐ TELE-PHONE ☐ WIRE

CATEGORY ☐ MINIMUM ☐ MODERATE ☐ DELUXE

CLIENT

AGT.
HOTEL/MOTEL

TEL. NO.

AGENCY LIABILITY SUBJECT TO CONDITIONS ON REVERSE SIDE HEREOF

CONFIRMED RESERVATIONS FOR:

_____ ROOMS _____ PERSONS _____ NIGHTS

HOUR DAY DATE VIA FROM
ARRIVE
DEPART

_____ SINGLE _____ TWIN _____ DOUBLE _____ STUDIO _____ SUITE _____ SEE BELOW

☐ NO FACILITIES ☐ PRIVATE TOILET ☐ PRIVATE SHOWER AND TOILET ☐ PRVATE BATH AND TOILET

☐ NO MEALS(EP) ☐ CONTINENTAL BREAKFAST ☐ AMERICAN BREAKFAST

☐ DEMI PENSION (MAP) ☐ FULL PENSION(AP)

CONFIRMED FOR HOTEL BY _____ DATE _____

ROOM RATE $_____

NO. OF NIGHTS _____

WHEN VALIDATED THIS VOUCHER HAS A VALUE OF
$

EXCLUDING TAXES AND CHARGES FOR SERVICE AND PERSONAL INCIDENTALS

PLEASE REPLY BELOW AND RETURN GREEN COPY TO TRAVEL AGENCY

☐ Quote rates in U.S. Dollars or specify currency exchange rate _____
☐ Advise cancellation date without penalty_____
☐ State if reservations are guaranteed _____ YES _____ NO
☐ May agency deduct commission if fully prepaid _____ YES _____ NO

COMM. $ _____

DEPOSIT _____

HOTEL/MOTEL TO COLLECT FROM CLIENT $ _____

Reply by Hotel/Motel:

THIS BOX FOR AGENCY USE ONLY
CK.   DATE
NO.   SENT

By _____ Date _____

Figure 13.5. Travel agency form for requesting hotel/motel accommodations. Efforts to standardize a single form and its use have been unsuccessful. *Courtesy: Willow Press, Inc., Syosset, N.Y.*

The procedure rarely works so well. First of all, the agency does not send the check. The agency may not have the check to send. A corporate account, for example, is customarily settled after the trip, not before. So rather than being prepaid, the guest tenders nothing more than an IOU (the agency's coupon or voucher), naively expecting hotel credit for payment made to the agency. Unless a good credit relationship has been established with the travel agency, this arrangement is obviously not to the hotel's liking. The hotel finds itself in the position of servicing the guest while attempting to collect from a third party. Quite naturally, it refuses to accept the agency's voucher unless the credit relationship exists beforehand. The problems are compounded by the fact that some hotel rates are noncommissionable (as when travel agents are permitted to quote corporate rates for the hotel), and certain hotels refuse to pay any commissions at all.

Two special circumstances exacerbate what is a touchy situation to begin with. First is the guest who leaves early and wants a rebate from the hotel, which has not yet been paid by the agency. Second is the overseas voucher. Efforts at broadening the international market have brought vouchers in different shapes, colors, and languages to front desk personnel who are unfamiliar with any language other than English.

Even in the United States, there is no uniformity of voucher and one agency's coupon hardly resembles another. Efforts by organizations such as the American Society of Travel Agents (ASTA) and the Hotel Sales Managers Association (HSMA) to standardize reservation forms have not been effective. Results might come from ASTA's more recent efforts to negotiate with the AH&MA. Actually, ASTA has its own voucher, but using it entails a fee payable to the Association's marketing services. Until there is success at the national level, little can be expected from the international standardized voucher that is being developed by the International Hotel Association and the Universal Federation of Travel Agents Association. Guaranteeing payments may make the voucher more palatable to the hotel industry; that's how the credit card companies make the guaranteed reservation successful.

The Agency Voucher

Whatever standardization has been achieved — and it hasn't been much — comes from the ability of the larger chains to influence the marketplace. Like the auto rental companies, almost every hotel chain has its own voucher form. Hilton, for example, developed a voucher-check for travel agencies to use. Requests for accommodations are made on a multicopy packet printed by the hotel and including a check payable to the hotel for the amount of the room less commission. The agency's voucher is this check, and this check-voucher is the request for accommodations. The packet is designed to reduce correspondence, but the check must still precede the guest! By holding the check at the

front office until the guest arrives, the hotel reduces the paperwork to that of a nonagency reservation. It does leave the checks collectability unresolved, however.

Figure 13.6 illustrates Holiday Inns' tour voucher. The agent prepares the packet, including perhaps several Holiday Inn stops, and sends one of the carbon forms along with the net balance (room rate less commission) to Memphis, the company's headquarters. Reservations are made at each of the participating inns. The guest's copy of the voucher is tendered in payment at each stop for one night. Eventual reimbursement is made from Memphis to each inn upon proper invoicing. Whatever procedure, the principle is the same: the travel agent pays the hotel in advance. It's different with the airlines.

Airline travel vouchers work much the same way. The airline is the agency and the guest carries the airline's MCO (Miscellaneous Charge Order) voucher, which looks very similar to an airline ticket (figure 13.7). Hotels accept airline vouchers on good faith and credit; advance payment is not required. That luxury is not possible with travel agencies. Estimates place the number of travel agencies at about 15,000 and the casualty factor is high enough to make front office credit managers cautious of open credit. Although the numbers are not as great, deregulation has brought about some airline bankruptcies and a closer examination by the hotels of the MCO vouchers.

Some chains are now selling packages of 100 or 1,000 vouchers to tour operators for a set price. Each voucher is redeemable for one night's lodging with no concern for the value of the voucher versus the value of the room. Distinctions in rate variations are ignored; each property is reimbursed a given amount, but the deal works wonders for the chain's cash flow. It also helps the international traveler who gets a run-of-the-house rate regardless of currency fluctuations between nations.

Figure 13.6. Holiday Inn travel vouchers are redeemable at local inns, which bill central headquarters for collection. *Courtesy: Holiday Inns, Inc., Memphis, Tenn.*

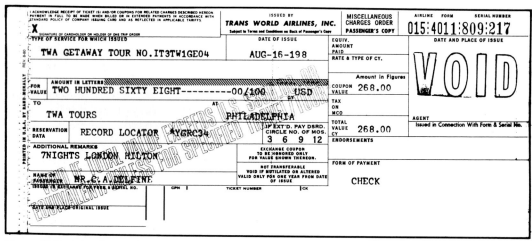

Figure 13.7. Miscellaneous Charge Order used by airlines acting in a travel agency capacity. *Courtesy: Trans World Airlines, Inc.*

Credit Rating

There are problems even when the credit relationship is firmly established. If the hotel is fully booked and unable to honor the reservation on the day of arrival, the guest finds himself with no room and no money. Anticipating that the room was to be fully paid, many are unprepared for the additional cash demands of taking rooms elsewhere. It is a question of which is more surprising to the guest, the lack of a room even though a confirmed reservation is in hand or the refusal of the hotel to refund the deposit, which is still in the hands of the agency.

Problems may also arise if there is a change in the length of stay. For example, if the guest remains less than the planned stay, the hotel must rebate the agency, not the guest. That, too, is beyond the guest's comprehension. If the guest stays longer than anticipated, the excess is collected from the guest and the commission on that extra amount is sent to the agency.

Unless the check is held with the reservation until the guest arrives, the final balancing takes place in the back office city ledgers. If the deposit was prepaid and credited to an agency account, the departing guest's folio is transferred to the city ledger, where it is charged (balanced) against that agency account. If the deposit has not been prepaid, the folio is transferred to the city ledger and the agency is billed. In both cases, the guest gets full credit for the coupon, which shows the payment to the agency and not the net amount after commission.

Holding the agency's check until the guest arrives makes some sense, although it appears to be poor money management. Unless there is a great sum tied up in undeposited checks or unless the travel agency has a poor credit reputation, there may be more wisdom in holding the checks than in depositing them. The clerical savings will be significant: no need

to maintain and post agency accounts in the back office; cancellations are easily handled by returning the original check; and a good deal of record verification is reduced because the check and the coupon are processed together.

Whether the check precedes or follows the guest, there is a difference between the check and the coupon value in the amount of the commission. That difference, usually 10 percent of room charges, is the agency's fee. It is an operating expense to the hotel and a credit to the account receivable. In other words, the account receivable is paid in full although the cash received is 10 percent less than the amount due.

MECHANICS OF THE ENTRY

City ledger charges at the front desk derive from one of two situations. Either nonguests make charges to a credit card or to a city account with the hotel, or registered guests transfer their active folios to the city ledger when checking out. Either way, charges are posted directly to the city ledger only when the city ledger is at the front desk. When the city ledger is away from the front office, which is usually the case, the mechanics of the entry must overcome the physical gap between the front office, where the charge originates, and the back office, where the account is kept. This is primarily a communication problem. It is the type of communication problem that computers have solved, as chapter 9 explained.

Nonregistered Guests

Charges for nonregistered guests invariably originate in the dining room or lounge. Every credit card payment must be verified promptly either by comparison to lists of cancelled or expired cards or by direct-dial telephone to

WATS numbers as discussed in the preceding chapter. The hotel's own alphabetical list of city accounts is cross-referenced numerically and filed in some accessible place like the front office. Computerized city ledgers flash the name on a CRT screen and speed the process dramatically.

The city vouchers, including the signed charge records of the private credit card companies, are separated at the front desk from the vouchers of registered guests and processed in one of several ways, depending on the size of the city ledger volume. Excessive volume decentralizes the process. Then each departmental cashier is responsible for tallying and forwarding the slips to the accounting office rather than processing them through the front desk.

When city charges number as few as, say, ten per day, they are accumulated and held for the night audit. The auditor enters each on a line of the hand transcript (a nightly listing of accounts receivable) as if it were an individual folio account. The night audit sheet thereby becomes the record of original entry. It may also become the final record; that is, the city ledger of a very small hotel. Using the vouchers in support of the transcript, it is possible to eliminate the city ledger accounts because there are so few to keep track of.

An intermediate step makes use of a memo record like the one in figure 13.8. City ledger activities are recorded there and the net totals only are entered on the transcript for each of the several categories. Individual account postings are made the following day in the accounting office. Contra accounting entries being made in totals on the transcript. For example, in figure 13.8, the contra entries for credit cards would be food sales, beverage sales, or transient accounts receivable. The contra entry for advance deposits would be cash. Obviously, city entries that involve cash, either receipts or disbursements, appear on the front office cash sheet. It would not be possible to reconcile the cash drawer without them.

City Ledger Totals

Date ____________________

Advance Deposits

$ ____________________

____________________ + or −

____________________ + or −

____________________ + or −

Total $ ____________

Credit Cards

$ ____________________

____________________ + or −

____________________ + or −

____________________ + or −

Total $ ____________

City Ledger Other

$ ____________________

____________________ + or −

____________________ + or −

____________________ + or −

Total $ ____________

Figure 13.8. City ledger memorandum record used by the front office during the day and left for the night auditor.

City Ledger Journal

When the number of city entries increases, the audit and memo journals, as described above, are replaced with a city ledger journal. Then,

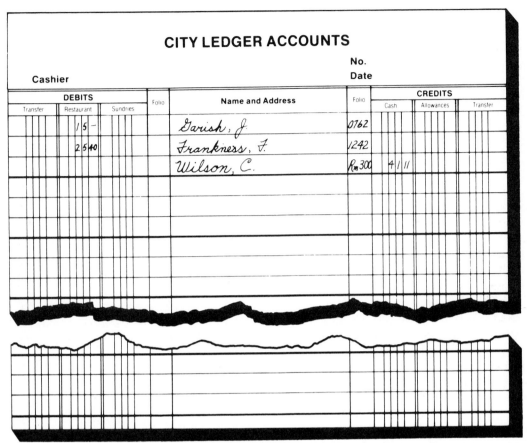

CITY LEDGER ACCOUNTS

Cashier

No.

Date

DEBITS			Folio	Name and Address	Folio	CREDITS		
Transfer	Restaurant	Sundries				Cash	Allowances	Transfer
	1 5 —			*Garish, J.*	0762			
	2 5 40			*Frankness, F.*	1242			
				Wilson, C.	Rm 300	4 1 11		

Figure 13.9. The city ledger journal is maintained at the front office as a communication device to the back office. Debit and credit headings refer to account receivable.

instead of waiting for the night auditor to journalize the entries, they are recorded during the day as the vouchers are generated. Like any accounting journal, the city ledger journal accumulates entries of like kind. In this way, city transactions are posted as one total to the audit rather than individually.

The debit and credit identification on the journal (figure 13.9) refers to accounts receivable and not to the column names of the form.

That is, an entry in the restaurant column means a charge (debit) to the receivable and not a charge to the restaurant column in which it is recorded.

The column names are the contra entries. In this case, a credit to restaurant sales. Similarly, a credit in the cash column means a credit to the guest account (a reduction of the due balance) and a debit to cash, which is recorded on the front office cash sheet and deposited in the usual manner. Since the debit and credit columns of the city journal do not refer to the same transaction, they would not equal in totals at the end of the day.

Sometimes, city accounts are accumulated on a special front office posting machine that is used for city accounts only, and the machine totals and tape become the journal record.

The city journal is delivered daily to the accounting office along with the city vouchers. These are checked against the journal entries and arranged alphabetically to speed posting to the alphabetically maintained city ledger. With a completely computerized system, city charges recorded by the front office are switched over to a back office module at the close of each day. Similarly, the arrival of an advanced deposit removes the figure from the city ledger and simultaneously adds it to the newly arrived transient folio. All computer systems are not so interfaced and the transfer between city and transient ledger must still be done by hand in many places.

Batch Handling

As the volume of city transactions grows, it becomes impractical to send every transaction through the front office so the billing clerk can record each entry in the city ledger journal. Instead, the vouchers are separated by type: MasterCard, Diners' Club, House Accounts, etc., and batched. A careful examination of figure 13.10 illustrates the procedure. For example, MasterCard drafts are accumulated, totaled, recorded on, and enclosed in the envelope (figure 13.10 lower left). Other credit cards are handled similarly, but transferred guest accounts, which are posted individually, are journalized individually on the left side of the envelope, which is used as a city ledger journal.

The summary section of the envelope is the audit information and is the same data that would appear on the transcript if one were being prepared. Total debits, credits, and balance today represent changes in city accounts receivable. Charges are divided among the shifts to facilitate error location and audit.

Vouchers are posted to city accounts the following day, but only true city accounts will be individually posted. The hundreds, perhaps thousands, of charges from the credit card companies are summarized on appropriate transmittal forms (figure 13.11). The total of each form, usually limited to 100 individual charges, is posted to the credit card company's city account and copies of the transmittal form are used to support the total figure. Receipts from the credit card companies are credited to the city accounts to keep the balances current. These receipts may or may not be processed through the front office cashiers.

Charge backs by the credit card companies are usually maintained in a second city account to distinguish them from the standard credit card charges. Thus, upon notification of the disallowed amount, the standard account will be credited, reduced, and a new individual city account will be debited, increased. The new account may eventually be written off as a bad debt when the probability of collection grows small.

Registered Guests

Registered guests become city guests when they transfer their active folios to the city ledger. Until then, charges are handled in the usual manner for posting transient charges. Vouchers that arrive after the transfer are late charges. Late charges and skippers are treated as previously explained.

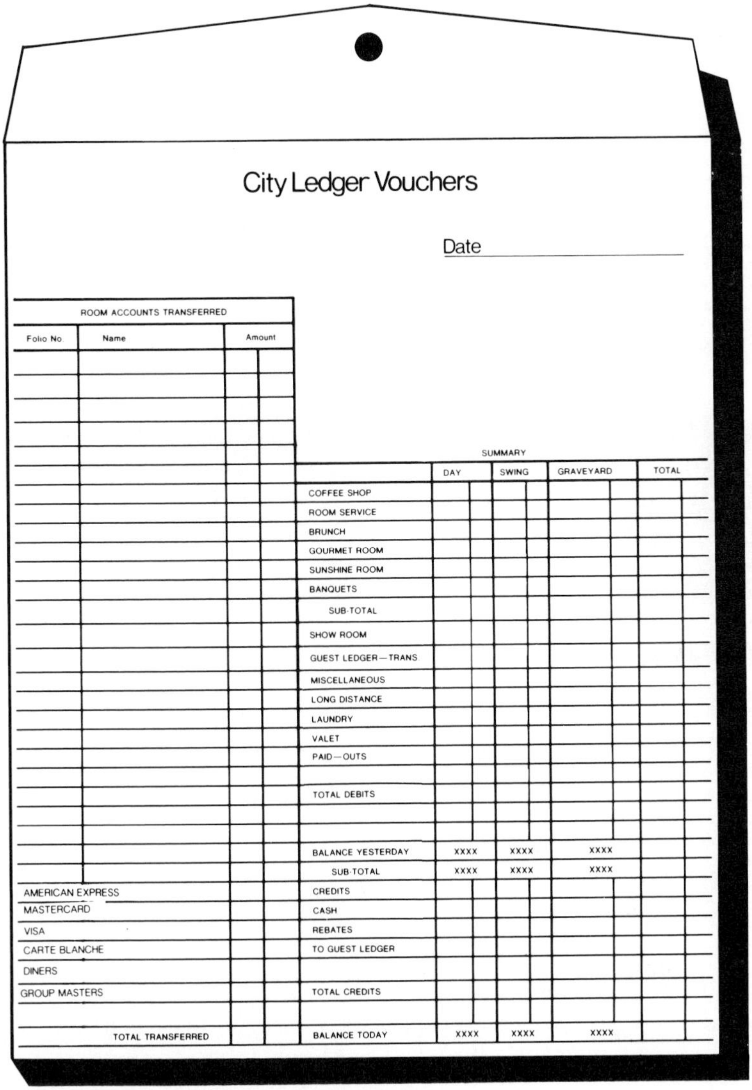

City Ledger Vouchers

Date _____

ROOM ACCOUNTS TRANSFERRED		
Folio No	Name	Amount

SUMMARY

	DAY	SWING	GRAVEYARD	TOTAL
COFFEE SHOP				
ROOM SERVICE				
BRUNCH				
GOURMET ROOM				
SUNSHINE ROOM				
BANQUETS				
SUB-TOTAL				
SHOW ROOM				
GUEST LEDGER — TRANS				
MISCELLANEOUS				
LONG DISTANCE				
LAUNDRY				
VALET				
PAID — OUTS				
TOTAL DEBITS				
BALANCE YESTERDAY	XXXX	XXXX	XXXX	
SUB-TOTAL	XXXX	XXXX	XXXX	
CREDITS				
CASH				
REBATES				
TO GUEST LEDGER				
TOTAL CREDITS				
BALANCE TODAY	XXXX	XXXX	XXXX	

AMERICAN EXPRESS
MASTERCARD
VISA
CARTE BLANCHE
DINERS
GROUP MASTERS

TOTAL TRANSFERRED

Figure 13.10. City ledger envelope for summarizing the various classifications of the city ledger and for conveying the vouchers to the back office.

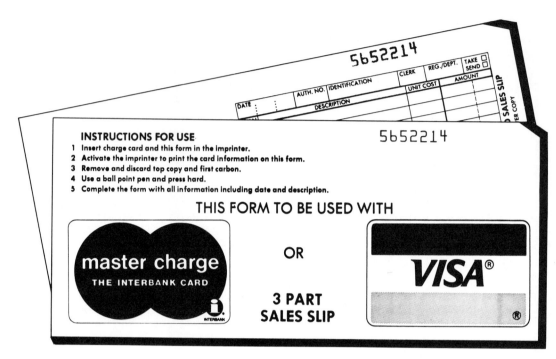

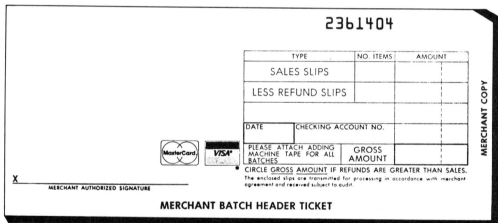

Figure 13.11. Guest charge slip (top) and summary transmittal form with which the merchant makes a deposit. *Courtesy: First Interstate Bank of Nevada, Las Vegas.*

Individual city accounts are subsidiary accounts of the master city ledger account maintained in the general ledger, just as the transient accounts in the front office bucket are subsidiaries of the transient control account in the general ledger. As the night audit reconciles the transient folios, so an abstract of individual city accounts is compared to the general ledger account monthly. Similarly, the advance deposit account must be reconciled periodically with the individual advance deposit reservations in the front office.

Transfer to City Ledger

Previous paragraphs refer to the transfer *of* the active folio *to* the city ledger. This terminology is confusing at times. What appears on the guest folio as a transfer *to* (city ledger) shows on the city ledger as a transfer *from* (guest ledger). Since the account receivable is normally a debit (charge) balance, the transfer *to* represents a credit, a reduction, in the guest ledger and the transfer *from* represents a debit, an increase, in the city ledger. Similar terminology is used when the charge balance is transferred to the guest ledger from the city ledger.

In other words, guests who check out owing the hotel (debit balance account), pay by national credit card. This zeroes out the guest account by a credit, called *transfer to city ledger*. Now the balance owed appears in the city ledger payable by the national credit card company. Since it is owed to the hotel, it is a debit city ledger account, appearing there as a result of a debit *transfer from transient ledger.*

Language gets twisted when the balance being transferred is a credit instead of a charge. It is not possible then to transfer *to* city ledger on the guest folio because a *to* transfer would be an additional credit. Rather, a *from* transfer (a debit) is needed on the folio even though the direction of the transfer is toward (*to*) the city ledger. Likewise, the new city account

would show the transfer as a *to* (credit transfer), although the actual direction would have been from the active guest folio. Because of this confusion, it is better to refer to transfers as debits, increases to the account receivable, or credits, decreases from it.

A transfer to the city ledger occurs at the time of checkout. It may be one of several credits used to balance out the active folio, including cash and allowances. At the same time, a new account is opened in the city ledger by means of the debit transfer there. Actually, new accounts are being opened in the city ledger less and less. The handful of major credit cards, which are already being used, easily accommodate new guests with new charges.

For the individual city account still being opened, banquets for example, active folio cards are being used as both the city ledger account and the city ledger statement that is mailed to the guest. There has even been some success with different colored headings on these mailings; faster collections come from colored headings than from those printed in the usual black ink. Taking a tip from the billing side, some hotels send special colored checks for their travel agency commissions. They hope to alert the agency to their prompt payment, and thus encourage new business.

Transient folios that are transferred to the city ledger need a balancing credit figure to show the closing of the folio. If the transfer is to a credit card company, which is then responsible for payment, the transfer credit posting appears on the folio in the usual manner (figure 10.5). If the transfer merely shifts the balance to the guest's city account, or a company account, the posting is often placed out of alignment. The appearance of the folio then seems less settled, which of course it is.

Transfer from City Ledger

Occasionally, a debit balance is transferred from the city ledger to the active account of a guest who has recently registered. This means a credit transfer in the city ledger and a debit transfer on the guest folio.

City transfers more often involve credit balances, since they are advance deposits being held for guest arrivals. Then the city ledger is debited to balance off the credit and the transient folio is credited to show the unused balance of the deposit (figure 10.4).

A city ledger journal entry is made for these transfers, and the daily totals are included in the city ledger balance when the night audit is completed. Regardless of the direction of the transfer, the amount, or the ledgers involved, debit transfers must always equal credit transfers. That axiom of equality serves to keep the accounts receivable reconciled throughout the entire hotel, as we see next in the process called the night audit.

QUERIES AND PROBLEMS

1. Explain how the following transfers should be handled. Be specific, citing the location of the entry, the ledger or ledgers involved, and the debit or credit requirements.
   a. A transient guest checks out using a national credit card.
   b. The president and treasurer of a small company check in for a business meeting. The hotel has been carrying the unpaid balance of a charge generated by these officers at their last business meeting about three months ago.
   c. A couple depart and request that the balance of their folio be charged

to the couple's parents, who are registered in another room. The parents concur.
   d. An association completes its meeting and the association executive, after reviewing the balance due, requests billing to the company's headquarters.

2. In terms of the front office and of the city ledger, explain the quick check-out system being used by numerous hotels and chains.

3. In terms of the front office and of the city ledger, explain how a reservation request from a travel agent is processed if (1) the agency has a good working relationship with the hotel, including a good credit rating, and the guest pays the agency; (2) the agency has no credit rating with the hotel, and the guest pays the agency; (3) the guest makes no payment to the agency.

4. In accounting entries, explain the following events.
   a. The hotel and the advertising media (radio station) agree to exchange guest room accommodations for air time.
   b. The hotel receives notice that its advertising was played on the air.
   c. The radio station trades some of its room accommodations to a record company (a third party) for tapes. Paying with the due bill that has passed into the hands of this third party, representatives of the record company use the rooms provided under the trade contract.

14

The Mechanical Night Audit

THE AUDITOR AND THE AUDIT

The final watch of the hotel day is that of the night audit, beginning somewhere between 11 P.M. and midnight. In a small hotel the auditor relieves the entire desk, filling the jobs of room clerk, cashier, telephone operator, and auditor. The audit staff of a large hotel may consist of a senior night auditor, two or three assistants who also handle the cashier's duties, and one or two food and beverage auditors. And even then they don't relieve the rest of the desk, which remains fully staffed.

The size of the audit crew depends upon the number of tasks being performed and the volume of guest charges. Some hotels are busy regardless of the number of rooms actually occupied. It is a matter of size — large hotels offer more services that create more postings — and clientele. Guests who use facilities (food, beverage, valet, golf) create charges that need auditing. A busy night spot in the hotel means more desk activity during the early

morning hours and less time for the auditor to devote to the business at hand. Simply put, the larger the hotel and the busier the desk, the fewer rooms each auditor can handle.

Contrary to the title, the night auditor need not be a trained accountant and is an auditor only by the broadest definition. An auditor is an appraiser-reporter of the accuracy and integrity of records and financial statements. One type of auditing, internal auditing, involves procedural control and an accounting review of operations and records. Internal auditing also reports on the activities of other employees. It is this final definition that best explains the role of the hotel night auditor.

No special knowledge of accounting or even of bookkeeping's debits and credits is required of the night auditor. Having this knowledge is helpful and desirable, but it is sufficient for the auditor to have good arithmetic skills, self-discipline, and a penchant for detailed work. Auditors must be careful, accurate, and reliable. The latter trait is an especially redeeming one because the unattractive working hours makes replacements difficult to recruit and almost impossible to find on short notice.

Even if the auditor does not assume the other front office tasks, as is the case with large properties, he or she must be conversant with the duties of all personnel since it is their work being audited. Where these tasks are taken on, the auditor is likely to be the sole responsible employee on duty and assumes the position of night manager whether the title is there or not. Mature judgment and experience are needed to carry out these nonaudit functions in the best interests of the house. The combination of audit skills, working hours, and responsibility merit a higher salary for the night auditor than for the average room clerk, but the spread is not noticeably large.

A Trial Balance of Receivables

A periodic reconciliation of accounts receivable is undertaken by every business that extends credit. The sum total of each individual debtor is compared to the cumulative balance of accounts receivable. Most businesses make this reconciliation monthly and some less frequently than that. Hotels do it nightly. Whereas nonhotel businesses can delay the reconciliation until errors are uncovered, hotels face a new day with more charges and more credits and with new arrivals and new departures whether or not the previous day is reconciled and whether or not the departures are properly billed. Therefore, a detailed analysis of charges, rather than a mere verification by totals, is prepared nightly.

This daily reconciliation of account receivable charges is the night audit. Since each new charge changes the account receivable balance, the audit is necessarily prepared when changes in the records are infrequent — in the early morning hours when most guests are in bed.

Cash sales do not pass through the front desk as earlier chapters have stressed. Cash sales are reviewed by the day audit. Only charge items — account receivable sales — are recorded at the front desk and thence through the night audit. They are then reviewed as part of the day audit and combined there with cash sales, ultimately to be recorded into the permanent books of account.

Every sale to or collection from an account receivable has two parts. Sales increase both hotel income and accounts receivable. (Cash sales, which also increase income for each department, are not recorded on guest folios.) Collections decrease the balance of the receivables but increase the amount of cash on hand. (Cash collections from receivables who are paying their outstanding accounts should not be confused with cash receipts from cash sales made in one of the dining rooms or lounges.) Verifying these changes in accounts receivable, in cash, and in hotel income is the purpose of the audit.

In summary, the night audit makes certain that guest charges are correctly posted to guest folios and that the sale that caused the guest charge is correctly credited to departmental income.

THE AUDIT PROCEDURE — DEBITS

Before the audit proper can begin, all of the work that is about to be audited must be finished. Earlier watches may not have completed the postings (chapter 10), leaving them for the auditor to do. Additional vouchers may arrive during the early portion of the auditor's watch and these, too, are posted before the audit begins. Vouchers that arrive at the desk after the close of the day are saved until after the audit and then posted as part of the following day's charges. Management sets a time that officially closes the day for record purposes, the *close-out hour.* That hour depends a great deal on the closing hours of the lounges, room service, and other dining facilities, but it cannot be too late without putting undue pressure on the auditing staff.

Auditors can handle more rooms if the previous shift, the swing shift, finished all of its own work and postings. Indeed, the swing shift can help the auditor by transcribing the folios onto the transcript sheet when a hand audit is used. Some swing shifts go as far as posting room charges and "footing" (totaling) some of the folios. This is possible only with a hand audit and only when there is very little activity during the closing portion of the swing shift.

Posting the Room Charges

After all the departmental vouchers are posted, the auditor removes the folios from the bucket (figure 10.2). Care must be exercised in going through the bucket, for both humidity and static electricity make the smaller folios hug the larger cardboard dividers and the account is easily overlooked. The auditor posts the room rate, the tax, and the telephone charges, using the rate that is on the folio heading and watching for rate changes that may have been made during the day. Taxes are charged at the legally required percentage and local telephone chits are charged at multiples of the local call rate. Telephone deregulation has changed telephone charges and procedures as chapter 16 explains.

Daily columns are footed on the hand-prepared folios, and the new balances are carried forward to the top of the next day's column, as is shown in figure 10.3. On machine-prepared folios, the old balance is picked up and the new balance is then automatically printed after the room charges, room taxes, and local telephone calls have been posted (figure 10.1).

Paid-in-advance room charges may or may not already be posted to the folio. In some instances, the guest is given a receipt for the payment and the cash is posted to the folio later, after the folio has been typed. Room charges are then posted by the auditor. In other cases, the folio is immediately prepared for the paid-in-advance guest and both the room charge and the cash credit are posted. The guest receives one copy, and the single hotel copy in the well alerts the auditor to the earlier room posting made by the cashier. Integrated computer systems input the data during the registration. Guests paying in advance go to the cashier's window where a receipted bill is provided. The entry remains in computer memory until the night audit.

It was noted in the chapter on registration that some of the rooms will have two or three folios from persons sharing the quarters. Each card will be charged with its proportionate share, except those marked "Info" or "No Rate"(NR) will have no posting at all.

Posting the room charge is a tedious and time-consuming task. Each folio, whether hand or machine posted, must be removed from the well. Each must be posted with the rate, tax, and telephone charges, if any. Each must be totaled. The hand-prepared folio is faster on the posting and slower in the totaling. The machine-prepared folio is slower on the posting but totals automatically. Automatic folio alignment is a standard feature on the new machine models, which speeds up the posting process (figure 10.4). Corrections on the hand folio are easily made with an eraser, but those on the machine require a good deal of thought and reposting.

Posting room charges with the computer requires none of this. First of all, there is no bucket and there are no folios. Time is saved just in not removing 500–1,000 folios from the well. Room charges with the appropriate tax have been programmed into the computer. Memory knows how much each room is to be billed and the proper tax is automatically computed. Individual postings and totaling are not required. Activating the rooms program brings all the accounts receivables up to date in memory, although most hotels will also get a night printout, a *hard copy,* for emergency backup.

Distributing the Charges
The Machine Audit

By this point in the day, hundreds or even thousands of charges will have been made against guests' accounts. Included in these charges are food, beverage, long-distance telephone calls, laundry, valet, cash advances, ski tows, golf greens, sauna baths, and the like. Added to the day's list are the room, tax, and local telephone charges just completed by the night auditor. If the amount of charges in each of these departments is to be reconciled with the records maintained by the departmental cashiers, it is necessary to separate charges by departments as well as by guests. That dual separation is the key to understanding the night audit, which reconciles both individual guest folios and distinct departmental incomes.

The front office posting machine makes this distribution automatically. As each charge is posted to the folio by the cashier, it is accumulated just like a cash register. Assume, for example, that a $9 beverage charge is posted to room 818. At the same time that the $9 is recorded on the folio of 818 (making the first separation, by room), it is added to all previous beverage charges. The total is accumulated in the machine and read as needed (making the second separation, by type of income). The beverage key, like other departmental keys, is functional, either mechanically or electronically. When struck, the key activates the machine, which does several jobs at once. It posts to the folio; it validates the voucher by printing across it; it prints on the audit tape so that individual entries can be traced during the night audit; and it accumulates the totals of charges made to each de-

partment. Room number keys and dollar amount keys are not functional and they will not activate the machine when depressed.

By separating the charges by department as well as by individual folio, the machine does some of the auditor's work even before the shift begins. All one need do is read the machine totals, which are printed on a special form—a D card (figure 14.1). The D card, which has identified the audit for so long, is not part of a computer audit although the term remains in the professional jargon. The process is more involved with the hand-prepared folio since there is no machine to accumulate separate totals or distribute the charges by departments. That important and time-consuming step is left for the auditor.

The Hand Audit
The completed hand folios, with the room and telephone charges posted and the balances footed, are copied one by one onto a large sheet called the *transcript.* Each horizontal line on the folio (room, room tax, food, etc.) has a corresponding vertical column on the transcript (figure 14.2). As each folio is transcribed to the transcript, departmental charges are being separated by columns. Totaling the individual columns produces a departmental charge figure similar to that accumulated by the posting machine. Although the preparation of the hand transcript is tedious, departmental charges are readily visible (figure 14.2), an advantage not provided by the machine audit tape (figure 14.3), or computer memory.

Figures that appear on the folio top to bottom are copied onto the transcript left to right. All folio figures are recorded, including the opening balance and closing totals. This thorough recording makes possible a verification of the addition on the folios, as we shall see later.

The accounts are listed in the same room number sequence in which they come from the bucket. As the night auditor moves down

D—NIGHT AUDITOR'S MACHINE BALANCE NO. 1722

DATE 10/31

DEPARTMENT	DATE	DESCRIPTION	ET TOTALS	CORRECTIONS	MACHINE TOTALS	
ROOM	OCT 31	ROOM	9078.00	32.50	* 9,110.50Z	
TAX	OCT 31	TAX	544.68	1.95	* 546.63Z	
TELEPHONE	OCT 31	PHONE	18.20	.80	* 19.00Z	
LONG DISTANCE	OCT 31	LDIST	258.31	4.46	* 262.77Z	
LAUNDRY	OCT 31	LNDRY	37.25		* 37.25Z	
VALET	OCT 31	VALET	-0-		* .00Z	
GARAGE	OCT 31	G'RAGE	-0-		* .00Z	
TELEGRAM	OCT 31	TELGM	-0-		* .00Z	
BEVERAGE	OCT 31	BEVGE	459.75		* 459.75Z	
MISCELLANEOUS	OCT 31	MISC	47.92		* 47.92Z	
RESTAURANT	OCT 31	RSETR	1711.64	73.51	* 1,785.15Z	
TRANSFER CHARGE	OCT 31	TR.CH.	75.53		* 75.53Z	
PAID OUT	OCT 31	PD.OUT	105.84		* 105.84Z	
TOTAL DEBITS			12337.12			
TRANSFER CREDIT	OCT 31	TR.CR.	5005.00		* 5,005.00Z	
ADJUSTMENT	OCT 31	ADJ	59.62		* 59.62Z	
PAID	OCT 31	PAID	1825.86		* 1,825.86Z	
TOTAL CREDITS			6890.48			
NET DIFFERENCE			5446.64			
OPENING DR BALANCE			16338.83			
NET OUTSTANDING			21785.47			
TOTAL MCH DR BALANCE	OCT 31		22501.64		*22,501.64Z	
TOTAL MCH CR BALANCE	OCT 31	IN.CR.	716.17		* 716.17Z	
NET OUTSTANDING			21785.47			
CORRECTIONS	OCT 31	CORR	-0-	113.22	* 113.22Z	

DETECTOR COUNTER READINGS

AUDITOR'S CONTROL 1722

MACH NUMBER 4

☑ DATE CHANGED

☑ CONTROL TOTALS AT ZERO

☑ MASTER TAPE LOCKED

☑ AUDIT CONTROL LOCKED

AUDITOR

George F. Hogan

Figure 14.1. Night auditor's D report: posting machine totals are verified against departmental control sheets, and net accounts receivable is verified against machine totals.

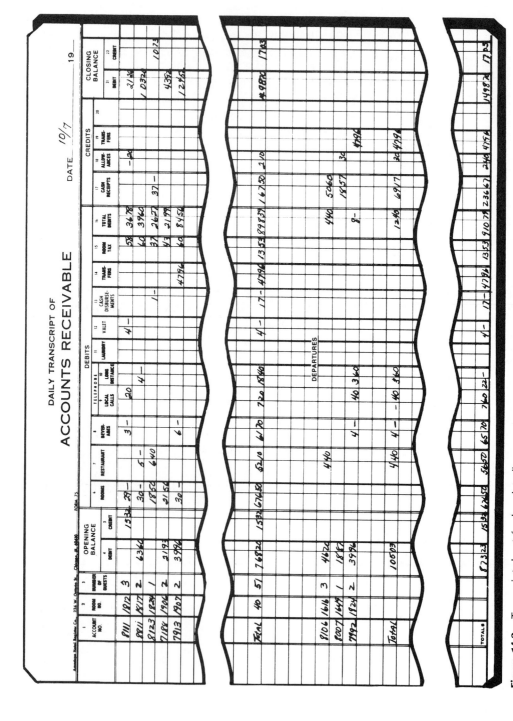

Figure 14.2. Transcript sheet for hand audit: column totals are verified against departmental control sheets, and totals are cross-footed. The first entry corresponds to figure 10.3.

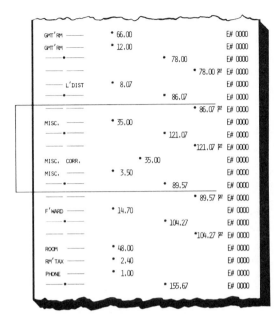

GMT'RM ────	• 66.00		E# 0000
GMT'RM ────	• 12.00		E# 0000
──•────		• 78.00	E# 0000
		• 78.00 ꟼ	E# 0000
────L'DIST	• 8.07		E# 0000
────────		• 86.07	E# 0000
		• 86.07 ꟼ	E# 0000
MISC. ────	• 35.00		E# 0000
──•────		• 121.07	E# 0000
		•121.07 ꟼ	E# 0000
MISC. CORR.	• 35.00		E# 0000
MISC. ────	• 3.50		E# 0000
──•────		• 89.57	E# 0000
		• 89.57 ꟼ	E# 0000
F'WARD ────	• 14.70		E# 0000
──•────		• 104.27	E# 0000
		•104.27 ꟼ	E# 0000
ROOM ────	• 48.00		E# 0000
RM'TAX ────	• 2.40		E# 0000
PHONE ────	• 1.00		E# 0000
──•────		• 155.67	E# 0000

Figure 14.3. A section of the machine audit tape showing, left to right: departmental description, charge column, credit column, new balance, old balance, operator's identification, and room number. This tape corresponds to figure 11.3.

the transcript, column headings get farther and farther away from the lower horizontal lines. Mistakes are more likely to be made at the bottom of the sheet, so a transcript ruler is used. This device consists of nothing more than the column headings pasted onto a piece of heavy cardboard. By using the transcript ruler below the next horizontal line, the auditor substantially reduces the possibility of posting to the wrong column.

After the transient guests are listed, departures and city ledger accounts (including late charges), if any, are recorded, usually on separate transcript sheets (figures 14.2 and 14.4). When a city ledger journal (figure 13.9) is used, the city ledger entry on the transcript may be no more than one or two lines reflecting in totals the individual items on the journal.

Although departures are also listed in room number order, certain departures can be combined to save time and space. Early departures rarely generate additional charges on their last day. They pay the same amount as the day's opening balance. In this case, the opening balances of all early departures are totaled and listed on one line along with the cash credit that balances their accounts. Early departures have no departmental charges on

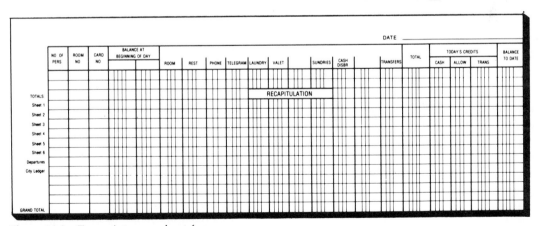

Figure 14.4. Transcript recap sheet for recapitulating the several sheets of the hand audit.

the day of departure. Therefore, the work of itemizing each departure can be eliminated and the audit speeded up. Where this technique is used, departures have two subdivisions: one line for all early departures combined and one line each for departures not among the early group.

Front office machines accumulate figures up to 100,000 or more, but a transcript holds only forty to sixty folios. Eight transcript sheets are not uncommon even for a hotel of 200 to 250 rooms if there has been a large turnover that day. Although each sheet is totaled and balanced, it is the final total that the auditor uses to reconcile with the departmental control sheets. The totals of the several transcript sheets are combined and a grand total is obtained on still another sheet called a *recap* (recapitulation). The recap (figure 14.4) may be a special form that includes some of the reports the auditor prepares, or it may merely be another transcript sheet combining totals from the other pages.

All the work is done in pencil. Correcting errors is the whole idea behind the audit and pencil makes it easier to do. Hand-prepared folios are also kept in pencil so that errors on both them and the transcript are corrected with an eraser. Sometimes the beginner forgets that the transcript is merely a summary of the transactions. Correcting errors on the transcript is only the first step. Corrections must also be made on the original records: folios, departmental sales sheets, and vouchers.

Machine corrections are not so easily made; errors cannot be erased. There is no provision in the machine for deleting figures, only for accumulating them. Individual folios are another matter, however. These are corrected by subtracting the amount of error with a subtract from balance or correction minus key and reposting the correct charge. Both figures, the correct one and the incorrect one, go into the machine, causing an imbalance with

the departmental totals by the amount of the error. Whether the amount posted is too large or too small, the incorrect amount is subtracted from the folio and the proper figure reposted. Figure 14.3 illustrates a correction as it appears on the tape. Note the bracketed area illustrates a $35.00 Misc posting added to an opening balance of $86.07. The posting should have been $3.50, so from the new incorrect balance of $121.07 is subtracted the incorrect $35.00 before the $3.50 posting is made.

A similar correction is made when a wrong functional key is depressed, charging the wrong department. Again, the amount is subtracted from the folio and reposted correctly. (Charges that are posted to the wrong folio are corrected by a transfer so long as the amount and department charged are correct.)

Thus even before the night auditor comes on duty, a great many procedural errors will have been corrected. Figure 14.5 illustrates the correction sheet that is completed each time one of the posting clerks repairs a mistake made with the posting machine. The total of these corrections is subtracted by department from the machine totals on the D card (figure 14.1), and the net is used to reconcile with the departmental control sheets. (Printed machine totals less corrections equaling the handwritten net totals of figure 14.1.)

The correction sheets themselves become a source of error when the clerks forget to record the mistakes.

Proving the Charges

At the close of the official day, each department sends its *departmental control sheet* (also called the *departmental sales sheet,* or the *departmental sales journal)* (figures 10.7 and 14.6) to the night auditor. Departments that close early in the day take care of this at that time. For those that remain open after the close-out hour, a new control sheet is started and sub-

CORRECTION SHEET

MACHINE NO._____
(WRITE SMALL AND NEAT)

CASHIER:—ENTER BELOW MEMORANDA ON OVERCREDITS, OVERCHARGES AND WRONG DEPARTMENT KEY REGISTRATIONS. TO BE USED IN CONNECTION WITH DR. AND CR. CORRECTION SLIPS. ONE SHEET DAILY FOR EACH MACHINE.

ROOM NO.	VOUCHER NO.	NAME	AMOUNT POSTED	CORRECT AMOUNT	AMOUNT OF ERROR	DEPT. KEY DEDUCTION	EXPLANATION OF ERROR	OPER-ATOR
0000	7121	Goodbridge	35 –	3 50	35 –	Misc.	Slide	E

Figure 14.5. Correction sheet for use with the machine audit; see also figure 14.3.

sequent vouchers are recorded on it before they are sent to the desk for posting. These later vouchers are the ones held by the auditor until the audit is complete, so they will be posted on the same accounting day as the control sheet on which they are recorded.

Unless the departmental cashier has already done so, the auditor will total the control sheet (figure 14.6).

Proving Departmental Charges

The proof of all the operating departments may be discussed as one. Although the form of the control sheet differs somewhat in the several departments (in some instances only the cash register tape, or only the total, is available), the method of proof is identical from department to department.

Vouchers from the various departments arrive at the desk all during the day. As each is posted, it is validated by the machine or with a rubber stamp in the case of hand-prepared folios. The different checks (vouchers) are sorted by department, and different colored vouchers make the job easier to do. Sorted into pigeonholes, the vouchers remain at the desk for use by the auditor. An adding machine tape is taken on each group of checks, getting a total by department. If each watch tapes the totals of its own shift, the auditor need only tape the grand total.

Three different totals are available to the auditor for each department. First is the total of the individual checks (vouchers) that arrived periodically during the day. Next is the total of charges made by the departmental cashier, as shown on the departmental sales record. Finally, there is the departmental column on the transcript (or motorized key on the machine) showing the total posted to the folios. All three totals must be equal!

Errors

Should the three totals be equal, the auditor moves on to the next department, beginning the audit in earnest when one of the figures

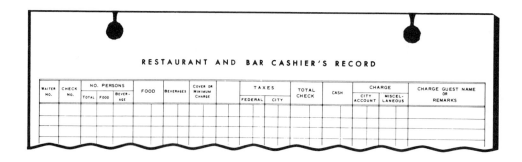

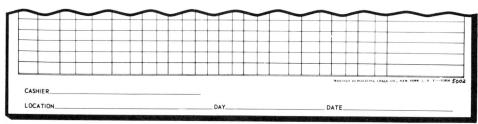

Figure 14.6. Typical departmental control sheet. See also figure 10.7.

fails to reconcile. If two of the three totals agree, the search is concentrated on the unequal total, among several likely causes.

Mistakes in mathematics account for a large portion of the errors; these include "slides," or misplaced units (19.67 written as 196.70), and the transposition of figures (19.67 written as 19.76). Subtracting one total from the other uncovers most mathematical errors. If the difference is evenly divisible by 9, the error is likely to be a slide or transposition, whereas differences that are multiples of ten (1, 10, 100, etc.) are usually simple mistakes in addition.

When the control sheet figure is larger than the other two balances, the auditor searches for a lost check. If the check was posted and then lost, the check (voucher) total will be the smallest of the three totals. Too small a transcript figure suggests that a folio was left in the well or that an omission was made in transcribing the folio. Simple oversights seem

less simple in the early morning hours. Then, a check omitted from the departmental control sheet or a voucher filed before it was posted mean long minutes of searching for the weary auditor.

Vouchers posted to the correct department but to the wrong guest account will not be evident to the auditor. All three totals will agree even though the wrong guest account is charged. This is not so with the reverse situation—when the charge is made to the proper folio but to the wrong department. Then the audit total will be out of balance with the voucher total and the total of that particular departmental control sheet. Of course, the other department—the one that received the extra posting—will also be out of balance by the same amount, which is a clue to the error.

Hand-prepared transcripts have an error all their own. A posting, any posting made during the day by the posting clerk, can accidentally be made in a previous day's column of the folio. It is not discovered until the audit and is difficult to locate even then. Having been posted to the previous day, which was already totaled, it does not even appear on the current day's transcript.

Machine-prepared folios have their own version of this error — an omission from the correction sheet, which makes the final figure on the D card higher than the totals on the control sheet and vouchers. And there always remains the possibility of a machine posting error that is not discovered and not corrected by the clerk who makes it. This is, of course, the real reason for the audit.

The final objective of the night audit is not to reconcile the three balances; nor is it to uncover posting errors, find omissions, or prove mathematical totals. The audit is designed to correct all errors and not just errors on the transcript, the D card, the vouchers, or the control sheets. These are only means of correcting the folios and reconciling them with the charges of the several departments.

Proving Room Charges

Unlike the other operating departments, room charges originate with the desk. There are no vouchers to be verified, but there is a type of departmental control sheet. Room income, house count, and room count are verified by means of this room count sheet. Room count — the number of rooms occupied — and house count — the number of guests registered — also appear on the hand transcript (figure 14.2). Unlike the machine-prepared audit, folios are listed individually on the transcript. This makes it possible to obtain the two statistics from the latter but not from the former. Since room count sheets seem to duplicate the transcript, they are omitted from the front office procedure of small hotels but at the cost of some internal control.

The Room Count Sheet

Several names, including the *daily rooms report* and the *room charge sheet,* are given to this form. It is completed by one of the swing shift room clerks before the shift closes, or by the night clerk if one remains with the auditor. The room count sheet (figure 14.7) is prepared from the room rack and is nothing more than a permanent record of that rack.

Recorded on each room rack slip (plate 1) are the number of persons in the party, the rooms they are occupying, and the rate being paid. This information is copied onto the room count sheet and subtotals are obtained for each floor. The grand total of room income is then compared to the room income figure derived by the audit, just as other departmental incomes are compared to the control sheets. Difficult errors are traced by reconciling the audit and the rack floor by floor, since subtotals are available for each.

Room count sheets are usually printed specially for each hotel. Having columns of the sheet printed in the same sequence as rows of the rack speeds up the copying procedure from rack to sheet. Room numbers are preprinted so that only the number of persons in the party and the rate need be transcribed. The arrival hour, indicated by a meal symbol (chapter 18), is also recorded in American plan hotels. Blank spaces indicate vacant rooms.

Correcting errors is the objective here, as it is with every other part of the audit. A discrepancy creeps in when the room count sheet is prepared relatively early in the evening and not updated when a late arrival checks in.

Less common, but equally troublesome, is the rare weekly bill. If the folio charge for the last day of a special weekly rate is posted net, rather than gross less an allowance, room income on the room count sheet will be larger (taken from the rack) than the audit figure (taken from the folio). Package plans are a

Figure 14.7. The room count sheet provides a permanent record of the room rack.

OCCUPANCY AND ROOM REVENUE REPORT — **Hotel Gary** — DAY _Monday_ DATE _9-18-_

EAST WING

ROOM	No Guests	RATE	ROOM	No Guests	RATE	ROOM	No Guests	RATE	ROOM	No Guests	RATE	ROOM	No Guests	RATE	ROOM	No Guests	RATE	ROOM	No Guests	RATE	ROOM	No Guests	RATE
3101			3319			3615			3910			4206			4501			4719			5016		
3102			3320			3616			3912			4207			4502			4720			5017		
3103			S3322	4	80	3617			3914			4208			4503			S4722			5018		
3104			3401			3618			3915			4210			4504			4801			5019		
3105			3402	2	66	3619			3916			4212			4505			4802			5020		
3106			3403	2	66	3620			3917			4214			4506			4803			S5022		
3107			3404			S3622			3918			4215			4507			4804			5101		
3108			3405	2	68	3701			3919			4216			4508			4805			5102		
3110			3406			3702			3920			4217			4510			4806			5103		
3112			3407			3703			S3922			4218			4512			4807			5104		
3114			3408	1	58 −	3704			4001			4219			4514			4808			5105		
3115			3410			3705			4002			4220			4515			4810			5106		
3116			3412	3	72	3706			4003			S4222			4516			4812			5107		
3117			3414	1	59 50	3707			4004			4301			4517			4814			5108		
3118			3415	3	66 −	3708			4005			4302			4518			4815			5110		
3416			3416			371..																		
3312			3606	2	66	3903			S4122			4418			4712			5007					
3314			3607	2	66	3904			4201			4419			4714			5008					
3315			3608	3	71	3905			4202			4420			4715			5010					
3316			3610	1	66	3906			4203			S4422			4716			5012					
3317			3612			3907			4204						4717			5014					
3318			3614			3908			4205						4718			5015					
TOTAL			TOTAL	57	3731 02	TOTAL			TOTAL			TOTAL			TOTAL			TOTAL			TOTAL		

variant of this. If the final night on a special marketing package is free, the rack and the transcript may differ.

Part-day guests present problems since they check out before the room count sheet is prepared. Although these day guests are no longer in the rack, their folios add room income to the audit and the difference needs reconciling. The same is true with a late checkout who pays a late check-out premium. Clerks leave pickup notices for the night clerk for each day rate or stayover (the check-out hour) charge incurred that day. Records of room and rate changes (figure 9.3) are also left for the auditor, since a failure to complete these on all the records is still another error that needs attention.

Sleepers are discovered by the room count sheet and the housekeeper's report. Sleepers are guests who have checked out but are still being carried in the rack. There is an obvious loss of income if the rack shows an empty room occupied and, thus, not available for resale. Assigning a guest to an already occupied room is the opposite side of the coin. The room count sheet reveals situations of this type, where there is no rack slip, and enables the auditor to make repairs before an embarrassing incident takes place. Room count sheets and housekeepers' reports notwithstanding, sleepers and their corresponding folios are sometimes carried a day or two beyond actual departure, requiring a room allowance to correct.

The Housekeeper's Report

Just about every hotel/motel uses a housekeeper's report as a means of communication between the desk and the linen room. It is a rather standardized report, varying only slightly from hotel to hotel and then chiefly in its frequency of preparation. Housekeeping forwards it to the desk as early in the day as possible. In large hotels with heavy traffic, a

HOUSEKEEPER'S DAILY REPORT

Kayco Form No. 1209

DATE __10-6__ 19___

ROOM NO.	OCCUPIED	VACANT	BAGGAGE	BED USED	ROOM NO.	OCCUPIED	VACANT	BAGGAGE	BED USED	ROOM NO.	OCCUPIED	VACANT	BAGGAGE	BED USED
2529	/				3517	/				4211	s/o			
2530	/				3518	/				4212	s/o			
2531	c/o				3519	/				4213		/		
2532		/			3520	/				4214	P			
2533			B		3521		/			4215				/
2534		/			3522	c/o				4216		/		
2535		/												

Figure 14.8. The housekeeper's report flows from the linen room to the front desk.

second report is made in the afternoon. Although not common, some hotels have three housekeeper's reports per day.

Using a generally accepted set of symbols, the housekeeper tells the front office the condition of guest rooms as reported by the floor attendants. For example, occupied rooms are indicated on the report by a check mark or line (figure 14.8). *Sleep outs,* rooms with baggage but no occupants, are flagged with the letter *B,* baggage. The opposite situation, occupied rooms with no baggage or only light baggage, is shown with an *X* mark. Vacant rooms that are ready for sale are shown as a *V* or slanted line, a half of a *V,* or sometimes by no symbol at all. Vacant rooms that are out-of-order use the standard *000* but it may be shortened to two zeroes or even one. Other symbols are *c/o,* checkout; *s/o,* stayover; and *P,* permanent guest, which is sometimes noted as *R,* resident guest. OK means the room has been made up and inspected. If the report also

indicates the number of persons occupying the room, the desk can uncover cases where guests are trying to avoid full payment.

Other symbols used and seen on the housekeeper's report include: vacant dirty rooms, *VD;* occupied dirty rooms, *OD;* double locked rooms, *DL;* and stayovers with no service (do not disturb), *SNS.* Many of the letter symbols came from EDP room status programs, which cannot use nonalphabetic symbols.

The housekeeper's report is compared to the night clerk's report or directly to the room rack. Printing the housekeeper's report in the same order as the clerk's report and/or the room rack facilitates the comparison. Discrepancies are investigated by the front office, the housekeeper, or the credit manager's staff. Credit is especially interested in light baggage reports, discrepancies in the number of occupants, and in skippers. This report also uncovers sleepers, as just explained, and *whos* (rack shows vacant but room is occupied). The desk's immediate job is identifying the who — who is it? In extreme cases, this takes an awkward call to the occupants and a direct inquiry as to their identity.

The difference between the housekeeper's report and the rack is often nothing more than human error. Housekeepers on the floors complete a miniature housekeeper's report in their own sections and these are transcribed onto the full report with all the possibilities of error. As frequently as not, the floor reports are scraps of paper instead of printed forms (figure 14.9). Reading and writing are not strong points in employees of this department and errors are common enough.

Technical situations give the appearance of errors when there are none. For example, guaranteed reservations show occupied in the rack although the room may be unused if the guest was a no-show. The room and rack reflect a similar discrepancy if the guest has left the hotel taking his or her luggage but plans to return to the room.

Other errors are caused by the difficulty of getting the information. Insistence that the housekeeper's report be at the desk by an early hour forces housekeeping to disturb the guests still in bed. "Just checking," the floor housekeeper tells irate occupants. This abusive practice and a change in the original intent of the report has reversed its flow. It is now frequently prepared by the desk for the housekeeper.

Using the Report. Reporting discrepancies is the beginning of the process, not the end. Someone must confirm the situation and evaluate it. What does it mean, for example, if the floor attendant, who was assigned to clean an occupied room, reports the room vacant? Or reports it as a sleep out (baggage in the room, but the beds are unused)? Situations that flag the desk's attention include double locked

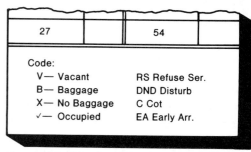

Figure 14.9. The floor housekeeper's report is prepared on the floor and sent to the linen room.

rooms (DL) or do not disturb rooms (DND) that remain unchanged between the morning and afternoon housekeeper's reports. These will be NS (not serviced) or guest refused service (RS) rooms. But management will need to decide whether to act then or wait a few more hours. Few hotel managers will allow the day to pass without calling the room, and if there is no answer, entering the room accompanied by hotel security or housekeeping.

Internal control is limited in a small hotel, where the desk is staffed by one person who sells the room, collects the money, and posts the record. The housekeeper's report was originally furnished to the auditor. Having a second party compare the rack report to the independently prepared housekeeper's report established a degree of internal control. It is still important for the small hotel! As front offices grow larger and departmentalize, the internal control function of the housekeeper's report diminishes. So does the reason for disturbing the sleeping guests.

In many hotels, the desk now prepares the report for the housekeeper, calling it a Room Occupancy Status Report and delivering it as the day begins. This speeds up the work of the linen room. Floor attendants are assigned and they can begin work immediately. With an early room count, the housekeeper calls in extra staff or cancels scheduled workers, if the union contract allows. Computer scheduling of room cleaners is a grand by-product of EDP installations. Additional information is communicated: which rooms had complaints overnight that need attention in the light of morning.

The afternoon housekeeper's report goes the usual route from the linen room to the desk. Although the redirected morning report is less apt to alert the desk to trouble spots, it can still work that way. However, the afternoon report has always been the major one for uncovering sleepers, skippers (DNCOs, Did Not Check Out), and whos, and there is no change in it.

The Formula Computation

A simple computation, much like a perpetual inventory formula, is still another means of verifying room count, house count, and room income (figure 14.10).

The computation is made three times, once for each statistic. In each instance, the opening balance is yesterday's audit figures, that is, the closing balance of the previous day's computation. Arrivals, departures, and changes are added or subtracted according to the formula. The closing balance should then equal the corresponding figures on the room count sheet and the audit. The units being added or subtracted are dollars, persons, or rooms, depending upon which computation is being made (figure 14.11, lower right).

The formula is more a tool of the day, or income, auditor, who verifies the accuracy of departmental records, than of the night auditor, who merely reconciles the given record with charges made to guest accounts.

Arrivals, Departures, and Changes

Once the figures are obtained, the mathematics of the formula are basic and the terms are easily understood. Arrivals are checkins; departures are checkouts; and changes are the net of plus and minus moves.

Arrivals are derived by adding the appropriate squares on the registration cards. The dollar amount of arrivals, for example, is the sum of the room rates recorded on each of the registration cards for that day—a simple adding machine procedure. Persons and room arrivals are counted in the same manner. When registration cards are stapled to the folios, as they frequently are, the information is not available to complete the formula. In that case, arrivals are journalized on an arrival sheet that shows the same three facts contained on the registration cards: the size of the party, the number of rooms taken, and the rate (figure 14.11). (Stapled to the folio, registration cards also provide a quick signature reference for guests requesting check-cashing privileges.)

Departures are computed similarly; an adding machine tape is made from the folios of the day's departures for the three figures. This information may be duplicated on a departure sheet (figure 14.11), but a departure sheet is prepared only when registration cards

	The Computation Formula		
	Room Count	House Count	Room Income
Opening Balance	840	1062	$17,420
+ Arrivals	316	391	8,010
= Total	1,156	1,453	$25,430
− Departures	88	122	1,640
= Total	1,068	1,331	$23,790
± Changes	+6	−2	+173
= Closing Balance	1,074	1,329	$23,963

Figure 14.10. Mathematical verification of the room-rack totals by independent computations.

are not stapled to the folio. Some means of communication is needed for the cashier to pass the checkout to the clerk. If there is no light board in a noncomputerized desk and no registration card to pull from the folio, a departure form is completed for communication purposes. The format is the same as for the arrival sheet. Information from this form can replace the folio totals in the formula. Registration cards that have been attached to the folios cannot be used in the formula because room and rate changes may have been made since the card was completed. By listing every departure on the cash sheet, whether cash is received or not, small hotels eliminate the departure record entirely.

Changes are recorded on a journal sheet (figure 14.11), or they are totaled from the individual change slips (figure 9.3) that were prepared during the day. Either plus changes are added with arrivals and minus changes subtracted with departures or the plus and minus changes are netted and the difference added to or subtracted from the totals. The change journal makes changes easier to visualize but duplicates the information on the change slips.

Since the formula is a part of the income audit and since internal controls can be relaxed as the number of employees and the separation of their duties increases, the formula is less important to large hotels than to small ones. As with so many other procedures, the same holds true for computerized hotels. Reconciling the transcript and the room count sheet (the room rack) is the purpose for the arrival, departure, and change report and its formula computation. Since computer memory holds all of that information, preparing the report has no practical significance with a computer.

Proving Room Tax

Room tax is charged as a percentage of room rate, and that percent is set by local or state governments. Posted along with the room charge, there is neither voucher nor control sheet for the tax. The tax figure is reconciled by multiplying the total room revenue by the sales tax percentage. The product should agree with the tax column of the transcript or machine key, more or less. We say more or less because the amount of tax is rounded off plus

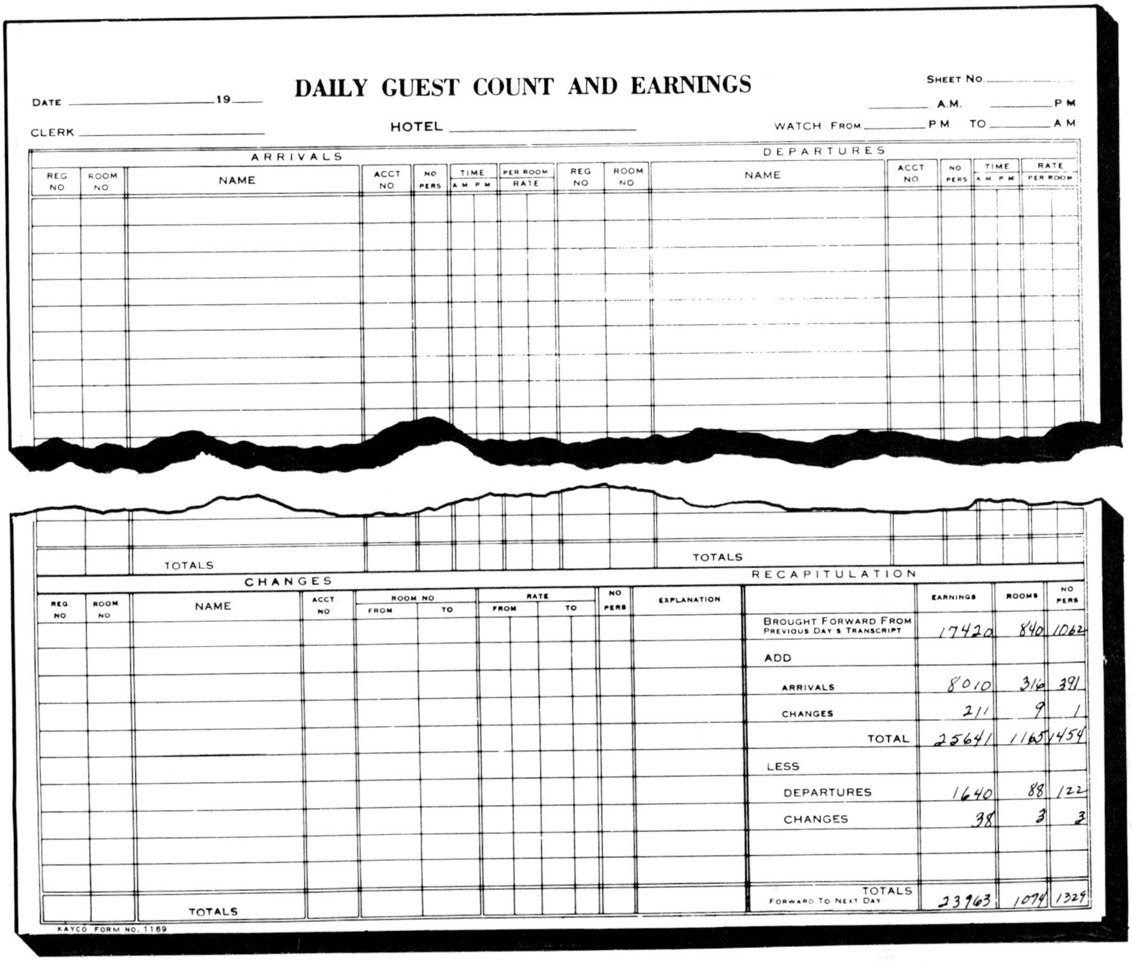

DAILY GUEST COUNT AND EARNINGS

DATE _____ 19 ___   SHEET NO _____

CLERK _____   HOTEL _____   _____ A.M.   _____ P.M

WATCH FROM _____ P.M. TO _____ A.M

ARRIVALS

REG. NO	ROOM NO	NAME	ACCT NO	NO PERS	TIME A M P M	PER ROOM RATE

DEPARTURES

REG NO	ROOM NO	NAME	ACCT NO	NO PERS	TIME A M P M	RATE PER ROOM

TOTALS   TOTALS

CHANGES

REG. NO	ROOM NO	NAME	ACCT NO	ROOM NO FROM	TO	RATE FROM	TO	NO PERS	EXPLANATION

TOTALS

KAYCO FORM NO. 1169

RECAPITULATION

	EARNINGS	ROOMS	NO PERS
BROUGHT FORWARD FROM PREVIOUS DAY'S TRANSCRIPT	17420	840	1062
ADD			
ARRIVALS	8010	316	391
CHANGES	211	9	1
TOTAL	25641	1165	1454
LESS			
DEPARTURES	1640	88	122
CHANGES	38	3	3
TOTALS FORWARD TO NEXT DAY	23963	1074	1329

Figure 14.11. Arrival, departure, and change
sheet with mathematical verification similar to
figure 14.10.

or minus on each folio. A $47.50 room rate taxed at 3 percent is charged at $1.43, one-half cent more than the actual mathematics. Repeat this many times and the total collected equals something more than 3 percent times the total room rate. The difference between the true tax and the amount collected accrues to the hotel in a few jurisdictions but must be paid to the taxing authority in most.

With a computer, the tax computation is an integral part of the room posting. Of course, neither the room nor the tax appears on an EDP folio until the guest departs. At departure, they are printed as totals for the entire stay, rather than a separate line for each day (figure 10.5).

THE AUDIT PROCEDURE — CREDITS

Cash

Two cash columns on the transcript (keys on the machine) receive the night auditor's attention: cash receipts and cash disbursements. Errors uncovered by the audit help reconcile turn-ins left unbalanced by the front office cashiers.

Front office cash sheets serve as departmental control records. The disbursement column on the transcript must agree with the paid-outs shown on the cash sheets. In addition, guest paid-outs have supporting vouchers, which are also reconciled. House paid-outs are not recorded on the cash sheets, and the supporting house vouchers are turned in as part of the day's cash count.

Receipts are balanced in the same way. Audit totals (hand transcript or D Card) are reconciled with the sum of the cash receipts shown on all the front office cash sheets. The night auditor may not have use for a cash sheet. This is true even when the auditor assumes cashiering responsibilities during the

watch. Desk activity is light during this shift, so the auditor often "sells" transactions to the incoming shift. This is possible whenever the cash received applies to the following day's audit, as with an early morning departure. Transactions that apply to the day under audit — that is, before the closeout hour — should not be postponed by "selling" them to the following shift. Although few in number, such transactions require the night auditor, who is also covering the desk, to open a separate cash sheet and include it along with the others.

As a matter of security, the night bank is very small. This is not a problem since the number of cash transactions handled during the shift is also small.

A and B Cards

Clearing the totals of the posting machine each night permits a new accumulation to be made the following day. Only the auditor has the keys to do this. However, posting clerks can take subtotals at any time without clearing the machine balances. This is necessary if the cashiers are to balance their banks when the shifts change.

The cashier who begins the new day finds the cash receipts and paid-out keys at zero. This is tested by printing the subtotals on the audit tape. If the keys have balances, the amounts are "purchased" from the night auditor, as explained, or the night auditor makes the turn-in with his or her own cash sheet. Other receipts and payments are then posted throughout the first watch.

At the end of the first shift, the two cashiers (outgoing and incoming) subtotal the receipts and paid-out keys on cash report A and cash report B (figure 14.12). Except for the sequence of lines, opening and closing lines being reversed on each, the two reports are identical. This permits the outgoing shift to post its closing balance on one card while the

A—CASH REPORT—FRONT OFFICE REGISTERS

On Duty 7 P.M.   Off Duty 11 P.M.   Cashier _Charles_   Machine No. 3

RECEIVED (Cash Cr)		DATE	DEPARTMENT	BALANCE	DIFFERENCE	MACH. TOTALS
CASH	CLOSING 1	JAN1	PAID			3,184.61
	OPENING 2	JAN1	PAID	135.23	x x x x x	3,049.38
	3					
DISBURSED	4					
	CLOSING 5	JAN1	PdOut			* 864.05
	OPENING 6	JAN1	PdOut	56.90		* 807.15
	7					
	CLOSING 8	JAN1	TELC'M			* 19.30
	OPENING 9	JAN1	TELC'M		——	* 19.30
	10					
	CLOSING 11					
	OPENING 12					
	13					

B— CASH REPORT – FRONT OFFICE REGISTERS

On Duty 12:30 A.M.   Off Duty 7:PM A.M.   Cashier _Baker_   Machine No. 3

RECEIVED (Cash Cr)		DATE	EXPLANATION	BALANCE	DIFFERENCE	MACH. TOTALS	
CASH	OPENING 1	JAN1	PAID			1,924.30	E# – ●
	CLOSING 2	JAN1	PAID	1125.08	x·x·x·x·x	3,049.38	E# – ●
	3						
DISBURSED	4						
	OPENING 5	JAN1	PdOut			* 283.49	E# – ●
	CLOSING 6	JAN1	PdOut	518.66		* 807.15	E# – ●
	7						
	OPENING 8	JAN1	TELC'M			* 16.50	E# – ●
	CLOSING 9	JAN1	TELC'M	2.80		* 19.30	E# – ●
	10						
	OPENING 11						
	CLOSING 12						
	13						

A—CASH REPORT—FRONT OFFICE REGISTERS

On Duty 7 P.M.   Off Duty 12:30 P.M.   Cashier _Able_   Machine No. 3

RECEIVED (Cash Cr)		DATE	DEPARTMENT	BALANCE	DIFFERENCE	MACH. TOTALS
CASH	CLOSING 1	JAN1	PAID			1,924.30
	OPENING 2			1924.30	x x x x x	
	3					
DISBURSED	4					
	CLOSING 5	JAN1	PdOut	288.49		288.49
	OPENING 6					
	7					
	CLOSING 8	JAN1	TELC'M	16.50		* 16.50
	OPENING 9					
	10					
	CLOSING 11					
	OPENING 12					
	13					
	CLOSING 14					
	OPENING 15			304.99		
	16		BALANCE	1619.31		
CORRECTIONS	17	SUBTRACT Cash Cr Deductions				
	18					
	19	ADD	DE			
	20		DE			
	21		DE			
	22		DE			
	23		NET			
	24			1619.31		

CASHIER TOTALS OF ABOVE KEYS MUST BE IMPRINTED ON FORMS A AND B IN PRESENCE OF ONCOMING CASHIER (SEE CORRECTION SHEET)

Figure 14.12. Cash A and B reports are used by cashiers in sequence to complete the turn-ins at the end of their watches.

opening balance of the incoming shift is being recorded on the other. Although there are usually only three shifts daily, this system accommodates an indefinite number of turnovers, with the new shift taking the next A or B card in sequence.

Several functional keys may be needed for paid-outs. There may be a separate key for tips, for newsstand, for laundry, for valet, and so on. Each key would be totaled to complete the cashing out procedure and, thus, the several lines for disbursements on the A and B reports. In contrast, there is but one line for receipts at the desk, collections on account.

The net of each cash key is determined by subtracting the opening balance from the closing balance and recording the difference. (The opening balance of the first shift is zero.) Subtotals of the several paid-outs are accumulated and the sum of the disbursements subtracted from cash receipts. It is possible, of course, that paid-outs could exceed receipts, resulting in a due bank.

The difference between receipts and disbursements is adjusted by corrections to obtain the true turn-in. Like other machine postings, errors on the cash keys cannot be erased from the accumulated totals. Such posting errors are recorded during the shift on the correction sheet (figure 14.5) and adjusted on the A and B reports (figure 14.12, line 17). Overposting the cash receipts key requires a subtraction from the total, and overposting the paid-out keys requires an addition to the total. The figure thus obtained is the net receipts before overages and shortages.

In summary, the cash paid-out column (debit) and the cash receipts column (credit) of the transcript (figure 14.2) must agree in total with the corresponding figures on the front office cash sheets. These transcript columns are represented by one or more keys on the posting machines (figure 14.12).

Allowances

Allowances are one of the three credit columns (or keys) that appear in the night audit. Cash receipts, one of the other credits, was just discussed and transfers, the final credit, follows.

Individual allowance vouchers are accumulated at the front desk and left for the night auditor. There is no other record maintained at the front office. Verification of the allowance portion of the audit merely requires the audit total (column or machine) to be reconciled with an adding machine tape of the individual vouchers. If the vouchers are maintained in numerical sequence, a missing one will be evident and the auditor can undertake an appropriate search. Each voucher, other than local telephone calls, should carry the signature of an authorized member of management.

Certain types of allowances may be accumulated on one allowance voucher. Local telephone allowances are the best example. Some hotels account for the difference between the amount collected from a travel agent (room rate less agent's commission) and the amount allowed to the guest against the account (the full room rate) by means of allowances. Using another technique, cash or checks in the amount of the travel agent's commission are added to the guest folio to balance the account. It is from the source of that money, say petty cash, that the expense of the commission is charged to the books of account.

Transfers

Every transfer involves two accounts (although both may be accounts of the same person), since the balance is removed from one account and added to the other. As we have already learned, transfers can take place between ledgers, as when a departing guest moves a transient account to the city ledger by means of a credit card.

Debit and credit transfers are reconciled together. Since each debit transfer requires an individual credit transfer, accounts are audited by comparing total debit transfers to total credit transfers. A discrepancy between the totals must be located and corrected. Search and correction are facilitated by the presence of a city ledger journal or of a transfer journal, in which every transfer has been recorded.

Every transfer has an equal debit and an equal credit, but both sides of the entry may not be apparent to the crew at the desk. Such is the case when one portion involves the transient ledger, which is at the front office, and the other portion the city ledger, whose postings occur in the back office.

VERIFICATION OF BALANCES

At this point, verification of nearly all the transcript columns (or machine totals) in figures 14.1 and 14.2 have been discussed. Room charges are tested against the room rack, and room taxes are tested against the room charges. Departmental charges of all types, from dining room to sauna, are proven with the departmental vouchers and departmental sales sheets, where maintained. Cash receipts and paid-outs rely on the front office cash sheets for proof. Allowances are compared to the total of the day's rebate vouchers, and transfer debits and credits are reconciled against each other. Only the balance columns remain to be explained.

The Hand Audit
Opening Balance

The opening balance of one accounting day is the closing balance of the previous accounting day. This is true of all accounting work, not of

receivables alone. Therefore, the first two columns of the transcript — opening balance debit and credit — are compared to the last two columns of the previous day — closing balance debit and credit. (The previous day's transcript or D card is always returned to the night auditor following the day audit.)

Several mistakes cause an imbalance between the opening and closing figures. Since the previous day's balance was part of a completed and balanced audit, search for errors should concentrate in today's transcript. A folio accidentally left in the well and not transcribed onto the transcript or posting machine makes today's opening balance smaller than yesterday's closing. Frequently, the problem is a slide or transposition of figures made when the transcript was copied from the folio.

The problem could be the folio itself. When the previous day's audit was completed, the closing balance on the hand-prepared folio may have been correct but the balance brought forward (today's opening) may have been in error. Slides and transpositions are common causes for such differences, but it also might be that an error discovered by yesterday's audit was not corrected on the folio.

Should a superficial inspection fail to uncover the error, a line by line comparison of the two transcripts becomes necessary. The transcript sequence will be similar but not identical. Differences will be due to checkouts that have taken place overnight, room changes that have been made, and new arrivals. Obviously, new arrivals have no closing balance on yesterday's transcript nor opening balance on today's.

Machine audits do not reconcile the opening balance figure separately. All the mathematics are reconciled in one step as part of the closing balance. We shall examine that shortly.

Total Charges

The total charge column is located between the debit and credit sides of the transcript (figure 14.2, column 16). It is used merely for mathematical convenience. Therefore, it is the only column that is not verified by comparison to some other form. It is subject, rather, to a mathematical proof. The sum of the total charge column should be the same as the sum of all the previous columns combined. That is to say, the sum of the opening balance column plus the sum of the rooms column, plus the tax column, the food, beverage, and telephone columns, etc., should equal the sum of the total charge column. Let's see why.

First of all, the total charge column is peculiar to the hand transcript; it is not part of a machine audit. After the night auditor foots the debit portion of the individual folios (figure 10.3), he or she records the total and subtracts the credits, if any, to obtain the closing balance. The folio is then *copied* onto the transcript and the total charge figure is recorded in the total charge (debit) column (figure 14.2, column 16). This column should be the sum of the previous columns since the total charge line on the folio, from which the total debit column was copied, was the sum of the charges that were transcribed onto the several transcript columns.

Using the axiom of the whole being equal to the sum of its parts, the total charge column can be used to prove and correct the addition on each folio. The folios were added individually and transcribed onto the transcript. If the total debits column of one folio line is equal to the sum of the preceding columns, then the sum of the total debits column should equal the sum of all the preceding column totals. If it does not, there is a mathematical error in one of the lines because the total cannot be something different from the sum of its parts. Each line must be re-added until the error is discovered. *Since each line represents a folio, the*

mistake must be traced to and corrected on the folio as well as on the transcript. Failing to do this is one cause of an imbalance between today's opening transcript balance, which was prepared from the noncorrected folio of yesterday, and yesterday's closing balance, computed from a corrected transcript.

The recap sheet (figure 14.4) is balanced the same way, except errors are pinpointed by verifying each transcript sheet before summarizing it on the recap.

Because the opening balance has two parts, debit and credit, the one is subtracted from the other before being added to the other column totals to derive the total charge figure. However, the audit is sometimes prepared without the opening balance columns (4 and 5) at all, as it is in our illustration (figure 14.2). In this case, the total charge column (16) really means the total charges made against guests on that particular day. This method is perfectly acceptable if the folio is designed to add the day's charges without the opening balance. Then the opening balance is verified as part of the closing balance.

Closing Balance

Proving the closing balance is just more of the same procedure. The auditor starts with the total charge column that has just been verified. Credits (cash, allowances, and transfers) are subtracted from it and the closing balance obtained in two parts, debit and credit.

The reason for this procedure goes back again to the folio, on which credits are subtracted from the opening balance plus total daily charges to obtain the closing folio balance. (If the credits exceed the debits, the closing folio balance is a credit instead of the more usual debit.) This information is *copied* onto the transcript, so the mathematical check of the credit totals is the same as that used to verify the total charges.

Since there are three credits (cash, allowances, and transfers) and two parts to both the opening and the closing balances, the equation reads:

Opening Balance (Debit-Credit)
+ Daily Charges
= Total Charges
− Credits
= Closing Balance (Debit-Credit)

Another Verification Technique

The proof changes if the audit is done under an alternative method. Yesterday's balance is taken from the audit of yesterday and all of the departmental charges are posted to today's transcript from the departmental charge vouchers and charge sheets. *Nothing is copied* from the folios under this method! The closing debit and credit balances are obtained in the usual manner, subtracting the sum of the several credits from the sum of the several debits. Note the difference: the mathematics are done on the transcript.

In the process being described, the mathematical balance of the transcript sheet merely means the transcripts are in balance. It is necessary to run an adding machine tape of the folios' closing balances. If the two are not in agreement, a search is made for the unbalanced folio and its representative line on the transcript (either could be wrong) and the corrections are made.

This is different and much slower than the traditional audit, where folios are copied onto the transcript so there is immediate agreement between the transcript's closing balance and that of the folios. Errors uncovered during the audit still need correcting on the individual folios, of course.

The Machine Balance

Balancing the machine is something entirely different from balancing the hand transcript, on which the mathematics are done manually.

After the auditor has verified all the departmental totals, but before recording room charges, taxes, and local telephone calls, he or she locks down a key on the NCR machine called the Trial Balance Key. This key accumulates totals in the same manner that the functional departmental keys accumulate departmental figures. Before the room rate is posted to each folio, the folio balance is picked up, that is, recorded. The amount of the pickup is accumulated by the Trial Balance Key. When the room rate, tax, and local calls are added, the total of all accounts receivable is available. That's because the pick up balance includes all the previous account receivable activity, and thereby represents the closing account receivable balance.

As part of the D report of the audit, the total machine debits and credits are combined for the net accounts receivable outstanding (figure 14.1). This closing balance is compared to the total of the departmental charges and credits, as netted, plus yesterday's closing balance from yesterday's D report. The two should equal (figure 14.1). That is, yesterday's balance of accounts receivable ($16,338.83 in the illustration) plus today's charges minus today's credits ($12,337.12 − $6,890.48 = $5,446.64) should equal the sum of all the balances picked up from the accounts receivable folios, the net of machine debits ($22,501.64) and credits ($716.17).

Yesterday's Closing Balance of Accounts Receivable	$16,338.83
Plus Today's Charges	12,337.12
Total	$28,675.95
Minus Today's Credits	6,890.48
Equals Today's Closing Balance	$21,785.47

This total is the same total shown in the machine in figure 14.1.

Machine Debit Balance	$22,501.64
Less Machine Credit Balance	716.17
Equals Today's Closing Balance	$21,785.47

This is the same formula as is used for the hand transcript: opening balance plus charges (that is, total charges) minus credits equals closing balance. Semiweekly or even nightly, an adding machine tape is taken of all the folios in the well and the sum of these balances is compared to the final balance of the D report for that day, a procedure that is similar to the individual listing of folios on a transcript. This must be done nightly with those posting machines that have no trial balance key to lock down, the NCR Class 5, for example. On the other hand, the Micros of figure 10.4 features a continuous trial balance.

Cash System of Accounting

Accounts receivable — the charge guest — has been the premise for all the discussion concerning the night audit. Even paid-in-advance guests are seen as guests who prepay their accounts rather than guests who purchase rooms for cash. This is not true of every hotel; many operate on a cash system in which income is recorded only when the cash is received. There are no accounts receivable. Neither is there credit nor credit cards. This may be as much a marketing decision as an accounting one, for savings in credit and credit card costs can be translated into lower priced rooms and broader market appeal. Nevertheless, it is possible to have a cash system of accounting and still allow guests to accrue charges.

Under the usual procedure, the one that has been described throughout this chapter, income is charged nightly. Room sales are recorded on both the folio and the night audit. The audit then becomes part of the bookkeeping procedure that records the sale as income for the day in question. There is nothing like that under the cash system. Income is recorded when the cash is received whether that is the day of arrival, the day of departure, or an intervening day. An audit of receivables is not prepared although individual guest charges may be accumulated on folios.

Figure 14.13 illustrates the type of cash sheet-transcript used with a cash system of recordkeeping. Lacking a transcript, the cash sheet is used to distribute income by departments. The distribution is made at checkout from the folio on which the charges have been accumulating during the guest's stay. Thus, the cashier might record several days of room charges or telephone charges or any other charges, distributing the cash received among the several departments. For accounting purposes, there is a debit to cash and a credit to each of the incomes regardless of which day they occurred. How different this procedure is from the transcript procedure in which each day's income is charged against accounts receivable and the entry on departure is a debit to cash and a credit to accounts receivable.

For accounting purposes, it is awkward to make cash advances for a guest — a tip, for example — when there is no account receivable to charge. This is handled by an *Advances to Guests* account. All advances for guests are charged to this account and all subsequent collections of the loan are credited there, too. The account "washes" (that is, comes to zero), balanced by the two entries. The debit originates at the time of the advance on the cash payments side of the front office cash sheet. Upon payment, the credit goes on the cash received side (figure 14.13): cash advances collected. With the transcript system, accounts receivable is debited when the loan is made and credited when it is repaid. Since a cash system has no accounts receivable, the Advances to Guests account is created.

OTHER WORK OF THE NIGHT AUDITOR

Depending on the size of the operation and the amount of front desk work assigned, the auditor may be able to handle additional duties. Most of these are so standardized that they are considered to be part of the audit.

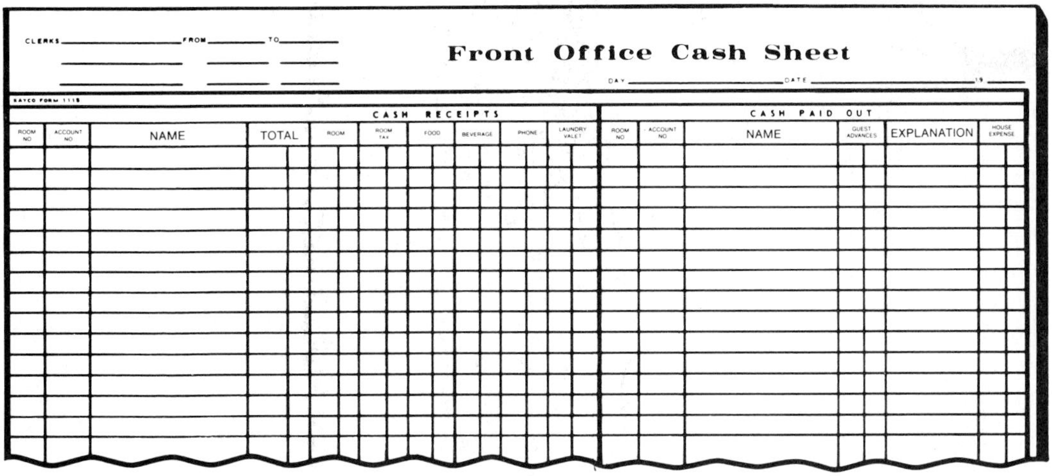

CLERKS ______ FROM ______ TO ______

Front Office Cash Sheet

DAY ______ DATE ______ 19 ______

RAYCO FORM 1115

CASH RECEIPTS										CASH PAID OUT					
ROOM NO	ACCOUNT NO	NAME	TOTAL	ROOM	ROOM TAX	FOOD	BEVERAGE	PHONE	LAUNDRY VALET	ROOM NO	ACCOUNT NO	NAME	GUEST ADVANCES	EXPLANATION	HOUSE EXPENSE

Figure 14.13. Front office cash sheet for cash systems that record income only when the cash is received. Compare to figures 11.1, 11.2, and 14.2.

Other duties are special projects given to the auditor as a means of increasing productivity during the many slow evenings of low occupancy.

Register Readings

Reading the registers of dining rooms and lounges that close after the accounting department has left for the day is standard operating procedure. The night auditor clears the registers, resets the dates, and takes the tapes, which are identified and dated. Used tapes are replaced with new rolls. These readings are turned in to the accounting office to be used in the income audit.

The night auditor clears the front office posting machines and replaces the audit tape there as well. If new tapes are needed during the day, someone from the accounting office handles the job. Cashiers do not have keys to the audit tape.

Weekly Bills

Although the number of weekly guests is declining, there are still occasions and hotels that cater to the long-term stay. The folio balance is carried from the old folio to the new one. The "From Bill Number . . . To Bill Number" of the hand-prepared folio is done by a transfer credit/transfer debit on the posting machines. Bills are also carried forward with the posting machines whenever the twenty-four lines are full. Guest copies of the folios are placed in room mailboxes as notice of payment due. An unnumbered folio card will be used for the second week by those hotels that maintain numbered folio and registration cards in one packet.

Bills are also prepared for express checkout guests if the hotel is using that system. Departing guests, regardless of how long they have been registered, alert the desk of their intent to use the express checkout the next day. The auditor prepares the folio, which is delivered to the guest rooms (under the door) in some hotels.

Credit Alert

Weekly bills that remain unpaid three days after billing are listed by the night auditor on a report to the credit manager. An additional list is prepared for those persons whose balance has reached a given cumulative figure, perhaps $500, or those who have accrued an unusually large amount in one day, perhaps $250. These amounts vary, of course, with the class of the hotel. These figures might also trigger an immediate rendering of the bill by the night auditor.

Some credit managers have the night auditor obtain through direct-dial information the telephone number of each walk-in, or suspicious walk-in, listed on the arrival sheet of that day. Although the absence of such a number is inconclusive in itself, it is an additional fact for the credit department in making its evaluation of the guest.

Night Manager

Unless the hotel is large enough to justify a night manager, this job will fall to the night auditor. The same range of problems faced by the day manager is involved, but to a lesser degree. Emergencies, credit, mechanical breakdowns, accidents, and deaths are some of the situations encountered by the night auditor.

Few hotels of less than 300 rooms employ a night engineer. Yet management has generally been lax in preparing the night auditor-manager for the problems that arise in this area of responsibility. Fire, plumbing problems, power failures, elevator mishaps, and boiler troubles are frequent, if not common, matters that take the auditor's time.

Less serious but equally time-consuming are guest relations: a noisy party going into the early hours of the morning; the victorious football team evident in the lobby; visiting conventioneers in the eleventh floor suite; paid reservations yet to arrive and the hotel 100 percent occupied; a sick guest. Such are the nonaccounting matters for which the night auditor is responsible.

Security or incident reports may be filed by the auditor or it may be a cooperative job with the security person. Without that help, the auditor may even walk security rounds and fire watch.

Reports

Several of the numerous reports completed by the night auditor have already been discussed. Included among these are the security or incident report, the register reading reports, and the credit reports. More common than these are the statistical reports that follow from the night audit. The night clerk's report to the manager is an interim analysis of the audit that is furnished the manager while the day audit is being completed. Room statistics and changes in accounts receivable are the kinds of information furnished. Chapter 17 discusses these statistics in detail.

Similarly, chapter 15 extends the reporting concept of the night audit. The electronic audit is primarily a report audit. The mechanical audit, which this chapter has discussed, is more in keeping with the procedural emphasis described in the opening paragraphs of this chapter. The mechanical audit is designed to correct the human errors that are bound to occur when hundreds of pieces of paper are handled daily. The electronic audit has no such need since all of the paperwork has been eliminated. It concentrates, instead, in preparing the numerous management reports that allow front office management to concentrate less on procedure and more on concept.

QUERIES AND PROBLEMS

1. Explain the similarities and interrelationships among the room count sheet (or daily rooms report); the housekeeper's report; the formula computation for arrivals, departures, and changes; and the night audit.

2. Is the transcript in balance? If not, what error or errors might account for the discrepancy? What percent of sales tax is being charged in this community?

Allowances	$100.00
Telephone	670.70
Transfers To	395.05
Rooms	9,072.00
Cash Advance	444.25
Debit Transfer	395.50
Beverage	1,920.00
Credit Card Charges	14,482.07
Cash	10,071.22
Closing Balance	3,670.41
Opening Balance	48,341.50
Rooms Tax	725.76
Food	3,000.10
Closing Balance	43,007.33
Opening Balance	185.00
Total Charges	64,384.81

3. Both the hand-prepared audit and the machine-prepared audit reconcile departmental charges to guest folios. Explain why the hand-prepared audit uses a spread sheet (transcript), but the machine-prepared audit does not. Focusing just on that statement, what are the advantages or disadvantages of each system?

4. In general journal form, using the figures of question 2 above, prepare a sales journal entry showing debit and credit items. Remember that if question 2 is in balance, this entry will balance; if question 2 is not in balance, this entry will not balance either.

15

The Electronic Night Audit: Computer Reports

Today's quickening appetite for technology and systems contrasts sharply with yesterday's disinterest and obtuseness. Basic changes in concept and structure preceded the computer's transformation to a management tool. Computers were seen initially as a means of electronic filing, as a new method of handling the mass of paper being generated by ever larger hotel properties. Fittingly, the beginning came at the start of the front office sequence: reservations. Chapters 3 and 4 describe the shift from paper processing to systems management. Reservation computerization has changed marketing strategies, introduced new business partners, restructured whole organizations, and necessitated a flow of management reports.

The same is happening at the other end of the front office sequence, at the night audit. It too has undergone first mechanical and then conceptual changes. Less and less a tool of internal audit, more and more a means of management reporting, the night audit would certainly change names were it not for tradition. Night audits no longer audit the internal errors of a human-based system. They focus, instead, on reporting the data of an almost error-free computer system.

Understanding the why and wherefore of the night audit's new role requires an understanding of the technological developments that have taken place in this industry along with other parts of American life. Some of the changes impact directly on the night audit, as this chapter explains. Other changes, although equally exciting, affect the night audit less directly, as the next chapter explains.

Selecting the verb tense that best describes electronic data processing in innkeeping is imprecise. The industry lies on the cusp of computer change. For some functions in some hotels, the future tense, "will," is the best to use. Where the pace of electronic conversion has been very rapid and very successful, descriptions might even be couched in past terms. Most fall somewhere in between with some new procedures on-line and some others still to come.

THE STATE OF THE ART

In one way the hotel industry, which is almost as old as history itself, has just come of age. Large manufacturers now see the hotel as a buyer of goods as well as a seller of services. Hotel's new buying power is a by-product of its shift from small, privately held businesses to large, publicly financed corporations. As hotels become an industry of capital investment, they become a buyer of capital goods. This new role has provided other industries with the economic justification for researching and developing new products designed primarily for the growing hotel market. Sometimes, unfortunately, the initial product is more the manufacturer's creation than a child of the user. That's what happened at first with EDP, electronic data processing, in the hotel industry.

Electronic data processing is a technological refinement of automatic data processing, which is, in turn, an improvement over manual processing. In each case, reduced handling of data is the objective. Automatic and electronic systems minimize manual handling by recording each transaction only once in machine-usable form. The data may then be processed numerous times without additional handling. Increased accuracy as well as increased speed results.

Consider the case of a restaurant check signed by a guest in the dining room. Information on the check is computed and recorded by the server, the dining room cashier, the front office posting clerk, the front office cashier, the night auditor, the day auditor, and finally the general accountant. Some of the re-recording can be done with duplicate postings or carbons, but each separate transcription slows the process and increases the chance of error. Although the audit trail is easy to follow, much of the work being audited obviously comes from the very procedure itself — errors introduced at the several stops along the trail. Automatically processing the information reduces recordkeeping to one time, improves accuracy, and permits the use of the data for additional purposes. It does not eliminate the need for an audit trail, however.

Although EDP is exciting in potential, its introduction into the front office has been slow and cautious. Except for a few notable exceptions, the industry has proceeded with prudence. The AH&MA's first survey of hotel technology (1976) reported few computer installations and most of those used key punch. It was first thought that several hotels might share a common processing facility. Later, time-sharing plans were advocated with each user transmitting data to a computer center. Neither idea materialized, but the headquarters of multi-property companies have begun to fill that role.

Many of the early reasons for avoiding computers are still voiced, but they are much less valid today. True, small properties still dominate the industry (figure 1.1), but the shift has become very apparent in the last decade. Besides, the price and size of the equipment have been substantially reduced. True, personal attention does characterize the service industries, but a good computer system increases the time that employees can spend with the guests. True, front office procedures are peculiar to the hotel business, but software companies have zeroed in on these special needs.

Incentive to change to computer systems received its biggest boost from the demise of the electromechanical equipment, including the NCR 2000 and 4200 models. Although these machines haven't been manufactured for years, the 1980 survey of technology by the

AH&MA reported 8,000 of them still in use, or some three-fourths of the properties that responded to the survey. Fortunately, the end of the electromechanical era coincided with the computer industry's shift from a hardware to a software emphasis. Since so many companies were already making good hardware, competition for the software market, including the hotel front office, became more intense.

Turnkey, off-the-shelf programs that are readily adaptable to every hotel, replaced the costly individualized programs that had contributed to the industry's slow entry into the arena. Turnkey companies now dominate the hotel computer field. Under the turnkey concept, a single vendor supplies both the hardware and the software, although the vendor may specialize in one segment and actually acquire the other ware from a second vendor. The seller also integrates the computer into the hotel's system, trains the staff, and maintains the installation.

Parts of the EDP System

Data equipment (hardware) cannot function without direction. Direction comes from a program (software), which tells the hardware what is wanted and how to go about finding it. Instead of being activated by keys and motor bars like an electromechanical front office machine, the computer operates electronically from a set of instructions given to it as a program. As the task given to the machine varies, so does the program that is used. The same hardware can carry out several functions from the same data. Information from the dining room check can process the account receivable, update the food and beverage inventory, and analyze the purchasing habits of the customers provided the system has been properly programmed with the necessary

software. And that software, designed for the special needs of the hotel industry, has been a long time in coming.

The delay in getting EDP into the hotel business may prove to be a blessing. Although the industry has been spared the difficult developmental periods, it will still benefit from the improvements in both hardware and software. These later-day computers consume (input), consider (process), and react upon (output) data at an amazing speed. They do it much faster than the input/output equipment (typewriters, printers) that translates the information between the operator and the machine. Many of the recent innovations in hardware have been in this peripheral input/output equipment.

The Punch Card

"Do not fold, spindle or mutilate" is a phrase that has earned a permanent place in our language. The punch card to which it refers was the first means of computer input and the first type of computer memory. The data, that restaurant charge discussed earlier, for example, was encoded on cards, which were then fed into one of several machines. Using the machine-readable code of the cards, the equipment reproduced other cards, sorted the data by categories, collated the cards, and printed out the restructured data. Hotels never really got into this phase of the computer's evolution.

Punch cards (paper tape too) remained the basic input media during the next developmental phase. Cards were accumulated and then processed in batches periodically as the particular information was needed. The ancillary equipment was a punch machine to convert the data into machine-readable language and a reader to reconvert the processed data back into human-readable language.

This era of the early 1960s was one of record processing more than information processing. Equipment was still bulky and expensive. It was yet unable to do the communicative tasks that the hotel industry needed. These were to come a decade later along with the reduced costs of integrated circuits, chips. Although some hotels tried these second and third generation computers, much to their sorrow, the industry as a whole waited.

Stored Memory

Today's computer is a far cry from the punched cards and the paper tape. It stores in memory both the program that processes it and the data being processed. The information is held in electronic or magnetic memory rather than on cards or paper tape. Just as the input evolution has been punch card, paper tape, typewriter, magnetic tape, and voice; so the storage permutation has been punch card, paper tape, magnetic tape, floppy discs, cassettes, and silicone chips.

Improvements in storage capabilities have shrunk the central processing unit (CPU), which is the working nucleus of the computer, from a stand-alone main frame of large dimensions to a microcomputer whose CPU functions are miniaturized on a printed circuit board. Miniaturization has blurred the long-used distinction that defined a main frame as one so large that it needed to be carried by an elephant; a minicomputer as one that required two burly men; and the micro as one that could be carried under one's arm. Microcomputers are usually self-contained, including the keyboard, the CRT, the printer, and some sort of external memory, frequently a floppy disk.

Memory is measured in kilobytes (K), although each K is actually more than 1,000 bytes, and kilobytes are comprised of bits, which is the basic memory unit. A byte is 8 or 16 bits. Memory capacity is split into two parts.

ROM and RAM are shorthand for read-only-memory and random-access-memory. ROM is an internal recall that enables the equipment to communicate with the user. Random-access-memory houses the data being processed and stores the programs that manipulate that data. ROM and RAM differ technically, but new chips are combining the advantages of each.

Storage is in the central processing unit (figure 15.1), or externally (on cassettes, discs, or tapes) when the data being stored exceeds the kilobyte capacity of the CPU. As needed, the central processing unit gets immediate access to the external memory, giving rise to the "random access" terminology.

The increasing capacity and accessibility of CPU and external storage partially explains the hotel industry's acceptance of computers. Enlarged memory meets the innkeeper's inordinate demand for on-line data. Billing, reservations, and credit identification are examples of the types of information that hoteliers call forth on real time. Increased storage on real time and hotel computerization have coincided and the reason is apparent.

Peripheral Equipment

Peripheral equipment, the means of getting the data into and out of the stored memory, has improved along with the basic computer. At one time, only cards or tape could be used to communicate with the equipment. Typewriters (data entry stations) were used next to feed information into the hardware and to get back answers from the computer (figure 15.2). Still more rapid communication was furnished by the cathode ray tube (CRT), which provided a video display, hence VDT, video display terminal (figure 3.3).

Now new point-of-sale devices are appearing: electronic cash registers connected directly to computer memory; magnetic ink readers for credit cards and security uses; tele-

Figure 15.1. Components of a computer installation showing (left to right): printer, video display terminal, input keyboard, disc drive, and central processing unit. *Courtesy: Sperry-Univac, Bluebell, Penn.*

phone interfacing; and sensors and thermostats for temperature and safety controls. Still serving where hard (permanently printed) copy is needed — departments such as housekeeping prefer hard copy materials — is the high speed printer (figure 15.3).

New optical input devices are capable of reading typewritten characters and indications are that they soon will read handwritten data as well. Optical input equipment goes under the abbreviation of OCR, optical character recognition or optic card reader. Voice activated and voice response computers are awaiting on the horizon. Touch sensitive devices that require no keyboard and optical scanners that read palmprints and fingerprints have already been introduced.

In every case, the input/output devices are less efficient than the computer itself. This is true with card packs, paper tapes, typewriters, OCRs, CRTs, and even the printers. The time lag between the peripheral equipment and the central processing unit enables the computer to handle several jobs at once — multiprogramming. It works on the second job while the first one, which has been completed by the computer, is being processed by the slower output devices. Remember, the computer operates in microseconds! Multiprogramming makes possible the use of many input/output locations (terminals) throughout the hotel. Of course, minicomputers are not able to handle the large number of terminals that a main frame services.

Figure 15.2. An alpha numeric input/output station; input is entered on the typewriter keyboard; output is through the printer. (A 10 key numeric pad on the right.)   *Photo by Ken Firestone.*

Figure 15.3. High speed printers, can be located anywhere in the system, but certainly at the cashier's window for processing folios.
Courtesy: ECI, EECO Computer, Inc., Santa Ana, Calif.

On-line

With stored memory, the input and output equipment communicate directly with the computer. The information goes back and forth as the operator waits and then the system is said to operate in "real time." Off-line systems shuttle information to storage before it is processed by the computer.

For an example, let us return to the dining room check being charged to a guest's room. On-line, the dining room cashier uses an input device to feed the information directly into computer memory, where it is immediately recallable. The system is off-line if the terminal in the dining room merely activates a card punch in the front office, or if the voucher goes to the front office manually and the data is entered there. The charge is filed by room number much like a folio is filed in the cashier's bucket. It is not placed in the computer memory until the night audit unless the guest leaves and requests a statement. In either case, it is processed with all the other departmental charges accumulated that day for that room. It is not immediately recallable from memory, and between batch runs it provides no more current information than a manual system.

Obviously, punch cards were the media for off-line storage. They were replaced by disc files and disc packs that still handle off-line needs. Off-line systems still service situations in which time is not critical: city ledger billing, payroll, advance reservations, registration card analysis, and the like. On-line systems are best for tasks that need immediate attention: transient ledger billing, credit checks, room requests for walk-ins, and the like.

On- and off-line is sometimes confused with shared and dedicated line. A dedicated line is used for one purpose: the lobby function board; a time and temperature display; a display of airline schedules. Shared lines are the more common, being used for reservations, registration, and most of the front office functions.

On the other hand, there are some on-line systems that are not quite on-line. These are *store and forward* systems, of which reservations are the best example. The local hotel takes reservations for itself and other members of the chain. These are stored in the local computer. Periodically, the information is forwarded to the system computer for a worldwide update. The system computer calls for the information when the lines are least busy.

Off-line systems produce backup materials that can be used to recreate the data in case of a breakdown. Every system is haunted by the fear of a computer malfunction. Fortunately, there have been outstanding improvements in hardware technology and the concern for *downtime,* the period during which the equipment is inoperative, is no longer a major criteria in selection. Still, disaster drills must be part of management's exigency plans, enabling the operation to adjust and function even when the computer is down.

Technical advances like these have brought the hotel industry to the threshold of the computer era. And while much has been accomplished, the hotel business has not yet crossed over.

The Threshold of Change

The decade of the 1970s brought giant technological steps to the computer industry and to its ability to service the hotel/motel market. All the major chains entered the computer age. Marriott installed a remote reservation system in 1975; Sheraton's first rooms management computer went into the Waikiki Beach in 1971. And a reluctant hospitality industry was presented with an inescapable fact: third and fourth generation computers were cheaper than ever; their adaptability to the hotel/motel industry was better than ever. And the minicomputer made it possible.

Minicomputers are small, but complete, data processing systems, but each self-contained unit can be interfaced with every other unit station. Thus the term derives: distributive data processing. Low cost has been the major appeal, but there is also the freedom of proceeding cautiously. Hoteliers are not forced to make a one-time commitment involving hugh sums of money. Computerization can be tested in small portions. One segment of the hotel's system can be put into a computer configuration at a time: back office; reservation; room status; billing. The financial burden is less, but so too is the trauma of simultaneously converting every function of the hotel's record system. And if it works, each separate segment can be married to the previous installation until there is one integrated whole.

Separating the whole into parts leaves the appearance of incompleteness. This is the real state of the industry's effort to computerize. During this period of introduction and adaptation, individual hotels are apt to have one portion computerized, say room status, but not another — reservations being processed manually. Another hotel might have a central reservation system for the chain but hand record reservations within the one house.

Similarly, different vendors proffer different modules to fit the front office functions. The quality of one module, say charges and posting, varying among the manufacturers. And there are no assurances that the producer of the best module in charges and postings will also have the best module in, say, registration. Partial systems do not lend themselves to noticeable savings in labor nor to substantial improvements in guest service.

In waiting for the romantic period of electronic data processing to pass, hoteliers have obtained a workable and economical tool for operational procedures and management decision making. Few would take exception to a forecast of unlimited potential as the industry crosses into the computer age.

A Vertically Integrated Business

Today's traveler views the trip as a total experience rather than a series of separate events. In that context, hotels are one unit of the package. Interface, long a term of the computer field, has appeared as part of travel/tourism terminology. It represents the integration of the reservation, transportation, and destination industries. As segments of these industries grow more interdependent, the industries themselves are drawn closer together. This movement has both caused and resulted from increased computer use.

Evidence is accumulating to indicate the direction of the merger. It is a vertical integration of the four or five major parts of the travel package. At one end is the booking agency, travel agent, wholesaler, or group mover. At the other end is the destination, either the hotel itself or a Disneylike complex with the hotel an intermediate service. In between are credit institutions and transportation agencies, air and land. Each depends upon the other for growth and survival; it is a marriage of need not one of mere convenience.

Many reasons lie behind the assimilation and many minute steps will occur before the process is complete. Hotels' need for capital has already been recited. The airlines' need for passenger service at destinations, particularly overseas, is also well known.

Other equally important developments are less apparent. Wholesale travel agencies have acquired resort properties as destination sites for their tour and incentive groups. Disney has combined the hotel and destination park in Florida, remedying thereby its oversight in California. Marriott's venture into the hotel-park combination lends further validity to the concept. Travel wholesalers have chartered fleets of aircraft and the airlines promote destination areas, booking hotel and auto reservations to boot. American Express has recently acquired one of the nation's largest travel agencies, and Hilton's reservation system sells Budget rent-a-car. The trend is obvious although the pace is erratic. The major impetus must come from the airlines, which are just now testing the full meaning of deregulation. Even without them, there will be an integrated travel structure of sorts. The computer will see to that.

Computers have a place in the hotel business even if the service and organizational revolutions that the author foresees never come about. Management has already begun to reduce front office paperwork and further reductions can be effected without major conceptual changes. Computers have moved from the back office to the front office. Beyond the front office are additional possibilities, but these must wait, as must innkeeping's vertical interface with the rest of the travel industry, until the computer has gained status in house.

EDP IN HOTELKEEPING

Once across the threshold of change, computers take on an increasingly important role in management decision making and control. Such an emphasis is already evident in the night audit. No longer concerned with the reconciliation of charges and departmental incomes,

the thrust of the computerized audit is management reporting. Personnel and equipment that were dedicated to the search for errors in transcribing and posting have been freed for other assignments. Data gathering and presentation are high on the priority list.

The functional application of EDP in hotelkeeping has been the topic of previous chapters: reservations, registration, communication, billing, etc. Vast quantities of data are assimilated by the computer as it carries out its functional procedures. Restructured, this data becomes the source of a variety of management reports. Some reports are called for during the day to serve as tactical tools; some are produced exclusively during the audit for strategic planning. Most reports are common to every hotel and are part of the usual turnkey package. A report generating module allows management to create its own reports as special needs dictate.

Every computer installation is not generating all the reports that this chapter reviews. Few systems are so fully operative; that deficiency has been noted before. The balance of the computer discussion is part fact and part speculation, therefore. Speculation in terms of what a mature electronic system will provide when it is properly integrated into a hotel that is vertically interfaced with the rest of the travel industry.

Reservations

A computerized reservation system benefits every member of the chain, company stores and franchisees alike. No one begrudged the large capital investments needed to make the systems work nationally and then internationally. That's why reservations were the foothold of the earliest computer efforts; which is logical since reservations are the beginning of the travel sequence. Reservation records become the basis for all subsequent procedures and data processing.

Making the Reservation

Today's guest calls the reservation into a telephone operator, who communicates with the computer by means of typewriter and CRT (figure 3.2). Conceivably, the guest will eventually do this unaided at reservation sites in airline terminals or at special computer centers that will be strategically located throughout the city. It is equally conceivable that the reservation computer will someday respond to the spoken voice and take in-WATS telephone inquiries without an operator on duty.

Electronic mail sent from home and reservations confirmed through the TV set are also being visualized. Pilot programs using the TV set as a catalog have already been tested successfully. Adding travel data and hotel reservations to these pilot programs is not a large conceptual jump. In-home computers capable of direct message transmission to hotel computers or indirectly to printers for hard copy requests are also reasonable expectations for the coming decades.

Only recently have the first steps been completed to interface the airline and hotel reservation systems (Westin Hotels and United Airlines, for example), but it is the beginning of an integrated reservation grid that portends the overall vertical assimilation described earlier in the chapter (figure 3.4).

Reservation Reports

Speedy completion of the routine, repetitive tasks required of reservations is only part of the computer's appeal. Information is the other part and it is the catchword of data processing. Without information the reservation system is incomplete.

The reservation manager must know the number of rooms sold and the number available by type, rate, and accommodations. He or she must know arrivals, departures, stayovers, cancellations, out-of-orders, and walk-ins. And the information must be available in a modified density chart like that in figures 4.5 and 4.8.

Additional information adds to the value of the data system. Which rooms are most popular and at which rates? Do no-show factors vary with the season and the day of the week? If so, by how much? How many rooms in which categories are turnaways? How many reservations were walked? How many were initiated by travel agents? How many in-WATS calls? Questions of this type make the computer as much a tool of management decision making as a technique of operations.

An alphabetical list of arrivals (figures 5.7 and 15.4) is an example of the latter. It reduces the number of lost reservations and facilitates the recognition of VIPs and DGs. It helps the headwaiter(waitress) in an AP dining room plan seating arrangements and helps the bell captain schedule a crew. It identifies the group affiliation of each guest, thereby improving reservation and billing procedures. Keeping track of reservations made against a group commitment is difficult without a computer. Yet, both the group's executive and the hotel's sales manager need to know how many and which rooms of the block reservation have been committed. Adjustments can be made at any given time: more rooms reserved, some rooms released, a new mailing prepared for the apathetic membership.

Because both kinds of information are available so rapidly, it may be difficult to demarcate the operational services of the computer from the data it provides for long-range decision making. Either can be displayed on a CRT or preserved on hard copy for slower digestion and evaluation. Placed on a permanent copy the information becomes a report. Although the capacity of individual programs determines the specific reports, reservation programs in general provide for the following. They do so even if reservations is the only front office function computerized.

```
A R R I V A L   R E P O R T

                                                                              PAGE: 1

                         TRAVEL                    NO OF  NO OF
         ROOM# RESV# VIP COMP AGENT  NAME          ROOMS  GUESTS  DEPART  GROUP  SOURCE
               A0016  -          -   ABBOTT, ALLAN    1      1    10/31/          MAIL
               A0083  -          -   ABELL, STEPHEN   1      1    10/31/          PHONE
               A0085  -          -   ADELMAN, STANLEY 1      1    10/31/          PHONE
               A0013  -          -   AKERS, PAUL      1      1    11/02/  IAHA
               A0059  -          -   ALAVEREZ VICTOR  1      1    11/04/          MAIL
               A0084  -          -   ALEXANDER, KATHE 2      2    11/02/  IAHA    MAIL
               A0023  -          -   ALLEN, JONATHAN  1      1    11/05/          PHONE
               A0007  -          +   ANDERSEN, JERRY  2      3    11/02/          TOUR FACT
               A0072  +          +   ANDREWS, RUSSELL 2      3    11/09/          CAL TOURS
               A0086  -          -   ARMSTRONG, RONALD 3     6    10/31/          PHONE
               A0024  -          -   ATKINSON, TIMOTHY 1     1    11/02/  IAHA
               A0090  -          -   AYERS, CONNIE    2      4    11/05/          PHONE
               A0012  -          -   BABCOCK, MARY    1      1    11/03/  IAHA
               A0017  -          -   BAILEY, CHARLES  1      1    11/02/  IAHA    PHONE
               A0022  -          -   BARKER, DUANE    1      2    11/02/  IAHA    PHONE
               A0030  -          -   BATES, SUSAN     1      1    11/02/          PHONE
               A0075  -          -   BAXTER, NORTON   1      1    10/31/          PHONE
               A0008  - RFB      -   BELL, JAMES      2      2    11/04/          KNOX
               A0014  -          -   BENSON, JERRY    1      2    11/01/          PHONE
               A0089  -          -   BERGER, JAMES    1      2    10/31/          PHONE
               A0028  -          -   BLOCK, STANLEY   1      1    11/04/  IAHA    PHONE
          151  A0025  -          -   BLOOM, MICHAEL   1      2    11/04/          PHONE
               A0018  -          -   BOLLINGER, EDITH 2      2    11/04/          MAIL
               A0076  -          +   BOWERS, CHERYL   2      4    11/04/          TOUR FACT
```

Figure 15.4. Alpha arrival list: all the anticipated arrivals for the day are listed alphabetically. See also figures 5.6 and 5.7. *Courtesy: Knox Data, Van Nuys, Calif.*

Arrivals Report: an alphabetical list of the day's expected arrivals, individually and by groups. Special information about the guest and special services requested by the guest are identified (figure 15.4).

Cancellation and Change Report: a list of reservation cancellations for the day or reservation changes and cancellations for a later date.

Central Reservations Report: an analysis of reservations made through the central reservations system, including numbers, kinds, rates, and fees paid. Should include a regret factor

(i.e. 73 percent; 73 regrets per 100 reservations accepted) and a comparison of changes in regrets between years.

Convention (Group) Delegates Report: a compilation of group (and tour) room blocks reserved, the number of rooms booked, and the number still available by rate category and name of group. Also called a Group Pick-up Report after delegates begin arriving.

Daily Analysis Report: one or more reports on the number and percentage of reservations, arrivals, no-shows, cancellations, walk-

```
FORECAST REPORT
02/14  6:30 PM
FR-PAGE   1   RUN  4
WITH MODIFICATIONS

            ARRIVALS    DEPART     STAYOVERS   RMS  SOLD  UN-SOLD    # GUESTS    # GPS   EXPECTED
DATE        DEF  TEN    DEF  TEN   DEF   TEN    RES  ALL   RES  ALL   DEF   TEN   AR DP   REVENUE

02/14       290  52     712  23    184  -23     474  503   714  685   544   49    5  1   19450.70
TUE           342         735        161        40%  42%              593          14

02/15       624  18     155  22    319    7     943  968   247  222   1204  43    2  5   44618.70
WED           642         177        326        79%  81%              1247            
                                                                                   11

02/16       116   5     156  12    787   13     903  921   287  269   1184  31    0  3   41208.43
THU           121         168        800        76%  77%              1215            
                                                                                    8


AVG ROOM RATE:  44.01
```

Figure 15.5. Reservation forecast. DEF means definite; TEN means tentative; and the figure below is the sum of the other two. RMS RES is the sum of arrivals and stayovers; SOLD ALL also includes the tentatives. #GPS is the number of groups arriving (AR) and departing (DP). See also figure 5.8. *Courtesy: ECI, EECO Computer, Inc., Santa Ana, Calif.*

ins, and early arrivals by source (travel agency, hotel rep, sales office, housing bureau, reservation center) and by type of guest (tour, convention, package, full rack, special rates).

Deposit Report: a categorization of reservations by deposit status—deposits requested and received, deposits requested and not received, deposits not requested. It could be treated as an exception report, depending on the hotel's policy of requesting, or not requesting, deposits. (Helpful in planning cash flows.)

Forecast Report: one of a variety of names (extended arrival report, future availability report) for projecting reservation data forward over short or long durations (figure 15.5).

Occupancy Report: a projection within the computer's horizon of expected occupancy by category of room. (Helpful with the broader forecast report for work force planning and budget preparation.)

Overbooking (or Walk) Report: a list of reservations walked, including their identification in detail (name and address, company affiliation, travel agency involved); the number of walk-ins denied; and the number and identification of reservations farmed out to other properties.

Regrets Report: a report on the number of room requests denied because of a capacity house. (Valuable data to support loan requests for additional rooms.)

Figure 15.6. Video display unit supplies the clerk with all the information needed for reservations, registration, and assignment. *Courtesy: ECI, EECO Computer, Inc., Santa Ana, Calif.*

Registration and Assignment

Most of today's reservation systems are part of the registration procedure, the room assignment, and the folio preparation, because the same information appears on all three records. Improvements in manual systems have focused on reducing the number of times this basic information is copied and recopied. With computer memory, that number is down to rock bottom—once.

Reservation information is furnished to the clerk on a CRT unit (figure 15.6). In addition to the basic data supplied to the hotel by the guest, the clerk might be given a guest history, a credit rating, a VIP alert, and a recommended room assignment. Until people become as automated as the system, it is difficult

to conceive a preassignment of rooms. Guest comings and goings are too unpredictable to program. Recommended assignments will be made by the computer at the time of the guest's actual arrival. The computer will weigh the known facts (rooms still on reservation, rooms on change, vacant rooms, and guests who have paid but not yet departed) and come up with a suggested room number. Energy conservation, wear and tear on room furnishings, and special requests from the guest could all be evaluated in the assignment.

Projecting still further, the guest alone will read the room status on a CRT and then complete the assignment on a self-service basis. Paying the charge with cash or credit card will release the key allowing the guest to be self-roomed. Hyatt is already experimenting with the idea. Until it becomes widespread, room selection remains a joint effort of the desk clerk and the computer reference.

Registration cards are still used, but they will be limited in the future to those jurisdictions that make registration a prerequisite to guest status. Pressure on legislatures will force changes in even this requirement when computer use becomes widespread enough. Arriving guests will offer the information verbally while the clerk records it on an input terminal. As the facts are fed into the computer, they will appear on a CRT unit for immediate verification by the guest.

A charge plate, prepared by the computer while the guest registers, will be used one day as identification for charging services in the various public rooms and for accessing tennis courts, the pool, and other recreational areas. This plate is to be the room key as well. Conventioneers will use the ID for convention registration, identification, and booth attendance.

An additional step is foreseeable if the projection is carried still further into the future. A set of baggage plates will be punched out along with the charge plate. These tags will be attached to the luggage and will guide the bags electronically through an internal delivery system that deposits the baggage in the guest's room. This is done now, of course, with key envelopes (figure 6.15) for group arrivals.

Room Status

Room status is an essential component of registration and assignment. Although many installations separate one from the other in developing computer capability, their unity is quite essential to the effective operation of both. The communication link between housekeeping and the desk, is improved substantially with input/output terminals in the linen room and on each sleeping floor. The telephone actually represents an input terminal in each guest room. (In-room computers are now being installed in guest rooms as a

marketing device, but they will undoubtedly serve a dual purpose one day soon.) For now, the floor attendant, without the assistance of the telephone operator, dials a simple numerical code into the computer to report the status of the room.

Having immediate access to the status of the house enables the desk to do a better job of reception and selling. CRTs can be made to display the highest priced rooms first. Rush priorities on unmade rooms can be communicated to housekeeping quickly so that waiting VIPs or guests holding reservations for limited accommodations can be roomed with a minimum of delay.

Housekeeping uses EDP to establish work priorities and improve productivity. Vacant rooms are serviced immediately while anticipated departures are held until after checkout. Room status is available floor by floor, permitting a more efficient assignment of housekeeping personnel. The computer keeps track of the floor housekeepers who dial in by telephone as each room is finished (figure 15.7). Daily job assignments can be computer programmed. Hard-copy lists of the rooms and their status are furnished to the employee at the start of the shift. The printout could be made to include special assignments (window washing), special services (a sick guest), as well as daily routine tasks or important employee messages (figure 15.8).

Computer programs can also include provisions for repair and maintenance orders noted by the supervisors making room inspections. The condition of each room is checked by a floor inspector after the room cleaner has finished but before the room is released to the desk.

Reports

An entirely new list of reports is generated for the management of the rooms division of the front office. Like those of the reservations report list, many of these are displayed period-

```
            MAID-ROOM SCHEDULE              01:53 PM NOV 11

NAME                          NUMBER  57  DUTY H  MESSAGE SIGNAL OFF
      NUMBER OF ROOMS ASSIGNED    0      BEGINNING ROOM NUMBER
ROOM U-R  IN      OUT    SL HK  CO  ROOM U-R   IN      OUT    SL HK  CO
  1200 A  9:35A   9:49A  SG OK  SO  1209 A                    SD D   SO
  1201 A  9:50A  10:14A  SS OK  SO  1210 A   8:44A   9:02A    SD OK  SO
  1202 A 11:50A  12:12P  SS OK  SO  1211 A   1:13P   1:48P    OK I   OK
  1203 A  9:20A   9:35A  SS OK  SO  1212 A   9:03A   9:19A    SG OK  SO
  1204 A 10:54A  11:17A  SM OK  SO  1213 A   1:48P             OK 57 DO
  1205 A 11:17A  11:50A  SD OK  SO  1214 A                     OK D  DO
  1206 A 10:31A  10:54A  SS OK  SO  1215 A                     OK D  DO
  1207 A 10:14A  10:31A  SS OK  SO
  1208 A 12:12P   1:13P  OK OK  OK

                                              END DISPLAY
```

Figure 15.7. A schedule of each floor attendant is tracked by the property management system allowing management to monitor productivity or to communicate with the floor attendant.
Courtesy: Holiday Inn Center Strip, Las Vegas, Nev.

ically throughout the day as the need arises. At least one hard copy of each would be part of the day's permanent record. Listed alphabetically, they are:

Arrival List: a list of the day's actual arrivals either alphabetically or in room number sequence including number of persons in the party, geographic origin, estimated departure date, and group affiliation, if any.

Block Report: a supplement to the Room Status Report showing the actual rooms blocked, the length of the block, and either the reason for it or the party to be accommodated.

Change Report: an identification of room changes, rate changes, and changes in the number of persons in the party or their identification. The report is an integral part of the night audit.

Departure Report: a computerized form of the departure sheet (figures 14.11 and 15.9).

DNS Report: a listing of guests who registered, but did not stay; not an everyday occurrence.

Expected to Depart Report: a list of guests who indicated the date being displayed as their departure date. The converse would be a stayover report.

Flag Report: a periodic printout of rooms flagged for special attention by the desk.

House Use Report: a summary of rooms occupied by hotel personnel; apt to remain unchanged day to day.

```
HOUSEKEEPING ASSIGNMENT LIST
02/14
PAGE   1

     MAID           1
     ROOM          TIME        NBR    BED
    NUMBER       CLEANED       GST    TYPE              NOTES
      775                       1     KG
      776                       1     TW
      778                       1     TW
      821                       2     DB
      822                       2     TW
      823                       2     DB
      824                       2     TW
      826                       2     TW
      828                       2     TW
      830                       2     TW
      832                       2     TW
      834                       2     TW
      836                       1     TW
      838                       2     TW
      840                       2     ST

SPECIAL MESSAGE TO MAIDS: MEETING IN REVERE ROOM AT 5:15 PM.

TODAYS MESSAGE: REPLACE AIRLINE BROCHURE TODAY
```

Figure 15.8. Hardcopy assignment lists are provided for the floor attendant each morning and may include special tasks or messages. Time cleaned is entered by the attendant; NBR GST is the number of guests in each room. *Courtesy: ECI, EECO Computer, Inc., Santa Ana, Calif.*

Late Checkout Authorization Report: a summarization of the authorizations granted by the desk for late departures without charge.

Late Checkout Report: an after-the-fact compilation of late departures that can prove valuable in reservation estimates and scheduling the housekeeping staff.

Length of Stay Report: an identification of guests who have been in the house for the specific number of days requested by the user. Arrival and estimated departure dates, guest name, and group identity are usually included.

Newspaper Distribution Report: a sequential list of the occupied rooms that should receive free newspapers. It might be the entire hotel, or just the concierge floor. If several different regional newspapers are distributed, the guest's home town could be identified on the list so that, if available, the newspaper originating from that area could be provided.

```
ACTUAL DEPARTURE GUEST LIST BY NAME
08/06
PAGE  1

ROOM#  QNAME   ARV DATE NAME                          CITY, STATE              #GUEST

1811   TELLI   07/29    BRYANT, MR. ARTHUR                                        1
2410           08/05    BURGGREN, EUGENE (90)         NEWPORT BEACH, CA.          1
1912           08/05    CADE, M/M JAMES (92)          CHANDLER, TX 75701          2
 603   TJSN6   08/02    CHESTNUT, MRS F               NET RATE                    1
 814           08/04    DAHL, MR. TERRY (92)          DEERFIELD, IL 60015         1
3003           08/01    DEANE, M/M J                  LARAMIE, WYO 82070          2
 905   TELLI   07/25    ELLIOTT, MS M & MS B          ROME, GA 30161              2
3103   CFOOD   07/30    GRAYBILL, M/M D               GREENSBURG, PA 15601        2
1904           07/30    HOBGOOD, M/M R. E. (92)       BIRMINGHAM, AL              2
1202           08/02    HUI, M/M K. C.                                            2
2703           08/01    KAPOS, MR ERVIN (92)          ARLINGTON, VA 22209         1
2308   TELLI   07/29    KEEL JR., M/M CAREY                                       2
1515           08/04    LEE, MRS IA                                               1
1705           08/04    LIEW, MRS SOON RE                                         1
2714           08/05    MANABE, M/M SHOZO/FAM                                     5
 611           07/17    MERTENS, M/M BUD              HONOLULU, HI 96815          2
1407           08/01    NUMATA, MRS. T (93)                                       2
1705           08/04    PAIK, MRS KYUNG SOON                                      1
 918           08/04    PARKER, M/M DOUGLAS           LINTHICANE MD               2
1201           08/05    SATHRE, M/M G                 THERMOSA BEACH CA 90245     2
1816           07/31    SPADE, MARIE G (90)           PARK RIDGE, IL 60068        1
 711           07/23    WACHI, MR. BOB                HON., HI 96815              1
2407   TELLI   07/29    WEBSTER, MR ROGER                                        1
2407   TELLI   07/29    WEBSTER, MR RONNIE                                       1
1508           07/28    WILLHITE, M/M L (92 DC)       BAKERSFIELD, CA 93301       2
3106   TELLI   07/29    WOODWARD, M/M LARRY                                       2

TOTAL NUMBER OF ROOMS   24              TOTAL NUMBER OF GUESTS   43
```

Figure 15.9. Alpha departure list: the actual
departures for the day are listed alphabetically.
QNAME is a group identification.   *Courtesy: ECI,*
EECO Computer, Inc., Santa Ana, Calif.

No-Show Report: an enumeration of no-show reservations supplemented by any information on credit standing—advance deposit, guaranteed reservation, credit card number, or travel agency referral.

On-Change Report: a status of vacated and on-change rooms that could be assigned, although waiting guests would not normally be taken to unmade rooms.

Out-of-Order Report: a list of specific rooms that are out of order, the reason for the downtime and the date they are likely to be returned to use.

Pick-up Report: an accumulated list of names and room numbers picked up by members of a specific group against their block. Also see Convention Delegates Report.

Rate Analysis Report: a distribution of rates by category—reservations, walk-ins, travel-agency made, res system, hotel sales department, packages, company-made, etc.

Room Productivity Report: an evaluation of housekeeping's productivity in total and by individual room cleaner allowing different weights to different room conditions, e.g., checkout versus stayover.

Room Section Report: a hard copy report provided to the floor housekeeper at the start of the day showing condition of rooms, priority of work assignment and special tasks to be performed (figure 15.8).

Room Statistics Report: a list of rooms, available and occupied, by categories (complimentary, permanent occupancy, etc.), with corresponding rate statistics.

Room Status Report: an identification by floors of the status of all rooms at the particular time of the report — occupied, vacant, on-change, blocked, expected departure, etc.

Special Services Report: a list by room number of those special services requested and provided by the housekeeping department.

Suite Report: a detailed rundown on the status of all suites including petit suites.

VIP Report: a list of distinguished guests and very important persons, including casino high rollers, for management's attention.

Billing

Electronic billing systems contain built-in controls; the kinds of controls that manual systems expect the supervisors to exercise. POS terminals monitor food and beverage vouchers for room number, registration status, and guest name. Incorrect information will clear a manual system and then rely on a reconciliation after the fact. Inaccurate or incomplete checks are rejected by the computer at the point of sale. So, too, are improper room identifications or rooms that have been flagged as paid in advance. More sophisticated terminals incorporate a signature verification capability. There have also been some attempts at using the key tag as a coded identification. When the charge is accepted, it appears directly in front of the guest on a CRT screen. Customers are familiar with this technique in cash registers, so it helps build guest confidence in the equipment.

Similar safeguards are programmed into the terminals. Audit trails are established by identifying each transaction. The source of the transaction (each terminal is coded), the identification of the cashier, and the voucher identification, where available, are required for each posting. Moreover, the computer is programmed to print out a nightly report of all folios that have been modified in some manner. (Unlike electromechanical machines, computers furnish a clean folio to the guest without corrections to confuse the reader.) Rate variances work in the same manner. Computers reject other than the programmed rate unless a variance code, which becomes part of the variance report, is activated.

Checkout

Arrival and departure lines are the bane of hotel guests. Computer installations have alleviated the problem somewhat. One innovation uses swing terminals that function either as a registration station or checkout window depending upon the traffic flow. There are no folios with the computer, no posting machines to be reconciled by floor during the night audit, and, hopefully, shorter lines. Preprinting the accounts of anticipated departures the night before; eliminating the clerk's need to search for late charges; and an almost instantaneous printout should reduce the check-out line dramatically.

The final guest statement is prepared from memory storage. The printout is rapid, from ten to fifteen folios per minute. More important to the speed of the check-out line, guests at some hotels can inspect their bills on CRTs before they approach the cashier's window. Private booths—not featured anywhere yet—would permit a leisurely examination without delaying other guests. The inspection could even be made in the guest's own room with the TV set replacing the CRT. Flight information is already being displayed on the TV screen.

Some hotels are also installing in-room computers. So the next step is clear: the guest inspects the folio on the TV screen, inputs a credit card number into the room computer, and waits for a printed receipt. The guest can check out without stopping at the desk. No need to return the key, for it too is a disposable computer blank (figure 16.13).

Once the departing guest has settled the account through payment or city ledger transfer, no further charges by that guest are possible. The computer will reject the charge plate, if one is being used, or the guest's identifying number (room number plus several letters of the last name), if that is being used. Old and new occupants of the same room are thus distinguishable.

Late charges are possible, nevertheless. Small volume departments, valet for example, cannot economically justify a computer terminal. They still forward vouchers to the desk or to strategically located terminal stations for posting. Even so, there is less grief with a computer. The computer folio remains open for late charges even though the guest has departed. The late charge can be posted as a trailer to the closed folio and transferred to city ledger or to the appropriate credit card if the original settlement was made that way. Wireless communication, say, from a distant club house, is being tried as a means of further reducing late charges.

Group members can also be more readily identified for billing purposes. Although each member accumulates charges separately, the total can be called up at the cashier's terminal for review or payment by the group executive if the charges are to be settled in one billing.

The Night Audit

The night audit offers the most spectacular demonstration of electronic data processing. Only those who have machine posted hundreds of folios or hand copied pages of transcripts can appreciate the savings in time and annoyance. In ten to fifteen minutes, the tedious tasks of posting 1,000 room rates and taxes, balancing the folios, and totaling the charges are finished. Labor-saving, the oft-touted but rarely delivered advantage of computer installations, is evident in the night audit, if anywhere. Since a minimum crew is always needed, the greatest labor savings are in the largest hotels. There is more than a reduction in numbers. Those who remain are able to take on additional tasks in the time that is freed up by the computer.

The computer has altered the mechanics of the audit, its purpose and scope. Audits have traditionally concentrated on errors and reports. The errors were themselves a function of the system. Computerized posting has a series of built-in safeguards, as explained earlier. Many errors are caught by the computer, which simply rejects the posting. The search for careless posting errors, which is the largest block of auditor's time, is eliminated with a computer audit. Staff time can go into informational reporting and analyses rather than into classifying and sorting vouchers.

Night Audit Reports

The ease of running a computerized audit explains the proliferation of night audit reports. Unless management remains selective, an array of reports, involving expensive machine time, labor, storage, and paper costs — computers are great paper eaters — is spewed out. Experienced management requires fewer hard copy reports, relying more on the screen for decision making.

Criteria used by one management for its reports are not necessarily the same as that used by another. More and more, all management has begun to request reports by exception. Only that information which digresses from the expectation is reported. A Room Rate Variance Report exemplifies the technique. The report flags special rates only: rates that have been charged at prices other than those pro-grammed into the system. Reports by exception alert management to problem areas without requiring the time-consuming inspection of normal data. Some examples of exception reporting follow.

Allowance Report: identifies by name, room number, and purpose those allowances authorized, and by whom.

Cashiers' Overage and Shortage Report: pinpoints by stations cash overages and shortages that exceed a predetermined norm.

Check-cashing Report: spotlights excessive check cashing, by both the number of checks and the amount. Used by the credit manager throughout the day.

Comps Report: comparable to an Allowance Report. Includes individual amounts and totals as a percentage of departmental sales.

Credit Limit Report: flags folios that exceed predetermined standards, including total dollars outstanding, charges incurred within a given time period (three hours, six hours, one day), or other criteria established by the credit manager.

No Luggage Report: another credit report listing occupied rooms in which there is no luggage. (See also figure 14.8.)

Room Rate Variance Report: compares actual rates charged by room to standard rate schedule, and identifies the authority (sales manager, casino executive, front office manager, etc.) granting the variance.

Room Tax Exempt Report: lists room charges exempt from sales tax, and explains why; or removes tax when it is included in the price, as with a package sale.

Skipper Report: provides room identification, dollar amount, and purported name and address along with any other credit information.

Write-off Report: lists daily write-offs, usually late charges, whose accounts receivable balance is less than a specified amount.

Reports by exception meet only part of the hotel's reporting needs, management reporting. Record reporting, a printout of the day's accounting records, is not ignored merely because the records are computer gathered. A permanent record base is still needed. If for no other reason, as a safeguard against machine malfunction. Permanent, hard-copy reports, many resembling the materials prepared by a traditional, noncomputer audit, are printed out nightly. A list of these follows.

Two security steps are also taken nightly. Usually, but not always, all of the folios are printed after the night audit is completed. This saves time for guests who depart with no charges the next day. The folios are also available in case a major failure renders the system inoperative. As a second precaution, the data is reproduced on a back-up disc and filed for two or three days. The information is easily retrieved if a temporary computer failure erases the data from the current disc.

Some systems disconnect the computer during the night audit run. Postings, POS input, and even registration may not be available during rate posting and folio update. Other companies tout the fact that the system is never down. Shutting down the terminals during the audit is somewhat like the close-out hour. It assures a consistency of records within each day.

With that consistency, all the reports that have been reviewed, and other reports as well, are generated daily, including those appropriate to the night audit. Throughout this text, the listing has been generic. Therefore, specific titles associated with marketing efforts by different software manufacturers may not be readily evident.

Alpha List: alphabetically lists the entire guest population (figure 15.10). It may be a special list or a part of the Guest Ledger Summary. The guest list is sometimes prepared in room number sequence (figure 15.11), making it a modified room count sheet (figure 14.7).

City Ledger Transfers: itemizes all the accounts by name, room number, address, and amount that were transferred to city ledger that day (cf. figure 13.9).

Concessionaire Charges: categorizes guest charges accepted by the front office for each concessionaire.

Convention Use Report: summarizes the room use of conventions by individual group to justify the number of complimentary rooms (usually one comp per fifty rooms used) granted.

Credit Card Report: reports and separates, by type of card, amounts and identities of credit card charges by both registered and nonregistered guests.

Daily Revenue Report: analyzes revenue totals from all sources including the minor departments, by outlet and means of payment. Comparable to a hand audit "D" report, and sometimes called that (figure 15.12).

Departmental Sales Journal: shows in detail the individual transactions of each department, which comprise the total daily revenue. (Comparable to the vertical columns of a hand transcript.) (figure 15.13.)

ROOM#	ROOM#	NAME	ACCT #	ARRIV-DEPRT	GROUP#	V	PKG	RATE	ADDLRATE	A-FOLIO	B-FOLIO	TOTAL	AMTOVER
		*ELI LILLY	E00112	09/11-09/13	E00112			0.00	0.00	0.00	0.00	0.00	0.00
		*EVAN PRODUCTS	E00133	09/11-09/12	E00133			0.00	0.00	0.00	0.00	0.00	0.00
		*FORD MMOTOR CO.	F00080	09/05-09/07	F00080			39.00	0.00	378.11	0.00	378.11	278.11
		*GROUP XX	GRP200	09/09-09/10	GRP200			0.00	0.00	0.00	0.00	0.00	0.00
		*NATL HOME FURNISHING ASSN.	N00022	09/10-09/13	N00022			0.00	0.00	0.00	0.00	0.00	0.00
		*PEAR BUREAU	P00118	09/10-09/11	P00118			0.00	0.00	0.00	0.00	0.00	0.00
		*SOCIAL-STATE TECH WORKSHOP	S00034	09/07-09/12	S00034			39.00	0.00	165.36	0.00	165.36	65.36
		*WIRE ROPE CORP	W00121	09/12-09/13	W00121			0.00	0.00	0.00	0.00	0.00	0.00
417		ADHHUS, DAN	12281	08/23-09/12				0.00	0.00	0.00	0.00	0.00	0.00
323		ALEXANDER, JAN	13905	09/07-09/12				39.00	0.00	0.00	0.00	0.00	0.00
		ARVIDSON, CURT	15140	09/12-09/14				0.00	0.00	0.00	0.00	0.00	0.00
		BACK OFFICE USE ONLY........	7286	08/06-09/12				0.00	0.00	0.00	0.00	0.00	0.00
433		BACKWATER, CHIEF	15794	09/08-09/12				39.00	0.00	238.06	0.00	238.06	138.06
400		BAILEY, BILL	12601	09/08-11/18		VA		39.00	0.00	165.36	0.00	165.36	65.36
		BANDY, MR. T.	15673	09/12-09/13				0.00	0.00	0.00	0.00	0.00	0.00
		BARRETT, MR. J.	11876	09/12-09/13		TA		0.00	0.00	0.00	0.00	0.00	0.00
		BARRINGTON, JOHN	15727	09/12-09/14				0.00	0.00	0.00	0.00	0.00	0.00
230		BARTH, JOHN	14962	09/07-09/12				39.00	0.00	257.30	0.00	257.30	157.30
		BARTHOLOMEW, ADINA	13838	09/12-09/13				0.00	0.00	0.00	0.00	0.00	0.00
		BEISTLINE, E.	15324	09/12-09/13		TA		0.00	0.00	0.00	0.00	0.00	0.00
529		BELK, WILLIAM	14896	09/08-09/12				200.00	0.00	932.90	0.00	932.90	832.90
		BLUM, MR. R.	15624	09/12-09/13		TA		0.00	0.00	0.00	0.00	0.00	0.00
		BRADY, KEN & HOFFSOMNER, KARL	12688	09/12-09/13				0.00	0.00	0.00	0.00	0.00	0.00
310		BRINISU, L.	12488	09/08-09/12				44.00	0.00	186.56	0.00	186.56	86.56
134		BROWN, TOM A.	15566	09/06-09/12				45.00	0.00	286.20	0.00	286.20	186.20
341		BUEHNER, M/M HENRY	10606	09/08-09/12			MC	39.00	0.00	165.36	0.00	165.36	65.36
409		BURKART, ALAN	13871	09/06-09/12	K00109			39.00	0.00	248.04	0.00	248.04	148.04
544		BURT, J.	15711	09/06-09/12				40.00	0.00	262.60	0.00	262.60	162.60
		BUTLER, N.	13095	08/27-09/12				39.00	0.00	0.00	0.00	0.00	0.00
407		BYINGTON, BILL	15104	09/06-09/12	F00080			39.00	0.00	206.70	0.00	206.70	106.70
		BYORICK, FRANK	12669	09/12-09/13	W00121			0.00	0.00	0.00	0.00	0.00	0.00
422		BYRD, J.	15345	09/06-09/12				39.00	0.00	195.52	0.00	195.52	95.52
		CAMERON, MR. JACK	6453	09/12-09/13		TA		0.00	0.00	0.00	0.00	0.00	0.00
		CAMPBELL, M/M H.	6760	09/12-09/13				0.00	0.00	0.00	0.00	0.00	0.00
132	302	CANTER, ELMER	13163	09/07-09/12				0.00	0.00	0.00	0.00	0.00	0.00

Figure 15.10. Guest ledger summary (alpha order) is a computerized version of the horizontal lines of the hand transcript. *Courtesy: Online Distributed Processing, Inc., Los Angeles, Calif.*

```
GUEST LEDGER SUMMARY
03/29
GS-PAGE   1
FOR: ALL GUESTS

ROOM    NAME                    FOLIO    BEG BAL   CHARGES  TRANSFERS   END BAL

    502 DALTON, MARTY           101844      .00     47.73    47.73-       .00
    503 JOHN, ELTON             101851      .00       .00      .00        .00
    504 BORGES, BION            101852      .00       .00      .00        .00
    505 DOSENHIMER, HARRY       101853      .00       .00      .00        .00
    506 CANTON, BRUCE           101845      .00       .00      .00        .00
    507 JAMISON, JOANNA         101854      .00       .00      .00        .00
```

```
        JETSET STOPOVER          101736    49.50-      .00      .00      49.50-
        TRANSFER--DO NOT POST    100010      .00       .00      .00        .00
        FOUR SISTERS GROUP       101733    75.00-      .00      .00      75.00-
        SNT SANFLEUR HI TOUR     101592    92.43-      .00      .00      92.43-
        MR. WAYNE WILLIAMS       100014   253.18       .00      .00     253.18
        MR. CHUCK WILLIAMS       100016   287.72       .00      .00     287.72

TOTALS                                  67,002.74            2,265.40-

                                                   2,528.54          67,265.88
```

Figure 15.11. Guest ledger summary in room number sequence (cf. 15.10). Also provides, like the "D" card (figure 14.1), an opening balance of receivables, total charges and credits, and a closing balance, $67,265.88.   *Courtesy: ECI, EECO Computer, Inc., Santa Ana, Calif.*

```
DAILY REVENUE REPORT--08/06/

                             GUEST  INTER   CREDIT   CITY     TOTAL
REVENUE SUMMARY      CASH    LEDGER HOTEL    CARDS  LEDGER

ROOM REVENUE
  REGULAR ROOMS       .00      .00    .00      .00     .00       .00
  EXTRA EARNINGS      .00      .00    .00      .00     .00       .00
  ADV DEP. RET        .00      .00    .00      .00     .00       .00
  ROOM REVE TOTALS    .00      .00    .00      .00     .00       .00

FOOD REVENUE
  TERRACE GRILLE    45.70   666.24    .00    68.00     .00    779.94
  BAGWELL'S 2424    30.00   177.26    .00    92.00     .00    299.26
  THE COLONY          .00   124.50    .00    30.00     .00    154.50
  ROOM SERVICE        .00    47.70    .00      .00     .00     47.70
```

```
FOOD OUTLET TIP      15.50    251.15    .00    41.50     .00    308.15

BEV OUTLET TIP         .00     27.75    .00      .00     .00     27.75

**TOTAL TIPS**       15.50    278.90    .00    41.50     .00    335.90

PAID OUTS              .00      2.50    .00      .00     .00      2.50

*BALANCE TOTAL*     116.15  2,528.54    .00   378.48     .00  3,023.17

BANQUET ADV. DEPOSITS            .00            .00
AMERICAN EXPRESS             -751.49         751.49
BANK AMERICARD FOLIO       -1,146.81       1,146.81
CASH FOLIO                    -64.05
CARTE BLANCHE FOLIO         -146.63         146.63
CITY LEDGER FOLIO              .00                      .00
DINERS CLUB                 -115.44         115.44
MASTER CHARGE                -40.98          40.98
PREPAID DEPOSITS APPLIED       .00
(COMMISSION WITHHELD TODAY     .00)

        TOTALS              263.14    .00  2,579.83     .00

GUEST LEDGER BAL PREV DAY  67,002.74

GUEST LEDGER BAL FOR TODAY 67,265.88
```

Figure 15.12. Daily revenue report summarizes revenue from all sources (cash and credit) for each location in the hotel. Format resembles the ''D'' card and totals include the guest ledger balances, $67,265.88. Daily revenue report is the source of the sales journal entry. *Courtesy: ECI, EECO Computer, Inc., Santa Ana, Calif.*

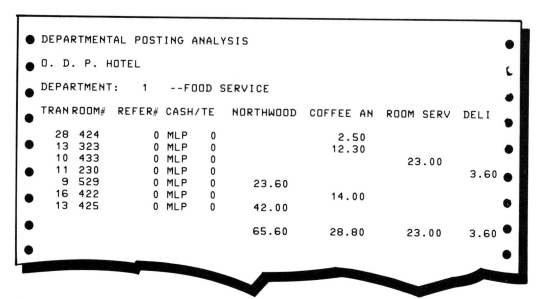

```
● DEPARTMENTAL POSTING ANALYSIS

● O. D. P. HOTEL

● DEPARTMENT:    1    --FOOD SERVICE

  TRAN ROOM#   REFER# CASH/TE   NORTHWOOD   COFFEE AN  ROOM SERV  DELI
     28  424        0 MLP   0                    2.50
●    13  323        0 MLP   0                   12.30
     10  433        0 MLP   0                                23.00
●    11  230        0 MLP   0                                           3.60
      9  529        0 MLP   0       23.60
●    16  422        0 MLP   0                   14.00
     13  425        0 MLP   0       42.00

●                                   65.60       28.80       23.00    3.60
```

Figure 15.13. Food service departmental sales journal is a computerized version of the food column of the hand transcript. *Courtesy: Online Distributed Processing, Inc., Los Angeles, Calif.*

Departure Report: lists the day's departures alphabetically (alpha list in computer jargon) (figure 15.9) or by room number. (Comparable to the departure sheet of noncomputerized systems.)

Due Bill Report: shows due bill number, company, and department(s) against which charges were made.

Floor Report: flags credit card users whose balances are approaching the hotel's floor limit for that particular credit card company.

Guest Ledger Summary: displays the daily activity for both the A and B folios of individual guest accounts — opening balance, charges and credits, and closing balance. (Comparable to the horizontal lines of a hand transcript.) Figure 15.10 illustrates the Alpha Trial Balance.

In-house Listing: lists alphabetically the room numbers of stayover guests. (Comparable to the first three columns of a hand transcript.)

Late Charge Report: identifies large late charges that were transferred to city ledger that day.

Night Auditor's Report: statistically analyzes room sales, occupancy figures, and rate ratios in totals and by type of room. (Comparable to the hand prepared night auditor's report, figure 15.14.)

Posting Report: displays all posting activity by an individual POS terminal. (Comparable to a departmental control sheet.)

Room and Rate Change Report: summarizes room and/or rate changes made throughout the day. (Comparable to a change sheet.)

Night Clerk's Report and Forecast

			Three Day Forecast	
Number of Rooms	669			
No. House Use	10	Wed	A.M. Occ	506
Total Available	659		Plus Arr	216
Rooms Out-of-Order	0		Total	722
Rentable Rooms	659		Less Dep	107
Comp Rooms Occupied	8		P.M. Occ	615
Group Rooms Occupied	336		Expected-Percentage Today	93%
Occupied-(all others)	162			
Total Rooms Occupied	506			
Total Rooms Vacant	153	Thurs	A.M. Occ.	615
			Plus Arr	107
Cancellations	32		Total	722
No. of No-Shows	23		Less Dep	145
No. of Walk-ins this Date	19		P.M. Occ.	577
			Expected-Percentage Tommorrow	87%
Total Comp Guests	11			
Total Group Guests	526			
All Other Guests	172			
Total No. of Guests	709	Fri	A.M. Occ	577
Holiday Package	18		Plus Arr	349
Aver. Rate Per Guest	$20.98		Total	926
Aver. Room Rate	$29.40		Less Dep	218
Percentage of Occ (%)	76.7%		P.M. Occ	708
Total Revenue (plus tax)	$14,876.60		Expected-Percentage Third Day	107%

Figure 15.14. Night clerk's report and forecast is prepared by the desk with pencil or computer to be in the manager's office at the start of the new day.

Room Revenue (Posting) Report: a printout of the room posting program showing each room and the rate and tax posted for the night. Room revenue can be obtained floor by floor. (Comparable to a room count sheet.)

Transaction Report: sequential display of all postings to all accounts in numerical order of the transaction; if transactions are not numbered, the sequence is chronological with the time of the posting included.

A night audit check list is part of the night auditor's task. Although not a report in the real sense of the word, this internal document lists all the reports that need to be prepared nightly, or periodically, and their distribution. Multiple copies might be needed. With management's call for more and more reports, it's the only way the auditor can keep track.

More reports, and better reports because there is a qualitative as well as a quantitative increase, is but the threshold of change. Improved technology has introduced the computer into areas of innkeeping that only recently have become of concern to management. Guest security and energy conservation are among these. They are new areas of attention, unlike the telephone which is also getting some very close inspection. Although the causes lie outside the realm of computerization, the focus is on computer miniaturization and the coining of smart switch terminology.

QUERIES AND PROBLEMS

1. Differentiate on-line computer systems from off-line computer systems from systems that store and forward. Limited resources always force management choices: in which front office functions would each of the systems perform best at the most economical cost?

2. What are the similarities and what are the differences between noncomputer night audits and those performed with a computer? Explain in terms of purposes, procedures, and results.

3. Report generation is the forte of the modern hotel computer system. Identify and discuss one report from each of the four divisions of the front office system: reservations; registration and assignment; billing; and the night audit.

4. What impact does a vertically integrated travel industry have on the computerization of the hotel element? And vice versa: what does the increasing computerization of the hotel industry suggest about the degree of vertical integration that the travel industry will sustain?

16

The Smart Switches

High technology is the byword of the era. High tech has been embraced by the whole travel industry, including those hoteliers who just a few years ago were passive onlookers. Doing business in such an environment means adopting old processes to new as quickly as possible. The changeover has been advanced by deregulation, by reduced equipment costs, and by improved profit projections. These loosely related components vectored in on the hotel business several years into the decade of the 1980s. Everything seemed to come together then, helped along by the quality and price of the high tech product: the microprocessor. Microprocessors are integrated circuits, smart switches, that perform a variety of operations. Their interconnecting capability and versatility offer the hotelier one of the few opportunities to hold down operating costs and improve efficiency without sacrificing guest service. Automation — automation of records, of telephones, of security, of maintenance — is the byword of the next era in hotel computerization, as the smart switches are interfaced into property management systems. All the distinctions will blur, and telephones, management information systems, and technical capabilities will become one.

THE TELEPHONE: SOME OLD; SOME NEW

If the computer, with its marvelous innovations and new management systems, has failed to sweep the industry in a pell-mell fashion, how do we explain the preeminence of the telephone, which has been around since Bell's 1876 patent: three generations. The parent recounts memories of the first telephone; the offspring clearly remembers the advent of the television set; and the grandchild will some day recall the time when there were no computers. Because the old and the new have many similarities, the old hat telephone impacts as heavily on hotelkeeping as does the modern computer.

Early computers were behemoths, filling large buildings with their mass. Telephone lines were the conduits of communication. As technology improved both the computer and the telephone, distinctions between them narrowed. Microprocessors carry out computer functions and communicate directly to the user. Microprocessors in telephones communicate to the user and carry out computer functions. Through technology, the telephone has grown smart and the computer has grown small.

Some Old

Love-hate best describes the relationship that once existed between the hotel and telephone industries. Recently, a new relationship has emerged but has not yet crystallized. As associates, the two industries provided a superior level of service; as adversaries, they argued about the level of commissions: saying, for example, that 5 cents was an inadequate (or adequate) reimbursement to hotels for guest credit card calls. Their interdependence was reinforced by state and federal legislation which is no longer a controlling factor. Eventually, the hotel and telephone industries may be competitors.

Within a short span of time, three traumas touched the telephone industry. The large, integrated Bell system was dissolved and its long-line service separated from its local operations. Competition from other manufacturers and service companies was invited in, which weakened the monopoly still further. And hotels were permitted once again to levy their own fees on calls originating on their premises.

What's Being Replaced?

As a utility, the telephone company has been controlled by many state and federal commissions, which established and enforced various rate structures. Consequently, there were, and

still are, different rates for intrastate calls (those taking place within the state) and for interstate calls (those that pass from one state to another). Rates on intrastate calls vary from state to state since each commission is free to act independently of its neighbor.

Interstate Calls

Interstate calls were regulated until 1981 by the FCC (Federal Communications Commission). Under its regulations hotels could not charge a fee for placing and handling interstate calls. Consequently, most telephone companies, and this includes all of the Bell system, paid the hotel a commission (generally 15 percent) on interstate calls. A different commission was paid for interstate calls charged to telephone credit cards and for collect calls or those charged to a third party. The point is that no fee was added to the guest's interstate telephone charge by the hotel under penalty of federal law.

When the telephone company quoted charges, the hotel added the federal tax and billed the guest for the total, but no more. The hotel collected from the guest, paid the telephone company on the basis of a monthly billing, and received a commission from the company on the same basis. The size of that commission was the point of contention between the hotel industry and the telephone companies, but, as we shall explain, this is no longer the case.

On January 1, 1982 the telephone companies ceased paying hotel commissions because the FCC ruled that hotels could make their own surcharges, just as they had done prior to 1944. A stroke of the pen undid a thirty-eight-year experiment. Uncertainty was the hotel industry's first reaction, and that motivated the AH&MA to negotiate with the Bell system a delay in implementation. Bell's announcement to discontinue commissions was not mandated by the FCC; it was a business decision made by Bell. A gutsy decision if the telephone dollar estimate of 1.5 billion (times the 15 percent rate) being handled by the hotel industry is an accurate one.

Teleplan. Teleplan, which involves overseas calls (international), is more new than old, having been introduced by the Bell system in 1975. FCC regulations govern surcharges on overseas calls originating in the United States, but obviously not on calls originating in other nations. Teleplan is a voluntary agreement to cap the international surcharge fee on guest calls. Marketing pressure, and marketing pressure alone, brought about the change. AT&T agreed to advise international travelers of participating hotels if the hotels agreed to surcharge limits.

Unlike the U.S. hotels prior to deregulation, overseas properties have long considered the telephone department as a profit center. A flood of complaints poured into AT&T as international business and tourism swelled, bringing an increase in the number of intercountry calls. First-time callers were nonplussed at huge service charges that were as much as five times the telephone charge. A $20 call might be billed at $100.

Logically enough, the first participants were the international U.S. chains, whose guests were primarily Americans calling back home. Hilton International was the first to join. Other American companies followed, building competitive pressure on non-U.S. chains, national tourist offices, and hotel associations. Impetus for Teleplan membership also came from an increasingly sophisticated caller. Guests placed short calls to the United States (most places have no three-minute minimum) and had the calls returned at U.S. rates. Or they used credit cards (much lower surcharges) or called from outside the hotel at telephone centers.

Reduced surcharge fees, maximum fees, and advertised rates have been the results. Not that overseas costs have been standardized;

merely that they have been capped. In some instances, the charge is a low percentage (20 to 25 percent of the telephone charge) and a high maximum (10 to 15 U.S. dollars). Other hotels have reversed the approach, charging upward of 100 percent of the call but a maximum of two dollars to ten dollars. Marriott has a daily maximum surcharge regardless of the number of calls made.

The international level of consumer awareness is just beginning to be felt in deregulated domestic calling.

Intrastate Calls

Intrastate regulations lack uniformity since the communications commissions of each state are free to act independently, and they do. Control varies from the very precise schedule put forth, until recently, by states like New York to practically no regulations at all, as in Nevada. Some states allow a surcharge to be added to local or intrastate toll calls as the hotel's fee for telephone service. Some telephone companies pay a commission on intrastate calls, usually with a maximum fee per call, just as they do with interstate calls. Some states allow both the surcharge and the commission. Depending on state jurisdiction and the policy of a particular hotel, charges to guests for local calls range from nothing to almost one dollar.

State communication commissions reacted to the FCC's decision allowing the resale of interstate calls by deregulating intrastate legislation. Many no longer regulate the hotel's surcharge for intrastate calls. A truly historical change when one considers that New York, long the leader in this type of regulatory control, had the policy in place since 1920. Now, perhaps, New York State will lead the reverse trend.

Deregulation has not changed the issue, only the approach to recovering the costs of telephone usage both as a business expense and as a guest service. A different solution was tried in 1969. Incoming Message Service (IMS) was conceived as a means of offsetting the traditional operating loss of the telephone department. Hotels began levying a fee of 1 to 3 percent of room charges on all guests as a means of recovering telephone costs that were not otherwise charged for: calls between rooms, incoming calls, and message services. Legal action was initiated by the attorney general of New York State, among others, in a class action that argued IMS was a hidden charge. The suit was upheld and the hotels involved were ordered to repay the fees improperly collected.

Other equally unsuccessful efforts to balance the telephone deficit have abounded, including the creation of a telephone answering business through the hotel switchboard. More often, cost cutting was the focus: fewer trunk lines; equipment inventories carefully made (monthly charges reflect the number of instruments and trunk lines being rented); comparison of charges made to guests against the telephone company's bill; and the like. Solutions have awaited deregulation and the resale of telephone charges at ceilings limited only by competition. A domestic teleplan may soon be in the works.

Let us review the old billing procedures before examining the new direction and new equipment being thrust upon the telephone division of the front office.

HOBIC

After decades of use, HOBIC was suddenly rediscovered by a hotel industry searching for a response to the recent deregulation in the telephone industry. In reacting to what was going to be, discussion focused on what had been, on HOBIC. HOBIC, *Hotel Outgoing Billing Center*, or *HOtel Billing Information Center*, or any other definition that one encounters, is an acronym for the telephone company's long-distance, and long-provided, network.

With HOBIC, the guest direct dials long-distance calls from the room telephone. The first digit dialed, 8, tells the system that long distance is going through. Digit 1, or digit 0 to get the operator, follows; then comes the number to be called. The HOBIC computer holds that number until the telephone company's operator intercepts. For digit 1 calls, the interception is merely to get the guest's room number. Zero digit intercepts are for person-to-person calls, third-party calls, credit card calls, and collect calls. All calls are intercepted and become operator-assisted calls for rate determinations.

New equipment, Universal HOBIC, records the guest number automatically and eliminates the operator assistance on direct-dial (DD) calls. This major technical advance enables the telephone company to automatically charge the call back to the hotel. But without operator intervention, the hotel does not receive a record from the telephone company until the end of the month, so the guest call would be free. The hotel companies are using the technology to be free of the HOBIC system; free to shop elsewhere for long-distance lines.

The Billing Procedure

Necessitated by technical improvements, several billing procedures have evolved. Regardless of the system in use, however, the aim has been prompt and correct billing on the guest folio at the front office.

Traffic Sheet. Before automation, the guest's request was completed by the hotel operator, who either dialed the local call or passed the guest on to the telephone company operator for a long-distance connection. Where the system is still used, the hotel operator completes a charge voucher. Local calls are a fixed amount if set by state commission; long-distance (LD) charges are relayed over the telephone line by the telephone company op-

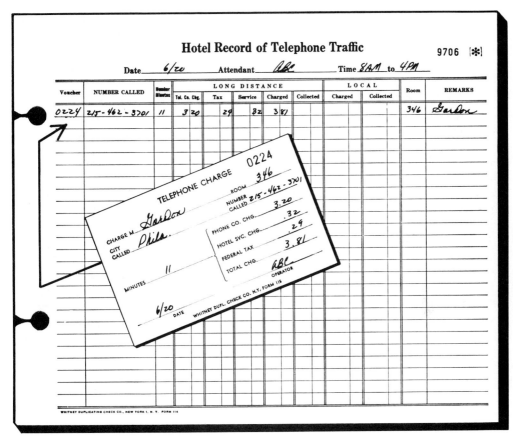

Figure 16.1. The telephone traffic sheet with charge voucher has been replaced by the HOBIC teletype printer (figure 16.2) in all but the smallest hotels and communities.

erator. Heretofore, that amount has been based on time and distance. Local and LD vouchers, usually different colors, go by pneumatic tube (figure 9.4) to the billing clerk for posting to the folio. A traffic sheet (figure 16.1) is maintained by the hotel operator as an internal control device (departmental control sheet) for the night audit. The telephone company's monthly bill to the hotel is also verified against the control sheet.

Local telephone charges are accumulated at the top or side (figures 10.3 and 11.3, Tues.) of the individual guest folio. These are nor-

mally posted only once daily by the night auditor. During the day they are recorded in the appropriate block by having one stroke represent each local call.

Automation. So many technological innovations have been introduced by the telephone companies of the nation, that only the smallest of hotels still rely upon the system of vouchers and traffic sheets just outlined. Direct-dial telephones eliminated much of the bookkeeping tasks inherent in the voucher and traffic sheet. Modern telephone equipment has mech-

Figure 16.2. The HOBIC printer provides direct communication between the telephone company and the front desk, furnishing a permanent record of calls and charges (see figure 16.5). *Courtesy: Centel, Las Vegas, Nev.*

anized the billing system even as it has made available a wide range of additional services. On the surface, modernization has meant touch-tone dialing, handsome consoles, and colored telephones. But more has taken place behind the scenes than on the desk tops. Without an operator, guests can call each other; place direct-dial local and long-distance calls; reach various departmental services by "one-pull" (one-digit) dialing—4 for the bell desk, 5 for housekeeping, 6 for room service, etc.—and even transfer incoming calls to another room number.

Progress came in stages: guests began to direct dial the telephone company operators and LD charges were relayed by teletypewriter directly to the front office, bypassing the hotel operator altogether. Transmission time for these HOBIC teletypewriters (figure 16.2) is less than one minute after completion of the call. Duplicate printings are often provided. One voucher is perforated so that each charge can be separated and posted to the individual folio. The other roll is a permanent departmental sales record, a modern version of the traffic sheet. It constitutes the total LD charges for the day and is especially helpful in verifying the telephone company's monthly billing.

Still another stage of development allowed the guest to bypass the telephone company operator and dial directly into the HOBIC system. Universal HOBIC equipment identifies the room number and the billing goes directly into the teletype system. The next stage is complete automation. The guest direct dials and the charges are returned into the hotel's computer system without teletype printout or any input being required by the hotel staff. Moreover, the number called can be printed on the folio or shown on a CRT by the cashier's stand in case the guest challenges the charge as being in error.

Local calls have gone through the same automation, with call accounting providing local call records as well as long-distance ones. Progress is uneven, so some hotels still use the telephone meter. Each completed call is automatically recorded on a register, a piece of equipment that monitors calls by room number. This register is located in the front office near the posting clerk (figure 16.3). Guests are charged for the number of calls between the opening balance on the meter (recorded on the folio at the time the guest arrived) and the closing balance at departure.

With the meter board, there is no record of the telephone number that was called, so an allowance is usually granted when the guest disputes the amount of local charges. But this also holds true for the voucher system. To save operator time, local vouchers rarely contain guests' names. It is impossible to determine whether the current guest or the former occupant actually made the call. New equipment now enables the desk to disconnect service between the time one guest departs and another takes the room.

There is a general movement toward eliminating local telephone charges altogether, but it may not be sustained under the costs associated with deregulation. Increased room rates would accomplish the same thing and do away with a source of guest irritation and hotel expense. If it is possible to quote the time and number called, and it is possible with the smart switches, the guest's memory will be refreshed and the number of protested calls minimized. Guests are especially forgetful when a telegram appears on the folio as a long-distance charge, since they don't make the association immediately.

Calls within the hotel between guests or various hotel personnel are not billed by the telephone company and, therefore, are not billed by the hotel to its guests.

Interconnect

Some attribute the rapid advances in telephone equipment to the increased competition allowed by the 1968 Carterfone court decision as implemented by the FCC. The ruling opened the way for Mr. Carter and others to attach privately owned equipment to telephone lines. Thus for the first time, it became possible for hotels to buy their own telephone equipment and interconnect it with the lines of the telephone system. Heretofore, all telephone equipment within the hotel was rented from the telephone company for as long as the hotel was in business. Now it was possible to buy the equipment, and after a payoff of, say, ten years, to own it. On balance, however, neither system has proven to be substantially better than the other.

A lack of service — local telephone companies will not repair interconnect equipment — proved to be the first disadvantage as new, untested companies rushed into the field. Competition has shaken out most of the weak entries. Additional considerations make interconnect good for one innkeeper and not for another. Included among these are: the income tax impact of lease rentals versus purchase contracts, including cash flow ramifi-

Figure 16.3. Meter boards for recording local telephone charges were outdated quickly by rapid technological improvements.

cations; availability and costs of later technological improvements; training of employees; speed and capability of restoration following a disaster; and others.

Competition for the hotel business grew steadily from the Carterfone decision. The floodgates were opened wider by the almost simultaneous, but unrelated, decisions to deregulate Bell and allow hotel resale of telephone charges.

Some New

Hoteliers are reluctant to admit it, but much of what happens in the business of hotelkeeping is thrust upon the industry from without. This is most apparent in the front office's new telephone department. The newness is not of the hotel's doing. It comes from regulatory deemphasis, from competition between nonhotel entities, and from rapid technological advances in electronics. As a result, hotel telephones are now providing new services for old demands and making a profit to boot.

The Meaning of the Ruling

The FCC's decision means different things to different properties, which is, of course, the purpose of deregulation and increased competition. Some hotel companies will pursue the opportunity aggressively and make the telephone department a new profit center. Others will be unable to take advantage of the situation because of the large capital investments required. Some will rush in with untested equipment; others will wait to see if competition drives down telephone earnings and undermines the very optimistic projections that early pro formas forecast.

Resale

Removing the restriction on telephone surcharges seems clear on the surface. Hotels are not required to charge, and there is no ceiling if they elect to do so. The excitement within the industry is directed more toward the purchase of the call than its resale. How can costs be reduced so that a small surcharge means substantial profits? It is the alternative cost factor that has changed the situation in the forty years since interstate surcharges were first eliminated.

Reselling without concern for reduced costs, and therefore without concern for new equipment, is a transitional approach for many properties and the ultimate decision for numerous mom-and-pops. HOBIC equipment is retained and a percentage fee, maybe the old 15 percent, is added as the hotel's charge. Adding a flat usage fee or a usage fee in conjunction with a sliding percentage sale are variations of the basic decision. Overall, both the change in system and the income garnered are small.

A measured approach like this will increase the cash flow, but is unlikely to make telephones a profit center since labor, maintenance, depreciation, etc., are legitimate charges against the sales. Resale for profit requires the hotel to file a 214 certificate with the FCC and to keep it current annually. Large chains and affiliations have the legal talent to do this and moved in quickly. For smaller operators, it is another hurdle and another incentive to go slowly.

The FCC does not require that telephone tariffs be posted. Market conditions and an alert consumer demand otherwise. Unreasonable surcharges will swing the telephone user, especially the business traveler, toward credit card calls. With credit card calls, there are no charges to surcharge, and hotels will fall into the trap being set by Bell system's advertising for greater credit card usage.

Resale strategy must convince users that hotel fees are competitive. Competitive enough to draw callers away from credit card and collect calls, which now total approximately 50 percent of hotel telephone business. Increased volume is needed to fund increased equipment. Failing to attract the nonrevenue users, a tariff may need to be levied on credit card and collect calls. The industry has never done this, and the strategy might backfire. Carrot — reduced LD charges — and stick — tariffs on nonrevenue calls — might prove the best strategy overall.

Call Accounting

Call accounting is the jargon used to identify the in-house billing systems that are replacing HOBIC. At the heart of the system is a microprocessor that identifies the source of outgoing calls. It is the type of equipment allowed by the Carterfone decision. The telephone companies' (Bell, General Telephone, Centel, etc.) operators no longer intercept calls to get guests' room numbers. Instead, the calls go as direct-dial calls, which are considerably less than operator-assisted calls. Thus, the cost to the hotel is less, almost a 50 percent savings.

AIOD (automatic identification of outward dialing), another term of the jargon, is what the microprocessor does. It is not new equipment, and it isn't even new for the hotel business. AIOD has been in overseas hotels for some time because those properties needed more rapid accounting than their host telephone companies were supplying. Domestic hotels have discovered AIOD because it is now possible to eliminate HOBIC and to profit thereby. HOBIC's demise would not be 100 percent since person-to-person calls and international calls still require operator intervention.

At its simplest, call accounting allows the hotel to earn the difference between the cost of the direct-dial sale (using AIOD equipment) and the selling price, which it retails at operator-assist levels (the old HOBIC rates). HOBIC rates are not the retail floor. Hotels may resell at any price and may be forced to do so by industry competition and by competition from the telephone companies.

Employing a minimum amount of new technology, call accounting (AIOD) is a passive approach to deregulation. Call accounting takes advantage of the Carterfone decision and the FCC's removal of billing restraints. The hotelier using only AIOD overlooks the competitive advantages accruing from the dismantling of the Bell network and the appearance of equally strong purveyors.

Linkage

Adopting AIOD and profiting from the cost-sale spread may be all that individual managers elect to do. Some will do even less, being satisfied with a percentage of the HOBIC line with no investment risk. Others will do more by taking advantage of the coincidental change in long-distance competition, but they will need to invest more as well, by buying least cost routers (LCRs).

LCRs, also called ARSs (automatic route selectors), choose the least expensive of several alternative lines that competition has created. Calls can be routed with the telephone company using the traditional message telephone service (MTS) lines or using the telephone company's WATS lines at a lesser cost. Or the telephone company can be ignored and the message sent over one of the numerous voice transmission services being offered by independent common carriers. With LCR equipment, each call is evaluated by the smart switches and shunted over the most economical route. The equipment is expensive, so the more calls being made — the larger the hotel and the more commercial its clientele — the more rapidly the equipment cost is amortized and the greater is the justification for its purchase.

Each property must be evaluated separately. Resorts have lighter telephone use than commercial houses. They have fewer wake-up calls to justify automation; they have more reservations than walk-ins, and thus less need for immediate room status capability; and finally, they are farthest from urban centers where service for self-owned telephone systems is based. Resorts might better buy their LCR and AIOD equipment, if at all, from their local telephone companies, which have also entered the business of competing with themselves.

WATS. Like so much of the telecommunication field, *Wide Area Transmission Service* (sometimes called *Wide Area Telephone Service*) is putting on a new face. The original concept of one flat monthly fee, for which the user could talk indefinitely, has been replaced with several new criteria.

Intra- and Interstate WATS have also been merged into one Expanded WATS. Outgoing WATS lines and incoming WATS lines (for travel agency use, for example) remain separate, as do the seven WATS zones that comprise the WATS system in the United States. (Figure 16.4 illustrates the six mainland zones.)

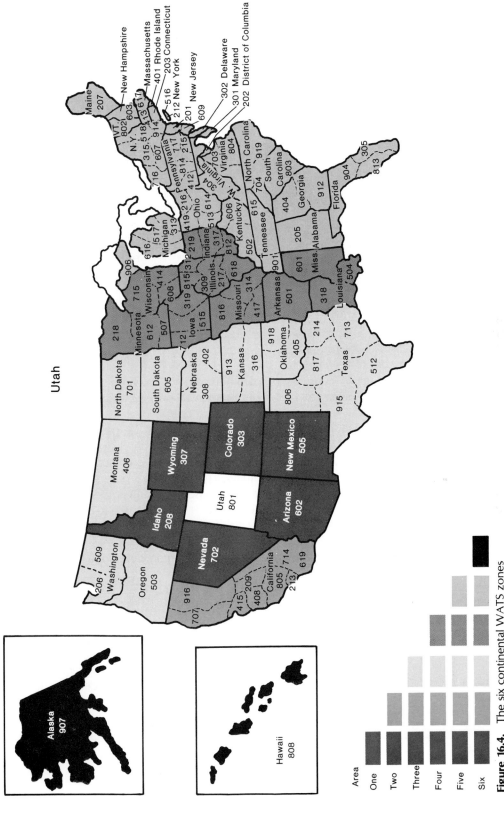

Figure 16.4. The six continental WATS zones currently applicable for the Utah Service Area. WATS service to higher numbered zones includes service to all lower zones.

WATS can be purchased in bands or zones radiating from the user's point to cover parts or all of the nation. The farther the reach, the higher the charge.

WATS charges are no longer flat monthly fees as they once were; charges are now based on increments of time. The rates vary according to the time of day and day of the week. In this respect, WATS has grown closer to the MTS lines.

Resale WATS is still another pricing alternative. Hundreds of companies have gone into the resale of WATS lines. They buy long-distance lines at quantity discounts and resell to customers at less than AT&T's charges. This practice may prove as discriminatory as the flat monthly rate (both putting small users at a disadvantage) and follow it to oblivion.

For cost efficiency in a call accounting system, WATS offers several selections for routing equipment. Depending upon the time of day or day of the week, regular WATS might be selected; first-band, second-band, etc., WATS might be the choice; or the selection could be shared-WATS lines. Indeed, the Automatic Route Selector might select another common carrier altogether, ignoring both Bell's WATS and MTS lines.

Other Carriers. Bell telephone competitors began selling and installing Private Branch Exchange (PBX) equipment after the 1968 Carterfone decision, which was followed by a similar ruling in Canada. The PBX, or switchboard, connects the numerous internal lines of the hotel — the Las Vegas Hilton has over 4,000 telephone lines and handles about 30,000 calls daily — to the outside telephone system.

Competition and new technology brought rapid changes to the electromechanical boards (PABX, Private Automatic Branch Exchanges) that were commonplace during the 1960s. Within a very few years, smart switches, Electronic Private Automatic Branch Exchanges

(EPABX), were being installed almost exclusively. Unlike the dumb switches of the pre-electronics age, smart switches have microprocessors that carry out a myriad of tasks.

The potential of the new switchboards remained untapped until the need for call accounting arose. With smart switches in place, additional equipment like automatic identification of outward dialing (AIOD) or least cost routers (LCR) can be installed with less cost and difficulty. Smart switches allow the newest PBXs to function with AIOD and LCR as integral parts of the equipment. Additional property management capability can also be handled through the smart boards.

The new switching equipment supplemented by the new call accounting equipment opened up other systems of telephone linkage. No longer limited to AT&T, hoteliers began to shop the other common carriers. One chain, Holiday Inn, established its own common carrier, the wholly owned subsidiary HI-Communications, Inc. Other common carriers include International Telephone and Telegraph (ITT), which is the parent of Sheraton Hotels; Western Union; Starnet Corporation; and Southern Pacific Communications among others. The automatic route selecting equipment accesses one of the other common carriers, if that is what's chosen to handle the call, by dial-up or tie lie (a leased circuit). Price is the main consideration when making the selection, be it a common carrier or a WATS line of AT&T.

Implementation

The deregulated environment of telecommunication presages for other areas of the hotel (travel and credit to start with) the same hard decisions that management now faces for the telephone department. After decades of impotence, hoteliers can finally do something — or not do something — about a department they have bewailed for so long. Like all management decisions, it is an issue of some complexity. The uncertainties of guest reaction, of market impact, of licensing, of capital commitment, of return on investment, and of vendor's promises need to be weighed and balanced.

Holding close to the status quo is the simplest decision. Service charges, the old 15 percent perhaps, can be added to long-distance charges, and a small room rate increase, one dollar perhaps, can be levied to cover local costs. Without commission from the telephone company, other service calls will be provided without charge.

In contrast, a capital investment large enough to automate the entire system can be made. Then there will be separate billing for local, intrastate, interstate, international, credit card, third-party, and HOBIC calls. A complete system will do more than account for the calling. It will search among the various telephone service vendors for the least cost method of sending the signal.

The equipment will recognize the room number when the guest dials, listen for the code and call number, search the access lines (WATS or private carrier), calculate the cost, and store the data until called for in the posting sequence. That takes a huge memory; there are some 10,000 different routing codes alone, and a big cost. For the big hotels the pay back is very rapid, but projections assume no customer resistance and little competition from the telephone utilities. Most vendors are so certain of the profit potential that they install with little investment from the hotel, taking their return from a share of the cost savings.

Simply accounting for all the calls that often slip through a HOBIC system will help turn the department into the black. And the system does account. Charges are either printed out for manual input into the billing systems (figure 16.5), or the information is interfaced with the billing computer. Like a POS terminal, there are

no vouchers, no departmental control sheets, and no lengthy audit verifications. Charges are printed on demand or at checkout. (Most print out periodically just to prove that they're functioning.) Of course, the telephone company no longer reimburses for skippers and no longer collects the federal tax.

Available at day's end is a list of calls (figure 16.5), which can be used for several purposes (the same purposes as the hand prepared traffic sheet, figure 16.1). Charges coming from the call carrier(s) can be verified monthly. Guest complaints can be met with proof of the number called. This needn't wait until the end of the day; the number called is available at any time either through a computer display or through the periodic printout of the call accounting system. There are in-house uses as well: daily departmental totals for audit and journalizing, and a record of administrative use by the several departments authorized to call out.

Other Uses for the Switch

Once in place, the smart switch of a modern telephone system becomes the smart switch of a modern telecommunication system. Numerous microprocessors in numerous pieces of equipment enlarge the scope of the telephone and the supplemental services that it performs.

Wake-up Calls and Message Service
The computer has upgraded the quality of wake-up calls. Service slipped in this area after the advent of the direct-dial telephone. Fewer operators are needed to handle an automatic switchboard, so there are fewer available when dozens of wake-up calls are scheduled simultaneously. First, the operator must answer the call requesting the wake-up: then record the request on a call sheet, a form (figure 16.6) with time columns that enables the op-

```
              PLACE CALLED      NUMBER      TIME  MIN  TYP  CLASS

A 2-22  WICHITA       KS   316  555-5020   0747    2   1      B    .43
A 2-22  VAN NUYS      CA   213  555-7487   0916    2   1      K    .97
A 2-22  LEWISTON      ME   207  555-6141   1628   12   1      K   6.13
A 2-22  CHICAGO       IL   312  555-5134   1832    7   1      S   1.96
A 2-22  CANOGAPARK    CA   213  555-4815   1935   14   1      S   3.39
A 2-22  PHOENIX       AZ   602  555-4958   0810    2   1      K    .97
A 2-22  ROOPVILLE     GA   404  555-4422   0806    3   1      K   1.52
A 2-22  NO HOLLYWD    CA   213  555-9540   0908    1   1      K    .58
A 2-22  GREELEY       CO   303  555-5876   1750   38   1      S   9.91
A 2-22  STPETERSBG    FL   813  555-1411   1620    4   1      K   2.21
A 2-22  OCILLA        GA   912  555-7464   1238    1   1      K    .64
A 2-22  HUNTITNBCH    CA   714  555-7243   1801    5   1      S   1.28
A 2-22  CANOGAPARK    CA   213  555-4815   1114    8   1      K   3.31
A 2-22  CODY          WY   307  555-2245   1131    5   1      K   2.34
A 2-22  DRAPER        UT   801  555-5093   1745    3   1      S    .85
A 2-22  BOULDER       CO   303  555-1181   0902    7   1      K   3.20
A 2-22  LONG BEACH    CA   213  555-8832   1747    8   1      S   1.98
A 2-22  BAMMEL        TX   713  555-7580   0811    7   1      K   3.28
A 2-22  GREELEY       CO   303  555-7067   1723   10   1      S   2.69
A 2-22  FORD CITY     PA   412  555-9600   1656   12   1      K   4.56
A 2-22  LITTLETON     CO   303  555-9999   1331    2   1      K   1.05
A 2-22  LOS ANGELES   CA   213  555-7784   2245    6   1      S   1.51
A 2-22  HUNTITNBCH    CA   714  555-7711   1317    3   1      K   1.36

                    *** N24 ***
```

Figure 16.5. A printout of long-distance calls as generated by the hotel's call accounting system. *Courtesy: Centel, Las Vegas, Nev.*

erator to bunch calls by quarter-hours; and eventually ring the room the following morning.

Calling begins ten minutes before the scheduled time and continues up to ten minutes late. Some hotels have furnished in-room alarm clocks as a solution. Computer-directed automatic telephone calls with a prerecorded message (weather or breakfast by room service) are replacing the reminder clock, the call list, and the busy operator.

Facilities in several Tokyo hotels enable the guest to dial in the morning call by room telephone using a code number followed by the wake-up hour. For example, dial 4-0715 (7:15 A.M.) or 4-1915 (7:15 P.M.). At the given hour, hundreds of rooms are awakened by the sounds of the koto and chirping birds. "Ohayo gozaimasu and good morning, honored guests," it announces.

Automatic wake-up systems periodically print confirmations for the telephone operator. Rooms that fail to respond after three automatic calls can be handled personally by the human operator. Security is dispatched when the guest cannot be roused. If more service is desirable, the wake-up system prints a list of anticipated calls fifteen to thirty minutes be-

Date _____				Personal Call List			
7.30	Name	**7.45**	Name	**8.00**	Name	**8.15**	Name

Figure 16.6. A morning call sheet for recording the guest name and the hour at which the call is to be placed. This manual system is being replaced by automatic call systems and in-room clocks.

fore the actual call. Room service or bellservice then delivers coffee and newspaper to the room about the time the automatic call is going through.

Messages also work in the other direction. Calls to room service display the guest room number and name, allowing an extra sense of identity. If room service or any other department is closed, the calls are automatically shunted to the operator rather than leaving the call unanswered.

In-coming messages to the guest have also been automated. The message waiting light, a red lamp on the telephone, actually goes back three decades. Modern versions allow the message to be stored in computer memory for several weeks. As the industry moves toward in-room computers, we can expect that message to be printed in the room awaiting the guest's return. Written messages will aid the hearing-impaired, although federal regulations even now require telephone equipment to be compatible with hearing-aid equipment. Guests might choose not to receive the messages, just as they now choose not to accept telephone calls, even from the telephone operator. Emergency situations permit the override of any do-not-disturb mechanism.

Communications. Almost daily it seems, the ubiquitous microprocessor takes on more of the communication services. CRTs and telephones are just the iceberg tip of a coming era of direct guest-computer communications. Full implementation awaits the technical development of verbal input/output devices. Computers will assume more and more of the duties now performed by clerks, cashiers, and telephone operators.

Even now, except for security, CRTs could be located in the lobby. Callers who were on the premises could find the guest's room number themselves and save that switchboard traffic. City-wide electronic telephone directories are presently being tested. Still further automation is undoubtedly coming in the form of self-activating computers that respond to the human voice and complete the call automatically.

Figure 16.7. The switchboard of one of the world's largest hotels. *Courtesy: MGM Grand Hotel, Las Vegas, Nev.*

Now available is a page-and-park feature. Requests to page guests are taken by the telephone operator who assigns the page to the smart switch. The page is removed from the switchboard, music is cut in for the caller (although the music may be irritating, it indicates the connection is still there), and the page continues for thirty to sixty seconds. If unanswered, the page returns to the operator, who reports back to the caller (figure 16.7).

In-coming calls to guest rooms work much the same. Once the operator rings the guest room, the call is removed from the switchboard. If there is no answer after six or eight rings, the call returns to the operator, who then responds to the caller.

Call sequencers have gained favor, if not throughout the entire hotel, at least in the reservation office. When all the incoming lines are busy, the sequencer answers the next call. A recorded message tells the guest that the call is being placed in sequence and music or a sales message is cut in. Flashing lights on the call board alert the operator to the waiting sequence. The microprocessor furnishes data on the number of calls per hour, the length of wait, and other information for management planning.

Communications of all types can be beamed to the guest through the TV screen or on CRTs conveniently located throughout the hotel. Major roads and maps of the city could be available at the turn of a dial. Road and weather conditions and the status of flights from local airports could be reported. Advertising messages and operating hours of various services could be furnished for the guest's convenience and the hotel's benefit. Dining room menus will be shown on public CRTs and personal messages relayed through the TV screen in the room. The Sheraton Washington has installed VDTs at strategic locations within the convention area. Meeting rooms, exhibitor rosters, hospitality suites, and other directory information that is not confidential is available without operator delay or paid staff in information booths.

Telephones are being used for emergencies, automatically dialing and relaying recorded messages to areas or specific floors of the hotel threatened by disaster. Room status, communications for housekeeping, energy control, indeed, all of the functions of the modern computer discussed in the previous chapter and more can be integrated into the hotel's telephone lines, including tasks ranging from the mundane of telephone conferencing to the esoteric of tee-off scheduling for the golf course.

Several obvious developments in domestic use will soon find their way to the hotel room. Rapid re-dial of busy signals using one or two keys, and speed dialing of frequently called numbers, which would be on the telephone faceplate or indexed into the system, are almost ready to be introduced. Some properties already have emergency systems that signal the operator when the telephone receiver is knocked off the hook.

Earth station and satellite communication have had more verbal attention than substantive action. Holiday Inns' HI-NET system has been at the forefront, but Marriott and Hilton have started to put money on the line. Costs are considerable. If limited to teleconferencing, progress will be slow. General adoption awaits several developments that can spread the cost over more than one use.

Reservations, which now rely on costly telephone lines (AT&T, Western Union), might be handled by satellite. Technically, reservation data – any data for that matter – can be sent between the unused lines of a video signal. Enlarging the entertainment network through proprietary satellite and earth stations would allow the reservation or call accounting systems to tag along. Document facsimile, where the actual document is reproduced at the other end, and electronic blackboards and document display in conjunction with video conferencing are other uses. Put into place, they will spread the cost of satellite communications and accelerate the introduction of teleconferencing.

Early installations have been comprised of receivers only. Interactive transreceivers may be economically feasible only if the installation costs are shared. The sharing might be among chain members, but costs are so great that it might take several chains to share, or more likely, a cooperative venture between hotel and airline companies. Raising again the specter of vertical integration.

A different type of integration has taken place within the hotel itself. In addition to telephone functions, smart switches have been broadened to include energy management, fire safety, and better security systems.

SECURITY AND KEYS

Security-conscious Americans carry their concerns into the nation's hotels and motels. And well they should, for clever thieves (after easy cash and credit cards) and clever news media (after easy stories) have focused there as well. It isn't fluff that makes the AAA include security protection as part of its rating system. Guests are worried about the safety of their hotel environments. So are innkeepers as they face new court challenges to old standards of security and responsibility.

Street crimes become the innkeeper's responsibility once they enter the hotel. In several highly visible suits, courts have stretched the hotel's responsibility for the guest's luggage and person. Going so far in several states as to rule that the standard key and knob system that hotels have installed for decades is no longer adequate security.

Industry response has been strong, aimed at keeping hotel crime below the level of street crime. Success in achieving that goal has resulted from improved technology and upgraded security efforts. Although security involves surveillance, intrusion detection, fire prevention, employee screening, and numerous other concerns, initial efforts have been directed toward lock and key security. It's here that some of the smart switches hold the greatest promise.

Keys

Hotel rooms didn't always have keys. They served no purpose when the room was occupied by several strangers. Things aren't quite as simplistic today. The hotel is a microcosm of a society preoccupied by keys. Easy access to the hotel building presents some special security problems, but the room key remains a weak link in a very fluid situation. If for no other reason, the sheer number of keys presents a security problem: there are two to four keys for every room, plus those uncountable numbers used to secure supplies and materials throughout the building.

Key loss is staggering. Key losses have been estimated at twelve to fifteen keys per room per year. Recomputed, that creates a rule of thumb of one key per room each month, although some hotels experience a rate as high as five per month. Replacement costs are proportional. It has been estimated that Holiday Inns spend a million dollars annually replacing locks. The cost of returning keys by mail is equally expensive, with postage running about 75 cents each—if the key even comes back, that is. A recent test by the AH&MA brought back only 30 percent of the keys mailed. There is a market for keys ($500–$1,000 for a master key), and the postal employees as well as the hotel's own employees know it. Forced entry into guest rooms is almost unknown because access through stolen, duplicated, or master key blanks is so easy. One group of blitzers (six-to-ten person units) "did" nearly 200 rooms in Anaheim, California in one morning. And *Los Angeles Magazine* reported the capture of one individual who had master keys for seventeen hotels.

There is a need for change, and a change is coming with the advent of the smart switch lock system.

The Old Systems

Control of hotel keys begins with an understanding of the kind and number of keys available. Most key systems are comprised of four or five keys. The single guest key, which would be used in a lock like the one shown in figure 16.9, is used for the individual guest room. It opens no other room regardless of the size of the hotel. Two or three of the guest room (or change) keys are available for user distribution (figure 9.8) with an equal number in reserve (figure 16.8). Rigid knobs on the corridor side of the guest room door prevent access to the room except by this key. And once the door is locked from within, all but emergency keys are shut out.

Figure 16.8. Reserve supply of keys exacerbates security control but is unavoidable with a standard key system if guest access is to be maintained.

Locking the door trips a signal that tells the floor attendant that the room is occupied. This device is disappearing. Signal systems of all types: do not disturb signs, lock signals, light systems, room service trays left in the corridor, signals on latches, and message notes on the door tell the thief as well as the housekeeper if anyone is occupying the room. The Peninsula Hotel in Hong Kong has a room-occupied light that is activated by the lock. Security suggests that the signal be in the linen closet, not in the corridor.

Burglars have been known to enter a room marked by the guest to be made up, change the sign to do not disturb, and finish their business in peace. Thieves will also enter when they hear the shower running; knowing that the occupant is in the bath allows the intruder to work with some immunity in the room. For a similar reason, entries are often attempted while the guest is asleep. Burglars have an edge when they know where their victims are. Estimates suggest that one in every three guests fails to double lock the door.

A guest might have several keys on the hotel key chain. In addition to the room key, an elevator key might be issued for access to the concierge floor. There might be a key for an in-room bar or a stocked refrigerated cabinet. Liquor charges are controlled by state law and the ultimate format (credit card, perhaps) of this key isn't yet resolved. In-room safes (figure 6.13) also have keys as do special security closets within the room.

Room cleaners carry pass keys (submaster keys), which are issued from and returned to the linen room daily. Each pass key, or section key (sometimes area key), controls the room cleaner's section of the floor, usually twelve to eighteen rooms. Since the pass key fits no other subset, both the hotel and the individual room cleaner are protected. Well-trained employees of every department refuse guests' requests to be admitted to certain rooms and use their pass keys for this purpose only after proper authorization is obtained from the desk or linen room.

Room cleaners must not permit guests without identification, that is a room key, to enter open rooms where they are working. Similarly, rooms must not be left unlocked if the room cleaner is called away before the room is completed. Locked drop boxes welded to the room cleaner's cart reduces a very common source of lost keys. Obviously, then, the room cleaner's own keys should not be hung on the cart or left in the door or remain unattended in the floor linen closet. Floor housekeepers must be constantly trained to stay on the alert. For every pathetic-guest-in-the-wet-bathing-suit ruse that is uncovered, thieves will create another equally appealing stunt.

Room cleaners sign in and out for their pass keys. Floor design or work assignment make pass keys (submasters) impractical at times. Then the room cleaner is issued a master key.

Master Keys

The master key (or floor key) controls all the rooms on a given floor and incorporates several pass keys. One master may cover several small floors, however. The floor inspector and other appropriate supervisors have master keys, which might be issued singly or in sets. It is this key, not the pass key, that controls the locks between connecting rooms if these are key locks rather than snap locks.

Limited access is the best means of controlling master keys. If one is needed, a whole ring of them shouldn't be issued. Master keys and grand masters are great temptations for insiders, who can dispose of them readily. It takes a little more effort, but a good key thief can reproduce the master key by dismantling the locks from a half-dozen rooms or so, and the thief does it at the cost of six check ins.

Certain department heads, like the chief engineer and the housekeeper, carry grand-master keys. (The Bellcaptain is a proprietary name of an in-room vending machine. Hence, the Bellcaptain's key is the key for that particular machine and not a special key entrusted to the hotel's bell captain.) Any guest room, except those locked from within, can be opened with the grandmaster. There is a trend, however, to sectionalize this key in order to minimize cost and vulnerablity in the event of loss. As additional protection, master keys of all levels function from the outside only. Hotel employees cannot lock themselves into guest rooms.

The house emergency key, the great grandmaster, unlocks every door, even those locked from within and even if the guest key is still in place. If the grandmaster is sectionalized, this E-key would be the only key to open every guest room. It could be used as a lock-out key, but since it is preferable to keep the great grandmaster under the jurisdiction of top management, the credit manager usually has a separate lockout key. Lockouts are extreme measures anyway, so most hotels try to avoid them by a direct interview with the guest.

E-keys should be kept under dual lock in the main safe (they should not be carried around), with one key to the safe under the accountant's or cashier's control and the other the responsibility of a line manager. Neither E-keys nor master keys, or any keys for that matter, should be carried off the property.

Key Security

Although key security has always been of concern to hotel managers, it is receiving special attention these days as crime rates climb and hotel guests become the victims. The key and the lock are only parts of a total key security system, which should minimize the number of master keys and maximize the flexibility of replacing locks. Room accessibility must be balanced by a security system that restricts unauthorized visitors. Security deals as much with people and procedures as with locks and keys. Control must be established over the myriad of employees who have legitimate access to keys. That includes all the front office and uniformed service personnel, the housekeeping staff, and the maintenance crews — well over half of all the employees in the hotel. Control must be established on the distribution of keys to the vast number of guests who make legitimate demands for access to their rooms. And finally, control must be established on the keys themselves.

Most guests keep their keys until check out, although it once was customary to return the key to the desk immediately. The change reflects, no doubt, the delay in retrieving keys from the desk. Keeping the key also eliminates the hazard of getting up to the room only to discover that the clerk had given out the wrong key. Proper desk procedure includes verifying the key number being issued since keys are often misfiled in the rack. Most of all, it mirrors a shift in the service concept that asks the guest to do more.

That's not true in certain foreign lands. Very heavy tags are used on keys in Europe, especially in countries behind the iron curtain. Rarely does the guest carry such large keys away, but the practice leads to those frequent calls at the key desk that American hotels wish to eliminate. It is not a problem in several Chinese hotels; they just don't have keys.

Good key security invariably focuses back on the front desk. Clerks must never issue keys without verifying the guest's identity, a procedure that takes but seconds with a rack or a computer. Still, in the pressure of the rush hours, many keys are issued with abandonment. Almost anyone can request a key and get it. At one time, a copy of the room rack slip was attached to the key rack, enabling the clerk to check identity before handing out keys. High labor costs have taken their toll on this particular procedure.

Key identification has been tightened to improve security. Heretofore, keys were completely identified as to room number, hotel, and address. For a while, the name and address were replaced by a post office box number, making it more difficult for finders to identify the hotel. That difficulty is mere illusion when the hotel is the only one in town or where the key numbering system is very distinct, as with keys having E or W numbers, east or west wings, or when the same box number appears on the stationery. And it is altogether meaningless when the key thief obtains the key right in the hotel, sometimes right off the desk. Quick retrieval of keys left on the desk or pushing them into the key slot is part of security training.

Security, along with increased mail costs, has encouraged hotels to drop identification tags altogether. The address is either contained on a larger key head or is not given at all. The former reduces the weight for mailing but eliminates the possibility of rotating locks without rekeying, since the room number is recorded on the key and not on a changeable tag. With the address eliminated, the guest must either return the key at his own expense or not at all. Replacing the key may actually be cheaper for the hotel than paying the postage, which it now does by special postal arrangements on keys mailed without an envelope.

Hyatt adopted a unique coding system that eliminated the room number from the key. Arriving guests are given the room number and the coded key in the rooming slip (figure 6.20), which the guest is asked to retain. Should the guest forget, the front office has a cross-reference list of room numbers and key codes.

Changing the master reference allows the coded key to be rotated with its corresponding lock.

Some hotels have colored markers that are activated in each compartment of the key rack when the key is issued. If the flag is still up when the old room rack slip of a departed guest is circulated, maintenance is alerted and the room lock is changed.

At one time or another, every hotel manager must have considered setting a deposit on each room key. Fourth- and fifth-class hotels frequently require a deposit for keys, as do some of the Out Islands of the Bahamas. In the majority of hotels, however, the mechanics of a deposit, the negative guest reaction, and the difficulty of determining the right amount to motivate the guest without irritation cause the idea to be rejected. Be that as it may, an automatic key deposit refund machine is available for motels that require a deposit, but close the desk at certain hours.

Training hotel personnel such as cashiers and the uniformed services to retrieve keys from departing guests is the approach that is getting most of the attention. Hotels are finally taking security seriously and that attitudinal shift must be instilled in the staff, who may otherwise treat key security rather nonchalantly. Procedural changes have been implemented. Guests' room numbers and names are no longer shouted out during routine front office business or when calling for the front. All deliveries throughout the hotel: packages, flowers, or whatever, must be made by authorized hotel employees only.

Physical alterations emphasize the personnel changes. Lobby designs (figure 2.7) now consider security. Lobby message boards have been replaced by in-room telephone message lamps because the board announces to the room thief which guests are likely to be away. Key drop boxes with printed reminders by exit doors, in courtesy buses, and even at the airport is another technique. At the least, and especially with new hotels, key heads should read, "Do Not Duplicate," and key manufacturers should agree not to make distribution of the hotel's key blank within a radius of several hundred miles of the property. Blanks are available with a common head shape that does not identify the make of lock. Or what about a sign that reads, "You're not checked out until your key's checked in"? Trained, conscientious, and loyal employees are one component of an effective security system. Good hardware is the other.

Key Hardware

Reported guest room losses are estimated at $400 per room per year. Unreported losses are somewhere between five to ten times that figure, which is more than the cost of computerizing lock systems. That is strong economic motivation for hoteliers to consider new locks and hardware of all kinds. Added incentive comes from court decisions that make the key-in-knob lock suspect as a security device. Key-in-knob snap locks are especially susceptible to manipulation by plastic cards. Inexpensive anti-shim devices are being installed as an interim move to convert the latch bolt into a type of mortise lock.

A mortise lock with the lock and the knob as separate parts provides even greater security. The deadbolt (figure 16.10) portion of any lock should be no less than five-eighths of an inch square and protrude into the frame at least one-half inch. A deadbolt (deadbolt means a key is required; the door does not latch automatically) provides effective security if the lock is brass and not merely a brass-colored pot metal.

Among the simple pieces of hardware being introduced are peepholes (observation ports), a code requirement in some jurisdictions, and chain latches. Latch guards are either the chain and slide variety or a simple cable

Figure 16.9. Key in knob locks are being reinforced with anti-shim devices and mortise locks for added security. *Courtesy: Schlage Lock Company, San Francisco, Calif.*

Figure 16.10. Extra security is offered by the mortise, deadbolt lock. Rekeying is done in this style by replacing the interchangeable core cylinder by means of a control key. *Courtesy: Schlage Lock Company, San Francisco, Calif.*

chain looped from the door stud over the knob. Even though these devices (or others like Charlie-bars on sliding doors) are provided, some guests opt not to use them. Reminders attached to the outside door, notices on the rooming slips, and bureau cards try to convince the guest to participate in his or her own security.

Doors, along with their frames, hinges, and pins, must be heavy and solid, especially those on motel units that open onto a parking lot. Space between the door frame (or door jamb) and the wall stud allows the frame to be spread, disengaging the lock. To fill this space, wooden spacers must be secured when the hinges are attached, or mortar inserted if the door jamb is attached to a masonry wall. Hinges and pins should be inside the room so the door cannot easily be removed, and all security devices should be cleared first with the local fire marshall.

The New Systems

Once the door has been secured, management can turn its attention to the locks. Two major breakthroughs in lock systems herald a new era in guest room security. One effort has concentrated in improving the basic mechanical lock. The other takes advantage of smart switch technology, introducing the electronic lock.

One system that didn't work, because it relied too heavily on the guest, was tried in the Americana in New York. Nothing was special about the lock and key. The guest carried a coded card that was the feature of the security system. The card was to be inserted in a unit attached to the television set within twenty seconds after entering the room. It was too great a burden for the guest. Few bothered to deactivate the system and dozens of false alarms were sounded.

Mechanical Locks

Great strides in the improved quality of mechanical locks make them a viable alternative to electronic substitutes. That was not the forecast when electronic locks were first introduced. Now, innkeepers cannot seem to distinguish electronic from mechanical locks according to a series of AH&MA surveys. The use of card keys in both systems undoubtedly accounts for some of the confusion.

Figure 16.11. Rekeying of this deadbolt lock is done externally by changing the key, not the tumbler core, using two different keyways for the master and guest keys.   *Courtesy: Winfield Locks, Inc., Costa Mesa, Calif.*

Changing locks originally meant just that, shifting the actual lock from one room to another. Relocating pin tumbler locks, in which the key is adapted to the tumbler combination, is costly and time consuming. Security generally involves a total rekeying every eight to ten years rather than periodically interchanging tumblers. New technology has changed the method of rotating mechanical locks.

One system uses a removable lock core. With a twist, a control key removes the whole pin-tumbler combination (figure 16.10), allowing it to be used in some other housing, and replaces it with a different core using a different key. The lock housing remains intact. It is a rapid and effective means of rotating locks for either emergency situations or periodic replacements.

The other innovation is even simpler. The change is made in the tumblers without removing the core. It is the key, not the tumbler, that is replaced (figure 16.11). Initially, of course, a new cylinder is put into the current mortise hardware. Thereafter, rekeying is done from the corridor without removing the tumblers, the core, or the hardware. Master keys are rekeyed separately (figure 16.11), controlling service access apart from guest access.

Rekeying time is less than one minute for both the guest key and the master key according to the manufacturer. Missing guest keys can be changed individually, and master keys to sections of the hotel, periodically. Keys are not discarded; they are reused. Since they are unmarked, keys that are carried away are lost unless the guest foots the postage costs. A removable, colored room number disc snaps in and out of the key, which permits the key to be used in other rooms. Changing disc colors distinguishes previously used keys from the combination currently in use.

Card-access keys are not limited to electronic locks, but have proved quite satisfactory with mechanical locks. One design, in which a magnetic strip is imbedded in plastic (somewhat like a military dog tag), has proven quite popular for sliding glass doors. Guests exit and enter the garden, athletic area, or pool directly and still maintain security.

Marrying the card-access system and the easy rekeying system offers still another alternative: the combination keycard and cylinder. Hotel personnel access the room by means of the mortise lock with careful control maintained on the number and accessibility of master and submaster keys. Guests enter with the plastic keycard. The combination for that keycard is entered into the lock by a code card from within the room.

Electronic Locks
Electronic security systems relate room access to room status. The hotel industry has not yet realized the full potential of electronic locks, but improved room status systems facilitates the move toward improved electronic locking systems using common memory and wiring

Figure 16.12. Combinations for individual room card keys are processed at the console in the front office. Each guest has a disposable key and the combination is changed between occupants.
Courtesy: Uniqey America, Inc., New York, N.Y.

and vice versa. Most electronic lock systems are being installed into new properties; wiring between the desk console and the room lock is a costly affair in existing structures. (Power failures—blackouts and brownouts—caused considerable havoc with early systems that lacked backup power or battery-operated emergency systems.)

Arriving guests are given a plastic card that is prepared by a computer (figure 16.12). The "key" is coded to match the combination en-

tered in the computer console by the clerk. There are literally millions of combinations possible. The computer selects a combination at random or the guest furnishes an anniversary or birthdate. The punched card is inserted in a slot by the bedroom door and if it agrees to the combination in the computer the door opens (figure 16.13). If not, the desk is signalled and security crews are dispatched. The lock emits a clicking signal if the key is inadvertently left in the keyport.

Figure 16.13. The guest inserts the special plastic key (see figure 16.12) prepared at the time of check in and gains access to the room. *Courtesy: Uniqey America, Inc., New York, N.Y.*

New keys are easily made, either as replacements for lost keys or for each new occupant of the room. The card that is carried away — bringing us full cycle, for the hotel now includes its name, address, and telephone number — is a public relations and advertising novelty. At least at this time it is a novelty since only a few dozen hotels have installed an electronic lock system.

There are several variations of electronic lock systems. Some systems are battery operated and some are hard wired. Some systems use a plastic key and some a traditional metal key. In some systems the guest carries a key and in some systems the lock is opened by a sequence of numbers tapped into a keypad by the door. The key could be activated by holes punched into the plastic or by a magnetic strip embedded within the card. Some systems interface with existing computer capacity and some require extra processors, printers, terminals, and space. Access by service personnel, including housekeeping,

is controlled by some systems and not by others. "Once-only" keys limit staff access to the room to once per day. Entry cards limited to a specific set of rooms are changed and issued daily.

Despite the many differences, electronic lock systems are conceptually the same. A new key that is computer coded is issued for each guest; the key codes are entered at either the front office or at the guest lock. Lost keys are replaced with new combinations, which include so many possibilities as to preclude duplication. Guest access can be restricted easily in cases of poor credit or lock-out procedures. Although employee entrance (housekeeping, repair, etc.) is still necessary, it too can be restricted and controlled by using separate memory systems.

The matter of guest security is so serious that the march toward better security systems, of which room keys are but a part, goes unabated. Three distinct factors influence the rate of change-over. The first factor is the rate of new construction since present technology is more easily incorporated into new buildings. The second factor is the rate of computerization throughout the industry since one computer system should be able to handle all the hotel's needs. And the third factor is the smart switch that contains some cross-over capability in other areas of security and energy. Multiple use helps to justify and to amortize the costs of computer installation.

Cross-Over Capability

Although the computer's initial acceptance as a basic tool was slow in coming, its broad adaptation has been almost immediate. Once installed, management realized the range of possible uses. The unanticipated severity of energy and security needs and a desire to get the most economical performance from the investment has focused management's attention on these other areas.

Energy-saving installations range from individual room control to the control of the entire hotel system. With individual room control, smart switches turn off lights, heat (or air conditioning), TV, and bathroom heat lights whenever the guest leaves the room. Although not as dramatic, some installations have the clerk activate the turn-off system from the desk as the guest checks out.

On a much broader scale, microprocessors monitor the hotel's entire energy system: from hot water to central air conditioning; from elevator usage to laundry consumption. Peak electrical loads are regulated by switching various pieces of equipment off and on. (Electric bills are based in part on these peak loads.) Public rooms and corridors can be monitored to reduce energy consumption when these areas are not in use. Rooming programs can recommend to the clerk those assignments that will lessen energy consumption based on the time of the year and the level of occupancy.

Energy control systems rely on sensors, which activate when the event takes place: guest leaves the room, banquet hall begins to fill, etc. Security devices operate in the same manner, sensing changes in the environment. Heat and smoke detectors maintain fire watch, and motion and pressure sensors detect intruders. Additional security is available through television cameras and employee identification devices, which can be made part of the employees' payroll clock system. Emergency paging in every guest room can be an adjunct to many wake-up systems. A prerecorded message — so the voice will be calm and not affected by the events — giving emergency evacuation instructions can be played into every room or into specific sections of the hotel depending upon the circumstances.

It is impossible to estimate the direction of computer development during the next two or three decades, but expectations for the cross-over capabilities of the smart microprocessors are great. The pace of adoption will increase as more uses are added to those already visualized: front office applications, security, entertainment, energy conservation, and teleconferencing.

Tomorrow's Horizon

Tomorrow's horizon is the electronic age. Society has already dubbed it that; an appellation that for the hotel industry is but father to the wish. Technology is posed on the brink of many startling discoveries. Miniaturized circuits and laser beam telegraphy are but the start of a new round of computer innovation that will make electronics an integral part of tomorrow's society. As such, the computer, and the systems that it breeds, cannot help but be an equally important constituent to the hotel of the future.

As is the case today, the thrust of development will be external to the hotel industry. Areas directly and indirectly related to the operation of the hotel will feel the impact of technological and conceptual change. The vertical integration of the travel industry will speed along the automatic reservations and the electronic fund transfers that are already on the horizon.

It has been suggested that many of the things predicted for the computer could be done today by hand if labor costs were less prohibitive. They will be less costly by data processing because many of the services will be a by-product of idle computer time. Credit and marketing will be secondary beneficiaries of computer installations. Reservations, registration, and billing are the more immediate needs. Even here, very few of the present installations are complete. Some systems do parts of one job and some do parts of another. There is almost no interface between components; point-of-sale terminals are still rare. Until all of these are married, the computer's presence at the front desk will be impalpable. When the pressures that were outlined throughout this text come to bear upon the hotel, the computer will become all-ubiquitous; the distinctions between computers, telephones, and smart switches will disappear. And the front office will never again be the same.

QUERIES AND PROBLEMS

1. "Intrastate" and "interstate" were important distinctions to users of the two previous editions of this text. Why was it necessary to make that distinction? Is the difference as important today? Explain.
2. Identify by name the several keys that comprise the system of most hotels. Explain who has access to which keys and what purpose is served by each level of key. How does the system work if the mechanical lock and key is replaced by the computer and the computer key card?
3. Telephone regulations began to change in the late 1960s. Three governmental rulings had major impact, separately and jointly, on the telephone departments of U.S. hotels. What were these three changes and how did each alter the way in which the telephone department operates?
4. What does the author mean by the chapter's title, "Smart Switches"? What smart switches are now in place in the hotel business? What use do you foresee for smart switches during the next decade?

17

Statistics

Planning and control, two of management's chief functions, depend upon the manager's knowledge of the hotel. That knowledge is obtained in part through statistical reports and analyses, which provide information for establishing standards, making comparisons, and drawing conclusions. Statistics reduce the diversity of the day's activities to succinct and manageable bits of information, which are usually presented numerically but not always. With this specific information, management draws general inferences and makes decisions in the face of uncertainties.

Although a profitable operation requires management's attention to the entire hotel, this chapter, as part of a front office text, treats front office figures only. This is not a serious shortcoming since the figures produced by the front office are among the most important and are the basis for much of the other data. Even those hotels doing a minimal amount of statistical work compute front office figures. After

all, the sale and occupancy of rooms is the chief determinant of volume, expenses, and profits in the other operating departments. For this reason, most operating ratios are expressed either in relation to room sales or on a cost per room basis, although a ratio to total sales is another commonly used relationship. The reason for this is that, with the exception of the direct operating expenses of the restaurant, the operating expenses of hotels are governed by the size, class, and occupancy of the hotel, all factors in room sales.[1]

After the data has been gathered and collated, it must be communicated from the statistician to the operating manager. This is done by means of reports, of which the daily report to the manager is the most common. It should be obvious, but often is not, that the accumulation of information and the preparation

1. E. Horwath, L. Toth, and J. Lesure, *Hotel Accounting*, 4th ed. (New York: The Ronald Press Co., 1978), p. 350.

of reports is useless if the information is ignored or if the reports are assigned to the wastebasket.

THE MEANING AND USE OF STATISTICS[2]

Statistics are merely special ways of grouping data in an orderly and usable manner. Statistics are the facts expressed in dollars, cents, or numbers. For example, instead of itemizing:

Guest A	Room 597	$50.25
Guest B	Room 643	$48.75
Guest C	Room 842	$59.25

and so on, one might say there are 220 guests in 189 rooms paying a total of $9,158. A great deal of information has been grouped, classified, and presented to become a statistic.

Is the sale of 189 rooms good or bad? *Good* and *bad* are relative terms, of course, and answering the question necessitates a comparison. This can be a comparison to last month's figures or to last year's. Comparing this operation to another hotel in the chain or to regional and national averages is another approach. Absolute comparisons are difficult since businesses vary in size and scope. Variations in different operations or in the same operation over time must be recognized. This can best be done by expressing one statistic in relation to another. This relationship is called a *ratio*. It facilitates the comparison and communication of information much as the batting average of a baseball player does (three hits in four times at bat).

The 189 occupied rooms can be expressed in relation to the number of rooms that the hotel has to sell — 270. This particular ratio

2. Jerome Vallen *et al., The Art & Science of Managing Hotels, Restaurants, Institutions,* 2d ed. (Rochelle Park, N.J.: Hayden Book Company, Inc., 1978), pp. 83–85.

is called the *percentage of occupancy.* Ratios are frequently given in percentages but they are also expressed as a direct relationship, 189 to 270, or as a turnover, the division of one figure into the other with the answer expressed as a number of times. For business statistics, there is considerable value in presenting ratios as percentages. With 100 cents in a dollar, the decimal figure can be read either as part of a dollar or as a percent when multiplied by 100.

Expressing the amount of rooms sold in relation to the potential number that could be sold:

$$\frac{\text{Number of Rooms Sold}}{\text{Number of Rooms Available for Sale}} = \frac{189}{270} = 70\%$$

is more meaningful than merely giving the number of rooms sold as 189. One hotel can be contrasted with another, with the national picture, or with business during a previous period in the same hotel. It may be that another hotel has sold 300 rooms today. Does this mean that the second is more fully occupied than the first? Certainly 300 rooms is more than 189. But what if the second hotel has 500 rooms for sale? Then it is operating at 60 percent occupancy (300/500) and is not doing as well with its potential as its competitor.

Ratios lend themselves to misinterpretation. An observed relationship between two figures does not necessarily imply cause and effect. An increase in the percentage relationship between room sale dollars and foreign dollars circulating in the city is not basis enough for using one to explain the other.

The Uniform System of Accounts

The financial statements of the hotel, as prepared by the accounting office, are the raw material for statistical analysis. Financial statements are incomplete unless the relationships hidden in the mass of figures are computed and interpreted. Computing these ratios is a simple, mathematical function. Interpreting their meanings and deciphering their impact on management decisions is the real challenge and the ultimate purpose of statistical presentations.

If the statistical work is to have value, the figures on which it is based must be as accurate and consistent as possible. That is the objective of the *Uniform System of Accounts for Hotels*, which is nothing more than a uniform system of recordkeeping. The classification of accounts and the composition of the records are standardized; terminology and presentation are regulated. Unlike the many office procedures that have been described for the various sizes, classes, and types of hotels, the industry attempts to speak a common statistical language.

Although the Uniform System has undergone several revisions since its introduction in 1925 by the New York City Hotel Association, it has retained its basic purposes. In the words of the preface, the system offers a "simple formula for the classification of accounts . . . and . . . a standard, uniform method of presenting financial results."[3] Uniformity assures comparability between individual properties, throughout the industry, and over time within the same hotel. It makes possible the accumulation of meaningful national, regional, and local statistics by which the measure of management efficiency and the location-correction of operational weaknesses are facilitated.

The Uniform System is, in fact, a media of communication, a common tongue. Standardized terminology and precise definitions permit comparisons and evaluations. Technical terms and industry jargon are used with confidence. A reasonably high degree of reliability

can be expected from ratios derived from accounting records whose contents are uniformly prescribed. The Uniform System shows which departments are carrying their own weight and which are riding on the coattails of better-managed divisions. If the basis of operation is similar from hotel to hotel, executives become functional more rapidly when they take new positions.

Since hotel operations often vary from hotel to hotel, examining the credibility and consistency of the figures is the first step in using them for comparisons. Take service charges, for example. Changing tax rules on tips suggest an increased use of service charges in the United States. Moreover, many chains are now international in scope, operating in countries where service charges are used. Uniform comparison is just not possible if one hotel making the service charge uses it to reduce payroll costs while another records the charges as an income.

Limitations notwithstanding, the system has had the wholehearted endorsement of the entire industry. Indeed, the idea has fathered several offspring. Not only is there a uniform system for motor inns, *The Uniform System of Accounts for Motels, Motor Hotels and Small Hotels* (American Hotel & Motel Association), but for restaurants and clubs as well.

The Meaning of Average

In statistics a whole set of possibilities is represented in one value called an *average*. For example, average annual occupancy for U.S. hotels in the 300–600 room range is 69 percent. That one figure represents all the hotels of this description during every day of the year. It would be an unbelievable coincidence if any one hotel met that measure. The average figure merely conveys the characteristic that describes the general circumstances or the central value, if the observations are mathematically listed.

3. Used with the permission of the Hotel Association of New York City, Inc.

The average must reflect all the values that can be observed. To the degree that it does this, it characterizes the entire set. Three different measures are used in an effort to best describe the central characteristic: the *mode*, the *mean*, and the *median*. Two of these are used in hotel statistics and one of them, the mean, is the computation that most of us recognize as the average. Misuse or misinterpretation of the terms will offset any degree of statistical certainty contributed by the *Uniform System of Accounts*.

The mode is that figure that occurs most often in the series. It is the typical value, the one in fashion, the most common, the a la mode of menu terms. Ninety-five percent is the mode of figure 17.1 because that value appears more than any other. There is little application of the mode to front office statistics, so it receives no further attention in this chapter.

The Arithmetic Mean

The *arithmetic mean* is the average that most laypersons know and the only measure of central tendency to which the statistician applies the term *average*. It is computed by adding the individual items and then dividing the total by the number of items in the group. Figure 17.1 represents the occupancy for a given week, so the divisor is 7 (the number of days in the week) and the average occupancy 71.1 percent, 498 ÷ 7.

The arithmetic mean is easy to understand and use and easy to derive. The result can be arithmetically computed, hence the *arithmetic mean*, and thus capable of algebraic manipulations. It is easily distorted by extreme figures, either at the high or low range, and this is its chief weakness. This is especially true when the size of the sample is small, as in figure 17.1. A simple illustration points out the problem. Average six figures, five of them with a value of 2 and one of them with a value of 110. The

Day of the Week	Occupancy %
Monday	95
Tuesday	100
Wednesday	88
Thursday	95
Friday	60
Saturday	10
Sunday	50
Total	498

Number of Items 7
Average Percentage
of Occupancy . . . . .71.1% Mean
Item That Appears
Most Often . . . . .95% Mode

Figure 17.1. Hypothetical occupancy for an urban hotel illustrates the meanings of mean and mode.

mean is 20 even though five of the six figures are 2's. (Here the mode would be more representative.) Excepting this weakness, the arithmetic mean is the best of the three measures of average.

The Moving Average

The *moving average* is a special application of the arithmetic mean. It is applied to time series to smooth out short-term irregularities and present the reader with a long-term trend line (figure 17.2). Statistically, it has the same advantages as the simple mean: it is easily computed and easily understood. The moving averages of two front office ratios, average rate and percentage of occupancy, are carefully tracked by industry watchers.

Using a twelve-month moving average, an annual cycle, eliminates seasonal fluctuations or other short-term deviations. Each point on the line is the arithmetic mean of the preceding twelve months. For each new computation, the first month of the sequence is dropped and the most recent month is added in its place. The mean for the next twelve

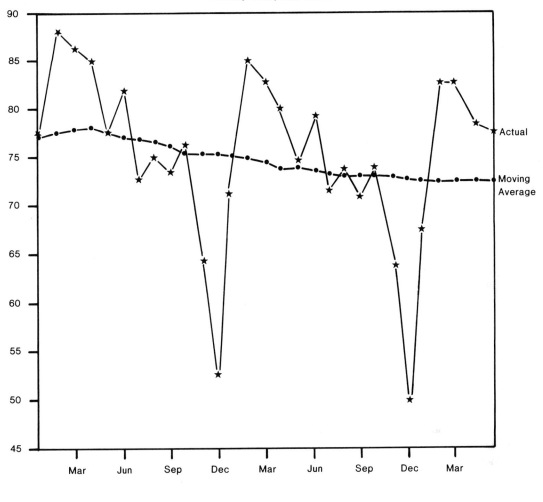

Monthly Occupancy Rates

Legend: ✳━━━✳ Actual

●━━━● Moving Average

Figure 17.2. When plotted on a graph, the moving average smooths out periodic fluctuations and points up the trend.   *Courtesy: Laventhol & Horwath, and Lodging, November, 1981, p. 27.*

months is then computed. If the first computation included the figures of January through December, the second computation would be February through the new January, the third computation March through February, and so on. Since each monthly mean includes only one new figure along with eleven old ones, changes come slowly.

The Median

The value of the median depends on its position in the array of statistics rather than on the value of the observations, which is the case with the mean. To locate the median, values must be arranged in order by magnitude. The median is the midpoint. Half the values are larger than the median and half are smaller (figure 17.3). The items in figure 17.1 have been rearranged in figure 17.4 to identify the midpoint.

The median is as easy to describe as the mean, but unlike the mean it is not pulled from its central location by unusual values on the extremes. It is a value of order, not quantity; a value of position, not size. Consequently, the median remains unaffected by changes in quantity. In this respect it is superior to the mean. In figure 17.4, for example, Saturday night's occupancy could increase from 10 percent to 87 percent without altering the value of the median. The mean, on the other hand, would increase by 11 percentage points.

Another advantage of the median is the ease of locating it when the series cannot be measured quantitatively. Conversely, unlike the mean, which is capable of algebraic manipulations, the median permits no further mathematical computations.

Percentiles

As the median divides the array of numbers into two equal parts, other points divide the series into different proportions. Three points separate the list into four parts — *quartiles*; nine

Median of Net Profit Margins		
Hotels and Casinos		Net Profit Margin
Hilton		15.6
Resorts International		8.8
MGM Grand		6.3
Holiday Inns		5.2
Median	4.5	
Marriott*		3.8
Caesars World		0.1
Ramada		def
Del E Webb		def

*Has no casinos

Median for All Leisure Industries Including Hotels and Gaming	
	5.3

Sample Medians for Other Industries	
Electrical Utilities	11.2
Drugs	9.6
Telecommunications	8.7
Banking	5.4
Fast Food	3.9
Apparel	2.9
Steel	0.7
Airlines	def

Median for All Industries (listing is incomplete; segments shown will not compute to the median of the complete list)	
	3.4

Figure 17.3. Medians of net profit margins contrast the performance of individual hotel firms and of the industry as a whole. *Courtesy: FORBES Magazine, January 3, 1983, pp. 208–12, 224–25.*

points, into ten parts — *deciles*; 99 points, into 100 parts — *percentiles*. Quartiles are the most important for hotel statistics. They fix the range of distribution, showing the spread of the middle half of the array, which falls between the lower and upper quartiles (figure 17.4). Op-

Day of the Week		Occupancy %
Tuesday		100
Monday	Quartile - - - - - - - -	95
Thursday		95
Wednesday	Median	88
Friday		60
Sunday	Quartile - - - - - - - -	50
Saturday		10

Mid-Half

Figure 17.4. Locating the median and the quartiles by arraying the figures in order of magnitude.

erational comparisons include the median and quartile range in most of the annual studies (figure 17.5).

HOTEL STATISTICS

Over the years, a number of ratios have come to form the basic guideposts by which hoteliers measure business volume and efficiency. Some deal with the front office exclusively, some with the other operating departments, and some with the overall picture. Use of many of the measures is so widespread that reference is made to them in an abbreviated, professional jargon. "Cost" is one of these. It is the relationship of cost of food consumed to total food sales. This ratio is also known as food cost, food percent, food cost percent, and others.

Occupancy, meaning the percentage of occupancy, is the front office counterpart to cost. Like all the statistics and ratios of the front office, it relates to the sale and use of guest rooms. Occupancy measures both the use factor of the hotel's facilities and the skill of the front office staff in meeting its basic selling responsibility. It reflects the pattern of the business as well as its general level of activity. Put another way, room statistics show the pattern

of rooms sold and not sold, and the latter can be just as enlightening. Indeed, it has been suggested that a percentage of vacancy would be more telling than a percentage of occupancy.

Percentage of Occupancy

As previously explained, the relationship of the number of rooms sold to the number of rooms that could have been sold if there were enough customers is called the percentage of occupancy:

Number of Rooms Sold (Room Count)
Number of Rooms Available for Sale

This ratio measures the marketing success of the sales department and acts as a barometer of volume for the operating departments that depend on room occupancy to generate business for them. It is the hotel's "share-of-the-market" statistic. Generally, the larger the hotel and the larger the city in which it is located, the larger the percentage of occupancy.

Break-even points, that level of volume in which there is neither profit nor loss, are expressed in occupancy percentages. Because hotels have a high percentage of fixed and semifixed costs, a large percentage of incre-

	Under 150 Rooms			150-299 Rooms		
	Lower Quartile	**Median**	Upper Quartile	Lower Quartile	**Median**	Upper Quartile
General Statistics						
Percentage of Occupancy	60.5%	**70.9%**	78.9%	64.8%	**74.2%**	82.0%
Percentage of Double Occupancy	27.3	**40.0**	62.3	24.1	**32.8**	45.8
Average Room Rate	$22.41	**$24.45**	$27.96	$22.57	**$26.10**	$29.35
Income Before Fixed Charges						
Ratio to Room Sales	36.1%	**42.2%**	49.6%	40.5%	**46.1%**	55.5%
Ratio to Total Sales	19.8%	**25.4%**	34.7%	24.3%	**29.1%**	35.8%
Number of Times Average Rate Earned	81	**111**	136	95	**126**	158
Sales and Payroll						
Food Sales						
Ratio to Room Sales	28.7%	**37.2%**	53.4%	28.1%	**36.4%**	49.7%
Beverage Sales						
Ratio to Food Sales	26.7	**42.7**	68.4	35.7	**47.2**	63.9
Telephone Sales						
Ratio to Room Sales	3.4	**4.2**	5.4	4.5	**5.1**	6.0
Ratio to Total Sales	2.0	**2.7**	3.5	2.5	**3.1**	3.9
Telephone Department Loss—						
Ratio to Room Sales	(1.7)	**(1.0)**	(.3)	(1.5)	**(.7)**	N
Ratio to Total Sales	(1.1)	**(.6)**	(.1)	(.9)	**(.5)**	N
Rentals and Other Income—						
Ratio to Room Sales	.6	**.9**	1.5	.7	**1.3**	2.3
Ratio to Total Sales	.3	**.6**	1.0	.4	**.8**	1.3
Ratio to Total Sales						
Cash Payroll	22.9	**24.8**	27.4	22.1	**24.5**	28.1
Employee Benefits	3.7	**4.4**	6.0	4.1	**4.9**	7.1
Net Payroll and Related Expenses	27.4	**29.2**	33.2	26.6	**29.6**	34.1
Rooms Department						
Ratios to Room Sales						
Payroll and Related Expenses	16.3	**19.4**	22.4	15.8	**17.5**	19.6
Commissions (including travel agents)	.1	**.2**	.4	.1	**.3**	.6
Contract Cleaning	.1	**.2**	.3	.1	**.2**	.3
Linen	.6	**.9**	1.3	.5	**.8**	1.2
Laundry and Dry Cleaning	.4	**.9**	2.5	.3	**1.1**	1.8
Operating Supplies	1.4	**1.8**	2.2	1.3	**1.6**	1.6
Other Operating Expenses	.4	**.9**	1.5	.3	**.9**	1.6
Reservation Expense	.6	**.8**	1.4	.5	**.8**	1.3
Uniforms	N	**.1**	.1	.1	**.1**	.2
Total Expenses	22.4	**25.5**	28.9	21.0	**23.4**	26.9
Departmental Income	71.2	**74.5**	77.6	73.1	**76.6**	79.0
Ratio of Departmental Income to Total Sales	40.0	**47.7**	58.3	41.2	**47.0**	53.2

N Negligible amount.

Figure 17.5. Annual hotel statistics provide medians and quartile distribution in the 1979 study, *U.S. Lodging Industry.* *Courtesy: Laventhol & Horwath.*

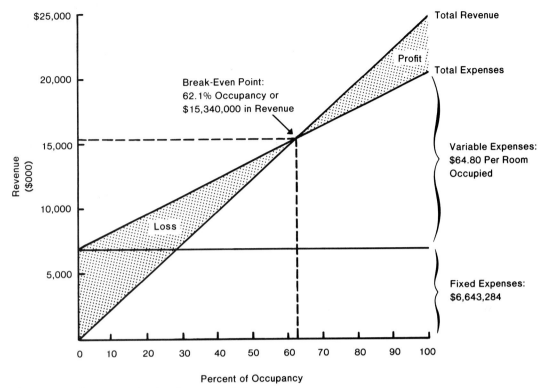

Figure 17.6. Representative break-even analysis computation for 600 rooms. Illustration appears in *U.S. Lodging Industry, 1983.* *Courtesy: Laventhol & Horwath.*

mental revenue flows to profits once the break-even point is achieved (figure 17.6). Occupancy patterns also provide data for marketing decisions and capital improvements.

Contrary to first assumptions, the value of the denominator, "number of rooms available for sale," does change over time. Guest rooms are gradually converted into storage space, rental space, and other uses. Certain rooms in very old hotels are no longer marketable. A spread appears between the number of rooms available for sale and the actual number of rooms in the hotel. Many years ago, Boomer suggested that this relationship should be about

95 percent.[4] Over time, the hotel's advertising might fall prey to consumerism if it continues to represent the original number of rooms rather than the actual number of some years later.

As chapter 1 noted, the older the hotel, the smaller this ratio of usable rooms to total rooms because fewer rooms are available for sale. The reasons are apparent. Space is requisitioned by departments that were short-changed by the original design or were

4. L. Boomer, *Hotel Management*, 3d ed. (New York: Harper & Bros., 1938), p. 48.

unanticipated at that time. No hotel of twenty years ago provided computer storage space. Few hotels built during Prohibition anticipated cocktail lounges and not very many hotels being built today provide for gaming casinos, which may well be the source of much of the revenue ten years hence. But a decline in available rooms is also a function of business volume. High occupancy makes each room important, but low occupancy encourages the conversion of rooms that are unneeded anyway. Executive housing is one such conversion. Management personnel live in as part of the compensation package.

The validity of the occupancy ratio depends in part upon the treatment of out-of-order rooms. If out-of-order rooms are subtracted from the number of rooms available for sale, the percentage of occupancy increases because the divisor is made smaller. This is valid if measuring the sales ability of the front office is the only purpose of the ratio. After all, room clerks cannot sell rooms that are not usable. It is a different situation altogether if the occupancy ratio is a measure of room utilization. Then out-of-order rooms must be included in the total available figure regardless of the reason for their unavailability. It makes no difference in measuring utilization if the room is out-of-order for repairs, renovations, temporary occupancy by hotel staff, fire or pet damage, etc. The reasons are of concern for management but the availability figure remains intact.

The numerator of the fraction, "number of rooms sold," is open to similar mathematical sleight of hand. This part of the occupancy ratio, also called room count, is verified by the night audit, through the night clerk's report. But it, too, can be shaded; sometimes inadvertently and sometimes intentionally but always with a change in the final occupancy figure.

Day rate occupancy is generally omitted from the room count unless the amount is substantial. Some hotels list day rates separately and some include them as part of the regular count. Including them obviously improves the percentage of occupancy and explains the success of some hotels, airport properties particularly, in exceeding the 100 percent daily figure.

Infrequent, but substantial, changes in the number of rooms sold occur during emergencies. Nonsleeping rooms (public parlors, dining rooms, and meeting rooms) are occupied by dozens or scores of persons. This dormitory style, which might even be intentional in places like ski resorts, needs some evaluative weight to determine a fair figure for the number of rooms sold. It has been suggested that every unit of three to five persons so accommodated should be valued as one occupied room. Rooms available would, of course, remain unchanged for that day or period. Occupancy would then exceed 100 percent, as it does during storms or other natural and man-made emergencies.

Counting parlors (part of a parlor/bedroom suite) that are rented as bedrooms is another method of increasing room count. The same end is accomplished by removing the parlor from the rooms available figure, if it was there at the beginning, because the connecting bedroom is occupied by a party that does not take the parlor. This variation between the number of rooms available and the number sold is a common programming problem when suites are included in a computer system. It carries over into house count when one person in a two-room suite is counted as two persons because the computer requires a duplicate (or triplicate) entry to close both (or three) rooms of the suite.

Consistency is needed if nothing else. Are parlor suites counted as one or two units when it comes to defining availability and room count? What about day rates? permanent guests? comp rooms?

Comp rooms add to the confusion. Is a complimentary room a room sold? If not, should the number of rooms available for sale be reduced by the number of comps? As with day rates, the amounts are usually so small that they are negligible. This is not so with casino hotels, which assign large blocks of rooms for casino comps when legally allowed to do so. A true measure of occupancy is difficult when from 10 percent to 20 percent of the hotel is complimented. It is even more difficult when a given percentage of available rooms is held at all times for casino use. Such rooms may stay vacant overnight although noncasino guests are turned away in large numbers. A similar practice occurs in noncasino hotels that hold rooms for possible emergencies only to have the day pass with the room still vacant.

Once the proper components of the ratio are resolved, the computation can be applied to all types of rooms or rate classes. The occupancy percentage for lanai rooms can be compared to that of the petite suites; the occupancy ratio of $80 rooms contrasted to those in the $50 range, and so on.

Percentage of Double Occupancy

As room count designates the number of rooms occupied, so house count designates the number of guests using those rooms. This leads to another ratio, a measure of the number of rooms occupied by more than one person. Although actually a ratio of multiple occupancy, *double occupancy* is the more common term. The percentage of double occupancy is:

$$\frac{\text{Number of Guests} - \text{Number of Rooms Sold}}{\text{Number of Rooms Sold}} =$$

$$\frac{220-189}{189} = 16.4\%$$

This ratio relates the number of guests to the number of rooms actually occupied. (Whatever comp and day rate rules apply to room count should apply equally to house count.) All multiple occupancies are assumed to house only two persons. Three, four, and five in a room are not differentiated and this makes the ratio somewhat inflexible. If ten rooms were occupied by twenty persons, double occupancy would be 100 percent whether the extra persons were spread evenly throughout the house or all were housed dormitory style in one room. Since estimating labor needs in the several departments is a major use of this statistic, this inaccuracy is not too serious. Twenty guests need the same amount of dining room service whether occupying one room or twenty. That is, one guest spending $80 needs less labor scheduled than four guests spending $20 each.

Another representation expresses the ratio on a per room basis. Then double occupancy equals 1.164 persons per room sold:

$$\frac{\text{Number of Guests}}{\text{Number of Rooms Sold}} = \frac{220}{189} = 1.164$$

Percentage of Bed Occupancy

This European measure is almost never found in the United States. This is unfortunate since the ratio is not without merit. Also known as *guest occupancy* or *sleeper occupancy, bed occupancy* measures the utilization of beds in the same manner that room occupancy measures room usage. It is a qualitative measure, so bed usage and room usage are not the same. Although bed occupancy measures persons in the beds, it is not the double occupancy of American statistics. Bed usage is related to beds available, and this makes the ratio more like the room occupancy relationship:

$$\frac{\text{Number of Beds Sold}}{\text{Number of Beds Available for Sale}} = \frac{220}{405} = 54\%$$

Like the room occupancy figures, inconsistencies creep into the computations. Double beds, twin beds, queens, and kings are counted as two in setting the denominator of the fraction. However, sometimes they are not. They are counted as one if sold as singles when no other singles are available. Other bed configurations (hide-a-beds, sofa-beds) confound the computation. Everything that was said about comps, day rates, and suites applies to the bed occupancy computation with one addition: bed occupancy must also provide for cots and rollaways. This means the denominator of the fraction changes practically every day.

Hoteliers use the ratio to measure the efficiency of the sales, reservation, and front office departments. For example, as the house nears capacity, single reservation requests should be refused in favor of doubles. Bed occupancy will show whether this is being done. Theory doesn't always work well in fact, which accounts for the general absence of the bed occupancy computation. If throughout the day the room clerk knew who (number and composition of the party) was coming and at what time, room assignments could be made or room requests refused to maximize the use of the bed configuration (single, double, queen, etc.). Put in realistic terms: should a single guest be turned away in mid-afternoon in the hope of filling that family room with four persons before the day is out?

Comparing the percentage of occupancy with the percentage of bed occupancy does give, nevertheless, some idea of the number of double rooms being sold as singles. Illustrations in this chapter have shown room occupancy at 70 percent and bed occupancy at 54 percent. (Seventy percent room occupancy usually equals about 50 percent bed occupancy.) This says that the proportion of single rooms to double rooms that was sold is actually larger than the proportion of single rooms to double rooms that is available for sale. That is, single rooms are being sold in greater proportion to those available than are

double rooms. Knowing this aids rate structuring and room furnishing. It provides direction for major renovations or planned additions. Tied to density charts and room reservation forecasts, bed occupancy figures offer another tool for evaluating the room product and the sales mix.

Tourism statistics utilize bed availability figures in another way: The Organization for Economic Cooperation and Development publishes bed statistics to indicate the available sleeping space in tourist destination countries. The OECD distinguishes between hotel beds and beds available in other, supplemental accommodations.

Sales per Occupied Room

Sales per occupied room, long called the average room rate, is the second most frequently computed ratio after occupancy. Room income, which is a composite of occupancy and class, serves as the numerator for this group of computations. Whereas occupancy figures are expressed as percentages, room rate ratios appear as a per unit basis: either per room or per guest.

The average room rate is the rate earned per day per room occupied. It is an arithmetic mean, found by using the following formula:

$$\frac{\text{Room Income}}{\text{Number of Rooms Sold (Room Count)}} =$$

$$\frac{\$9,158}{189} = \$48.46$$

Average room rates have been rising for a half century. That comes as no surprise since room revenue is the hotel's major source of income and the means by which rising expenses are offset. It must be remembered, therefore, that increases over time may reflect nothing more than inflationary pressures. Average rates are subject to misinterpretation unless consideration is given to the declining value of money. Sometimes several rate increases have taken place within one year. That's consistent with the changes in overall price levels and the close correlation between the consumer price index and the average sale per occupied room.[5]

Average room rate is standard terminology for the hotel industry and has been part of its vocabulary for a long time. As its computation indicates, average room rate is actually the value of room sales per room occupied. It is not an average of room rates. Use of the term "average" here has the same inherent weakness that was explained earlier. It is very unlikely that any one room actually sells for this amount. There is confusion in the use of the term, which the guest understands to be the price charged the public and the industry understands to be the income generated by each occupied room. The industry's computed average room rate is obviously not the same average room rate that is advertised in the brochures. For this reason, and especially in this day of consumerism, there is likely to be a greater and greater use of the term "income (or sales) per room occupied," rather than "average room rate."

If the hotel has a wide range of rates, the income per occupied room tends toward the lower half of the range between the lower and upper quartiles. Lower priced rooms are more popular and these sell first when occupancy, the demand for rooms, is low. Thus, low income per occupied room has come to be associated with low occupancy. This generalization does not hold true when the rate range is restricted or when the market is skewed in favor of the affluent buyer.

Double occupancy also affects income per occupied room. Since the denominator of the average room rate fraction is the number of rooms sold, it remains constant irrespective of changes in the percentage of double occupancy. But higher double occupancy means more room income, which increases the numerator and so the income per occupied room. Such changes can be misleading to the hotel manager. If the tour market, which is almost always double occupancy, makes up a good portion of the total market, sales per occupied room may remain relatively high even though the hotel is slipping in its competitive edge. A very large tour business usually has the opposite effect. Commanding a large purchasing power, tour operators are able to bargain rates down. Hotels that are dominated by the tour operator find their income per occupied room actually lower than their minimum quoted rack rate, but occupancy levels might be quite high. High double occupancy benefits the other operating departments, so management might be happy with the trade off.

Many factors influence the sales per occupied room figure, including double occupancy, discounts and advertising specials, the level of occupancy, the amount of convention business, the type of guest, and the size of the hotel. The larger the hotel, the larger its average room rate figure. Still, the rooms department of any hotel must contribute proportionately to total revenue. If that contribution is low relative to national averages and if the percentage of occupancy is high relative to the same figures, the inference is that the average room rate is too low.

Other Sales Ratios

Two additional rate ratios are the sales per available room (average rate per available room is the old terminology):

$$\frac{\text{Room Income}}{\text{Number of Rooms Available}} = \frac{\$9,158}{270} = \$33.92$$

5. Eric Green, "The Facts Behind International Statistics," *Panorama*, Second Quarter, 1981, No. 12, p. 25.

and the sales per guest (average rate per guest is the old terminology):

$$\frac{\text{Room Income}}{\text{Number of Guests}} = \frac{\$9,158}{220} = \$41.63$$

The mathematics are the same for these and the average room rate. Only the denominator of the fraction changes. Unless the house is 100 percent full, the sales per available room must always be smaller than the sales per room sold. Or mathematically, the sales per room sold multiplied by the percentage of occupancy equals the sales per available room, $48.46 × 70 percent = $33.92. The income per guest also declines as the percentage of double occupancy increases.

The average rate per guest is more significant to the American plan operator than to an EP counterpart. AP rates include values for both food and lodging. Reductions allowed for double occupancy, or even those allowed for less desirable rooms, have a smaller impact on sales per occupied room computations because of the proportionately large, unaffected portion relating to the meal value.

Number of Times the Average Rate Was Earned

This is a special measure developed by Laventhol & Horwath in their search for better bases of comparing the operating results of different hotels.[6] It is a qualitative measure as are all the average room ratios in contrast to the quantitative measures of the occupancy figures.

There is a presumption that a larger hotel is going to do better. Therefore, operating comparisons must give consideration to the size of the hotel, and the comparison of operating income must be made on a per room basis. (Operating income is net income from all operating departments except store rentals

6. Horwath, Toth, and Lesure, *Hotel Accounting*, p. 356.

and before fixed costs like taxes, interest, insurance, and depreciation. This income before fixed charges was once called *house profit.)* Since a hotel with high rates should earn more than one with low rates, the comparison should be the house profit per room relative to the sales per room. Simply put, a large hotel with a hefty rate should show profits in operations all across the house.

1. Number of Available Rooms	270	
2. Average Room Rate	$48.46	
3. House Profit	$1,372,011	
4. House Profit Per Available Room (Item 3 Divided by Item 1)	$5,082	(recognizes size)
5. Number of Times Average Rate Is Earned (Item 4 Divided by Item 2)	105[7]	(recognizes rate)

Other Statistics

Several other statistics are usually presented in front office reports although the occupancy and rate figures are by far the most common. Although the following list is not exhaustive, it suggests the direction that might be taken.

Potential Gross Revenue Ratio

Financial institutions and appraisers use the potential gross revenue ratio more than operational managers do. As an "occupancy" percentage, it reflects unrecorded sales and thus serves as a special tool for absentee owners as well. The ratio expresses actual room income as a percentage of the maximum possible income from the sale of rooms:

$$\frac{\text{Room Income}}{\text{Potential Optimum Revenue}} = \frac{\$9,158}{\$13,125} = 69.8\%$$

7. Laventhol & Horwath's most recent annual study puts this figure at 100 as the median for independent hotels and 119 for chain-affiliates. See also figure 17.5.

	Number of Rooms	Number of Beds	Price at Optimum	Potential Optimum Revenue
Twins	100	200	$60	$ 6,000
Doubles	20	40	50	1,000
Singles	145	145	40	5,800
Twin Doubles	5	20	65	325
	270	405		$13,125

Average Optimum Room Rate: $\dfrac{\$13,125}{270} = \$48.61$

Figure 17.7. The average optimum room rate is derived from potential optimum revenue, assuming every room and every bed is occupied.

Since the potential optimum revenue assumes the sale of every room and every bed, it is more optimistic than optimum. In this respect the ratio is like the percentage of bed occupancy. Even with a full house, it is almost impossible to sell every bed. Guests do not arrive in the proper sequence nor accommodate their party size to the needs of the hotel. A modified denominator, "expected possible revenue," is sometimes substituted to come closer to reality.

The potential gross revenue ratio solves the problem of comparing room rates over time when an increase in rates has altered the basis. Rather than comparing average room rates in dollars, the comparison is between potential sales in each of the periods expressed in percentages.

Once the potential optimum revenue is computed (figure 17.7) an average optimum room rate can be derived by dividing by the number of available rooms. Then it is a simple matter to compare the actual average daily room rate to the optimum average daily room rate:

$$\frac{\text{Actual Average Daily Room Rate}}{\text{Optimum Average Daily Room Rate}} = \frac{\$48.46}{\$48.61} = 99.7\%$$

If the answer is 100 percent or better, the desk is selling up. More likely it is less than 100 percent, which is another way of saying that a larger percentage of lower priced rooms are being sold than those rooms represent to the entire room inventory. This could be either lower priced rooms or rooms with provisions for double occupancy going as singles.

Length of Guest Stay

Guest day, guest night, room night, and *bed night* are all terms for the stay of one guest for one night. A visitor (or tourist) night is the same term used in tourism statistics. Thirty guests staying for one night or one guest staying for thirty nights equal the same thirty guest days (nights).

Increasing mobility, a national sense of impatience, and better transportation facilities have contributed to guests' transiency. Even overseas trips are of shorter duration. Apparently, the number of guest nights per stay is declining although there are no statistical studies similar to the occupancy and rate figures to support this observation. One reason for the shortage of information is the lack of simple formula. Computing the month's guest nights is easy enough; the house count for the period is added up. But it is not possible to know how many different persons were involved unless

Class of Guest	Length of Stay	Number of Guests	Weighted Product
A	1 night	55	55
B	2 nights	380	760
C	3 nights	70	210
D	4 nights	20	80
E	5 nights	5	25
5	15 nights	530	1,130

Average Length of Stay:

Simple average $15 \div 5 = 3$ nights
Weighted average $1,130 \div 530 = 2.1$ nights

Figure 17.8. Weighted average gives importance to the value of the items and not merely to the number of items.

that number is individually recorded. That information must be taken from the individual registration card or folio and that becomes time consuming on a continuing basis. A good computer program makes it easier. One shortcut divides the number of guests, excluding permanent guests, by the number of arrivals.

Knowing the average length of stay aids the forecaster. It serves reservation projections and can be an indicator of poor employee attitudes or a warning of facilities that are no longer competitive. If nothing else, the average length of stay helps decide how often sheets are to be changed — they are not changed daily everywhere — and what inventory or rental arrangements are needed to provide that service. Whereas occupancy percentages are the usual break-even measures of commercial hotels, room nights are the usual measure for American plan hotels. Income from meals is an integral part of the American plan figures and occupancy computations alone do not provide that information.

Length of stay is sometimes computed by a weighted average rather than by an arithmetic mean. Figure 17.8 illustrates how this procedure gives value to each figure relative to its importance or weight.

Nature of the Market

Knowing the origin of the guest and the reason for the visit goes far toward explaining many guest characteristics, including the likely length of stay. The distance traveled, and the activities planned set good statistical definitions of who the "average" guest is.

Guests can be geographically defined by one of three methods; distance from the hotel, regions or areas of the country, and specific locations such as major cities. Modern marketing techniques look to the front office for still further demographic information. Management wants to know the age range of its clientele, the sex, the income levels, the educational achievement, the composition of the traveling party, and other data. Having this qualitative information improves decisions on

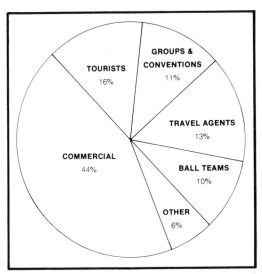

Figure 17.9. Pie chart provides visual contrast to the proportionate values that make up the whole; in this illustration, percentage of registrations by type of guest is shown.

such diverse matters as advertising and credit policies. It helps management decide questions like type of entertainment and availability of foreign-language-speaking employees.

When the clientele is known (the market mix) decisions on types of accommodations, rate structures, and levels of service come easier. Tourists seek different facilities than business persons. Transient visitors do not need the same things that permanent guests do. Package plans require double occupancy but conventioneers often want singles. A simple chart reflecting the purpose of the guests' trips is shown in figure 17.9. It is one tool in the statistical kit.

With the ease of computer-derived figures on the near horizon, we can anticipate that statistics, old ones and new ones yet to be developed, will become an even more important source of interpretative information for management decision making.

QUERIES AND PROBLEMS

1. Textbook discussions always provide the mathematical values for making statistical assumptions and computations. However, someone must determine those figures in real life. What are the sources (forms or procedures) of these front office statistics?
   Number of rooms available for sale
   Number of rooms occupied
   Number of guests
   Number of dollars of room sales
   Number of dollars of room allowances
2. Using the terms given in problem 1 above, create five front office ratios and explain in nonmathematical terms the meaning of each. Which are quantitative measures and which qualitative?
3. Uniformity of measure and of ratio analysis is essential for comparative work and decision-making. But results can be altered, and front office statistics can reflect different values by merely including or excluding certain circumstances or by viewing those circumstances differently. Cite at least three examples and explain how each changes the value of the front office statistic.
4. Examine copies of the annual studies prepared for the same year by Laventhol & Horwath and by Pannell Kerr Forster & Company. Compare five – ten different ratios.
   a. What is the explanation for the variation between them?
   b. What is the explanation for the variation between any given hotel's figures and those provided by either one of the reports?

Supplemental Chapter

18

The American Plan

The billing procedures that were outlined in past chapters need some modification when it comes to the American plan. The major differences are room and meal charges, which appear on the folio as one item.

Although few hotels offer the American plan and fewer still require guests to buy it, well-known exceptions come immediately to mind. Grossinger's in the Catskills has not only succeeded with the American plan, it has done so with kosher food. And the Greenbrier in White Sulphur Springs, West Virginia has been merchandised so well that the modified American plan is seen to be an advantage rather than a limitation. And for the hotel, it is an advantage — a decided one.

Good food promotes room sales and increased room sales means, in turn, increased revenue for the dining room. Not only are total sales greater, but cost-saving projections, which reduce waste in buying, production, and labor, are more accurate when it is known that every guest will take all three meals in the hotel.

Additional savings can be made with the smaller menus used in American plan dining rooms. Meals that guests pay for but do not eat, called *breakage,* improve the profit picture still further. Breakage is one of the major reasons guests dislike the American plan; no one likes paying something for nothing. The breakage that is disdained as part of the American plan becomes quite marketable when disguised in an EP package plan. It is the relative costs, of course. Guests don't mind losing a drink, or a greens fee, or an unused historic tour (all of which might be in a package) as much as they begrudge the loss of a meal under an AP plan. Everyone eats, so a meal that is lost at the hotel must be bought somewhere else. It's double payment. Not so with a greens fee, which is lost because the guest doesn't play golf.

Changing eating habits have been a major cause for the decline in the American plan. Food is at the heart of this type of hotel and that is the very thing that has been in the forefront of America's cultural changes. The national trend is toward food that is easily and quickly prepared and easily and quickly consumed. Although there are differences of degree, the changes apply equally well to leisure dining as to standup sandwich snacking. To many persons, much of the American plan seems to be a relic of another age.

The hotels themselves contributed to the decline of the American plan. Rigid meal hours developed breakage profits at the expense of guest dissatisfaction. Strict rules of dress encouraged guests to stay away from midday meals rather than undertake several clothing changes. Unimaginative menus spelled disaster to a captive audience.

Automobiles also contributed to the decline. Isolated resorts were no longer distant from other dining facilities. The availability of other establishments made the American plan seem restrictive. Resorts introduced the modified American plan to increase their flexibility without surrendering all the advantages of the full American plan.

Hotel markets are not monolithic. Where the location of the property and the nature of the clientele permit, the American plan continues to operate successfully. But if the plan is no longer in decline, neither is it in a period of growth.

THE AMERICAN PLAN DAY

Unlike the European plan, which measures a guest day by an overnight stay — and this, too, is changing — the American plan measures a day in terms of meals and lodging. American plan guests are entitled to three meals along with the night's lodging.

Since meals are critical to the day's measure, a meal code facilitates the interpretation of arrival and departure times. Registration cards are meal coded and time stamped (figure 7.1) at registration. The time stamp alone is insufficient, for many guests who arrive during the meal hour have eaten prior to arrival. The meal symbol appears on the registration card, the rack slips (plate 1, room 902), and the folio. It improves communication between the room clerk, who checks in the guest, and the cashier, who completes the folio several days later when the guest leaves.

Arrival Code

Long usage has pretty well standardized the meals symbols, so that:

"B" means arrival before breakfast
"L" means arrival before lunch
"D" means arrival before dinner
"SL" means sleep only, arrival after dinner

An arrival of "7/9/L" is one who checks in on July 9 before luncheon. Since luncheon, dinner, and lodging are furnished on the day of arrival, this guest is entitled to breakfast on the day of departure. Three meals and a night's lodging are furnished each full day that the guest remains. On the day of departure, whether it is the day following arrival or several days later, sufficient meals are provided to complete the three-meal sequence.

Guests who arrive after the dining room has closed for the evening meal are marked "SL" (sleep, no meals). Other symbols used to indicate this late arrival are "R" (room only) or sometimes "X." An arrival time of "7/9/SL" entitles the guest to three meals on the day of departure. Similarly, an arrival of "/B" means no meals on the final day. Some guests elect to take more than the three meals and others less than the full American plan day. Both of these situations require special handling on the folio.

Departure Code

Departure times are less critical entries than arrival times. Time stamping the folio may suffice because the guest is actually leaving and no further communication among desk personnel is anticipated. Nevertheless, a second set of symbols is often used to designate meal departures. Whereas the first set uses the abbreviations to indicate arrival, before the meal, the second set uses them to indicate departure, after the meal. So that:

"B/B" means departure before breakfast
"B" means departure after breakfast
"L" means departure after luncheon
"D" means departure after dinner

The three basic meal symbols do not provide for the period before breakfast as they did not for the "SL" period under the arrivals. "B/B" (before breakfast) fills that need. Figure 18.1 illustrates several measures of the American plan day.

THE AMERICAN PLAN CHARGE

The American plan includes lodging and meals, but the two rates are not quoted separately. Although only a total figure appears on the folio, anyone with a modicum of mathematical ability can make the separation, especially if both AP and EP rates are being quoted.

Guests stay more or less than a full American plan day and must either be charged for or given credit for the difference, which makes it necessary to assign a value to each meal. Some AP hotels, however, make a flat daily charge with no consideration for meals taken or missed, but even under those circum-

Arrival	Departure	Time
3/25/D	3/26/L	1 Full AP Day
8/1/SL	8/4/D	3 Full AP Days
6/11/B	6/13/B/B	2 Full AP Days
5/10/L	5/12/L	More than 2 Full AP Days
9/19/D	9/20/B	Less than 1 Full AP Day

Figure 18.1. Measuring the full AP day, which includes breakfast, luncheon, dinner, and lodging.

stances management would wish to separate room and meal charges internally for operational purposes.

Distributing the Total Charges

In distributing the charge between meals and rooms, it is well to remember that the guest's ability to eat is not determined by the rate paid. A guest paying $82 per day is not eating half of that being consumed by a $164 per day guest. Variations in rate thus apply to variations in the quality of the room, not in the quantity of food consumed. Guests pay a higher rate for a better room. The meal allocation remains the same from guest to guest and variations in the rate are assigned to the room charges. This holds true for seasonal rate adjustments as well. Seasonal reductions (or increases) in rate affect room income not food revenue.

Conference centers are the exception. Full AP rates with a flat room rate per person is the typical conference center charge. The center, of course, isn't a resort, and the rooms are almost identical.

This method of distributing the rate becomes more obvious when room rates and food charges are derived separately and then combined to set the total rate. Room rate derivations were discussed previously and these do not change merely because the hotel is American plan. If the room rate is determined to be from $65 to $80 and the food is set at $20 per day,[1] the American plan quote will be from $85 to $100 per person per day.

There is no reduction for the food portion of double occupancy as there is for the room portion, since the second guest eats as much as the first. Children sharing their parents' rooms are often an exception. They are sometimes charged half price on the American plan. Each hotel defines a child differently, the definition ranging from less than five years of age to less than twelve years of age.

Rates reflect competition as well as cost, and this is no different for an American plan hotel. However, within the total rate, too large an allocation to food sales makes the dining room appear unrealistically profitable. Too small an allocation drops meal prices below the competition. Although outside guests can be charged a meal rate different from house guests, it is easier if the figures are the same, and they should be if the distribution is realistic.

Distributing the Meal Charges

Once the meal portion has been determined, it is subdivided among the three meals (two meals for modified American). Thus, the $20 rate might be split into breakfast at $3, luncheon at $5, and the $12 balance to dinner. Again, market situations, menu offerings, and costs determine the division.

For mathematical ease, the allocation is sometimes made equally. One third of meal income is assigned to each of the three meals.

---

1. Food cost per day per person must be determined. Assume $8. If management seeks a 60 percent gross profit on food sales, food cost is 40 percent of sales. If 40 percent of food sales equals $8, then food sales must be $20: the cost of food sold ÷ food sales = food cost percentage, or

$$\frac{\$8}{x} = 40\% \ (0.40)$$

$$x = \$20$$

Some properties include lodging and split the total rate into quarters, one to each meal and one to lodging. Not only is this practice absurd, but it creates an untenable position for the clerk trying to explain how it works. Another variation is one-fifth to each of the three meals and two-fifths to the room rate. This is no better, for what explanation is there when the guest is paying $80 per day and the breakfast charge is $16. Especially if the neighboring room is $120 per day and that breakfast $24!

Charging for Sales Taxes

Sales taxes get special attention under the American plan in those states where food is exempt from the tax. A clear division between meals and lodging is necessary since the law usually requires the tax to be collected directly from the guest and only on that portion of the charge that is room rate. Where such legislation exists, it may be desirable to separate room and meal charges on the folio.

Charging for Gratuities

Although not a common practice, including gratuities in the rate quote is far more frequent in American plan than in European plan hotels. This practice originates with the general procedure of negotiating a gratuity for all meal functions whether American or European plan. There is no consistency from hotel to hotel, however. Some charge a flat percentage, usually 15 percent, on the full AP rate whereas others levy the percentage on only the meal portion of the rate. Sometimes the gratuity is included only on group and convention business and sometimes on the social guests as well (figure 18.2).

Assessing the percentage is only the start of the gratuity problem. The internal division among the hotel staff is a completely unresolved area of hotel operations. Management

Service Charge Arrangements.

To all guests:
Many Greenbrier guests have requested to have gratuities handled automatically.

Therefore, for your convenience, we have instituted a service charge of $5.00 per guest, per day. This charge will be added to your room account to take care of gratuities for all dining room personnel serving breakfast and dinner. (Waiters, waitresses, roll girls and busboys.) Also included in the service charge are room maids, including night time turn-down service. (A nominal service charge applies for parlors.)

On all a la carte checks, fifteen percent will be added for beverage service, wine, luncheon, buffet or room service. (Minimum of 50¢ per room service order.) The entire check can be charged to your room account.

To reward an individual for superior service, you may leave cash or indicate "additional tip" on the check, while noting the amount. This will be added to your room account.

Please note: no arrangements have been made for bellmen, doormen, bath or swimming pool attendants, limousine drivers, valet, porters or locker attendants. You may take care of them at your discretion.

Figure 18.2. How much to tip? Typical card provided for American plan guests. *Courtesy: The Greenbrier, White Sulphur Springs, W.Va.*

sometimes keeps part of the money for itself. Even when this is not the case, misunderstanding and conflict over the proper distribution is widespread. The most logical distribution becomes less so upon investigation. True, bellpersons can share based on the number of guests roomed; floor attendants on the number of rooms cleaned; waiters and waitresses on the number of covers handled. Equating the work of the bellperson to the waiter/waitress or to the floor attendant is the real difficulty. Is one bag carried equal to one cover served or to one room cleaned? And what of the desk clerk, the telephone operator, the houseman, the bus and pool attendants? How are these jobs to be measured? Do supervisory employees like the inspector, the bell captain, and the headwaiter or hostess share? If so, in what proportion? No wonder gratuities have become a negotiable item in union contracts and remain a source of much internal irritation.

Changing social attitudes supported by more stringent definitions of what is included in the minimum wage and how much it should be are apt to bring service charges to the entire industry, EP as well as AP hotels. This would make moot the whole tip and gratuity question. Major conventions are already including blanket tips (figure 18.3). With more and more union contracts including provisions for guaranteed tip income, the concept of an all-inclusive service charge is not far away and is being hastened by the large tour and travel agencies and the incentive tour packagers. With tour or package plans, guests do not tip individually since a blanket gratuity is paid. Hotel management can take the initiative too, as the Grand Hotel in Mackinac, Michigan has done by being one of the first no-tip hotels. The more federal legislation that bears on tipping, the faster the flat service charge will replace the discretionary gratuity.

AMERICAN PLAN RECORDS

American plan hotels use the same front office forms that European plan hotels use. Small variations exist in the format of the registration card and folio rather than in their purposes.

How Much Shall We Tip?

The tradition of tipping has become a deeply entrenched American custom. The extent of the gratuity given for good service is a very personal affair for individual decision.

It is because we are so frequently asked that we have published this information for your convenience.

Convention guests please check. Your committee may have arranged for tips to be added to your bill. However, the cocktail waiters and waitresses are not included in convention gratuities.

Waiters and Waitresses

Breakfast . . . . $.50 to $.75 daily per person
Dinner . . . . $1.50 to $1.75 daily per person

A la carte Services

Food and Beverages . . 15% to 20% of your check

We respectfully suggest that gratuities be given after each meal since you may not have the same personnel each time (this also applies to the children's dining room).

Thank You
For letting us be your HOST.

Figure 18.3. Guests are concerned about when, how much, and whom to tip. *Courtesy: Host Enterprises, Inc., Lancaster, Pa.*

Registration Cards

AP registration cards always include the meal of arrival and frequently the meal of anticipated departure. When there is more than one plan, the plan that the guest selects must be indicated. The number of persons in the room is shown with the particular plan, as "3AP" (three persons, American plan; sometimes "3FAP," full American plan), "2EP" or "1MAP." The number and plan of each party appears on the registration card, the room rack slips (plate 1, room 902), and the guest folio. No designation is needed if only one plan is offered. This is true whether the single offering is American or European plan. Confusion about the plans, if any, lies more often with the guest than with the hotel staff (figure 18.4).

Folios—the First System

American plan folios differ in two respects from those of European plan houses. First, there may be a special allowance item for meals, distinct from the general allowance provision. Second, room and meals appear as one item. This is so even though room and meal incomes are split on the accounting records. One charge is posted by the night auditor for room and meals in the same manner that the room charge alone is posted on the EP folio (figure 18.5).

There are two methods of recording American plan charges on the folio. Under the first system, guests are charged a full day's rate when they arrive regardless of the number of meals eaten during that first day. Each subsequent day is charged in full. If the final meal completes the full American plan day, there is no folio entry on the day of departure. If the final meal extends the stay beyond a full AP day, there is an extra charge. If the final meal does not complete the full day, there is an allowance, but not always.

Allowance for Meals Missed

Meals missed at the end of the stay should not be confused with meals missed during the stay. Almost no hotel gives allowances for the latter, but some provide for the former. Indeed, they should. Guests generally arrive in the late afternoon, "/D," after a day on the road. They generally depart in the morning, "/B," in order to get in a good day's drive. Luncheon is fre-

The Arizona Biltmore

You are on the European Plan, which means no meals are included in your room rate.

Gratuities throughout the hotel are at your own discretion.

Enjoy your stay with us! If we may assist you in any manner, please do not hesitate to ask.

Western International Hotels / Partners in travel with United Airlines

The Arizona Biltmore

You are on the Modified American Plan, which means your breakfast and dinner are included in your room rate.

Meals may be taken in any dining outlet other than the Orangerie Restaurant. The Orangerie is strictly a European Plan dining room, and therefore no credit will be extended to our Modified American Plan guests.

A daily service charge covering food service and maid service is being added to your room account.

Beverage service, Orangerie dining, and other service personnel gratuities are at your discretion.

Enjoy your stay with us! If we may assist you in any manner, please do not hesitate to ask.

Western International Hotels / Partners in travel with United Airlines

The Arizona Biltmore

You are on the Full American Plan, which means your breakfast, lunch and dinner are included in your room rate.

Meals may be taken in any dining outlet other than the Orangerie Restaurant. The Orangerie is strictly a European Plan dining room, and therefore no credit will be extended to our Full American Plan guests.

A daily service charge covering food service in the meal plan areas and maid service is being added to your room account.

Beverage service, Orangerie dining, and other service personnel gratuities are at your discretion.

Enjoy your stay with us! If we may assist you in any manner, please do not hesitate to ask.

Western International Hotels / Partners in travel with United Airlines

The Arizona Biltmore

You are on the Modified American Plan, which means your breakfast and dinner are included in your room rate.

Meals may be taken in any dining outlet other than the Orangerie Restaurant. The Orangerie is strictly a European Plan dining room, and therefore no credit will be extended to our Modified American Plan guests.

A service charge of 15% of the meal rate will be added to your room account. This covers the gratuities for the food service personnel.

Beverage service, Orangerie dining, and other service personnel gratuities are at your discretion.

Enjoy your stay with us! If we may assist you in any manner, please do not hesitate to ask.

Western International Hotels / Partners in travel with United Airlines

Figure 18.4. Complete information minimizes the confusion about plans and dining rooms.
Courtesy: Arizona Biltmore, Phoenix, Ariz.

quently missed and provision should be made for that fact. (This is still another reason for the introduction of the modified American plan.)

The amount of the allowance varies. It may be a complete allowance or it may be a percentage of the charge, frequently 50 percent. A full allowance creates a European plan, in effect, and no allowance makes for an unhappy guest, although the guest may stay and have the meal. Giving a full allowance for adequate notice of departure, say at the time of arrival, and 50 percent when the notice is short strikes a compromise.

Figure 18.6 illustrates the allowance computation. The example is one of a late arrival and a departure before dinner on the check-out day. The dollar distribution that was suggested several pages back is being used in the illustration. Dinner is the meal missed. At $12 per person, with two in the party, the total dinner charge is $24. At 50 percent, the allowance is $12.

Meal allowances are made by the front office cashiers based on the arrival and departure hours. Their authority is limited to meal allowances; other allowances still need the attention of the assistant manager.

Charge for Extra Meals Taken

When the guest's stay extends beyond the full American plan day, extra meals are charged according to the price schedule. The $20 rate

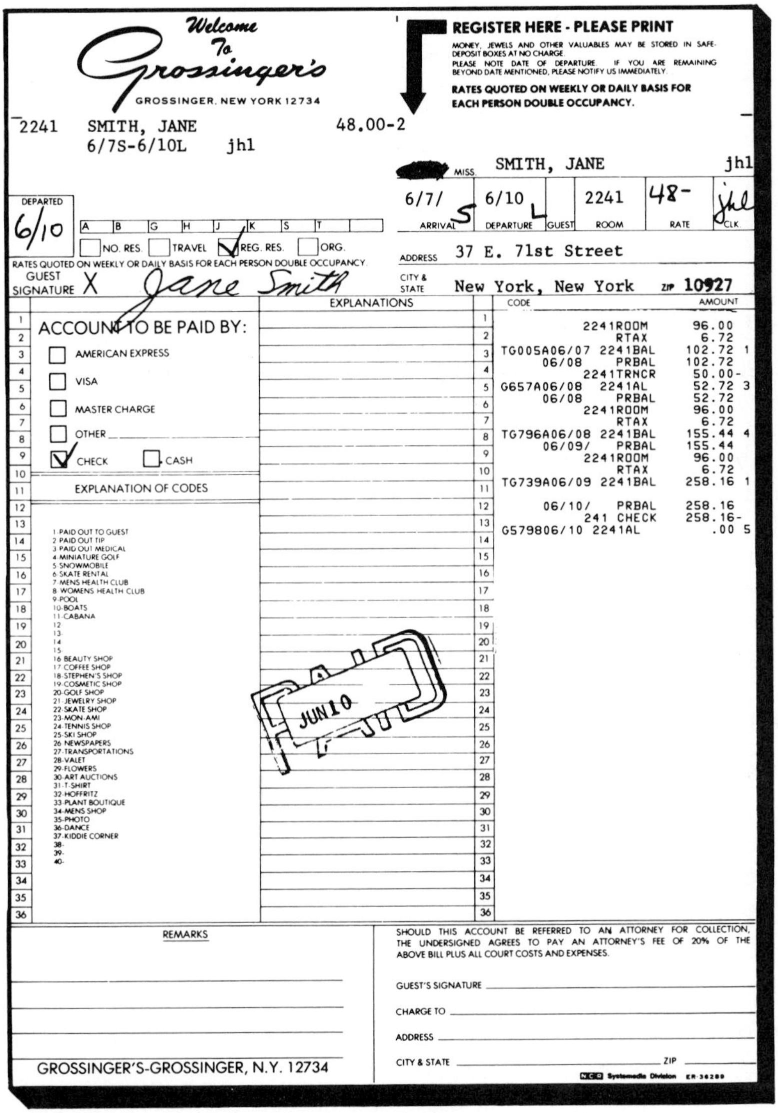

Figure 18.5. Combined American plan folio and registration card. Note meal symbols on arrival and departure dates, and the one daily posting for both room and meals ($48 per person per day). *Courtesy: Grossinger's, Grossinger, N.Y.*

```
Given:     Arrival 3/11/R
           Departure 3/14/L
           AP Rate $180 Double Occupancy
Charge:    3/11: $180
           3/12: $180
           3/13: $180
           3/14: $12 Credit Allowance
                 (2 dinners at $12
                 each × 50%)
```

Figure 18.6. Room rate computation under the American plan where a 50 percent allowance is granted for final meal(s) missed.

that was used heretofore included $3 for breakfast, $5 for luncheon, and $12 for dinner. Since the checkout precedes the night audit, the extra meal charge is posted by the front office cashier just as a late room charge would be in a European plan hotel. It appears on the folio as part of the room rate and in the audit as part of the room and board charges.

This additional charge should not be confused with another type of meal charge that actually appears on the folio as "Extra Meals." Extra meals are posted in much the same way that a meal charge is handled in a European plan hotel. The posting goes to the extra meal account rather than to the restaurant account. A visitor would be the source of such a charge. When a guest entertains a nonguest for meals, the additional charge appears as extra meals on the guest's folio.

Special items appear on American plan menus on traditional nights: lobster on Fridays and steak on Saturdays. On other nights, these items and others like them are not available on the general menu. They are sometimes available by special order. But, if so, it is at an extra charge. A voucher for this additional service is prepared by the dining room, signed by the guest, and posted as an extra meal charge. Income generated by this procedure is never enough to offset the loss of guest goodwill. Management should either make the rates high enough to offer these items nightly or not offer

them at all. Figure 18.4 illustrates another method of handling this. One dining room is designated European plan only. It offers a broader menu. Persons who eat there know in advance that their meals will not be covered under the AP plan.

Tray Service

Room service usually contains hidden charges. An extra 50 cents or more is added to the normal menu price for room service in an attempt to recover the extra cost of service. This device is not available to the American plan hotel because meals being delivered to the room are not priced separately. Instead, a flat charge of several dollars per person is made and euphemistically called *tray service*. This charge is initiated by the room service department and posted to the folio as either tray service or extra meals.

A Second Method of Recording AP Charges

Under this alternative procedure, guests are charged only for those meals actually taken, beginning with the day of arrival. This contrasts with the first method, by which a full day's charge is posted immediately regardless of the actual meals received the first day. Obviously, allowances are eliminated with this technique. Since charges are made only for meals taken, no credits are needed to offset excessive charges. Any meal taken on the day of departure will require a posting whether it completes a full AP day or whether it is more than or less than a full AP day.

So long as a 100 percent allowance is granted for meals missed, this procedure is easier to administer and easier for the guest to understand. It becomes awkward when the allowance is less than 100 percent and is not recommended under those circumstances. Assume, for example, that a guest arrives before lunch "/L," and departs the following morning before breakfast "B/B." Using a 50 percent allowance, there would be a charge for half the price of the missing breakfast. Under the first system, in which the charge is made on the first day, the missed meal appears as a 50 percent refund on the final day. Guests find this much more acceptable than under the alternative system, in which the 50 percent appears on the final day as a charge rather than a refund.

The alternative method is especially difficult when meal charges are based on values like 20 percent for each meal and 40 percent for lodging. Using a 50 percent allowance figure, an $80 single rate would generate an $8 charge even though the guest had no breakfast. It would be $16 if there were breakfast. Couples face the ridiculous figure of a $16 no-breakfast charge and a $32 charge if they elect to eat. This is an impossible situation to explain but one that actually happens in some hotels.

Many hotels, Grossinger's included, make no provision for meals missed. There is no allowance for any meal, including those at the end of the stay. There is, therefore, no provision for allowances and no special problems in American plan billing. The guest is billed every night similar to the billing under a European plan system. Control on meals taken is only for extra meals, which are charged for. Eating less than the number of meals permitted is the guest's decision, but the hotel makes no allowance for it.

Selecting the right system for the right hotel is decided more by marketing needs than by front office procedures.

Dining Room Procedures

Since meals are an integral part of the American plan, good communication between the dining room and the front desk is a necessity. This is no less so with the front office and the kitchen, since many advantages of the plan depend upon front office projections. Arrivals and departures are relayed to the maitre d' on an individual name basis but furnished to the kitchen as a total meal projection. Projections are made daily and updated on a meal-to-meal basis as the number of arrivals, departures, and stayovers becomes known. Each rack slip shows the anticipated departure date, including the meal, and these provide a substantially accurate forecast when reservations and estimates of outside diners are included.

House Guests

Although the host(ess) receives a list of daily arrivals, guests are given an introductory card to the dining room as they check in. The names of last minute walk-ins are telephoned to the dining room so the maitre d' will not be taken by surprise. Although the introductory form may be nothing more than a carbon prepared as part of the rooming slip, it is sometimes a separate form (figure 18.7). It is a historical curiosity that many of these cards still contain reference to the chauffeurs and maids who traveled with the families that once comprised the social clientele of the American plan house. Computers offer a startling contrast. With them, all departments have access to the memory bank. Rather than an introductory card, the host(ess) can display the list of new arrivals on the dining room's CRT.

In many, but not all, American plan dining rooms, guests are assigned a permanent table with a permanent server for their entire stay. The longer the stay and the higher the rate, the better the table assignment. Whenever possible, the dining room makes the assignments in advance from the list of anticipated arrivals after deleting probable departures.

Large AP hotels may have two seatings in the dining room, much as is done aboard ship. It takes a nimble host to juggle the house guests and outsiders between the two seatings. There is more flexibility when permanent table as-

```
┌─────────────────────────────────────────────────────┐
│                  HOTEL GUEST CARD                     │
│        _____           │
│                                                       │
│                                                       │
│     Name _____    │
│                                                       │
│     Room Number_____ Date_____      │
│                                                       │
│     Probable Length of Stay _____      │
│                                                       │
│     PLAN—( ) American  ( ) European  ( ) Modified     │
│                                              American  │
│     Please present this card the first time in dining room │
└─────────────────────────────────────────────────────┘
```

Figure 18.7. Dining room introduction cards (may be copies of the rooming slip) are being replaced with CRTs.

signments are not used. It is obvious that a permanent table cannot be assigned to an outside diner until the house guest has eaten. The dining room staff likes the floating assignment, too, because tips are lower per meal when the guest has the same server for a long period of time. This is another reason for adding the gratuity to the room charge. The floating arrangement may require special notice to the guest (figure 18.3).

Transient Restaurant Guests

Very few American plan dining rooms still limit service to house guests only. Indeed, some AP dining rooms service house guests almost incidentally to a large transient traffic. In most instances the dining room is a balance between the two and the menu reflects it, although sometimes two menus are prepared. The menu without prices is presented to house guests and the other is presented to transients. Omitting prices encourages guests to order in all price ranges. There is some indication that AP guests pick the more expensive entrees when prices are included on the menu.

The host(ess) needs to pay special attention to the two types of guests. House guests should not be billed except for extra meals, and the bill for transient guests should not be overlooked. Permanent table assignments minimize the chance for error, but the control can be easily established with the food checker in the kitchen.

At one time transient guests purchased meal tickets at the front desk before dining. They received a dining room introduction card like that of the house guest. This one-price policy discourages outside guests and it is rarely seen today.

Especially where there are no permanent table assignments, servers must be told which guests are house and which transient. Different colored checks can be left on the table by the headwaiter(waitress). The dining room introduction card can also be used for this purpose. With a floating table assignment, the card is placed on the table of house guests. In case of permanent table assignments, it is removed from the table to point out transient guests using a house guest's regular table.

A greater effort is needed to sell the advantages of the American plan. Too often it appears as just the opposite to the guest, especially where both European and American plans are offered. Extra meals are charged AP guests in full, and meals missed are allowed at only a percentage of their value. The advantage of the American plan should be demonstrated unequivocally. High-priced entrees should be available to AP guests. Extra meals and meals beyond the full AP day should be on a lower price schedule for AP guests than for EPs or walk-ins. A dine-around plan, which allows guests to eat in several different dining rooms of the hotel or to dine in any of several cooperating hotels, is a conscientious effort to emphasize the advantage of the American plan.

The Night Audit

Very few changes are needed to adapt the night audit to the American plan. Separating the single folio charge into room and meal designations is the major shift. Tray service and extra meal accumulations must also be provided for. Although AP and EP guests are not separated during the audit or in the well, a separate house count is usually obtained for each plan being offered.

Room charges, including AP meals, are verified against the room count sheet as before. Since the room income contains meal charges for guests who remain beyond the full AP day, the room count sheet will be verified with the transcript's subtotal of active guests, rather than the grand total, which includes checkouts. When a posting machine is used, these additional meals are subtracted from the machine total to reconcile with the rack. An additional verification is made by multiplying the number of American plan guests by the daily meal charge ($20 in our discussion) to test the total of American plan board.

Neither of these proofs is possible with the alternative method of charging. Under this plan, the board total will reflect only those meals taken on that date. This total cannot be verified by multiplying the number of AP guests by $20. Verification with the room count sheet is not possible either because the rack reflects quoted rates and not actual charges of that day.

The alternative method provides a truer daily income picture, but the first method of billing can be adjusted to obtain the same figure if the need is there. Actually the meal value is somewhat arbitrary anyway and the differences will balance out over time as reflected in the to-date figures. If a true daily figure is essential, actual food revenue can be computed by subtracting unearned food income from the total audit figure. For example, a guest who arrived before dinner "/D," has unearned luncheon and breakfast charges in the amount of $8; $3 for breakfast and $5 for luncheon. If there were 300 such guests, $2,400 worth of food sales would be unearned for "/D" arrivals. Similar computations can be made for "/L" arrivals and "/SL" arrivals. The total unearned figure is thus available. This allows the total meal income (total AP guests times $20) to be reduced by the unearned meals, and the true daily food revenue is thus obtained.

Night auditors have one additional duty in the AP situation that has no computer. A meal information sheet is prepared for the food checker to start the next day. A room count sheet is used. Beside each room number on the meal information sheet, the auditor furnishes the number of guests and their plan. It is the food checker's responsibility to keep the form current with arrivals and departures during the day. This is one of the many tasks that a computer system eliminates.

The night auditor, or the day auditor if the task is handled then, must be aware of the distribution of travel agency fees under the American plan. The agency has traditionally received its 10 percent on both the lodging and food portions of the total charge. One large resort recently announced it would pay commissions hereafter on room charges only, just as European plan hotels do.

When cashiers in the front office sell AP meal tickets, the total appears on the receipts side of the front office cash sheet and is included with the turn-in, subject to audit, like any other money.

Modified American Plan

The modified American plan offers no additional problems. All that has been said about the American plan can be adopted to the modified plan as well. Indeed, because this plan eliminates the middle meal, it means less recordkeeping and fewer allowances than the full American plan.

Continental plan (European plan plus breakfast) is handled exactly like the European plan in every way. Costs of continental breakfasts are not separately charged and are recovered as part of the overall room rate like any other expense.

———————

In an industry as rich in tradition and as diverse as that of innkeeping, the American plan must be seen for what it actually is. It is not an anachronism, but a rather vivid portrayal of the multifarious entity that is hotelkeeping. Variation and sensitivity to the different pieces that interlock the hospitality mosaic help explain the inability of any one voice to interpret the whole industry. Indeed, no single voice can even summarize one portion of the whole. For every futurist who prophesies the demise of the mom-and-pop, there is a new purchaser of a small motel. For every expert who foretells of the computerized, nonpersonalized front office, there is a repurchase of pads and pads of hand transcripts. And for each entrepreneur who builds a $200,000 per room hotel, another creates a compartmental hotel.

Students of the industry must keep apace: watching for change and searching for the societal shifts that, in the final analysis, will account for the shape and direction of tomorrow's hotel.

QUERIES AND PROBLEMS

1. Argue the pros and cons for granting an allowance, in full or in part, for meals missed at the conclusion of a stay at an American plan resort.
2. Discuss the outlook for the American plan portion of the U.S. hotel industry during the next decade.
3. How much does each guest owe if the European rate on all rooms is $80 and the American plan charge is an additional $25 ($5 for breakfast, $7 for luncheon, and $13 for dinner). State sales tax is 3 percent of room charge. Make one computation using a 50 percent meal allowance and one computation assuming no allowance at all. Check-out hour is noon; late charge is an additional $20.

Guest	Day of Arrival	Day of Departure
A-2EP	3/2 8PM	3/4 6AM
B-1AP	3/2/R	3/4/B
C-2AP	3/2/L	3/6/B
D-1EP	3/2 6AM	3/3 8PM
E-3AP	3/2/B	3/5/L

4. Costs and competition are calling for an increase in rates at this American plan hotel. The sales executive suggests an $8 across-the-board increase, which is 8 percent of the hotel's average room rate. The food and beverage manager urges that a larger credit, $4 more per day, be assigned to the food account. The rooms manager supports a small increase to the food charge of each guest and the application of a sliding scale to the rooms portion of every room. The accountant is unconcerned how the increase is obtained so long as it averages between $6 and $10 per person per day. Which suggestion(s) do you as the general manager adopt? Why?

Glossary

Italics identify those words in each definition which are themselves defined elsewhere in the Glossary.

"A" card A form used with front office posting machines to reconcile and report cash at the close of the first shift and alternate shifts thereafter; *see* **"B" card.**

account (card) *See* **guest bill.**

account receivable A company, organization, or individual, registered or not, who has an outstanding bill with the hotel.

accounts receivable ledger The aggregate of individual *account receivable* records.

adds Last minute *reservations* added to the reservation list on the day of arrival.

adjoining rooms Rooms that abut along the corridor but do not connect through private doors; cf. *connecting rooms.*

advance deposit A deposit furnished by the guest on a room *reservation* that the hotel is holding.

advances *See* **cash paid-outs.**

affiliated hotel One of a chain, *franchise,* or *referral* system, the membership of which provides special advantages, particularly a national reservation system.

after departure (AD) A *late charge.*

afternoon tea A light snack comprised of delicate sandwiches and small sweets served with tea, or even sherry.

agency ledger A division of the *city ledger* dealing with *travel agency* accounts.

AIOD Telephone equipment that provides *Automatic Identification of Outward Dialing* for billing purposes.

allowance A reduction to the *folio,* as an adjustment either for unsatisfactory service or for a posting error. Also called a *rebate.*

American Hotel & Motel Association (AH&MA) A federation of regional and state associations composed of individual hotel and motel properties throughout the Americas.

American plan (AP) A method of quoting room *rates* where the charge includes room and three meals.

American Society of Association Executives (ASAE) An organization of the professional executives who head the nation's numerous associations.

American Society of Travel Agents (ASTA) A professional association of retail *travel agents* and wholesale tour operators.

arrival, departure, and change sheet A form on which all guest *check ins, check outs,* and *changes* are recorded; sometimes three separate forms.

arrival time That hour by which the guest specifies he or she will arrive to claim the *reservation.*

available basis only Convention reservations that have no claim against the *block* of convention rooms because the requests arrived after the *cutoff date;* condition under which most special rates are allowed, no reservations permitted. *See* **blanket reservation.**

available rooms The number of guest rooms the hotel has for sale: either the total in the hotel or the number unoccupied on a given day.

average (daily) room rate The average (daily) *rate* paid by guests; computed by dividing room revenue by the number of rooms occupied. More recently called sales per room occupied.

back to back A sequence of consecutive *group* departures and arrivals usually arranged by tour operators so rooms are never vacant; a floor plan design that brings the piping of adjacent baths into a common shaft.

bank Coins and small bills given to the cashier for making change.

bank cards Credit cards issued by banks, usually for a smaller fee than that charged by *travel and entertainment cards.*

batch processing A computer procedure that collects and codes data, entering it into memory in batches; cf. *on-line computer.*

"B" card A form used with front office posting machines to reconcile and report cash at the close of the second shift and alternate shifts thereafter; *see* **"A" card.**

bed and board Another term for the *American plan.*

bed and breakfast (B&B) Lodging and breakfast offered in a domestic setting by families in their own homes; less frequently, the *Continental plan.*

bed board A board placed under the mattress to provide a firmer sleeping surface.

bed night *See* **guest day.**

bed occupancy A ratio relating the number of bed spaces sold to the number available for sale.

bell captain The supervisor of the bellpersons and other uniformed service personnel; a proprietary in-room vending machine.

bell captain's log *See* **callbook.**

bellstand The bellperson's desk located in the lobby close to and visible from the front desk.

Bermuda plan A method of quoting room *rates* where the charge includes a full breakfast as well as the room.

best available A *reservation* requesting (or a confirmation promising) the best room available or the best room to open prior to arrival.

blanket reservation A *block* of rooms held for a particular *group* with individual members requesting assignments from that block.

block A restriction placed in a *pocket* of the *room rack* to limit the clerk's discretion in assigning the room; a number of rooms reserved for one *group.*

book To sell hotel space, either to an individual or to a *group* needing a *block* of rooms.

box Reservation term that allows no *reservations* from either side of the boxed dates to spill through; cf. *sell through.*

breakage The gain that accrues to the hotel or tour operator when meals or other services included in a *package* are not used by the guest.

brunch A meal served after breakfast but before lunch and taking the place of both.

bucket *See* **cashier's well.**

budget motel *See* **limited service.**

cabana A room on the beach (or by the pool) separated from the main *house* and sometimes furnished as a sleeping room.

café complet Coffee snack at midmorning or midafternoon.

callbook The bellperson's record of calls and activities.

call sheet The form used by the telephone operator to record the room and hour of the *morning call*.

cancellation A guest's request to the hotel to void a *reservation* previously made.

cash advance *See* **cash paid-outs.**

cash disbursement *See* **cash paid-outs.**

cashier's report The cash *turn-in* form completed by a departmental cashier at the close of the *watch*.

cashier's well The file that holds the guest *folios*, often recessed in the counter top; also known as *bucket or pit*.

cash paid-outs Monies disbursed for guests, either advances or loans, and charged to their accounts like other departmental services.

cash sheet The *departmental control form* maintained by the front office cashier.

cathode ray tube (CRT) A television screen that displays information put out by the computer; also called a VDT, *video display terminal*.

central processing unit (CPU) The *hardware/ software* nucleus of the computer that performs and monitors the essential functions.

change Moving a party from one guest room to another; any change in room, *rate*, or number of occupants.

charge back Credit card charges refused by the credit card company for one reason or another.

check in All the procedures involved in receiving the guest and completing the registration sequence.

check out All the procedures involved in the departure of the guest and the settlement of the *account*.

check-out hour That time by which guests must vacate rooms or be charged an additional day.

city ledger An *accounts receivable ledger* of nonregistered guests.

city ledger journal The form used to record transactions that affect the *city ledger*.

Civil Aeronautics Board (CAB) Federal agency responsible for regulating U.S. air service. Destined to be eliminated by deregulation.

class The quality of hotel with *average room rate* the usual criterion.

close of the day An arbitrary hour that management designates to separate the records of one day from those of the next.

closet bed *See* **Murphy bed.**

colored transparency A colored celluloid strip placed in the *room rack pocket* as a *flag* or indicator of room status.

commercial hotel A *transient hotel* catering to a business clientele.

commercial rate A reduced room *rate* given to businesspersons to promote occupancy.

commissionable An indication that the hotel will pay *travel agents* the standard fee for business placed.

comp Short for complimentary; accommodations — and occasionally food and beverage — furnished without charge.

company made (reservation) A *reservation* guaranteed by the arriving guest's company.

concession A hotel tenant whose facilities and services are indistinguishable from those hotel-owned and operated.

concierge A European position, occasionally found in U.S. hotels, responsible for handling guests' needs, particularly those relating to out-of-hotel services; designation of the sleeping floor where these services are offered.

confirmed reservation The hotel's agreement, usually in writing, to the guest's *reservation* request.

connecting rooms *Adjoining rooms* with direct, private access making use of the corridor unnecessary.

Continental plan A method of quoting room *rates* where the charge includes a continental breakfast (sweet roll and coffee) as well as the room rate.

convention rate *See* **run-of-the-house rate.**

convertible bed *See* **sofa bed.**

corner (room) An *outside room* on a corner of the building having two *exposures.*

correction sheet A form used with front office machines to record posting errors for later reconciliation by the *night auditor.*

cot *See* **rollaway bed.**

coupon A checklike form issued by *travel agencies* to their clients and used by the clients to settle their hotel accounts. Also called a *voucher.*

credit An accounting term that indicates a decrease in the *account receivable*; the opposite of *debit.*

cutoff date That date on which the unsold *block* of reserved convention rooms is released for general sale.

cutoff hour That time at which the day's unclaimed *reservations* are released for sale to the general public.

daily rooms report *See* **room count sheet.**

day rate A reduced charge for occupancy of less than overnight; used when the party arrives and departs the same day.

"D" card The form on which the totals of the front office posting machine are printed for use in the *night audit.*

debit An accounting term that indicates an increase in the *account receivable*; the opposite of *credit.*

deluxe A non-U.S. designation implying the best accommodations; unreliable unless part of an official rating system.

demi-pension (DP) A non-U.S. method of quoting room *rates* similar to the *MAP* but allowing the guest to select either luncheon or dinner along with breakfast and room; also called *half pension.*

density board (chart) A *reservation* system where the number of rooms committed is controlled by type: *single, twin, queen,* etc.

departmental control form A form maintained by each *operating department* for recording data from departmental *vouchers* before forwarding them to the front desk for posting.

deposit reservation *See* **advance deposit.**

destination hotel The objective of — and often the sole purpose for — the guest's trip; cf. *transient hotel.*

did not stay (DNS) Means the guest left almost immediately after *registering.*

difference returnable *See* **exchange.**

dine-around plan A method of quoting AP or MAP room rates that allows guests to dine at any of several independent but cooperating hotels.

display room *See* **sample room.**

double A bed approximately 54 inches by 75 inches; the *rate* charged for two persons occupying one room; a room with a double bed.

double-double *See* **twin-double.**

double occupancy Room occupancy by two persons; a ratio relating the number of rooms double occupied to the number of rooms sold.

double occupancy rate A *rate* used for tours where the per person charge is based on two to a room.

double-up A designation of *double occupancy* by unrelated parties necessitating two *room rack slips.*

downgrade Move a *reservation* or registered guest to a lesser accommodation or *class* of service; cf. *upgrade.*

downtime That time span during which the computer is inoperative because of malfunction or preemptive operations.

ducat *See* **stock card.**

due back *See* **exchange.**

due bank *See* **exchange.**

due bill *See* **trade advertising contract.**

duplex A two-story *suite* with a connecting stairwell.

early arrival A guest who arrives a day or two earlier than the *reservation* calls for.

economy class *See* **tourist class.**

efficiency Accommodations that include kitchen facilities.

electronic data processing A data handling system that relies upon electronic (computer) equipment.

ell A wing of a building usually at right angles to the main structure.

en pension *See* **full pension.**

European plan (EP) A method of quoting room *rates* where the charge includes room accommodations only.

exchange The excess of cash *turn-in* over net receipts; the difference is returnable (due back) to the front office cashier; also called *due back, due bank,* or *difference returnable.*

executive room *See* **studio.**

exposure The direction (north, south, east, or west) or view (ocean, mountain) that the guest room faces.

extra meals An *American plan* charge made for dining room service over and above that to which the guest is entitled.

family plan A special room *rate* that allows children to occupy their parent's room at no additional charge.

family room *See* **twin-double.**

fam trip Familiarization trip taken by *travel agents* at little or no cost to acquaint themselves with *properties* and destinations.

farm out Assignment of guests to other *properties* when a full *house* precludes their accommodation.

first class A non-U.S. designation for medium-priced accommodations with corresponding facilities and services.

flag A device for calling the room clerk's attention to a particular room in the *room rack.*

flat rate *See* **run-of-the-house rate.**

floor key *See* **master key.**

floor release limit The maximum amount of charges permitted a credit card user at a given *property* without clearance; the limit is established for the property not for the user.

folio *See* **guest bill**; a folio is also called an *account card.*

forecast A future projection of estimated business volume.

forecast scheduling Work schedules established on the basis of sales projections.

forfeited deposit A *reservation* deposit kept by the hotel when a *no-show* fails to cancel the reservation; also called a lost deposit.

franchise An independently owned hotel or motel that appears to be part of a chain and pays a fee for this right of identity.

free sale Occurs when a *travel agent,* airline, or other agency commits hotel space without prior confirmation with *the property.*

from bill number . . . to bill number A cross reference of *account* numbers when the bill of a guest who remains beyond one week is transferred to a new *folio.*

front The next bellperson eligible for a *rooming* assignment or other errand apt to produce a gratuity.

front office A broad term that includes the duties and functions involved in the sale and service of guest rooms as well as the physical front desk.

full day The measure of a chargeable day for accounting purposes; three meals for an *AP* hotel, overnight for an *EP.*

full house Means 100 percent occupancy, all guest rooms sold.

full pension A European term for the *American plan.*

full service Means a complete line of services and departments are provided, in contrast to a *limited service* hotel or motel.

futon A Japanese sleeping arrangement made of many layers of cotton-quilted batting that is rolled up when not in use.

garni A non-U.S. designation for hotels without restaurant service, except for *continental* breakfast.

general cashier The chief cashier with whom deposits are made and from whom *banks* are drawn.

general manager (GM) The hotel's chief executive.

grandmaster One key that opens all guest rooms except those locked from within; *see also* **house emergency key.**

graveyard A work shift beginning about midnight.

greens fee A charge for the use of the golf course.

group A number of persons with whom the hotel deals (reservation, billing, etc.) as if they were one party.

guaranteed reservation Payment for the room is promised even if the occupant fails to arrive.

guest account *See* **guest bill.**

guest bill A special form used by hotels for keeping *transient account receivable* records; different forms used with hand-prepared and machine-prepared systems; also known as a *folio* or *account card.*

guest check The bill presented to patrons of the dining rooms and bars and often used as the departmental *voucher.*

guest day (night) The stay of one guest for one day (night); also known as a *room night* or *bed night.*

guest elevators The front elevators for the exclusive use of the guests; employees are not permitted except for bellpersons when accompanying the guest to or from a room; cf. *service elevators.*

guest history (card) A record of the guest's visits including rooms assigned, *rates,* special needs, and credit rating.

guest ledger The accounts of registered guests as distinct from *city ledger* accounts; also known as the *rooms ledger* or *transient ledger.*

guest night *See* **guest day.**

guest occupancy *See* **bed occupancy.**

guest service area *See* **front office.**

half-board *See* **modified American plan.**

half pension *See* **demi-pension.**

hard copy Computer term for material that has been printed rather than merely displayed.

hardware The physical equipment (electronic and mechanical) of a computer installation and its peripheral components; cf. *software.*

hideabed *See* **sofa bed.**

high tea A fairly substantial late afternoon or early evening meal.

HOBIC An acronym for Hotel Outgoing Billing Center, the telephone company's long-distance hotel network.

hollywood bed *Twin* beds joined by a common headboard.

hollywood length An extra long bed, about 80 inches to 82 inches instead of the usual 75 inches.

hospitality suite (room) A facility used for entertaining, usually at conventions, trade shows, and similar meetings.

hostel An inexpensive but supervised facility with limited services catering to young travelers on foot or bicycle.

hotelier French for innkeeper.

hotel manager *See* **resident manager.**

Hotel Sales and Marketing Association International (HSMAI) An international association of hotel sales and marketing managers.

hot list A list of lost or stolen credit cards furnished to hotels and other retailers by the credit card companies.

house A synonym for hotel, as in house bank, house count; *see also* **(the) property.**

house bank *See* **bank.**

house call Telephone call made to the outside by a member of the staff for company business and not subject to charge.

house count The number of registered guests.

house emergency key One key that opens all guest rooms including those locked from within, even those with the room key still in the lock, also called the great grandmaster.

housekeeper's report A *linen room* summary of the status of guest rooms, used by the front desk to verify the accuracy of the *room rack.*

house laundry A hotel-operated facility in contrast to an *outside laundry* with which the hotel might contract.

house profit The net profit before income taxes from all *operating departments* except store rentals and before provision for rent, taxes, interest, insurance, and depreciation; renamed by the 1977 edition of the *USA*, ``total income before fixed charges.''

house rooms Guest rooms set aside for hotel use and excluded, therefore, from *available rooms.*

housing bureau A city-wide reservation office, usually run by the convention bureau, for assigning *reservation* requests to participating hotels during a city-wide convention.

Hubbart Room Rate Formula A basis for determining room rates developed by Roy Hubbart and distributed by the *American Hotel & Motel Association.*

imprest petty cash A technique for controlling petty cash disbursements by which a special, small cash fund is used for minor cash payments and periodically reimbursed.

incentive (group, guest, or trip) Persons who have won a hotel stay (usually with transportation included) as a reward for meeting and excelling their sales quotas or other company-established standards.

inclusive terms Phrase that is sometimes used in Europe to designate the *American plan.*

independent A *property* with no chain or *franchise* affiliation, although one proprietor might own several such properties.

information rack An alphabetic listing of registered guests with a room number cross reference.

in-season rate A *resort's* maximum rate, charged when the demand is heaviest, as it is during the middle of the summer or winter; cf. *off-season rate.*

inside call A telephone call that enters the switchboard from inside the hotel; a telephone call that remains within the hotel; cf. *outside call.*

inside room A guest room that faces an inner courtyard or light court enclosed by three or four sides of the building.

inspector Supervisory position in the housekeeping department responsible for releasing *on-change* rooms to ready status.

interface Computer term designating the ability of one computer to communicate with another.

interstate call A long distance call that crosses state lines.

intrastate call A long distance telephone call that originates and terminates within the same state.

in-WATS *See* **Wide Area Telephone Service.**

IT number The code assigned to an inclusive tour for identification and *booking.*

junior suite One large room, sometimes with a half partition, furnished as both a *parlor* and a bedroom.

king An extra long, extra wide *double* bed about 78 inches by 80 inches.

lanai A Hawaiian term for veranda; a room with a porch or balcony usually overlooking gardens or water.

last The designation for the bellperson who most recently completed a *front*.

late arrival A guest with a *reservation* who expects to arrive after the *cutoff hour* and so notifies the hotel.

late charge A departmental charge that arrives at the front desk for billing after the guest has *checked out*.

late checkout A departing guest who remains beyond the *check-out hour* with permission of the desk and thus without charge.

least cost router (LCR) Telephone equipment that routes the call over the least expensive lines available. Also called automatic route selectors (ARS).

light baggage Insufficient luggage in quantity or quality on which to extend credit; the guest pays in advance.

limited service A hotel or motel that provides little or no services other than the room; a *budget hotel* (motel); cf. *full service*.

linen closet A storage closet for linens and other housekeeping supplies usually located conveniently along the corridor for the use of the housekeeping staff.

linen room The housekeeper's office and the center of operations for that department, including the storage of linens and uniforms.

lockout Denying the guest access to the room, usually because of an unpaid bill. A key of that name.

log A record of activities maintained by several *operating departments*.

lost and found An area, usually under the housekeeper's jurisdiction, for the control and storage of lost-and-found items.

maid's report A status-of-rooms report prepared by the floor housekeeper and consolidated by the *linen room* to create a *housekeeper's report*.

mail and key rack A piece of front office equipment where both mail and keys are stored by room number.

maitre d' The shortened form of maitre d'hotel, the headwaiter.

market mix The variety and percentage distribution of hotel guests: conventioneer, tourist, businessperson, etc.

master account One *folio* prepared for a *group* (convention, company, tour) on which all group charges are accumulated.

master key One key controlling several *pass keys* and opening all the guests rooms on one floor; also called a *floor key*.

menu An array of function choices displayed to the computer user who selects the appropriate function.

message lamp A light on or near the telephone, used to notify an occupant that the telephone operator has a message to relay.

minor departments The less important *operating departments* (excluding room, food, and beverage) like valet, laundry, and telephone.

miscellaneous charge order (MCO) Airline *voucher* authorizing the sale of services to the guest named on the form, with payment due from the airline.

modified American plan (MAP) A method of quoting room *rates* in which the charge includes breakfast and dinner as well as the room.

mom-and-pop A small, family owned business with limited capitalization in which the family, rather than paid employees, furnishes the bulk of the labor.

morning call A *wake-up* telephone call made by the telephone operator at the guest's request.

Ms An abbreviation used to indicate a female guest whose marital status is unknown.

Murphy bed A standard bed that folds or swings into a wall or cabinet in a closetlike fashion.

NCR 2000 A front office posting machine manufactured by the NCR Company; no longer in production.

NCR 4200 A front office posting machine manufactured by the NCR Company and usually called a "42"; no longer in production.

NCR paper No carbon required: paper is specially treated to produce copies without carbon.

night audit A daily reconciliation of *accounts receivable* that is completed during the *graveyard watch*.

night auditor The person or persons responsible for the *night audit*.

night clerk's report An interim report prepared by the *night auditor* or night clerk and used until the day audit has been completed.

no reservation (NR) *See* **walk-in**.

no-show A *reservation* that fails to arrive.

occupancy, percentage of A ratio relating the number of rooms sold to the number *available for sale*.

off line *See* **batch processing.**

off-season rate A reduced room rate charged by *resort* hotels when demand is lowest; cf. *in-season rate*.

off the street (OS) *See* **walk-in.**

on change The status of a room recently vacated but not yet available for new occupants.

one- (two-) pull dialing One (two) digit telephone dialing that connects the caller to hotel services like room service, bellstand, etc.

on-line computer Computer facilities hooked directly to input and output devices for instantaneous communication.

operating departments Those divisions of the hotel directly involved with the service of the guest, in contrast to support divisions like personnel and accounting.

out of order (OOO) The room is not available for sale because of some planned or unexpected shutdown of facilities.

outside call A call that enters the switchboard from outside the hotel; a call that terminates outside the hotel; cf. *inside call.*

outside laundry (valet) A nonhotel laundry or valet service contracted by the hotel in order to offer a full line of services; cf. *house laundry.*

outside room A room on the perimeter of the building facing outward with an *exposure* more desirable than that of an *inside* room.

out-WATS *See* **Wide Area Telephone Service**.

over and short A discrepancy between the cash on hand and the amount that should be on hand.

overbooking Committing more rooms to possible guest occupancy than are actually available.

override Extra commission above standard percentage to encourage or reward quantity bookings; process by which the operator bypasses certain limits built into the computer program.

overstay A guest who remains beyond the expiration of the anticipated stay.

package A number of services (transportation, room, food, entertainment) normally purchased separately but put together and marketed at a reduced price made possible by volume and *breakage.*

paid in advance A room charge that is collected prior to occupancy; it is the usual procedure when a guest has *light baggage*, and with some motels, it is standard procedure for every guest.

paid-outs *See* **cash paid-outs.**

parlor The living room portion of a *suite.*

part-day rate (guest) *See* **day rate.**

pass key A submaster key limited to a single set of rooms (12–18) and allowing access to no other.

PBX *See* **private branch exchange.**

penthouse Accommodations, usually *suites*, located on the top floor(s) of the hotel.

percentage of occupancy *See* **occupancy**.

permanent (guest) A resident of long-term duration whose stay may or may not be formalized with a lease.

petite suite *See* **junior suite**.

petty cash *See* **imprest petty cash.**

pickup The procedure used with front office posting machines to accumulate the *folio* balance by entering the previous balance into the machine before posting the new charges; the figure so entered.

pit *See* **cashier's well.**

plan The basis on which room *rate* charges are made; *see* **American plan** and **European plan.**

plus, plus Shorthand for the addition of tax and tip to the check or price per cover.

pocket A portion of the *room rack* made to accept the *room rack slips* and provide a permanent record of accommodations and *rates*.

point-of-sale terminal (POS) A computer term for input equipment immediately accessible to the place of sale for *on-line* input.

preassign *Reservations* are assigned and specific rooms *blocked* before the guest arrives.

preregistration A procedure in which the hotel completes the registration prior to the guest's arrival; used with *groups* and tours to reduce congestion at the front desk, since individual guests do not then register.

private branch exchange (PBX) A telephone switchboard.

projection *See* **forecast.**

(the) property Refers to the hotel, including its personnel and physical facilities.

queen An extra long, extra wide *double bed* about 60 inches by 80 inches.

quote To state the room *rate* or other charges.

rack *See* **room rack.**

rack rate The standard *rate* established for and quoted from the *room rack*.

rate The charge made by the hotel for its room.

rate cutting A *rate* reduction that attracts business from competitors rather than creating new customers or markets.

rebate *See* **allowance.**

recap A summary (*recap*itulation) of the *transcript* sheets to obtain the day's grand totals.

Red Book A publication of the *American Hotel & Motel Association* geographically listing and briefly identifying member hotels, their facilities, and rates.

referral A *reservation* system for *independently* owned properties developed to counter the reservation advantages of the chains and their *affiliates*.

registered, not assigned (RNA) A guest who has *registered* but is waiting for a specific room assignment until space becomes available.

register(ing) The procedure by which the arriving person signifies an intent to become a guest by completing and signing the *registration card*; the name for a book which served at one time as the registration card.

registration card (reg card) A form completed by the guest at the time of arrival giving name, address, and sometimes business affiliation.

reminder clock A special alarm clock that can be set forty-eight times at fifteen-minute intervals, used chiefly for *wake-up calls*.

reservation A mutual agreement between the guest and the hotel, the former to take accommodations at a given time for a given period and the latter to furnish the same.

reservation rack An alphabetic list of anticipated arrivals with a summary of their needs, filed chronologically by date of arrival.

residential hotel A hotel catering to long-term guests who have made the property their home and residence. *See also* **permanent guest.**

resident manager Hotel executive responsible for the front of the house, including *front office,* housekeeping, and uniformed services; sometimes called hotel manager or house manager.

resort A hotel that caters to vacationing guests providing recreational and entertainment facilities; often a *destination hotel.*

rollaway bed A portable utility bed approximately 30 inches by 72 inches; also called a *cot.*

room charge sheet *See* **room count sheet.**

room count The number of occupied rooms.

room count sheet A permanent record of the *room rack* prepared nightly and used to verify the accuracy of room statistics.

rooming (a guest) The entire procedure by which the desk greets and assigns new arrivals and the bell staff directs them to their rooms (rooms them).

rooming list The list of names furnished by a buying *group* in advance of arrival and used by the hotel to *preregister* and *preassign* the party.

rooming slip A form issued by the desk to the bellperson and left by the bellperson with the guest for verification of name, *rate,* and room.

room inspection report A checklist of the condition of the room prepared by the *inspector* when the room cleaner has finished cleaning.

room night *See* **guest day.**

room rack A piece of front office equipment representing the guest rooms in the form of metal *pockets* in which colors and symbols identify the accommodations.

room rack slip (card) A form prepared from the *registration card* identifying the occupant of each room and filed in the *pocket* of the *room rack* assigned to that guest.

rooms available *See* **available rooms.**

room service Food and beverage service provided in the privacy of the guest room by a designated (room service) waiter or waitress.

rooms ledger *See* **guest ledger.**

rule-of-thumb rate A guideline for setting room rates with the hotel charging $1 in rate for each $1,000 per room construction costs.

run-of-the-house rate A special *group* rate generally the midpoint of the *rack rate* with a single, flat price applying to any room, *suites* excepted, on a *best available* basis.

ryokan A traditional Japanese inn.

safe-deposit boxes Individual sections of the vault where guests store valuables and cashiers keep *house banks.*

sales per occupied room *See* **average room rate.**

sales rack The front office space for the storage and control of *stock cards* (*ducats* or *sales tickets*).

sales ticket *See* **stock card.**

salon The European designation for *parlor.*

sample room A guest room used to merchandise and display goods, usually in combination with sleeping accommodations.

season rate *See* **in-season rate.**

sell through Denoting days for which no reservation arrivals are accepted; reservations for previous days will be accepted and allowed to stay through the date; cf. *box* date.

sell up Convince the arriving guest to take a higher priced room than was planned or reserved.

service charge A percentage (usually from 10 percent to 20 percent) added to the bill for distribution to service employees in lieu of direct tipping.

service elevators Back elevators for use by employees (room service, housekeeping, and maintenance, etc.) on hotel business and not readily visible to the guests; cf. *guest elevator.*

shoulder Marketing term designating the period between peaks and valleys; the time on either side of the in-season.

siberia Jargon for a very undesirable room, one sold only after the *house* fills and then only after the guest has been alerted to its location or condition.

single A bed approximately 36 inches by 75 inches; a room with accommodations for one; occupancy by one person; the *rate* charged for one person.

sitting room *See* **parlor.**

size The capacity of the hotel as measured by the number of guest rooms.

skip *See* **skipper.**

skipper A guest who departs surreptitiously leaving an unpaid bill.

sleeper A departed guest whose *room rack slip* remains in the *rack* giving the appearance of an occupied room.

sleeper occupancy *See* **bed occupancy.**

sleep out A room that is taken, occupied, and paid for but not slept in.

slide The transcription error caused by a misplaced decimal, as when 362 is written 3620.

sofa bed A sofa with fixed back and arms that unfolds into a standard *single* or *double bed*; also called a *hideabed*.

software The programs and routines that give instructions to the computer; cf. *hardware*.

special attention (SPATT) A label assigned to important guests designated for special treatment.

split rate Division of the total room *rate* charge among the room's several occupants.

split shift A work pattern divided into two working periods with an unusually long period (more than a rest or meal time) between.

spread rate Assignment of group members or conventioneers using the standard rate distribution, although prices might be less than rack rates; cf. *run-of-the-house rate*.

star rating An unreliable ranking (except for some well-known exceptions) of hotel facilities both in the United States and abroad.

star reservation Indicates the arrival of an important guest — a *VIP*.

stay Any guest who remains beyond a one night stay; an anticipated checkout who fails to depart; *stayover*.

stayover An anticipated checkout who remains beyond the stated date of departure; any guest who remains overnight.

stock card A colored card of heavy paper with code designations representing the *room rack pocket* and used when the *room rack* is inaccessible to the room clerk; also called a *ducat*.

studio A bed approximately 36 inches by 75 inches without headboard or footboard that serves as a sofa during the day; the room containing such a bed.

suite A series of *connecting rooms* with one or more bedrooms and a *parlor*; suites occasionally include additional rooms like a dining room. *See* **hospitality suite.**

summary transcript *See* **recap.**

supper A late night meal; or the evening meal when the midday service is designated as dinner.

swing The work shift between the day shift and the *graveyard* shift, usually starting between 3 P.M. and 4 P.M.

TelAutograph A proprietary piece of communication equipment that transcribes written messages.

time stamp A clock mechanism that prints date and time when activated.

to-date Designates a cumulative amount; the sum of all figures in the current period (usually monthly or annually) including the day or date in question.

tour group *See* **package.**

tourist class A non-U.S. designation for *limited service* hotels whose accommodations frequently lack private baths; also called *economy class*.

trade advertising contract An agreement by which hotel accommodations are swapped for advertising space or broadcast time; also called a *due bill*.

traffic sheet A *departmental control form* used by the telephone department.

transcript A form used by the *night auditor* to accumulate and separate the day's charges by departments and guests.

transcript ruler The headings of a transcript sheet attached to a straight edge and used as a column guide at the bottom of the long *transcript* sheet.

transfer An accounting technique used to move a figure from one form to another, usually between *folios*; the movement of guests and/or luggage from one point to another, e.g., from the airline terminal to the hotel.

transfer folio A special, unnumbered *folio* used to carry the guest's account beyond the first week when the original folio was numbered and cross referenced to the *registration card*.

transfer from The *debit* portion of a *transfer* between accounts or ledgers.

transfer journal A front office form used to record *transfer* entries between different accounts or different ledgers.

transfer to The *credit* portion of a *transfer* between accounts or ledgers.

transient guest A short-term guest; *see* **transient hotel**.

transient hotel A hotel catering to short-stay guests who stop en route to other destinations; cf. *destination hotel*.

transient ledger *See* **guest ledger**.

transmittal form The form provided by national credit card companies for recording and remitting credit card charges accumulated by the hotel.

transposition A transcription error caused by reordering the sequence of digits, as when 389 is written as 398.

travel agent (TA) An entrepreneur who *books* space and facilities for clients in hotels and public carriers and receives a commission for placing the business; hotels usually pay 10 percent.

travel and entertainment card A credit card issued by a proprietary company other than a hotel for which the user pays an annual fee.

Travel Industry Association of America (TIA) A nonprofit association of many travel related agencies and private businesses working to develop travel and tourism in the United States.

tray service The fee charged *American plan* guests for *room service*.

tub *See* **cashier's well**.

turn away To refuse *walk-in* business because rooms are unavailable; the guest so refused.

turn-downs An evening service rendered by the housekeeping department, which replaces soiled bathroom linen and prepares the bed for use.

turn-in The sum deposited with the *general cashier* by the departmental cashier at the close of each shift.

turnkey A facility (computer, franchise, entire hotel) so complete that it is ready for use at the turn of a key.

twin A bed approximately 39 inches by 75 inches to sleep one person; a room with two such beds.

twin-double Two *double* beds; a room with two such beds capable of accommodating four persons.

twins Two *twin* beds.

understay A guest who *checks out* before the expiration of the anticipated stay.

Uniform System of Accounts for Hotels (USA) A manual of accounting terms, primarily incomes and expenses, to assure industry-wide uniformity in terminology and use.

United States Travel and Tourism Administration (USTTA) A division of the Department of Commerce responsible for promoting travel to the United States. Successor to the United States Travel Service (USTS).

upgrade Move a *reservation* or registered guest to a better accommodation or class of service; cf. *downgrade*.

use rate *See* **day rate**.

user friendly Computer design, application, and implementation that minimizes the user's fears, encouraging purchase and use of the equipment.

vacancy Occupancy of less than a *full house* so rooms are available for sale.

very important person (VIP) A reservation or guest who warrants *special attention* and handling.

video display terminal (VDT) *See* **cathode ray tube.**

voucher The form used by the *operating departments* to notify the front desk of charges incurred by a particular guest; form furnished by a *travel agent* as a receipt for a client's advance *reservation* payment. *See* **coupon.**

wake-up call *See* **morning call.**

walk (a guest) To turn away guests holding confirmed *reservations* due to a lack of available rooms.

walk-in A guest without a *reservation* who requests and receives accommodations.

walk-through A thorough examination of the *property* by a hotel executive, *franchise* inspector, prospective buyer, etc.

watch Another term for the work shift.

WATS *See* **Wide Area Telephone Service.**

who An unidentified guest in a room that appears vacant in the *room rack.*

wholesaler An entrepreneur who conceives, finances, and services *group* and *package* tours that he or she promotes (often through *travel agents*) to the general public.

Wide Area Telephone Service (WATS) Long-distance telephone lines provided at special rates — even wholesaled — to large users; multiple lines may be purchased at multiple charges; separate charges are levied for incoming and outgoing WATS lines.

youth hostel *See* **hostel.**

zero out To balance the *account* as the guest *checks out* and makes settlement.

Bibliography

The ABCs of Travel. New York: Public Transportation and Travel Division. Ziff-Davis Publishing Co., 1972.

Abraben, E. *Resort Hotels.* New York: Reinhold Publishing Co., 1965.

Abrams, Samuel, *et al. Basic Concepts of Antitrust Law.* Egg Harbor, N.J.: Hotel Sales Management Association (International), 1977.

Arthur, R., and Gladwell, D. *The Hotel Assistant Manager.* 3d ed. London: Barrie & Rockliff, 1975.

Astroff, Milton, and Abbey, James. *Convention Sales and Services.* Dubuque: Wm. C. Brown Company Publishers, 1978.

Axler, Bruce. *Room Care for Hotels and Motels.* Indianapolis: ITT Educational Publications, 1974.

————. *Focus on . . . Security for Hotels, Motels, and Restaurants.* Indianapolis: ITT Educational Publications, 1974.

Barba, Stephen. "Operating the Traditional American Plan Resort." *The Practice of Hospitality Management,* ed. Pizam, Lewis, and Manning. Westport: Avi Publishing Co., Inc., 1982.

Beavis, J. R. S., and Medlik, S. *A Manual of Hotel Reception.* 2d ed. London: William Heinemann Ltd., 1978.

Berman, Shelley. *A Hotel Is a Place.* . . . Los Angeles: Price/Stern/Sloan, Publishers Inc., 1972.

Boomer, Lucius. *Hotel Management.* New York: Harper & Bros., 1938.

Booz, Allen & Hamilton, Inc. *External Reservation Services Analysis.* New York: American Hotel & Motel Association, 1970.

————. Under the direction of the Cornell School of Hotel Administration. *Operation Breakthrough, An Approach to Hotel/Motel Operations in 1978.* New York: American Hotel & Motel Association, 1969.

Browning, Marjorie. *Night Audit Procedure.* Columbus: The Christopher Inn, March 1, 1969.

Bucher, A. F. *101 Tips on Check Cashing.* New York: Ahrens Publishing Co., Inc., circa 1930.

Burstein, Harvey. *Hotel Security Management.* New York: Praeger, 1975.

Buzby, Walter J. *Hotel and Motel Security Management.* Los Angeles: Security World Publishing Co., 1976.

Chandler, Raymond. *Trouble Is My Business.* New York: Ballantine, 1972.

Coltman, Michael M. *Hospitality Management Accounting.* Boston: CBI Publishing Company, Inc., 1978.

Compton, Richard. *City Ledger Accounting for the Small Hotel Using IBM Equipment*. Ithaca: Unpublished Masters Thesis, 1967.

Convention Liaison Manual. 3d ed. No city: Convention Liaison Council, 1980.

Dahl, J. O. *Bellman and Elevator Operator*. Stamford: The Dahls, 1933. Revised by Crete Dahl.

———. *Room Clerk's Manual*. Stamford: The Dahls, 1933. Revised by Crete Dahl.

Deveau, Jack, and Penraat, Jaap. *The Efficient Room Clerk*. New York: Learning Information, Inc., 1968.

Dukas, Peter. *Hotel Front Office Management and Operations*. 3d ed. Dubuque: Wm. C. Brown Company Publishers, 1970.

Dunn, David. *Front Office Accounting Machines in Hotels*. Ithaca: Unpublished Masters Thesis, June 1965.

———. *Operations Manual for the Front Office*. Ithaca: The Statler Club, Cornell University, September 1961.

Dunseath, M., and Ransom, J. *The Hotel Bookkeeper Receptionist*. London: Barrie and Rockliff, 1967.

End, Henry. *Interior Book of Hotels and Motor Hotels*. New York: Whitney Library of Design, 1963.

Expense and Payroll Dictionary. New York: Prepared for the American Hotel & Motel Association by Laventhol and Horwath, 1979.

Fay, C.; Rhoads, R.; and Rosenblatt, R. *Managerial Accounting for the Hospitality Service Industries*. 2d ed. Dubuque: Wm. C. Brown Company Publishers, 1976.

Fidel, John. *Hotel Data Systems*. Revised Ed. Albuquerque, September 1972.

Front Office and Reservations. Burlingame, Ca.: Hyatt Corporation, 1978.

Front Office Courtesy Pays. Small Business Administration, U.S. Government Printing Office, 1956.

Front Office Manual. New York: New Yorker Hotel, 1931.

Front Office Manual: Franchise Division. No city: Sheraton Hotels & Inns, Worldwide, no date.

Front Office Operations Manual (of the) Hotel McCurdy, Evansville, Indiana. No city: Research Bureau of the American Hotel Association, April 1923.

Front Office Procedures. East Lansing: Educational Institute of the American Hotel & Motel Association, 1976.

Front Office Selling. East Lansing: Educational Institute of the American Hotel & Motel Association, no date.

Front Office Selling "Tips." New York: Hotel Sales Management Association, 1960.

Glossary of Hotel/Motel Terms. New York: Hotel Sales Management Association, 1970.

Goodwin, John, and Rovelstad, James. *Travel and Lodging Law: Principles, Statutes, and Cases*. Columbus, Ohio: Grid Publishing, Inc., 1980.

Gray, William S., and Liguori, Salvatore C. *Hotel & Motel Management & Operations*. Englewood Cliffs, New Jersey: Prentice-Hall, Inc., 1980.

Guest Relations Training for Front Office Cashiers. Boston: Sheraton Corporation of America, 1961.

A Guide to Terminology in the Leisure Time Industries. Philadelphia: Laventhol & Horwath. No date.

Hall, Orrin. *Motel-Hotel Front Office Procedures*. Hollywood Beach, circa 1971.

Hamilton, Francis. *Hotel Front Office Management*. Miami, 1947.

Haszonics, Joseph. *Front Office Operation*. New York: ITT Educational Services, Inc., 1971.

Heldenbrand, H. V. *Front Office Psychology*. Evanston: John Willy, Inc., 1944. Republished by American Hotel Register Company, Chicago, circa 1982.

Hitz, Ralph. *Standard Practice Manuals for Hotel Operation, I, Front Service Division*. 2d ed. New York: Harper & Bros. Publishers, 1936.

Horwath, E.; Toth, L.; and Lesure, J. *Hotel Accounting*. 4th ed. New York: The Ronald Press, 1978.

The Hotelman Looks at the Business of Meetings. St. Paul: 3M Business Press, 1968.

Hubbart, Roy. *The Hubbart Formula for Evaluating Rate Structures of Hotel Rooms*. New York: American Hotel & Motel Association, 1952.

Hudson, Holton. *What is a Motel/Hotel Worth?* No city: Author published, 1976.

Implications of Microcomputers in Small and Medium Hotel & Catering Firms. Prepared for the Hotel and Catering Industry Training Board by the Department of Hotel, Catering, and Tourism Management, University of Surrey, Guildford, Surrey, November 1980.

Kasavana, Michael. *Effective Front Office Operations.* Boston: CBI Publishing Co., Inc., 1981.

———. *Hotel Information Systems.* Boston: CBI Publishing Company, Inc., 1978.

Lattin, Gerald. *Modern Hotel and Motel Management.* 3d ed. San Francisco: W. H. Freeman and Co., 1977.

Lawrence, Janet. *Room Sales and Reception Management.* Boston: The Innkeeping Institute of America, 1970.

Lefler, Janet, and Calanese, Salvatore. *The Correct Cashier.* New York: Ahrens Publishing Co., 1960.

Lundberg, Donald. *The Hotel and Restaurant Business.* 4th ed. New York: CBI — Van Nostrand Reinhold Co., 1984.

———. *Front Office Human Relations.* Distributed by NU-PAK, PO Box 379, San Marcos, Calif., 1979.

Lundberg, Donald, and Kane, V. *Business Management: Hotels, Motels, and Restaurants.* Tallahassee: Peninsular Publishing Co., 1952.

Martin, Robert. *The Executive Housekeeper's Handbook.* Minneapolis: Alpha Editions, 1981.

Medlik, S. *The Business of Hotels.* London: William Heinemann Ltd., 1980.

———. *Profile of the Hotel and Catering Industry.* 2d ed. London: William Heinemann Ltd., 1979.

Meek, Howard B. *A Theory of Room Rates.* Ithaca: Cornell University, Department of Hotel Administration, June 1938.

A Meeting Planner's Guide to Master Account Billing. Developed by the Insurance Conference Planners, and published by The Educational Institute of the American Hotel & Motel Association, May 1980.

Metelka, Charles. *Dictionary of Tourism.* Wheaton, Ill.: Merton House Publishing Co., 1981.

Miller, Floyd. *Statler.* New York: The Statler Foundation, 1968.

Ministry of Tourism. *The Front Desk Business.* Toronto: Ontario Ministry of Tourism, 1978.

Moreo, Patrick J. *Night Audit Workbook.* Minneapolis: Burgess Publishing Co., 1980.

NCR Hotel On-line System (HOST). Dayton: The National Cash Register Company. No date.

Ogilvie, A.W.T. *Lecture Outline in Front Office.* No city: American Hotel Association, 1923.

Operating Instructions for Guest Account Posting. Dayton: National Cash Register Co. No date.

Pfeiffer, W.; Voegele, M.; and Wolley, G. *The Correct Service Department for Hotels, Motor Hotels, Motels, and Resorts.* New York: Ahrens Publishing Co., 1962.

Podd, G., and Lesure, J. *Planning and Operating Motels and Motor Hotels.* New York: Ahrens Publishing Co., 1964.

Relieving Reservation Headaches. East Lansing: Educational Institute of the AH&MA, 1979.

Renner, Peter. *Basic Hotel Front Office Procedures.* Boston: CBI Publishing Company, Inc., 1981.

Resale in the Lodging Industry: A Bell System Perspective. Nashville: AH&MA Mid-Year Meeting, April 1982.

Room Clerk, The Man Up Front. Temple, Tx: Motel/Motor Inn Journal, 1977.

Rosenzweig, Stan. *Hotel/Motel Telephone Systems: Opportunities Through Deregulation.* East Lansing: The Educational Institute of the American Hotel & Motel Association, 1982.

Ross, Bruce. *Hotel Reservation Systems Present and Future.* Ithaca: Unpublished Masters Monograph, May 1977.

Sapienza, Dunnovan L.; Abbey, James R.; Vallen, Jerome J. *Readings in the Art & Science of Managing Hotels/Restaurants/Institutions.* Rochelle Park, N.J.: Hayden Book Company, Inc., 1977.

Saunders, K. C. *Head Hall Porter.* London: Catering Education Research Institute, 1980.

Self, Robert. *Long Distance for Less.* New York: Telecom Library, Inc., 1982.

Sherry, John. *How to Exclude and Eject Undesirable Guests.* Stamford: The Dahls, 1943.

Sicherman, Irving. *The Investment in the Lodging Business.* Scranton, Pa.: Sicherman, 1977.

Sikich, Franklin. *Let's Get the Money Inn.* Dallas: Texas Hotel and Motel Short Course, July 1977.

Starting and Managing a Small Motel. Small Business Administration, U.S. Government Printing Office, 1963.

The State of Information Processing and Related Technology in the Hotel/Motel Industry. New York: American Hotel & Motel Association, 1976.

The State of Technology in the Lodging Industry. New York: American Hotel & Motel Association, 1980.

Successful Credit and Collection Techniques. East Lansing: Educational Institute of the American Hotel and Motel Association, 1981.

Tarbet, J. R. *A Handbook of Hotel Front Office Procedure.* Pullman: Student Book Corporation, circa 1955.

Tarr, Stanley, and Fay, Clifford. *Basic Bookkeeping for the Hospitality Industry.* East Lansing: Education Institute of the American Hotel & Motel Association, 1976.

Taylor, Derek, and Thomason, Richard. *Profitable Hotel Reception.* New York: Pergamon Press, 1982.

Trends in the Hotel-Motel Business. New York: Pannell Kerr Forster & Co., Various years.

Tucker, Georgina, and Schneider, Madelin. *The Professional Housekeeper.* Boston: CBI Publishing Company, Inc., 1975.

Uniformed-Service Training. Boston: Sheraton Corporation of America, 1960.

Uniform System of Accounts and Expense Dictionary for Motels, Motor Hotels, Small Hotels. New York: American Hotel & Motel Association, 1962.

Uniform System of Accounts for Hotels. 7th ed. New York: Hotel Association of New York City, Inc., 1977.

U.S. Lodging Industry. Philadelphia: Laventhol & Horwath, Various years.

Vallen, Jerome J.; Abbey, James R.; and Sapienza, Dunnovan L. *The Art & Science of Managing Hotels/Restaurants/Institutions.* Rochelle Park, N.J.: Hayden Book Company, Inc., 1977.

White, P., and Beckley, H. *Hotel Reception.* 3d ed. London: Edward Arnold, 1978.

Witzky, Herbert. *Practical Hotel-Motel Cost Reduction Handbook.* New York: Ahrens Publishing Co., Inc., 1970.

Yellowstone Park Company Cashier Training Program. Yellowstone: Yellowstone Park Co., 1978.

Yuen, Ronald. *The Historical Development of Computers in the Hotel Industry.* Ithaca: Unpublished Masters Monograph, May 1979.

Index